GENERAL INDEX

TO THE

DOCUMENTS

OF THE

STATE OF NEW YORK.

PREPARED, AND PUBLISHED PURSUANT TO A RESOLUTION OF THE SENATE,

BY

T. S. GILLETT.

ALBANY:

WEED, PARSONS AND COMPANY.

1860.

"IN SENATE, April 10, 1857.

"*Resolved*, That a general index of the documents and laws of this state, to and including 1857, be prepared by T. S. Gillett, in the same general form of convenience for reference, as the index prepared by P. B. Prindle in 1841; that he cause five hundred copies to be printed and bound, and that fifty copies be placed in the Senate and Assembly libraries, for the use of the Legislature, and the balance to be distributed as provided by chapter 258, of the Laws of 1845.

"By order of the Senate,

"S. P. ALLEN,

"*Clerk.*"

INDEX

TO THE

DOCUMENTS

OF THE

STATE OF NEW YORK,

FROM 1777 TO 1857, INCLUSIVE.

[The letters S and A respectively stand for Senate and Assembly Documents.]

A.

		Doc.	Vol.	No.
	ABBOT, NERUM.			
1835.	Report on petition for compensation for damages to his lands by the Chemung canal, ...	A	2	115
	ABBOTT, NIRUM.			
1847.	Report on petition of, ...	A	7	206
1849.	Report of committee on grievances on petition of, ...	A	2	61
	ABDUCTION.			
1857.	Or enslavement of citizens of this state, communication from governor relative to, ...	A	1	47
	ABLEMAN, S.			
1846.	Report of commissioners of land office on petition of, ...	A	5	191
	ABOLITIONISTS.			
1836.	Proceedings of the legislature of Alabama relative to, ...	A	3	209
1836.	do do North Carolina, ...	A	1	22
1836.	do do Kentucky, ...	S	2	79
1836.	do do Georgia, ...	A	3	109
1836.	do do Michigan, ...	S	2	77
1836.	do do Mississippi, ...	A	4	301
1836.	do do Virginia, ...	A	4	246
1836.	do do South Carolina, ...	S	1	1

		Doc.	Vol.	No.
	ABOLITION OF CAPITAL PUNISHMENT, *see* Capital Punishment.			
	ABOLITION OF SLAVERY, *see* Slavery.			
	ABORIGINAL HISTORY OF THE STATE.			
1846.	Memorial of H. R. Schoolcraft and others relative to,..........	S	2	55
	ABRAHAM, CHARLES AND JOHN.			
1845.	Report of the committee on the judiciary on the bill authorizing the change of name of,................................	A	3	59
	ABSCONDING, CONCEALED AND NON-RESIDENT DEBTORS, *see* Debtors.			
	ACADEMIES, &c.			
1834.	Under the charge of the regents of the university, report relative to the purchase of books, &c., for the use of,...........	S	1	44
1837.	Report of amount of appropriations made to,..................	S	1	32
1838.	Report on petition to prohibit praying, &c., in,...............	A	2	55
1838.	Report recommending an increase of the annual sum now distributed by law among,..................................	A	5	236
1851.	Report on memorials from colleges and,.......................	S	2	49
1851.	Instructing teachers, report of committee on literature, ...	S	2	58
1857.	Report of the comptroller, in reply to resolution relative to loans to colleges and,......................................	A	3	155
	ALBANY INSTITUTE:			
1834.	Petition of, for aid,.......................................	S	1	15
	ALEXANDER HIGH SCHOOL:			
1831.	Report on petition to incorporate,...........................	A	4	319
	ALFRED ACADEMY:			
1856.	Report on petition of,......................................	A	4	133
	AVON ACADEMY:			
1845.	Report of regents of the university relative to an act to consolidate certain school districts with, &c.,....................	S	3	105
	BROOKLYN INSTITUTE:			
1845.	Annual report of trustees of, ...	A	4	94
1848.	Annual report of, ...	A	6	199
1849.	Annual report of,..	A	5	235
1858.	Annual report of trustees of, ...	A	3	76
	BUFFALO FEMALE SEMINARY:			
1830.	Report on petition to incorporate,...........................	S	2	161
	DE RUYTER INSTITUTE:			
1849.	Petition of Messrs. Bently, Sears, Enos and others, in behalf of agricultural department of, ...	A	2	78
	ERASMUS HALL ACADEMY:			
1832.	Report on petition of, relative to distribution of literature fund,.	A	2	59
	FAIRFIELD ACADEMY:			
1850.	Report on the application of trustees of,.....................	A	2	63
	FREE ACADEMY OF NEW YORK:			
1850.	Report on memorial of,.......................................	S	3	90
	GENESEE WESLEYAN SEMINARY:			
1844.	Report of the comptroller on,................................	A	3	38
1844.	Report of committee on colleges, &c., on the petition of, ...	A	3	92

Year	Subject	Doc.	Vol.	No.
	GREENBUSH AND SCHODACK ACADEMY:			
1836.	Report on petition for a portion of the literature fund, ...	A	4	218
	HAMILTON ACADEMY:			
1830.	Report on petition of, relative to the distribution of the literature fund, ...	S	4	304
1840.	Report on petition for the establishment of a department in, for the education of common school teachers, ...	S	2	58
	HUDSON RIVER AGRICULTURAL SEMINARY:			
1837.	Report on petition for aid to the, ...	A	2	60
	JEFFERSON ACADEMY:			
1833.	Report on petition for aid to, in Schoharie county, ...	A	3	260
	MEXICO ACADEMY:			
1856.	Report on loaning money to, ...	A	4	107
	MIDDLEBURY ACADEMY:			
1834.	Report on bill for the relief of, ...	A	4	368
	MOUNT PLEASANT ACADEMY:			
1835.	Report on memorial for relief, ...	A	2	132
	OGDENSBURGH ACADEMY:			
1843.	Report of committee on literature, on petition of, ...	S	1	32
	ONONDAGA COUNTY INSTITUTE:			
1849.	Memorial of, in relation to free schools, ...	A	3	115
	REDHOOK ACADEMY:			
1830.	Report of the regents of the university relative to the exclusion of the, from the distribution of the income of the literature fund, ...	A	4	310
	RENSSELAER INSTITUTE:			
1848.	Report of committee on agriculture on petition of, ...	A	6	192
	RUTGERS' FEMALE INSTITUTE:			
1838.	Report on petition to incorporate, ...	A	6	302
	ST. LAWRENCE ACADEMY:			
1845.	Report of regents of university concerning the, ...	A	5	158
1849.	Report of committee on colleges, academies and common schools, on petition of trustees of, ...	A	1	34
	SHERBURNE UNION ACADEMY:			
	Report on memorial of, ...	S	4	127
	TROY FEMALE SEMINARY:			
1852.	Report on memorial of Emma Willard, ...	A	1	74
1852.	Report on memorial of Emma Willard, ...	A	5	117
	UNION ACADEMY:			
1831.	Report on petition to raise money by tax for the benefit of, ...	A	3	262
	UNION HALL ACADEMY:			
1830.	Report relative to the exclusion of the, from the distribution of the income of the literature fund, ...	A	4	320
1832.	Report on petition of, relative to the distribution of the income of the literature fund, ...	A	2	59
1846.	Report of regents of university relative to, ...	A	5	141

		Doc.	Vol.	No.
	ACCIDENTS.			
1856.	Memorial of R. H. Walworth for a law relative to,	S	1	37
	ACCOUNTS WITH THE UNITED STATES, *see* United States.			
	ACKER, ABRAHAM.			
1845.	Report of committee on privileges, &c., on the case of,	A	1	21
	ACKLEY, ELIPHALET.			
1839.	Report on petition of the widow and heirs of, for remuneration for certain land for taxes,	A	5	303
1840.	Report of committee on claims on the same,	A	6	237
1841.	Report of attorney-general on the same,	S	1	29
	ADAMS, ALSON.			
1856.	Report on petition of,	A	3	56
1857.	Report of committee on claims favorable on petition of, for payment of money due,	A	2	123
1858.	Report on claim of,	A	4	125
	ADAMS, CHRISTOPHER.			
1848.	Report on petition of,	A	3	109
	ADAMS, HORACE, AND ELIPHALET SEARS.			
1852.	Report on petition of,	A	2	29
1853.	Report of committee on claims, on petition of, for relief,	S	2	44
1857.	Report of committee on claims favorable on petition of, for further compensation,	A	2	112
	ADAMS, JOHN Q.			
1848.	Report respecting address commemorative of services of,	A	3	122
	ADAMS, MARCUS.			
1847.	Report on petition of,	A	8	248
1848.	Report on petition of,	A	3	84
1832.	ADAMS, PARMENIO, *see* Genesee County, &c.			
	ADAMS, STEPHEN, AND OTHERS.			
1847.	Report on petition of,	A	2	92
	ADAMS, TOWN OF.			
1854.	Report of committee on charitable and religious societies relative to First Methodist Episcopal Church in,	A	2	58
	ADDINGTON, S. H., AND OTHERS.			
1833.	Report on petition for compensation for damages to their lands by the Erie canal	A	3	229
	ADJUTANT-GENERAL.			
	N. F. BECK:			
1830.	Annual report of,	A	3	201
	M. H. WEBSTER, ACTING:			
1831.	Annual report of,	A	1	16

ADJUTANT-GENERAL—*continued.*

Year		Doc.	Vol.	No.
	JOHN A. DIX:			
1832.	Annual report of,	A	2	60
1832.	Report on petition to reduce the number of parades of the militia,	S	1	4
1832.	Report on petition of the fourth brigade of artillery, for a change in one of the companies of said brigade,	A	3	220
1833.	Annual report of,	A	2	84
1833.	Report of, relative to certain books received from the secretary of war,	A	3	153
1833.	Report on petition of Gilbert D. Dillon,	S	2	101
	LEVI HUBBELL:			
1834.	Annual report of,	A	3	172
1834.	Memorial of, for an addition to the pay of his department,	A	1	32
1834.	Report of committee on the same,	A	1	31
1835.	Annual report of,	A	3	211
1836.	Annual report of,	A	3	200
	THOMAS W. HARMAN:			
1837.	Annual report of,	A	1	12
	ALLAN MCDONALD:			
1838.	Annual report of,	A	2	50
1839.	Annual report of,	A	2	27
	RUFUS KING:			
1839.	Report of, on petition of Gen. Corss and others,	A	6	394
1840.	Report of, transmitting the reports of the presidents of courts-martial in New York,	S	3	88
1840.	Annual report of,	A	3	80
1841.	Annual report of,	A	2	50
1841.	Report of committee on the militia, on petition to increase the salary of,	A	2	152
1842.	Annual report of,	A	2	4
1842.	Annual report of,	A	2	41
1842.	Report on petition of Thomas Averill,	A	7	153
1842.	Report relative to staff-officers in 29th division and 49th brigade,	A	7	157
	LYMAN SANDFORD:			
1843.	Annual report of,	A	2	24
	ARCHIBALD C. NIVEN:			
1844.	Annual report of,	S	1	5
1845.	Annual report of,	A	1	3
1845.	Communication from, relative to troops at Hudson,	A	1	16
	THOMAS FARRINGTON:			
1846.	Report of comptroller relative to moneys paid to, and attorney-general,	S	1	28
1846.	Annual report of,	A	1	6
1846.	Report of, in answer to a resolution of the assembly,	A	5	184
1847.	Annual report of,	A	1	39
1847.	Report of, as to organization of New York volunteers,	A	2	80
1847.	Report of, as to vacancies in offices of volunteer regiments in Mexico,	A	6	151
	SAMUEL STEVENS:			
1848.	Annual report of,	A	2	54
1848.	Report on memorial of Titus Gazynski and others,	A	5	177
1849.	Annual report of,	A	2	88
1849.	Report of, in answer to a resolution of assembly, relative to non-commissioned officers and privates of the 1st division of militia,	A	2	45
1850.	Annual report of,	A	4	51

ADJUTANT-GENERAL—*continued.*

		Doc.	Vol.	No.
	L. WARD SMITH:			
1851.	Annual report of,..	A	1	7
1851.	Annual report of,..	A	1	9
1851.	Report on the cost of the militia system,....................	S	2	28
1852.	Annual report of,..	A	1	7
	ROBERT E. TEMPLE:			
1853.	Annual report of,..	S	1	28
1853.	Report of the, in answer to a resolution in relation to clerks in his office,..	S	2	47
1853.	Report of the commissioners and, appointed to codify and amend the militia laws,..	S	2	66
1854.	Annual report of, ...	A	1	17
1854.	Communication from, relative to commutations in New York,...	S	2	72
	J. WATTS DE PEYSTER:			
1855.	Annual report of,..	A	1	15
	ROBERT H. PRUYN:			
1856.	Annual report of,..	A	4	155
	FREDERICK TOWNSEND:			
1857.	Annual report of,..	A	3	195
1858.	Annual report of,..	A	1	16

ADSIT, A. M.

1845.	Report of committee on grievances on petition of,.............	A	4	136

ADULTERY AND SEDUCTION.

1840.	Report on petition for a law for the punishment of,............	A	3	68
1840.	Report on petition for a law for the punishment of,............	A	8	333
1842.	Report of committee on petition for law to punish, ...	A	7	159
1843.	Report on petitions for a law more effectually to punish, &c.,...	A	5	134
1844.	Report of committee on the judiciary on petition for the suppression of,..	A	3	63
1847.	Report of committee on grievances relative to,.................	S	2	68

ADVERSE CLAIMS, *see* Claims, Adverse.

AGASSIZ, PROFESSOR.

1847.	Report on letter of,..	S	4	155

AGENTS, CONSIGNEES AND FACTORS.

1830.	Memorial of merchants of New York for a law to prevent abuses in the disposition of goods in the hands of,.................	S	1	46
1830.	Report of committee on the judiciary on the same,............	S	1	55
1830.	Remonstrance against the passage of the bill concerning,.......	S	2	105

AGRICULTURE.

1833.	General report on subject of,................................	A	4	312
1834.	do do (Mr. Sudam),..........	S	2	97
1838.	do do (Mr. L. F. Allen), and bill to improve,	A	4	161
1839.	do do (Mr. C. E. Clarke),................	A	5	273
1840.	do do (Mr. J. Johnson),.	A	8	352
1841.	Report on communication from the American Institute on the subject of (Mr. Johnson),..................................	A	6	217
1842.	Report relative to amending act to promote,....	A	5	91
1842.	Report on the transactions of the state and county societies,....	A	6	131
1843.	Report of the committee on,................................	S	1	46

AGRICULTURE—*continued.*

Year	Subject	Doc.	Vol.	No.
1844.	Report of the committee on, on that portion of governor's message respecting,	A	5	115
1844.	Report of the committee on, on petition of agricultural society of Erie county,	A	7	198
1845.	Report of committee on, on so much of governor's message as relates to,	S	2	60
1845.	Report of committee on, on so much of governor's message as relates to,	A	6	200
1846.	Report of committee on, on so much of governor's message as relates to,	A	5	146
1846.	Report of committee on, on so much of governor's message as relates to,	A	5	148
1846.	Report of committee on, recommending the printing of the annual report of the American Institute,	A	6	200
1848.	Report of committee on, on petition of Rensselaer Institute,	A	6	192
1849.	Report of committee on,	A	5	212
1850.	Discoveries by R. Comstock,	A	3	23
1850.	Commissioners' report,	A	3	30
1850.	Report of committee on memorial of State Agricultural Society,	A	4	56
1850.	Resolution of the legislature of Rhode Island on the subject of,	A	8	180
1852.	*See* memorial of emigration and agricultural association,	S	1	19
1853.	Report of minority of committee on, in relation to the incorporation of the People's College,	A	2	38
1853.	Minority report,	A	2	42
1853.	Report of committee to establish an agricultural college, &c.,	A	2	36
1853.	Report of committee on, authorizing the Rensselaer County Agricultural Society to hold and convey real estate,	S	1	4
1855.	Report of committee, on petition of T. S. Lambert and others, in reference to stocking waters with fish,	A	5	142
1857.	Report on "an act to enable the Warren County Agricultural Society to draw their proportion of public money from the state,"	A	3	191
1857.	Report of committee on, favorable, on petition and bill, to furnish a library of agricultural books to each school district,	A	3	173

AGRICULTURAL COLLEGE AND EXPERIMENTAL FARM.

Year	Subject	Doc.	Vol.	No.
1847.	Report of committee on colleges, &c., relative to,	A	6	153
1847.	Report of committee on agriculture, relative to,	A	6	169
1847.	Report of committee on colleges, &c., relative to establishment of and workshop, and promotion of agricultural and mechanic arts	A	7	187
1850.	Report of special committee,	A	5	104
1851.	Report of majority of committee on agriculture, relative to,	A	2	33
1851.	Minority report of same committee,	A	4	116
1852.	Report on governor's message relative to,	A	5	100
1853.	Report of committee on agriculture to establish an,	A	2	36
1855.	Report of committee on finance on petition for aid to,	S	2	61
1855.	Memorial of trustees of,	A	3	64
1856.	Report relative to,	S	1	23
1856.	Report of committee on finance on petition relative to,	S	1	26
1858.	Report of trustees of,	A	4	154

AGRICULTURAL DEPARTMENT, *see* Academies—De Ruyter Institute.

AGRICULTURAL SCHOOLS.

Year	Subject	Doc.	Vol.	No.
1833.	Report on memorial of the New York State Agricultural Society, for the establishment of,	S	2	79
1834.	Report of committee on agriculture on the same,	A	4	311
1834.	Report of joint committee of senate and assembly on the same,	S	2	97
1834.	Report of committee on agriculture, on the same,	S	2	110
1849.	Memorial of N. Y. State Agricultural Society for establishment of,	A	2	65
1849.	Report of committee on agriculture respecting, &c.,	A	5	212

AGRICULTURAL SCHOOLS—*continued.*

		Doc.	Vol.	No.
1850.	Memorial,	A	5	86

AGRICULTURAL SOCIETIES.

1838.	Report on establishing,	A	4	161

AGRICULTURAL SOCIETY, NEW YORK STATE.

1842.	Transactions of, and county agricultural societies,	A	6	131
1843.	Report of,	S	2	63
1843.	Annual report of,	S	3	63
1844.	Annual report of transactions,	A	4	100
1845.	Annual report of transactions of the year 1844,	S	3	85
1846.	Report of, for 1845,	S	4	105
1847.	Report of,	A	5	150
1848.	Report of,	A	4	125
1849.	Memorial of committee of, for the establishment of a state agricultural school,	A	2	65
1850.	Report of committee on agriculture on memorial of,	A	4	56
1850.	Annual transactions,	A	7	175
1851.	Annual report of,	A	6	150
1852.	Transactions of,	A	6	126
1853.	Transactions of,	A	6	112
1854.	Annual report of,	A	6	151
1855.	Report of select committee on communication from, in relation to entomology,	A	5	137
1855.	Annual report of,	A	6	145
1856.	Communication from, respecting noxious insects,	A	5	207
1856.	Communication of corresponding secretary of,	A	7	217
1857.	Transactions of,	A	4	213
1857.	Transactions of,	A	5	213
1858.	Annual report of,	A	5	161

For COUNTY AGRICULTURAL SOCIETIES, *see* the respective counties.

AGRICULTURAL STATE CONVENTION.

1837.	Resolution of, recommending the establishment of agricultural societies,	S	1	26
1837.	Resolution of, for aid in the cause of agriculture,	A	3	167

AGRICULTURAL STATE INSTITUTION.

1833.	Bill to incorporate,	A	4	312

ALABAMA, STATE OF.

1833.	Resolution of the legislature of, in relation to the tariff laws and the doctrine of nullification,	A	4	274
1836.	Correspondence between the governor of, and the governor of New York, in relation to the demand for the surrender of R. G. Williams, a fugitive from justice,	S	1	1
1836.	Resolution of the legislature of, in relation to the abolitionists,	A	3	209
1838.	Resolution of the legislature of, for the annexation of Texas to the United States,	A	5	218
1841.	Resolution of the legislature of, relative to protection of American industry,	A	3	57
1841.	Resolution of the legislature of, relative to the controversy between Georgia and Maine,	A	4	125
1841.	Communication from the secretary of state of, relative to an exchange of supreme court decisions with the several states,	A	4	138
1842.	Resolutions of general assembly of, relative to public lands,	A	2	43
1842.	Resolutions of general assembly of, relative to public lands,	S	1	19
1842.	Resolutions of general assembly of, relative to the admission of Texas into the Union,	A	2	48

Year	Subject	Doc.	Vol.	No.
	ALABAMA, STATE OF—*continued.*			
1852.	Resolutions of general assembly of, relative to the admission of Texas into the Union,	S	2	25
1843.	Joint resolution of legislature of,	S	3	88
1856.	Resolutions of,	A	4	117
	ALABAMA, TOWN OF.			
1832.	Report on petition for a new town from part of the,	A	2	57
1846.	Report of the canal board on the petition of citizens of,	A	4	136
1847.	Report on the petition of inhabitants of,	A	2	59
1848.	Report of committee on claims on petition of inhabitants of,	A	2	26
	ALBANY AND SCHENECTADY TURNPIKE COMPANY.			
1831.	Report on petition of, to amend the act of the last session relative to,	A	2	132
1832.	Report on petition of, to allow the Mohawk and Hudson railroad to construct a branch road, &c.,	A	1	36
1833.	Report on petition to increase the capital stock and to increase the rates of toll,	S	2	69
1852.	Report on application of, to abandon part of their road,	A	5	110
	ALBANY, CITY OF.			
1851.	Report of select committee on bill relative to,	A	4	114
1851.	Report of minority committee relative to bill concerning,	A	4	114
	ALBANY REPUBLICAN ARTILLERY:			
1843.	Report of the select committee on the petition of the same for leave to erect a monument in the Capitol Park to the memory of the late Colonel John Mills,	A	5	145
	ARBOR HILL IN:			
1830.	Report on petition for a grant of land on, for religious and benevolent purposes,	A	4	352
	ARSENAL:			
1858.	Report of commissioners in relation to,	S	3	122
	AUCTIONS:			
1832.	Report on petition to restrain the sale of books at daylight,	A	1	39
	BASIN AND PIER:			
1830.	Report on petition relative to an opening in the north end of the pier,	A	2	83
1831.	Report on petition to construct a bridge across the opening in,	A	2	94
1835.	Report relative to the improvement of the navigation of the basin,	S	2	71
1835.	Report of the canal commissioners on the same,	S	2	76
1836.	Report on the petition for an opening in the pier between Columbia and State streets,	S	2	75
1837.	Report on petition of the common council to amend the law relative to the navigation of,	A	3	281
1838.	Report relative to widening the pier,	S	2	50
1840.	Report on petition of the common council to amend the law relative to the navigation of,	A	4	150
1843.	Report of the select committee on the basin,	A	5	177
1844.	Report of the committee on the judiciary on the memorial of the corporation of, praying for relief in relation to the basin assessment,	A	7	192
1845.	Report of canal board relative to basin,	S	2	83
1845.	Report of canal board, on petition of G. W. Stanton and others, relative to excavating,	S	4	83
1846.	Report of committee on finance relative to basin,	S	4	116

ALBANY, CITY OF—*continued.*

		Doc.	Vol.	No.
1848.	Report of committee on claims on petition of mayor, &c., relative to basin, ...	A	3	66
1848.	Report of proprietors of pier, ...	A	5	142
1848.	Report on law, ...	A	5	145
1849.	Report of select committee on the excavations in, ...	S	1	7
1849.	Communication from comptroller in relation to removing wrecks in basin, ...	S	1	18
	BEEF AND PORK, INSPECTOR OF:			
1830.	Philo Booth, annual report of, ...	A	2	160
	BEER:			
1835.	Report of select committee in relation to the manufacture of, ...	S	2	88
	BRIDGE OVER THE HUDSON RIVER AT:			
1835.	Report on petition for, ...	A	4	363
1841.	Majority report on petition for, ...	A	6	200
1841.	Minority report on petition for, ...	A	6	253
1845.	Memorial of corporation of Troy concerning the, ...	A	3	72
1845.	Report of the majority of committee on roads and bridges against,	A	6	198
1845.	Report of the minority of committee on roads and bridges in favor of, ...	A	6	199
1848.	Report of committee on roads and bridges on bill to, ...	A	5	149
1852.	Report on, ...	A	5	114
1856.	Testimony relative to, ...	A	5	196
1856.	Testimony relative to, ...	A	5	206
1856.	Report relative to, ...	S	2	56
1857.	Report of committee on roads and bridges, relative to, ...	A	3	203
1857.	Testimony relative to, ...	A	3	203
	BRIDGE OVER WATER STREET IN:			
1846.	Report of committee on canals relative to, ...	A	4	128
	CAPITOL, *see* Capitol.			
	CHARTER ELECTIONS, INSPECTORS OF:			
1831.	Report concerning, ...	A	2	116
	CHARTER OF:			
1834.	Report of attorney-general on bill to amend the, ...	A	2	123
	CHARTER OFFICERS:			
1834.	Remonstrance against altering the time of electing, ...	A	4	357
1838.	Report on petition to change the time for the election of, ...	A	6	305
	CLERGY OF:			
1838.	Communication from, accepting the invitation to open the morning sessions with prayer, ...	S	1	6
	COMMON COUNCIL:			
1830.	Report on petition of, on various subjects, ...	A	3	221
1837.	Report on petition of, to borrow money to aid in the construction of the Albany and West Stockbridge railroad, ...	A	3	256
1839.	Report on petition of, to borrow money to aid in the construction of the Albany and West Stockbridge railroad, ...	A	3	155
1839.	Report on petition of, to borrow money to aid in the construction of the Albany and West Stockbridge railroad, ...	A	4	189
	COMMON SCHOOLS IN:			
1830.	Moneys, report on petition to amend the law apportioning, &c., ..	S	4	323
1831.	District No. 6, report on petition to raise money by tax to build a school-house in, ...	A	1	17

ALBANY, CITY OF—*continued.*

Year	Subject	Doc.	Vol.	No.
1832.	District No. 2,	A	4	300
1840.	Report on petition to separate the male and female departments in the,	A	6	244
	CONVICT LABOR:			
1843.	Resolutions on the subject of, adopted at a meeting of the mechanics in,	A	5	156
	COUNTY POOR:			
1837.	Report on petition to continue an act relative to support of the,	A	3	191
	COURT OF OYER AND TERMINER:			
1830.	Report on petition of William Campbell, for pay for services as crier of the,	A	4	365
	CRIMINAL COURT:			
1830.	Report recommending the organization of a,	A	3	221
	DISTRICT ATTORNEY OF:			
1838.	Report relative to the salary of,	A	3	68
	DOMESTIC DISTILLED SPIRITS, INSPECTORS OF:			
1831.	Stephen W. Johnson, annual report of,	A	2	155
1832.	Stephen W. Johnson, annual report of,	A	2	145
1834.	James Buckbee, annual report of,	A	3	245
1834.	do do	A	4	346
1836.	do do	A	3	190
1839.	do do	A	4	220
1840.	do do	A	5	189
	ELECTIVE FRANCHISE:			
1844.	Report of committee on privileges and elections on the petition of citizens of, for the passage of a law requiring a residence of twenty days in a ward to entitle a person to exercise the,	S	4	132
	EXCHANGE COMPANY:			
1837.	Report on petition to incorporate the,	A	1	43
	FIREMEN:			
1833.	Report on petition to amend the law relative to the,	A	2	74
	FLOUR, INSPECTORS OF:			
1830.	Jasper S. Keeler, annual report of,	S	1	64
1831.	do do	A	2	162
1832.	do do	A	2	89
1833.	do do	A	4	290
1834.	Erastus Miller, annual report of,	A	3	140
1835.	do do	A	3	203
1836.	do do	A	3	191
1837.	do do	A	2	145
1838.	do do	A	3	156
1839.	do do	A	4	219
1840.	do do	A	8	358
1843.	Annual report of,	A	5	187
1844.	do	A	7	173
1845.	do	A	3	49
1846.	do	A	6	220
	GAS LIGHT COMPANY:			
1833.	Report on petition to incorporate,	A	2	58

ALBANY, CITY OF—*continued.*

		Doc.	Vol.	No.
	GREEN HIDES AND SKINS, INSPECTOR OF:			
1832.	A. Comstock, annual report of,	S	1	18
1833.	do do	S	2	66
1835.	do do	A	5	398
1836.	do do	A	4	316
	HARBOR MASTER:			
1837.	Report on petition for the appointment of a,	A	4	292
1838.	Barnum Whipple, annual report of,	S	1	20
1839.	do do	S	1	25
1840.	do do	A	4	133
1841.	Seleck Whitney, do	A	4	126
1843.	Annual report of,	A	5	186
1847.	Annual report of,	A	1	38
1848.	Report of,	A	5	184
1849.	Report of,	A	5	231
1850.	Annual report of,	A	8	187
1857.	Annual report of,	A	3	207
1858.	Annual report of,	A	4	150
	HOPS, INSPECTOR OF:			
1830.	John C. Donnelly, annual report of,	A	2	191
1831.	do do	A	2	161
1845.	Report of,	A	4	145
	HORSE RACING AND TROTTING:			
1845.	Report of committee on charitable and religious societies, on bill to prevent, on Albany and Troy road, &c.,	S	3	88
	HOSPITAL:			
1853.	Annual report of governors,	A	3	71
	INSTITUTE, *see* Academies, &c.			
	INTEREST, RATE OF:			
1833.	Remonstrance of citizens of, against the bill to return the,	S	2	76
	JAIL AND WORK-HOUSE:			
1834.	Report on bill in relation to,	A	1	35
1839.	Report on petition of the supervisors to repeal part of the law relative to,	A	6	362
	JURORS:			
1836.	Report on petition to compensate them,	A	3	202
	JUSTICE OF THE PEACE FOR THE FIFTH WARD:			
1836.	Report on petition of the grand jury to abolish the office,	A	4	316
1837.	Report on petition to extend the powers of the,	A	3	248
1838.	do do do	A	6	338
1839.	do do do	A	5	306
	LEATHER, INSPECTORS OF:			
1831.	George Charles, annual report of,	A	2	176
1832.	do do	A	2	165
1833.	do do	A	2	45
1834.	do do	A	3	151
1834.	do do	A	4	335
1835.	do do	A	2	73
1836.	do do	S	1	43
1837.	do do	A	2	67
1838.	do do	A	3	128
1839.	do do	A	4	194

ALBANY CITY OF—*continued.*

Year	Entry		Doc.	Vol.	No.
1840.	George Charles, annual report of,		A	4	152
1832.	A. Russell,	do	A	2	107
1833.	do	do	S	2	51
1834.	B. Van Benthuisen,	do	A	3	154
1835.	do	do	A	3	179
1836.	do	do	A	3	159
1837.	do	do	A	2	65
1838.	do	do	S	2	37
1839.	do	do	S	1	43
1840.	do	do	S	2	43

LUMBER, INSPECTORS OF :

Year	Entry		Doc.	Vol.	No.
1830.	Report on petition for an additional one,		A	3	212
1834.	Report on petition to increase the number of,		A	4	262
1837.	S. V. R. Ableman, annual report of,		A	2	91
1839.	John Burlison,	do	A	3	143
1840.	do	do	A	3	79
1832.	B. C. Capron,	do	A	2	141
1833.	do	do	A	1	15
1834.	do	do	A	2	89
1834.	do	do	A	4	259
1835.	do	do	A	1	50
1836.	do	do	S	1	39
1837.	do	do	S	1	42
1838.	do	do	S	2	55
1839.	do	do	S	2	52
1837.	Daniel P. Clark,	do	A	2	59
1838.	do	do	A	4	189
1839.	do	do	A	2	54
1840.	do	do	A	1	9
1830.	A. H. De Witt,	do	A	2	141
1831.	do	do	A	2	184
1832.	do	do	A	3	225
1835.	Asa Fassett,	do	A	1	44
1836.	do	do	A	3	150
1837.	do	do	A	2	138
1838.	do	do	A	3	154
1838.	William B. Gourlay,	do	S	2	54
1839.	do	do	S	2	51
1840.	do	do	S	1	7
1830.	Isaac P. Hand,	do	A	2	139
1831.	do	do	A	2	124
1832.	do	do	A	2	85
1833.	do	do	A	2	93
1834.	do	do	A	3	133
1835.	do	do	A	1	30
1836.	do	do	A	2	95
1838.	do	do	S	1	33
1839.	do	do	S	2	34
1837.	Lawrence Hallenbake,	do	A	3	162
1838.	do	do	S	1	28
1839.	do	do	A	5	311
1840.	do	do	A	8	359
1832.	H. M. Hopkins,	do	S	1	14
1834.	do	do	A	2	92
1834.	do	do	A	4	344
1835.	do	do	S	1	42
1837.	Erastus Hunt,	do	A	3	237
1835.	Peter Lansing,	do	A	3	196
1836.	do	do	A	3	170
1834.	Garrit Lansing, Jr.,	do	A	4	258

ALBANY, CITY OF—*continued.*

		Doc.	Vol.	No.
1834.	Garrit Lansing, Jr., annual report of,	A	4	361
1830.	William P. Lansing, do	A	2	150
1831.	do do	A	1	42
1832.	do do	A	1	50
1833.	do do	A	2	96
1834.	do do	A	3	232
1834.	do do	A	4	322
1835.	do do	A	1	53
1836.	do do	A	2	46
1837.	do do	A	2	153
1839.	John T. Maher, do	A	4	177
1840.	do do	A	5	196
1830.	Henry Salisbury, do	A	2	140
1831.	do do	A	2	185
1832.	do do	A	2	112
1833.	do do	A	2	94
1834.	do do	S	1	45
1835.	do do	S	1	52
1836.	do do	S	1	9
1837.	do do	S	1	41
1838.	do do	S	2	46
1839.	do do	S	2	46
1840.	do do	S	3	84
1837.	Nelson Salisbury, do	A	2	64
1838.	do do	S	1	31
1839.	do do	S	2	48
1840.	Peter G. Sharp, do	A	5	162
1830.	Hosea Spencer, do	A	2	149
1838.	Daniel W. Tallcott, do	S	1	27
1839.	do do	S	1	26
1840.	do do	A	5	193
1834.	George R. Vanderlip, do	A	3	152
1835.	do do	A	1	29
1836.	do do	A	2	93
1837.	do do	A	2	96
1838.	do do	S	2	41
1839.	do do	S	2	47
	MAYOR'S COURT:			
1839.	Report on petition to change the time for holding the,	A	5	294
	MECHANICS:			
1843.	Resolutions on the subject of convict labor adopted at a meeting of,	A	5	156
	MEDICAL COLLEGE, *see* Medical Colleges.			
	ORPHAN ASYLUM:			
1832.	Report on petition for aid to,	A	2	121
1847.	Majority report on bill relative to,	A	7	217
1847.	Minority report on bill relative to,	A	8	259
	PENITENTIARY:			
1853.	Report of committee on state prisons relative to the,	A	2	52
1853.	Report of minority of committee on state prisons, in relation to the,	A	2	52
	POOR-HOUSE:			
1832.	Report on petition of supervisors to raise money to build,	A	2	93
	POOR, SUPPORT OF:			
1832.	Report on petition of the common council to make the city a separate district for the,	S	1	38

ALBANY, CITY OF—*continued.*

Year	Subject	Doc.	Vol.	No.
	POT AND PEARL ASHES:			
1830.	B. Van Benthuisen, annual report of,	A	2	85
1831.	do do	A	2	74
1832.	do do	A	2	108
1833.	do do	A	2	78
1831.	Jason Rudes, do	A	2	74
1833.	do do	A	2	78
1834.	do do	A	3	149
1834.	do do	A	4	340
1835.	do do	A	2	84
1836.	do do	A	3	158
1837.	do do	A	2	122
1838.	do do	S	1	28
	RACE-COURSE AND HORSE FAIR:			
1833.	Report on petition for a,	A	2	75
	SHIP CANAL from, to Lake Ontario, *see* Ship Canal.			
	SHIP CANAL from, to New Baltimore:			
1833.	Petition of E. C. Genet and others for a,	S	1	24
1833.	Report of committee on canals on petition for,	S	2	80
	SIDEWALKS AND STREETS:			
1836.	Report on petition of the common council for power to cause an assessment of the expense of cleaning to be made, and that it be a lien upon the lots assessed,	A	4	245
	STATE HALL, *see* State Hall.			
	STATE PRISON LABOR:			
1843.	Resolutions adopted at a meeting of mechanics and citizens of, on the subject of,	A	5	156
	STAVES AND HEADING:			
1830.	Inspector-general J. Radcliff, report of,	A	2	133
1831.	do do	A	1	57
1832.	do do	A	2	66
1833.	do do	A	2	72
1834.	do do	A	3	171
1835.	do do	A	4	275
1836.	do do	A	4	282
1837.	do do	A	3	213
1839.	Culler-general J. Radcliff, report of,	A	6	334
1840.	Culler-general J. N. Bates, report of,	A	8	355
	TAXES IN:			
1830.	Report on petition to extend the time for the collection of,	A	3	262
1832.	do do do	A	3	217
1835.	do do do	A	3	220
1837.	do do do	A	3	208
	TITLE TO CERTAIN LANDS:			
1842.	Report of the judiciary committee on the petition relative to,	A	7	177, 181
	VAN RENSSELAER GUARDS IN:			
1838.	Report on petition for certain privileges and exemptions,	A	2	42
	WATER STREET.			
1846.	Report of committee on canals respecting a bridge over,	A	4	128

ALBANY, CITY OF—*continued.*

		Doc.	Vol.	No.
	WATER WORKS COMPANY:			
1830.	Report on petition to incorporate a,	S	3	202
1831.	Report on petition to incorporate a,	A	3	195
1831.	Remonstrance of the "Albany Water Works Company," against incorporating a second one,	A	3	218
	WHARFAGE:			
1850.	Report of committee on,	S	3	91
	YOUNG MEN'S ASSOCIATION:			
1835.	Report on bill to incorporate,	A	2	80
	ALBANY COUNTY.			
	DISTRICT ATTORNEY OF:			
1838.	Report relative to the salary of,	A	3	68
	INSPECTOR'S REPORTS, *see* Albany City.			
	JAIL AND WORK-HOUSE:			
1834.	Report on bill concerning,	A	1	35
1839.	Report on petition of supervisors to repeal part of the law relative to the,	A	6	362
	LANDS:			
1842.	Majority report relative to titles to certain, in Schoharie and,	A	7	181
1842.	Minority report on same subject,	A	7	177
	MANOR OF RENSSELAERWYCK:			
1835.	Report on a resolution to inquire whether ground rents, quarter sales, &c., are subject to taxation,	S	2	83
1840.	Report of comptroller relative to paying the militia called out to assist the sheriff, &c.,	S	3	67
1840.	Report on bill for the payment of the militia,	A	5	175
1840.	Landlord and tenant, report of the commissioners appointed to effect a settlement of the disputes between,	A	7	261
1844.	Report on the petition of sundry residents of, praying for certain modifications of the law respecting the rights of, &c.,	A	7	183
1844.	Report of select committee on above petition,	A	7	189
1840.	Manor difficulties, governor's message respecting the,	S	3	70
1840.	Report in relation to the,	A	6	271
1845.	Report of select committee on so much of governor's message as relates to,	A	6	222
1846.	Report of select committee on so much of governor's message as relates to,	A	5	156
1850.	Manorial lands, report of committee on,	S	3	96
1850.	Report of select committee on,	A	3	24
1851.	Report of attorney-general on the subject of,	S	2	27
1852.	Report on petition of tenants upon, for relief,	A	5	92
1853.	Report of attorney-general respecting titles to,	A	3	59
1850.	Manorial suits, report of attorney-general relative to,	S	1	26
1850.	Manorial tenants, report of select committee on petition of,	A	5	80
1850.	Report on petition of, for relief,	A	5	92
1850.	Manorial titles, resolutions relative to,	S	3	84
1851.	Report on bill to stay proceedings,	S	1	9
1851.	Attorney-general's report,	S	2	27
1853.	Report of attorney-general in answer to a resolution relative to,	A	3	59
	See Landlord and Tenant, Rent, &c.			
	POOR:			
1837.	Report on petition to continue an act relative to the support of,	A	3	191

ALBANY, COUNTY OF—*continued.*

Doc. Vol. No.

POOR-HOUSE:

1832. Report on petition to raise money to build,.................. A 2 93
1831. Report on petition of the supervisors for a law authorizing the supervisor, justices of the peace and town clerk to audit the accounts of all charges payable by their respective towns,.... A 1 30

SHERIFF OF:

1840. Report relative to paying the militia called out to assist the,.... S 3 67

ALBANY TO OWEGO.

1835. Report on petition for a McAdam road from,.................. A 5 387

ALBERTY, J. & J. W.

1854. Report of committee on claims on petition of,................ A 3 99

ALBRIGHT, HARRISON.

1855. Report of committee on claims relative to,.................... A 1 17
1855. Report of attorney-general relative to claim of,............... A 5 124
1856. Report of committee on claims on petition of, for relief,....... A 3 80

ALEXANDER, HENRY P., AND OTHERS.

1849. Report of committee on canals, on bill for relief of,............ A 2 63

ALEXANDER, SAMUEL, AND H. DICKINSON.

1843. Report commisioners of land office on petition of, ... S 3 106

ALEXANDRIA, DISTRICT OF COLUMBIA.

1842. Proceedings of municipal council of, in favor of retrocession of, to Virginia,.. A 4 53

ALEXANDRIA, TOWN OF.

1838. Report on petition to extend the time for collection of taxes in,.. A 3 90
1830. Report on petition to divide the,............................ A 8 356

ALFRED, TOWN OF.

1832. Report on petition for the division of the, ... A 3 266

ALIEN AND SEDITION LAWS.

1833. Resolution of Virginia and Kentucky of 1798, and Mr. Madison's report on the Virginia resolution of 1799, &c., ... S 2 41

ALIEN PASSENGERS.

1845. Report on the memorial from New York relative to,............ A 6 216
1850. Communication in regard to, ... A 5 99

ALIENS.

1833. Report on bill concerning, ... A 4 326
1848. Report on bill to allow, to hold real estate,.................... A 5 168
1854. Report of majority and minority of committee on, on petition of John O'Brien,.. A 1 39
1854. Report of majority and minority of committee on, on petition of John O'Brien,.. A 2 44
1854. Report on petition of James Hay,............................ A 3 93

ALIENS—*continued.*

		Doc.	Vol.	No
1857.	Committee on petitions of, report of, favorable on petition of Hanna S. Carter for escheated lands,	A	2	83
1857.	Committee on petitions of, report of, favorable on petition of heirs of Horatio A. Griffin for escheated lands,	A	3	146
1857.	Committee on petitions of, report of, favorable on petition of James Robb for power to hold land,	A	2	84
1857.	Committee on petitions of, report of, favorable on petition of Agnes C. Turner for escheated lands,	A	2	62

ALIENS, RESIDENT.

1838.	Report on bill to enable them to hold real estate,	A	3	129

ALLEGANY, COUNTY OF.

1831.	Report on petition for a new county from parts of Genesee and,	A	2	105
1831.	Report on petition to change the name of,	A	2	128
1831.	Report on petition to reduce the elections in, to one day,	A	4	359
1831.	Report on petition to raise money to build a bridge across Genesee river,	A	4	285
1833.	Report on petition to authorize the board of supervisors of, to raise money to build a bridge across Genesee river, in the town of Hume,	A	4	256
1837.	Petition of inhabitants of, for an investigation into the malpractices of banks, and remonstrating against the chartering any bank bank to be located in said county,	A	2	130
1837.	Petition of inhabitants of, for an extension of the banking system, &c.,	A	3	195
1837.	Petition of inhabitants of, for a bank at Cuba,	A	3	200
1839.	Report on petition for a new county from parts of Genesee and,	A	6	393
1840.	Report on petition for an investigation of the title of the trustees of the Pulteney estate to certain lands in,	A	6	232
1840.	Report of attorney-general on the same,	A	8	342
1849.	Report for new county from parts of Steuben and,	A	3	136
1855.	Report of select committee in relation to division of,	A	5	141
1857.	Report favorable on petition for a new county from parts of Steuben and,	A	3	157
1858.	Report of select committee on removal of county seat of,	A	1	29

DODGE'S CREEK:

1831.	Report as to declaring it a public highway,	A	4	326

JAIL IN:

1831.	Report on petition to extend the jail limits in,	A	3	221
1840.	Report on petition to raise money to build,	S	4	128
1840.	Report on petition to compel the supervisors to raise money to build,	A	8	332
1848.	Report on petition of inhabitants of, for	A	3	108

POOR-HOUSE:

1832.	Report on petition of Jno. Lloyd for the appointment of commissioners to settle his accounts for building the,	A	3	241

ALLEGANY RESERVATION.

1846.	Message of governor relative to Indians on,	S	2	57

ALLEGANY RIVER.

1832.	Report on petition for a ferry across the,	A	2	151
1834.	Resolution relative to the improvement of the navigation of, from Pittsburgh, Pa., to Olean,	S	1	48

ALLEGANY RIVER—*continued.*

		Doc.	Vol.	No.
1836.	Communication from B. Chamberlain in relation to the navigation of,	S	2	76
1838.	Report relative to the continuation of the Erie canal to the,	A	5	243
1858.	Report relative to a bridge across,	A	3	75

ALLEN, AUGUSTUS.

1858.	Report on petition for relief of,	A	3	59

ALLEN, DOTY, AND OTHERS.

1831.	Report on petition for the pre-emptive right to certain lands,	A	3	230
1832.	Report of select committee on the same,	A	3	195
1832.	Report of surveyor-general on the same,	A	3	235
1833.	Report of surveyor-general on the same,	A	2	46

ALLEN & HECOX.

1831.	Report on petition for extra compensation for work done on the Oswego canal,	S	1	42
1841.	Report of committee on canals on the same,	S	1	57

ALLEN, HIRAM.

1854.	Report on petition of,	A	2	73
1855.	Report of commissioners on claims on petition of,	A	2	34

ALLEN, ISAAC, AND OTHERS.

1832.	Report on petition for compensation for damages to their lands by the Erie canal,	A	2	119
1833.	Report of the committee on claims on the same,	A	4	261
1834.	Report of the committee on canals on the same,	A	2	67

ALLEN, LEWIS F., AND OTHERS.

1841.	*See* City Bank of Buffalo,	A	7	290

ALLEN, NECHO.

1831.	Report on petition relative to a ferry across Lake Champlain,	A	3	220

ALMOND, TOWN OF.

1832.	Report on petition for a new town from part of,	A	3	266
1840.	Report on petition to annex part of, to the town of Burns,	A	8	316

ALVORD, HARVEY, AND OTHERS.

1845.	Report of committee on claims on bill from the assembly for the relief of,	S	3	98

AMENDMENTS OF THE CONSTITUTION, *see* Constitution.

AMERICAN AND FOREIGN BIBLE SOCIETY.

1845.	Report of the minority of the committee on charitable and religious societies on the petitions for incorporating,	A	3	39
1845.	Report of a majority of committee on same,	A	3	38

AMERICAN ART UNION, *see* New York.

AMERICAN ASSOCIATION FOR THE ADVANCEMENT OF SCIENCE, *see* New York.

AMERICAN COLONIZATION SOCIETY, *see* Colonization Society, American.

		Doc.	Vol.	No.
	AMERICAN GEOGRAPAHICAL AND STATISTICAL SOCIETY, *see* New York.			
	AMERICAN GEOLOGICAL SOCIETY, *see* Geological Society, American.			
	AMERICAN INDEPENDENCE.			
1853.	Message of the governor in relation to a convention at Philadelphia, respecting the erection of a monument in Independence Square, ...	A	4	89
1853.	Report of select committee on reference of governor's message, relative to a memorial, commemorative of,.................	A	4	102
	AMERICAN INSTITUTE, *see* New York.			
	AMERICAN SEAMEN'S FRIEND SOCIETY, *see* New York.			
	AMERICAN TRACT SOCIETY.			
1847.	Report of officers and directors of, relative to certain operations,	A	2	75
	AMHERST AND CLARENCE, TOWNS OF.			
1831.	Report concerning the burying grounds in the, ...	A	4	291
	AMPHLETT, JOHN, AND ISAAC J. FORBES.			
1837.	Report on petition to confirm their title to certain land, ...	A	4	319
	AMSDEN, AMORY, *see* Canals.			
	AMSDEN, MANLEY, AND OTHERS.			
1838.	Report on petition for compensation for damages to their lands by the Troy dam, ...	S	2	40
	AMSDEN HYDROSATIC SCALE, *see* Canals.			
	AMSTERDAM BRIDGE COMPANY.			
1830.	Statement of the affairs of the, ...	S	1	25
	AMSTERDAM, TOWN OF.			
1838.	Report on petition to extend the time for the collection of taxes in, ...	A	3	67
	ANATOMY, STUDY OF.			
1832.	Report on petition for legal provision for supplying medical schools with subjects for the,..............................	A	3	246
1838.	Report on petition of citizens of Troy relative to,..............	A	6	301
	ANDERSON, HOLBROOK.			
1835.	Report on petition of, for a law authorizing John Johnson, an Indian, to convey to him certain land, ...	A	2	75
	ANDREWS, JAMES M., *see* Chancery, clerk in.			
	ANDREWS, MARCUS.			
1830.	A sub-contractor on the Erie canal, report on petition for relief,	A	4	355
	ANGELICA, TOWN OF.			
1832.	Report on petition for a new town from part of, ...	A	3	266

		Doc.	Vol.	No.
	ANTHONY AND FIERO.			
1850.	Report on claim,	A	3	33
	ANTHONY, MICHAEL.			
1830.	Report on petition of, for compensation for damages done by the army of the United States upon a farm,	A	2	89
1832.	Report on petition of, for compensation for damages done by the army of the United States upon a farm,	A	2	89
1841.	Report on petition of, for compensation for damages done by the army of the United States upon a farm,	A	1	20
	ANTIQUARIAN AND HISTORICAL COLLECTIONS, *see* Natural History; Regents of the University.			
	ANTIQUARIAN SOCIETY OF MASSACHUSETTS.			
1839.	Circular from,	A	3	118
	ANTI-RENT, *see* Albany, City of; Landlord and Tenant.			
	APPEALS, COURT OF, *see* Court of Appeals.			
	APPORTIONMENT.			
1842.	[Ex. Sess.] Act of congress for the apportionment of representatives, &c.,	A	7	195
1842.	[Ex. Sess.] Resolutions protesting against action of congress on the subject of apportioning representatives, &c.,	A	7	196
1846.	Report of attorney-general on,	A	4	122
1846.	Report of minority of committee on,	A	6	203
1847.	Report on bill to district state,	S	3	106
1856.	Communication from attorney-general relative to ratio of representations in county divisions,	S	2	68
1857.	Answer of the attorney-general to resolutions relative to districting the state,	A	1	9
1857.	Report of minority of select committee in relation to districting the state,	S	3	98
1858.	Law of 1857, opinion of attorney-general relative to,	A	1	21
1858.	Of members of assembly, report of majority on bill to amend laws of 1857 relative to,	A	4	93
1858.	Of members of assembly, report of a minority (Mr. Barnes), on bill to amend laws of 1857, relative to,	A	4	105
1858.	Of members of assembly, report of minority (Mr. Fullerton), on same,	A	4	106
	APPRAISERS OF CANAL DAMAGES, *see* Canal Appraisers.			
	APPRENTICES.			
1832.	Report on ameliorating the condition of,	A	4	308
	AQUEDUCT, CROTON, *see* New York.			
	ARCULARIUS, HENRY, *see* Commissary-General.			
	ARKANSAS, STATE OF.			
1838.	Resolution of the legislature relative to the public lands,	A	6	365
	ARLINGTON, TOWN OF.			
1832.	Report on petition to change the name of the,	S	1	43
	ARMS AND MILITARY STORES.			
1842.	Message of governor relative to,	S	2	27

		Doc.	Vol.	No.
	ARMSTRONG, JABIN.			
1857.	Report of committee on claims favorable on petition of, for damages by diversion of water from mill,	A	1	24
	ARNOTT, JOHN, AND LYMAN COVELL.			
1840.	Report on petition for compensation for the loss of their boat on the Erie canal,	S	1	15
	ARSENALS, STATE.			
1838.	Governor's message concerning the breaking open of the, at Watertown, Elizabethtown and Batavia,	A	5	217
1838.	Report on same,	A	5	241
1838.	Report of commissary-general relative to the arms taken from the,	A	6	308
1849.	Report of commissary-general respecting,	A	5	238
	BUFFALO:			
1840.	Report on petition for an,	A	6	251
	CANANDAIGUA:			
1833.	Report on petition for the sale of the,	A	4	328
	MALONE:			
1851.	Report of committee on sale of lot at,	S	1	14
	NEW YORK:			
1833.	Report on petition for an appropriation for certain improvements to the,	A	2	64
1834.	Removal of, and the erection of a new one, report of Mr. Ruggles on the subject,	A	4	389
1835.	Removal of, and the erection of a new one, report of Mr. Judd on the subject,	A	4	372
1840.	Erection of a new one, report of Mr. Overbagh relative to the,	A	4	148
1841.	Erection of a new one, report of commissary-general relative to the,	A	2	18
1831.	Report on petition for a release of a part of the lot, to the lying-in hospital,	A	3	275
1833.	Report on petition for a release of a part of the lot, to the corporation, &c.,	A	4	248, 275
1845.	Resolutions relative to new,	A	3	62
1848.	Report of commissioners of land office as to cost of completing,	S	2	54
1849.	Communication from attorney-general respecting sale to corporation of the city of New York of the site of,	A	3	143
1849.	Communication from attorney-general in answer to resolution of assembly respecting sale of site of, to the corporationof New York,	A	5	211
1849.	Report of committee to superintend erection of,	A	1	29
1849.	Report of select committee of New York delegation against bill relative to,	A	3	137
1856.	Sale of,	A	5	194
	PEKIN:			
1841.	Report on petition for the location of an,	A	6	196
	ARTILLERY.			
	4th BRIGADE:			
1832.	Report on petition for a change in one of the companies of said brigade,	A	3	320
	9th BRIGADE:			
1831.	Report on petition to reduce the number of parades, &c.,	A	2	182
	1st REGIMENT OF HORSE:			
1835.	Report on petition for certain exemptions,	A	2	112

Year	Subject	Doc.	Vol.	No.
	ASHES, POT AND PEARL.			
1845.	Report of committee on manufactures adverse to the bill concerning inspectors of, &c.,	S	2	69
	ASHFORD, TOWN OF.			
1830.	Report concerning town officers of the,	A	4	411
	ASIATIC CHOLERA, *see* Cholera.			
	ASSEMBLY.			
1833.	Confidential journal of proceedings of, in relation to the application for the Tompkins County Bank,	A	3	143
1834.	Rules and orders of the,	A	1	7
1835.	do	A	1	3
1836.	do	A	1	10
1837.	do	A	1	17
1837.	Report of committee appointed to revise rules and orders,	A	1	11
1839.	do do do	A	3	156
1840.	do do do	A	1	1
1835.	Rule 38th, report of committee on the judiciary relative to amending,	A	1	62
1838.	Rule 23d, report on proposed amendments to,	A	6	336
1842.	Official list of members,	A	1	3
1842.	Rules and orders, report of select committee on,	A	1	6
1842.	Committees of,	A	1	8
1842.	Members, boarding-houses, &c.,	A	1	9
1842.	General orders of,	A	5	103
1842.	General orders of,	A	7	170
1843.	Official list of members of,	A	1	1
1843.	Standing committees of,	A	1	5
1843.	General orders,	A	3	47
1844.	Official list of members of,	A	1	1
1844.	Standing committees of,	A	1	8
1844.	Members and officers of,	A	1	11
1844.	General orders,	A	5	104
1844.	General orders	A	6	144
1845.	Official list of members of,	A	1	1
1845.	Rules and orders of,	A	1	5
1845.	Standing committees of,	A	1	13
1845.	List of officers and members of the house,	A	1	15
1845.	General orders of,	A	5	166
1845.	Statistics of,	A	6	205
1845.	General orders of,	A	6	223
1846.	Official list of members of,	A	1	1
1846.	Rules and orders of,	A	1	2
1846.	Standing committees of,	A	1	11
1846.	List of members and officers of,	A	1	15
1846.	Report of attorney-general as to right of county judge to take testimony relative to contested seats in,	A	2	30
1846.	Annual report of statistics of,	A	6	205
1847.	Official list of members of,	A	1	1
1847.	Standing committees of,	A	1	7
1847.	List of members and officers of, with residence, &c.,	A	1	8
1847.	General orders of, resolution relative to printing,	A	4	101
1847.	List of members and officers of, with statement of bills and business of,	A	7	184
1848.	Official list of members of,	A	1	1
1848.	Rules and orders of (1847),	A	1	2
1848.	Standing committees of,	A	1	8
1848.	Rules and orders of (1848),	A	1	6
1848.	List of members and officers of,	A	1	9

ASSEMBLY—*continued.*

Year	Subject	Doc.	Vol.	No.
1848.	58th rule of,	A	2	24
1848.	General orders and business of,	A	5	135
1848.	Statistics of,	A	5	188
1848.	Assault on member of, report as to,	A	6	213
1849.	Official list of members of,	A	1	1
1849.	Rules and orders of last,	A	1	3
1849.	Rules and orders of present,	A	1	4
1849.	Standing and select committees of,	A	1	9
1849.	Members and officers of, &c.,	A	1	11
1849.	Members and officers of, with place of birth, &c.,	A	3	126
1849.	Report relative to select committees,	A	8	261
1850.	Official list of members, &c.,	A	1	3
1850.	Rules and orders of,	A	1	12
1850.	Committees, select,	A	3	21
1850.	Standing committees of,	A	4	54
1850.	Standing committees of,	A	4	55
1850.	Members and officers, with place of residence, &c.,	A	4	57
1850.	General orders,	A	5	77
1850.	General orders,	A	5	83
1850.	Report of attorney-general as to pay of committees during recess,	A	5	110
1851.	List of members, &c.,	A	1	1
1851.	Rules and orders of last,	A	1	3
1851.	Standing committees,	A	1	5
1851.	Rules and orders adopted,	A	1	14
1851.	General orders,	A	3	81
1851.	Standing committees,	A	5	141
1851.	Rules and orders, extra session,	A	5	142
1851.	Members and officers of, &c.,	A	3	85
1852.	List of members, &c.,	A	1	2
1852.	Rules and orders of,	A	1	12
1852.	Standing committees of,	A	1	5
1852.	List of members and officers of, with residences, &c.,	A	1	13
1852.	Joint rules of, and senate,	A	2	36
1852.	General orders of,	A	2	52
1852.	List of bills, in committee of the whole, and unacted on March 20, 1852,	A	3	95
1852.	See report of comptroller in answer to resolution of assembly in relation to refunding to the clerk of, amount advanced for postage stamps, &c.,	A	5	124
1852.	List of members, with places of birth, &c.,	A	7	128
1853.	Members of, with counties and districts,	A	1	2
1853.	Rules and order of, as amended,	A	1	7
1853.	List of officers of, with county represented, place of residence, &c.,	A	1	9
1853.	Standing committees of,	A	1	11
1853.	Rules and orders as finally adopted January 12, 1853,	A	1	12
1853.	Joint rules of, and senate, as amended by the senate,	A	2	17
1853.	Members of, with officers, place of birth, &c.,	A	2	41
1854.	Members of,	A	1	1
1854.	Rules and orders of,	A	1	2, 6
1854.	Standing committees of,	A	1	8
1854.	Members and officers of, residences, &c.,	A	1	13
1854.	Calendar of bills,	A	2	68
1854.	Calendar of bills,	A	3	109
1854.	Statistics of, relative to,	A	3	124
1855.	Rules and orders of, for 1855,	A	1	2, 6
1855.	Committees of,	A	1	9
1855.	Members and officers of, with boarding places,	A	1	24
1855.	Calendar of business pending in,	A	2	54
1856.	Members of, list of seventy-ninth session,	A	1	2
1856.	Rules of,	A	1	5
1856.	List of members,	A	1	6

ASSEMBLY—*continued.*

Year	Subject	Doc.	Vol.	No.
1856.	Report of select committee on rules of,	A	3	13
1856.	Report in relation to sick members,	A	4	179
1856.	Members and officers, statistics relating to,	A	5	190
1857.	Report of select committee on rules of,	A	1	6
1857.	Rules and orders of,	A	1	7, 24
1857.	Rules and orders of,	A	1	25
1857.	Standing and select committees of the,	A	1	8, 13
1857.	Members, officers and reporters of the,	A	1	11
1857.	Library of, report of librarian relative to copies of Revised Statutes in,	A	1	33
1857.	Joint rules of the senate, for 1857,	A	1	34
1857.	Clerk of, report of, in reply to resolution relative to printing and distribution of documents,	A	2	115
1857.	Members and officers of, statistical list of,	A	3	192
1858.	List of committees,	A	1	8
1858.	Rules and orders of, adopted February 5, 1858,	A	1	11
1858.	List of members of,	A	1	14
1858.	Members of, opinion of attorney-general as to residence and election of,	A	3	54
1858.	Report of majority on bill to amend laws of 1857, relative to apportionment of members of,	A	4	93
1858.	Minority report (Mr. Barnes), on same,	A	4	105
1858.	Minority report (Mr. Fullerton), on same,	A	4	106
1858.	Members and officers of, statistical list of,	A	4	142

For JOINT RULES OF, AND SENATE, *see* Legislature.

ASSEMBLY CHAMBER.

Year	Subject	Doc.	Vol.	No.
1832.	Report relative to furnishing it with curtains,	A	3	274
1832.	Report of secretary of state relative to the archives of the,	A	4	302
1834.	Report on petition of Jno. Torrey in relation to heating and ventilating the,	A	4	388
1835.	Report on petition of Jno. Torrey in relation to heating and ventilating the,	A	5	399
1843.	Report of committee on public printing, on the report of select committee on the arrangement of the seats in the same,	A	2	27
1843.	Report of a majority of select committee on the arrangement of seats in same,	A	3	55
1849.	Report of select committee on cause of damp atmosphere within,	A	2	44
1850.	Report of committee on expiring laws relative to granting use of, to Gerrit Smith,	A	5	112

ASSEMBLY DISTRICT COURTS.

Year	Subject	Doc.	Vol.	No.
1858.	Report on bill to establish,	A	4	110

ASSEMBLY DISTRICTS.

Year	Subject	Doc.	Vol.	No.
1849.	Report of committee on judiciary, relative to setting off portions of towns in one, to other towns in other districts,	A	3	138

ASSESSMENT LAWS, *see* Taxes, &c.

Year	Subject	Doc.	Vol.	No.
1842.	Report on the memorial of Peter A. Jay and others, of New York, relative to, and accompanying documents,	S	4	100
1850.	Report on governor's message relative to, and collection of taxes,	S	1	19
1851.	Report of committee,	S	2	44
1858.	Reports of railroad companies of the state relative to,	S	2	68
1858.	Report of comptroller relative to,	S	2	95
1858.	Opinion of attorney-general on law of 1857,	A	1	21

ASSESSORS.

Year	Subject	Doc.	Vol.	No.
1838.	Report on petition for the election of, for 3 years, &c.,	A	6	357
1839.	Report on petition for the election of, for 3 years, &c.,	A	3	79

		Doc.	Vol.	No.
	ASSESSORS—*continued.*			
1840.	Report on petition to amend the law relative to the duties and oath of,	A	5	170
	ASSISTANT REGISTER IN CHANCERY, *see* Chancery.			
	ASSOCIATIONS FOR BANKING, *see* Banks—General Banking Law.			
	ASSOCIATIONS, INDUSTRIAL, *see* Industrial Associations.			
	ASTOR, JOHN JACOB.			
1830.	Communication from the attorney-general relative to the trial of one of the causes on the claim of, to certain lands in Putnam and Dutchess,	S	1	5
1830.	Opinion of the Supreme Court of the United States in relation to the same,	S	4	347
1830.	Report of comptroller of amount paid counsel in defending the titles of certain persons to lands derived from the state, against the claim of,	A	4	380
1831.	Communication from the attorney-general in relation to the claim of,	S	1	2
1831.	Communication from Smith Thompson relative to the trial of one of the causes on the claim of,	S	1	24
1831.	Report of attorney-general on the communication from Smith Thompson,	S	1	28
1831.	Memorial of Edmund C. Genet relative to the claim of,	S	1	29
1831.	Memorial of Edmund C. Genet relative to the claim of,	S	1	77
1832.	Communication from the attorney-general in relation to the claims of,	A	2	149
1832.	Communication from the comptroller relative to the issue of stock to,	A	3	205
1832.	Report of select committee on the communication from the comptroller,	S	2	96
	ASTOR LIBRARY, *see* New York.			
	ASTRONOMICAL OBSERVATORY, NEW YORK, *see* New York.			
	ATHENS AND CATSKILL TURNPIKE COMPANY.			
1832.	Report on petition to incorporate the,	A	2	155
	ATHENS, TOWN OF.			
1838.	Report on petition from, relative to fishing in Murderer's creek in,	A	3	62
	ATHOL AND WARRENSBURGH, TOWNS OF.			
1833.	Report on petition for aid to build a bridge across the Hudson river between,	A	3	157
1833.	Report of committee on finance on the same,	S	2	117
1834.	Report of committee on roads and bridges on the same,	A	3	168
1835.	Report of committee on roads and bridges on the same,	A	2	126
	ATKINSON, T. F. G. AND W. (Aliens.)			
1830.	Report on petition to sell and convey real estate,	A	1	44
	ATLANTIC STEAM NAVIGATION COMPANY.			
1845.	Report of committee on trade and manufactures on petition of,	A	6	232
	ATLAS AND MAP OF THE STATE.			
1830.	Report of surveyor-general relative to the publication of an,	A	2	189
1857.	Report of state engineer and surveyor, in reply to resolution relative to,	A	2	114

		Doc.	Vol.	No.
	ATLAS, STONE & CLARK'S.			
1839.	Report on petition for aid to their,	A	4	168
	ATTACHMENTS.			
1839.	Against absconding, concealed and non-resident debtors, report on a resolution to amend the law relative to,	A	5	302
	ATTORNEY-GENERAL.			
	GREENE C. BRONSON:			
1830.	Communication from, relative to the boundary line between this State and New Jersey,	S	1	4
1830.	Communication from, in relation to the trials on the Astor claim,	S	1	5
1830.	Report of, on bill concerning Wm. P. Perce, a debtor imprisoned at the suit of the people of this state,	A	2	193
1830.	Report of, on the law regulating the practice of physic and surgery,	A	2	198
1830.	Report of, on petition of Gideon Castle,	A	3	233
1830.	Report of, on bill to divide the town of Huntington,	A	4	392
1830.	Report of, on a resolution of assembly as to the constitutionality of increasing the rates of toll on the canals, and the duties on salt and goods sold at auction,	S	4	344
1830.	Report of, on the charges against the Grand Chapter of Free-masons,	A	4	417
1831.	Communication from, relative to the suit instituted by New Jersey on the boundary question,	A	1	3
1831.	Report on petition of Zebulon Barker and others,	A	2	73
1831.	Report on petition of S. Barnum relative to the Neversink Navigation Company,	A	2	188
1831.	Report on petition of Abijah Hunt,	A	4	300
1831.	Report on bill concerning Richmond county,	A	3	225
1831.	Communication from, in relation to the Astor claim,	S	1	2
1831.	Report of, on the letter of Smith Thompson,	S	1	28
1832.	Report concerning the Cayuga marshes,	A	1	6
1832.	Communication from, in relation to the Astor claim,	A	2	149
1832.	Report of, concerning lotteries,	A	4	292
1832.	Report of, relative to the power of the legislature over corporations,	S	1	8
1832.	Report of, relative to the salaries of the bank commissioners,	S	1	9
1832.	Report of, relative to grants of land under water,	S	1	45
1832.	Report of, relative to the Astor claim,	S	2	54
1832.	Report of, relative to taxes upon incorporated companies,	S	2	103
1833.	Report of, relative to repealing charters by two-thirds, or a majority vote,	S	1	8
1833.	Report of, relative to the assessment of taxes on incorporated companies,	S	1	9
1833.	Report of, relative to the election and qualification of justices of the peace,	S	1	10
1833.	Report of, on the eligibility of members of the legislature as senators in congress,	S	1	18
1833.	Report of, relative to the exemption of real estate of corporations from taxation,	S	1	33
1833.	Report of, on a resolution to examine and report whether any further legislation is requisite to protect the titles and secure the public property constituting the canals,	A	1	10
1833.	Report of, relative to the common school fund lands at Fort Covington,	A	2	41
1833.	Report of, concerning lotteries,	A	1	13
1833.	Report of, on petition of J. Chapman,	A	2	99
1833.	Report of, on petition of J. A. Farrell,	A	3	184
1833.	Report of, on petition of Lucas Elmendorf, and the first South-western Turnpike Company,	A	3	101
1833.	Report of, on bill for the election of a recorder in Cazenovia,	A	3	227

ATTORNEY GENERAL—*continued.*

Year	Report	Doc.	Vol.	No.
1833.	Report of, on petition of the president of the Neversink Navigation Company,	A	4	262
1833.	Report of, on increasing the jurisdiction of circuit judges,	A	4	293
1833.	Report of, on vacancies in the office of justices of the peace,	A	4	300
1834.	Report of, on petition of Reuben Wells,	A	2	53
1834.	Report of, relative to ferries,	A	2	61
1834.	Report of, relative to the suit of Alvah Beebe against the speaker of the last house of assembly,	A	3	135
1834.	Report of, relative to the taxation of debts owing to the Connecticut school fund,	A	3	137
1834.	Report of, on petition of Ephraim Bogardus,	A	3	156
1834.	Report of, on petition of William Gilliland,	A	4	285
1834.	Report of, relative to the Montezuma Turnpike Bridge Company,	A	4	342
1834.	Report of, on bill for the relief of Enos Stone and others,	A	4	381
1834.	Report of, relative to the proof of wills, executors and administrators, guardians and wards, and surrogates' courts,	S	7	118
1834.	Report of, on bill to amend the charter of the city of Albany,	S	2	123
1835.	Report of, relative to incorporations for manufacturing purposes,	S	1	4
1835.	Report of, relative to the contracts for the labor of convicts in the state prisons,	A	2	106
1835.	Report of, on petition of Samuel Kelly and others,	A	3	234
1835.	Report of, on petition of E. Smith Sweet,	A	3	262
1835.	Report of, concerning the New York and Harlem Railroad Company,	A	4	329

SAMUEL BEARDSLEY:

Year	Report	Doc.	Vol.	No.
1836.	Report of, on petition of Archibald Campbell,	S	2	108
1836.	Report of, relative to the Farmers' Fire Insurance and Loan Company,	A	4	311
1837.	Report of, on the bill authorizing county judges to inspect turnpike roads, and to locate gates on,	S	2	47
1837.	Report of, on petition for a new county from parts of Madison, Otsego and Chenango,	A	2	131
1837.	Report of, on bill to authorize the business of banking,	A	4	303
1837.	Report of, in relation to limited partnerships,	A	4	304
1838.	Report of, in relation to the Onondaga salt springs,	S	2	60
1838.	Report of, on petition of Isaac Brown, Jr.,	A	3	145
1838.	Report of, on petition of John Shirland,	A	5	272
1839.	Report in relation to the reward for the arrest of Thomas Rector,	A	2	38
1839.	Report of, relative to the bail of Wm. Van Nortwicke,	A	3	123

WILLIS HALL:

Year	Report	Doc.	Vol.	No.
1839.	Report of, in relation to the erection of new counties from contiguous territory lying in different senate districts,	A	4	227
1840.	Report of, on petition of Jacob Vanderheyden,	A	4	149
1840.	Report of, relative to the title of the trustees of the Pulteney estate to lands in Allegany and Steuben,	A	8	342
1841.	Report of, on petition of the widow and heirs of Eliphalet Ackley,	S	1	29
1841.	Report on petition of William Boggs and others,	S	1	38
1841.	Report of, relative to assessing lands ceded to the United States,	A	5	145
1841.	Report of, relative to the Phœnix Bank,	A	6	236
1841.	Report of, on petition of Janet Hay, or McAndrew and others, for escheated land,	A	7	268

GEORGE P. BARKER:

Year	Report	Doc.	Vol.	No.
1843.	Report on a resolution of the assembly on the petition of P. Maine,	A	3	58
1843.	Report on a resolution of the assembly in relation to state prison contracts,	A	5	169
1844.	Report of, of the amount of printing done for his office,	S	2	68
1844.	Report of, in answer to a resolution of the assembly of January 27, 1844,	A	3	48

ATTORNEY GENERAL—*continued.*

Year	Subject	Doc.	Vol.	No.
1844.	Report of, in answer to a resolution of the assembly of February 10, relative to the manufacture of ingrain and Brussels carpeting,	A	3	75
1844.	Report of, in answer to a resolution of the assembly of March 19, 1844, relative to the commencement of a suit against some person holding land by deed or contract from the heirs or trustees of the Pulteney estate,	A	6	145
1844.	Report of, on the act for the relief of Orris Hamilton,	S	1	14
1845.	Report of, in answer to a resolution,	A	5	159
1845.	Report of, in answer to a resolution relative to the New York and Erie Railroad Company,	A	6	204
1845.	Report of, in answer to a resolution referring the petition of John Roof,	A	7	240
1845.	Report of, on the petition of John H. T. Smith,	S	1	20
1845.	Report of, on the bill from the assembly, entitled an act to amend an act entitled an act relative to incorporations for manufacturing purposes, passed March 22, 1811,	S	2	59
1845.	Report of, on the petition of John Morin and others, heirs of Charles McKnight, deceased,	S	2	63
1845.	Report of, on the bill entitled an act to erect the county of Schuyler, &c.,	S	2	66
	JOHN VAN BUREN:			
1846.	Report of comptroller relative to moneys paid to, and adjutant-general,	S	1	28
1846.	Report of, amount received by him for extra services,	S	1	36
1846.	Report of comptroller, relative to extra allowances made to,	S	2	63
1846.	Report of, claims against the state for extra services,	S	3	95
1846.	Report of comptroller relative to payments to, for extra services,	S	3	102
1846.	Report of, in answer to a resolution of the assembly of February 17th,	A	4	111
1846.	Report of, in answer to a resolution relative to apportionment of members of the convention,	A	4	122
1846.	Report of, in answer to a resolution relative to the petition of A. Campbell and others,	A	5	161
1846.	Report of, in answer to a resolution of the 26th of March,	A	5	167
1846.	Report of, on petition of citizens of Troy,	A	5	167
1846.	Report of, in answer to a resolution of the 26th of March,	A	5	196
1846.	Report of committee of conference on bill relating to,	A	6	209
	AMBROSE L. JORDAN:			
1847.	Report of, in answer to a resolution,	S	1	28
1847.	Communication from, relative to power of the legislature to appoint committee to investigate affairs of free banks,	A	4	106
1848.	Report of, as to right of county judge to take testimony relative to contested seats in assembly,	A	2	30
1848.	Report of, as to constitutionality of a general act of appropriation,	A	2	52
1848.	Report of, as to claim of S. G. Gage,	A	3	118
1848.	Report of, relative to the Cayuga Bridge Company,	A	5	140
1848.	Report of, on petition of first Christian society of Oneida Indians,	S	2	35
1848.	Communication from, in relation to location of Hudson railroad through state lands at Sing Sing,	S	2	64
1849.	Communication recommending measures in relation to the introduction of disease and pauperism from foreign countries,	S	3	76
1849.	Report of, on the constitutionality of erecting the new counties of Patterson and Unadilla, from parts of different senate and assembly districts,	A	3	123
1849.	Report of, relative to a bridge in the town of Day,	A	3	181
1849.	Communication from, relative to marine hospital fund,	A	5	206
1849.	Communication from, respecting sale of site of old arsenal to corporation of New York,	A	5	211

ATTORNEY GENERAL—*continued.*

Year	Entry	Doc.	Vol.	No.
	LEVI S. CHATFIELD:			
1850.	Report in relation to savings' banks,	A	3	28
1850.	Report on non-resident lands,	A	3	39
1850.	Report on division, alteration and erection of towns and counties,	A	5	82
1850.	Report on law for preserving the public health,	A	5	126
1850.	Report on free school law,	A	5	107
1850.	Report as to pay of committees during recess,	A	5	110
1850.	Report on claim of W. W. Niles,	S	2	61
1850.	Report on manorial suits,	S	1	26
1851.	Report on enlargement of state canals,	S	3	68
1851.	Report on manorial lands,	S	2	27
1851.	Communication in relation to commissioners of the canal fund,	A	2	30
1851.	Report as to attempt at bribing,	A	6	159
1852.	*See* report of secretary of state respecting books purchased by the,	A	5	120
	OGDEN HOFFMAN:			
1853.	Report of the, in answer to a resolution of last year respecting clerks in his office,	S	2	61
1853.	Report of the treasurer in relation to fees paid into the treasury since January 1st, 1848, by the,	A	2	16
1853.	Report of the, in answer to a resolution of the assembly of February 18, 1853, concerning titles to manorial lands,	A	3	59
1853.	Report in answer to a resolution in relation to a certain note,	A	4	85
1853.	Report of, in reference to claim of David Jones,	A	5	118
1854.	Communication from, relative to certain acts,	A	3	78
1854.	Report of fees paid in by,	S	1	10
1854.	Report of fees paid in by,	S	1	28
1854.	Opinion of, relative to toll bridge, &c.,	S	2	87
1854.	Opinion of, relative to grants of land under water,	A	3	105
1854.	Opinion of, relative to judgments against state prison agents,	A	3	121
1854.	Opinion of, relative to regulation of ferries,	A	4	131
1855.	Communication from, in answer to resolution,	S	1	21
1855.	Communication from, in relation to suit against Geo. W. Newell,	A	5	122
1855.	Opinion of, as to judgments against state prison agents,	A	2	28
1855.	Claim of Harrison Albright,	A	5	124
	STEPHEN B. CUSHING:			
1856.	Communication from,	A	4	153
1856.	Communication from,	A	5	186
1856.	Communication from, relative to ratio of representation in county divisions,	S	2	68
1857.	Reply of, relative to power of appointment,	S	2	71
1857.	Reply of, to resolution inquiring what statutes are in force regulating the sale of intoxicating liquor,	A	1	39
1857.	Reply of, to resolution relative to districting the state, &c.,	A	1	9
1857.	Reply of, to resolution relative to suits on canal contracts,	A	1	16
1857.	Communication from the, relative to suits against commissioners of loans,	A	1	19
	LYMAN TREMAIN:			
1858.	Opinion of, relative to assessment law of 1857,	A	1	21
1858.	Opinion of, relative to a certain provision of the constitution,	A	1	22
1858.	Opinion of, relative to the residence and election of members of assembly,	A	3	54
1858.	Report of, relative to the constitutionality of an act to incorporate colleges, &c.,	A	1	41
1858.	Report of, relative to the constitutionality of laws making streams public highways,	A	4	112
1858.	Report of committee on the judiciary, in relation to salary, fees and perquisites of the,	S	3	138

ATTORNEY GENERAL—*continued.*

		Doc.	Vol.	No.
1858.	Communication from, relative to appointment of Metropolitan police,........	S	2	41
1858.	Communication from, in relation to pay of expenses of justices and judges of the supreme court,........	S	2	38
1858.	Communication from, in reference to appointing loan commissioners by governor,........	S	2	47
1858.	Communication from comptroller and, relative to suit of Munson J. Lockwood,........	S	2	85

ATTORNEYS.

1847.	Resolution offered by Mr. Bascom as to fees of, &c.,........	A	1	37

AUBURN STATE PRISON, *see* State Prisons.

AUBURN, VILLAGE OF.

1834.	Report on petition to alter the boundaries of,........	A		234
1834.	St. Peter's church in, report on petition to change the name of,..	S	1	12
1839.	First society of the Methodist Episcopal church in, report on petition to confirm acts and doings of said society,........	A	5	316
1840.	Report on petition of citizens of, for the removal of the dam across Owasco outlet, adjacent to the state prison,........	A	7	301

INSPECTOR OF SOLE LEATHER, *see* Cayuga County.

AUCTION DUTIES.

1832.	To be restored to the general fund, resolution for the same,.....	S	2	70
1832.	To be restored to the general fund, resolution for the same,.....	S	2	100
1833.	Report of secretary of state, relative to the publication of said amendment,........	S	1	14
1833.	Report of committee on the judiciary on the same,........	S	2	45
1834.	Resolution to restore the, to the general fund,........	A	3	131
1835.	Report of secretary of state relative to the publication of said amendment,........	A	1	42
1835.	Report of committee on the judiciary on the same,........	A	1	49
1835.	Resolution and recital relative to the same,........	A	1	59
1834.	Report of comptroller of amount received from,........	A	2	66
1839.	Report of comptroller of amount accrued to the state since the year 1812,........	S	3	76
1830.	Report of attorney-general as to constitutionality of increasing,	S	4	344
1845.	Report of the comptroller relative to,........	A	6	208
1849.	Report of minority of committee on ways and means respecting,	A	3	192
1849.	Report of committee on trade and manufactures, respecting,....	A	5	218

AUCTIONEERS.

1830.	Report on bill respecting sales by,........	A	4	381

AUCTIONEERS IN NEW YORK, *see* New York.

AUCTIONS.

1831.	Report on petition of citizens of Rochester concerning,........	A	2	151
1831.	Report on petition of citizens of Ogdensburgh to regulate sales at,	A	1	12

AUCTIONS, PETTY.

1830.	Report of select committee as to restraining them,........	A	2	72

AUDITOR-GENERAL.

1851.	Report of, on the cost of the militia system,........	S	2	28

AUDITOR OF CANAL DEPARTMENT, *see* Canal Department, Auditor of.

		Doc.	Vol.	No.
	AUGUSTA, TOWN OF.			
1831.	Report on petition of settlers on the school lot in,	A	1	10
	AUGUSTINE, PETER.			
1832.	An Indian, report on petition to sell real estate,	A	2	150
	AURELIUS, TOWN OF.			
1834.	Report on petition of the vestry of St. Paul's church in, to change the name of said corporation,	S	1	12
	AURORA, TOWN OF.			
1837.	Report on petition relative to certain roads in the,	A	2	62
	AUSTIN, EUSEBIUS.			
1830.	Report on petition for aid, to enable him to support an insane son,	A	4	429
	AUSTIN, ORRIN.			
1850.	Report on claim,	S	1	14
	AVERILL, JAMES.			
1834.	Report on petition for compensation for damages by the Erie canal,	A	3	167
	AVERILL, JAMES, AND JACOB H. FAILING.			
1835.	Report of canal board on petition for compensation, for damages by the Erie canal,	A	2	94
1835.	Report of committee on grievances on the same,	A	4	365
	AVERILL, LOUIS, AND OTHERS.			
1847.	Report on petition of,	S	4	114
	AVERILL ORE BED.			
1858.	Report of inspectors of state prisons relative to,	S	2	92
	AVERILL, THOMAS.			
1842.	Report of committee on militia on petition of,	A	7	136
1842.	Report of Mr. S. E. Church on petition of,	A	7	139
1842.	Report of adjutant-general on petition of,	A	7	153
	AVERY, DANIEL. (Commissioner of loans for Cayuga county.)			
1833.	Report on petition of, relative to the sale of certain land,	S	2	75
1834.	Report of committee on claims to the sale of certain land,	S	1	33
1837.	Report of committee on grievances to the sale of certain land,	A	2	152
	AVERY, SAMUEL.			
1858.	Report on claim of,	A	3	63
	AVON, TOWN OF.			
1835.	Report on petition from the, for a modification of the election law,	A	2	119
	AXON, ROBERT.			
1851.	Report of commissioners on petition for damages, in consequence of being thrown from a bridge on Black River canal,	S	1	71

		Doc.	Vol.	No.
	AYLESWORTH, MARCUS.			
1846.	Communication from governor on petition of,	A	6	208

B.

	BABCOCK, B. W.			
1837.	Report on petition for extra allowance for work done on the Chenango canal,	A	3	187
1839.	Report of committee on claims on the same,	A	3	100
	BABCOCK, JOHN C.			
1833.	Report on petition to change the name of his son,	A	2	121
	BABCOCK, JOHN H., AND OTHERS.			
1849.	Report of committee on claims of,	A	1	27
1849.	Report of committee on canals on petition of,	A	3	121
1852.	Report on petition of,	A	2	47
	BABCOCK, LUKE P.			
1856.	Report on petition of,	S	1	13
1856.	Report of canal board on petition of,	S	2	51
	BABCOCK, L. P., AND OTHERS.			
1851.	Report of committee on claims on petition of,	S	3	65
1854.	Report on petition of,	A	3	79
1855.	Report of committee on claims in reference to petition of,	A	3	75
	BABCOCK, S., AND OTHERS.			
1846.	Report of committee on public lands on petition of,	A	3	87
	BABCOCK, VARNUM.			
1847.	Report on petition of,	S	4	126
	BABCOCK, VARNUM M.			
1848.	Report on petition of,	A	2	39
	BACKUS, LEVI S.			
1838.	Report on petition for aid to enable him to furnish educated mutes with a newspaper published by him,	A	5	263
1839.	Report of select committee on the same,	A	3	160
	BACON, HOSEA.			
1858.	Report of committee on claims on petition of,	A	4	103
	BACON, IRA.			
1833.	Report on petition to construct a dam across Genesee river,	A	1	31
	BACON, NATHANIEL, AND OTHERS.			
1833.	Report on petition relative to the last will, &c., of D. Bacon,	A	4	265
	BADGER, SAMUEL, AND OTHERS.			
1830.	Report on petition to build a dam across Susquehannah river,	A	1	60
1841.	Report on petition to extend an act authorizing them to build a dam across Susquehannah river,	A	7	287

		Doc.	Vol.	No.
	BADGER, WILLIAM L.			
1836.	Report on petition to change his name,......................	A	2	105
	BADGLEY, A. T., AND OTHERS.			
1845.	Report committee on grievances on petition of, ...	A	5	179
	BAILEY, BENAJAH P., *see* Robert Land and others.			
	BAILEY, HORACE.			
1843.	Report of committee on canals on his petition,....	A	2	29
	BAILY, ERASTUS.			
1830.	Report on petition for the privilege of erecting mills on the Genesee river, ...	A	4	375
1833.	Report on petition to build a boat lock in Genesee river,.......	A	2	88
	BAINBRIDGE, TOWN OF.			
1843.	Resolution of the annual town meeting of, transmitted by governor, ...	A	5	138
	BAIN, PETER, AND OTHERS.			
1845.	Report of the committee of the land office on petition of,........	A	1	18
	BAKER & CHEESBRO.			
1842.	Report of committee on claims on petition of, for relief,........	S	3	63
	BAKER, BRAYTON & CO.			
1842.	Report of committee on claims on petition of,..................	S	3	63
1843.	Report of committee on claims on petition of,.................	A	3	84
	BAKER, CHARLES, AND OTHERS.			
1831.	Report on petition for damages to their lands by the Champlain canal,..	A	2	158
1833.	Report of committee on claims for damages to their lands by the Champlain canal,..............................	A	2	130
1833.	Report of canal commissioners for damages to their lands by the Champlain canal, ...	S	2	114
1834.	Report of committee on claims for damages to their lands by the Champlain canal, ...	A	2	101
1836.	Report of committee on grievances for damages to their lands by Champlain canal,..............................	A	2	53
1838.	Report of committee on grievances for damages to their lands by the Champlain canal, ...	A	3	65
1839.	Report of committee on grievances for damages to their lands by the Champlain canal, ...	A	2	44
1840.	Report of canal commissioners for damages to their lands by the Champlain canal, ...	A	3	72
	BAKER, HENRY.			
1852.	Report on petition of the representatives of deceased,..........	S	2	64
1854.	Report on petition of representatives of,.....................	S	1	53
1855.	Report of committee on claims on petition of representatives of,..	A	2	45
	BAKER, OLIVER.			
1846.	Report of canal board on petition of,........................	A	4	115

BAKER, WILLIAM. (Canal Commissioner.)

		Doc.	Vol.	No.
1840.	Report on petition for an investigation of the charges against,...	A	4	102

BALCHER AND SCHMIDT.

1851.	Report of committee on ways and means on claim of,..........	A	4	97

BALCOM, LUKE, AND OTHERS.

1837.	Report on petition for extra allowance for work done on the Chenango canal,....................................	A	2	101
1838.	Report of select committee for extra allowance of work done on the Chenango canal,....................................	A	3	134
1839.	Report of committee on claims for extra allowance for work done on the Chenango canal,....................................	A	2	53
1840.	Report of committee on claims for extra allowance for work done on the Chenango canal,....................................	A	4	119

BALCOM, R.

1846.	Report of committee on the judiciary on petition of, relative to the supreme court,....................................	A	3	64

BALDWIN, A. C. & E. T.

1844.	Report of the canal board on the petition of,..................	A	3	43

BALDWIN AND STILLWELL.

1844.	Report on a bill to confirm the acts of,......................	S	2	83

BALDWIN, CALVIN.

1839.	Report on petition for pay for building a bridge over the Hudson river in Warren county,....................................	A	5	298

BALDWIN, CHARLES A., *see* Luke Balcom and others.

BALDWIN, HARVEY.

1850.	Report on petition for dam at Baldwinsville,..................	A	3	47
1856.	Report on petition of, &c.,....................................	S	1	35
1857.	Report on claim of,....................................	S	1	6

BALDWIN, HARVEY, AND OTHERS.

1855.	Report of committee on claims in reference to petition of,......	A	3	76

BALDWINSVILLE.

1835.	Report relative to tolls on the canal around the falls at,........	A	3	232
1836.	Report relative to tolls on the canal around the falls at,........	A	3	141
1836.	Bridge across the Seneca at, report on petition to raise money to build a,....................................	A	3	149
1850.	Report in relation to improvement,..........................	S	3	94

BALDWIN, W., AND OTHERS.

1852.	Report on petition of,....................................	S	2	51

BALDWIN, WILLIAM.

1849.	Report of committee on claims on petition of,.................	A	3	163
1856.	Report on petition of,....................................	S	2	48

BALDWIN, WM. W., AND CATHERINE V. S.

1852.	Report on petition of, for relief,..............................	A	2	79

BALLOT BOXES, GLASS.

Year	Subject	Doc.	Vol.	No.
1857.	Report of committee on grievances in favor of,	A	3	197

BALL, SILAS.

Year	Subject	Doc.	Vol.	No.
1857.	Report of committee on claims favorable on petition of John A. Dodge, attorney of, for payment of interest on protested draft,	A	2	128

BALL, THOMAS, AND MARY.

Year	Subject	Doc.	Vol.	No.
1844.	Report of commissioners of the land office on the petitions of,	A	5	112

BANK COMMISSIONERS.

Year	Subject	Doc.	Vol.	No.
1831.	Annual report of,	A	1	59
1832.	do	A	2	70
1833.	do	A	2	69
1834.	do	A	2	102
1835.	do	A	2	74
1836.	do	A	2	80
1837.	do	A	2	78
1838.	do	A	3	71
1839.	do	A	3	101
1840.	do	A	2	44
1841.	do	A	3	64
1832.	Salaries of, report of attorney-general relative to the payment of the,	S	1	9
1834.	Salaries of, report of committee on petition to increase the salaries of the,	A	1	27
1833.	Report of, in relation to bank dividends,	A	4	252
1833.	Report of, giving the name of stockholders in the several banks, etc.,	A	2	89
1834.	Report of amount of dividends made by the banks under their inspection,	S	1	32
1835.	Report of, relative to unclaimed dividends in banks,	A	2	139
1838.	Report of amount of unredeemed bank notes under $5,	S	1	19
1838.	Report of amount of loans and dividends to stockholders of banks, &c.,	S	2	44
1838.	Communication from, in relation to an error in said report,	S	2	53
1838.	Report of investigation of the Jefferson County, Commercial Bank of Oswego, Livingston County, Chautauque County, Commercial of Buffalo, Bank of Orleans, Wayne and Saratoga County Banks,	A	2	13
1839.	Report of, concerning the Brooklyn Bank,	S	3	84
1839.	Special report of,	A	4	225
1841.	Report of, in relation to the Wayne County Bank, &c.,	A	5	172
1842.	Annual report of,	A	2	29
1842.	Message of governor returning bill appointing John G. Blauvelt,	S	4	83
1843.	Annual report of,	A	2	34
1843.	Report of committee on banks and insurance companies on bill to abolish said office,	A	5	154

BANKING DEPARTMENT OF COMPTROLLER'S OFFICE.

Year	Subject	Doc.	Vol.	No.
1839.	Communication from the comptroller relative to the appointment of a committee to examine the accounts of,	A	4	169
1841.	Report of committe appointed to examine the accounts cf,	A	5	151
1842.	Report of joint select committee appointed to examine accounts of,	A	1	7
1843.	Report in relation to the accounts of the treasurer, and on so much as relates to the banking department,	A	1	13
1843.	Canal department, treasury and, report of joint committee to examine their condition,	A	2	18
1844.	Canal department, treasury and, report of joint committee to examine their condition,	A	1	9

BANKING DEPARTMENT OF COMPTROLLER'S OFFICE—*continued.*

Year	Subject	Doc.	Vol.	No.
1845.	Canal department, treasury and, report of the joint committee to examine their condition,	A	1	4
1846.	Canal department, treasury and, report of joint committee to examine their condition,	A	1	7
1847.	Report of committee of the assembly, appointed to examine accounts of treasurer, and canal and,	A	1	21
1848.	Annual report as to examination of,	A	3	65
1850.	Report of comptroller as to expenses,	A	5	85
1851.	Report of committee to examine accounts,	A	2	23

BANKING DEPARTMENT, SUPERINTENDENT OF.

Year	Subject	Doc.	Vol.	No.
1852.	Annual report of,	A	1	9
1853.	Annual report of,	A	1	6
1853.	Report of committee to examine accounts of,	A	1	8
1854.	Report of, relative to bank at Oswego,	S	1	58
1854.	Report of committee on banks, on communication from,	S	2	96
1854.	Annual report of,	A	1	15
1854.	Annual report of committee to examine accounts of,	A	1	25
1855.	Annual report of,	A	1	10
1855.	Report of committee to examine accounts of treasurer, &c.,	A	1	11
1856.	Annual report of,	A	1	4
1856.	Annual report of committee to examine accounts of,	A	4	173
1857.	Annual report of,	A	1	5
1857.	Report in reply to resolution relative to Lewis County Bank and the bank fund,	A	1	21
1857.	Report in reply to resolution relative to expenses of,	A	3	202
1858.	Report of commissioners to examine securities in, for the fiscal years ending 30th September, 1856 and 1857,	S	1	14
1858.	Report of commissioners to examine securities in, for the fiscal years ending 30th September, 1856 and 1857,	S	2	104
1858.	Annual report of,	A	1	4
1858.	Report in reply to a resolution,	A	1	24
1858.	Communication from, showing withdrawal of securities, &c.,	A	1	38
1858.	Report relative to savings banks,	A	1	39

BANK OF THE UNITED STATES, *see* United States Bank.

BANKRUPT LAW.

Year	Subject	Doc.	Vol.	No.
1840.	Report of committee on the judiciary relative to a,	S	1	24
1840.	Message from the governor transmitting the proceedings of a meetings of citizens of New York in relation to a,	S	3	78
1840.	Resolution offered by Mr. Grout relative to a,	A	4	117
1840.	Report of committee appointed to inquire into the correctness of the Senate Journal of March 21, relative to the passage of the resolutions for a,	S	4	127
1841.	Report of select committee on the subject of a,	A	4	92

BANKS.

Year	Subject	Doc.	Vol.	No.
1832.	List of.	A	3	229
1833.	Memorial of citizens of Utica against incorporating more,	S	2	72
1833.	List of,	A	3	137
1833.	List of,	A	3	207
1834.	List of,	A	2	56
1834.	List of,	A	2	324
1836.	List of,	A	2	66
1836.	Report relative to requiring them to receive bills of all solvent banks in this state in payment of debts, &c.,	A	3	134
1841.	Report on bill to prevent fraudulent practices in the management of,	A	6	214
1841.	Resolution to appoint a committee to inquire whether any of the			

BANKS—*continued.*

Year	Subject	Doc.	Vol.	No.
	banks in Albany or New York have been engaged in creating unnecessary alarm or distrust in the solvency of the,	S	2	48
1842.	Report of committee on, and banking fund,	A	7	187
1845.	Report of committee on, relative to,	S	3	97
1847.	Number and condition of new,	A	7	199
1848.	Report of committee on, respecting so much of governor's message as relates to,	S	1	27
1849.	Report of select committee on so much of governor's message as relates to,	A	3	141
1850.	Report of committee on,	S	1	25
1850.	Majority report of committee on banks and insurance companies on governor's message,	S	2	53
1850.	Minority report on same,	S	2	54
1855.	Report of committee on, in answer to resolution of assembly,	A	2	55
1856.	Act relative to banks, &c.,	S	2	47
1848.	Banking institutions, report of committee on banks, &c., as to formation of,	A	3	70
1853.	Banking privileges, message of the governor returning bill in relation to, with his objections,	A	5	113
1854.	Banking purposes, act to authorize corporations for,	A	4	128
1830.	Charters, report as to what banks have acceded to the provisions of the act renewing their,	A	2	71
1841.	List of, with amount of capital, and the time when their charters will expire,	A	5	184
1841.	Currency and report concerning (Mr. Kelsey),	A	7	301
1847.	Free banks, communication from attorney-general relative to power of the legislature to appoint a committee to investigate affairs of,	A	4	106
1848.	Funds in deposit, report relative to,	A	5	182
1854.	Funds, report of committee on, relative to surplus,	A	2	61
1852.	Loans to, report of commissioners of canal fund relative to,	S	2	81
1855.	Mortgages, report of committee on, in relation to, as a basis for banking,	A	3	70
1837.	Paper money, report relative to reducing the amount of, in circulation and increasing the proportion of metallic currency,	A	4	302
1849.	Public money, report of commissioners of canal fund relative to deposits of, in,	A	1	31
1830.	Public moneys deposited in, comptroller's report on a resolution of assembly relative to,	A	4	382
1839.	State stocks, report on bill allowing banks to deal in,	S	3	87
1846.	State stocks in trust for, report of comptroller relative to,	A	6	202
1837.	Taxation of, for the enlargement of the Erie canal, report on bill,	A	4	316
1830.	Taxes, statement of amount of, paid by,	A	1	32
1835.	Tax on, for highway labor, report on the expediency of a,	A	3	189
1856.	Trust companies, report of committee on, relative to certain,	S	3	101
1857.	Trust companies, report relative to condition of incorporated,	S	4	163

BANK FUND:

Year	Subject	Doc.	Vol.	No.
1842.	Report of committee on, and banks,	A	7	187
1847.	Report as to payments made by banks to,	S	4	145
1848.	Answer of comptroller to resolutions concerning	S	2	41
1849.	Stock of, in the canal department, report of the commissioners of the canal fund as to,	S	2	35
1857.	Report of superintendent of banking department in reply to resolution relative to,	A	1	21

BANKING SYSTEM:

Year	Subject	Doc.	Vol.	No.
1830.	Proposed by Mr. Speaker Root,	A	1	22
1830.	Report thereon,	A	1	26
1832.	Report of committee on banks on the,	A	2	74
1832.	do	S	1	22
1834.	do (Mr. Edmonds),	S	1	108

BANKS—*continued.*

Year	Subject	Doc.	Vol.	No.
1834.	Report of committee on banks on the (Mr. Morris),	A	3	163
1835.	Report of committee on banks on the (Mr. Edmonds),	S	1	27
	CAPITAL, INCORPORATED :			
1832.	Amount of, in the county,	A	1	15
1834.	Amount of, in the state,	A	2	66
1836.	Amount of, in the state,	A	2	66
1836.	Amount of, at different periods,	A	2	102
1834.	Amount of, in the state,	A	1	56
1841.	Amount of, in the state,	A	5	184
1851.	Report of comptroller relative to, and names, &c., of incorporated banks and other corporations,	A	3	87
	DIVIDENDS AND DEPOSITS :			
1838.	Report of bank commissioners relative to dividends,	A	4	252
1834.	Bank commissioners' report of amount of dividends under their inspection,	S	1	32
1834.	Bank commissioners' report of amount of unclaimed,	A	2	139
1852.	Report of commissioners respecting unclaimed,	A	7	127
1852.	Report of select committee in relation to gratuities being given to obtain deposits,	S	3	98
1556.	Report of committee on, relative to payment of interest on deposits, &c.,	S	2	58
1858.	Report of majority relative to unclaimed,	A	4	126
1858.	Report of minority relative to unclaimed,	A	4	140
	GENERAL BANKING LAW :			
1837.	Petition for a,	S	1	10
1837.	Report on petition for a (Mr. Young),	S	2	55
1837.	Report of attorney-general on the constitutionality of the,	A	4	303
1837.	Report of select committee on bill to create,	A	4	318
1838.	Report on the subject of a (Mr. Patterson),	S	2	122
1838.	Report on the subject of a (Mr. Young),	S	2	42
1838.	Report on the subject of a (Mr. Young),	S	2	68
1840.	Resolution offered by Mr. Roosevelt in relation to the associations under the,	A	1	28
1840.	Opinion of the supreme court relative to the constitutionality of the,	A	3	65
1840.	Resolution directing the comptroller to give a full statement of notes delivered to each association for circulation, &c.,	A	1	28
1841.	Associations and individual bankers under the, report giving the names of those who have failed to redeem their notes on demand,	S	2	53
1846.	Report of committee on banks, &c., on bill to amend,	A	3	72
1849.	Report of committee on banks and insurance companies on the propriety of amending, so as to admit the deposits of United States stocks as a basis of circulation,	S	1	22
1849.	Report of committee on banks, &c., relative to re-organization of, whose charters are about expiring under the,	A	3	141
	INVESTIGATION OF :			
1835.	Resolution calling on the governor for any information he may possess in relation to improper practices of banks,	A	1	60
1835.	Interrogatories addressed to banks,	A	2	96
1835.	Report of committee appointed to investigate certain charges against the,	A	3	229
1837.	Resolution to appoint a committee to investigate charges of malpractices of (Cutting),	A	1	34
1837.	Resolution to appoint a committee to investigate charges of malpractices of (Roosevelt),	A	1	42

BANKS—*continued.*

		Doc.	Vol.	No.
1837.	Resolution to appoint a committee, to investigate charges of malpractices of (Cutting),	A	1	46
1837.	Petition of citizens of Allegany for an investigation of,	A	2	130
1837.	Report of select committee appointed to investigate,	A	3	243
1837.	Report of select committee appointed to investigate,	A	4	328

See also Commercial Bank, Albany; Chautauque County Bank; City and Commercial Banks, Buffalo, Erie county; Jefferson County Bank; Brooklyn Bank, Kings county; Bank of Dansville and Livingston County Bank, Livingston county; Dry Dock Company, Manhattan Company, Phenix and Seventh Ward Banks, New York; Oneida County Bank; Orleans County Bank; Sacketts Harbor and Oswego County Banks, Oswego county; Saratoga County Bank, and Wayne County Bank.

NOTES:

		Doc.	Vol.	No.
1835.	Redemption of, at par in New York, report on the subject of the (Mr. Wilkinson),	A	3	189
1836.	Report of amount of their issues on the 1st January, 1836, &c.,	S	1	33
1837.	Resolutions for the redemption of, at par in New York,	A	1	27
1837.	Post, petition to allow them to issue,	A	4	293
1837.	Post, petition to allow them to issue,	A	4	294
1837.	Report on the same,	A	4	309
1838.	Of foreign banks whose charters have expired, report relative to,	A	5	224
1838.	Of foreign banks, report on authorizing the banks of this state to receive the,	A	5	265
1838.	Of specie paying, resolution relative to collecting the revenues in,	A	6	328
1839.	Report relative to extending the circulation of the,	A	4	222
1839.	Report on bill to regulate the value of (Mr. Kellogg),	A	4	223
1840.	Report of minority of committee on petition for the redemption of, at par in New York,	A	4	146
1840.	Report of committee of conference on bill for same object,	A	8	325
1842.	Report of committee on banking, &c., on petitions relative to safety fund circulating, &c.,	A	7	148
1844.	Report of committee on banks, &c., on the bill to compel all banks to redeem their, in the city of New York,	A	5	127
1845.	Report of the comptroller in answer to a resolution of the assembly relative to the issue of registered,	A	5	161
1845.	Par redemptions of, report of the committee on banks, &c., in relation to,	S	3	89
1845.	Report of the comptroller relative to agents for the redemption of, &c.,	S	3	100
1846.	Par redemptions, report of majority of committee on,	A	4	131
1846.	Par redemptions, report of minority of committee on,	A	5	145
1847.	Report as to asking issues of,	S	4	123
1848.	Petition for redemption of, in New York,	A	3	56
1848.	Petition for redemption of, in New York,	A	3	86
1848.	Reports as to issues of,	A	3	91
1848.	Report as to limiting issues of,	A	3	116
1850.	Report in relation to redemption of,	A	8	185
1851.	Report in relation to destruction of,	A	5	138
1853.	Report of committee on banks and insurance companies, on petitions praying for an enlargement of the basis of circulation,	A	2	46

SAFETY FUND:

		Doc.	Vol.	No.
1830.	Report in relation to the expediency of amending the law relative to,	A	2	129
1831.	Report relative to enlarging the powers of the comptroller relative to,	S	1	36
1832.	Memorial of the New York banks relative to the investment of the,	S	1	55
1832.	Report on the same,	S	2	71
1832.	Report of the comptroller relative to the disposition of the,	S	1	23

BANKS—*continued.*

Year	Subject	Doc.	Vol.	No.
1832.	Report of the comptroller relative to the disposition of the,	A	3	248
1833.	Report of amount paid toward the, and relative to the investment of,	S	1	19
1833.	Report in relation to the investment of the,	S	2	47
1833.	Not subject to, report on the expediency of altering the charters of such banks so as to subject them to the liabilities of that act,	S	2	99
1833.	Bank commissioners' report of amount of dividends and profits of the,	A	4	252
1834.	Resolution requiring them to have at all times one-fifth of their capital in specie,	S	1	8
1834.	Report of comptroller of amount paid toward, and relative to the investment of the,	S	2	62
1835.	Report of comptroller of amount paid toward, and relative to the investment of the,	S	2	48
1837.	Report relative to enlarging the, &c. (Mr. Powers),	S	1	38
1839.	Report of amount paid by each bank to the, and the dividend made thereon to each bank,	A	4	161
1841.	Report of bank commissioners in answer to a resolution of assembly relative to the,	A	5	172
1842.	Report of committee on banks on condition of,	A	7	187
1848.	Report in relation to rebate of interest to,	S	2	56
1848.	Report of committee on banks and insurance companies in relation to payments to,	S	3	56
1851.	Report of committee on banks and insurance companies as to contribution to,	S	2	39
	SAFETY FUND BANKS:			
1842.	Report relative to circulating notes of,	A	7	148
1845.	Report of committee on banks, &c., on the affairs of the receivers of the several insolvent,	S	3	118
1853.	Report of committee on banks, &c., on reference of the resolutions calling for information concerning,	A	4	81
	SMALL BILLS OF:			
1833.	Report on bill to prevent the circulation of (Mr. Morris),	A	3	215
1834.	Report on bill to prevent the circulation of (Mr. Bowne),	A	3	178
1835.	Resolution offered by Mr. Edwards relative to the circulation of,	S	1	26
1838.	Report on petition to repeal the law prohibiting the issue of,	S	1	10
1838.	Report of bank commissioners of amount of unredeemed,	S	1	19
1838.	Report of committee of conference on the bill to repeal the law prohibiting the issue of,	S	2	38
1839.	Report on bill to repeal the law prohibiting the issue of,	A	2	19
	SPECIE PAYMENTS:			
1838.	Message from governor in relation to the resumption of,	S	2	70
1838.	Message from governor relative to the bill authorizing the suspension of,	S	2	71
1838.	Report on bill to repeal the suspension law,	A	5	246
1838.	Report on the subject of the resumption of (Mr. Birdseye),	A	6	352
1838.	Senate bill, with amendments of the assembly,	A	6	354
1838.	Bill to facilitate the resumption of,	A	6	354
1838.	Report of committee of conference on the bill to facilitate the resumption of,	A	6	358
1838.	Report on bill to facilitate the resumption of (Mr. Birdseye),	A	6	344
	STOCK:			
1830.	Memorial of mechanics of New York against repealing the law imposing a tax on,	A	3	272
1834.	Preamble and resolutions relative to the sale of, at auction,	A	1	12
1834.	Report thereon,	A	3	136
1838.	Distribution of, investigation by the bank commissioners in relation to the,	A	2	23

BANKS—*continued.*

		Doc.	Vol.	No.
	STOCKHOLDERS IN:			
1830.	List of, in the New York banks, not residing within the county of New York, with the amount of stock holden by them, and their residence respectively, ...	A	3	232, 277
1833.	List of, with the amount of stock held by them, &c., ...	A	2	89
1838.	Loans and discounts to, &c., amount of, ...	S	2	44
1838.	Communication from the bank commissioners relative to an error in the above report, ...	S	2	53
1849.	Report of committee on banks and insurance companies on so much of governor's message as relates to individual liability of, ...	S	2	42
	ALBANY COUNTY:			
1838.	Albany City Bank, annual report of unclaimed dividends and deposits, ...	S	1	18
1839.	Annual report of unclaimed dividends and deposits, ...	S	1	10
1840.	do do	S	3	80
1841.	do do	S	1	13
1842.	do do	S	1	14
1836.	Bank of Albany, annual report of unclaimed dividends and deposits, ...	A	2	43
1837.	Annual report of unclaimed dividends and deposits, ...	A	1	26
1837.	Report of amount of notes in circulation, ...	A	1	23
1838.	Annual report of unclaimed dividends and deposits, ...	A	2	35
1839.	do do	A	2	50
1840.	do do	A	1	16
1841.	do do	A	2	21
1842.	Report of unclaimed dividends and deposits, ...	A	2	33
1843.	Annual report of, ...	A	5	186
1843.	Report of, in relation to its funds and property, ...	A	5	187
1845.	Annual report of, ...	A	1	17
1847.	do	A	6	175
1848.	Report of, ...	A	6	203
1836.	Canal Bank, annual report of unclaimed dividends and deposits,	A	2	92
1837.	Annual report of unclaimed dividends and deposits, ...	A	2	92
1838.	do do do	A	3	155
1839.	do do do	A	5	276
1840.	do do do	A	2	34
1841.	do do do	A	4	103
1842.	Report of unclaimed dividends and deposits, ...	A	4	56
1843.	Annual report of, relative to unclaimed dividends and deposits, ...	A	5	195
1844.	Annual report of, ...	A	6	158
1845.	do	A	6	220
1849.	Report of receiver of, in compliance with resolution of the assembly, ...	A	3	185
1849.	Report of receiver of, ...	A	5	222
1849.	Report of committee appointed to investigate affairs, ...	S	2	62
1849.	Report on the affairs of, ...	S	2	63
1830.	Commercial Bank, annual report of th condition and affairs of,	A	2	166
1831.	Annual report of the condition and affairs of, ...	A	2	160
1833.	do do	A	2	134
1833.	Remonstrance against being subject to the safety fund law, ..	S	2	111
1834.	Annual report of, ...	A	1	50
1835.	Annual report of, ...	A	3	199
1836.	Investigation, report of select committee, ...	S	2	94
1836.	Documents accompanying the same, ...	S	2	95
1836.	Report of select committee on communication from Lewis Benedict, ...	S	2	96
1836.	Additional testimony relative to the official conduct of Isaac W. Bishop, ...	S	2	101

BANKS—*continued.*

Year	Subject	Doc.	Vol.	No.
1836.	Additional testimony relative to the investigation,	S	2	102
1836.	Report of select committee in the case of John W. Edmonds,	S	2	104
1836.	Communication from John I. Mumford and Isaac W. Bishop,	S	2	107
1836.	Annual report of,	A	3	160
1837.	do	A	3	163
1838.	do	A	4	186
1839.	do	A	4	209
1841.	do	A	4	121
1842.	Report of unclaimed dividends and deposits,	A	5	90
1843.	Report in relation to certain moneys deposited in, part of the net proceeds of the sales of public lands of the United States,	A	5	144
1843.	Annual report of,	A	5	184
1845.	Annual report of,	A	5	163
1836.	Mechanics and Farmers' Bank, annual report of unclaimed dividends and deposits,	A	1	24
1837.	Annual report of unclaimed dividends and deposits,	A	1	15
1838.	do do do	A	2	56
1839.	do do do	A	2	20
1840.	do do do	A	2	38
1841.	do do do	A	3	53
1842.	Report of unclaimed dividends and deposits,	A	2	35
1843.	Report of unclaimed dividends and deposits,	A	5	194
1845.	Annual report of,	A	3	54
1846.	do	A	1	16
1846.	do	A	1	17
1847.	do	A	7	176
1848.	Report of,	A	6	204
1838.	New York State Bank, annual report of unclaimed dividends and deposits,	A	5	211
1839.	Annual report of unclaimed dividends and deposits,	A	4	178
1840.	do do do	A	2	59
1841.	do do do	A	4	93
1842.	Report of unclaimed dividends and deposits,	A	4	75
1843.	Report of, in relation to its funds and property,	A	5	193
1849.	Watervliet Bank, communication from receiver of,	A	5	204
1849.	Report of the receiver of,	A	5	227

See Banks, Savings.

CAYUGA COUNTY:

Year	Subject	Doc.	Vol.	No.
1832.	Cayuga County Bank, report on petition to incorporate,	A	2	104
1841.	Annual report of unclaimed dividends and deposits,	S	2	38

CHAUTAUQUE COUNTY:

Year	Subject	Doc.	Vol.	No.
1832.	Chautauque County Bank, bank commissioners' report of investigation of,	A	2	23

COLUMBIA COUNTY:

Year	Subject	Doc.	Vol.	No.
1830.	Hudson River Bank, report on petition to incorporate,	S	4	292
1837.	Report of unclaimed divideds and deposits,	A	1	13
1838.	do do do	A	3	66
1839.	do do do	S	1	10
1840.	do do do	S	3	74

DELAWARE COUNTY:

Year	Subject	Doc.	Vol.	No.
1832.	Delaware County Bank, report on petition to incorporate,	A	2	126

DUTCHESS COUNTY:

Year	Subject	Doc.	Vol.	No.
1856.	Bank of Fishkill, report of the committee on ways and means on the petition of the president and directors of, relative to a certain claim,	A	3	16

BANKS—*continued.*

Year	Subject	Doc.	Vol.	No.
1830.	Bank of Poughkeepsie, report on petition to incorporate,.......	S	4	383
1836.	Report of unclaimed dividends and deposits,............	A	2	51
1840.	Dutchess County Bank, annual report,.....	A	3	207
1832.	Annual report,......................................	A	2	230
1833.	do	A	3	213
1834.	do	A	3	251
1835.	do	A	4	267
1836.	do	A	4	214
	ERIE COUNTY:			
1831.	Bank of Buffalo, report on petition to incorporate,............	S	1	43
1841.	City Bank, report of register in chancery in relation to the affairs of the,..	A	4	87
1841.	Communication from register in chancery transmitting sundry documents, &c.,............................	A	4	108
1841.	Communication from W. L. Marcy, receiver, in relation to,..	A	4	144
1841.	Communication from W. L. Marcy, receiver, in relation to,..	A	5	159
1841.	Report on petition of L. F. Allen, J. H. Lathrop and Stephen White, for an investigation into their acts and proceedings as connected with the,................................	A	7	290
1846.	Purchasing assets of, report of comptroller in answer to a resolution relative to,....	A	4	120
1838.	Commercial Bank, bank commissioners' report of investigation of,	A	2	23
1830.	Mechanics' Bank, report on petition to incorporate,............	S	4	338
1857.	Walter Joy's Bank, report of committee on judiciary relative to,	A	3	186
	ESSEX COUNTY:			
1837.	Essex County Bank, report of unclaimed dividends and deposits,	A	1	35
	GREENE COUNTY:			
1836.	Catskill Bank, annual report of unclaimed dividends and deposits,	A	3	124
1837.	Annual report of unclaimed dividends and deposits,.......	A	3	218
1837.	do do do	A	2	38
1839.	do do do	S	1	10
1840.	do do do	S	1	22
1841.	do do do	A	3	58
1842.	Report of unclaimed divideds and deposits,...............	A	2	20
1843.	Report of, in answer to a resolution of assembly of 27th February,..	A	4	117
1843.	Annual report of,..................	A	5	180
1844.	Report of,..	A	7	179
1844.	Annual report of,..................................	A	7	180
1845.	Annual report of,..................................	A	4	113
	Farmers' and Mechanics' Bank, Catskill, report on petition to incorporate,......................................	S	4	386
1831.	Tanners' Bank, report on petition to incorporate,..............	S	1	43
1836.	Report of unclaimed dividends and deposits,.............	S	1	42
	HERKIMER COUNTY:			
1831.	Herkimer County Bank, report on petition to incorporate,......	S	1	16
1848.	Mohawk Valley Bank, petition of as to par redemption, in New York,..	A	3	86
	JEFFERSON COUNTY:			
1837.	Jefferson County Bank, memorial of a majority of the commissioners appointed to distribute the increased capital of,...	A	4	285
1837.	Affidavit of N. M. Woodruff, one of the commissioners,....	A	4	299
1837.	Memorial of majority of the commissioners,...............	A	4	322
1837.	Report of select committee on the investigation of,........	A	3	284
1837.	Additional testimony,..................................	A	4	326
1837.	Affidavits of L. Paddock and N. M. Woodruff,............	A	4	305
1838.	Bank commissioners' report of investigation of,..........	A	2	23

BANKS—*continued.*

		Doc.	Vol.	No.
1837.	Sackets' Harbor Bank, report of select committee recommending the repeal of the charter of,	A	3	243
1837.	Memorial of the directors of, against the repeal of the charter,	A	4	296
1837.	Testimony relative to the issuing of checks by the,	A	3	245
1837.	Additional testimony,	A	4	297
1837.	Additional testimony,	A	4	298
1838.	Report on petition to recharter,	A	5	278
	KINGS COUNTY:			
1838.	Atlantic Bank, report on bill for the relief of,	A	3	92
1836.	Brooklyn Bank, annual report of unclaimed dividends and deposits,	A	1	26
1839.	Petition of F. C. Treadwell for an investigation of,	A	3	83
1839.	Report of bank commissioners in relation to the,	S	3	84
1835.	Long Island Bank, report of the affairs and condition of,	S	2	63
	See Banks, Savings.			
	LEWIS COUNTY:			
1857.	Lewis County Bank, report of superintendent of banking department in reply to resolution relative to,	A	1	21
	LIVINGSTON COUNTY:			
1845.	Bank of Dansville, report of committee on the judiciary, on the memorial of R. L. Dorr and others relative to the,	A	1	17
1846.	Report of majority of committee on banks, &c., relative to,	A	6	224
1846.	Report of minority of committee on banks, &c., relative to,	A	6	225
1847.	Petition of Richard W. Porter, director of, and others, for investigation of the affairs of, &c.,	A	2	79
1847.	Remonstrance of cashier of, denying charges in petitions for investigation of the affairs of said bank,	A	2	93
1847.	Report of select committee to inquire whether affidavit of John Gilman in the matter of, had been improperly taken from the files,	A	4	125
1847.	Report of committee on banks and insurance companies on petitions for investigating affairs of,	A	4	145
1830.	Livingston County Bank, report on petition to incorporate,	S	4	307
1838.	Bank commissioners' report of investigation of the,	A	2	23
	MADISON COUNTY:			
1831.	Madison County Bank, report on petition to incorporate,	S	1	43
	MONROE COUNTY:			
1835.	Bank of Rochester, annual report of,	S	2	26
1838.	Report of unclaimed dividends and deposits,	S	1	18
1839.	Report on petition to extend the charter,	A	2	57
1841.	Report of unclaimed dividends and deposits,	A	3	85
1836.	Bank of Monroe, report of unclaimed dividends and deposits,	A	1	28
1838.	Report of unclaimed dividends and deposits,	A	3	105
	MONTGOMERY COUNTY:			
1831.	Montgomery County Bank, report on petition to incorporate,	S	1	43
1838.	Report of unclaimed dividends and deposits,	S	1	18
	NEW YORK:			
1830.	Report of amount of stock held by persons residing out of the state, &c.,	A	3	232
1830.	Report of amount of stock held by persons residing out of the state, &c.,	A	3	277
1832.	Report on several applications for,	S	1	32
1832.	Memorial of, relative to the investment of the bank fund,	S	1	55
1832.	Report on several applications for,	S	1	22

BANKS—*continued.*

Year	Entry	Doc.	Vol.	No.
1857.	American Exchange Bank, report of, in reply to a resolution,...	A	3	208
1857.	Report of, in reply to resolution of inquiry,...............	A	3	209
1836.	Bank of America, report of unclaimed dividends and deposits,..	S	1	45
1838.	Report of unclaimed dividends and deposits,..............	S	1	18
1842.	Annual report of,..................................	S	2	36
1844.	Report of unclaimed dividends,.........................	S	1	8
1843.	Bank of New York, annual report of,.......................	A	5	185
1843.	Annual report relative to unclaimed dividends and deposits,	A	5	185
1830.	Butchers' and Drovers' Bank, report on petition to incorporate,	S	4	385
1836.	Report of unclaimed dividends and deposits,............	A	2	56
1837.	do do	A	2	82
1838.	do do	S	1	18
1839.	do do	S	1	10
1840.	do do	S	1	19
1841.	do do	S	1	8
1842.	Annual report of,..................................	S	1	12
1844.	Report of unclaimed dividends and deposits,.............	S	1	10
1847.	Central Bank, report on application of,....................	S	4	141
1856.	Chatham Bank, report in reference to, ...	A	4	171
1857.	Report of committee on state prisons, favorable on petition of for payment of money loaned,....................	A	2	142
1830.	Chemical Manufacturing Company Bank, annual report of, ...	A	3	251
1832.	Annual report of,..................................	A	2	161
1833.	Annual report of,..................................	A	3	170
1833.	Remonstrance of, against being subject to the safety fund law,	S	1	102
1833.	Remonstrance of, against being subject to safety fund system,	S	2	102
1834.	Annual report of,..................................	A	4	305
1835.	do	A	4	304
1836.	do	A	4	221
1837.	do	A	3	232
1838.	do	A	5	249
1839.	do	A	5	277
1840.	do	S	4	97
1841.	do	A	4	137
1842.	do	A	7	135
1831.	City Bank, report on petition to reduce the capital of,.........	A	4	304
1841.	Commercial Bank, report of unclaimed dividends and deposits,..	S	1	15
1843.	Report of the receiver of the,..........................	A	4	75
1830.	Delaware and Hudson Canal Company [*see* Canals], report of comptroller on petition of, for power to sell certain land,	S	1	21
1830.	Report of comptroller relative to the stock issued to the,...	S	2	198
1830.	Report of comptroller relative to the stock issued to the,...	S	4	317
1839.	Report relative to the issue of bank notes not payable on demand, ...	S	2	49
1849.	Report of comptroller relative to stocks issued to,.........	S	2	41
1830.	Dry Dock Bank, annual report of,..........................	A	1	62
1831.	Annual report of,..................................	S	1	76
1832.	do	A	3	218
1833.	do	A	4	280
1834.	do	A	3	240
1835.	do	A	1	31
1836.	do	A	1	28
1837.	do	A	1	16
1838.	Report of committee appointed to investigate the affairs of,..	A	6	318
1839.	Annual report of,..................................	A	6	344
1840.	do	A	1	7
1841.	do	A	4	112
1842.	Annual report of unclaimed dividends and deposits, ...	A	4	52
1843.	Annual report of,..................................	A	5	189
1844.	do	A	7	181
1845.	do	A	5	171

BANKS—*continued.*

		Doc.	Vol.	No.
1847.	Dry Dock Bank annual report of,	A	7	179
1848.	Annual report of,	A	6	209
1833.	Fulton Bank, remonstrance of, against being subject to the safety fund law,	S	2	104
1833.	Remonstrance of, against being subject to safety fund system,	S	2	140
1836.	Report of unclaimed dividends and deposits,	S	1	40
1836.	Greenwich Bank, report of unclaimed dividends and deposits,	A	1	37
1837.	Report of unclaimed dividends and deposits,	S	2	53
1838.	do do	S	1	18
1839.	do do	S	1	10
1840.	do do	S	3	79
1841.	do do	A	3	71
1842.	Annual report of unclaimed dividends and deposits,	S	1	15
1843.	Annual report of unclaimed dividends and deposits,	A	5	192
1842.	Lafayette Bank, annual report of unclaimed dividends and deposits,	S	1	10
1832.	Leather Manufacturers' Bank, report on petition to incorporate,	S	2	95
1832.	Memorial of the committee of the association applying for the,	S	2	104
1838.	Report of unclaimed dividends and deposits,	A	2	40
1839.	do do do	A	4	167
1840.	do do do	A	1	20
1841.	do do do	A	2	48
1842.	do do do	A	2	34
1843.	Annual report of,	A	5	198
1845.	do	A	1	9
1846.	do	A	1	21
1847.	Annual report of unclaimed dividends and deposits,	A	6	172
1848.	Report of,	A	6	209
1848.	Annual report of,	A	6	210
1836.	Manhattan Company Bank, report on petition for an investigation of the affairs of,	A	4	308
1837.	Report of unclaimed dividends and deposits,	A	1	39
1838.	do do do	A	2	49
1840.	do do do	A	5	199
1841.	do do do	A	5	59
1839.	Report of unclaimed items of interest on canal stock in the,	A	3	134
1842.	Annual report of,	A	2	40
1843.	do	A	5	179
1845.	do	A	6	219
1846.	do	A	1	18
1847.	do	A	7	177
1848.	do	A	6	207
1836.	Mechanics' Bank, report of unclaimed dividends and deposits,	A	2	59
1837.	Report of unclaimed dividends and deposits,	A	1	22
1840.	do do do	A	2	56
1841.	do do do	S	1	27
1843.	Annual report of, in relation to its funds and property,	A	5	202
1844.	Annual report of,	A	6	159
1847.	Annual report of,	A	6	174
1838.	Mechanics' and Traders' Bank, report of unclaimed dividends and deposits,	A	3	96
1838.	Merchants' Bank, report of unclaimed dividends and deposits,	S	1	18
1839.	Report of unclaimed dividends and deposits,	S	1	10
1841.	Report of unclaimed dividends and deposits,	S	1	26
1844.	Annual report of,	A	7	167
1845.	do	A	5	184
1846.	do	A	1	17
1848.	do	A	6	206
1840.	Merchants' Exchange Bank, report of unclaimed dividends and deposits,	A	5	207
1841.	Report of unclaimed dividends and deposits,	A	2	49

BANKS—*continued.*

Year	Subject	Doc.	Vol.	No.
1843.	Merchants' Exchange Bank, annual report in relation to its funds and property,	A	5	191
1845.	Annual report of,	A	5	170
1846.	do	A	1	17
1847.	do	A	7	178
1848.	do	A	6	208
1856.	Morris Canal and Banking Company, report of judiciary committee on bill,	S	2	95
1836.	National Bank, report of amount of bills in circulation,	A	2	78
1836.	Report of unclaimed dividends and deposits,	A	3	206
1838.	do do do	S	1	18
1839.	do do do	A	3	126
1841.	do do do	A	3	80
1842.	Annual report of,	S	2	40
1833.	North River Bank, annual report of,	S	2	42
1834.	Annual report of,	S	2	56
1835.	Annual report of,	S	1	18
1839.	Report on petition to increase its capital and extend the charter of,	A	5	266
1841.	Minority report on bill to recharter,	A	6	231
1842.	Report of minority committee on banking and insurance companies on petition for recharter of,	A	4	79
1838.	Phenix Bank, report of the investigation of certain charges against,	A	5	281
1839.	Report of unclaimed dividends and deposits,	A	3	82
1840.	do do	S	1	23
1841.	do do	S	1	10
1841.	Report on bill to reduce the capital of,	A	6	205
1841.	Report of attorney-general in relation to the proceedings instituted against the,	A	6	236
1842.	Annual report of unclaimed dividends and deposits,	S	1	17
1843.	Annual report of unclaimed dividends and deposits,	A	5	182
1844.	Annual report of,	A	7	180
1834.	Seventh Ward Bank, report of committee appointed to inquire into the practices resorted to for the purpose of procuring the charter of,	S	1	47
1834.	Letter from James Perkins,	S	2	94
1834.	Letter from I. D. Brown,	S	2	73
1834.	Letter from R. D. Dodge,	S	2	80
1834.	Letter from Levi Ridder,	S	2	89
1834.	Letter from David Russell,	S	2	64
1836.	Tradesmen's Bank, report of unclaimed dividends and deposits,	A	1	27
1838.	Union Bank, report of unclaimed dividends and deposits,	S	1	23
1841.	Report of unclaimed dividends and deposits,	S	1	11
1842.	Annual report of unclaimed dividends and deposits,	S	1	13
1843.	Annual report of the,	A	5	201

ONEIDA COUNTY:

Year	Subject	Doc.	Vol.	No.
1855.	Bank of Whitestown, report of committee on claims in reference to claim of,	A	4	94
1831.	Oneida Bank, report of select committee on petition for an investigation of,	S	1	35
1837.	Report of majority and minority of the committee on petition to repeal the charter of,	S	2	58
1837.	Affidavits of stockholders of,	S	2	61
1848.	Petition of, for redemption of notes in New York city,	A	3	56
1850.	Petition of, for par redemption in New York,	S	1	24
1841.	Utica, Bank of, report of unclaimed dividends and deposits,	A	3	63
1836.	Branch of, at Canandaigua, report of unclaimed dividends and deposits,	A	2	57
1836.	Report of amount of bills in circulation,	A	2	58
1836.	Ontario Branch, at Utica, report of unclaimed dividends and deposits,	A	1	35

BANKS—*continued.*

Year	Subject	Doc.	Vol.	No.
1841.	Ontario Branch, at Utica, report of unclaimed dividends and deposits,	S	1	12
	ONONDAGA COUNTY:			
1832.	Onondaga County Bank, report of unclaimed dividends and deposits,	A	3	116
1832.	Salina, Bank of, report on petition to incorporate,	A	4	323
	ONTARIO COUNTY:			
1838.	Geneva, Bank of, report of unclaimed dividends and deposits,	A	1	12
1842.	Annual report of unclaimed dividends and deposits,	S	1	7
1843.	Annual report of,	A	5	199
1845.	Annual report of,	A	4	104
1847.	Annual report of unclaimed dividends and deposits,	A	2	91
1848.	Annual report of,	A	6	205
1836.	Ontario Bank, report of unclaimed dividends and deposits,	A	4	212
1838.	Report of unclaimed dividends and deposits,	A	3	84
1836.	Branch of, at Utica, report of unclaimed dividends and deposits,	A	1	35
1841.	Report of unclaimed dividends and deposits,	S	1	12
1836.	Utica, Branch of, report of unclaimed dividends and deposits,	A	2	57
1836.	Report of amount of bills in circulation,	A	2	58
	ORANGE COUNTY:			
1836.	Orange County Bank, report of unclaimed dividends and deposits,	A	2	49
1838.	Report of unclaimed dividends and deposits,	A	3	136
1836.	Newburgh, Bank of, report of unclaimed dividends and deposits,	A	2	60
1840.	Report of unclaimed dividends and deposits,	A	1	19
	ORLEANS COUNTY:			
1838.	Orleans County Bank, Report of investigation of the charges against,	A	5	256
1838.	Bank commissioners' report of investigation of,	A	2	23
	OSWEGO COUNTY:			
1838.	Commercial Bank, bank commissioners' report relative to the distribution of the stock of the,	A	2	23
	OTSEGO COUNTY:			
1830.	Otsego County Bank, report on petition to incorporate,	S	4	384
	RENSSELAER COUNTY:			
1836.	Bank of Troy, report of unclaimed dividends and deposits,	A	1	33
1836.	Merchants and Mechanics' Bank, report of unclaimed dividends and deposits,	A	1	25
1837.	Report of unclaimed dividends and deposits,	A	2	143
1838.	Report of unclaimed dividends and deposits,	A	4	184
	See Banks, Savings.			
	ST. LAWRENCE COUNTY:			
1836.	Ogdensburgh Bank, report of unclaimed dividends and deposits,	S	1	57
1841.	Report of unclaimed dividends and deposits,	S	1	21
	SARATOGA COUNTY:			
1830.	Saratoga County Bank, report on petition to incorporate,	S	3	281
1837.	Report of select committee relative to the sale by Mr. Young of his stock in the,	S	2	66
1838.	Bank commissioners' report of investigation of,	A	2	23
	SCHENECTADY COUNTY:			
1834.	Schenectady Bank, report on bill to incorporate,	A	4	390
1836.	Report of amount of bills in circulation,	A	2	47
1836.	Report of unclaimed dividends and deposits,	A	1	36
1838.	Report of unclaimed dividends and deposits,	S	1	18

Year	Subject	Doc.	Vol.	No.
	BANKS—*continued.*			
1839.	Schenectady Bank, report of unclaimed dividends and deposits,	S	1	10
1840.	Report of unclaimed dividends and deposits,	S	4	112
1841.	do do	S	1	17
	ULSTER COUNTY:			
1831.	Ulster County Bank, report on petition to incorporate,	S	1	43
	WASHINGTON COUNTY:			
1830.	Washington and Warren Bank, report of the comptroller in relation to the returns of the,	A	4	370
1836.	Whitehall, Bank of, report of unclaimed dividends and deposits,	A	1	40
1840.	Report of unclaimed dividends and deposits,	A	5	212
1841.	Report of unclaimed dividends and deposits,	A	4	90
1842.	Report of unclaimed dividends and deposits,	A	4	59
1843.	Annual report of,	A	5	190
1845.	Annual report of,	A	5	180
	WAYNE COUNTY:			
1838.	Wayne County Bank, bank commissioners' report of investigation of,	A	2	23
1841.	Bank commissioners' report of, in answer to a resolution of assembly,	A	5	172
	WESTCHESTER COUNTY:			
1848.	Bank of New Rochelle, answer to a resolution of assembly calling for information respecting,	A	5	217
1855.	Sing Sing Bank, report on claim of,	A	5	201
1856.	Report on claim of,	A	5	202
1842.	Westchester County Bank, report of unclaimed dividends and deposits,	A	2	49
	YATES COUNTY:			
1831.	Yates County Bank, report on petition to incorporate,	S	1	43
	BANKS, SAVINGS.			
1846.	Report of committee on banks and insurance companies relative to, at Buffalo and Rochester,	A	2	54
1846.	Report of committee on banks and insurance companies relative to, at Rochester,	A	3	68
1848.	Report of committee on banks, &c., relative to bill for incorporating,	S	2	59
1850.	Report of attorney-general in relation to,	A	3	28
1851.	Majority report of committee on judiciary on,	A	2	39
1851.	Minority report of committee on judiciary on,	A	2	40
1845.	Report of committee on banks relative to, in New York and Kings county,	S	2	57
1856.	Report of committee on banks relative to,	S	3	107
1856.	Report of secretary of state relative to,	A	3	60
1857.	Report of standing committee on banks relative to,	S	4	160
1858.	Report relative to,	A	1	39
	ALBANY SAVINGS BANK:			
1830.	Annual report of,	A	4	443
1832.	do	A	4	320
1833.	do	A	4	308
1835.	do	A	5	397
1836.	do	A	4	305
1837.	do	A	4	290
1838.	do	A	6	339
1839.	do	A	6	361
1840.	do	A	8	330

BANKS, SAVINGS—*continued.*

		Doc.	Vol.	No.
1841.	Annual report of,	A	5	176
1842.	Annual report of,	A	4	63
1843.	Report of unclaimed dividends and deposits,	A	5	202
1844.	Report of unclaimed dividends and deposits,	S	2	61
1847.	Annual report of,	A	2	88
	BOWERY SAVINGS BANK:			
1836.	Annual report of,	S	1	53
1837.	do	S	1	18
1838.	do	S	2	39
1839.	do	S	1	17
1841.	do	S	1	24
1842.	Report of,	S	2	37
1842.	Annual report of,	A	4	54
1842.	Report of,	A	4	55
1843.	Report of unclaimed dividends and deposits,	A	5	197
1844.	Annual report of,	A	6	161
1845.	do	S	3	119
1845.	do	A	5	187
1848.	do	A	6	196
	BROOKLYN SAVINGS BANK:			
1830.	Annual report of,	A	4	
1832.	do	A	2	70
1833.	do	A	3	233
1834.	do	A	4	306
1835.	do	A	4	335
1836.	do	A	4	235
1837.	do	S	2	51
1838.	do	A	5	248
1839.	do	S	3	61
1840.	do	A	6	249
1841.	do	A	4	129
1842.	do	A	4	55
1843.	Annual report of unclaimed dividends and deposits,	A	3	67
1844.	Annual report of,	S	2	57
1845.	Annual report of,	A	5	164
1847.	Annual report of,	A	6	173
	BUFFALO SAVINGS BANK:			
1846.	Report of committee on banks, &c., relative to,	A	2	54
1847.	Annual report of,	A	8	232
1848.	Annual report of,	A	6	200
	GREENWICH SAVINGS BANK:			
1834.	Annual report of,	A	2	89
1835.	do	S	2	50
1836.	do	S	2	69
1838.	do	S	2	43
1839.	do	S	1	24
1840.	do	S	3	76
1841.	do	S	1	28
1841.	Report of unclaimed dividends and deposits,	S	1	9
1842.	Annual report of,	S	2	46
1844.	do	S	1	33
1845.	do	S	3	120
	ITHICA SAVINGS BANK:			
1843.	Annual report of,	A	5	196
1847.	Annual report of,	A	4	148
	MECHANICS' AND TRADERS' SAVINGS INSTITUTIONS, N. Y.:			
1852.	*See* report of minority on bill to incorporate,	A	2	40

BANKS, SAVINGS—*continued.*

		Doc.	Vol.	No.
	NEW YORK BANK OF SAVINGS:			
1830.	Annual report of,	S	2	185
1830.	Report on petition for an extension of its powers relative to the investment of the money of depositors,	S	3	203
1832.	Annual report of,	A	3	255
1833.	do	S	2	63
1834.	do	S	2	71
1835.	do	S	2	72
1836.	do	S	1	54
1837.	do	S	1	31
1838.	do	S	2	71
1839.	do	S	3	62
1840.	do	S	3	95
1836.	Communication from trustees of, in relation to the law relative to unclaimed dividends and deposits,	S	1	1
1842.	Annual report of,	S	2	48
1843.	Annual report of,	A	2	54
1843.	Annual report relative to unclaimed dividends and deposits,	A	3	64
1844.	Annual report of,	S	2	89
1845.	do	S	3	121
1848.	do	S	3	78
	ONTARIO SAVINGS BANK:			
1834.	Annual report of,	A	4	270
1835.	do	S	2	87
1845.	do			
	POUGHKEEPSIE SAVINGS BANK:			
1841.	Report of unclaimed dividends and deposits,	S	1	16
	ROCHESTER SAVINGS BANK;			
1846.	Report of committee on banks, &c., relative to,	A	3	68
	SCHENECTADY SAVINGS BANK.			
1834.	Annual report of,	A	4	390
1836.	do	S	1	41
1837.	do	S	1	43
1838.	do	S	2	47
1839.	do	S	2	45
1840.	do	S	4	109
1841.	do	S	1	30
1842.	do	S	2	29
1844.	do	S	1	32
1848.	do	A	6	202
	SEAMAN'S BANK FOR SAVINGS:			
1831.	Annual report of,	S	1	21
1832.	do	A	3	247
1833.	do	S	2	81
1834.	do	S	2	53
1835.	do	A	3	186
1836.	do	A	3	164
1837.	do	A	3	180
1838.	do	A	5	210
1839.	do	A	4	175
1840.	do	A	5	195
1841.	do	A	4	114
1842.	do	A	4	74
1843.	do	A	5	188
1844.	do	A	7	165
1845.	do	A	5	167
1847.	Annual report of, to July, 1847,	A	2	90
1848.	Annual report of,	A	6	198

BANKS, SAVINGS—*continued.*

		Doc.	Vol.	No.
	STATE TRUST AND SAVINGS BANK:			
1852.	Report on act incorporating the, at Buffalo,	S	1	40
	TROY SAVINGS BANK:			
1830.	Annual report of,	A	4	420
1831.	do	A	4	344
1832.	do	A	4	286
1833.	do	A	4	292
1834.	do	S	2	124
1835.	do	S	2	81
1836.	do	S	2	90
1837.	do	A	4	300
1838.	do	A	6	312
1839.	do	A	6	354
1840.	do	A	7	307
1841.	do	S	3	73
1836.	Report of unclaimed dividends and deposits,	S	1	32
1837.	do do do	A	1	29
1838.	do do do	A	3	72
1839.	do do do	A	2	56
1840.	do do do	A	1	23
1841.	do do do	A	2	35
1839.	Report on petition to amend the charter of the,	A	3	73
1842.	Annual report of,	S	4	99
1842.	do	A	2	25
1843.	do	A	5	183
1844.	do	A	7	168
1844.	Report of,	A	7	172
1845.	Annual report of,	A	3	53
1845.	22d annual report of,	A	6	213
1848.	Annual report of,	A	6	201
	UNION SAVINGS BANK, ROCHESTER:			
1855.	Report of minority of committee relative to,	S	3	70
	UTICA SAVINGS BANK:			
1839.	Report on petition to incorporate,	A	2	65
1841.	Annual report of,	S	1	22
1842.	do	S	2	47
1844.	do	A	7	171
1845.	do	A	5	181
1847.	Annual report of unclaimed deposits and its affairs,	A	2	87

BANT, JOANNA, *see* Eliza McCarthy.

BAPTIST MISSIONARY CONVENTION, STATE.

1844.	Report of committee on charitable and religious societies on the bill relative to,	S	2	67

BARBER, HIRAM.

	Report on petition for a lease of surplus water of the Glens Falls Feeder dam,	A	3	259

BARBER, JOSIAH.

1845.	Report on the petition of,	S	3	101

BARCLAY, ANTHONY.

1849.	Report on petition of,	S	2	59

BARCLAY, HENRY.

		Doc.	Vol.	No.
1831.	Report on petition to build a bridge over Esopus creek,	A	2	159
1832.	Report on petition to build a bridge over Esopus creek,	A	1	25

BARCLAY, LAWRENCE.

1834.	Report on claim for work done on the Cayuaga and Seneca canal,	A	4	366
1834.	Report of committee on claims,	A	4	379
1835.	do do	A	3	247
1836.	do do	A	2	68

BARD, SAMUEL W.

1835.	Report on petition to allow him to maintain a ferry across the Hudson between Rockland and Westchester,	A	4	313

BARDWELL & BRAYTON.

1830.	Report on petition for extra compensation for work done on the Erie canal,	A	4	319
1831.	Report of committee on grievances on the same,	A	1	28
1831.	Report of canal board, on the same,	A	3	203
1833.	Report of select committee, on the same,	A	2	129

BARGY, PETER, Jr.

1837.	Report on petition for extra allowance for work done on the Chenango canal,	A	4	313
1837.	Report on petition for extra allowance for work done on the Chenango canal,	A	4	320
1840.	Report of committee on claims on the same,	A	6	263
1841.	Report of canal board on the same,	A	5	162
1841.	Report of canal board on the same,	A	5	178
1843.	Report of canal board on petition of P. Cagger, administrator of,	A	5	135
1852.	Report on petition of P. Cagger, administrator of, deceased,	A	2	75

BARHYDT, JOHN S. M.

1852.	Report on petition of,	S	2	62

BARKER & STROUD.

1837.	Report on petition for extra compensation for work done on the Chenango canal,	A	1	44

BARKER, OLIVER.

1849.	Report on petition of,	S	1	16

BARKER, TOWN OF.

1840.	Report on petition to annex part of, to the town of Greene,	A	6	273

BARKER, Z., AND OTHERS.

1831.	Report on petition relative to certain lands escheated to the state on the death of John G. Leake,	A	2	73

BARNES & HINMAN.

1842.	Report of canal board on petition of,	A	5	119
1845.	Report of canal board on petition of,	A	3	73
1845.	Report of the canal board on the petition of,	A	3	79

BARNES, DAVID, AND PLINY JENNINGS.

1830.	Report on petition for bounty land,	A	4	406
1831.	do do	A	3	269
1832.	do do	S	1	42

BARNHARDT, WILLIAM G., AND OTHERS.

		Doc.	Vol.	No.
1851.	Appraisement of damages,	A	1	8
1855.	Report of committee on claims on petition of,	A	4	99

BARNHART, JACOB, AND OTHERS.

1853.	Report of commissioners of land office on resolution referring matter of,	A	2	34
1853.	Report of committee on public lands on the petition of,	A	3	58

BARNHART, W. G.

1850.	Report on claim,	A	6	160

BARNHART, W. & GEO., AND OTHERS.

1853.	Report of committee on public lands on petition of, for relief,	A	3	58
1854.	Report on petition of,	S	1	32

BARNUM, MERRILL, AND McDONALD.

1842.	Report of claim committee on petition of,	A	5	111

BARNUM, S., AND H. HOWELL.

1831.	Report on petition to be released from a judgment in favor of the state,	A	2	189
1832.	Report of select committee on the same,	A	4	293
1832.	Report of committee on finance on the same,	S	2	111

BARR, THOS. J.

1856.	Report relative to seat contested by,	S	3	98

BARRETT, SOLOMON, JR.

1836.	Report on petition of, to furnish a copy of his grammar to each of the common schools,	S	2	105

BARRON, QUARTUS H., AND OTHERS.

1839.	Report on petition to occupy certain land for the use of a rail-road,	A	3	157

BARRON, WM.

1849.	Report on petition of, for relief,	A	3	133

BARRY, JOHN A.

1840.	Report on petition of, for an impeachment of Judge Inglis,	A	8	348

BARTHOLOMEW, PETER, *see* New York Poudrette Company.

BARTLETT & STEWART.

1854.	Report on petition of,	A	2	48

BARTLETT, C., AND OTHERS.

1839.	Report on petition of,	A	3	107

BARTLETT, JEFFERSON, AND OTHERS.

	Report on petition for a grant of surplus water of the Chemung canal,	A	2	91

BARTLETT, M. R.

Year	Subject	Doc.	Vol.	No.
1830.	Memorial of citizens of Utica relative to his school manual, ...	A	1	65
1830.	Report of committee on colleges, &c., on, ...	A	4	131

BARTON, BENJAMIN, AND OTHERS.

Year	Subject	Doc.	Vol.	No.
1834.	Report on petition relative to certain land in Lewiston, ...	A	1	28
1834.	Report of committee on public lands on the same, ...	A	1	49

BARTON, BENJAMIN, AND AUGUSTUS PATER.

Year	Subject	Doc.	Vol.	No.
1836.	Report concerning an execution against, ...	S	1	17

BARTON, MICHAEL H.

Year	Subject	Doc.	Vol.	No.
1830.	Report on petition to change his name, ...	A	2	32

BARTON, THEO. D.

Year	Subject	Doc.	Vol.	No.
1855.	Report of committee on claims on petition of, ...	S	1	15

BARTON, THEODORE R.

Year	Subject	Doc.	Vol.	No.
1854.	Report on petition of, ...	A	1	24

BASTIDO, LEWIS, & N. B. KINGSLAND.

Year	Subject	Doc.	Vol.	No.
1846.	Report on petition for relief of, ...	S	4	129

BATAVIA TO BROCKPORT.

Year	Subject	Doc.	Vol.	No.
1830.	Report on petition to lay out a road from, ...	A	2	164

BATAVIA, VILLAGE OF.

Year	Subject	Doc.	Vol.	No.
1835.	Report on petition to relinquish certain lands in, to the Holland Land Company, ...	A	1	14
1838.	Arsenal at, message from the governor relative to the breaking open of the, ...	A	5	217

BATES, FRANCIS, AND OTHERS.

Year	Subject	Doc.	Vol.	No.
1849.	Report of committee on petition of, ...	A	1	18

BATES, LORENZO.

Year	Subject	Doc.	Vol.	No.
1846.	Report of committee on claims on petition of, ...	A	2	39
1847.	Report on petition of, ...	A	4	115
1852.	Report on bill for relief of, ...	A	2	48

BATH AND CROOKED LAKE RAILROAD, *see* Railroads.

BATH AND LAKE ERIE TURNPIKE.

Year	Subject	Doc.	Vol.	No.
1831.	Report on petition to abolish part of the, &c., ...	A	3	256
1833.	Report on petition to repeal the charter of the, ...	S	2	105
1833.	Report on petition for a new license to erect toll gates on ten miles of the, ...	S	2	110
1834.	Report on petition that the west ten miles may be made a public highway, ...	A	3	202

BATH AND SUSQUEHANNAH TURNPIKE ROAD.

Year	Subject	Doc.	Vol.	No.
1838.	Report on petition to lay off part of said road into road districts,	A	6	355

BATTLE, JAMES, AND OTHERS.

Year	Subject	Doc.	Vol.	No.
1835.	Report on petition to change their names, ...	A	1	25

BAXTER, ASA.

		Doc.	Vol.	No.
1846.	Report of commissioners of land office on petition of,...........	A	3	85
1846.	Report of committee on public lands,.......................	A	5	179
1847.	Report on petition of,................................	S	4	117
1848.	do	A	2	41
1850.	do	S	1	35
1850.	do	S	3	35

BAXTER, SUBMIT, AND OTHERS.

		Doc.	Vol.	No.
1857.	Report of commissioners of land office in reply to resolution relative to claim of,....................................	A	3	182

BEACH, CHAPMAN & McOMBER.

		Doc.	Vol.	No.
1839.	Report of canal commissioners in relation to certain work done on the Erie canal by,..............................	S	2	40
1840.	Report of committee on claims,..........................	A	3	87

BEACH, E., *see* Otsego and Schoharie Railroad.

		Doc.	Vol.	No.
1854.	Report on petition of,................................	A	3	108
1855.	Report of committee on claims in reference to petition of,......	A	4	101
1856.	Report on petition of,................................	S	2	60
1857.	Report on claim of,................................	S	1	23

BEACH, HORACE.

		Doc.	Vol.	No.
1847.	Report on petition of,................................	A	8	246

BEACH & HEWETT.

		Doc.	Vol.	No.
1847.	Report as to damages of,................................	S	4	150

BEACH, JOHN, *see* John Phillips and John Beach.

BEACH, NELSON J.

		Doc.	Vol.	No.
1851.	Communication in relation to canal enlargement,..............	A	3	63

BEADLE, LOAMMI.

		Doc.	Vol.	No.
1841.	Report on petition for relief,..............................	S	2	62

BEARDSLEE, LOVINIA.

		Doc.	Vol.	No.
1846.	Report of canal commissioners on petition of,................	A	2	48

BEARDSLEY, JOHN, AND LUTHER PARDEE.

		Doc.	Vol.	No.
1835.	Report on petition for compensation for damages to their lands by the Minden dam,....................................	A	4	361
1835.	Report on the same,....................................	A	5	393

BEARDSLEE, L. AND J. J.

		Doc.	Vol.	No.
1836.	Report on petition for compensation for damages to their lands by the Minden dam,....................................	S	1	63

BEARDSLEY, SAMUEL, *see* Attorney-General.

BEARS, BOUNTY ON.

		Doc.	Vol.	No.
1834.	Report on petition from the town of Florence relative to,.......	A	4	316
1835.	Report on petition from the town of Florence relative to,.......	A	1	43

BEAUMONT, A. L., AND OTHERS (contractors on the Erie canal).

		Doc.	Vol.	No.
1838.	Report on petition for relief,	A	3	121
1838.	do	A	5	215
1839.	do	A	4	239

BEAVERKILL SWAMP AND PACAMA VALLEY.

		Doc.	Vol.	No.
1848.	Report as to draining,	A	2	34

BECK, LEWIS C.

		Doc.	Vol.	No.
1832.	Report of, relative to the adulteration of potash,	A	3	260

BECKER, HENRY (a revolutionary soldier).

		Doc.	Vol.	No.
1830.	Report on petition for bounty land,	A	3	213
1831.	Report on petition for bounty land,	A	3	227

BECKER, PETER.

		Doc.	Vol.	No.
1852.	Report on petition of,	A	2	38

BEEBE, ALONZO.

		Doc.	Vol.	No.
1837.	Report on petition to confirm his official acts as a justice of the peace,	A	1	20

BEEBE, ALVAH.

		Doc.	Vol.	No.
1833.	Confidential journal of the proceedings of assembly in relation to,	A	3	143
1833.	Report of select committee,	A	3	155
1833.	Report of select committee,	A	3	169
1833.	Answer of, to the several interrogatories addressed to,	A	3	171
1834.	Report of attorney-general concerning the suit brought by, against the speaker of assembly,	A	3	135

BEEBE, ELISHA, AND N. TOWER.

		Doc.	Vol.	No.
1831.	Report on petition of, relative to the sale of certain land,	A	2	112

BEEBE, LEWIS, AND J. CHAPMAN.

		Doc.	Vol.	No.
1833.	Report on petition for extra compensation for work done on the Erie canal,	A	3	222
1834.	Report of committee on claims on the same,	A	1	43

BEEBE, LEWIS, AND OTHERS.

		Doc.	Vol.	No.
1854.	Report on petition of,	A	1	38
1855.	Report of committee on claims on petition of,	A	5	125
1856.	Report on petition of,	A	4	151
1857.	Report of committee on claims favorable on petition of, for further compensation,	A	1	41

BEEBE, LEWIS, AND WILLIAM THOMPSON.

		Doc.	Vol.	No.
1839.	Report on petition for extra compensation for work done on the Erie canal,	A	2	61
1839.	Report of committee on claims,	A	3	103
1839.	Report of canal commissioners,	A	6	372
1840.	Report of committee on claims,	A	2	45
1841.	Report of committee on claims,	A	3	54

BEEBE, THOMPSON & Co.

		Doc.	Vol.	No.
1846.	Report on petition for relief of,	S	1	26

BEECHER & HOSMER.

		Doc.	Vol.	No.
1850.	Report of committee on grievances on claim of, ...	A	5	89

BEEKMAN AND PAWLING TURNPIKE.

1830.	Report on petition to amend the charter of, ...	A	4	416

BEERS, JAMES E.

1847.	Report on petition of John R. Heywood, of Westchester, to be admitted to seat occupied by, ...	A	1	29

BEET ROOT.

1848.	Report of the American Institute relative to the manufacture of sugar from the, ...	A	4	134

BELLINGER, FREDERICK.

1833.	Report on petition for a grant of surplus water of the Erie canal,	A	4	265

BELLMONT.

1857.	Report of committee on roads and bridges on "An act for the laying out and constructing a road from Clinton Prison to town of," &c., ...	A	2	129

BENEDICT, LEWIS.

1855.	Report of commissioners of canal fund in reference to award to,	A	4	114

BENJAMIN, GAMALIEL.

1856.	Report on petition for relief, ...	A	3	58

BENNETT, ROSWELL G.

1857.	Report of committee on claims favorable on petition of, for damages by leakage and overflow of Genesee Valley canal, ...	A	2	121

BENNINGTON, TOWN OF.

1838.	Report on petition from, relative to one day elections, ...	A	6	317

BENOIT, LEWIS (an alien).

1831.	Report on petition to hold real estate, ...	A	2	148

BENTHAM, JEREMY.

1837.	Defense of usury, ...	S	1	6

BENTLEY, WM.

1843.	Report of canal board on petition of, ...	A	4	97

BENTLY, D., AND OTHERS.

1854.	Report on petition of, ...	A	3	113

BENTON, LEWIS.

1843.	Report of committee on claims on petition of, ...	A	3	73

BENTON, POSTERITAS POPE.

1835.	Report on petition to change name of, ...	A	2	147

BERESFORD, S. B.

		Doc.	Vol.	No.
1856.	Report of select committee on petition of,	S	2	64

BERGEN, JACOB, AND THOMAS SMITH.

1830.	Executors of the last will, &c., of John Bergen, report on petition of,	A	4	426

BERGEN, TOWN OF.

1854.	Report of committee on charitable and religious societies relative to First M. E. Church in,	A	2	50

BERKSHIRE, TOWN OF.

1831.	Report on petition for the division of,	A	3	266

BERLIN AND POESTENKILL TURNPIKE COMPANY.

1834	Report on petition to extend their road,	S	2	57

BERN, TOWN OF.

1849.	Report on petition for a fire engine company in,	A	6	390

BERRY, MR.

1856.	Report of, against senate bill 176,	A	5	203

BERZEE, MOSES.

1857.	Report on claim of,	S	1	38

BESTOW, JOB, *see* J. Clary.

BETHLEHEM, TOWN OF.

1832.	Report on petition to extend the time for the collection of taxes in,	A	3	182
1832.	Report on petition to reunite the,	A	4	332
1833.	Report on petition to reunite the,	A	2	131
1839.	Report on petition to extend the time for the collection of taxes in,	A	4	250

BETTINGER, MARTIN, AND DAVID LOBAN.

1838.	Report on petition for compensation for damages by the Erie canal,	A	5	288

BETTING ON ELECTIONS.

1839.	Report relative to prohibiting,	A	6	203

BETTS, CHARLES L.

1838.	Report on petition to change his name,	A	2	53

BEVIN, JOHN L., AND OTHERS.

1838.	Contractors on the Chenango canal, report on petition for relief,	A	6	316

BEVINS, JOHN L.

1844.	Report of canal board on petition of,	A	1	25

BEVINS, THOMAS.

1854.	Report on petition of,	A	1	34

BIBLE, *see* American and Foreign Bible Society.

1838.	Report on petition to prohibit the reading of, in academies, schools, &c.,	A	2	55

BICKNELL, JOSEPH.

		Doc.	Vol.	No.
1844.	Report on petition of heirs of,......	S	2	60

BIG CHAZY RIVER.

1851.	Report of committee on railroads respecting drawbridge over,...	A	5	145
1852.	Report relative to improving navigation of,......	A	2	57

BIGELOW, HORACE.

1833.	Report on petition to confirm his acts as justice of the peace,....	A	2	114

BIGELOW, JOHN L.

1839.	Report on petition for extra allowance for work done on the Kingsley Brook reservoir,......	A	2	22
1849.	Report of select committee on petition of administrators of, &c.,	A	3	157

BIGELOW, OTIS, AND OTHERS.

1837.	Report on petition concerning the Seneca river towing path,.....	A	2	114

BIGHAM, ANDREW.

1852.	Report on petition of, for relief,......	A	2	83

BIGHAM, A. T. & A.

1845.	Report of committee on grievances on petition of, ...	A	5	179

BIG SALMON RIVER.

1836.	Report relative to fishing in,......	A	3	183

BILLE, STEEN.

1847.	Communication from, relative to conciliation courts,......	S	3	98

BINDING, *see* Printing.

BINGHAM, A., AND OTHERS.

1845.	Report of committee on grievances on petition of,......	A	5	179

BINGHAM, ELIJAH.

1840.	Report on petition for pay for services as a surgeon in the last war,......	A	4	126

BIRD, WILLIAM A., AND OTHERS.

1836.	Report on petition of, relative to the surplus waters of the Black Rock dam,......	A	4	223
1841.	Report of canal board,......	S	2	57

BIRDSALL, BENJAMIN, AND OTHERS.

1849.	Report of secretary of state, relative to report of commissioners of land office, on petition of,......	A	3	162

BIRDSALL, HORACE, AND OTHERS.

1842.	Memorial of, for corporation to complete the canals,......	A	7	160

BIRDSEYE, VICTORY, *see* William Morgan.

BIRTHS, MARRIAGES AND DEATHS.

1846.	Report on petitions for registration of,......	S	4	81
1847.	Report on registry of,......	S	1	8
1848.	Report of secretary of state,......	S	3	73
1849.	Report relative to,......	S	3	86

BIRTHS, MARRIAGES AND DEATHS—*continued.*

		Doc.	Vol.	No.
1852.	Report of secretary of state respecting,........................	S	1	50
1852.	Report of secretary of state respecting his report of,..........	S	1	51
1858.	Report of select committee on the registration of,.............	S	2	81

BISHOP, EDSON.

1855.	Report of canal commissioners in respect to claim of,..........	A	4	92
1855.	Report of committee on claims, on petition of,................	S	1	16

BISHOP, ISAAC W., *see* Commercial Bank investigation.

BISSELL, D. P.

1847.	Memorial of, relative to report of select committee of 1846, for investigating canal frauds,..............................	S	3	109

BISSELL, I., Jr.

1831.	Report on petition of the executors of the last will, &c., of,....	A	4	347

BLACK, JOHN H.

1849.	Report of judiciary committee on petition of, for a divorce,.....	A	2	66

BLACKMAN, A. S., AND OTHERS.

1834.	Proposition of, to build a prison for female convicts,..........	S	2	84

BLACKMAN, CHARLES.

1847.	Report on petition of,..	A	7	220

BLACKMAN, CHARLES, AND OTHERS.

1846.	Report of committee on grievances on petition of,.............	A	2	84

BLACK RIVER.

1836.	Bridge across at Fish Island, report on petition for,.....	A	4	276
1837.	Report on petition of the Dexter Company, relative to the injuries they will sustain by diverting the waters of, to supply the Black River canal and Erie canal feeder,........................	A	3	205
1840.	Bridges across, report on petition from the towns of Champlain, Wilna, Pamela and Le Ray for a loan to build,..............	A	8	336
1850.	Report of committee on claims on bill for damages for diversion of water,..	S	3	78
1850.	Report of canal board on supplying with water,..............	S	3	98
1854.	Communication from auditor relative to improvement, ...	S	2	79
1855.	Water rights, report of select committee in relation to,.........	A	5	128
1856.	Report of committee to investigate grievances of owners of water rights on,..	A	4	125
1856.	Report of committee on petition of supervisors and others, for the construction of a bridge over,........................	A	4	130

BLACK RIVER CANAL, *see* Canals.

BLACK RIVER COTTON AND WOOLEN MANUFACTURING COMPANY.

1833.	Report concerning, ...	S	1	21

BLACK ROCK.

1835.	Ferry at, report on petition of Donald Frazier for an extension of the lease of, ...	A	3	240
1836.	Bridge across the Niagara at, report on the petition of Wm. H. Lacey to build,..	A	4	333
1839.	Harbor, report of A. Barrett, civil engineer, in relation to,......	S	2	54

BLACK ROCK—*continued.*

Year	Subject	Doc.	Vol.	No.
1840.	Harbor, report of canal board relative to the pier at,	A	8	312
1840.	Forts at, communication from Gouvernier Kemble relative to,	A	6	268
1843.	Report of canal board relative to property shipped and left at,	A	5	148
1843.	Report of commissioners of land office on the documents referred to them by the assembly relative to ceding certain lands at, to the United States for military works,	A	5	662
1847.	Report relative to bill entitled an act to provide for draining certain lands near Skajaquada creek in town of,	A	1	27
1847.	Report of commissioners of land office to permit board of supervisors of Erie county to take stone from public lands in,	A	1	44
1849.	Harbor, report of the canal board on,	S	2	33
1850.	Strike on canal at,	A	5	93
1851.	Harbor, report of canal board on removal of obstructions,	A	3	90
1857.	Harbor, report of auditor in reply to resolution relative to leases of surplus waters of,	A	3	204
	Surplus water at, *see* Wm. A. Bird and others.			

BLACK ROCK AND NIAGARA FALLS RAILROAD, *see* Railroads.

BLACK ROCK LAND AND RAILROAD COMPANY.

Year	Subject	Doc.	Vol.	No.
1836.	Report on petition of, to lay down piers in the Black Rock harbor,	A	3	115

BLAIR, GEORGE (an alien).

Year	Subject	Doc.	Vol.	No.
1839.	Report on petition of, relative to certain real estate,	A	5	295

BLAISDELL, WESLEY, AND OTHERS.

Year	Subject	Doc.	Vol.	No.
1840.	Report on petition to annul certain provisions of a will,	A	4	135

BLAKE, DOMINICK T.

Year	Subject	Doc.	Vol.	No.
1830.	Report on petition that the state purchase copies of his Digest of Criminal Law,			

BLAKELEY, JOHN (an alien).

Year	Subject	Doc.	Vol.	No.
1839.	Report on petition to confirm his title to certain land,	A	2	70

BLAKIE, I. & J. (aliens).

Year	Subject	Doc.	Vol.	No.
1832.	Report on petition of,	A	3	233

BLAKELY, MARIA, AND R. COLDEN.

Year	Subject	Doc.	Vol.	No.
1847.	Devisees of Maria H. Williamson, report on petition of,	A	2	94

BLATCHFORD, JANE.

Year	Subject	Doc.	Vol.	No.
1850.	Report of committee on commerce and navigation on petition of,	A	6	141, 143

BLAUVELT, JOHN G., AND ANDREW PARSONS (executors, &c., of John O'Neil, deceased).

Year	Subject	Doc.	Vol.	No.
1842.	Report of executive committee on petition of,	S	3	72

BLEECKER, BARENT, AND JOHN R.

Year	Subject	Doc.	Vol.	No.
1836.	Report on petition of, relative to the aqueduct over Oriskany creek,	S	1	64

BLENHEIM AND FULTON, TOWNS OF.

Year	Subject	Doc.	Vol.	No.
1833.	Report on petition from, relative to the hunting of deer,	A	3	176
1835.	Report in relation to the instruction of the,	A	5	394
1835.	Report relative to the enumeration of the,	A	1	65

BLIND.

INSTITUTION FOR, NEW YORK:

Year	Subject	Doc.	Vol.	No.
1833.	Report on petition for aid,	A	2	123
1834.	Memorial of the managers of, for aid,	S	1	28
1834.	Report on memorial for aid,	A	3	114
1834.	Report on bill in aid of,	A	4	392
1835.	Report on petition for aid,	A	5	394
1837.	First annual report of the,	A	3	199
1838.	Second annual report of the,	A	5	268
1839.	Third annual report of the,	A	4	226
1840.	Fourth annual report of the,	A	6	243
1841.	Fifth annual report of the,	A	6	213
1840.	Report of secretary of state concerning the,	A	5	172
1841.	Report on petition for aid to,	A	7	260
1842.	Annual report of,	A	4	77
1843.	do	A	4	88
1844.	do	A	3	57
1845.	Report of managers of,	S	1	18
1845.	Annual report of the managers of,	A	3	45
1845.	Report of committee on charitable and religious societies on the petition of,	A	4	92
1846.	Report of managers of,	S	1	38
1846.	Annual report of,	A	3	61
1846.	do	A	5	140
1847.	do	A	2	50
1848.	do	A	3	59
1849.	Thirteenth annual report of managers of,	A	2	84
1849.	Report of secretary of state, in answer to a resolution of assembly, respecting appointment of trustees of,	A	3	109
1850.	Annual report of,	A	4	76
1851.	Petition of managers of,	A	2	34
1851.	Annual report of,	A	3	49
1852.	Report of,	S	2	88
1853.	Annual report of,	S	2	54
1854.	do	S	2	108
1855.	do	S	3	75
1856.	Twentieth annual report for,	A	5	200
1857.	Annual report of managers of,	A	3	196
1858.	Annual report of managers of,	A	3	79

BLISS, NEZIAH, AND OTHERS.

Year	Subject	Doc.	Vol.	No.
1853.	Resolution of Mr. Beekman, on petition of,	S	2	68

BLOOD, HAIGHT & CADY.

Year	Subject	Doc.	Vol.	No.
1846.	Report of committee on claims on petition of,	A	4	107
1847.	Report of committee on claims on petition of,	A	1	28

BLOOMFIELD.

Year	Subject	Doc.	Vol.	No.
1832.	Northeast Congregational Society, report on petition to change the name of,	A	4	328

BLOOMFIELD, JOSEPH E., *see* Oneida Lake Canal Company.

Year	Subject	Doc.	Vol.	No.
1833.	Report on petition of, relative to the surplus waters of the canal at Utica,	S	2	112

BLOOMINGDALE ASYLUM, *see* New York.

BLOOMINGDALE ROAD, *see* New York.

BLOUNT & TRAVIS.

Year	Subject	Doc.	Vol.	No.
1854.	Report on petition of,	S	2	106

Year	Entry	Doc.	Vol.	No.
	BLUNT, EDWARD.			
1853.	Petition of, relative to life insurance companies,...............	A	5	121
	BOARDMAN, DANIEL.			
1831.	Report on petition of, relative to the sale of certain land for taxes,	A	2	115
	BOARDS OF SUPERVISORS, *see* Supervisors.			
	BOGARDUS, EPHRAIM.			
1834.	Report on petition for indemnification for costs in defending two ejectment suits, &c.,......................................	A	3	156
1834.	Report of committee on claims,..................................	A	3	220
1835.	do do	A	2	160
1836.	do do	A	2	69
	BOGART, H. H., AND OTHERS, *see* Dresden Manufacturing Company.			
	BOGART, H. H.			
1835.	Report on his claim for the construction of fences on the Crooked Lake canal,..	A	4	283
	BOGART, WILLIAM H.			
1853.	Compiler of the Digest of Claims, communication from,........	S	1	6
1855.	Index to legislative documents,..........	S	1	33
	BOGGS, WILLIAM, AND OTHERS.			
1841.	Report on petition for a grant of escheated land,...............	S	1	38
	BOLER, ANTONIO ALEXANDER (an alien).			
1835.	Report on petition to take and hold real estate,................	A	1	48
	BOLTON, JOHN, *see* President Delaware and Hudson Canal Company.			
	BOND, BARNARD.			
1842.	Report of canal board on petition of,........................	A	5	93
	BOND, BARNET.			
1830.	Report on petition for damages to his boat and cargo on the Champlain canal,...	A	2	180
1838.	Report on petition for damages to his boat and cargo on the Champlain canal,...	A	3	73
1841.	Report on petition for damages to his boat and cargo on the Champlain canal,...	A	4	122
1847.	Report on petition of, ...	A	7	210
	BOONVILLE, VILLAGE OF.			
1839.	Report on petition for a road from, to Salisbury,..............	A	5	325
1846.	Report of the surveyor-general in reply to a resolution relative to state lands lying near the proposed railroad and slack water navigation from Port Kent to,..............................	S	3	88
	BOSTON CORNER, MASS.			
1849.	Petition of inhabitants of district of, for annexation to State of New York, ...	A	2	54
1849.	Report on annexation of district of, to State of New York,......	A	3	194

BOTANIC PHYSICIANS, &c., *see* Thomsonian Physicians.

		Doc.	Vol.	No.
1830.	Report on petition to allow them to practice and to receive pay for their services,	A	2	110
1830.	Statement of the articles used by,	A	2	182

BULLARD, JOSEPH:

1834.	A report on petition of, to allow him to collect pay for his services,	A	3	206

BOTANIC PRACTICE.

1835.	Report on petition to repeal the laws restraining,	A	3	190
1833.	Report concerning the,	A	3	198

BOTANIC SOCIETY OF CATLIN.

1834.	Report on petition to incorporate,	A	2	95

BOTANIC SOCIETY, 1ST GENESEE UNION.

1833.	Report on petition to incorporate,	A	3	174
1834.	Report on petition to incorporate,	A	3	236

BOUCK W. C. (Canal Commissioner.)

1840.	Report on petition for an investigation of certain charges against,	A	4	102

BOUGHTON, REUBEN H., *see* Davis Hurd.

BOUGHTON, SENECA.

1852.	Report on petition of,	S	2	61

BOUNDARY COMMISSIONERS.

1858.	Communication from, in answer to a resolution of the house,	A	3	74
1858.	Report of the, in answer to a resolution of February 8, 1858,	A	4	148

BOUNDARY LINE.

Between Maine and New Brunswick, *see* Northeastern Boundary.
Between New York and Connecticut, *see* Connecticut.
Between New York and New Jersey, *see* New Jersey.

BOUNTY LANDS, *see* Lands, Military Bounty.

BOURON, JOHN S.

1858.	Report on claim of,	A	3	82

BOWERY FIRE INSURANCE COMPANY, *see* Insurance Companies.

BOYD, JOHN H.

1845.	Report of committee on claims in relation to the relief of,	S	1	27

BOYER, JOSEPH.

1837.	Report on petition to confirm his official acts as commissioner of deeds,	A	1	18

BOYES, W., *see* W. McComb.

BRADT, JAMES F.

1834.	Report on petition for compensation for damages by the Erie canal,	A	3	225

BRADT, JAMES F.—*continued.*

		Doc.	Vol.	No.
1835.	Report on petition for compensation for damages by the Erie canal,	A	3	250

BRADWAY, I.

		Doc.	Vol.	No.
1832.	Report on petition to continue a ferry across Schoharie creek,...	A	4	277

BRADY, JAMES.

		Doc.	Vol.	No.
1848.	Report on petition of,....................................	A	2	50
1849.	Report of committee on canals on petition of,................	A	1	37
1856.	Report on petition for relief,................................	A	3	79

BRADY, JAMES, AND PATRICK FITZSIMMONS.

		Doc.	Vol.	No.
1841.	Report on petition for moneys due on a contract for work on the Erie canal,..	A	6	248
1842.	Report of canal board on petition of,......................	S	4	86, 93
1843.	Report of committee on claims on petition of,................	S	1	16
1845.	Report of committee on grievances on petition of,............	A	3	56
1846.	Report of committee on claims on petition of,................	A	1	29
1847.	Report of committee on claims on petition of,................	A	1	23
1850.	Report on petition of,......................................	S	3	77
1851.	Report of committee on petition for canal damages,...........	S	2	47

BRADY, PATRICK.

		Doc.	Vol.	No.
1857.	Report of committee on claims favorable on petition of, for relief from contract on Champlain canal,....................	A	2	97

BRAINARD, CHAUNCEY.

		Doc.	Vol.	No.
1836.	Report on petition for the payment of certain costs,............	S	2	84

BRALEY, NATHANIEL.

		Doc.	Vol.	No.
1857.	Report of committee on claims favorable on petition of, for damages by overflow and breaks of Erie canal,..............	A	2	104

BRAN AND SHORTS.

		Doc.	Vol.	No.
1839.	Report on petition to repeal the law regulating a standard measure for,..	A	6	366

BRANDRETH, BENJAMIN.

		Doc.	Vol.	No.
1856.	Memorial of,..	S	1	4
1856.	Privileges and elections, report of committee on, on seat contested by, ...	S	2	89

BRANTINGHAM, TOWN OF.

		Doc.	Vol.	No.
1832.	Report on petition to change the name of,....................	A	2	86

BRAYTON AND CHESEBROUGH.

		Doc.	Vol.	No.
1844.	Report of committee on claims on petition of,................	A	3	88

BRAYTON AND OTHERS, *see* Baker, Brayton & Co.

BRAYTON, FRANCIS L.

		Doc.	Vol.	No.
1847.	Report of committee on canals on petition of,.....	A	2	82

BRAYTON, HARVEY, AND OTHERS.

		Doc.	Vol.	No.
1854.	Report of committee on petition of,.........................	A	1	12

BRAYTON, THOMAS L.

		Doc.	Vol.	No.
1847.	Report on petition of,	A	7	220

BRAYTON, THOMAS R., AND THOMAS W. CHESEBRO.

1844.	Report of canal board on petition of,	A	3	54

BRAYTON, W., *see* Bardwell and Brayton.

1839.	Report on petition for repairing canal fences,	A	5	269
1839.	do do do	A	5	290
1841.	do do do	A	4	118

BREAD, DANIEL (an Indian).

1832.	Report on petition for relief,	A	4	298

BREED & CO., *see* Geer, Kasson and Breed.

BRENARD, ISAAC G.

1856.	Report on petition for relief,	A	4	144

BRENT, DANIEL (United States Consul at Paris).

1840.	Communication from, in relation to the conveyance of real estate,	A	4	132

BREWERTON.

1838.	Report on petition to cause the Oneida river to be made navigable for steamboats from Three River Point to,	A	5	232

BREWERTON BRIDGE COMPANY.

1851.	Report of committee,	A	2	29

BREWSTER, SAMUEL S.

1850.	Report on memorial,	A	5	135

BRICE, J. R.

1846.	Report of judiciary committee on petition of,	A	3	70

BRIDGES.

1838.	Report relative to amending the Revised Statutes relative to,	A	5	207
1849.	Report of commissioners of the code concerning highways and ferries and,	A	1	12
1854.	Communications relative to commutations for,	A	2	52
1855.	Report of minority of select committee on bill to authorize additional sums to be raised for, and roads,	A	2	48

BRIDGES ON THE CANAL, *see* Canal Bridges.

BRIGHAM, STEWART & CO.

1850.	Report on claim,	A	5	90

BRIGHTON AND PITTSFORD.

1835.	Report relative to the use of canal water at, for hydraulic purposes,	A	2	83

BRIGHTON, TOWN OF.

1822.	Report on petition for the division of the,	A	3	273
1839.	Report on petition for the division of the,	A	3	85

BRIGGS, LYDIA.

		Doc.	Vol.	No.
1835.	Report on petition for an appropriation to pay an assessment for draining the Cayuga marshes,...........................	S	3	94

BRIGGS, THOMAS.

		Doc.	Vol.	No.
1851.	Report of committee on claims on petition of, for canal damages,..	S	3	29

BRIGGS, THOMAS, AND EBEN WORDEN.

		Doc.	Vol.	No.
1846.	Report of committee on claims on petition of,.................	S	1	31
1847.	Report of canal board respecting testimony taken in case of,.....	A	1	34

BRINGHAM, STEWART & CO.

		Doc.	Vol.	No.
1850.	Report of committee on canals on petition of,.................	A	5	90

BRINTNALL, HIRAM & JOSIAH, AND OTHERS.

		Doc.	Vol.	No.
1847.	Report of committee on claims on petition of,.................	A	2	74

BRISTOL AND RENSSELAERVILLE TURNPIKE COMPANY.

		Doc.	Vol.	No.
1837.	Report on petition of,....................................	S	1	30

BRISTOW, LYDIA (an alien).

		Doc.	Vol.	No.
1831.	Report on bill for the relief of..............................	S	1	26

BRISTOW, THOMAS, LYDIA & W. R.

		Doc.	Vol.	No.
1831.	Report on petition to vest in them the title to certain land in Brooklyn,.........	A	1	58

BRITTON AND TOWNSEND.

		Doc.	Vol.	No.
1858.	Report on claim of,.......................................	A	4	90

BRITTON, SURRANUS.

		Doc.	Vol.	No.
1849.	Report of committee on claims on petition of,.................	A	3	163
1857.	Report of committee on canals favorable on petition of, for payment of work done,......................................	A	2	144

BROADALBIN, TOWN OF.

		Doc.	Vol.	No.
	Report on petition to annex part of, to the town of Perth,.......	A	6	244

BROCKPORT, VILLAGE OF.

		Doc.	Vol.	No.
1830.	Report on petition for a road from, to Batavia,...............	A	2	164
1835.	Hook and ladder company in, report on petition to organize,....	A	4	292

BROCKWAY, MOSES, AND OTHERS.

		Doc.	Vol.	No.
1832.	Report on petition for remuneration for improvement on lots 64 and 28 Freemason's patent,...............................	A	4	295
1833.	Report on petition for remuneration for improvement on lots 64 and 28 Freemason's patent,...............................	S	2	60

BRODHEAD, J. ROMEYN.

		Doc.	Vol.	No.
1842.	Communication from Governor transmitting correspondence from,	S	4	88
1842.	Report of on Colonial History,..............................	A	1	2

BRODHEAD, J. ROMEYN—*continued.*

		Doc.	Vol.	No.
1842.	[Ex. Sess.] Historical agent, communication from, to the Governor,	A	7	195
1845.	Agent to procure and transcribe documents in Europe, final report of, relative to the Colonial History of this State,	S	1	47
1846.	Memorial of, relative to the Aboriginal History of the State,	S	2	55

BRODOCK, GEORGE H., AND OTHERS.

1858.	Report on claim of,	A	4	92

BROMAN, C. M.

1851.	Majority report on petition to discharge sureties of, as treasurer of Onondaga county,	A	3	51
1851.	Minority report on petition to discharge sureties of, as treasurer of Onondaga county,	A	3	50

BRONSON, A.

1847.	Report on petition of,	S	2	41

BRONSON, ALVIN, *see* Oswego Canal Company.

BRONSON, ALVIN, AND OTHERS.

1844.	Report of commissioners of land office on petition of,	A	5	111
1848.	Report on petition of,	A	3	121

BRONSON, CASE & Co.

1856.	Report of judiciary committee on petition of,	S	2	79
1857.	Report on claim of,	S	1	27

BROOKHAVEN, TOWN OF.

1830.	Report on petition for the division of,	A	3	261
1831.	do	S	1	66
1832.	do	A	3	207
1841.	do	S	1	16

BROOKLYN.

1830.	Municipal court, report on petition to amend the law establishing,	A	3	244
1831.	Firemen, report on petition to reduce the term of service,	A	2	149
1831.	School district No. 1, report on petition to sell their school-house and lot, &c.,	A	2	177
1833.	Taxes, report on petition to extend the time for collecting,	A	1	6
1833.	Auction sales in, report on petition to amend the law relative to,	A	2	43
1834.	Incorporation of, memorial for the,	A	1	36
1834.	Incorporation of, remonstrance of common council of New York against,	A	3	175
1834.	Incorporation of, memorial of a convention of delegates of the several towns in Kings county in relation to,	A	3	183
1835.	Taxes unpaid, report on petition to authorize the collection of,	A	4	375
1836.	Taxes unpaid, report on petition to authorize the collection of,	A	2	64
1838.	Harbor masters, report relative to the fees of,	A	2	47
1838.	Greenwood cemetery, report on petition to incorporate,	A	6	334
1839.	Corporation of, report on petition of, for aid to the Long Island Railroad Company,	S	3	67
1839.	Taxes, report on petition to extend time for collecting,	A	1	14
1840.	Water line in the sixth ward, report on petition of Cyrus P. Smith and others,	A	3	62
1849.	New charter of, remonstrance from delegates from eighth and ninth wards of, against,	A	1	28

BROOKLYN—*continued.*

		Doc.	Vol.	No.
1849.	Communication from minority of committee appointed to forward a copy of proposed new charter for,	A	1	32
1849.	Secretary of navy, communication from, respecting the purchase of certain land adjoining the navy yard,	A	5	237
1850.	Report of committee on trade and manufactures on petition of gas company in,	S	1	22
1850.	Letter from secretary of navy in regard to certain lands,	A	4	54
1850.	Bulkheads and wharves,	A	6	141
1850.	Common schools and board of education, report of select committee on,	A	6	156
1850.	Report on wharfage in, and New York,	A	6	162
1850.	Letter of secretary of navy in regard to certain lands,	A	6	171
1850.	Report in regard to ceding certain lands to the United States,	A	8	183
1851.	Report on union with New York and Williamsburgh,	S	3	74
1854.	Remonstrance of common council against interference, &c.,	S	1	44
1855.	Report on petitions relative to excavations in,	S	2	50
1856.	Report of committee on laying out street and constructing a canal therein,	A	4	106
1856.	Tenement houses, report on,	A	5	199
1856.	Police, minority report in relation to,	A	5	209
1856.	Dispensary, annual report for 1855,	A	4	116
1857.	Report of majority of committee on incorporation of cities and villages, relative to the police departments of New York and,	A	2	127
1857.	Report of minority of committee on same subject,	A	3	149
1857.	Report of select committee appointed to examine tenant houses in New York and,	A	3	205
1858.	Assessment bill, report of committee of conference on,	A	4	104
1858.	Williamsburgh, and the town of Bushwick, report of committee on the incorporation of cities and villages, on the bill to amend the act to consolidate,	S	2	100

BANKS, *see* Banks, Kings County ; and Banks, Savings.
FERRIES, *see* New York Ferries.
INSPECTORS OF LUMBER, &c., *see* Kings County.
INSURANCE COMPANIES, *see* Insurance Companies.
RAILROADS, *see* Railroads.
LANDS UNDER WATER, *see* I. G. Hicks and O. Jackson.

BROOME COUNTY.

		Doc.	Vol.	No.
1833.	Report on petition for an application for the improvement of a road in, leading to a mineral spring in said county,	S	2	56
1834.	Report on petition of the supervisors of, relative to the payment of a loan,	A	3	130
1834.	Report on petition of the supervisors of, relative to the payment of a loan,	A	3	160
1834.	Report on petition of the supervisors of, relative to the payment of a loan,	A	3	160
1834.	Dam across the Susquehannah river in, report on petition to erect a,	A	3	159
1842.	Petition of the New York and Erie Railroad Company, respecting the different lines surveyed in Sullivan and, for the location of their road,	S	3	58
1847.	Report of commissioners of land office on petition of certain Indians relative to land in,	A	7	215

BROTHERTOWN INDIANS, *see* Indians, Brothertown.

BROWN, BILLINGS, AND OTHERS, *see* Burlington.

BROWN, CONRAD, AND OTHERS.

		Doc.	Vol.	No.
1846.	Communication from secretary of state relative to claim of,	A	4	132

BROWN, DAVID, AND OTHERS, *see* New York Marine Dry Dock Company.

BROWN, ELIAS.

		Doc.	Vol.	No.
1846.	Report of canal commissioners on petition of,	A	1	22

BROWN, ISAAC, Jr.

		Doc.	Vol.	No.
1836.	Report on petition for compensation for land taken for the Nine Mile Creek feeder,	S	2	78
1837.	Committee on claims,	A	2	112
1838.	Attorney-general,	A	3	145
1838.	Committee on claims,	A	4	175

BROWN, J. D.

		Doc.	Vol.	No.
1834.	Communication from, relative to the Seventh Ward Bank,	S	2	73

BROWN, JONATHAN, AND OTHERS.

		Doc.	Vol.	No.
1838.	Report on petition for compensation for damages to their lands by the Chemung canal feeder,	A	5	292

BROWN, JOSEPH.

		Doc.	Vol.	No.
1833.	Report on petition to confirm his title to certain land,	A	4	286

BROWN, LEVI.

		Doc.	Vol.	No.
1852.	Report on petition of, for relief,	S	4	37

BROWN, MARCUS.

		Doc.	Vol.	No.
1843.	Report of committee on claims on the petition of,	S	1	22
1844.	do do	A	5	112
1845.	do do	A	4	130
1846.	do do	A	2	42
1847.	Report on petition of,	A	1	19
1848.	Report on petition of,	A	5	185
1849.	Report of committee on claims on petition of,	A	2	53
1852.	Report on petition of, for relief,	A	2	76
1852.	Affidavits relative to the claim of,	A	5	96
1856.	Report on petition of,	S	2	72
1857.	Report on claim of,	S	2	58

BROWN, MATTHEW, AND OTHERS (sureties of C. Van Slyck).

		Doc.	Vol.	No.
1838.	Report on the petition to be released from a certain judgment,	A	6	364
1839.	Report on the petition to be released from a certain judgment,	A	3	111
1842.	Report of committee on grievances on petition of,	A	7	140
1843.	Report of committee on grievances on their petition for relief,	A	2	23

BROWN, MERRIT H., AND OTHERS.

		Doc.	Vol.	No.
1849.	Report of committee on claims on petition of,	A	3	129

BROWN, NEAL.

		Doc.	Vol.	No.
1832.	A canal contractor, report on petition for extra allowance,	A	3	194
1833.	Canal commissioners,	S	2	116
1833.	Committee on claims,	A	2	57
1834.	Committee on claims,	A	1	44

BROWN, OLIVER.

		Doc.	Vol.	No.
1857.	Report of committee on claims favorable on petition of, for damages by break in Erie canal,	A	1	56

BROWN, PELEG, AND OTHERS.

		Doc.	Vol.	No.
1832.	Report on petition for remuneration for improvements on certain lands in Freemason's patent,	A	4	295

BROWN, SOLOMON.

		Doc.	Vol.	No.
1843.	Report of committee on claims on his petition.	A	4	97
1843.	Report of committee on claims on his petition,	A	2	20
1845.	Report of canal board on the petition of,	A	3	36

BROWN, THOMAS.

		Doc.	Vol.	No.
1844.	Report of canal commissioners on petition of,	S	3	101

BROWN, T. J.

		Doc.	Vol.	No.
1855.	Report of committee on claims in case of,	A	2	51

BROWNVILLE AND HOUNSFIELD, TOWNS OF.

		Doc.	Vol.	No.
1836.	Report on petition to raise money to build a bridge across Black river at Fish island,	A	4	276

BRUCE, PACKARD.

		Doc.	Vol.	No.
1847.	Reports as to allowance to,	A	2	61
1847.	Report on petition of,	A	1	41
1849.	Report on petition of,	S	2	38

BRUNDAGE, B. S.

		Doc.	Vol.	No.
1830.	Report on petition of, relative to the mortgage given by him to George McClure,	S	1	27

BRUNGES, ANNA C.

		Doc.	Vol.	No.
1855.	Report of committee on public lands on petition of,	A	5	127

BRUNJES, ANNA C.

		Doc.	Vol.	No.
1856.	Report on petition of, for relief,	A	3	76

BRUSSELS CARPETING.

		Doc.	Vol.	No.
1844.	Report of attorney-general in reply to a resolution of the assembly of February 10, relative to the manufacture of,	A	3	75

BRUYN, JANSEN.

		Doc.	Vol.	No.
1844.	Report on petition of,	S	2	53

BUCHANAN, THOMAS E., AND H. CARD.

		Doc.	Vol.	No.
1851.	Report of committe on grievances on petition of, for canal damages,	A	3	82

BUCKDORF, JACOB.

		Doc.	Vol.	No.
1834.	Report on petition to be refunded certain moneys paid for toll,	A	4	274

BUELL, N.

		Doc.	Vol.	No.
1847.	Report of canal board on petition of,	A	7	213

BUELL, WILLIAM.

		Doc.	Vol.	No.
1834.	Report on petition to authorize the commissioners of the canal fund to pay the expense of certain suits,	A	4	318
1835.	Report on the same,	S	2	34

BUELL, WILLIAM—*continued.*

		Doc.	Vol.	No.
1846.	Report of committee on claims on petition of,	A	2	40
1846.	Reports on the bill for relief of,	S	4	119
1846.	Report of committee on claims on petition of,	S	4	126
1847.	Report on petition of,	A	6	171
1847.	Memorial of,	S	3	94
1851.	Petition for relief for canal damages,	A	2	44
1851.	Report of committee on claims,	A	3	74
1852.	Report on petition of, for relief,	S	1	17

BUEL, WILLIAM, AND T. C. PETERS.

		Doc.	Vol.	No.
1850.	Memorial in relation to agricultural colleges,	A	6	158

BUFFALO AND BATAVIA RAILROAD, *see* Railroads.

BUFFALO AND BLACK ROCK RAILROAD, *see* Railroads.

BUFFALO AND HORNELLSVILLE RAILROAD, *see* Railroads.

BUFFALO AND NEW HAMBURGH TURNPIKE.

		Doc.	Vol.	No.
1839.	Report on petition to incorporate,	S	1	16
1832.	Report on petition to incorporate,	A	3	516

BUFFALO AND NIAGARA FALLS RAILROAD, *see* Railroads.

BUFFALO AND ROCHESTER PACKET BOAT COMPANY.

		Doc.	Vol.	No.
1839.	Report on petition to be refunded certain moneys paid for canal tolls,	A	3	162
1839.	Report on petition to be refunded certain moneys paid for canal tolls,	A	4	210

BUFFALO, CITY OF.

		Doc.	Vol.	No.
1830.	Road from, to Cattaraugus creek, report on petition for a State road, &c.,	A	3	224
1831.	Fire department, report on petition to raise money to purchase engines, &c.,	A	4	322
1831.	Roads and bridges in the Buffalo Creek Reservation, report of comptroller on the bill concerning,	A	6	198
1834.	Road from Abbott's Corners, report on petition to raise money by tax to improve a,	A	4	313
1834.	Burial Ground Association, report on petition to incorporate,	A	4	375
1836.	Marine hospital, report relative to certain lands claimed by,	A	4	319
1837.	Marine railway, report on petition to increase the capital of,	A	3	197
1839.	Canal basin, Main and Hamburgh streets, report of canal commissioners relative to,	A	6	363
1840.	Report of the survey of,	A	6	257
1840.	Arsenal at, report on petition for,	A	6	251
1842.	Report of select committee relative to excise in,	A	2	46
1843.	Remonstrance of common council of,	A	3	44
1843.	Report of committee on grievances on bill for relief of,	A	3	48
1843.	Report of canal board in answer to a resolution of the assembly calling for information in relation to property shipped and left at,	A	5	148
1847.	Report on petition from, relative to Erie canal,	A	7	205
1847.	Report on petition of E. Pierson for floating dry dock at,	A	2	63
1848.	Report of committee on roads and bridges on a resolution of common council of,	S	1	11
1849.	Report of canal board on the construction of the works at,	S	1	26
1850.	Strike on canal at,	A	5	93
1854.	Dispensary, memorial of,	S	1	16

BUFFALO CITY—*continued.*

		Doc.	Vol.	No.
1856.	Report on petition of citizens of, to be annexed to adjoining towns, ...	A	3	88
1858.	Report on petition of charitable institutions located in, ...	A	4	108

BANKS, *see* Banks, Erie County; and Banks, Savings.

INSURANCE COMPANIES, *see* Insurance Companies.

MEDICAL COLLEGES, *see* Medical Colleges.

SEMINARY, *see* Academies, &c.

REPORTS OF INSPECTORS OF PROVISIONS, *see* Erie County.

BULL, A.

1847.	Report on petition of,..	A	7	213

BULL, GEO. W.

1851.	Report in relation to charges, ...	S	2	60

BULL, WILLIAM.

1843.	Report of committee on claims on petition of,................	S	1	31
1854.	Report on petition of,.......................................	A	2	45
1857.	Report of committee on claims adverse on petition of, for damages by falling of a bridge over the Erie canal,..................	A	1	56
1857.	Report of committee on claims adverse on petition of, for damages by falling of a bridge over Erie canal,........................	A	3	156

BULLARD, JOSEPH (a botanic physician).

1834.	Report on petition to authorize him to collect pay for services, &c.,	A	3	206

BUMP, JOHN.

1845.	Report on petition of,..........	A	4	141

BUMPUS, NATHAN, AND OTHERS.

1835.	Report on claim of, on lots 24 and 68, Freeman's patent,.......	A	2	137
1836.	Report on claim of, on lots 24 and 68, Freeman's patent, ...	S	2	91

BURCH, JOHN.

1844.	Report of the committee on claims on the petition of,..........	A	5	139
1845.	Report of the canal board on the petition of,..................	A	4	102

BURCH, RUSSELL B.

1847.	Report on petition of,.......................................	A	7	225

BURCHARD, NATHAN (attorney for the Oneida Indians).

1841.	Communication from, in relation to his salary,................	A	4	139

BURCKLE, CHRISTIAN J.

1837.	Report on petition for the conveyance to him of certain land, ...	A	3	216

BURDICK, HUBBARD.

1845.	Report of canal board on petition of,........................	A	6	217
1846.	Report of committee on claims on petition of, ...	A	2	32
1847.	Report on petition of,..	A	2	66
1848.	Report on petition of,..	A	2	37
1849.	Report of committee on claims on petition of,.................	A	2	97
1850.	Report of committee on canals on petition of,.................	A	4	75
1850.	Report on claim of,...	A	5	79

	BURDSELL, BENJ., AND OTHERS.	Doc.	Vol.	No.
1849.	Report of secretary of state relative to petition of, ...	A	3	162
	BURLINGHAME, PLATT.			
1858.	Report of committee on claims on petition of, ...	A	4	147
	BURLINGTON, ELIJAH, AND OTHERS.			
1840.	Report on petition to confirm their title to certain land, ...	S	3	66
1840.	Report on petition to confirm their title to certain land, ...	S	4	124
	BURLINGTON GREEN, VILLAGE OF.			
1832.	Report on petition to incorporate a fire company in, ...	A	4	297
	BURLINGTON WATER WORKS COMPANY.			
1837.	Report on petition of Billings Brown to incorporate, ...	A	4	286
	BURNETT, GEN. WARD B.			
1858.	Report of committee on militia and public defence on the bill to pay moneys to, ...	S	2	101
	BURNHAM, NOAH.			
1835.	An insane person, confined in Cayuga county jail for murder, report concerning, ...	A	3	209
	BURNS, THOMAS.			
1854.	Report of committee on grievances on petition of, ...	A	1	34
	BURNS, TOWN OF.			
1840.	Report on petition to annex part of the town of Almond, ...	A	8	316
	BURR, LEVI S.			
1834.	Report of, for an investigation of the conduct of the officers of the Mount Pleasant prison, ...	A	3	211
	BURROW, ASA.			
1835.	Report on petition for compensation for damages to his land by the Erie canal, ...	A	4	348
1836.	Canal commissioners' report, ...	A	4	231
1836.	Report of the committee on grievances, ...	A	4	255
	BURROW, JABEZ (collector of canal tolls at West Troy).			
1835.	Report on petition to be relieved from the payment of certain money, ...	S	2	63
	BURROWS, ROSWELL S. AND LORENZO, AND OTHERS.			
1858.	Report of committee on petition of, for relief, ...	A	1	37
	BURT, D. G., AND WILLIAM HARRIS.			
1831.	Report on petition for compensation for damages to their lands by the erection of the Saratoga dam, ...	A	2	187
1832.	Report of committee on canals, ...	A	2	148
1838.	Report of committee on canals, ...	A	3	64
	BURT, HARRIET R.			
1849.	Report of commissioners of land office on petition of, ...	A	3	102

BURT, JUSTUS.

		Doc.	Vol.	No.
1830.	Report on petition for the repayment of certain money paid for land, ...	A	2	101
1830.	Commissioners of the land office, report on bill for the relief of,	S	2	156

BURTON, TOWN OF.

1840.	Report on petition relative to roads and bridges in the, ...	A	6	238

BURYING GROUNDS, *see* Cemeteries, &c.

1853.	Report of committee on medical societies and colleges in relation to the better protection of, ...	A	2	21

BUSH, WM., AND HENRY B. HEWETT.

1847.	Report of committee on claims on petition of, ...	A	8	230

BUSHWICK, TOWN OF.

1835.	Report on petition to extend the time for the collection of tolls in,	A	1	19
1837.	do do	A	1	33
1839.	do do	A	1	14
1858.	Report on the bill to amend the act to consolidate the cities of Brooklyn and Williamsburgh with, ...	S	2	100

BUTLER, NORMAN, *see* Johnson, Stiles, and Norman Butler.

BUTRICK, R. P.

1856.	Report on petition for relief, ...	A	5	192

BUTTERFIELD, CHAS. E.

1857.	Report of committee on claims adverse on petition of, for damages to horse and wagon, ...	A	3	160

BUTTERNUTS AND OTHER CREEKS.

1836.	Report of canal commissioners in relation to the waters of, ...	S	2	80

BUTTERNUTS AND SHERBURN TURNPIKE COMPANY.

1840.	Report on petition relative to the location of a gate on, ...	A	4	145

BUTTERNUTS, TOWN OF.

1838.	Report on petition relative to the appointment of a commissioner of deeds at, ...	A	5	226
1846.	Report of select committee on petition of inhabitants of, ...	A	5	194

BUTTERLY, JOHN M., & JOSEPH P. HEWETT.

1844.	Report of canal board on petition of, ...	A	5	134

BUTTRICK, RICHARD P.

1857.	Report of committee on canals adverse on petition of, for additional compensation, ...	A	1	45
1857.	Report of committee on canals adverse on petition of, for extra compensation, ...	A	2	87

BYNGTON, B.

1833.	Report on petition for a loan from the state, to aid him in the discovery of rock salt in Salina, ...	A	4	314

BYRAM RIVER.

		Doc.	Vol.	No.
1851.	Report on petition for a draw-bridge across,	A	5	146

C.

CABINET OF NATURAL HISTORY, *see* Natural History.

CADWELL, EBENEZER S., *see* Elijah Burlingham and others.

CADWELL, MATHEW, AND OTHERS.

1830.	Report on petition for a premium, provided they discover a coal mine within ten miles of the Erie canal,	A	2	175

CADY, BLOOD & HAIGHT.

1846.	Report of committee on claims on petition of,	A	4	107
1847.	Report on petition of,	A	1	28

CADY, HENRY, & J. M. KASSON.

1843.	Report of committee on claims on petition of,	S	1	36
1848.	Report of committee on grievances on petition of,	A	3	117

CADY, SHULER.

1851.	Report of committee on petition for canal damages,	A	3	23
1851.	Report on petition of, for canal damages,	A	3	73
1851.	Mr. Chamberlain's report, from committee on grievances, on petition of,	A	3	75

CAGGER, PETER.

1843.	Report of canal board on his petition, as administrator of P. Bargy, Jr., deceased,	A	5	135
1852.	Administrator, report on petition of,	A	2	75

CAIRO AND CATSKILL TURNPIKE COMPANY.

1831.	Report on petition to renew the charter of,	A	2	134

CALDWELL, G. & J. W.

1852.	Report on their petition,	A	2	71
1854.	Report on petition of,	S	2	69

CALDWELL, GEORGE.

1842.	Report of committee on claims on petition of,	S	3	57

CALDWELL, GEORGE & JOSEPH.

1853.	Report of committee on claims in relation to the claims of,	S	2	38

CALDWELL'S LANDING.

1835.	Report on petition for a ferry from, to Peekskill,	A	4	313

CALIFORNIA.

1849.	Report of select committee on so much of governor's message as relates to the introduction of slavery into, and New Mexico,	A	3	139

CAMBRIDGE AND WHITE CREEK.

1833.	Report relative to highway labor in,	A	2	79

CAMDEN, VILLAGE OF.

		Doc.	Vol.	No.
1841.	Report on petition to amend the charter of the,................	S	3	95

CAMERON, DANIEL.

		Doc.	Vol.	No.
1835.	Report on petition to confirm the last will, &c., of, &c.,.........	A	4	271

CAMERON, JAMES J , *see* Warren county, jailor of.

CAMERON, TOWN OF.

		Doc.	Vol.	No.
1831.	Report relative to the poor fund of the,.......................	A	4	297
1832.	Report on petition for the division of the,.....................	A	2	136
1838.	Report on petition to raise money to build a bridge across the Canisteo river,......................................	A	5	291

CAMILLUS, TOWN OF.

		Doc.	Vol.	No.
1839.	First Methodist Episcopal Society, report on petition to sell real estate, ...	A	4	235
1841.	Report on petition of inhabitants of, for the use of surplus waters of the canal at,......................................	A	6	206

CAMMERDON, JOHN.

		Doc.	Vol.	No.
1848.	Report on petition of,.....................................	A	5	143

CAMPBELL, A.

		Doc.	Vol.	No.
1846.	Report of attorney-general on the petition of,.................	A	5	161

CAMPBELL, ALEXANDER.

		Doc.	Vol.	No.
1849.	Report of canal board, transmitting petition and affidavits of,...	A	3	173

CAMPBELL AND MOODY.

		Doc.	Vol.	No.
1851.	Report of commissioners of the land office relative to the claim of,	S	2	45
1851.	Report of commissioners of land office on petition of,.........	S	3	45

CAMPBELL, ARCHIBALD.

		Doc.	Vol.	No.
1838.	Report on claim of,......................................	A	4	163
1840.	Report on petition relative to a piece of land claimed to be escheated to the state,..................................	S	3	69

CAMPBELL, ASA.

		Doc.	Vol.	No.
1835.	Report on claim of, for work done on the Erie canal,...........	A	2	98
1835.	Report on claim of, for work done on the Erie canal,...........	A	3	222

CAMPBELL, HARRIS.

		Doc.	Vol.	No.
1849.	Report of committee on claims on petition of, ...	S	2	68

CAMPBELL, JOHN A.

		Doc.	Vol.	No.
1858.	Report of committee on claims on petition of,................	S	2	64

CAMPBELL, JOHN J.

		Doc.	Vol.	No.
1832.	Report on petition for compensation for certain land sold by the surveyor-general, ...	S	2	97
1837.	Report of commissioners of the land office,....................	A	2	156
1837.	Report of committee on grievances,........................	A	3	178
1840.	Report of committee on claims,............................	A	6	225

CAMPBELL, JOSEPH, AND S. LITTLEFIELD.

		Doc.	Vol.	No.
1834.	Report on petition for compensation for damages by the Champlain canal,	A	4	266

CAMPBELL, SQUIRE, AND OTHERS.

1842.	Report on petition of,	A	5	116

CAMPBELL, W.

1830.	Report on petition for pay for services as crier of the court of oyer and terminer in Albany,	A	4	365

CANADA.

1853.	Report of auditor of canal department in relation to tolls and quantity of property going to and coming from,	S	1	29
1850.	Report of joint select committee on application of parliament of,	S	1	9
1851.	Resolutions of parliament of,	A	3	60

CANADICE, TOWN OF.

1834.	Report on petition for the division of the,	A	4	334

CANAJOHARIE.

1830.	Report on petition to confer additional powers on supreme court commissioner,	A	4	405
1840.	Report on petition to extend the time for the collection of taxes in,	A	5	181
1848.	Report on the annexation of, to Minden,	A	3	96

DEAF AND DUMB INSTITUTION, *see* Deaf and Dumb.

CANAJOHARIE AND CATSKILL RAILROAD, *see* Railroads.

CANAJOHARIE AND PALATINE BRIDGE COMPANY.

1832.	Report on petition to amend the charter of,	S	2	78
1832.	Report on petition to amend the charter of,	S	2	99
1847.	Report of, under resolution,	S	2	51

CANAL APPRAISERS.

1830.	Compensation for expenses of, &c.,	A	1	28
1837.	Report of the, relative to the applications of Nathan Hall, W. P. Couch, and W. Skillenger, for compensation for canal damages,	S	2	70
1838.	Report of the, of appraisal of damages on the Erie, Champlain, Chenango and Chemung canals,	A	5	201
1840.	Report of the, on petition of N. S. Howard,	A	4	128
1844.	Report of, on the memorial of land owners in Frankford, German-flats and Herkimer, on the subject of canal damages,	A	5	101
1845.	Report of comptroller in relation to the pay, &c., of,	S	2	74
1845.	Report of, on the petition of John Watkins,	A	3	41
1845.	Report of, on the petition of Joseph Demont, O. Tyler and E. Mynderse,	A	3	46
1847.	Report of, of allowance made to Patrick Bruce, for damages from building Genesee Valley canal,	A	2	61
1847.	Report of, of allowance made to Abraham V. Putman for damages in enlarging Erie canal,	A	2	98
1849.	Annual report of,	S	1	14
1849.	Report of, on the condition of books, records, &c., in their office,	S	1	28
1849.	Report of, on petition of Simon Matison,	A	3	145
1850.	Report of, of testimony taken in case of John Watkins,	S	2	63
1850.	Annual report of,	S	2	69
1851.	Annual report of,	S	2	41

CANAL APPRAISERS—*continued.*

		Doc.	Vol.	No.
1851.	Report of committee on canals on bill to authorize, to award damages,	S	2	69
1852.	Annual report of,	S	2	60
1853.	Report of the, in answer to a resolution of the assembly of 17th February, in relation to applicants for damages,	A	2	47
1853.	Annual report of, in relation to clerk hire,	S	2	40
1854.	Communication from, relative to claims of mill owners at Rochester,	A	2	63
1854.	Annual report of,	S	2	80
1854.	Annual report of,	S	3	80
1855.	Communication from, in reference to claim of George Folts,	A	4	82
1855.	Annual report of,	S	3	69
1856.	Report of, relative to Rochester mill owners' claims,	S	3	103
1856.	Annual report of,	S	4	106
1857.	do	S	2	75
1858.	do	S	2	40

CANAL BOARD.

		Doc.	Vol.	No.
1830.	Report relative to increasing the rates of canal tolls,	S	4	291
1830.	Report relative to the preference of packets in passing locks on the canal,	S	2	98
1830.	Report on petition of Daniel McInray for extra allowance,	A	2	104
1830.	Report on petition of Andrew P. Tillman for extra allowance,	A	3	240
1830.	Report of expenditures on the Erie and Champlain canals, the number of superintendents, &c.,	S	3	243
1831.	Report on petition of S. Bardwell and W. Brayton for extra allowance,	A	3	203
1831.	Report on claim of the Oswego Canal Company,	A	4	309
1831.	Report on petition of Allen & Hecox for extra allowance,	S	1	57
1832.	Report on petition of Holmes, Hutchinson and I. Trumpbour,	A	3	188
1832.	Report on petition of Neal Brown for extra allowance,	A	3	194
1832.	Report of amount of tolls received on packet boats and passengers for the last two years,	S	1	49
1831.	Report on bill to incorporate the Oneida Lake Canal Company,	S	1	64
1832.	Report on petition of Philip Ludington for a bridge across the canal,	S	2	75
1833.	Report of, relative to bridges and fences on the canals,	S	1	30
1833.	do damages by draining Tonawanda creek,	S	2	89
1833.	do Oneida Lake Canal Company,	A	3	196
1833.	do Cohoes Bridge Company,	A	4	243
1833.	do Cayuga inlet, improvement of,	A	4	244
1833.	Report of, on petition of Frederick Bellinger for a grant of surplus water,	A	4	265
1833.	Report of, on petition of Samuel Wilkes for damages to his boat, &c.,	A	4	273
1833.	Report of, on petition of D. & R. Gorton for damages to their mills, &c.,	A	4	321
1833.	Report of, relative to canal bridges,	A	4	317
1833.	Report of, relative to condition of the Erie canal in Herkimer county,	A	4	272
1833.	Report of, on petition of farmers and others, of western New York, in relation to combinations of forwarding companies, &c.,	A	4	320
1834.	Report on petition of Henry Thalemer for extra allowance,	A	4	338
1834.	Report on petition of Peter Failing and others for extra allowance,	S	1	26
1834.	Report on petition of Lawrence Barclay for extra allowance,	A	4	366
1834.	Report of, relative to the improvement of Cayuga lake,	A	4	348
1834.	Report of, relative to work done on the Oswego canal by Henry Hill and others,	S	2	102
1834.	Report of, on a resolution of the senate relative to terminating the Erie canal at Schenectady,	S	2	72

CANAL BOARD—*continued.*

		Doc.	Vol.	No.
1835.	Report of, on petition of Zebulon Douglass for extra allowance,..	A	4	354
1835.	Report of, on the claim of Samuel Farwell,..................	A	2	86
1838.	Report of, on the claim of Holmes Hutchinson,...............	A	2	140
1835.	Report relative to the construction of a ship canal from Lake Ontario to the Hudson river,............................	A	4	334
1835.	Report relative to the towpath bridge across the Mohawk, constructed by the Cohoes company,..............................	A	4	364
1836.	Report on the subject of supplying the Rome summit with water,	S	1	61
1836.	Report relative to the cost of the Champlain canal,............	S	2	72
1836.	Report on a resolution of the senate relative to the increase or diminution of business on the Erie canal in consequence of the construction of the lateral canals,..........................	S	2	81
1836.	Report and documents relative to the enlargement of the Erie canal,..	A	2	98
1836.	Report and documents relative to the enlargement of the Erie canal,..	A	2	99
1836.	Report on petition of the Black Rock Land and Railroad Company,..	A	3	115
1836.	Report on petition of W. A. Bird and others, for a grant of surplus water,..	A	4	228
1836.	Report on petition of Philip Schuyler relative to canal fences,...	A	4	234
1836.	do T. V. Van Nest for extra allowance,.......	A	4	269
1836.	do Isaac Vail for extra allowance,..........	A	4	230
1836.	Report of, concerning tolls on gypsum,......................	A	4	294
1837.	Report on bill for the relief of John A. Ehle and others,.......	S	1	36
1837.	Report on memorial of Pratt, Watson & Co., relative to a contract,	S	2	47
1837.	Report relative to the enlargement of the Erie canal,...........	S	2	53
1837.	Report on claim of Jacob Trumpbour,.........................	A	3	181
1837.	Report on petition of I. E. Hinman and H. W. Schroeppel for damages to their lands,.....................................	A	3	185
1837.	Report on petition of B. W. Babcock for extra allowance,.......	A	3	187
1837.	Report on petition of Arnold, Mason and F. Pratt, for extra allowance,..	A	3	219
1837.	Report on petition for a weigh-lock at Oswego,................	A	3	231
1837.	Report in relation to the estimated and actual cost of the canals that are finished, and the estimated cost of those unfinished,..	A	3	189
1838.	Report of, on petition of the Tioga Coal, Iron, Mining and Manufacturing Company,....................................	S	2	45
1838.	Report of, on petition of Plynn Darby for extra allowance,.....	A	4	193
1838.	Report of, on petition of Martin Bettinger and David Loban for damages to their lands,.................................	A	5	288
1838.	Report giving the names and compensation of officers employed on the canals,..	A	5	231
1839.	Report of, on petition of citizens of Lockport relative to a bridge over the Erie canal,.................................	S	3	88
1839.	Report of, on petition of John B. Ives, a canal contractor, ...	A	6	352
1839.	Report of, on petition of Moses Drake for canal damages,.......	A	6	368
1839.	Report relative to the enlargement of the Oswego canal, ...	A	6	357
1839.	Report relative to the enlargement of the Cayuga and Seneca canal,..	A	6	367
1839.	Report relative to the enlargement of the Erie canal from Utica to Syracuse,..	A	6	369
1839.	Report relative to leasing the surplus waters of the Oswego canal,	A	6	370
1839.	Report on petition for the reduction of the tolls on the Chenango canal, and the equalization thereof with the rates on the Erie canal,..	A	6	343
1839.	Report on a resolution of the assembly relative to the cost of the Genesee Valley canal,..................................	A	6	376
1839.	Report relative to supplying the Erie canal with water from Lake Erie to the Seneca river,................................	A	6	381
1839.	Report on a resolution of the assembly relative to the cost of the Black River canal,......................................	A	6	391

CANAL BOARD—*continued.*

Year	Subject	Doc.	Vol.	No.
1840.	Report of, relative to the survey of the branches of the Hudson river,	S	2	61
1840.	Report on bill for the relief of Samuel Farwell and others,	S	4	100
1840.	Report on petition of John Spencer and others for extra allowance,	A	6	258
1840.	Report relative to the occupancy of the pier of the Black Rock harbor,	A	8	313
1840.	Report of, giving the names and compensation of officers appointed by the canal board and canal commissioners,	A	8	318
1840.	Report as to changes of plan of locks, &c., on the Genesee Valley canal,	A	8	329
1840.	Report relative to the canal debts and revenues and the enlargement of the Erie canal,	A	7	306
1841.	Report on petition of Andrew P. Tillman for extra allowance,	S	2	42
1841.	do do W. A. Bird and others for a lease of surplus water,	S	2	57
1841.	do do Peter Bargy, Jr., for extra allowance,	A	5	162
1841.	do do Peter Bargy, Jr., for extra allowance,	A	5	178
1841.	do do W. W. Dygert for damages to his lands,	A	5	175
1841.	Report relative to the Scottsville Canal Association,	S	3	72
1841.	Report relative to the Oneida Lake canal and feeder, and Seneca River towing path,	S	3	76
1841.	Report on bill for the relief of James Germain,	S	3	77
1841.	Report on petition of Gerret Visscher and William Shepard, for such portion of the bed of the Erie canal as may be abandoned,	A	5	187
1841.	Report on petition of Samuel Farwell, for extra allowance,	A	5	194
1841.	do do John S. Tallman and J. Child, for interest on damages awarded to them,	A	6	216
1841.	do do Thompson Parkhurst, for pay for lands taken for the Erie canal,	A	6	220
1841.	do do Henry Heath, for damages by the Erie canal,	A	6	229
1841.	Report on the propriety of establishing a uniform rate of tolls on all the canals,	A	6	221
1841.	Report on petition for a bridge over the Mohawk, at or near the lower aqueduct,	A	6	223
1841.	Report on petition of Henry C. Stone, relative to a canal contract,	A	6	245
1841.	do do Patrick Fitzsimmons and James Brady,	A	6	248
1841.	do do Benjamin and Sarah Skinner, for damages, by the construction of the Chenango canal,	A	6	251
1841.	do do Joseph Long, for the same,	A	6	254
1841.	do do the Cohoes Company, relative to their bridge,	A	7	257
1841.	do do William Newton, for extra allowance,	A	7	270
1842.	do do Asa T. Smith,	S	2	31
1842.	do do Patrick Fitzsimmons and James Brady,	S	4	86
1842.	do do Patrick Fitzsimmons and James Brady,	S	4	93
1842.	do do Levi Casler,	A	5	84
1842.	do do Barnet Bond, for loss of boat and cargo,	A	5	93
1842.	do do William Finn,	A	5	100
1842.	do do William H. Gibson and John Mattemore,	A	5	102
1842.	do do Nelson and Phillips,	A	5	107
1842.	Report on petitions for, and remonstrance against the removal of Fort Millers dam,	A	5	114
1842.	Report on petition of Aaron Barnes and John E. Hinman,	A	5	119
1842.	do do James D. Treat and others,	A	7	132
1842.	do do Henry Heath,	A	7	150
1842.	do do William Paige,	A	7	164
1843.	do do David Murray,	S	1	28
1843.	do do Medad Pomeroy,	S	3	90
1843.	do do William Bentley,	A	4	91
1843.	do do Asa T. Smith,	A	4	108

CANAL BOARD—*continued.*

Year	Subject	Doc.	Vol.	No.
1843.	Report of, on petition of Peter Cagger, administrator of Peter Bargy, deceased, ...	A	5	135
1843.	Report of, in answer to a resolution of the assembly calling for information in relation to property shipped and left at Buffalo, Black Rock, Oswego, &c., ...	A	5	148
1844.	Report of, relative to allowances to contractors on suspended public works, ...	S	3	117
1844.	Report of, relative to the five combined locks at Lockport, ...	S	4	130
1844.	Report of, of damages awarded to contractors for breaches of contracts on the part of the state, in consequence of the suspension of the public works by the act of 1842, ...	A	1	2
1844.	Report of, transferring the annual report of the railroad commissioners, ...	A	1	6
1844.	Report of, on reference from the assembly of the petition of R. N. Cassler, ...	A	1	24
1844.	Report of, on reference from the assembly of the petition of John L. Bevins, ...	A	1	25
1844.	Report of, on reference of the petition of A. C. & E. T. Baldwin,	A	3	43
1844.	Report of, on reference of the petition of Thomas R. Brayton and Thomas W. Chesebro, ...	A	3	54
1844.	Report of, on the petition of Eggleston and Sanford, ...	A	3	69
1844.	Report of, in answer to a resolution of the assembly of January 31, 1844, ...	A	3	70
1844.	Report of, on the reference by the assembly of the petition of Yates and Vandebogert, ...	A	5	108
1844.	Report of, on the reference by the assembly of the petition of Thomas McLachlin, ...	A	5	109
1844.	Report of, on the petition of a number of residents of Oswego, Onondaga, &c., ...	A	5	114
1844.	R port of, on reference by the assembly of the petition of Benjamin H. Sage and William B. Williams, ...	A	5	121
1844.	Report of, on reference by the assembly of the petition of Robert Spoor, ...	A	5	128
1844.	Report of, on reference by the assembly of the bill for the relief of John Simons, ...	A	6	151
1844.	Report of, in answer to a resolution of the assembly calling for the testimony in the case of Robert Fero, ...	A	6	153
1844.	Report of, on the reference from the assembly of the petition of the citizens of Little Falls for the finishing of a bridge, ...	A	6	157
1844.	Report of, on the petition of John G. Wheelock and others, ...	A	7	203
1844.	Report of, on the petition of the common council of the city of Utica, ...	A	7	204
1845.	Report of, on the claim of Timothy Eddy, ...	S	1	34
1845.	Report of, in relation to the Albany basin, ...	S	2	83
1845.	Report of, on the bill entitled an act to authorize and require the canal commissioners to take charge of the side-cut canals in the village of Liverpool, ...	S	3	99
1845.	Report on bill from the assembly to provide for the removal of cases decided by, to Supreme Court, by certiorari, ...	S	3	103
1845.	Report of, on reference, of the petition of Solomon Brown, ...	A	3	36
1845.	do do do Hart and Candee, ...	A	3	55
1845.	do do do Barnes and Hinman, ...	A	3	73
1845.	do do do John Burch, ...	A	4	102
1845.	do do do James Stewart, ...	A	4	125
1845.	do do do John Bump, ...	A	4	141
1845.	do do do Joshua Reed, ...	A	5	156
1845.	do do do A. J. Yates, ...	A	5	191
1845.	do do do inhabitants of Verona,	A	5	193
1845.	Report of committee on canals on the bill to remove cases from, to the Supreme Court, ...	A	5	195
1845.	Report on petition of Ledyard and Matthews, ...	A	6	201
1845.	Report relative to locks on Genesee Valley canal, ...	A	6	202
1845.	Report on petition of J. P. Yates, ...	A	6	214

CANAL BOARD—*continued.*

		Doc.	Vol.	No.
1845.	Report on petition of H. Burdick, ...	A	6	217
1845.	Report on petition of J. Ingraham,.	A	6	218
1846.	Report of committee on canals on bill relative to,...............	S	4	128
1846.	Report of, on the petition of Lewis Bastido and N. B. Kingsland,	S	4	129
1846.	Report of, in relation to the claim of Andrew Rockwell,........	S	4	134
1846.	Report of, on reference of the petition of Asa T. Smith,........	A	2	49
1846.	Report of, on reference of the petition of Sanford & Eggleston,..	A	3	78
1846.	Report of, relative to the contract of John Ellis,...............	A	3	81
1846.	Report of, on petition of N. Schuyler,......................	A	4	98
1846.	do do C. P. Richardson and others,.........	A	4	103
1846.	do do Oliver Baker, ...	A	4	115
1846.	Report of relative to Florida bridge, ...	A	4	127
1846.	Report of, on petition of J. P. Veeder, ...	A	4	135
1846.	Report of, on petition of citizens of Alabama, Genesee county,..	A	4	136
1846.	Report of, relative to water power along Seneca river, ...	A	5	144
1846.	Report of, on petition of Silas Eggleston, ...	A	5	147
1846.	do do Jas. C. Ott,......................	A	5	151
1846.	do do John Hollister,......................	A	5	252
1846.	do do Learned & Johnson, ...	A	5	145
1846.	Report of, relative to weirs at Seneca lake,..................	A	5	166
1846.	Report of, relative to surplus waters from Chenango canal,......	A	5	195
1846.	Report of, on reference of the petition of George W. Hildreth,..	A	6	201
1847.	Report of, on the petition of H. C. Swift,....................	S	3	105
1847.	Report in answer to a resolution of the assembly relative to testimony taken in case of Briggs Thomas and Eben C. Worden,..	A	1	34
1847.	Report of, in answer to a resolution referring petition of Barhurd Bruce to them,......................................	A	1	41
1847.	Report of, on petition of inhabitants of town of Lenox, Madison county, relative to surplus water on Rome level, ...	A	4	109
1847.	Report of, relative to Hamburgh canal in Buffalo, and a bridge across Chenango canal at Elmira,........................	A	6	152
1847.	Report of, on petition of John Gibson, ...	A	7	195
1847.	Report of, on petitions for draining lands between Tonawanda and Elicott's creek, ...	A	7	198
1847.	Report of, on petition of James Folbs, for a bridge at Frankfort,	A	7	200
1847.	Report of, on memorial for enlargement of Erie canal and basins at Buffalo,..	A	7	205
1847.	Report of, relative to bill for relief of Abojiah Osborn,.........	A	7	209
1847.	Report of, on petition of N. Buell, ...	A	7	213
1848.	Report of, under a resolution relative to a petition for a law on canal damages, &c., ...	S	2	48
1848.	Report of, under a resolution relative to improvements at Squaw island, ...	S	2	57
1848.	Report of, relative to Genesee and Black River canals,..........	A	3	97
1848.	Report of, of 1847, and resolutions,......................	A	5	130
1848.	Report of, on petition of James Nichols, John C. Hoyt, &c.,.....	A	5	170
1848.	Report of, on memorial of E. W. Leavenworth, president of village of Syracuse,....................................	A	5	171
1848.	Report of, relative to diversion of waters of Genesee river,......	A	5	172
1848.	Report of, on petition of Robert Renwick, Jr., and Henry Marcy,	A	5	179
1848.	Report of, on petition of Robert McBride,..................	A	6	215
1849.	Report of, on the condition of the contracts of the proposed new works at Buffalo,...................................	S	1	26
1849.	Report of, in relation to the outlay that would be necessary to improve Black Rock harbor,...........................	S	2	33
1849.	Report of, relative to Fort Miller dam, ...	A	3	125
1849.	Report of, transmitting petition, &c., of Alexander Campbell, ..	A	3	173
1850.	Report in relation to Honeoye, Conesus and other lakes,........	S	1	40
1850.	Report on petition of John Harris and others in relation to Fort Miller's dam,....................................	S	2	66
1850.	Report on petition of Jared B. Moss,......................	S	3	86
1850.	Report in relation to improvement at Baldwinsville,...........	S	3	94
1850.	Report on supplying Black river with water,.................	S	3	98

CANAL BOARD—*continued.*

Year	Subject	Doc.	Vol.	No.
1850.	Report on petition of Elizabeth Granger and others,	S	3	102
1850.	Report of, in relation to claim of Anthony and Fiero,	A	3	33
1850.	Report in relation to canal at Geddes,	A	5	103
1850.	Report of, in relation to nuisance at Spencerport,	A	5	139
1850.	Report of, in relation to canal at Sodus,	A	6	151
1851.	Communication in relation to claim of Collins & Hitchcock,	S	1	18
1851.	Report in relation to lengthening lock on the Erie canal,	A	3	67
1851.	Report of, on the removal of obstructions in Black Rock harbor,	A	3	90
1852.	Communication from,	S	1	8
1852.	Report of judiciary committee relative to preamble and resolutions of the,	S	1	15
1852.	Auditor's report respecting extra allowance on contracts by,	S	1	23
1852.	To hear and determine the claim of A. Rockwell & Co.,	A	2	72
1853.	Report of auditor in answer to a resolution calling for proceedings of, respecting complaints or charges against canal superintendents,	S	3	71
1854.	Resolntion of, relative to grants of national land,	S	1	13
1854.	Communication from, under resolution,	S	3	62
1854.	Communication from, under resolution,	S	3	83
1854.	Resolution of, relative to reduction of tolls,	A	4	134
1854.	Auditor's report of claims made to,	A	5	148
1855.	Communication from, in relation to line of canal near Port Byron,	A	3	74
1855.	Communication from, in relation to line of Erie canal near Port Byron,	A	4	74
1855.	Report of, in relation to new feeder for Genesee Valley canal,	A	7	146
1856.	Report of majority of, relative to canal superintendents,	S	2	42
1856.	Report of minority of, relative to canal superintendents,	S	2	43
1856.	Report of, on petition of Luke P. Babcock,	S	2	51
1857.	Communication from, relative to Rochester mill owners,	S	1	12
1857.	Report of, relative to tolls,	S	4	127
1857.	Report of committee on claims favorable on petition of A. Y. Lansing for rehearing of claim by,	A	3	164
1857.	Resolution of, in favor of the reduction of tolls on certain articles,	A	3	187
1858.	Report of, relative to tolls on wheat and flour,	S	3	134
1558.	Report of proceedings of, relative to tolls on iron, &c.,	S	3	135

CANAL COMMISSIONERS.

Year	Subject	Doc.	Vol.	No.
1830.	Annual report, and report on the Chenango canal,	A	1	47
1830.	Report on petition of D. Stevenson, to be released from a canal contract,	A	1	60
1830.	Report on the subject of lowering Oneida lake,	A	1	63
1830.	Report relative to Fort Miller dam,	A	2	86
1830.	On petition of Joshua Howe, for damages by the canal,	A	2	109
1830.	On petition for a bridge across the canal at Utica,	A	3	275
1830.	Report relative to the improvement of the Hudson river with the steam dredging machine,	A	4	335
1830.	Report of, in relation to their proceedings in relation to the construction of the Chemung and Crooked Lake canals, with estimates of the cost and revenues of, &c.,	A	2	97
1830.	Report of S. Young, one of the, on the same,	A	2	195
1830.	Report on petition of Paisley Laing, for damages to his lands,	A	3	280
1830.	do do Ephraim Wemple, for damages to his lands,	A	4	331
1830.	do do A. Dailey and H. Fuller, for damages to their lands,	A	4	357
1830.	do do Jacob Vreeland and others, relative to the water privileges at the foot of Seneca lake,	A	3	284
1830.	do do Abraham Waggener for the construction of a bridge,	A	4	332
1830.	do do the president, &c., of the Florida Bridge Company, for authority to collect certain toll,	S	4	340

CANAL COMMISSIONERS—*continued.*

		Doc.	Vol.	No.
1830.	On the subject of canal bridges and fences,	A	4	334
1831.	Annual report of,	A	1	20
1831.	On petition of George Clarke for canal damages,	A	4	334
1831.	On Abraham Knapp for canal damages,	S	1	38
1831.	Of the survey of the Black River canal,	A	3	229
1831.	Of the survey of the Susquehannah and Chemung rivers,	A	3	278
1832.	Annual report of,	A	1	42
1832.	Report relative to the draining the Cayuga marshes,	A	2	51
1832.	Report on petition of A. Porter and others,	A	2	113
1832.	do do Isaac Allen and others for damages to their lands by the canal,	A	2	119
1832.	do do W. W. Case for damages to his boat and cargo,	A	2	120
1832.	do do R. Van Valkenburgh and others,	A	3	190
1832.	do do Henry Thalimer for extra allowance,	S	1	56
1833.	Annual report of,	A	2	36
1833.	Report relative to draining the Cayuga marshes,	A	3	192
1833.	Communication from, relative to appointing an additional commissioner,	A	3	220
1833.	Report of committee on canals on the same,	A	4	240
1833.	Report on petition of Luther Pardee and others for damages to their lands,	A	4	322
1833.	do do Ogden Mallory for extra allowance,	S	1	25
1833.	do do Augustus Porter and others,	S	1	29
1833.	do do Harvey Edwards and others,	S	2	73
1833.	do do E. Granger and William W. Chapin for damages to their lands,	S	2	78
1833.	do do Cornelius Marseles for pay for land taken for the Erie canal,	S	2	92
1833.	do do Peter Thalimer for extra allowance,	S	2	109
1833.	do do Joseph E. Bloomfield relative to a certain lease of surplus water,	S	2	112
1833.	do do John M'Intyre and others for damages to their lands,	S	2	114
1833.	do do Neal Brown for extra allowance,	S	2	116
1834.	Annual report of,	A	2	55
1834.	Report relative to the northern termination of Chenango canal,	A	1	25
1834.	do do improvement of the Erie canal at Rochester,	A	2	88
1834.	do do survey and reservoirs of the Chenango canal,	S	2	87
1834.	do do gifts, grants and donations for the Chenango canal, &c.,	S	2	85
1834.	do do surplus water at Lockville,	A	4	287
1834.	do do surplus waters of the Mohawk and Hudson rivers,	A	4	359
1834.	Report on the petition of the Buffalo and Black Rock Railroad Company,	A	2	84
1834.	Report on petition of the Cohoes Company for relief,	A	3	227
1834.	Report on bill for relief of the Cohoes Company,	S	2	95
1834.	Report on petition of Joseph E. Smith & Co. for extra allowance,	A	3	209
1834.	do do W. W. Case for damages to his boat and cargo,	A	3	249
1834.	do do William Jackson for damages to his lands,	A	4	271
1834.	do do Jacob Buckdorf, to be refunded certain moneys paid for tolls,	A	4	274
1834.	do do James H. Rathbone and others, for damages to their mills,	A	4	294
1834.	do do David H. Richardson, for a grant of surplus water,	A	4	298
1834.	do do Jacob Van Dam, for damages to his mills,	A	4	299
1834.	do do H. Hulburt and D. Porter, for extra allowance,	A	4	315

CANAL COMMISSIONERS—*continued.*

		Doc.	Vol.	No.
1834.	Report on petition of D. Tomlinson and others, relative to the condition of the canal near Schenectady,	A	4	327
1834.	do do Peter J. Enders, for damages to his lands,.	A	4	328
1834.	do do Aaron Parkhurst, for an allowance, &c.,...	A	4	329
1834.	do do William Young, for damages to his mills,..	A	4	330
1834.	do do Jeremiah Gillet, for damages to his mills,..	A	4	351
1834.	do do W. Gibbs, D. Earll & Co., for damages to their mills,........................	A	4	353
1834.	do do Joseph Waggoner, for damages to his lands,	A	4	383
1834.	do do E. S. Granger and others, for damages to their lands,........................	S	1	27
1834.	do do George L. Taylor, for damages to his lands,.	S	2	69
1834.	do do John Sweeting, for damages to his lands,..	S	2	70
1834.	do do Vincent Conkling, for a grant of surplus water,...........................	S	2	78
1834.	do do Harvey Edwards and others,............	S	2	79
1835.	Annual report of,..	A	2	85
1835.	Report on petition for a lock in the village of Oxford,..........	S	2	64
1835.	Relative to the Albany basin,...............................	S	2	76
1835.	Relative to the survey of the Black River canal,..............	A	1	55
1835.	Report on petition of Samuel Farwell, for extra allowance,......	S	2	84
1835.	Report on petition for the lease of the surplus water at Brighton and Pittsford,..	A	2	83
1835.	Report on petition of George Coryell and others, for damages to their lands,....	A	2	89
1835.	do do Vincent Conklin and Jefferson Bartlett, for a lease of surplus water,..............	A	2	91
1835.	Report on petition for a lock from the Chenango canal into the Chenango river, at or near Chenango Forks,................	A	2	93
1835.	Report on petition of James Averill and Jacob Failing for damages to their lands,......................	A	2	94
1836.	do do Asa Campbell, for pay for services on the canal,........	A	2	98
1835.	do do Simeon Matteson, for pay for services on the canal,..............................	A	2	101
1835.	do do Junius Rogers, for pay for services on the canal	A	2	121
1835.	do do Joseph E. Smith & Co., for extra allowance,	A	2	109
1835.	do do John Herkimer, for damages to his lands,.	A	2	116
1835.	do do Plynn Darby, for extra allowance, &c.,....	A	2	118
1835.	do do John W. Wisner, for extra allowance, &c.,..	A	2	120
1835.	Report relative to the enlargement of the Erie canal,...........	A	2	143
1835.	Report on petition of George T. & Henry Perry, for damages to their mills, &c ,....................................	A	3	226
1835.	Report on petition of H. H. Bogart, relative to the canal fences,..	A	4	283
1835.	Report of survey of the Genesee Valley canal,................	A	4	264
1835.	Report relative to the cost of canals and railroad,..............	A	4	296
1835.	Report relative to the inlet of Cayuga lake,....................	A	4	297
1835.	Report relative to level of the Crooked Lake canal,............	A	4	343
1835.	Report on petition of Stephen Tuttle and others, for relief,......	A	4	324
1835.	do do Peter J. Enders, for damages to his lands,..	A	4	325
1835.	do do M. H. Fairservice for pay for work done on the Erie canal,........................	A	4	231
1835.	do do W. H. Lacy, to construct a bridge at Black Rock harbor,........................	A	4	333
1835.	do do Bernardus J. Swartwout, for a grant of surplus water,..........................	A	4	341
1835.	do do Nathan Paddock, for damages to his mills,	A	4	344
1835.	do do J. N. Hicks and others, for the use of surplus water at Liverpool, to carry a pump to raise salt water,....................	A	4	347

CANAL COMMISSIONERS—*continued.*

Year	Subject	Doc.	Vol.	No.
1835.	Report on petition of Asa Burrows, for damages to his lands,...	A	4	348
1835.	do do Luther Pardee and others, for damages to their lands, ...	A	4	361
1836.	Annual report of,....	A	2	65
1836.	Report on petition of Luther Pardee and others, for damages to their lands, ...	S	1	63
1836.	do do Barent and John R. Bleecker, for damages to their mills,..	S	1	64
1836.	do do Isaac Brown, Jr.,......................	S	2	78
1836.	Report relative to the waters of Limestone, Butternuts and Chittenango creeks,..................................	S	3	80
1836.	Report relative to the survey of the Genesee Valley canal,......	A	1	42
1836.	Report on petition of Charles Orwan, for a grant of surplus water,	A	2	107
1836.	do do John Gregg, for a grant of surplus water,..	A	3	108
1836.	do do the contractors on the Chenango canal for relief,..............................	A	3	121
1836.	do do Abraham Waggoner, for damages to his mills,..............................	A	3	126
1836.	do do Joseph E. Smith & Co., for extra allowance,	A	3	128
1836.	do do W. Gibbs and others, for damages to their mills, &c.,..........................	A	4	220
1836.	do do Peter J. Enders, for damages to his lands,..	A	4	229
1836.	do do Asa Burrows, for damages to his lands,...	A	4	231
1836.	Report relative to the quality of the stone in the Onondaga quarries, ...	A	4	261
1836.	Report on petition of Oliver Culver, for a lease of surplus water, &c.,..........................	A	4	268
1836.	do do Westlake and McConnel, for extra allowance, ...	A	4	280
1836.	do do John G. Wheelock, for damages to his lands,	A	4	428
1836.	do do Morris F. Sheppard, relative to the surplus waters of the Crooked Lake canal,.....	A	4	299
1836.	Report relative to a wet dock and bridge company at Oswego,...	A	4	290
1837.	Annual report,..	A	2	73
1837.	Report on petition for the purchase of the Oneida lake canal and feeder, ...	S	1	16
1837.	Report on petition of Amaziah Stebbins, for extra allowance,...	S	1	17
1837.	Report of amount of money agreed to be paid for changing the termination of the Chenango canal, &c.,......	S	2	49
1837.	Report on petition of the Cohoes Company for a grant of a portion of the Erie canal, &c.,............	S	2	60
1837.	do do Barker & Stroud, and Gilbert & Sprague, for extra allowance, ...	A	1	44
1837.	do do John Gregg, for a grant of surplus waters..	A	2	77
1837.	do do Catharine Fridley, for damages to her lands,	A	2	99
1837.	do do A. Plantou, relative to his canal steamboat,	A	2	100
1837.	do do Otis Bigelow and others, *see* Seneca river tow path, &c.,......................	A	2	114
1837.	do do John N. De Graff,......................	A	3	179
1837.	Report relative to the improvement of the Cayuga inlet,........	A	2	90
1837.	do do using canal water to propel a salt punt at Liverpool,...........................	A	2	93
1837.	do do the construction of the Chenango canal,.....	A	3	201
1837.	do do the upper level of the Crooked Lake canal,..	A	3	203
1837.	Report on petition of Peter B. Ten Brook, for damages by the canal,..............................	A	3	206
1837.	do do John C. Wanmaker, for damages by the canal,..............................	A	3	207
1837.	do do citizens of Sherburne, to be released from their liabilities to the state,............	A	3	211
1837.	do do W. Newton, for extra allowance,.........	A	3	242

CANAL COMMISSIONERS—*continued.*

Year	Subject	Doc.	Vol.	No.
1837.	Report relative to the tow path bridge crossing the outlet of the Cayuga lake,........	A	3	250
1837.	Report on petition of Peter Bargy, Jr., for extra allowance, &c.,.	A	4	313
1837.	Report on petition of W. L. Crossitt and others, for extra allowance, ...	A	4	317
1838.	Annual report,........	A	3	61
1838.	Report on petition of Manley Amsden and others, for damages to their lands by the erection of the Troy dam,........	S	2	40
1838.	Report on petition of W. Hantley, to drain a swamp in the town of Manlius,........	S	2	59
1838.	Report relative to damages for private property taken for the Chenango canal,........	S	2	67
1838.	Report relative to a feeder from the Conesus outlet to the Genesee Valley canal,........	A	2	30
1838.	Report relative to lands overflowed by water on the Oswego canal,	A	3	42
1838.	Report relative to lands overflowed by water on the Tonawanda and Ellicott creeks,........	A	3	124
1838.	Report on petition of Page, Kellogg, Sage & Co., for extra allowance, ...	A	3	99
1838.	Report on petition of John Stewart, &c., and others, for extra allowance,........	A	3	121
1838.	Report on petition of Aaron Parkhurst and others for a grant of surplus water,........	A	4	197
1838.	Report on petition of Hiram Blanchard and others relative to the line of the Erie canal at Oriskany,........	A	5	225
1838.	Report in relation to appraisals for damages on the Erie canal, &c.,	A	5	201
1838.	do do the Chemung canal feeder,........	A	5	244
1838.	do do locks, &c., on the enlarged Erie canal,.....	A	5	251
1838.	do do bridges over the enlarged Erie canal,.......	A	6	298
1838.	do do the construction of same at West Troy level,	A	6	313
1838.	Report on petition of Jonathan Brown and others,........	A	3	292
1839.	Annual report, ...	A	3	86
1839.	Report on bill for the regulation of the water in the Cayuga and Seneca canal,........	S	2	44
1839.	Report on petition of Beach, Chapman & McOmber, for extra allowance, ...	S	2	40
1839.	Report of amount of work under contract on the Genesee Valley canal, &c.,........	S	3	69
1839.	Report relative to constructing the enlarged Erie canal, independent of the Niagara river,........	S	2	54
1839.	Report in relation to the Junction canal,........	S	3	90
1839.	Report on bill for the relief of Livingston Spraker and others,...	S	3	91
1839.	Report on petition of Susan Ogden and Mary Murray, proprietors of the dam at Mount Morris,........	S	3	95
1839.	Report on petition of John L. Bigelow for extra allowance, ...	A	2	22
1839.	do do W. Coleman and others for extra allowance,	A	2	25
1839.	do do Marlatt & Dunham for extra allowance,....	A	2	31
1839.	Report of, transmitting a report of estimates and map in relation to the Oneida river,........	A	2	59
1839.	Report on petition of Lewis Beebe and W. Thompson for extra allowance,........	A	2	61
1839.	Report on petition of Page, Kellogg, Sage & Co., and Clark, Strover & Sumner, contractors on the Glens Falls feeder, for relief,	A	2	69
1839.	Report on petition of I. P. Smith and others, contractors on the Erie canal, for relief,........	A	3	72
1839.	Report on petition of John B. Ives, a canal contractor on the Erie canal, for relief,........	A	3	95
1839.	Report of, relative to the extension of the Chenango canal,......	A	3	116
1839.	Report on petition of J. Child and others, that certain money paid for canal tolls may be refunded to them,........	A	3	132
1839.	Report on petition of Barzilla Richmond for a bridge across the Erie canal,........	A	3	137

CANAL COMMISSIONERS—*continued.*

		Doc.	Vol.	No.
1839.	Report on petition of Timothy Fenill and others for extra allowance,	A	3	142
1839.	Report on petition of citizens of Sherburne to be released from their liabilities to the state,	A	3	139
1839.	Resolution requiring the, to report the estimated cost of the enlargement of the Erie canal, &c.,	A	4	224
1839.	Report of estimated cost of the enlargement of the Erie canal, &c.,	A	6	339
1839.	Report relative to walling with stone the sides of the Erie canal,	A	4	238
1839.	Report on remonstrance of citizens of Oriskany relative to changing the route of the Erie canal,	A	4	261
1839.	Report on petition of Truman Jackson for damages to his lands,	A	4	263
1839.	Report of the estimated cost of the Genesee Valley and Black River canals,	A	6	267
1839.	Report of the estimated cost of the Genesee Valley and Black River canals,	A	6	360
1839.	Report on petition of W. Brayton and others relative to canal fences,	A	5	269
1839.	Report relative to the location of the lines of the Erie canal in the city of Rochester,	A	5	287
1839.	Report on petition of John Hadcock for damages to his lands,	A	5	308
1839.	Report on petition for the construction of a bridge across the Genesee river,	A	6	346
1839.	Report of amount derived from tolls upon passengers, furniture and baggage, with their opinion on the propriety of allowing parallel railroads to transport the same free of toll, &c.,	A	6	355
1839.	Report of, on petition of W. Finn for damages to his lands and fences,	A	6	358
1839.	Report relative to the proposed basin at Buffalo,	A	6	363
1839.	Report on petition of James Germain for damages to his mill,	A	6	371
1839.	do do Beebe, Thompson & Co., for extra allowance,	A	6	372
1839.	do do Gilbert Weeks to be indemnified for injuries received by falling from a wall constructed by the state,	A	6	379
1840.	Annual report of,	A		60
1840.	Report on the petition of the widow and heirs of Samuel Pike for damages to house, &c., by the canal,	S	1	25
1840.	Report on petition of W. Jackway for damages to his lands,	S	1	26
1840.	do do Susan Ogden and Mary Murray to have a bond canceled,	S	3	81
1840.	do do Jemima Rexford for a portion of the land occupied by the present Erie canal,	S	3	87
1840.	Report relative to the lands overflowed adjacent to Scajockety creek,	S	3	92
1840.	Report relative to leasing the surplus water of the Glens Falls feeder dam,	S	4	114
1840.	Report transmitting a report from H. S. Dexter in relation to hydraulic cement,	S	4	122
1840.	Report relative to the survey of the canal route from the Chemung canal to the state line,	A	1	32
1840.	Report on petition of W. Gay, Jr., for pay for lands taken for Genesee Valley canal,	A	2	37
1840.	Report on petition of C. Baker and others, for damages to their lands,	A	3	72
1840.	Report on petition of Henry Paddock and others, for damages to their lands,	A	4	158
1840.	Report on petition for the purchase by the state of the Oneida Lake canal and feeder,	A	3	81
1840.	Report transmitting reports of engineers relative to the condition of the Genesee Valley canal, and the mode of supplying it with water,	A	3	96
1840.	Report of the survey of the Conewango canal,	A	4	160
1840.	Report relative to improvement of the Chemung canal,	A	5	161

CANAL COMMISSIONERS—*continued.*

Year	Subject	Doc.	Vol.	No.
1840.	Report transmitting the report of survey in continuation of the Black River canal,	A	6	233
1840.	Report transmitting the report of the Main and Hamburgh street canal in Buffalo,	A	6	257
1840.	Report on petition of Daniel M'Inroy for extra allowance,	A	7	279
1841.	Annual report,	A	3	72
1841.	Report on petition of John Hadcock for damages to his lands,	S	2	40
1841.	do do Pharez Gould for certain land,	S	2	60
1841.	do do Hervey Luce for damages by the Chemung canal,	S	3	84
1841.	do do W. Z. De Zeng and others for damages to their lands,	S	2	62
1841.	Report of estimated cost of a canal from the head of Seneca lake to Havana,	S	2	50
1841.	Report on petition of Henry White and John Williams for a re-appointment,	A	3	76
1841.	do do W. Newton for extra allowance,	A	3	81
1841.	do do Luther Pardee and others for damages to their lands,	A	5	155
1841.	do do John Wright for the construction of a ditch near the Champlain canal,	A	5	156
1841.	do do David Fitzgerald to be indemnified against a certain judgment,	A	5	173
1841.	do do W. Sternbergh for extra allowance,	A	5	190
1841.	do do Robert Land and others for a reassessment of damages,	A	5	191
1841.	do do Silas Wallace and others for damages to their lands,	A	6	201
1841.	Report in answer to a resolution of assembly in relation to contracts on the canals,	A	6	203
1841.	Report on petition of inhabitants of Camillus for the use of surplus water,	A	6	206
1841.	Report on petition of Franklin Livingston and David B. King relative to an infringement of their patent right, &c.,	A	6	211
1841.	Report on petition for a bridge across the Otsquago creek on the south side of the Erie canal,	A	6	225
1841.	Report on petition for a side-cut from the Champlain canal at Stillwater,	A	6	232
1841.	Report on petition for the removal of the canal feeder dam on the Genesee river,	A	6	250
1841.	Report on petition for the removal of the canal feeder dam on the Genesee river,	A	7	274
1841.	Report on petition for adoption of Amsden's substitute for weigh-locks,	A	7	272
1839.	Accounts of the, report of the committee appointed to examine the,	A	1	8
1840.	Accounts of the, report of the committee appointed to examine the,	A	1	14
1841.	Account of the, report of the committee appointed to examine the,	A	5	151
1833.	Additional one, communication from the canal commissioners relative to appointing an,	A	3	220
1833.	Additional one, report of committee on canals on the same,	A	4	240
1836.	Salary of the, report on bill to increase the,	A	2	86
1840.	Bouck and Baker, report on petition for investigation of the charges against,	A	4	102
1842.	Report of, on petition of Ira Gould and others,	S	4	84
1842.	Annual report of,	A	2	24
1842.	Report of, in answer to resolution of assembly, calling for information relative to engineers in the employ of the state,	A	2	45
1842.	Report of, in compliance with resolution of assembly, January 25,	A	4	64

CANAL COMMISSIONERS—*continued.*

		Doc.	Vol.	No.
1842.	Report of, on petition of Luther Pardee and others,	A	5	101
1842.	Report of, on petition of inhabitants of Oswego county relative to dam at Oswego falls,	A	7	167
1842.	Report of, in relation to contracts on the canals,	A	7	173
1843.	Report of, on the petition of Jonas Ingraham and others,	S	1	11
1843.	Report of, relative to lot 63 in Tyre, Seneca county,	S	1	25
1843.	Report of, of the amount necessary to finish the Black River canal,	S	1	49
1843.	Report of comptroller relative to payment for services for non-acting,	S	1	45
1843.	Report of, on the petition of Nicholas Nicholson and Jon. Colton,	S	3	71
1843.	Report of relative to the Genesee Valley canal,	S	3	77
1843.	Report of comptroller relative to services of non-acting, and payment therefor,	S	3	80
1843.	Report of, in relation to the aqueduct across Schoharie creek, &c.,	S	3	94
1843.	Report of, in relation to the combined locks at Lockport,	S	3	98
1843.	Report of, in relation to the bridges between Little Falls and Utica,	S	3	105
1843.	Report of select committee relative to alleged abuses of,	S	3	118
1843.	Annual report of,	A	2	25
1843.	Report of, on the resolution of the assembly relative to Oneida creek feeder,	A	3	45
1843.	Report in answer to a resolution of the assembly in relation to the removal of the dam on the Oswego falls, and Horse Shoe dam,	A	4	93
1843.	Report on the resolution of the assembly in relation to the Cayuga and Seneca canal, and the outlet of Seneca lake,	A	4	102
1844.	Report of, on petition of Timothy Eddy,	S	1	48
1844.	Report of, relative to the number and names of engineers and assistant engineers employed on the unfinished works in 1842, 1843, &c.,	S	2	69
1844.	Report of the, relative to the Genesee Valley canal,	S	3	111
1844.	Report of the, relative to the Genesee Valley canal,	S	3	112
1844.	Report of, relative to the Jordan level of the Erie canal,	S	4	129
1844.	Annual report of,	A	1	16
1844.	Report of, on petition of John I. and Joseph T. Cook,	A	3	99
1844.	Report of, on reference by the assembly of the petition of Samuel Cheever,	A	5	130
1844.	Report of, in relation to the combined locks at Lockport,	A	5	131
1844.	Report of, on the petition of E. Remington and others,	A	5	132
1844.	do do R. N. Casler,	A	5	133
1844.	do do Gerrit C. Sweet,	A	5	137
1844.	do do John Merriam and others,	A	5	138
1844.	Report of, in answer to a resolution of the assembly of March 12, in relation to contracts made for enlarging Erie canal, &c.,	A	6	146
1844.	Report of, on petition of inhabitants of Watervliet for two bridges over canal at West Troy,	A	6	149
1845.	Report of, on petition of Walter S. Todd,	S	1	13
1845.	do do Chas. Stroud and others,	S	1	14
1845.	do do Jacob Vandermark and others,	S	1	15
1845.	Report of, answering a resolution of the senate relative to clerk hire, &c.,	S	1	19
1845.	Report of, answering a resolution of the senate relate to engineers, &c.,	S	1	23
1845.	Report of, on the petition of S. S. Riddle and others,	S	2	49
1845.	Report of, relative to obstructions in the Chemung canal near the inlet of Seneca lake, &c.,	S	2	55
1845.	Report of, relative to the new line of canal through the village of Rome, &c.,	S	2	70
1845.	Report of, relating to the preservation of the materials on the unfinished canals,	S	2	72

CANAL COMMISSIONERS—*continued.*

		Doc.	Vol.	No.
1845.	Report of, relative to the plan of constructing a reservoir on Mill creek to supply the Dansville branch of the Genesee Valley canal, &c., ...	S	2	75
1845.	Report of canal board on bill to authorize the, to take charge of the side-cut canals in village of Liverpool,........	S	3	99
1845.	Report of, on reference of the petition of Warren Granger,........	A	1	27
1845.	Annual report of,........	A	1	28
1845.	Report of, on reference of the petition of James Spraker,........	A	3	42
1845.	Report of, on reference of the petition of citizens of Troy relative to a side-cut in the Erie canal, ...	A	3	57
1845.	Report of, transmitting annual report of railroad commissioner,	A	3	63
1845.	Report of, in answer to a resolution of the assembly,........	A	4	101
1845.	Report of, in answer to a resolution of the assembly relative to Black River canal and feeder,........	A	4	131
1845.	Report of, on reference of the petition of J. Lafoy and J. W. Clemens, ...	A	4	132
1845.	Report of, in reference to the Dansville side-cut of the Genesee Valley canal,........	A	4	135
1845.	Report of, in answer to a resolution of the assembly relating to unfinished public works,........	A	5	150
1845.	Report of, relative to the expense of preserving unfinished public works on the Genesee Valley canal,........	A	5	154
1845.	Report of, in answer to a resolution of the assembly,........	A	6	207
1845.	do on reference, of the petition of C. J. Hill,........	A	6	209
1845.	do relative to the Erie canal enlargement,........	A	6	225
1845.	Report of, on the petition of sundry citizens of the county of Chemung, relative to the Cayuga and Seneca canal,........	A	7	246
1846.	Report of, in answer to a resolution relative to the best mode of repairing the canals, &c.,........	S	1	27
1846.	Annual report of,........	A	1	14
1846.	Report of, on reference of the petition of Elias Brown,........	A	1	22
1846.	do in answer to a resolution of the assembly,........	A	2	35
1846.	do on reference of the petition of Lovinia Beardslee,...	A	2	48
1846.	do in answer to a resolution of the assembly,........	A	2	52
1846.	do on reference of the petition of Platt Williams, ...	A	3	74
1846.	do in answer to a resolution of the assembly,........	A	3	88
1846.	do in answer to a resolution of the assembly, relative to doubling locks on Erie canal,........	A	4	110
1846.	do relative to lock at Tonawanda,........	A	4	117
1846.	do comptroller relative to expenses of,........	A	4	118
1846.	do giving names of superintendents,........	A	4	119
1846.	do in answer to a resolution of the assembly,........	A	5	150
1846.	do relative to supply of water on Rome level,........	A	5	171
1846.	do relative to superintendents of repairs,........	A	6	221
1847.	do in answer to a resolution of January 29th, 1847,.....	S	2	59
1847.	do on petition of John Swift,........	S	2	67
1847.	do on petition of Frazee & Foster,........	S	2	74
1847.	do on petition of Charles Ehle,........	S	2	76
1847.	do on petition of Joseph G. Case,........	S	2	77
1847.	do on petition of F. A. Spalding and others,........	S	3	85
1847.	do on petition of D. S. & S. B. Green,........	S	3	96
1847.	do on petition of Matthew C. Pitcher,........	S	4	124
1847.	do on bill for relief of Louis Averell and others,........	S	4	114
1847.	do of Jones, on public works and officers connected,....	S	4	125
1847.	do on petition of William and John James,........	S	4	140
1847.	Annual report of,........	A	1	20
1847.	Report of, relative to draining the Tonawanda level on Erie canal,	A	4	149
1847.	do on petition of H. B. Smith and others, for bridge in Rochester,........	A	7	221
1847.	do on petition of J. B. Moss,........	A	7	185
1847.	do as to moneys due Grant, Ryan and Turner,........	A	7	212
1847.	do relative to work put under contract on canals,........	A	7	208

CANAL COMMISSIONERS—*continued.*

Year	Title	Doc.	Vol.	No.
1848.	Annual report of,	A	2	16
1848.	Report on petition of inhabitants at Havana,	A	3	64
1848.	Report on petition of John Donnelly,	A	3	99
1848.	Report of, as to probable cost of completing Genesee Valley canal,	S	2	58
1849.	Report of, in relation to the length and width of chambers of enlarged Erie canal locks, &c.,	S	2	50
1849.	Report of, on the feasibility of constructing a basin at West Troy, or between that place and Albany,	S	2	65
1849.	Report of, in relation to constructing a basin in vicinity of lock No. 2, Erie canal,	S	3	71
1849.	Annual report of,	A	2	40
1849.	Statement from, relative to purchase of materials and tools,	A	2	55
1849.	Report of, in answer to resolution of assembly respecting expense of bringing into use one set of enlarged locks on Erie canal, from Syracuse to Buffalo,	A	3	116
1850.	Report of, as to supply of water between Tonawanda and Montezuma,	S	1	29
1850.	Report of, as to supply of water between Tonawanda and Montezuma,	S	2	41
1850.	Report of, on canals other than Erie,	S	3	83
1850.	Report of, on enlargement of canals other than Erie,	S	3	88
1850.	Report of, on Amsden's hydrostatic scale,	A	3	35
1850.	Annual report of,	A	3	45
1850.	Report of committee on canals on annual report of,	A	6	153
1851.	Report of, in answer to resolution from senate,	S	3	88
1851.	Annual report of,	A	2	26
1852.	Annual report of,	A	2	33
1853.	Report of, in relation to tolls received on Champlain canal for year ending January 1st, 1853, &c.,	S	1	20
1853.	Communication from, in answer to a resolution in relation to canal contracts,	A	2	18
1853.	Annual report of,	A	2	23
1853.	Communication from Hon. Henry Fitzhugh in reply to the preamble and resolutions offered in the assembly,	A	2	27
1853.	Communication from John C. Mather respecting the condition of a portion of the Champlain canal crossing the Mohawk,	A	4	110
1853.	Report of, relative to suspensions of navigation on Erie and Champlain canals,	A	5	128
1854.	Report of, under resolution,	S	2	90
1854.	Communication from, relative to commutations, &c.,	A	2	52
1854.	Annual report of,	A	2	65
1855.	Report of, on petition of Abraham Duell and others,	S	2	37
1855.	Annual report of,	A	2	32
1855.	Communication from, in reference to claim of Edson Bishop,	A	4	92
1855.	Communication in reference to canal at Geddes,	A	5	133
1855.	Report of, in relation to new feeder for Genesee Valley canal,	A	7	146
1856.	Annual report of, and auditor,	S	1	15
1856.	Report of, of eastern division relative to repairs and superintendence of,	A	3	31
1856.	Report of, of eastern division,	A	3	87
1856.	Annual report of,	A	3	100
1857.	Report of, and state engineer and surveyor relative to the enlargement of the Genesee Valley canal,	A	1	35
1857.	Report of commissioner Fitzhugh relative to the Chemung canal locks,	A	1	51
1857.	Report of, in reply to resolution respecting canal bridge at West Troy,	A	2	92
1857.	Report of commissioner Sherrill and the state engineer and surveyor in reply to resolution relative to condition of the Champlain canal,	A	2	116
1857.	Annual report of,	A	3	145
1858.	Annual report of,	A	1	20

CANAL DEPARTMENT.

Year	Subject	Doc.	Vol.	No.
1843.	Report relative to the condition of, &c.,	A	2	18
1844.	Annual report of joint committee of senate and assembly, appointed to examine the accounts of the treasurer and,	A	1	10
1845.	Report of comptroller relative to clerks in,	S	1	45
1845.	Report of joint committee to examine the condition of, and of banking department, and treasury,	A	1	4
1846.	Report of joint select committee relative to accounts of treasury, banking department and,	A	1	7
1847.	Report of assembly committee appointed to examine accounts of,	A	1	21
1849.	Bank fund stock in, report of commissioners of the canal fund relative to,	S	2	35
1851.	Report of committee to examine accounts of,	A	2	23
1853.	Annual report of joint committee to examine the accounts of,	A	1	8
1854.	Annual report of committee on accounts of, and banking department,	A	1	25
1856.	Annual report of committee to examine accounts of,	A	4	173
1858.	Report of commissioners to examine accounts of, and of treasurer,	S	2	79
1858.	Report of commissioners appointed to examine accounts of, and securities in the banking department for the two fiscal years ending with 30th day of September, 1856 and 1857,	S	2	104

CANAL DEPARTMENT, AUDITOR OF.

FRANCIS H. RUGGLES:

Year	Subject	Doc.	Vol.	No.
1849.	Annual report of, relative to expenditures on the canals,	A	1	30
1849.	Report of, on the tolls, trade and tonnage of the canals.	A	3	170
1849.	Communication from, relative to collection of canal tolls,	A	3	195
1850.	Annual report,	A	4	75
1850.	Report on $50,000 borrowed by commissioners of canal fund,	A	5	81
1850.	Report on tolls, trade and tonnage,	A	6	140
1851.	Annual report,	A	3	56
1851.	Digest of canal claims,	S	2	50

GEORGE W. NEWELL:

Year	Subject	Doc.	Vol.	No.
1852.	Report of, respecting inquiry of senate about extra allowance on contracts by the canal board,	S	1	23
1852.	Report of tolls, trade and tonnage of the canals,	S	3	94
1852.	Report containing estimates for expenses of the canals,	A	5	116
1852.	Report relative to expenditures on the canals,	A	5	125
1853.	Report of, in answer to a call of the senate in relation to the quantity of, and tolls on property going to and coming from Canada,	S	1	29
1853.	Report of, in answer to a resolution calling for reasons why certain claims paid from the treasury were not charged to the canal debt sinking fund,	S	2	51
1853.	Report of, in answer to a resolution calling for proceedings of the canal board in relation to complaints or charges against canal superintendents,	S	3	71
1853.	Communication from, in relation to the expenditures of the appropriation for the support and maintenance of the canals for the current fiscal year,	S	3	84
1853.	Annual report of the,	A	2	15
1853.	Report of the commissioners of the canal fund, with the annual report of,	A	2	15
1853.	Communication from, in relation to certain claims, for the allowance of which there is no authority of law,	A	3	56
1853.	Report of, in answer to a resolution calling for the salaries and expenses of travel of division and resident engineers,	A	3	73
1853.	Report of, in relation to expenditures on the canals,	A	4	105
1853.	Report of, of the tolls, trade and tonnage of New York canals,	A	4	107
1853.	Report of, in answer to a resolution of the assembly calling for information in relation to mileage of George Cole, engineer,	A	5	122

CANAL DEPARTMENT, AUDITOR OF—*continued.*

Year	Subject	Doc.	Vol.	No.
1853.	Report of auditor in relation to expenditures of appropriation for the support and maintenance of the canals for the current fiscal year,	A	5	126
	MARIUS SCHOONMAKER:			
1854.	Annual report of,	A	1	10
1854.	Report relative to salary, &c.,	S	1	36
1854.	Communication from, relative to claim of Harry Hall,	S	1	41
1854.	do under resolution,	S	1	45
1854.	do relative to fees paid certain persons,	S	2	63
1854.	do relative to contracts on Black river improvement,	S	2	79
1854.	do relative to certain claims,	S	2	85
1854.	do under resolution,	S	2	101, 110
1854.	do relative to commutations,	A	2	62
1854.	do do Edward Murray,	A	2	70
1854.	do do tolls on Oneida Lake canal, &c.,	A	2	74
1854.	do as to awards for damages, &c.,	A	3	114
1854.	do relative to a certain draft,	A	4	135
1854.	do under resolution,	A	4	141
1854.	Report of, of expenditures on the canals,	A	5	146
1854.	Report of, of claims made to canal board,	A	5	148
	WILLIAM I. CORNWELL:			
1855.	Report to commissioners of canal fund,	A	1	5
1855.	Report of testimony in case of Black River canal lettings,	A	1	8
1855.	Communication from, in answer to resolution in relation to work on section 370, Erie canal,	A	3	72
1855.	Report in reference to trade and tonnage of canals,	A	4	95
1855.	Report of minority of select committee on bill to elect by the people,	A	4	108
1855.	Report of fees received by,	A	5	116
1855.	Communication from, in reference to award to Hulburt and Vrooman,	A	5	138
1855.	Annual report relative to expenditures of canals,	A	7	147
	NATHANIEL S. BENTON:			
1856.	Report of, and commissioners of canal fund,	S	1	15
1856.	Communication from, in reference to state canals,	A	4	146
1857.	Annual report of,	S	1	10
1857.	Annual report of, showing expenditures on the canals,	A	3	175
1857.	Annual report of, on tolls, trade and tonnage of the canals,	A	3	185
1857.	Report of, in reply to resolution relative to leases of surplus waters of Black Rock harbor,	A	3	204
1857.	Communication from the, with resolution of the canal board, relative to the reduction of tolls on certain articles,	A	3	187
1858.	Annual report of, with commissioners of the canal fund,	S	1	7
1858.	Report of, relative to outstanding canal drafts,	S	2	109
1858.	Report of, in relation to tolls on the canals,	S	3	123
1858.	Report of, giving cost of each of the canals of this state, except the Erie and Champlain canals,	S	3	128
1858.	Report of, relative to canal expenditures,	A	4	145
1858.	Report of, relative to tolls, trade and tonnage,	A	5	155

CANAL FUND.

Year	Subject	Doc.	Vol.	No.
1842.	Report of comptroller relative to premiums paid on the stock of 1845 and loans of moneys of, to the banks,	S	3	62
1843.	Report of commissioners relative to loan of, to certain banks,	S	3	92
1846.	Report of majority of committee on ways and means relative to, and general fund,	A	5	189

CANAL FUND—*continued.*

		Doc.	Vol.	No.
1846.	Report of minority of committee on ways and means relative to, and general fund,	A	5	190
1847.	Report of comptroller relative to balance of,	S	4	132
1849.	Report of comptroller in answer to resolutions of assembly in reference to extinguishment of certain debts of,	A	1	13
1853.	Report of comptroller in answer to resolutions of assembly in reference to extinguishment of certain debts of,	A	1	33
1853.	Report of committee on finance in relation to certain expenses chargeable upon the,	S	1	10

CANAL FUND, COMMISSIONERS OF.

		Doc.	Vol.	No.
1830.	Annual reports of receipts and expenditures on the canals, &c.,	A	2	152
1831.	do do do	A	2	102
1832.	do do do	A	1	5
1833.	do do do	A	1	4
1834.	do do do	A	1	4
1835.	do do do	A	1	4
1836.	do do do	A	1	4
1837.	do do do	A	1	3
1838.	do do do	A	1	5
1839.	do do do	A	2	26
1840.	do do do	A	3	74
1840.	Communication from, in relation to their annual report,	A	3	69
1841.	Annual report of receipts and expenditures on the canals, &c.,	A	1	5
1832.	Report of amount of tolls collected on the canals for 1831, &c.,	A	1	38
1833.	do do do 1832, &c.,	A	3	173
1834.	do do do 1833, &c.,	A	3	107
1835.	do do do 1834, &c.,	S	2	58
1836.	do do do 1835, &c.,	S	2	70
1837.	do do do 1836, &c.,	S	2	52
1838.	do do do 1837, &c.,	S	1	35
1839.	do do do 1838, &c.,	S	1	27
1840.	do do do 1839, &c.,	S	3	63
1841.	do do do 1840, &c.,	S	2	65
1830.	Report of amount of damages awarded to owners of lands in the valley of Wood creek, for injuries to their lands,	S	4	360
1833.	Report on receipts and expenditures on the canals, from 1817 to 1832,	S	1	38
1833.	Report relative to loans for the construction of the Chenango canal,	S	2	120
1833.	Report relative to their contingent expenses, &c.,	A	4	270
1833.	Relative to allowances made to George W. Newell,	A	4	271
1833.	Report on bill authorizing a loan to the Junction Canal Company,	A	4	305
1833.	Report in relation to deficiencies in the revenues of the Chemung canal,	A	4	331
1834.	Report on petition of William Buell to be indemnified against certain costs,	A	4	318
1838.	Report of allowances made to the Chenango canal contractors,	S	2	64
1839.	Report on bill relative to the duties of,	S	3	81
1839.	Report giving the items of interest on canal stock in the Manhattan Bank,	A	3	134
1840.	Report on resolution of the senate, requesting them to communicate in what banks the money pledged for the redemption of the Erie and Champlain canal debt, and also the stock appropriated for the construction of the Black River canal, is deposited, &c.,	S	2	62
1840.	Report of moneys deposited in banks to their credit, the amount in each case, and the terms of such deposit,	A	6	224
1840.	Report relative to the expenditure of the $500,000 loan,	A	8	331
1841.	Report relative to notices for the redemption of canal stock, &c.,	S	2	55
1841.	Report relative to the tonnage of the Erie canal,	A	5	193

CANAL FUND, COMMISSIONERS OF—*continued.*

		Doc.	Vol.	No.
1841.	Report on the claim of David B. King and Franklin Livingston, for an infringement of their patent right,........	A	6	228
1842.	Annual report of, relative to tolls collected and property transported on the canals in 1841, ...	S	2	33
1842.	Report of, on resolution of senate relative to loan for the Chemung canal, ...	S	3	69
1842.	Annual report of,........	A	2	18
1842.	Mr. Hoffman's resolution calling on, for a statement of state debt,	A	2	23
1842.	Report in compliance with Mr. Hoffman's resolution,........	A	4	64
1843.	Annual report of,........	A	2	36
1843.	Annual report of,........	S	3	100
1843.	Report of relative to payments made for repairs and improvements on canals, to what banks loans were made, and the names of holders of canal stock which has been paid off or redeemed since February, 1842, &c.,........	S	2	70
1843.	Report relative to loans of canal fund to certain banks,........	S	3	92
1844.	Report of, of the printing done for their department,........	S	2	80
1844.	Annual report of,........	A	3	40
1844.	Report in answer to a resolution of the assembly,........	A	5	120
1845.	Report from, of the tolls, tonnage and trade of the New York canals, for 1844,........	S	2	115
1845.	Annual report of,........	A	5	165
1846.	Report of, relative to the tolls, tonnage, &c., of the canals, ...	S	2	59
1846.	Report of, relative to freight carried by railroads,........	S	3	78
1846.	Report of, in answer to a resolution calling for names of persons paid by canal superintendent at Syracuse,........	S	3	101
1846.	Annual report of,........	A	1	4
1846.	Report of, in answer to a resolution of the assembly,........	A	2	33
1847.	Report of, as to trade and tonnage of canals,........	S	3	90
1847.	Report of, under resolution of September 10, 1847,........	S	4	112
1847.	Report of, under resolution,........	S	4	151
1847.	Report of, in answer to a resolution as to toll derived from western trade in 1846,........	A	1	42
1847.	Annual report of,........	A	2	60
1848.	Report of, on trade and tonnage,........	S	2	50
1848.	Annual report of,........	A	1	11
1848.	Report of, in part compliance with a resolution,........	A	1	15
1849.	Report of, relative to the bank fund stock in the canal department,........	S	2	35
1849.	Report of, on resolution of inquiry relative to deposits of public money in banks of the state,........	A	1	31
1849.	Annual report of,........	A	2	100
1850.	Report in reply to resolution,........	S	3	97
1850.	Report of, in answer to resolution,........	S	5	97
1850.	Annual report of,........	A	4	69
1850.	Report of canal auditor on appropriation of $50,000, borrowed by,	A	5	81
1850.	Report of committee on canals on annual report of canal commissioners and,........	A	6	153
1851.	Annual report of,........	A	2	27
1851.	Communication from attorney-general and lieutenant-governor relative to, ...	A	2	30
1852.	Report relative to loans to banks,........	S	2	81
1852.	Annual report of,........	A	1	15
1853.	Report of, with annual report of auditor of canal department,..	A	2	15
1853.	Report of, in relation to appropriation of surplus revenues to claims arising prior to June 1st, 1846,........	A	5	125
1854.	Annual report of, &c.,........	A	1	10
1855.	Annual report of,........	A	1	5
1855.	Communication from, in reference to award to Lewis Benedict,..	A	4	114
1856.	Report of, and auditor,........	S	1	15
1857.	Annual report of, and auditor of canal department,........	S	1	10
1858.	Annual report of, with annual report of auditor of canal department,........	S	1	7

CANAL FUND, COMMISSIONERS OF—*continued.*

		Doc.	Vol.	No.
1858.	Report of, relative to moneys appropriated to canals, &c., ...	A	1	49
	ACCOUNTS OF THE:			
1839.	Communication from the comptroller relative to the appointing a committee to examine, ...	A	4	169
1839.	Report of committee appointed to examine, ...	A	1	8
1840.	do do	A	1	14
1841.	do do	A	5	151
1842.	Report of joint select committee appointed to examine, ...	A	1	4
1842.	Report of joint committee appointed to examine, and of treasurer,	A	7	4

CANALS.

		Doc.	Vol.	No.
1833.	Report of attorney-general on a resolution to inquire whether any further legislative aid is necessary to protect the titles, and secure the public property constituting the, ...	A	1	10
1836.	Report of the relative cost of, and railroads, ...	A	4	296
1837.	Report of estimated and actual cost of those that are finished, and the estimated cost of those unfinished, &c., ...	A	3	189
1842.	Report of committee on canals on petition of Arthur Tappan and others for the early opening of, ...	A	5	100
1842.	Reports in compliance with Mr. Swackhamer's resolution requiring information from railroad and canal companies, ...	A	7	144
				151, 161, 163, 164
1842.	Report of committee on canals in relation to the preservation of maps, plans, and models of the public works, ...	A	7	154
1842.	Memorial of citizens of Niagara county asking the incorporation of a company to complete, ...	A	7	160
1842.	Memorial for the incorporation of a company to complete, ...	A	7	162
1843.	Report of committee on canals in relation to grog-shops on state lands, on line of, ...	S	3	122
1843.	Report of minority of the committee on that portion of governor's message relative to the same, ...	A	5	168
1843.	Report of Mr. Murray, one of the committee on the same, on so much of the governor's message as relates to them, ...	A	5	170
1844.	Report of Mr. Denniston on the subject of, ...	S	3	98
1844.	Resolution relating to, ...	S	3	108
1844.	Report of attorney-general on the subject of damages on the suspended, ...	S	3	116
1844.	Report on the petitions relative to new line of, at Rome, ...	A	5	125
1844.	Report of committee on, on so much of the governor's message as relates to, ...	A	7	177
1845.	Report of canal commissioners relative to new line of, through Rome, &c., ...	S	2	70
1845.	Report of canal commissioners relative to preserving materials on unfinished, ...	S	2	72
1845.	Report of committee on, on the bill from the assembly relative to,	S	3	110
1845.	Unfinished public works, report of canal commissioner relative to,	A	5	150
1845.	Report of committee on, on so much of governor's message as relates to, ...	A	6	235
1845.	Message from the governor returning the bill relating to the canals,	A	7	251
1846.	Report of committee on, relative to the Niagara River Hydraulic Company, ...	S	1	30
1846.	Report of committee on, on petition for a, in Chemung county, ..	A	4	112
1846.	Supply of water at Rome level, report of canal commissioners relative to, ...	A	5	171
1846.	Materials at Lockport, report of committee on, relative to, ...	A	5	185
1846.	Report of committee on canals respecting water from Genesee river, ...	A	6	204
1847.	Report of committee on, relative to appropriations for, ...	S	2	52
1847.	Report of committee on canals on governor's message and bill for repairs, &c., of canals (majority), ...	S	2	63

CANALS—*continued.*

		Doc.	Vol.	No.
1847.	Report of committee on canals on governor's message and bill for repairs, &c., of canals (minority),	S	2	79
1847.	Minority report of committee on canals relative to unfinished works,	S	3	81
1847.	Report on public works and officers connected,	S	4	125
1847.	Report of canal balance,	S	4	132
1847.	Report of committee on, on so much of governor's message as relates to,	A	4	128
1847.	Report on Jordan level draining,	A	4	140
1847.	Report of committee on, on bill making appropriations for improvement of, and the prosecution of the public works, and amendments of senate thereto,	A	4	167
1848.	Report of canal board relating to damages,	S	2	48
1848.	Report of joint committee on,	A	5	146
1848.	Report on bill for protection of laborers on,	A	5	173
1849.	Report of committee on, on bill and petitions for the construction of a basin at West Troy,	A	3	171
1849.	Report of committee on, relative to apportionments and improvements,	A	3	178
1850.	Strike on, at Buffalo and Black Rock,	A	5	93
1851.	Annual report of state engineer and surveyor on,	A	3	45
1852.	Report of joint select committee on lettings,	A	3	89
1852.	Report of state engineer and surveyor on,	A	4	90
1853.	Report of auditor, with reasons why certain claim were not paid to canal debt sinking fund,	S	2	51
1853.	Report of state engineer and surveyor relative to cost of finishing,	S	2	64
1853.	Report of the comptroller in relation to the time when the state tax would be available for the improvement of,	A	1	14
1853.	Annual report of the state engineer and surveyor, in relation to, for 1852,	A	2	28
1853.	Report of committee on ways and means on the bill to provide means to pay present claims upon the treasury, to support the government, to carry on the public works, &c.,	A	2	48
1853.	Report of the minority on the same subject,	A	2	54
1853.	Report of comptroller in reply to a resolution of Mr. Burroughs respecting time when the state tax would be available for the improvement of the,	A	3	61
1853.	Report of committee on, in reference to so much of governor's message as relates to,	A	3	64
1853.	Report of comptroller as to when the state tax would be available for the improvement of,	A	5	114
1853.	Report of conference committee of senate and assembly on amendments to constitution in relation to,	A	5	116
1854.	Annual report of state engineer and surveyor relative to,	S	1	60
1854.	Report of committee on commerce and navigation on bills to incorporate companies to navigate, &c.,	A	1	16
1854.	Minority report on same bill,	A	1	32
1855.	Annual report of the state engineer and surveyor in relation to,	A	2	50
1856.	Report of committee on, in relation to payment for certain labor on,	A	4	127
1856.	Report relative to work, &c.,	A	4	169
1856.	Communication from auditor,	A	5	191
1857.	Report of committee on ways and means favorable on petition of Ela N. Merriam for payment of a canal draft,	A	1	50
1857.	Annual report of state engineer and surveyor relative to,	A	1	60
1858.	Annual report of state engineer on, for 1857,	S	1	15
1858.	Report relative to moneys appropriated to,	A	1	49
1858,	Report of state engineer relative to amount of money necessary to complete the unfurnished,	A	4	116
	BOATS:			
1830.	Packets, report relative to their preference in passing locks,	S	2	98

CANALS—*continued.*

		Doc.	Vol	No.
1830.	Packets, report relative to their preference in passing locks,.....	S	2	183
1841.	Report on petition for the adoption of Mr. Amsden's plan for weighing,..........	A	7	271
1841.	Report on petition for the adoption of Mr. Amsden's plan for weighing,..........	A	7	272
1849.	Report respecting Mr. Amsden's plan for weighing,...........	A	5	225
1850.	Report respecting Mr. Amsden's plan for weighing,...........	A	3	35

STEAMBOAT, *see* A. Plantou.

BRIDGES:

		Doc.	Vol	No.
1830.	Bridge at Utica, report on petition for,....................	S	3	274
1830.	Report of the canal commissioners on the subject of,..........	A	4	334
1833.	Report of canal board on the subject of,....................	S	1	30
1837.	Claims for building, report on petition for a general law authorizing the canal commissioners to settle, &c.,..............	A	3	220
1838.	Report of canal commissioners in relation to, over the enlarged Erie canal,..............	A	6	278
1839.	Report of the canal board on the same,.....................	S	3	88
1843.	Report of the canal commissioners relative to, between Little Falls and Utica,..............	S	3	105
1844.	Report of canal commissioners on petition of inhabitants of Watervliet for two, over canal at West Troy,..................	A	6	149
1844.	Report of the canal board on the reference from the assembly of the petition of the citizens of Little Falls for the finishing of a,	A	6	157
1847.	Report of canal board relative to a, across Chenango canal at Elmira,..............	A	6	152
1847.	Report of canal board on petition of James Folbs for a, at Frankfort,..............	A	7	200
1847.	Report of the canal commissioners on petition of H. B. Smith and others for, at Rochester,..............	A	7	221
1857.	Report of canal commissioners in reply to resolution respecting, at West Troy,..............	A	2	92

CONTRACTORS:

		Doc.	Vol	No.
1842.	Report of canal commissioners relative to,..................	A	7	173
1844.	Report of canal board relative to allowances to, on suspended public works,..............	S	3	117
1844.	Report of comptroller of the extra allowances made to,........	S	4	134
1844.	Report of canal board relative to damages awarded to, for breaches of contracts on the part of the state in consequence of the suspension of the public works by the act of 1842,.............	A	1	2
1844.	Report of committee on canals on petition of,................	A	6	147
1845.	Report of committee on canals on petition of,................	A	3	48
1851.	Report of committee on claims on petition of, on the Oswego canal,	A	2	31

CONTRACTS:

		Doc.	Vol	No.
1842.	Report of canal commissioners relative to,..................	A	7	173
1847.	Report of canal board relative to work put under,............	A	7	208
1852.	Auditor's report respecting extra allowance on, by canal board,..	S	1	23
1853.	Communication from the canal commissioners in answer to a resolution of the assembly in relation to,..................	A	2	18
1857.	Report of attorney-general in reply to resolutions relative to suits on,..............	A	1	16

DEBT, ERIE AND CHAMPLAIN:

		Doc.	Vol	No.
1833.	Receipts and expenditures from 1817 to 1832,................	S	1	38
1836.	For the construction of, and repairs of the Erie, Champlain and Oswego canals, resolution relative to the payment of,........	A	1	59
1839.	Amount of the, when due, &c.,..............................	A	6	388
1840.	Report of commissioners of the canal fund in relation to the redemption of the,..............	S	2	62

CANALS—*continued.*

		Doc.	Vol.	No.
1840.	Report of canal board relative to the, and revenues,	A	7	306
	ENGINEERS:			
1842.	Report of canal commissioners relative to, in the employ of the state,	A	2	45
1844.	Report of the canal commissioners of the number and names of engineers and assistants employed on the unfinished works in 1842, 1843, &c.,	S	2	69
1845.	Report of canal commissioners in answer to a resolution of the senate relative to engineers in employ of the state, &c.,	S	1	23
	ENGINEERS, DIVISION AND RESIDENT:			
1853.	Report of auditor of canal department in relation to salaries and expenses of travel of the,	A	3	73
	ENLARGEMENT:			
1850.	Report of canal commissioners on, of canals other than Erie,	S	3	88
1851.	Report of attorney-general on bill to provide for,	S	3	68
1857.	Report of majority of committee on canals relative to,	S	3	69
1851.	Report of the minority on same subject,	S	3	70
1851.	Communication from Nelson J. Beach relative to,	A	3	63
1853.	Majority and minority report on the amendment of the consitution relative to,	A	4	98, 99
1853.	Memorial of the Chamber of Commerce of New York in relation to,	A	4	100
1854.	Communication from state engineer and surveyor relative to,	S	2	109
1854.	Report of committee on, relative to, and certificates,	A	3	119
1855.	Communication from auditor in relation to work on section 370, Erie canal,	A	3	73
1856.	Report on the maintenance and,	A	3	90
1856.	Communication from auditor in relation to, and completion of,	A	4	146
	EXPENDITURES:			
1830.	Annual report of, for 1829,	A	3	208
1831.	do do 1830,	A	3	206
1832.	do do 1831,	A	1	9
1833.	do do 1832,	A	1	16
1834.	do do 1833,	A	2	75
1835.	do do 1834,	A	3	216
1836.	do do 1835,	A	4	211
1837.	do do 1836,	A	2	159
1838.	do do 1837,	A	1	6
1839.	do do 1838,	A	1	16
1840.	do do 1839,	A	4	131
1841.	do do 1840,	A	3	51
1843.	Annual report of comptroller relative to, for 1841,	A	3	63
1843.	Annual report of comptroller relative to, for 1842,	A	3	56
1844.	Annual report of comptroller on,	A	5	105
1845.	Annual report of comptroller relative to,	A	5	162
1846.	Annual report of comptroller on,	A	4	90
1846.	Report of majority of printing committee relative to printing annual report of comptroller on,	A	4	94
1846.	Report of minority of printing committee relative to printing annual report of comptroller on,	A	4	95
1847.	Estimate of,	S	2	43
1847.	Report of,	A	1	15
1847.	Report of, for certain years,	A	4	129
1847.	Report of committee on canals on report ofcomptroller relative to,	A	4	174
1848.	Annual report of comptroller relative to,	A	3	60
1849.	Annual report of auditor of canaldepartment relative to,	A	1	30
1852.	Auditor's estimates for,	A	5	116

CANALS—*continued.*

		Doc.	Vol.	No.
1852.	Auditor's report on,..........	A	5	125
1853.	Communication from auditor relative to, of the appropriation for the canals for the current fiscal year,..........	S	3	84
1853.	Report of auditor of canal department in relation to,..........	A	4	105
1853.	Report of auditor respecting,..........	A	5	126
1854.	Annual report of auditor relative to,..........	A	5	146
1855.	Annual report of auditor in relation to,..........	A	7	147
1856.	Annual report of auditor relative to,..........	A	5	213
1857.	Annual report of auditor concerning,..........	A	3	175
1858.	Annual report of auditor relative to,..........	A	4	145
	FENCES:			
1830.	Report of canal commissioners on the subject of,..........	A	4	334
1832.	Report of canal commissioners on the subject of,..........			
1833.	Report of canal board on the subject of,..........	S	1	30
1836.	Report of canal board on the subject of,..........	A	4	234
1839.	Report of canal commissioners on petition of W. Brayton and others, relative to,..........	A	5	269
1839.	Report of committee on claims on the same,..........	A	5	290
1841.	Report of committee on grievances on the same,..........	A	4	118
	FRAUDS:			
1847.	Memorials relative to,..........	S	3	93, 94
1847.	Report and resolution of committee on canals concerning report of select committee of 1846 to investigate, &c.,..........	A	2	78
1847.	Report of select committee of assembly of 1846, for investigation of,..........	A	3	100
1847.	Memorial of Holmes Hutchinson relative to report of select committee for investigating,..........	A	7	218
1851.	Report of select committee of assembly of 1846, for investigation of,..........	A	6	156
1851.	Report of select committee of assembly of 1846, for investigation of,..........	A	6	158
	HYDROSTATIC SCALE, AMSDEN'S:			
1841.	Report on petition for the adoption of,..........	A	7	271
1841.	Report on petition for the adoption of,..........	A	7	272
1849.	Report of canal commissioners respecting,..........	A	5	225
1850.	Report of canal commissioners relative to,..........	A	3	35
	LOCKS:			
1843.	Report of canal commissioners in relation to combined, at Lockport,..........	S	3	98
1844.	Report on the subject of closing the, on the Sabbath,..........	S	4	119
1844.	Report of canal board relative to the five combined, at Lockport,	S	4	130
1844.	Report of canal commissioners in relation to the combined, at Lockport,..........	A	5	131
1845.	Report of committee on canals relative to closing, on Sunday,...	A	4	148
1846.	Report of canal commissioners in answer to a resolution relative to doubling of, on Erie canal,..........	A	4	110
1848.	Report of canal commissioners relative to, at Tonawanda,......	A	4	117
1849.	Report of canal commissioners in relation to the length and width of chambers of enlarged, on Erie canal,..........	S	2	50
1849.	Report on the subject of closing, on Sunday,..........	S	2	6
1849.	Report of canal commissioners in answer to a resolution of the assembly respecting expense of bringing into use one set of enlarged, on Erie canal, from Syracuse to Buffalo,..........	A	3	116
1851.	Report of state engineer and surveyor relative to lengthening,..	A	3	67
1856.	Report of committee on canals relative to, on Chemung canal,...	A	4	132
1857.	Minority report of committee on canals relative to, on Chemung canal,..........	S	2	56

CANALS—*continued.*

		Doc.	Vol.	No.
1857.	Report of Canal Commissioner Fitzhugh relative to, on Chemung canal,	A	1	51
1858.	Report in answer to resolution relative to enlargement of, on Chemung canal,	S	3	133
1858.	Report of committee on canals relative to closing, on Sunday,	S	2	77
1858.	Minority report on same subject,	S	2	91
1858.	Report of state engineer and surveyor relative to, on Chemung canal,	S	3	124
1858.	Report of state engineer and surveyor relative to enlargement of, on Chemung canal,	S	3	133
1858.	Majority report relative to closing, on Sunday,	A	4	134
1858.	Minority report on same subject,	A	4	137
	NAVIGATION:			
1833.	Report relative to its preservation and management,	A	4	255
1835.	Communication from the canal board relative to the,	S	1	24
	OFFICERS:			
1838.	Report of the canal board giving the names and compensation of,	A	5	231
1840.	Report of the canal board giving the names and compensation of,	A	8	318
	PACKET BOATS:			
1830.	Report relative to their preference in passing locks,	S	2	98
1830.	Report relative to their preference in passing locks,	S	2	133
	RECEIPTS AND EXPENDITURES:			
1830.	Annual report of the commissioners of the canal fund,	A	2	152
1831.	do do do	A	2	102
1832.	do do do	A	1	5
1833	do do do	A	1	4
1834.	do do do	A	1	4
1835.	do do do	A	1	4
1836.	do do do	A	1	4
1837.	do do do	A	1	3
1838.	do do do	A	1	5
1839.	do do do	A	2	26
1840.	do do do	A	3	74
1840.	Communication in relation to their annual report,	A	3	69
1841.	Annual report,	A	1	5
	See Expenditures, Revenues.			
	REPAIRS:			
1846.	Report of committee on canals on an act to reduce expenses of,	A	5	173
1846.	Report of canal commissioners relative to the best mode of,	S	1	27
1846.	Report of committee on canals on bill to reduce expense of superintendence and,	S	3	104
1846.	Report of committee on canals on an act to reduce expenses of,	A	5	173
1846.	Superintendent of, report of canal commissioners relative to,	A	6	221
1847.	Majority report of committee on canals on so much of governor's message as related to bills for,	S	2	63
1847.	Minority report on same,	S	2	79
1847.	Report on bill, &c., for,	S	2	63, 79
1855.	Report of committee on canals relative to contracting,	S	3	73
1856.	Report of commissioner of eastern division relative to, and superintendence of,	A	3	31
	REVENUES:			
1832.	Resolution to amend the constitution in relation to,	S	2	70
1832.	do do do	S	2	100
1834.	do do do	A	3	131
1835.	do do do	S	2	35
1836.	do do do	S	1	48
1836.	Of the lateral canals, report of comptroller relative to,	S	1	58

CANALS—*continued.*

Year	Subject	Doc.	Vol.	No.
1840.	Report of canal board relative to, and debt,	A	7	306
1842.	Report of comptroller in reply to a resolution of the senate as to,	S	1	16
1848.	Committee on canals, report relative to appropriations of surplus, to unfinished works,	A	2	25
1848.	Report as to application of surplus,	A	5	137
1853.	Report of commissioners of the canal fund relative to appropriation of surplus, to claims arising prior to June 1, 1846,	A	5	125
1855.	Report relative to deficiency in,	S	3	74
	ROUTES, SURVEYS OF:			
1831.	Comptroller, report of items of amount paid the, &c.,	A	4	399
	STOCK:			
1839.	Report of unclaimed items of interest on, in the Manhattan Bank,	A	3	134
1841.	Erie and Champlain, report in relation to notices for the redemption of,	S	2	55
1845.	Report of comptroller relative to the issue and redemption of,	A	5	175
	SUPERINTENDENTS:			
1846.	Report of commissioners of canal fund in answer to a resolution calling for names of persons paid by, at Syracuse,	S	3	101
1846.	Report of canal commissioners in answer to a resolution giving names of,	A	4	119
1847.	Report of comptroller respecting amounts paid, &c.,	S	1	40
1853.	Report of auditor in reply to a resolution calling for proceedings of canal board respecting complaints or charges against,	S	3	71
1856.	Report of majority of canal board relative to,	S	2	42
1856.	Minority report,	S	2	43
	SYSTEM AND INTERNAL IMPROVEMENTS:			
1831.	Report on the subject of, (N. P. Tallmadge,)	S	1	32
1833.	do do (Mr. Stillwell,)	A	4	268
1834.	do do (Mr. Hubbard,)	S	2	55
1840.	do do (Mr. Lay,)	A	7	277
	TOLLS, TRADE AND TONNAGE:			
1830.	Report of canal board relative to increasing the rates of,	S	4	291
1830.	Report of the attorney-general as to the constitutionality of increasing the rates of,	S	4	344
1832.	Amount collected on packet boats and passengers for the last two years,	S	1	49
1832.	Amount collected in 1831, &c., report of commissioners of canal fund of,	A	1	38
1833.	Amount collected in 1832, &c., report of commissioners of canal fund of,	A	3	173
1833.	On flour and wheat, report of canal board on petition to modify the,	A	4	320
1834.	Amount collected from 1820 to 1834,	A	2	66
1834.	Amount collected in 1833,	A	3	107
1832.	Resolution to amend the constitution relative to,	S	2	70
1832.	do do do	S	2	100
1834.	do do do	A	3	131
1835.	do do do	S	2	35
1836.	do do do	S	1	48
1834.	Report relative to, on the canal around the falls at Baldwinsville,	A	3	232
1836.	Report relative to, on the canal around the falls at Baldwinsville,	A	3	141
1836.	Report of canal board relative to, on gypsum,	A	4	294
1832.	Amount collected, rates of, &c., in 1834, report of C. C. fund of,	A	1	38
1833.	do do 1832, do	A	2	173
1834.	do do 1833, do	A	3	107
1835.	do do 1834, do	S	2	58
1836.	do do 1835, do	S	2	70

CANALS—*continued.*

		Doc.	Vol.	No.
1837.	Amount collected, rates of, &c., in 1836, report of C. C. fund of,	S	2	52
1838.	do do 1837, do	S	1	35
1839.	do do 1838, do	S	1	27
1840.	do do 1839, do	S	3	63
1841.	do do 1840, do	S	2	65
1839.	Report on the petition for the reduction of, on the Chenango canal,	A	6	343
1840.	Report on petition for the reduction of, on coal and lead,	A	8	343
1841.	Report of canal board relative to uniform rates of, on all the canals,	A	6	222
1836.	Amount received on each of the lateral canals,	S	1	58
1842.	Annual report of commissioners of the canal fund relative to tolls collected and property trnasported on the canals in 1841,	S	2	33
1842.	Report of committee on canals on petition of Clinton Walworth for reduction of tolls on lead and copper,	A	7	158
1843.	Report of the comptroller respecting amount of tolls on passengers on the Erie canal,	S	1	21
1844.	Report of commissioners of land office, of the amonnt of tolls collected at Buffalo and Black Rock in 1840, 1841, 1842, &c.,	S	1	35
1844.	Report of the canal commissioners of the trade and tonnage of the canals, &c.,	S	4	118
1845.	Report of committee on canals relative to discriminating tolls on,	S	3	113
1845.	Report of commissioners of canal fund of tolls, tonnage and trade of New York canals, 1844,	S	3	115
1845.	Comptroller's report in relation to amount of tolls paid on Erie canal, on freight shipped to or from lateral canals,	S	3	116
1845.	Petition of inhabitants of western New York for a reduction of tolls on Oswego canal,	A	4	81
1845.	Remonstrance of citizens of Oswego against discriminating tolls on the Erie canal,	A	4	85
1845.	Report of committee on canals relative to discriminating tolls on the Oswego and Erie canals,	A	5	189
1845.	Minority report on same,	A	5	190
1846.	Report of commissioners of the canal fund of the tolls, tonnage, &c., on the canals,	S	2	59
1846.	Report relative to reduction of rates of,	S	3	89
1846.	Report of comptroller in answer to a resolution relative to tolls on Erie canal, &c.,	A	4	113
1847.	Report of comptroller as to amount of tolls and amounts paid superintendents on canals,	S	1	40
1847.	Trade and tonnage of,	S	3	90
1847.	Report on tolls of western trade,	A	1	42
1848.	Report of commissioners of canal fund respecting,	S	2	50
1849.	Report of auditor of,	A	3	190
1849.	Communication from auditor respecting collection of tolls,	A	3	195
1850.	Report of,	A	6	140
1851.	Annual report of auditor on,	A	3	56
1852.	Auditor's report on,	S	3	94
1853.	Report of canal commissioners relative to tolls received on Champlain canal during 1852, &c.,	S	1	20
1853.	Report of canal commissioners in relation to tonnage on Champlain canal,	S	1	20
1853.	Report of auditor in relation to tolls on property going to and coming from Canada,	S	1	29
1853.	Report of auditor of tolls, tonnage, &c.,	A	4	107
1854.	Report of auditor relative to, on Oneida Lake canal, &c.,	A	2	74
1854.	Report of canal board relative to reduction of,	A	4	134
1854.	Annual report of trade and tonnage,	A	5	145
1855.	Report of auditor in relation to trade and tonnage,	A	4	95
1856.	Annual report of auditor on,	A	5	212
1857.	Report relative to canal tolls,	S	4	127
1857.	Annual report of the auditor on,	A	3	185

CANALS—*continued.*

		Doc.	Vol.	No.
1857.	Resolution of canal board relative to reduction of tolls on certain articles,	A	3	187
1858.	Reply of the canal board to a resolution of the senate relative to,	S	3	113
1858.	Report of auditor relative to,	S	3	123
1858.	Report of canal board relative to tolls on wheat and flour,	S	3	134
1858.	Report of proceedings of canal board relative to tolls on iron, &c,	S	3	135
1858.	Annual report of auditor on,	A	5	155

For Tolls on Railroads, *see* Railroads.

Weigh Locks:

		Doc.	Vol.	No.
1841.	Report on petition for the adoption of Mr. Amsdem's substitute for,	A	7	271
1841.	Report on petition for the adoption of Mr. Amsden's substitute for,	A	7	272
1849.	Report of canal commissioners respecting Mr. Amsden's substitute for,	A	5	225
1849.	Report of canal commissioners respecting Mr. Amsden's substitute for,	A	3	95

Black River Canal:

		Doc.	Vol.	No.
1831.	Report of canal commissioners relative to the survey of the,	A	3	229
1831.	Proceedings of a meeting of delegates of the towns on the route of the, in relation to the construction of,	A	3	245
1831.	Report of committee on canals, on petition for the construction of,	A	4	287
1834.	do do do	A	4	273
1835.	do do do	S	2	77
1835.	do do do	A	2	150
1835.	Report of canal commissioners relative to the survey of,	A	1	55
1836.	Report of the majority of the committee on canals, on petition for,	S	1	36
1836.	Memorial of a convention of delegates from Oneida, Lewis, Jefferson and St. Lawrence counties,	S	1	21
1837.	Report relative to damages by diverting the waters of Black river to supply the,	A	3	205
1838.	Side-cut from, to Delta, report on petition for,	A	3	91
1839.	Side-cut from, to Delta, report on petition for,	A	2	68
1838.	Extension of, to Sacketts Harbor, report on petition for,	A	5	213
1839.	Extension of, to Sacketts Harbor, report on petition for,	A	4	197
1839.	Estimated cost of, report of canal commissioners relative to,	A	5	267
1839.	Estimated cost of, report of canal commissioners relative to,	A	6	360
1839.	Cost of, report of canal board on a resolution of assembly to inquire whether any alteration can be made to lessen the cost of,	A	6	391
1840.	Extension of, to Sacketts Harbor, report of a survey of a route,	A	6	233
1840.	Extension of to Sacketts Harbor, report on bill for the,	A	8	345
1841.	Extension of, to Sacketts Harbor, report on petition for the,	A	6	234
1841.	Contracts for the construction of, report of canal commissioners relative to,	A	6	203
1843.	Report of the canal commissioners relative to the amount necessary to finish the,	S	1	47
1845.	Report of canal commissioners in answer to a resolution of the assembly relative to, and feeder,	A	4	131
1845.	Memorial relative to completing,	A	5	151
1848.	Report relative to, and Genesee,	A	3	97
1855.	Report by auditor of testimony in relation to, lettings,	A	1	8

Cato Canal Company:

		Doc.	Vol.	No.
1830.	Report on petition to incorporate,	A	4	421

Cayuga and Seneca:

		Doc.	Vol.	No.
1831.	Deficiency in the revenue of, comptroller's report relative to the payment of certain money to the commissioners of the canal fund for the,	A	4	339

CANALS—*continued.*

		Doc.	Vol.	No.
1837.	Towpath bridge on, report relative to,..........................	A	3	250
1839.	Report of canal board on bill for the regulation of the water in,..	S	2	44
1839.	Enlargement of, report of canal board relative to,...............	A	6	367
1840.	Enlargement of, report of canal committee on,....................	A	5	177
1843.	Report of canal commissioners in relation thereto, and the outlet of the Seneca lake, in answer to a resolution of assembly of March 23, 1842,..	A	4	102
1845.	Report of the commissioners on reference of the petition of citizens of Chemung, relative to,..............................	A	7	246
	CHAMPLAIN CANAL:			
1830.	Report of expenses of, for the last year, the number of superintendents, &c.,...	S	3	243
1831.	Surplus water of, report on petition of John F. King, for the use of,	S	1	53
1833.	Receipts and expenditures of, report of the commissioners of the canal fund,..	S	1	38
1836.	Cost of construction and maintenance of,.........................	S	2	72
1838.	Report on petition for the survey of a route for a canal from the head waters of the Hudson to,..............................	A	5	238
1840.	Canal debt, report of commissioners of the canal fund relative to the redemption of,..	S	2	62
1841.	Side-cut from, into the Hudson river, at Stillwater, report on petition for,..	A	6	232
1846.	Report of Mr. Clark from the select committee appointed to inquire into certain expenditures, &c., on the northern section of, and Glens Falls feeder, &c.,................................	S	4	144
1850.	Report on proposition to enlarge,................................	A	5	129
1853.	Report of canal commissioners in relation to tolls received and tonnage employed,..	S	1	20
1853.	Communication from J. C. Mather respecting part of the, where it crosses,...	A	4	110
1853.	Report of canal commissioners relative to suspensions of navigation on, and Erie,...	A	5	128
1857.	Report of state engineer and surveyor and Canal Commissioner Sherrill, in reply to resolution relative to the condition of, ...	A	2	116
	CHEMUNG CANAL:			
1830.	Report of canal commissioners in relation to their proceedings in relation to the construction of, with estimate of cost and revenues,...	A	2	97
1830.	Report of S. Young, one of the canal commissioners, on the same,	A	2	195
1830.	Report of committee on canals (A. C. Paige), on the reports of the canal commissioners,................................	A	4	326
1833.	Deficiency in the revenues of the, report in relation to,.........	A	4	331
1835.	Tolls collected on certain articles, report in relation to,........	A	2	159
1839.	Extension of, to the Pennsylvania canal, governor's message relative to the,...	S	3	86
1836.	Extension of, to the Pennsylvania canal, report of joint committee on,..	S	3	112
1840.	Extension of, to the Pennsylvania canal, report of, survey of,...	S	1	2
1840.	Extension of, to the Pennsylvania canal, report of canal commissioners on survey of the,..................................	A	1	32
1840.	Extension of, to the Pennsylvania canal, committee on canals (Mr. Knibloe),..	A	7	287
1840.	Improvement of the, report of committee on canals (Mr. Moseley),	S	4	105
1840.	Improvement of the, report of canal commissioners in relation to the,...	A	5	161
1841.	Improvement of the, report relative to the estimated cost of a canal from Seneca lake to Havana,.........................	S	2	50
1841.	Improvement of the, report of committee on canals (Mr. Moseley),	S	2	61
1811.	Improvement of the report of committee on canals (Mr. Moseley),	A	5	174

CANALS—*continued.*

Year	Subject	Doc.	Vol.	No.
1842.	Report of the commissioners of the canal fund on resolution of the senate relative to loan for,	S	3	69
1842.	Report of comptroller in relation to the amount of premiums received on, and Chenango canal stocks,	S	4	87
1845.	Report of canal commissioners answering a resolution of the relative to obstructions in, &c.,	S	2	55
1850.	Report of select committee respecting,	S	3	105
1856.	Report of the state engineer and surveyor in relation to locks on,	A	4	113
1856.	Report relating to locks on,	A	4	132
1857.	Report of minority of standing committee on canals relative to locks on,	S	2	56
1857.	Report of state engineer and surveyor relative to,	S	3	87
1857.	Report of Canal Commissioner Fitzhurgh relative to locks on,	A	1	51
1858.	Report of state engineer and surveyor respecting locks on,	S	3	124
1858.	Report in answer to resolution relative to enlargement of locks on,	S	3	133
	Chemung Canal Feeder:			
1838.	Report of the canal commissioners of estimated expense of continuing said feeder to the junction of the Conhocton and Tioga rivers, &c.,	A	5	244
1839.	Extension of, report on petition for and against the,	A	4	198
1842.	Report of committee on canals on petition for the extension of,	A	7	188
	Chemung Canal, Surplus Waters of, *see* Jefferson Bartlett, Vincent Conkling, John Gregg and Charles Orwan.			
1834.	Report of canal commissioners in relation to,	A	2	91
1837.	Report of canal commissioners in relation to,	A	2	77
	Chenango Canal:			
1830.	Report of canal commissioners on petition for the construction of,	A	1	47
1830.	Report of committee on canals (Mr. Paige), for the construction of,	A	4	299
1831.	do do (Mr. Hubbard), for the construction of,	S	1	20
1832.	do do (Mr. Hubbard), for the construction of,	S	1	16
1832.	do do on bill for the construction of,	A	3	206
1833.	do do (Mr. Van Schaack), for the construction of,	S	2	44
1833.	do do (Mr. Stilwell), for the construction of,	A	1	26
1833.	Report of canal commissioners in relation to the loans for the construction of,	A	3	220
1834.	Report on petition for the termination of the, at Utica,	A	1	25
1834.	Report on petition for the termination of the, at Utica,	A	2	83
1834.	Petition from Oneida and Madison counties to change the termination of, to the Oneida creek,	S	2	61
1834.	Report of canal commissioners relative to gifts, grants and donations to,	S	2	85
1834.	Report of canal commissioners relative to survey and reservoirs of the,	S	2	87
1835.	Report on petition for a lock from, into the Chenango river,	A	2	93
1835.	Report on petition for a lock at the Oxford basin,	S	2	64
1835.	Report of comptroller in relation to stock issued for the,	A	5	381
1836.	Report on petition of citizens of Utica to be released from tax for changing the termination of,	A	2	88
1838.	Report on petition of citizens of Utica to be released from tax for changing the termination of,	A	2	33
1838.	Report on petition of citizens of Utica to be released from tax for changing the termination of,	A	4	194
1836.	Contractors on, report on petition of Joseph Saxton and others, for relief,	A	3	121

CANALS—*continued.*

		Doc.	Vol.	No.
1836.	Contractors on, report on petition of Joseph Saxton and others, for relief,	A	3	197
1837.	Report of amount of money agreed to be paid for changing the termination of,	S	2	49
1837.	Report of canal commissioners in relation to the construction of,	A	3	201
1837.	Sub-contractors, report on petition for extra compensation,	A	3	236
1837.	Report on petition of citizens of Sherburne to be relieved from certain liabilities in relation to the location of the, in said village,	A	3	211
1839.	Report on petition of citizens of Sherburne to be relieved from certain liabilities in relation to the location of the, in said village,	A	3	139
1839.	Report on petition of citizens of Sherburne to be relieved from certain liabilities in relation to the location of the, in said village,	A	4	217
1838.	Allowances made to canal contractors, report of,	S	2	64
1838.	Damages to private property taken for, report of canal commissioners relative to,	S	2	67
1839.	Extension of, to the Pennsylvania canal, governor's message relative to the,	S	3	86
1839.	Extension of, to the Pennsylvania canal, report of joint committee,	S	3	112
1839.	Extension of, to the Pennsylvania canal, report of committee on canals,	A	4	195
1839.	Extension to state line, near Tioga Point, canal commissioners' report of survey of,	A	3	116
1840.	Extension to state line, near Tioga Point, report of committee on canals (Mr. Moseley),	S	3	71
1839.	Reduction of tolls on, report on petition for,	A	6	343
1840.	Report relative to a deficiency of funds to pay damages awarded on the,	A	7	302
1842.	Report of comptroller relative to the amount of premiums received on, and Chemung canal stocks,	S	4	87
1843.	Report of the committee on canals, on petition of inhabitants of Oriskany Falls and vicinity, respecting moneys paid by them on account of locating, through said village,	A	4	105
1846.	Report of canal board respecting surplus waters from,	A	5	195
1847.	Report of canal board relative to bridge across, at Elmira,	A	6	152
	CONEWANGO CANAL:			
1838.	Report on petition for the survey of a route for,	A	5	243
1840.	Report of the canal commissioners of the survey of,	A	4	160
	CROOKED LAKE CANAL:			
1830.	Report of canal commissioners of estimated cost and revenues of, &c.,	A	2	97
1830.	Report of S. Young, one of the canal commissioners, relative to estimated cost and revenues of, &c.,	A	2	195
1835.	Report of canal commissioners in relation to summit level of, &c.,	A	4	343
1835.	Report on petition of owners of hydraulic works on the outlet of Crooked Lake,	A	4	369
1837.	Report of canal commissioners in relation to the upper level of the,	A	3	203
1855.	Report of state engineer in reference to improvement of,	A	5	117
	DELAWARE AND HUDSON CANAL, *see* Banks:			
1830.	Report on petition for power to sell certain land, &c.,	S	1	21
1830.	Report of comptroller relative to the stock issued to the,	S	2	198
1830.	Report of comptroller relative to the stock issued to the,	S	4	317
1831	Communication from the president of the, to the governor,	A	1	3
1834.	Report of committee on petition of citizens of Orange and Sullivan for relief from injuries sustained from the,	S	2	77
1839.	Report relative to the issue of bank notes not payable on demand,	S	2	49
1842.	Letter of president of, to the governor,	A	1	2

CANALS—*continued.*

		Doc.	Vol.	No.
1842.	Letter of president of, to the comptroller relative to,...........	A	7	162
1845.	Report of the comptroller relative to,........................	A	5	155
1848.	Report of committee on finance in relation to,................	S	2	43
1849.	Report of comptroller relative to stocks issued to,............	S	2	41
1852.	Report of company of, respecting violation of charter of the,...	A	2	60
1852.	Minority report of company of, as to violation of charter of,....	A	2	70
	ERIE AND CHAMPLAIN CANAL:			
1835.	Report of amount of moneys taken from the general funds and paid for the construction and support of, from 1816 to 1834,..	S	2	40
1840.	Debt of, report of commissioners of the canal fund as to what banks the money pledged for the redemption of the, is deposited, &c.,..	S	2	62
1841.	Notices for the redemption of, report of the commissioners of the canal fund relative to,..................................	S	2	55
1853.	Report of canal commissioners relative to suspensions of navigation on Erie,..	A	5	123
	ERIE CANAL:			
1834.	Aqueduct at Rochester, report of canal commissioners relative to rebuilding,..	A	2	88
1833.	Banks of, report on petition of citizens of Herkimer county relative to defects in,....................................	A	4	272
1837.	Branch from, to Catskill, report on petition for (H. Rogers),....	A	3	280
1828.	do do do do (L. F. Allen),...	A	5	212
1839.	do do do do (Mr. Lewis),....	A	4	251
1836.	Business on, report relative to increase or diminution of, by the construction of the lateral canals,........................	S	2	81
1834.	Condition of, near Schenectady, report relative to,............	A	4	327
1834.	Cost of constructing from Schenectady to Albany, &c.,..........	S	2	72
1847.	Contract, report respecting work under,......................	A	7	208
1841.	Contracts for the enlargement of, report of canal commissioners in answer to a resolution of assembly relative to the,.........	A	6	203
1843.	Contracts on the enlarged, report of the comptroller respecting, between Albany and Troy,................................	S	1	15
1844.	Contracts made for enlarging, &c., report of the canal commissioners in answer to a resolution of the assembly of March 12, relative to,..	A	6	146
1835.	Enlargement of, report of canal commissioners in relation to the,	A	2	143
1835.	Committee on canals (Mr. Wager),........................	A	3	254
1835.	Resolution offered by Mr. Thorn in relation to the,..........	A	4	340
1836.	Report on petition of common council of, for a direct route from Schenectady to Albany,........................	S	2	99
1836.	Supply of water for the Rome summit, report relative to,...	S	1	61
1836.	Report of canal board in relation to the,.................	A	2	98
1836.	Documents accompanying,..............................	A	2	99
1837.	Report of canal board in relation to the,.................	S	2	73
1837.	Remonstrance of inhabitants of Oneida against the,........	A	2	132
1837.	Tax on banks for the more speedy, report on bill,..........	A	4	316
1838.	Appraisers' report of damages by the,....................	A	5	201
1838.	At Oriskany, report on petition to change the route for the,..	A	5	225
1838.	Report of committee on canals on petition for,.............	A	5	245
1838.	Locks on the, report of canal commissioners relative to,.....	A	5	251
1838.	Bridges on the, report of canal commissioners relative to,...	A	6	298
1838.	At West Troy, report of canal commissioners relative to the construction of the,..............................	A	6	313
1838.	Committee on canals on the construction of the,..........	A	6	333
1838.	Contractors on the, report of canal commissioners on petition of, for extra compensation,.........................	A	3	131
1838.	Report of select committee on the same,..................	A	5	215
1839.	Report on propriety of constructing the, independent of the Niagara river,..	S	2	54

CANALS—*continued.*

Year	Subject	Doc.	Vol.	No.
1839.	Enlargement of, appraisal of property taken for, in the city of Rochester; *see* Hervey Ely and others.			
1839.	Resolution calling on the canal commissioners for estimates of the cost of the, &c.,	A	4	224
1839.	Expenses of, report of canal commissioners in relation to,	A	5	267
1839.	estimated cost and revenues of, report of canal commissioners,	A	6	339
1839.	Route of, through Oriskany, report on petition against changing the,	A	4	261
1839.	Location of, at Rochester, report relative to the,	A	5	287
1839.	Walling with stone the sides of the, report of canal commissioners on the expediency of,	A	4	238
1839.	From Utica to Syracuse, report on petition to lower the bottom of the canal, instead of raising the surface of the water,	A	6	369
1839.	Report relative to supplying the, with water from Lake Erie to the Seneca river,	A	6	381
1840.	Revenues, resolution calling on the canal board for estimates of future, &c.,	A	5	204
1840.	Debts and revenues, &c., report of canal board on a resolution of assembly,	A	7	306
1842.	Report of committee on canals on petition for speedy,	A	7	190
1843.	Report of committee on canals relative to a portion of,	S	3	102
1845.	Report of canal commissioners relative to,	A	6	225
1847.	Report of, on memorial for, and basins at Buffalo,	A	7	205
1847.	Proceedings of a meeting of citizens of Rochester, memorializing the legislature as to the speedy,	A	7	183
1851.	Report of committee on canals relative to governor's message respecting,	A	4	102
1853.	Report of majority and minority committee on amending constitution relative to the,	A	4	98, 99
1853.	Memorial of New York chamber of commerce,	A	4	100
1857.	Report of engineer and surveyor, at Port Byron, in reply to resolution relative to,	A	2	88
1858.	Reply of state engineer and surveyor to a resolution of the senate relative to securing six feet depth of water in the,	S	3	117
1840.	Expenditure of the $5,000,000 loan, report of commissioners of canal fund relative to the,	A	8	331
1852.	Feeder, report on petition of citizens of Rochester in relation to the,	A	5	109
1847.	Frauds on, report respecting,	A	3	100
1855.	Geddes, communication from canal commissioners in reference to,	A	5	133
1853.	Improvement of, and Oswego, message of governor relative to appropriations for,	S	3	67
1853.	Governor's message relative to appropriation for,	A	4	91
1844.	Jordan level of, report of canal commissioners in relation to,	S	4	129
1846.	Locks on, report of canal commissioners in answer to a resolution of the assembly relative to doubling,	A	4	110
1849.	Report of canal commissioners as to length and width of,	S	2	50
1849.	Report of canal commissioners in answer to resolution of assembly respecting expense of bringing into use one set of enlarged, on the Erie canal,	A	3	116
1851.	Report of the canal board in relation to lengthening,	A	3	67
1847.	Memorial relative to report on,	A	7	205
1853.	Navigation on, and Champlain, report of the canal commissioners relative to suspensions of,	A	5	128
1855.	Port Byron, communication from canal board relative to line of, near,	A	3	74
1853.	Port Byron, communication from canal board relative to line of, near,	A	4	74

CANALS—*continued.*

Year	Subject	Doc.	Vol.	No.
1855.	Port Byron, report of committee on petitions and remonstrances in reference to change of line near,............	A	5	132
1830.	Receipts and expenditures of, number of superintendents, &c.,..	A	3	243
1833.	From 1817 to 1832, report of the commissioners of the canal fund of,..	S	1	38
1844.	Rome, report of engineer relative to the enlarged,..............	S	3	110
1845.	Report of the canal commissioners relative to new line of, through, &c.,..	S	2	70
1846.	Rome level, report of canal commissioners relative to supply of water on,..	A	5	171
1855.	Section 370, communication from auditor in reply to a resolution respecting work on,................................	A	3	72
1845.	Side-cut in, report of the canal commissioners on reference of the petition of citizens of Troy relative to a,............	A	3	57
1850.	Sodus, report of canal board relative to, at,..................	A	6	151
1831.	Surplus water of, report of committee on canals relative to the use of the,..	A	4	355
1831.	At Lockport, *see* Lockport.			
1831.	At Watervliet, communication from Major Talcott relative to,	A	3	207
1831.	*See* Isaac Allen and others.			
1833.	*See* Frederick Bellinger.			
1833.	At Utica, *see* Joseph C. Bloomfield.			
1833.	At Lockville, report of canal commissioners concerning,....	A	4	287
1834.	At Macedon, report on petition of D. H. Richardson for a grant of,..	A	4	298
1835.	At Brighton and Pittsford, report on petition for a grant of,.	A	2	83
1839.	*See* Cyrus P. Dunham and others.			
1839.	*See* A. Parkhurst and John T. Dunn.			
1834.	At Schoharie creek dam, report on petition of John Enders for a grant of,..	A	3	237
1841.	Of Nine-Mile Creek feeder, report on petition of inhabitants of Camillus for a grant of,............................	A	6	206
1847.	Report of canal board on petition of town of Lenox relative to, on Rome level,......	A	4	109
1837.	Tolls, amount of diverted by the lateral canals,...............	S	2	73
1839.	On passengers, furniture and baggage, report of amount derived from, and on the propriety of allowing parallel railroads to transport the same free of toll, &c.,...........	A	6	355
1843.	Comptroller's report of the amount of, on passengers,......	S	1	21
1845.	Report of comptroller respecting amount of, paid on freight shipped to or from lateral canals,......................	S	3	116
1845.	Remonstrance of inhabitants of Oswego against proposed discriminating duties on,................	A	4	85
1845.	On Oswego and, report of majority of committee on canals relative to discrimination of,..........................	A	5	189
1845.	Report of minority on same subject,.....................	A	5	190
1846.	Report of comptroller relative to, &c.,....................	A	4	113
1847.	Tonawanda level on, report of the canal commissioners relative to draining the,.................................	A	4	149
1841.	Tonnage of the, report of the commissioners of canal fund respecting the,..	A	5	193
1842.	Erie Canal Enlargement and Black River and Genesee Valley Completion Company, memorial for the incorporation of,.........	A	7	160

Feeder Dam on the Genesee River:

Year	Subject	Doc.	Vol.	No.
1841.	Report of canal commissioners on petition for the removal of,..	A	6	250
1841.	Proceedings of a meeting of the citizens of Monroe county for the removal of,..	A	7	274

Genesee Valley Canal:

Year	Subject	Doc.	Vol.	No.
1835.	Report on petition for the immediate construction of,..........	S	2	78
1835.	Survey of a route for,......................	A	4	264

CANALS—*continued.*

Year	Subject	Doc.	Vol.	No.
1836.	Survey of a route for,	A	1	42
1836.	Report of committee on canals (Mr. Baland) on petition for,	A	3	140
1838.	Feeder from Conesus outlet to the, report of canal commissioners relative to,	A	2	30
1839.	Cost of, report of canal commissioners in relation to the, between the Allegany river and the point where the Dansville side-cut intersects the said canal,	S	3	69
1839.	Change of location of a part of, report of committee on canals on petition for,	A	4	176
1839.	Side-cut to connect with the Genesee river,	A	4	264
1839.	Estimated cost of, report of canal commissioners,	A	5	267
1839.	Side-cut to Dansville. report on petition for,	A	5	296
1839.	Alteration of the plan to lessen the cost of, report of canal board on a resolution of assembly,	A	6	376
1839.	Feeder to, report on petition for the construction of,	A	4	260
1840.	Condition of, and the mode of supplying it with water, reports of engineers in relation to,	A	3	96
1840.	Changes of the plan of locks, &c., under the act of May 1, 1839, report of canal board in relation thereto,	A	8	329
1841.	Substitution of a railroad for a portion of the, report of select committee on petition for,	A	5	199
1841.	Contracts for the construction of, report of canal commissioners in answer to a resolution of assembly relative to,	A	6	203
1842.	Report of committee on canals on petition for speedy completion of,	A	7	190
1843.	Report of the canal commissioners relative to,	S	3	77
1844.	Resolution relative to the completion of,	S	1	45
1844.	Report of canal commissioners relative to,	S	3	111
1844.	Report of canal commissioners relative to,	S	3	112
1844.	Report of committee on canals respecting the application of Frederick House and others to construct a slip and basin with the branch of, Dansville,	A	7	164
1844.	Affidavit in relation to the proposed connection of the Dansville side-cut with,	A	7	182
1844.	Further in relation to the Dansville slip and basin.	A	7	187
1845.	Report of canal commissioners relative to plan for constructing a reservoir on Mill creek, &c.,	S	2	75
1845.	Report of committee on canals relative to the berme bank of the Dansville branch of,	S	2	82
1845.	Report of committee on canals on bill from the assembly to authorize Charles Shepard and others, to connect a slip and basin with the Dansville side-cut of,	S	3	96
1845.	Report of committee on canals on petition of Charles Shepherd and others, relative to Dansville side-cut,	A	4	117
1845.	Report of canal commissioners in reference to, and Dansville side-cut,	A	4	135
1845.	Report of canal commissioners relative to preserving unfinished work on,	A	5	154
1845.	Report of canal board in relation to locks on,	A	6	202
1848.	Report of canal commissioners as to probable cost of completing,	S	2	58
1848.	Report as to, and Black River,	A	3	97
1855.	Reports of canal board, state engineer and surveyor and canal commissioners in reference to new feeder for,	A	7	146
1856.	Report on petition for an act of extension of,	A	4	160
1857.	Report relative to extension of,	S	2	53
1857.	Report of state engineer and surveyor respecting,	S	3	103
1857.	Report of state engineer and surveyor concerning,	S	4	114
1857.	Report of state engineer and surveyor and canal commissioners relative to the enlargement of,	A	1	35
	HAMBURGH CANAL, BUFFALO:			
1847.	Reports on,	A	6	152

CANALS—*continued.*

Year	Subject	Doc.	Vol.	No.
	JUNCTION CANAL:			
1833.	Report on bill granting a loan to,	A	4	305
1839.	Report of examination of, in reference to a purchase of the same by the state,	S	3	90
1839.	Report on petition for the purchase of, by the state,	A	4	188
1840.	Report on petition for the purchase of, by the state,	A	5	191
	ONEIDA LAKE CANAL COMPANY:			
1831.	Report on petition to incorporate the,	A	1	49
1831.	Report of canal board on bill to incorporate,	S	1	64
1833.	Report on petition for the pre-emptive right to certain land,	A	3	196
1837.	Purchase of by the state, report of committee on canals on petition for,	S	1	27
1837.	do do report of canal commissioners on petition for,	S	1	16
1838.	do do report of committee on canals on petition for,	A	5	252
1839.	do do report of committee on canals on petition for,	A	2	33
1840.	do do report of canal commissioners on petition for,	A	3	81
1840.	do do report of committee on canals on petition for,	A	5	165
1841.	Report of the canal board in relation to the petition for,	S	3	76
1854.	Report of auditor relative to tolls on, &c.,	A	2	74
	OSWEGO CANAL:			
1831.	Deficiency in the revenue of, report of comptroller relative to amount paid the commissioners of the canal fund for the,	A	4	339
1831.	Report of canal board on petition of the Oswego Canal Company for extra allowance for work done on said canal,	A	4	309
1833.	Surplus waters of the, report relative to leasing the,	S	2	57
1836.	Report in relation to sales of land near the, and the diversion of tolls from the Erie canal by said canal,	S	2	73
1838.	Lands overflowed by water on the, report of canal commissioners, &c.,	A	3	112
1839.	Enlargement of, report of canal board on petition for the,	A	6	357
1839.	Surplus waters of, report relative to leasing the,	A	6	370
1845.	Remonstrance of New York Chamber of Commerce against increase of tolls on,	S	2	61
1845.	Petition of inhabitants of western New York for reduction of tolls on,	A	4	81
1845.	Report of majority of committee on canals relative to discriminating tolls on, and Erie,	A	5	189
1845.	Report of minority of committee on canals relative to discriminating tolls on, and Erie,	A	5	190
1851.	Report of select committee on bill in relation to,	S	2	59
1851.	Report of committee on claims of contractors,	A	2	31
1851.	Report of committee on canals on petition for the enlargement of,	A	4	129
1853.	Message of the governor relative to appropriations for the improvement of, and Erie,	S	3	67
1853.	Message of the governor relative to making appropriations for the improvement of, and Erie,	A	4	91
	SACANDAGA CANAL:			
1837.	Report on petition for survey of a route for,	A	2	157
1840.	Report on petition for the construction of,	A	8	335
	SCOTTSVILLE CANAL ASSOCIATION:			
1841.	Report of canal board on bill for the relief of,	S	3	72

CANALS—*continued.*

	Sodus Canal:	Doc.	Vol.	No.
1850.	Report of canal board relative to,	A	6	151
1851.	Mr. Townsend's report on the renewal of the charter of,	A	3	64
1851.	Mr. Burrow's report on the same subject,	A	3	65

CANANDAIGUA.

1830.	Supreme court clerk's office at, report on petition for the removal of,	A	2	176
1832.	Hook and ladder company, report on petition to organize,	A	4	316
1833.	Arsenal at, report on petition for the sale of,	A	4	328

CANANDAIGUA AND GENESEE RAILROAD, *see* Railroads.

CANASTEO.

1855.	Report of select committee on formation of new county of,	A	5	141

CANDE, WILLIAM, AND SARAH HART.

1842.	Report of committee on claims on petition of,	A	5	104
1845.	Report of canal board on petition of,	A	3	55

CANDEE, WILLIAM, AND OTHERS.

1858.	Report of committee on claims on petition of,	A	3	64
1858.	Report on claim of,	A	4	119

CANFIELD, PALMER.

1833.	Memorial of, in relation to lotteries,	S	2	108

CANFIELD, T., *see* Moses Brockway.

CANISTEO RIVER.

1832.	Dam across, report on petition of Jared Ketchum to build,	A	2	87
1833.	Dam across, report on petition to authorize R. G. Gilman and Isaac Myers to build,	A	2	50
1835.	Dam across, report on petition of Wm. Woods to build,	A	1	38
1838.	Dam across, report on petition of Arthur Erwin to build,	A	6	327
1838.	Bridge across, report on petition of inhabitants of the town of Cameron to raise money to build,	A	5	291

CANISTEO, TOWN OF.

1838.	Report on bill to confirm the election of town officers, &c.,	A	5	255

CANTON, TOWN OF.

1837.	Academy in, report on petition for a tax for the benefit of the,	A	3	253
1849.	Report on bill to authorize the building of a plankroad in,	S	2	62
1850.	Report on bill to authorize road from, to Ogdensburgh, to borrow money,	S	1	13

CAPE MAY.

1856.	Resolution relative to a breakwater at,	A	5	185

CAPITAL PUNISHMENT.

1832.	Report on petition for the abolishment of (Mr. Stilwell),	A	3	187
1838.	do do do (Mr. Edwards),	S	2	97
1838.	do do do (Mr. Ogden),	A	5	293
1839.	do do do (Mr. M'Elrath),	A	6	378

CAPITAL PUNISHMENT—*continued.*

Year	Subject	Doc.	Vol.	No.
1840.	Report on petition for the abolishment of (Mr. Simmons),	A	8	363
1841.	do do do (Mr. O'Sullivan),	S	6	249
1842.	Remonstrance of inhabitants of Salina, against abolishing,	A	7	133
1842.	Memorial of inhabitants of Guilford for abolishing,	A	7	146
1842.	do relative to,	S	3	78
1842.	do relative to,	S	3	97
1842.	do of the inhabitants of Albany and Chenango counties relative to,	S	4	78
1842.	do of the inhabitants of Albany and Chenango counties relative to,	S	4	97
1842.	Remonstrance against abolishing,	A	7	133
1843.	Petition of A. G. Stevens and others, of Lockport, for the passage of a law to abolish,	A	3	59
1845.	Report of select committee on petition for abolishment of,	A	7	249
1846.	Report of majority of select committee relative to,	A	6	213
1846.	Report of minority on same subject,	A	6	214
1847.	Report relative to abolition of,	A	2	95
1848.	Reports on,	A	5	133
1848.	Reports on,	A	5	191
1849.	Memorial of H. W. Taylor on,	S	1	10
1851.	Report of select committee on,	A	4	109
1857.	Report of select committee in favor of abolishing,	A	3	170

CAPITOL.

Year	Subject	Doc.	Vol.	No.
1839.	Removal of the, report of select committee in relation to the,	A	6	400
1839.	do do the minority in relation to the,	A	6	401
1839.	do do the minority in relation to the,	A	6	402
1832.	Improvement of assembly chamber and repairing the, communication from the trustees relative to the expenditures for the,	A	3	196
1832.	Park fence, &c., report of committee on finance in relation to,	S	2	92
1833.	do do trustees of the, in relation to,	A	3	150
1833.	do do select committee on the report of trustees,	A	4	282
1834.	do do trustees in relation to the,	A	2	106
1834.	do do select committee in relation to,	A	3	205
1839.	Alterations in the, report of committee recommending,	S	3	105
1840.	do do expenditures for,	A	7	293
1841.	do do expenditures for,	A	3	73
1843.	Report on petition of the officers and members of the Albany Republican Artillery Company for leave to erect a monument in the park to the memory of the late Colonel John Mills,	A	5	145
1845.	Report of General Fonda on flag-staff on,	A	6	230
1846.	Report of select committee in favor of removal of,	A	5	153
1846.	Report of minority of select committee against removal of,	A	5	175
1848.	Report as to warming of,	A	2	29
1848.	Report relative to removing,	A	5	148
1851.	Report of select committee on bill to remove,	A	4	106

CARD, HENRY.

Year	Subject	Doc.	Vol.	No.
1851.	Report of committee on petition for canal damages,	A	3	82

CARLEY, JOSEPH.

Year	Subject	Doc.	Vol.	No.
1831.	Report on petition for bounty lands for revolutionary services,	A	4	333

CARLTON ISLAND.

Year	Subject	Doc.	Vol.	No.
1830.	Report on petition inhabitants of, for relief,	A	2	92

CARLTON, TOWN OF.

Year	Subject	Doc.	Vol.	No.
1836.	Report on petition for a new tax roll for the,	A	2	71

		Doc.	Vol.	No.
	CARMAN, DAVID.			
1831.	Report on petition for bounty lands for revolutionary services,..	A	4	315
	CAROLINE, STEAMBOAT, *see* Northern Frontier.			
	CARPETING.			
1844.	Report of the attorney-general on, &c.,......................	A	3	75
	CARR, JOHN, AND OTHERS.			
1841.	Report on petition for extra compensation for work done on the Champlain canal,....................................	A	3	75
	CARR, SALLY C.			
1854.	Report of committee on claims on petition of,................	A	3	83
1856.	Report on petition for relief of,............................	A	3	48
	CARROLL & COOK.			
1845.	Geological contract of, transmitted by the governor,...........	A	2	78
	CARSWELL, DANIEL.			
1830.	Report on petition for extra compensation for work done on the Champlain canal,....................................	A	1	40
	CARTER, ADONIJAH.			
1835.	Report on petition for relief on account of injuries received while doing military duty,..................................	A	3	217
1839.	Report on petition for relief on account of injuries received while doing military duty,..................................	A	3	265
	CARTER, HANNAH S.			
1857.	Report of committee on the petitions of aliens, favorable on petition of, for escheated lands,...........................	A	2	83
	CARTER, JOSEPH, AND OTHERS.			
1834.	Report on petition to be released from the payment of certain moneys due the state,................................	A	4	386
	CARTHAGE.			
	Extension of the Black River canal from, to Sacketts Harbor, *see* Black River canal.			
	CARVIS, JOHN.			
1846.	Report of committee on claims on petition of,................	A	3	73
	CASE, BRONSON & CO.			
1856.	Report on petition of,....................................	S	2	79
1857.	Report of standing committee on judiciary on petition of,.......	S	1	13
	CASE, JOHN.			
1833.	Report on petition for a divorce,............................	A	2	49
	CASE, JOSEPH G.			
1847.	Report on petition of,....................................	S	2	77
1858.	Report of committee on claims on petition of,................	A	4	88

CASE, W. W.

		Doc.	Vol.	No.
1832.	Report on petition for compensation for damages to his boat and cargo by weigh-lock at Rochester,...........	A	2	120
1833.	Report of committee on canals,..............................	S	1	22
1834.	Report of canal commissioners,..............................	A	3	249

CASLER, LEVI.

1842.	Report of canal board on petition of,........................	A	5	84

CASLER, LEVI, AND ALVAN RICHMOND.

1857.	Report of committee on claims favorable on petition of, to be released as sureties for John Uhle,........................	A	1	49

CASLER, R. N.

1844.	Report of canal board on petition of,.........................	A	1	24
1844.	Report of canal commissioners on petition of,.................	A	5	133

CASLER, SAGE & CO., *see* Sage, Casler & Co.

CASTILE, TOWN OF.

1832.	Report relative to the boundary line of,......................	A	2	172

CASTLE, GIDEON.

1830.	Report on claims of, to certain land,.........................	A	3	233
1830.	Report of committee on public lands on the same,.............	A	4	348
1831.	Report of committee on claims on the same,................ .	A	1	14
1831.	do do do	A	4	403
1832.	do do do	A	2	125

CASWELL, H.

1845.	Report of committee on canals in the case of,.................	A	6	238

CATHARINE, TOWN OF.

1833.	Report relative to highway labor in,..........................	A	4	254

CATHOLICS, ROMAN.

1853.	Report on petition of certain, relative to the education of their children,...	A	4	97

CATLIN, LEONARD.

1856.	Report of committee on claims on petition of,.................	A	8	66
1856.	Report on petition of, for relief,............................	A	3	32

CATLIN, THEODORUS, & FRED. GREEN.

1847.	Report on petition of,......................................	A	4	108
1848.	Report of committee on claims on petition of,................	A	3	114

CATLIN, TOWN OF.

1834.	Report on petition to incorporate a botanic society in,..........	A	2	95
1856.	Majority report on bill to alter boundaries of, and Veteran,.....	S	2	44
1856.	Minority report on same subject,............................	S	2	59

CATO CANAL COMPANY. *see* Canals.

CATSKILL.

1835.	Report on petition from, to raise money to rebuild bridges over the Kakerskill,..	A	4	373

CATSKILL—*continued.*

		Doc.	Vol.	No.
1837.	Dry Dock Company, report on petition to incorporate,..........	A	2	54
1837.	Schoharie creek, report on petition for a survey of,...........	A	3	280
1838.	Canal from, to the Erie canal above Schenectady, report on petition for,....................................	A	5	212
1839.	Canal from, to the Erie canal above Schenectady, report on petition for,....................................	A	4	251

BANKS, *see* Banks.

CATSKILL AND ATHENS TURNPIKE COMPANY.

		Doc.	Vol.	No.
1832.	Report on petition to incorporate,..........................	A	2	155

CATSKILL AND CANAJOHARIE RAILROAD, *see* Railroads.

CATSKILL AND ITHACA RAILROAD, *see* Railroads.

CATTARAUGUS COUNTY.

		Doc.	Vol.	No.
1831.	Court house and jail, report on petition to raise money by tax to complete,....................................	A	2	135
1836.	Bridges across Cattaraugus creek at Zoar, report on petition to raise money by tax to build,...........................	A	4	241
1836.	Bridges in town of Olean, report on petition to raise money by tax to build,....................................	A	4	274
1833.	Creek fishery, report on a petition for a law to protect the,......	A	4	248
1831.	Dodge's creek in, report as to declaring it a public highway,....	A	4	326
1837.	Petition of inhabitants of, upon the subject of banking,........	A	3	200
1838.	Justices of the peace in, (Reuben Cheney,) report on petition to confirm his official acts,................................	A	5	285
1839.	Supreme court commissioner, report on bill to appoint,.........	A	6	336
1842.	Report respecting the erection of a new county from parts of Chautauque, Erie and,................................	S	2	43
1845.	Report on same subject,......................................	S	1	30
1847.	Report relative to petition of supervisors of,.................	A	7	194
1853.	Report relative to the erection of a new county from parts of Chautauque, Erie and,................................	A	3	57

CATTARAUGUS RESERVATION.

		Doc.	Vol.	No.
1846.	Message of governor relative to Indians on,....................	S	2	57

CAUCUS RETURNS.

		Doc.	Vol.	No.
1846.	Abstract of,..	A	1	5

CAUGHNAWAGA INDIANS, *see* Indians—Caughnawagas.

CAULKING, EBENEZER.

		Doc.	Vol.	No.
1834.	Report on petition of, relative to the sale of certain land for the non-payment of principal and interest on,..................	S	1	17

CAULKINS & COLE.

		Doc.	Vol.	No.
1848.	Report of committee on claims on petition of,.................	A	2	44

CAYUGA BRIDGE COMPANY.

		Doc.	Vol.	No.
1848.	Report of attorney-general relative to,.......................	A	5	140
1855.	Report of committee on petition of,..........................	A	4	89
1857.	Report of committee on claims, adverse on petition of, for damages sustained by the construction of the Cayuga and Seneca canal,...	A	3	209

CAYUGA COUNTY.

Year	Subject	Doc.	Vol.	No.
1830.	Race course in, report on petition for a law to regulate, &c.,	A	3	275
1832.	Jail, report on petition to raise money by tax to build,	A	2	124
1833.	Jail, report on petition for a loan to complete,	S	1	13
1835.	Jail, report on petition relative to the situation of Noah Burnham, a prisoner, confined in,	A	3	209
1837.	Court-house, report on petition for a loan to complete,	A	1	21
1838.	Court-house, report on petition for a loan to complete,	A	2	46
1836.	Constables' fees, report on petition of board of supervisors for a law to regulate, &c.,	A	3	181

COMMISSIONERS OF LOANS IN, *see* Daniel Avery.

INSPECTORS' REPORT:

Year	Subject	Doc.	Vol.	No.
1831.	Beef and pork, annual report of George W. Gunn,	A	2	109
1832.	do do do	A	3	175
1833.	do do do	S	3	177
1835.	do do do	A	2	82
1836.	do do do	S	1	46
1837.	do do do	A	2	126
1838.	do do do	S	3	139
1839.	do do do	S	2	32
1840.	do do do	A	3	63
1831.	do do Zadock Hall,	A	3	202
1840.	do do Stephen Bouton,	A	5	201
1833.	Sole leather, annual report of A. Parsons,	S	2	67
1834.	do do do	S	2	77
1835.	do do do	S	2	61
1835.	do do H. R. Graves,	S	1	20
1837.	do do H. R. Graves,	S	1	40
1833.	do do David B. Wheeler,	S	2	46

SENECA CANAL, *see* Canals.

CAYUGA INDIANS, *see* Indians—Cayugas.

CAYUGA LAKE.

Year	Subject	Doc.	Vol.	No.
1833.	Inlet of, improvement of, report of canal board on petition for the,	A	4	244
1833.	Inlet of, improvement of, report of committee on canals, on petition for the,	A	4	267
1834.	Inlet of, improvement of, report of canal board on petition for the,	A	4	348
1835.	Inlet of, improvement of, report of canal commissioners relative to survey of,	A	4	297
1837.	Inlet of, improvement of, report of canal commissioners relative to survey of,	A	2	90
1839.	Outlet of, report on petition to repair the free bridge across,	A	4	234
1858.	Outlet of, report as to obstructions in the,	A	1	46

CAYUGA LAKE AND INLET.

Year	Subject	Doc.	Vol.	No.
1834.	Report relative to killing ducks in,	A	4	349

CAYUGA LAKE AND INLET STEAMBOAT COMPANY.

Year	Subject	Doc.	Vol.	No.
1830.	Report on petition to increase the capital of,	A	4	312

CAYUGA MARSHES.

Year	Subject	Doc.	Vol.	No.
1830.	Report of commissioners for draining the,	A	3	287
1830.	Report of comptroller on petition for an investigation of the expenditures and accounts of the commissioners appointed to drain the,	A	2	178
1831.	Report of commissioners asking for an additional appropriation,	S	1	45
1831.	Report of select committee on the same,	S	1	51
1831.	Report of comptroller in relation to the,	A	2	70

CAYUGA MARSHES—*continued.*

		Doc.	Vol.	No.
1831.	Report of select committee on the comptroller's report,	A	4	330
1832.	Report of attorney-general concerning the commissioners for draining the, and their treasurer,	A	1	6
1832.	Report of canal commissioners relative to the survey of the, &c.,	A	2	51
1833.	Report of James Geddes relative to draining the,	A	3	192
1840.	Report on petition for an extra appropriation to pay an assessment for draining the,	S	3	94
1852.	Report of commissioners respecting draining,	S	2	66
1853.	Report of committee relative to draining,	S	2	35

CAZENOVIA LAKE.

		Doc.	Vol.	No.
1839.	Report relative to fishing in,	A	4	164

CAZENOVIA, VILLAGE OF.

		Doc.	Vol.	No.
1833.	Report on petition to amend the charter of the,	A	3	227

CEMENT, HYDRAULIC.

		Doc.	Vol.	No.
1840.	Report of H. S. Dexter, in relation to,	S	4	123
1840.	Report on petition of E. C. Warner, to appoint a committee to examine a cement made by him, &c.,	A	7	297

CEMENT, HYDRAULIC, COMPANY.

		Doc.	Vol.	No.
1840.	At Laurenceville, upon petition to incorporate,	A	3	94

CEMETERIES, &c.

		Doc.	Vol.	No.
1842.	Report on petitions for law to protect the sanctity of the grave,	A	7	186
1853.	Report of committee on medical societies and colleges in relation to the better protection of public burying grounds,	A	2	21
1858.	Report on bill to prevent the desecration of graveyards and,	A	4	111

CENSUS.

		Doc.	Vol.	No.
1831.	State, for the years 1825 and 1830,	A	4	308
1832.	Of the several congressional districts, in 1820, 1825 and 1830,	S	1	65
1834.	State, for the years 1810, 1820, 1825 and 1830,	A	2	66
1836.	State, for 1835, secretary of state's report transmitting,	A	3	114
1835.	State, report as to requiring the blind inhabitants to be enumerated, &c.,	A	1	65
1841.	State, for 1840, letter from the marshal of the northern district in relation to the,	A	2	31
1841.	State, for 1840,	A	4	117
1845.	State, report of committee on Indian affairs, in relation to,	S	2	84
1846.	Indian, report of secretary of state relative to,	S	1	24
1851.	Seventh, communication from governor relative to,	A	6	157
1846.	State, report of, transmitted by secretary of state,	A	1	5
1851.	Communication from governor and secretary of the interior relative to,	S	2	63
1856.	State, for 1855, report of committee on,	A	4	165
1856.	Communication relative to,	S	1	8
1858.	Reports of, reply of secretary of state to resolution in reference to,	S	2	45
1856.	Communication from secretary of state relative to,	S	1	8

CENTERVILLE.

		Doc.	Vol.	No.
1832.	Congregational Society of, report on petition to sell certain lands,	A	4	323
1836.	Congregational Society of, committee on two-third bills,	A	3	111

CENTIGRADE THERMOMETER.

		Doc.	Vol.	No.
1842.	Report of regents of university relative to the,	S	4	94

		Doc.	Vol.	No.
	CENTRAL ASYLUM FOR THE DEAF AND DUMB, *see* Deaf and Dumb.			
	CERTIORARIS AND APPEALS FROM JUSTICES' COURTS.			
1833.	Report in relation to,........	A	4	273
1845.	Bill to remove cases decided by the canal board to the supreme court by, report of committee on finance relative to,..........	S	3	103
	CHAMBERLAIN, B.			
1836.	Letter from, in relation to the navigation of Allegany river,.....	S	2	76
	CHAMBERLAIN, C. T.			
1845.	Report of committee on claims, on petition of, ...	A	5	192
	CHAMBERLAIN, ENOCH, AND OTHERS.			
1849.	Report of committee on canals, on petition of,.................	A	3	197
	CHAMBERLAIN, JACOB.			
1849.	Report of committee on claims, on petition of, ...	A	3	114
	CHAMBERLAIN, ORRIN.			
1843.	Report of committee on claims, on his petition, ...	S	3	85
	CHAMPION, TOWN OF.			
1840.	Report on petition for a loan to build bridges across Black river,.	A	8	336
	CHAMPLAIN, TOWN OF.			
1836.	Report on petition to extend the time for the collection of taxes in,..........	A	3	112
	CHANCELLOR.			
1832.	Communication from the, in relation to the New York Life and Trust Company, ...	S	2	112
1834.	Communication from the, in relation to the New York Life and Trust Company, ...	S	2	59
1835.	Communication from the, in relation to the New York Life and Trust Company, ...	A	4	284
1836.	Communication from the, in relation to the New York Life and Trust Company, ...	A	3	143
1837.	Communication from the, in relation to the New York Life and Trust Company, ...	A	3	257
1838.	Communication from the, in relation to the New York Life and Trust Company, ...	A	6	353
1839.	Communication from the, in relation to the New York Life and Trust Company, ...	S	3	70
1840.	Communication from the, in relation to the New York Life and Trust Company, ...	A	8	353
1835.	Communication from the, relative to the re-organization of the court of chancery,..........	A	2	94
1836.	Communication from the, relative to the re-organization of the court of chancery,..........	A	4	222
1836.	Communication from the, relative to the re-organization of the court of chancery,..........	A	4	279
1836.	Communication from the, in relation to the business of his court,	S	2	74
1839.	Report of, on petition of H. Sniffen and wife for a divorce,......	A	5	304
1840.	Report of, on petition of H. Sternberg in relation to funds invested in chancery, &c., ...	S	4	102

CHANCELLOR—*continued.*

Year	Subject	Doc.	Vol.	No.
1840.	Communication from the, transmitting a catalogue of the library of the court of chancery,	S	4	121
1840.	Communication from the, transmitting a report of the clerk of 2d circuit,	A	5	187
1843.	Communication relative to the New York Life Insurance and Trust Company,	A	2	37
1843.	Report of, in answer to a resolution of the assembly respecting the amount of the fund of the court of chancery on the 1st of January, 1843,	A	3	57
1843.	Report of, in answer to a resolution of the assembly relative to dispatch of business in the court of chancery,	A	4	86
1846.	Report of, relative to notices required to be published in the state paper,	S	3	96
1847.	Communication from,	S	4	113
	VICE-CHANCELLOR:			
1830.	Report on bill to repeal so much of the Revised Statutes as gives to them exclusive jurisdiction in certain cases,	A	3	210
	VICE-CHANCELLOR, FIRST CIRCUIT:			
1831.	Report on petition for the appointment of a,	A	1	41
1839.	Petition from members of the bar relative to the business before the,	S	2	36

CHANCERY, CLERKS IN.

Year	Subject	Doc.	Vol.	No.
1843.	Report of,	S	3	81
	FIRST CIRCUIT, *see* Assistant Register.			
	SECOND CIRCUIT:			
1835.	Alexander Forbus, report of amount of fees received by him,	A	3	243
1836.	do report of amount of fees received by him,	A	2	45
1840.	do report relative to accounts and business of his office,	A	5	187
1840.	do relative to the bills filed for the foreclosure of mortgages, &c.,	A	4	118
	THIRD CIRCUIT, *see* Register.			
	FOURTH CIRCUIT:			
1835.	G. M. Davidson, report of amount of fees received by him,	A	3	245
1836.	do report of amount of fees received by him,	A	2	90
1840.	do report relative to bills filed for the foreclosure of mortgages, &c.,	A	3	90
1840.	do report relative to accounts and business of his office,	A	5	169
	FIFTH CIRCUIT:			
1835.	James Williams, report of amount of fees received by him,	A	3	240
1836.	do report of amount of fees received by him,	A	2	55
1840.	do report relative to bills filed for the foreclosure of mortgages, &c.,	A	5	178
1840.	do report relative to accounts and business of his office,	A	5	186
	SIXTH CIRCUIT:			
1835.	J. L. Woods, report of amount of fees received by him,	A	4	309
1840.	R. B. Monell, report of accounts and business of his office,	A	6	250
1840.	R. B. Monell, report relative to bills filed for the foreclosure of mortgages, &c.,	A	3	93

CHANCERY, CLERKS IN—*continued.*

		Doc.	Vol.	No.
	SEVENTH CIRCUIT:			
1835.	S. A. Goodwin, report of amount of fees received by him,......	A	3	244
1836.	do report of amount of fees received by him, ...	A	2	44
1840.	do report of accounts and business of his office, ...	A	5	206
1840.	do report relative to bills filed for the foreclosure of mortgages, &c.,..........................	A	5	213
	EIGHTH CIRCUIT:			
1835.	S. L. Selden, report of amount of fees received by him,........	A	3	249
1840.	do report of accounts and business of his office,......	A	6	219
1840.	do report on petition of, to be allowed to retain the amount of certain expenses of his office, out of the moneys received by him,..............	A	4	106
1846.	Report of, in answer to a resolution relative to the expenses of his office, during the year ending Dec. 31st, 1845, ...	S	2	48
	FEES OF:			
1835.	Report of Alexander Forbes, clerk of 2d district, of amount received by him,..	A	3	243
1836.	Report of Alexander Forbes, clerk of 2d district, of amount received by him,..	A	2	45
1835.	Report of G. M. Davidson, clerk of 4th district, of amount received by him,..	A	3	245
1836.	Report of G. M. Davidson, clerk of 4th district, of amount received by him,..	A	2	90
1835.	Report of Jas. W. Williams, clerk of 5th district, of amount received by him,..	A	3	240
1836.	Report of Jas. W. Williams, clerk of 5th district, of amount received by him,..	A	2	55
1835.	Report of I. L. Woods, clerk of 6th district, of amount received by him,..	A	4	309
1835.	Report of S. A. Goodwin, clerk of 7th district, of amount received by him,..	A	3	244
1836.	Report of S. A. Goodwin, clerk of 7th district, of amount received by him,..	A	2	44
1835.	Report of S. L. Selden, clerk of 8th district, of amount received by him,..	A	3	249
1836.	Report of I. Sutherland, clerk of 8th district, of amount received by him,..	A	1	23
1838.	Resolution to appoint a committee to ascertain the annual amount of,..	A	5	273
1838.	Report of committee appointed to ascertain the annual amount of,..	A	6	351
1839.	Report of select committee (Mr. Stout) in relation to,..........	A	4	186
1840.	Comptroller's report of the amount paid into the treasury, &c.,.	A	3	77
1842.	Report of comptroller relative to, ...	S	2	30

CHANCERY, COURT OF.

		Doc.	Vol.	No.
1831.	Report concerning the jurisdiction of, on sums less than $100, ..	S	1	48
1835.	Delays in the, the remedy, &c., report of the chancellor in relation to,..	A	2	95
1836.	Delays in the, the remedy, &c., report of the chancellor in relation to,..	A	4	222
1836.	Delays in the, the remedy, &c., report of the chancellor in relation to,..	A	4	279
1839.	Memorial of the New York bar, for the appointment of commissioners for the dispatch of the arrears of equity business.....	S	2	36
1842.	Act for the relief of,..	A	5	94
1843.	Report of chancellor relative to dispatch of business in, ...	A	4	86
1843.	Catalogue of the library of,.......................... ..	A	5	166

CHANCERY, COURT OF—*continued.*

		Doc.	Vol.	No.
	FORECLOSURE OF MORTGAGES IN:			
	Number of bills filed, number of decrees of sale, the number of sales under such decrees, costs allowed, &c.			
1840.	Report of clerk of 2d district,	A	4	118
1840.	do 4th district,	A	3	90
1840.	do 5th district,	A	5	178
1840.	do 6th district,	A	3	84
1840.	do 7th district,	A	5	213
1840.	Report of register,	A	5	166
1839.	Report of Mr. Edwards, in relation to the,	S	1	28
1839.	Report of Mr. Healy, in relation to the,	A	6	407
	FUNDS INVESTED IN:			
1838.	Register's report of amount of,	A	6	293
1838.	Assistant register's report of amount of,	A	6	356
1838.	Report of select committee in relation to,	A	6	356
1840.	Chancellor's report on petition of Herkimer Sternberg, relative to,	S	4	102
1840.	Report of clerk of the 2d district, with the master's report thereon,	A	5	187
1840.	do 4th district, do	A	3	90
1840.	do 5th district, do	A	5	186
1840.	do 6th district, do	A	6	250
1840.	do 7th district, do	A	5	206
1840.	do 8th district, do	A	6	219
1836.	Register's report of amount of,	A	4	300
1840.	Assistant register's report of,	A	7	281
1840.	Register's report of,	A	6	230
1843.	Report of chancellor relative to amount of, on 1st of January, 1843,	A	3	57
1847.	Report relative to,	S	4	120
1849.	Report on condition of,	S	3	73
1852.	Report relative to,	A	2	56
1856.	Report relative to,	S	3	113
	REORGANIZATION OF:			
1834.	Report of committee on the judiciary relative to the,	S	2	107
1836.	Resolution offered by Mr. Powers for the,	S	1	27
1836.	Resolution reported by the committee on the judiciary, for the,	A	4	265
1837.	Resolution offered by Mr. Bradish for the,	A	3	173
1837.	Resolution offered by Mr. Edwards for the,	S	1	13
1837.	Resolution offered by Mr. Patterson for the,	A	1	24
1838.	Resolution offered by Mr. Ogden for the,	A	5	267
1839.	Report and resolution by Mr. Edwards for the,	S	1	28
1839.	Resolution offered by Mr. Verplanck for the,	S	2	50
1839.	Resolution offered by Mr. Taylor for the,	A	1	15
1839.	Report of the committee on the judiciary, on the same,	A	3	93
1840.	Resolution proposed by Mr. Taylor for the,	A	3	60
1841.	Report and resolution by Mr. Simmons for the,	A	4	136
1841.	Report of select committee, on the same,	A	7	288

CHANCERY, REGISTER IN.

		Doc.	Vol.	No.
1832.	Report of amount of fees received by him,	A	3	203
1832.	Report of select committee in relation to his fees,	A	4	309
1835.	Report of amount of fees received by him,	A	3	238
1835.	do do	A	4	314
1836.	do do	A	2	96
1836.	Report of, relative to the funds in court of chancery,	A	4	300
1838.	Report of, relative to the funds in court of chancery,	A	6	296
1838.	Report relative to his loaning and using chancery funds,	A	6	356
1839.	Report of select committee in relation to his fees,	A	4	186

CHANCERY, REGISTER IN—*continued.*

		Doc.	Vol.	No.
1838.	Resolution to appoint a committee to ascertain the annual amount of his fees,	A	5	273
1838.	Report of said committee,	A	6	351
1840.	Comptroller's report of amount of fees paid into the treasury, &c.,	A	3	77
1840.	Report of, relative to the business and accounts of his office,	A	6	230
1840.	Report of, relative to bills filed for the foreclosure of mortgages, etc.,	A	5	166
1841.	Report of, relative to the affairs of the City Bank of Buffalo,	A	4	87
1841.	Report transmitting a petition and documents relative to the City Bank of Buffalo,	A	4	108
1843.	Report of,	S	3	81
1843.	Report of,	S	3	119
1846.	Report of, relative to clerks in his office,	S	1	39

FEES OF:

		Doc.	Vol.	No.
1832.	Report of select committee in relation to,	A	4	309
1832.	Report of James Porter of amount received by him,	A	3	203
1835.	do do do	A	3	238
1835.	do do do	A	4	314
1836.	do do do	A	2	96
1838.	Resolution to appoint a committee to ascertain the annual amount of,	A	5	273
1838.	Report of committee appointed to ascertain the annual amount of,	A	6	351
1839.	Report of select committee (Mr. Stout) in relation to,	A	4	186
1840.	Comptroller's report of amount paid into the treasury, &c.,	A	3	77
1845.	Report of comptroller relative to amount of, charged and not paid into the treasury since September 30, 1844,	S	2	48
1845.	Report of comptroller respecting, and salaries of,	S	2	50

CHANCERY, ASSISTANT REGISTER IN.

		Doc.	Vol.	No.
1835.	Report of amount of fees received by him,	A	3	246
1835.	do amount of fees and expenditures,	A	4	306
1836.	do do do	A	3	144
1836.	do do do	A	4	254
1838.	do relative to funds invested in the court of chancery,	A	6	297
1838.	Resolution to appoint a committee to ascertain the annual amount of fees received by him, &c.,	A	5	273
1838.	Report of the said committee,	A	6	351
1838.	Report relative to his loaning chancery funds,	A	6	356
1839.	Report in relation to his fees,	A	4	186
1840.	Comptroller's report of amount of fees paid into the treasury,	A	3	77
1840.	Report of, relative to business and accounts of his office,	A	7	281
1843.	do	S	3	81
1843.	do	S	3	119
1846.	do	S	1	39
1846.	do relative to clerks in his office,	S	2	54

FEES OF:

		Doc.	Vol.	No.
1835.	Report of John Walworth of amount of, received by him,	A	3	246
1835.	Report of John Walworth of amount of, received by him,	A	4	306
1836.	And expenditures, report of amount of,	A	3	144
1836.	And expenditures, report of amount of,	A	4	254
1838.	Resolution to appoint a committee to ascertain the annual amount of	A	5	273
1838.	Report of committee appointed to ascertain the annual amount of,	A	6	351
1839.	Report of select committee (Mr. Stout) in relation to,	A	4	186
1840.	Comptroller's report of amount paid into the treasury, &c.,	A	3	77
1845.	Report of comptroller relative to amount of, charged and not paid into the treasury since September 30, 1844,	S	2	48

CHANDLER, ABEL.

		Doc.	Vol.	No.
1845.	Report of committee on claims on bill for the relief of,	S	2	68
1845.	Report of committee on grievances on the petition of,	A	3	37

CHAPIN, CYRENUS.

		Doc.	Vol.	No.
1837.	Report on petition for the sale to him of certain lands to him at a stipulated price,	A	4	324

CHAPIN, W. W., *see* E. Granger.

CHAPLAINS, *see* Legislature, Chaplains of, &c.

CHAPLIN, LUCY.

		Doc.	Vol.	No.
1855.	Report of committee on claims on petition of,	A	4	81
1856.	Report on petition of, for relief,	A	3	97

CHAPMAN, BEACH AND McOMBER, *see* Beach, Chapman and McOmber.

CHAPMAN, DAN.

		Doc.	Vol.	No.
1837.	Report on claim for services during the revolution,	A	3	209
1838.	Report on claim for services during the revolution,	A	6	307

CHAPMAN, E., AND OTHERS, *see* Doty, Allen and others.

CHAPMAN, HIRAM, AND OTHERS.

		Doc.	Vol.	No.
1842.	Report of committee on claims on petition of,	A	7	147

CHAPMAN, I., *see* L. Beebe and I. Chapman.

CHAPMAN, NANCY.

		Doc.	Vol.	No.
1831.	An imprisoned debtor, report on petition of,	A	2	174

CHAPPELL, N.

		Doc.	Vol.	No.
1856.	Report of committee on petition for relief,	A	1	22

CHARGE D'AFFAIRES OF UNITED STATES AT PARIS.

		Doc.	Vol.	No.
1843.	Communication from, transmitted by governor,	A	4	119

CHARITABLE INSTITUTIONS.

		Doc.	Vol.	No.
1848.	Report as to receipts, &c., of,	A	5	139
	First Senate District:			
1841.	Report of commissioners on the condition of,	A	1	4
1842.	Report of committee relative to,	A	2	19
1843.	Report of commissioners of,	S	1	42
1844.	Report of state commissioners relative to the faithful expenditure of money for,	S	2	76
1845.	Report of commissioners appointed to supervise the expenditure of moneys raised and collected for certain,	S	2	62

CHARITABLE PURPOSES.

		Doc.	Vol.	No.
1856.	Report of commissioners on expenditures for state,	S	3	114

CHARITABLE SOCIETIES.

		Doc.	Vol.	No.
1848.	Report of minority of committee on bill for incorporating,	S	2	45

CHARITIES, PUBLIC.

		Doc.	Vol.	No.
1847.	Report concerning,	S	3	92

CHARLOTTE RIVER.

1838.	Report relative to fishing in,	A	6	340

CHARTERS, *see* Corporations.

CHASE, CHARLES G., AND OTHERS.

1847.	Report of committee on claims on petition of, for relief,	A	2	72

CHASE, ESTHER.

1831.	Report on claim of, to certain land sold by the surveyor-general by mistake,	A	2	78
1831.	Report on claim of, to certain land sold by the surveyor-general by mistake,	A	4	335
1834.	Report on claim of, to certain land sold by the surveyor-general by mistake,	A	4	291

CHAUTAUQUE COUNTY.

1830.	Jail in, report on petition to raise money by tax to build a,	A	4	397
1831.	Report on petition to amend the law relative to the,	A	3	210
1832.	do do raise money by tax to build a,	S	1	19
1834.	do do raise an additional sum to complete the,	A	3	246
1834.	Court-house, report on petition for a,	A	1	10
1834.	Report on bill to provide for the erection of the,	S	2	54
1832.	County buildings, report relative to the location of,	A	3	221
1831.	Division of, report on petition for the,	S	1	75
1838.	General sessions of the peace, report on petition to repeal an act relative to the,	A	1	1
1840.	Treasurer of, report of majority of select committee in relation to the,	S	1	31
1840.	Treasurer of, report of minority of select committee in relation to the,	S	1	32
1842.	Report concerning the erection of a new county from parts of Cattaraugus, Erie and,	S	2	43
1843.	Proceedings of democratic convention of,	A	5	178
1845.	Report respecting the erection of a new county from parts of Cattaraugus, Erie and,	S	1	30
1853.	Report on same subject,	A	3	57

BANKS IN, *see* Banks—Chautauque County.

CHAZY RIVER, BIG.

1851.	Report of railroad committee respecting draw-bridge over,	A	5	145
1852.	Report on petitions to improve navigation of,	A	2	57

CHEESBRO AND OTHERS, *see* Baker and Cheesbro.

CHEESEMAN, JOSEPH.

1835.	Report on petition to erect a dock adjoining his land in North Hempstead,	A	4	308

CHEEVER, SAMUEL.

1844.	Report of canal commissioners on petition of,	A	5	130

CHEMUNG AND SUSQUEHANNAH RIVERS.

1830.	Report of select committee relative to the survey of, and the connecting of the Otsego lake with the Erie canal, by canal or railroad,	A	1	63

CHEMUNG AND SUSQUEHANNAH RIVERS—*continued.*

		Doc.	Vol	No.
1831.	Survey of, report of canal commissioners in relation to the,.....	A	3	278

CHEMUNG COUNTY.

1837.	County buildings, majority report relative to the removal of,....	A	3	240
1837.	County buildings, minority report relative to the removal of,....	A	3	241
1837.	Poor-house, report on petition for a loan to build,..............	A	3	164
1840.	Poor-house system, report on petition to abolish the,...........	A	6	267
1845.	Report of the canal commissioners on reference of the petition of citizens of, relative to Seneca and Cayuga canal,............	A	7	246
1846.	Report of committee on canals on petition for a canal in,........	A	4	112
1846.	Report of committee on erection and division of towns and counties on petitions for a new county from parts of Otsego, Delaware and,..	A	4	97
1846.	Report of minority of committee on same,......................	A	4	105
1847.	Report on petition of citizens of, and Steuben, Tompkins and Yates counties, for erection of a new county,................	A	2	62
1847.	Minority report on same,...................................	A	2	81

CHEMUNG RIVER.

1833.	Report on petition to prevent fishing with seines in the,........	A	4	310
1837.	Dam across, report on petition for a, at or near "Upper Narrows,"	A	2	158

CHENANGO BRIDGE.

1845.	Report of judiciary committee on,............................	A	6	229
1845.	Report on the,..	A	6	239

CHENANGO COUNTY.

1837.	County buildings, report relative to the removal, and on petition to raise money to build a new court-house,............	A	2	70
1837.	Minority report on the same,............................	A	2	71
1839.	Report on petition for a loan to complete the,.............	A	3	92
1833.	Report on petition of commissioners for loaning money,........	A	3	187
1840.	Road in, report on petition to repeal an act to lay out a, passed May 25, 1836,..	A	4	145
1834.	Road from the valley of the, report on petition for a, to the Hudson river,...	A	6	363
1840.	New county from parts of, Otsego and Delaware, with the county seat at Unadilla, report on petition for,.....................	A	6	242
1837.	New county from, Madison and Otsego, report on petition for,...	A	2	131
1834.	Inspector of sole leather, annual report of George P. Hudson,...	S	2	93
1835.	do do do ...	A	4	328
1836.	do do do ...	S	1	50
1837.	do do do ...	A	3	269
1847.	Report of commissioners of land office on petition of Oneida and Onondaga Indians relative to land in Broome and,...........	A	7	215

CHENANGO FORKS.

1835.	Report on petition from, for a lock from the Chenango canal into the Chenango river,.....................................	A	2	93

CHENANGO RIVER.

1831.	Dam across, report on petition of Charles Sprague to maintain a,	A	3	232

CHENANGO, TOWN OF.

1832.	Report on petition for the division of the,....................	S	2	86

CHENEY, REUBEN.

		Doc.	Vol.	No.
1838.	Report on petition to confirm his official acts as a justice of the peace,	A	5	285

CHERRY VALLEY.

1840.	Road from, to Manheim Bridge, report on petition to repeal law to lay out a,	A	8	357

CHESEBRO, THOMAS W., AND OTHERS.

1844.	Report of canal board on petition of,	A	3	54

CHESEBROUGH, AND OTHERS, *see* Brayton and Chesebrough.

CHESTER, TOWN OF.

1856.	Report on petition of inhabitants of, and Pottersville,	A	3	64

CHIEF JUSTICE, *see* Supreme Court.

CHILD, JONATHAN, *see* Harvey Ely and others.

CHILD, JONATHAN, AND JNO. T. TALLMAN.

1841.	Report on petition for interest on damages awarded to them,	A	6	216
1841.	Report of committee on claims on the same,	A	6	246

CHILI, TOWN OF.

1840.	Bridge across Genesee river in, report on petition for a loan from the state to build a,	A	6	248

CHINA, TOWN OF.

1831.	Report on petition for the division of the,	A	2	191
1836.	First Congregational Society in, report on petition to sell real estate,	A	3	111

CHIPMAN, JEFFREY.

1833.	Report on petition relative to the election of justices of the peace,	A	1	35
1833.	Report of attorney-general,	A	2	99

CHITTENANGO AND OTHER CREEKS.

1836.	Report of canal commissioners in relation to the waters of,	S	2	80

CHITTENANGO, VILLAGE OF.

1830.	Literary institution, memorial of J. B. Yates in relation to,	S	1	39
1830.	Report of committee on literature on memorial of J. B. Yates,	S	2	124

CHOATE, BENJAMIN L.

1856.	Report on petion for relief,	A	4	176

CHOLERA, ASIATIC.

1832.	Message from the governor in relation to the,	A	4	330
1832.	Report on the subject of,	A	4	331
1832.	Report on the subject of,	S	2	115
1850.	Communication from governor,	S	1	36
1850.	Report of committee on medical societies and colleges concerning,	S	3	92

CHURCH, CALEB C., AND HARVEY NORTON.

1842.	Report on petition of,	A	2	44

CHURCH, PHILIP.

1833.	Report on petition of, to suspend the sale of certain land for non-payment of taxes,	A	4	289

CHURCH, PHILIP—*continued.*

		Doc.	Vol.	No.
1836.	Report on petition to be relieved from liability as security for Moses Van Campen, a commissioner of loans for Allegany county,	A	4	293

CHURCH, PHILIP, AND OTHERS, *see* New York and Erie Railroad Company.

CHURCH, SARAH.

1849.	Report of committee on judiciary on petition praying for appointment of special guardian for, with authority to sell certain real estate,	A	3	127

CHURCHES, &c.

1838.	Exemption of, from taxation, report concerning,	A	5	262

CICERO, TOWN OF.

1836.	Great marsh in, report relative to draining,	A	1	19

CIRCUIT CLERKS, *see* Chancery, &c.

CIRCUIT COURTS, SEVENTH DISTRICT.

1846.	Report of comptroller relative to expenses of,	S	1	35

CIRCUIT JUDGE.

	First Circuit:			
1832.	Ogden Edwards, report of amount of fees received by him,	A	2	163
	Second Circuit:			
1832.	C. H. Ruggles, report of amount of fees received by him,	A	3	193
	Third Circuit:			
1832.	J. Vanderpoel, report of amount of fees received by him,	A	2	122
	Fourth District:			
1832.	Esek Cowen, report of amount of fees received by him,	A	2	147
	Fifth Circuit:			
1832.	Nathan Williams, report of amount of fees received by him,	A	2	139
	Sixth Circuit:			
1832.	Robert Monell, report of amount of fees received by him,	A	2	135
	Seventh Circuit:			
1832.	Daniel Moseley, report of amount of fees received by him,	A	2	134
	Eighth Circuit:			
1832.	Addison Gardner, report of amount of fees received by him,	A	2	132

CIRCUIT JUDGES.

1833.	Report of attorney-general relative to the power of the legislature to increase the jurisdiction of,	A	4	293
1835.	Resolution to abolish the office of,	A	3	193
1835.	do do	A	4	337
1835.	do do	A	4	338
1835.	Report of select committee on the same,	A	4	370
1835.	Resolution to abolish the office of,	S	1	27
1837.	do do	A	1	24
1838.	do do	A	5	267
1839.	do do	S	2	50

CIRCUIT JUDGES—*continued.*

		Doc.	Vol.	No.
1839.	Resolution to abolish the office of,............................	A	1	15
1839.	Report of committee on the judiciary on the same,............	A	3	93
1840.	Resolution to abolish, &c.,..................................	A	6	270

CITIES.

		Doc.	Vol.	No.
1855.	Report of select committee relative to passage of bill to amend act respecting railroads in,....................................	A	5	136
1857.	Report of standing committee on banks relative to financial condition of,..	S	2	54

CITIES, MAYORS OF.

		Doc.	Vol.	No.
1836.	Resolution to amend the constitution so as to make them elective,	A	2	75
1837.	Resolution to amend the constitution so as to make them elective,	A	2	148
1838.	Communication from the secretary of state, relative to the publication of a proposed amendment,........................	A	2	28
1838.	Report of the committee on the judiciary on the report of the secretary of state, ...	A	3	110
1839.	Report of committee on the judiciary on the said amendment,...	A	3	96
1845.	Civil officers, report of secretary of state, of, ...	S	1	4

CIVIL PROCEDURE, *see* Code of Civil Procedure.

CIVIL SUITS.

		Doc.	Vol.	No.
1830.	Imprisonment in, report to amend the law in relation to, ...	A	2	132

CLAIMS.

		Doc.	Vol.	No.
1834.	Report on bill in relation to, adverse, ...	A	4	300
1844.	Digest of,...	A	6	140
1845.	Digest of,...	A	7	252
1846.	Digest of,...	A	6	210
1850.	Report of committee on, on improper presentation of, ...	S	1	27
1850.	Appendix to report of committee on,........................	A	4	61
1851.	Digest of, presented to the legislature since 1843, ...	S	1	5
1851.	Digest of, presented to the canal board, from its organization to March 1, 1851,..	S	2	50
1853.	Digest of, communication from the compiler,..................	S	1	6
1853.	Communication from auditor in relation to, for the allowance of which there is no authority of law,......................	A	3	56
1853.	Report of committee on, on general bill for the final settlement of,	A	4	87
1854.	Digest of,...	S	1	51
1854.	Communication from canal department relative to certain,......	S	2	85
1855.	Digest of, by W. H. Bogart, ...	S	1	11
1856.	Digest of, by W. H. Bogart,................................	S	3	109
1856.	Digest of, by H. C. Paige,..................................	A	1	14

CLANCY, DAVID.

		Doc.	Vol.	No.
1833.	Report on petition relative to, for the payment of certain surplus money received on the sale of certain land for taxes,.........	A	2	40
1833.	Report on petition relative to, for the payment of certain surplus money received on the sale of certain land for taxes,.........	A	2	67

CLARENCE, TOWN OF.

		Doc.	Vol.	No.
1841.	Burying grounds in, report concerning,......................	A	4	291

CLARK, AMBROSE, AND OTHERS.

		Doc.	Vol.	No.
1843.	Report of committee on claims on petition of,.................	A	5	173

CLARK, BENONI, *see* Sally L. Duval.

CLARK, CHESTER.

		Doc.	Vol.	No.
1844.	Report of committee on claims on petition of,	A	3	78

CLARK, CHRISTOPHER (Colonel).

1834.	Report on claim for services during the last war,	S	1	39

CLARK, GEORGE.

1831.	Report on petition for compensation for damages to his lands by the Erie canal,	A	4	334
1831.	Report of committee on claims,	A	4	352
1832.	Report of committee on canals,	A	3	226
1833.	Report of committee on claims,	A	4	264

CLARK, GUSTAVUS.

1854.	Report on petition of,	S	1	58

CLARK, JABEZ.

1858.	Report on claim of,	A	4	136

CLARK, JAS. R.

1849.	Report of committee on claims on petition of,	A	2	80

CLARK, JASON, AND OTHERS.

1852.	Report on petition of, for relief,	S	1	43

CLARK, JOHN (an alien).

1830.	Report on petition to hold real estate,	A	2	108

CLARK, LOT.

1831.	Memorial of, relative to surplus waters at Lockport,	A	2	91

CLARK, MERRITT.

1844.	Report of committee on claims on petition of,	A	3	90

CLARK, MERRITT, AND OTHERS.

1843.	Report of committee on claims on their petition,	A	5	173
1846.	Report of committee on claims on bill for relief of,	S	4	124
1846.	Report of committee on claims on petition of,	A	3	71

CLARK, RANSOM, AND DANIEL CORNELL.

1849.	Report of committee on claims on petition of,	A	2	87
1849.	Report of committee on claims on petition of,	A	3	158
1850.	Report of committee on internal affairs of towns and counties, on bill for relief of,	S	3	110
1850.	Report of select committee on bill for relief of,	A	3	26
1852.	Report on petition of,	S	1	14

CLARK, REED, AND OTHERS.

1843.	Report of committee on claims on petition of,	A	5	173

CLARK, SAMUEL.

1830.	Report on petition of the heirs of,	A	4	424

CLARK, STROVER AND SUMNER.

		Doc.	Vol.	No.
1839.	Report on petition for extra allowance for work done on the Glens Falls feeder,	A	2	69

CLARK, SYLVESTER.

1842.	Report of committee on claims on petition of,	A	2	21

CLARK, WILLIAM.

1838.	Report on petition to change his name,	A	5	294

CLARK, WILLIAM, AND DE WITT.

1839.	Contractors on the Chenango canal, report on petition for further compensation,	A	4	246

CLARY, JOSEPH.

1834.	Report on petition for pay for services as attorney in an ejectment suit, &c.,	A	3	189

CLAY, TOWN OF.

1830.	Report on petition to change the name of the,	A	3	248

CLEAVELAND, E., AND J. WHIPPLE.

1833.	Commissioners of loans for Madison county, report on petition of,	A	3	156

CLEAVELAND, MOSES.

1831.	Report on petition to compel the town of Salem to remunerate him for certain expenses incurred as a commissioner of highways,	A	4	313

CLEAVELAND, WILLIAM, AND OTHERS.

1857.	Report of committee on claims, favorable, on petition of, for damages by water from culvert,	A	2	82

CLEMENS, JOSHUA W.

1852.	Report on petition of,	A	2	54

CLEMENS, J. W., & J. LAFOY.

1845.	Report of the canal commissioners on petition of,	A	4	132
1850.	Report of committee on claims on petition of,	A	3	31
1855.	Report of committee of ways and means on petition of,	A	1	21

CLERGYMEN.

1830.	Report on petition to vacate the seat of the Hon. N. Fox, a member of the assembly, on account of his being a,	A	4	376
1838.	Exemption of, from taxation, report on petition to repeal the law relative to,	A	5	262
1839.	Exemption of, from taxation, report on petition to repeal the law relative to,	A	4	180
1840.	Exemption of, from taxation, report on petition to repeal the law relative to,	A	5	182
1831.	Exemption of, from taxation, report on petition to repeal the law relative to,	A	6	226
1838.	Report on petition to prohibit them from acting as inspectors of common schools, &c.,	A	5	262

CLERKS IN CHANCERY, *see* Chancery.

CLERKS OF THE SUPREME COURT, *see* Supreme Court.

		Doc.	Vol.	No.
	CLEVELAND, PALMER.			
1843.	Memorial of, in relation to the employment of state prison convicts,	A	5	159
	CLINTON COUNTY.			
1832.	Academy, report on petition of, relative to the distribution of the literature fund,	A	2	59
1833.	Common pleas, report on petition to abolish the January term,	A	2	83
1833.	Health law, report on petition that the amount expended under the, by said county, be refunded out of the state treasury,	A	1	33
1832.	Redemption of land sold for taxes, report on petition from, to amend the law relative to the,	A	1	27
1839.	Road in, from Plattsburgh west through the town of Saranac, report on petition for aid to improve a,	A	3	267
1831.	Report on the same,	A	3	267
1832.	Report on the same,	S	1	62
1832.	Road from Whitehall to the north bounds of, report on petition for aid to open and improve a,	A	3	253
1831.	Report on the same,	A	3	110
1830.	Franklin military road, report on petition to appoint commissioners to inspect the accounts of tolls received on the, &c.,	A	3	282
1843.	Report of committee on roads and bridges, on the petition of inhabitants of St. Lawrence, and for a wagon road,	A	4	84
1849.	Report of committee on roads and bridges, on petition of sundry citizens of, and Essex and Washington counties relative to road from Whitehall to Plattsburgh,	A	3	186
1854.	Report of committee on judiciary on petition of supervisors of,	A	3	122
	CLINTON, DE WITT.			
1839.	Governor's message recommending the erection of a monument to,	S	1	1
1839.	Report of select committee on the same,	A	4	215
	CLINTON, GEORGE.			
1839.	Report on the expediency of erecting a monument to,	A	6	392
	CLINTON PRISON, *see* State Prison, Clinton.			
	CLINTON, TOWN OF.			
1846.	Report on bill to confirm the election and official acts of the officers of,	S	3	75
	COAL.			
1830.	Report on petition of Matthew Cadwell and others for a premium, provided they discover a coal mine within ten miles of the Erie canal,	A	2	175
1840.	Report relative to reducing the canal tolls on,	A	8	343
	COAN, CLAUDIUS C.			
1843.	Report of committee on grievances on petition of,	A	3	68
1845.	Report of committee on claims on petition of,	S	1	35
	COBB, E. B.			
1834.	Communication from, relative to a state prison for female convicts,	S	2	103
	COBB, EDWIN H.			
1852.	Report on bill for relief of,	A	1	16

COBLESKILL, TOWN OF.

		Doc.	Vol.	No.
1845.	Report of select committee relative to turnpike road in,	A	4	103

COBURN, EDMUND.

1850.	Report of committee on claims on claim of,	A	5	113

COCHRAN, WILLIAM, AND OTHERS, *see* New York Trinity Church.

COCKET, S.

1831.	Report on petition to be restored to the rights of citizenship,	A	3	273

COCKETT, JOHN.

1835.	Report on petition to continue a dam across the Susquehannah,	S	1	17

COCKMAN, G. W., AND ELIZA.

1832.	Report on petition to change the name of,	A	2	123

CODD, MATTHEW.

1833.	Report on petition to change his name,	A	2	70

CODE, COMMISSIONERS OF.

1847.	Report of,	S	4	146
1848.	Report of, under resolution,	A	2	31
1848.	Report of, under resolution,	A	6	211
1848.	Communication from John A. Collin resigning office of,	A	2	28
1849.	Report of, relative to highways, ferries, &c.,	A	1	12
1849.	Report of comptroller in relation to moneys drawn by A. L. Robertson, one of,	A	2	42
1849.	Communication from A. L. Robertson,	A	2	46
1849.	Report of comptroller under resolution of assembly respecting expenses incurred under act appointing commissioners of practice and pleadings,	A	2	69
1849.	Communication from A. L. Robertson resigning his commission,	A	5	223
1849.	Communication from,	S	1	5
1850.	Amount paid them,	A	3	44
1850.	Communication from, in answer to resolution,	A	5	96
1850.	Report of,	A	6	149

CODE OF CIVIL PROCEDURE.

1850.	Report of commissioners,	A	2	16
1850.	Report of Mr. Graham, dissenting,	A	2	17

CODE OF CRIMINAL PROCEDURE.

1850.	Report of commissioners on practice and pleadings relative to,	A	2	18
1850.	Report of commissioners on practice and pleadings final,	A	3	19
1855.	Report of select committee on,	A	7	150

CODE OF PRACTICE AND PLEADINGS.

1848.	Report as to revision of,	A	5	183

COMMISSIONERS OF:

1847.	Report from, as to progress, &c.,	A	7	202
1847.	Report from, in answer to a resolution,	A	8	235
1848.	Report of, under resolution of 12th January,	A	2	17
1848.	Report of,	A 2	31, 6	211
1849.	Report of committee on judiciary on bill to continue in office,	A	2	47

CODE OF PRACTICE AND PLEADINGS—*continued.*

		Doc.	Vol.	No.
1849.	Report of minority of, on same bill,	A	2	51
1849.	Minority report respecting,	A	3	167
1848.	Report of comptroller respecting expenses incurred under act appointing,	A	2	69
1849.	Committee from,	S	1	6
1849.	Report of judiciary committee on,	S	2	67
1850.	Communication from comptroller on cost of printing and binding reports of,	S	1	33

CODY, BEAUMONT & HECOX.

1838.	Contractors on the Erie canal, report on petition for relief,	A	3	121
1838.	do do do	A	5	215
1839.	do do do	A	4	239

COFFIE, ELEANOR.

1830.	Report on petition for the release of certain land said to be escheated,	A	4	337

COFFIN, WILLIAM, AND OTHERS.

1847.	Report of committee on claims on petition of, for remuneration for loss sustained on stock issued for Chemung canal loan of 1841,	A	2	54

COGSWELL, JEREMIAH.

1838.	Report on petition for the relief of the family of, late a superintendent on the Erie canal,	A	5	258

COHOCTON, TOWN OF.

1833.	Report on petition to extend the time for the collection of taxes in,	A	2	127
1834.	Report on petition to annex part of, to the town of Dansville,	A	2	85

COHOES COMPANY.

1833.	Report on petition for damages by the canal,	A	4	243
1834.	Report on petition to construct a tunnel under the Erie canal, &c.,	A	3	227
1834.	Report on bill for the relief of,	S	2	95
1835.	Towpath bridge across the Mohawk, constructed by the, report concerning,	A	4	364
1837.	Report on petition for compensation for damages by the Erie canal, and for a grant of a portion of the Erie canal,	S	2	60
1841.	Report on petition to be relieved from the further care and protection of the towpath bridge connected with their bridge across the Mohawk,	A	7	257

COHOES, VILLAGE OF.

1836.	Inspector of wood and stone at, report on petition for an,	A	4	307

COLBURN, EDW. S.

1857.	Report of minority of judiciary committee,	A	3	62

COLDEN, R., AND MARIA BLAKELY.

1847.	Devisees of Maria H. Williamson, report on petition of,	A	2	94

COLD SPRING HARBOR.

1840.	Report on petition of John H. Jones to erect a wharf at,	A	7	283

COLE, AMOS.

		Doc.	Vol.	No.
1842.	Report on petition of,......................................	A	4	71

COLE AND CALKINS.

1848.	Report on petition of,......................................	A	2	44

COLE, ENOS.

1856.	Report on claim of,......................................	S	1	36

COLE, GEORGE.

1853.	Canal department, report of auditor in relation to mileage of,....	A	5	122

COLE, ISAAC J.

1830.	Report on petition to confirm his official acts as commissioner of deeds,......................................	A	4	363

COLE, MOSES, *see* William L. Crossett and others.

COLE, WILLIAM, AND OTHERS.

1839.	Report on petition for extra allowance for work done on the Erie canal,......................................	A	2	25

COLESVILLE, TOWN OF.

1840.	Report on petition to require the commissioners of common schools in, to give bonds, &c.,......................................	S	2	46

COLLEGES, &c., *see* Medical Colleges.

1837.	Report of amount of appropriations made to,....................	S	1	32
1838.	Report on petition to prohibit praying, &c., in,..................	A	2	55
1838.	Report recommending an appropriation for a limited time to,....	A	5	236
1846.	Report of committee on, on so much of governor's message as relates to,......................................	A	4	133
1850.	Report of committee on medical societies and colleges, see governor's message relating to colleges,......................	S	3	92
1851.	Report on memorial from academies and,....................	S	2	49
1851.	Report of committee on finance on appropriations to, and academies,......................................	S	2	49
1856.	Report of comptroller as to aid to,......................	S	1	32
1857.	Report of comptroller in reply to resolution relative to loans to academies and,......................................	A	3	155
1858.	Report of attorney-general respecting the constitutionality of an act to incorporate, &c.,......................................	A	1	41

AGRICULTURAL, *see* Agricultural College, State.

COLUMBIA:

1830.	Report of trustees of,......................................	A	3	286
1838.	Report recommending an appropriation to,....................	A	5	236
1839.	Report on petition for aid to,......................................	A	4	248
1841.	Communication from the president of,......................	S	1	2
1841.	Report on petition for aid to,......................................	A	4	124
1843.	Report of committee on petition of trustees of,..................	A	2	30
1855.	Report of select committee appointed to examine into affairs of,.	S	2	67

DE VEAUX:

1858.	Annual report of the, for orphans and destitute children,........	S	3	118

GENESEE:

1850.	Memorial of,......................................	A	5	86

COLLEGES, &c.—*continued.*

		Doc.	Vol.	No.
	GENEVA:			
1832.	Report on petition for aid,	A	4	329
1835.	Report on petition for power to confer the degree of "Doctor of Medicine,"	A	3	182
1836.	Message from the governor returning a bill in relation to,	S	2	110
1838.	Report recommending an annual appropriation to,	A	5	236
1841.	Medical department of, report on petition for aid to,	A	3	62
1848.	Report of committee on literature on petition of,	S	2	23
	HAMILTON:			
1830.	Report of regents of the university relative to the affairs, &c., of the,	A	4	373
1834.	Report on petition for aid,	S	2	60
1837.	Memorial of the trustees of, for aid,	S	1	15
1837.	Memorial of the trustees of, in relation to a petition from the students of,	A	3	268
1837.	Communication from C. O. Shepard relative to the memorial of trustees of,	A	4	311
1838.	Report recommending an annual appropriation to,	A	5	236
1848.	Report of committee on literature on petition of,	S	2	23
	HOBART FREE:			
1856.	Memorial of the trustees of,	A	3	94
1857.	Report of committee on claims favorable on petition of, for unpaid appropriation,	A	1	54
	LITERARY AND THEOLOGICAL INSTITUTION, HAMILTON:			
1840.	Report on petition to incorporate,	A	7	309
	MADISON UNIVERSITY:			
1847.	Report of committee on, on an act for relief of,	A	6	158
1848.	Report of committee on literature on petition of,	S	2	23
1843.	Report relative to,	A	3	111
1849.	Memorial in relation to,	S	2	37
1849.	Remonstrance against the repeal of an act relative to,	S	2	52
	METROPOLITAN:			
1852.	Minority report against a charter for,	A	2	87
	N. Y. UNIVERSITY:			
1831.	Memorial for the incorporation of the,	A	3	197
1838.	Report recommending an annual appropriation to,	A	5	236
1838.	Report on petition to be relieved from a judgment obtained by the agent of the state prison against the,	A	6	335
1839.	Report on petition to be relieved from a judgment obtained by the agent of the state prison against the,	A	4	254
1839.	Investigation of the, petition of George Zabriskie and others, for an,	S	3	92
1839.	Investigation of the, petition of Henry Tappan and others for an,	S	3	93
1839.	Investigation of the, memorial of a committee of the council of the,	S	3	94
1840.	Brief history of the origin and progress of the,	S	1	2
1840.	Report of the regents of the university relative to the,	S	1	10
1842.	Report of committee on petition of medical faculty of,	A	5	125
1849.	Report of committee on colleges, academies, &c., in relation to,	A	3	164
	PEOPLE'S:			
1853.	Report of minority of committee on agriculture in relation to incorporating,	A	2	38
1853.	Report of majority on same subject,	A	2	42

COLLEGES, &c.—*continued.*

		Doc.	Vol.	No.
	ROCHESTER UNIVERSITY:			
1851.	Memorial of trustees of,	A	3	68
1857.	Report of committee on ways and means on bill making appropriation to the,	A	3	148
	ST. LAWRENCE UNIVERSITY:			
1857.	Report of committee on ways and means on petitions for an appropriation to the,	A	2	143
	ST. PAUL'S:			
1840.	Report on petition to incorporate,	A	6	247
	UNION:			
1830.	Annual report of the trustees of,	A	4	306
1831.	do do	A	4	357
1832.	do do	A	3	271
1833.	do do	S	1	43
1834.	do do	A	3	198
1835.	do do	A	3	219
1836.	do do	A	4	238
1837.	do do	S	2	50
1838.	do do	A	5	247
1839.	do do	S	3	102
1840.	do do	S	3	96
1841.	do do	S	3	66
1842.	do do	S	3	56
1843.	Report of the trustees of, for the collegiate year ending July, 1842,	A	4	77
1844.	Annual report of trustees of,	A	3	80
1845.	Annual report of,	A	5	188
1846.	Annual report of trustees of,	A	4	129
1847.	Annual report of trustees of,	S	3	56
1849.	Report of trustees of, in answer to resolution of assembly,	A	5	213
1849.	Annual report of trustees of,	A	5	232
1850.	Report of majority of select committee,	A	6	146
1850.	Report of committee on colleges (Mr. Pruyn) on affairs of,	A	6	147
1851.	Annual report of trustees of,	A	5	145
1850.	Annual report of trustees of,	A	8	190
1851.	Report of comptroller in answer to a resolution relative to,	S	2	26
1851.	Report on the condition of,	S	3	71
1852.	Report of the commission on,	S	2	58
1853.	Report of a majority of the commissioners to examine the affairs of,	S	2	41
1853.	Memorial of trustees of (at end of report),	S	2	41
1853.	Memorial of president of (at end of report),	S	2	41
1853.	Resolution of Mr. Beekman on petition of Levinus Vanderheyden and others,	S	2	68
1853.	Annual report of,	A	5	134
1854.	Report of majority of committee of investigation into affairs of,	S	1	5
1854.	Annual report of trustees of,	A	4	142
1855.	Annual report of trustees of,	A	5	139
1858.	Annual report of,	A	4	128

COLLINS AND HITCHCOCK.

		Doc.	Vol.	No.
1851.	Report of canal board on claim for damages,	S	1	18
1851.	Report of committee on canals on petition of,	S	2	21

COLLINS, DAVID, AND OTHERS.

		Doc.	Vol.	No.
1856.	On petition of,	A	4	115

COLLINS, TOWN OF.

Year	Subject	Doc.	Vol.	No.
1831.	State road in, report on petition to discontinue a part of the, ...	A	4	284

COLLINS, WOOLSTON AND HUGHES.

Year	Subject	Doc.	Vol.	No.
1848.	Report on petition of, ...	A	5	174

COLMAN, WILLIAM, *see* John Carr and others.

COLONIAL HISTORY OF THE STATE.

Year	Subject	Doc.	Vol.	No.
1839.	Memorial of the New York Historical Society, for the appointment of an agent to transcribe documents in Europe relative to the, ...	A	3	153
1839.	Report of select committee on the same, ...	A	4	231
1842.	Committee from the governor relative to, ...	S	4	85
1842.	Mr. Brodhead's report on, ...	A	1	2
1842.	List of documents relative to, ...	A	7	195
1844.	Report of select committee relative to, ...	S	1	42
1845.	Governor's message transmitting the final report of the agent appointed to procure documents in Europe relative to, ...	S	1	47
1845.	Report of Mr. Folsom, from the select committee, on same subject, ...	S	3	111
1849.	Communication from secretary of state relative to manuscript documents in his possession, concerning and recommending their publication, ...	A	3	188
1851.	Communication from governor and secretary of state respecting,	A	3	66
1853.	Report of comptroller relative to expenses of, &c., ...	S	1	24
1853.	Report of secretary of state respecting, ...	S	2	43
1857.	Report of comptroller relative to cost of, and Documentary History, ...	A	1	10
1857.	Reply of secretary of state to resolution relative to, ...	A	2	70
1857.	Report of the comptroller in reply to resolution relative to cost of,	A	2	81
1857.	Report of secretary of state in reply to resolutions relative to printing, &c., ...	A	2	134
1851.	Communication of governor and secretary of state respecting, ...	A	3	66

COLONIZATION.

Year	Subject	Doc.	Vol.	No.
1852.	Report in relation to, ...	A	2	44

COLONIZATION SOCIETY, AMERICAN.

Year	Subject	Doc.	Vol.	No.
1830.	Resolution of the legislatures of Georgia and of Missouri relative to the constitutional power of congress to appropriate money to aid the, ...	A	1	13
1830.	Memorial of the, ...	S	4	333
1831.	Resolution of the legislature of Ohio relative to the constitutional power of congress to appropriate money to aid the, ...	A	3	233

COLONIZATION SOCIETY STATE.

Year	Subject	Doc.	Vol.	No.
1830.	Memorial of the, presenting the petition of the American Colonization Society, ...	S	4	333
1832.	Memorial of the, for aid, ...	S	2	89
1851.	Report of committee on charitable and religious societies on the memorial of, ...	A	3	71
1855.	Memorial of, relative to colored emigrants, ...	S	2	55
1856.	Minority report on bill to promote the objects of, ...	A	3	70
1856.	Majority report on same subject, ...	A	3	74

COLORED PERSONS.

Year	Subject	Doc.	Vol.	No.
1843.	Resolution of Georgia legislature respecting citizenship of, ...	A	3	51

COLORED PERSONS, FREE.

		Doc.	Vol.	No.
1840.	Report on petition to prevent kidnapping of,	A	8	341
1841.	Report on petition to extend the right of suffrage to,	A	5	183
1841.	Report on the resolutions proposed by Mr. Duer to extend the right of suffrage to,	A	5	181
1842.	Report of committee on petition to extend elective franchise to,	A	7	155

COLTON, GEORGE H., *see* William Gibbs and others.

COLTON, JOHN.

1843.	Report of canal commissioners on petition of,	S	3	71

COLTON, P. C.

1857.	Report of committee on claims on petition of, for damages by falling of a bridge across the Champlain canal,	A	2	102

COLUMBIA COUNTY.

1831.	Court of common pleas, report on petition to change the time of holding,	A	1	35
1834.	Court-house and jail, report on bill to provide for the erection of,	A	4	377
1836.	Report on petition to amend the law for the erection of,	A	4	270
1836.	Jail in, report on petition to raise money to convert the, into a city hall,	A	4	287
1832.	Bridges, report on petition to make certain bridges in, a county charge,	S	2	108
1840.	Assessment roll, report on petition to extend the time for delivering the, to collectors, &c.,	A	6	253
1837.	Dog tax, report on petition to amend the law,	A	1	47
1839.	Report on petition to repeal the same,	A	4	257
1831.	Inspector of beef and pork, annual report of E. Hayward,	A	2	156
1831.	do do Ichabod Rogers,	A	2	142
1833.	do do Ichabod Rogers,	A	3	167
1847.	Report of comptroller relative to expenditures of money in,	A	2	99
1858	Report relative to reimbursements of money to,	A	3	67

COLUMBUS, IRVING'S LIFE OF.

1833.	Report relative to the introduction of, into the common schools,	A	4	333

COMBS, SARAH.

1845.	Report of committee on aliens on the petition of,	A	3	47

COMMERCE AND NAVIGATION.

1854.	Report relative to law of 1801,	S	2	99

COMMISSARY-GENERAL.

1830.	Annual report,	A	2	200
1831.	do	A	2	122
1832.	do	A	2	58
1832.	Report relative to using the arsenal at Malone for a school-house,	A	3	231
1832.	Report relative to the arsenal lot in New York,	A	3	275
1832.	Report relative to the arsenal lot in New York,	A	4	275
1833.	Report on petition for the sale of the arsenal at Canandaigua,	A	4	328
1834.	Annual report,	A	2	79
1835.	do	A	1	28
1836.	do	A	1	17
1837.	do	A	1	32

COMMISSARY-GENERAL—*continued.*

		Doc.	Vol.	No.
1838.	Annual report,	A	2	48
1839.	do	A	2	40
1834.	Report relative to the attack on the arsenal in New York,	A	4	389
1834.	Communication from, relative to the Middlebury academy,	A	4	368
1835.	Special report relative to the issue of arms and stores to the troops called out to suppress riots in New York,	A	3	200
1838.	Report in relation to arms and ordnance unlawfully taken from the arsenals of this state,	A	6	308
1838.	Report of, to the governor, in relation to the ordnance on Navy island,	A	5	217
1840.	Annual report,	A	1	25
1841.	do	A	1	8
1840.	Report of, on petition for an arsenal at Buffalo,	A	6	251
1841.	Report of, relative to the construction of an arsenal in New York,	A	1	18
1842.	Annual report of,	A	5	80
1843.	do	A	2	40
1844.	do	A	3	50
1845.	Communication from governor transmitting report of,	A	3	51
1845.	Report of, relative to the expense of the troops at Hudson,	A	4	87
1845.	Annual report of,	A	4	99
1846.	Annual report of,	A	2	59
1847.	Report of,	A	4	110
1848.	Annual report of,	A	3	75
1848.	Report of arsenals,	A	3	75
1849.	Annual report of,	A	3	120
1849.	Report of, respecting the arsenals of the state,	A	5	238
1850.	Annual report of,	A	5	105
1851.	do	A	1	20
1853.	do	A	1	26
1854.	do	A	5	147
1855.	do	A	7	148
1856.	do	A	4	140
1858.	do	A	6	165

COMMISSIONERS OF CANAL FUND, *see* Canal Fund, Commissioners of.

COMMISSIONERS OF CODE, *see* Code, Commissioners of.

COMMISSIONERS OF DEEDS, *see* Deeds, Commissioners of.

COMMISSIONERS OF EMIGRATION, *see* Emigration, Commissioners of.

COMMISSIONERS OF HEALTH, *see* New York.

COMMISSIONERS OF LAND OFFICE, *see* Land Office, Commissioners of.

COMMISSIONERS OF LOANS, *see* Loans, Commissioners of.

COMMISSIONERS OF PILOTS, *see* New York.

COMMISSIONERS OF PRACTICE AND PLEADINGS, *see* Code of Practice and Pleadings

COMMON CARRIERS.

1847.	Report on petition of,	S	4	142

COMMON SCHOOLS.

Year	Subject	Doc.	Vol.	No.
1830.	Improvement of, petition of citizens of Rochester for the, ...	A	4	387
1833.	Irving's Columbus, report in relation to the introduction of, into the,..........	A	4	333
1834.	Under the charge of the regents, report relative to the purchase of books for, ...	S	1	44
1836.	Barrett's grammar, report on petition to supply each school with a copy of, ...	S	2	105
1838.	Praying, &c., in, report on petition to prohibit,..............	A	2	55
1839.	Report of superintendent of, relative to disturbances in,........	A	5	315
1845.	School fund, report of committee on colleges, &c., on the bill to increase, ...	A	5	177
1845.	Report of committee on colleges, &c., on so much of governor's message as relates to common schools, &c., ...	A	6	206
1846.	Report of committee on colleges, &c., on so much of governor's message as relates to common schools, &c.,..........	A	4	133
1846.	Common school system, report of select committee relative to,..	A	5	146
1850.	Majority report of committee on literature on bill to provide for support of common schools,..........	S	3	111
1851.	Webster's Unabridged Dictionary, report of committee on furnishing to, ...	S	3	81
1851.	Webster's Unabridged Dictionary, report of committee on furnishing to, ...	S	3	89
	Bills of Indigent Persons:			
1835.	Report relative to the payment of,..........	A	4	281
1835.	Report of superintendent of common schools on the same,......	A	4	317
1835.	Report of superintendent of common schools on the same,......	A	4	163
	Commissioners of:			
1830.	Appeals to, communication from the superintendent of common schools relative to the insufficiency of the law in relation to,..	A	4	377
1835.	Reports of, report relative to altering the time for making,......	A	2	110
1838.	Election of, for three years, report on petition for the,..........	A	6	357
1839.	Election of, for three years, report on petition for the,..........	A	3	79
1840.	To give bonds, report on petition to require them,..............	S	2	46
	County Superintendents:			
1847.	Committee on colleges, &c., report relative to salaries of,........	A	8	242
1847.	Report as to salaries due,..........	A	8	245
1856.	Select committee on memorial of,..........	S	2	71
	Deputy Superintendents of:			
1842.	Report of committee on petition to abolish the office, ...	A	7	168
1843.	Committee on colleges, &c., report on petitions for, and remonstrances against the repeal of so much of the act relative to common schools as directs the appointment of,..........	A	4	100
	District Libraries:			
1839.	Preservation of, report of superintendent of common schools relative to,..........	A	2	285
1840.	Returns of,..........	A	8	321
1841.	Harper's catalogue of,..........	S	1	2
1857.	Report of committee on agriculture favorable on petition and bill to furnish a library of agricultural books to each, ...	A	3	173
	Districts:			
1831.	Report on bill concerning school-houses in,..........	A	1	43
1834.	Report on petition that the law regulating the mode of settling disputes in, may be restored to its original provisions,........	S	1	43
1839.	Report on bill providing that the trustees of, residing in two or more towns may assess the taxable property therein,.........	A	5	291

COMMON SCHOOLS—*continued.*

Year	Subject	Doc.	Vol.	No.
1845.	Report of regents of the university on bill to consolidate certain, with Avon Academy, and for other purposes,	S	3	105
	EDUCATION:			
1837.	Majority report on bill to improve,	A	3	222
1837.	Minority report on bill to improve,	A	3	223
1840.	Report on bill to provide for the education of children of persons employed on the public works,	A	3	317
1846.	Memorial of citizens of Rochester relative to,	A	4	101
1852.	See memorial of E. Willard and others on female,	A	2	74
1852.	See memorial of E. Willard and others on female,	A	5	117
1853.	Instruction of Roman Catholic children, report relative to the, ..	A	4	97
	FREE SCHOOL LAW:			
1850.	Report of attorney-general,	A	5	107
1850.	Report of select committee,	A	6	150
1850.	Petition of inhabitants of Onondaga for repeal,	A	6	166
1851.	Report of majority of committee on colleges and schools on,	A	2	41
1851.	Report of minority on same subject,	A	2	42
	FREE SCHOOLS:			
1846.	Report of committee on colleges, academies and common schools relative to,	A	6	222
1849.	Memorial of Onondaga County Institute respecting,	A	3	115
1850.	Report on petition in regard to,	S	1	38
	INFANT SCHOOLS:			
1832.	Report on petition for a general act to incorporate,	A	4	327
	INSPECTORS OF:			
1832.	Report on petition to abolish the office of,	A	2	131
1838.	Report on petition to prohibit clergymen from acting as,	A	5	262
1838.	Election of, for three years, report on petition for the,	A	6	357
	LAWS OF:			
1848.	Report as to,	A	3	115
1852.	Report of the commissioners for codifying,	A	1	21
	MANUAL FOR:			
1830.	Bartlett's, petition of citizens of Utica for a law directing the purchase of one copy of, for each school district,	A	1	65
1830.	Report on the same,	A	4	431
1840,	Resolution directing the superintendent of common schools to offer a premium for,	A	4	116
	MONEYS, APPORTIONMENT OF:			
1830.	Report of superintendent of, relative to,	A	4	377
1831.	Report of committee on colleges, &c., on bill to amend the Revised Statutes in relation to the,	A	2	81
1839.	In Rockland, Kings, Oswego and Seneca, report of superintendent of, in relation to,	A	4	184
1840.	Report on petition for a portion of the, for the education of children on the public works,	A	8	317
1849.	Report of superintendent in answer to a resolution relative to, ..	A	1	14
	NORMAL SCHOOL:			
1844.	Report of committtee on colleges, &c., in regard to establishment of,	A	5	135
1845.	Report of executive committee of,	S	1	24
1846.	Report of executive committee of,	S	1	32
1846.	Report of executive committee in answer to a resolution,	A	5	168
1847.	Annual report of,	S	1	31

COMMON SCHOOLS—*contiued.*

		Doc.	Vol.	No.
1848.	Report of,	S	1	18
1849.	Annual report of,	S	1	8
1850.	Annual report of,	S	2	56
1851.	Annual report of the executive committee,	A	1	12
1852.	Report of executive committee of,	S	1	34
1852.	Report as to cause of panic at public exercises of,	A	5	119
1853.	Annual report of executive committee of,	A	2	20
1854.	do do	S	1	30
1855.	do do	S	1	20
1856.	Report of,	S	1	40
1856.	Annual report of,	S	3	40
1857.	Annual report of executive committee of,	A	1	26
1858.	Annual report of executive committee of,	A	1	25
	PUBLIC INSTRUCTION:			
1835.	Report and bill for the organization of a department of,	A	5	382
1838.	Report recommending the appointment of a president of, &c.,	A	5	236
1847.	Report of committee on colleges, &c., relative to,	A	8	254
	TEACHERS:			
1840.	Report on petition of trustees of Hamilton Academy for the establishment of a department for the education of,	S	2	58
1851.	Report of committee on literature relative to academies instructing,	S	2	58
	TEACHERS' INSTITUTES:			
1847.	Report relative to,	A	2	71
1852.	Report for a union,	S	2	82
	TEACHING:			
1835.	Improved manner of, petition of John Preston relative to an,	A	1	34
1835.	Report on the same,	A	1	63
	TOWN SUPERINTENDENTS:			
1849.	Report of superintendent of common schools relative to amount paid during the year to,	A	5	202
	VISITORS OF:			
1840.	Reports of the,	A	7	307
1841.	Reports of the,	A	5	153

COMMON SCHOOLS, SUPERINTENDENT OF.

		Doc.	Vol.	No.
	A. C. FLAGG:			
1830.	Annual report of the,	A	1	31
1831.	do do	A	1	15
1832.	do do	A	1	11
1833.	do do	A	1	17
1831.	Communication from, transmitting the annual report of the New York Institution for the Deaf and Dumb,	A	2	95
1832.	Communication from, transmitting the annual report of the New York Institution for the Deaf and Dumb,	A	2	101
1833.	Communication from, transmitting the annual report of the New York Institution for the Deaf and Dumb,	A	3	201
1830.	Annual report in relation to the deaf and dumb,	S	3	235
1832.	Annual report in relation to the deaf and dumb,	S	1	106
1830.	Report of the, relative to apportioning the school moneys,	A	4	387
1831.	Report of the, on petition of the trustees of school district No. 11 in Farmington,	A	4	302
	JOHN A. DIX:			
1834.	Annual report of the,	A	1	9

COMMON SCHOOLS, SUPERINTENDENT OF—*continued.*

Year	Subject	Doc.	Vol.	No.
1835.	Annual report of the,	S	2	66
1836.	do do	A	1	6
1837.	do do	A	1	6
1838.	do do	A	1	13
1839.	do do	A	1	17
1839.	Communication in relation to the,	A	3	152
1834.	Communication from, transmitting the annual report of the New York Institution for the Deaf and Dumb,	A	3	108
1835.	Communication from, transmitting the annual report of the New York Institution for the Deaf and Dumb,	A	4	288
1836.	Communication from, transmitting the annual report of the New York Institution for the Deaf and Dumb,	A	3	125
1837.	Communication from, transmitting the annual report of the New York Institution for the Deaf and Dumb,	A	4	291
1838.	Communication from, transmitting the annual report of the New York Institution for the Deaf and Dumb,	A	2	31
1839.	Communication from, transmitting the annual report of the New York Institution for the Deaf and Dumb,	A	4	201
1834.	Annual report in relation to the deaf and dumb,	S	1	41
1836.	do do do	S	1	47
1838.	do do do	S	1	25
1839.	do do do	S	2	31
1834.	Report of the, on petition of the trustees of school district No. 3 in the town of Gates, Monroe county,	A	2	52
1835.	Report of the, relative to the payment of school bills of indigent persons,	A	4	317
1836.	Report of the, on petition of Solomon Barrett, Jr., to supply each school with a copy of his grammar,	S	2	105
1837.	Report of the, in relation to a digest of decisions made by his predecessors and himself in matters of appeal,	A	1	5
1839.	Report of the, in relation to common schools,	S	3	98
1839.	do relative to school moneys in certain counties,	A	4	184
1839.	do relative to the preservation of district school libraries,	A	5	285
1839.	do relative to the powers of trustees of school districts,	A	5	291
1839.	do relative to the prevention of disturbances in common schools,	A	5	315
	JOHN C. SPENCER:			
1840.	Annual report of the,	A	4	120
1841.	Annual report of the,	A	4	100
1840.	Communication from, transmitting the annual report of the New York Institution for the Deaf and Dumb,	A	5	179
1841.	Communication from, transmitting the annual report of the New York Institution for the Deaf and Dumb,	A	5	157
1840.	Annual report in relation to the deaf and dumb,	A	5	172
1840.	Report in relation to the instruction of the blind,	A	5	172
1841.	Report transmitting the annual report of the New York Institution for the Blind,	A	6	213
1840.	Report of the, on petition of James L. Voorhees relative to school district No. 25 in the town of Lysander,	S	3	89
1840.	do on petition of T. Mowers, and others, relative to school district No. 1 in Gorham,	A	4	123
1840.	do transmitting reports of visitors of common schools,	A	7	307
1840.	do do returns of district libraries,	A	8	321
1841.	do do reports of visitors of common schools,	A	5	153
1841.	do petition of the trustees of school district No. 16 in New Berlin,	A	5	188
1841.	do respecting the distribution of school moneys in the city of New York,	S	3	86

COMMON SCHOOLS, SUPERINTENDENT OF—*continued.*

Year	Title	Doc.	Vol.	No.
1841.	Report of the, giving copies of certain reports respecting the schools of the Public School Society, and other schools,......	S	3	90
	SAMUEL YOUNG:			
1842.	Annual report of,..	A	1	12
1842.	Communication from, transmitting annual report of New York Deaf and Dumb Institution,............................	A	4	57
1842.	Communication from, transmitting annual report of New York Institution for the Blind,..................................	A	4	77
1842.	Report of, on petition of Squire Campbell and others,..........	A	5	116
1842.	Report of committee on petition to abolish office of deputy,....	A	7	168
1843.	Annual report of, with accompanying documents,.............	A	1	14
1843.	Communication from, transmitting the annual report relative to the Institution for the Instruction of the Deaf and Dumb,....	A	4	74
1843.	Communication from, transmitting annual report relative to the New York Institution for the Blind,.........................	A	4	88
1844.	Communication from, transmitting annual report relative to the Institution for the Instruction of the Deaf and Dumb,........	A	1	26
1844.	Annual report of, and documents, ...	A	2	34
	NATHANIEL S. BENTON:			
1845.	Annual report of, with accompanying documents,.............	A	2	30
1845.	Communication from, transmitting annual report relative to the Institution for the Instruction of the Deaf and Dumb,........	A	3	70
1846.	Annual report of,..	A	2	30
1846.	Report of printing committee on printing annual report of,.....	A	1	28
1847.	Report of committee on colleges, &c., relative to printing annual report of,..	A	1	9
1847.	Annual report of,..	A	1	10
	CHRISTOPHER MORGAN:			
1848.	Annual report of,..	A	1	5
1848.	Annual report of,..	S	3	79
1849.	Report of, relative to distribution of school moneys in certain cases,..	A	1	14
1849.	Annual report of,..	A	1	20
1849.	Report relative to amount paid during the past year to town superintendents of,..	A	5	202
1850.	Annual report of,..	A	4	50
1851.	Annual report of,..	A	1	21
	HENRY S. RANDALL:			
1852.	Annual report of,..	A	1	25
1853.	Annual report of,..	A	1	4
1853.	Report of, relative to school moneys due from city and county of New York,..	A	3	63
1853.	Communication from, relative to certain unpaid school moneys,..	A	5	127
	ELIAS W. LEAVENWORTH:			
1854.	Annual report of,..	A	1	7
1854.	Report relative to office of,..............................	S	1	39
	VICTOR M. RICE: *			
1854.	Communication from, under resolution of 24th March,........	S	1	29
1855.	Annual report of,..	A	1	7
1856.	Annual report of,..	A	3	65
	HENRY H. VAN DYCK: *			
1857.	Annual report of,..	A	2	95
1858.	Annual report of,..	A	1	6

* This office is now termed, Superintendent of Public Instruction.

COMPTROLLER.

SILAS WRIGHT, Jr.:

Year		Doc.	Vol.	No.
1830.	Annual report of,	A	1	48
1830.	Report of expenditures on the canals,	A	3	208
1830.	Report relative to George M'Clure's loan and B. S. Bundage's mortgage,	S	1	19
1830.	Report on petition of supervisors of Washington county to raise certain money by tax,	A	1	20
1830.	Report on petition of Delaware and Hudson Canal Company to sell certain land,	S	1	21
1830.	do do Delaware and Hudson Canal Company relative to transfer of stock issued to the,	S	2	198
1830.	do do Delaware and Hudson Canal Company relative to stock issued to the,	S	4	317
1830.	Report giving a statement of the Amsterdam Bridge Company,	S	1	25
1830.	Report relative to amount of compensation paid to canal appraisers,	A	1	28
1830.	Report of amount of taxes paid by banks, insurance, and other incorporated companies, in 1826 and 1827,	A	1	32
1830.	Report relative to balances due from county treasurers,	A	1	37
1830.	Report on petition of the administrators of Huet Hills,	S	1	42
1830.	Report relative to the loan to the Neversink Navigation Company,	A	1	49
1830.	Report relative to the amount of compensation and expenses paid the commissioners for building the Mount Pleasant prison,	A	1	52
1830.	Report relative to clerks and clerk hire in his office,	A	1	59
1830.	Report giving a list of the banks which have filed their assent to the provisions of the act renewing their charters,	A	2	71
1830.	Report on petition for an investigation of expenditures and accounts of the commissioners to drain the Cayuga marshes,	A	2	178
1830.	Report on petition of W. Young for compensation for surveying a route for a railroad from Boston to Hudson river,	A	2	181
1830.	Report giving the residence of stockholders in the New York banks, with amount of stock held by them,	A	3	232, 277
1830.	Report on bill concerning the sale of land for taxes,	A	3	239
1830.	Report relative to hospital moneys,	A	3	252
1830.	Report of amount paid special counsel in the Morgan trials,	S	3	254
1830.	Report of amount paid for defending the titles of certain persons to lands against the claim of John Jacob Astor,	A	4	380
1830.	Report relative to the returns of the Washington and Warren Bank,	A	4	370
1830.	Report on a resolution of assembly relative to the public moneys deposited in banks,	A	4	382
1831.	Annual report of,	A	1	37
1831.	Report on petition of John H. Johnson relative to the sale of certain land for taxes,	A	1	46
1831.	Report on petition of the supervisors of Washington county to credit the treasurer of said county for certain compound interest charged against him in the comptroller's office,	A	1	51
1831.	Report on the Cayuga marshes and swamp lands,	A	2	70
1831.	Report relative to the health department in New York,	A	2	127
1831.	Annual report of expenditures on the canals,	A	3	206
1831.	Report on petition of the settlers on the Cowasselon tract of land,	A	3	260
1831.	Report relative to the amount of the expenses of the last sale of land for taxes,	A	3	264
1831.	Report relative to the Port Kent and Hopkinton road,	A	4	283
1831.	Report on the Oldenbarneveld Manufacturing Company,	A	4	290
1831.	Report in answer to a resolution of the assembly in regard to the payment of certain sums of money,	A	4	339
1831.	Report relative to clerk hire in his office,	S	1	11
1831.	Report relative to lot No. 75 in the township of Lysander,	S	1	46
1831.	Annual report of,	A	1	4

COMPTROLLER—*continued.*

		Doc.	Vol.	No.
1832.	Report of expenditures on the canals,	A	1	9
1832.	Report of amount of bank capital in each county, &c.,	A	1	15
1832.	Report on petition to amend the law relative to the redemption of lands sold for taxes,	A	1	37
1832.	Report relative to the issue of stock to John Jacob Astor,	A	3	205
1832.	do do liability of the state for costs under the excise law,	A	3	210
1832.	do do an appropriation for clerk hire in his office, &c.,	A	3	236
1832.	do do the disposition of the bank fund, &c.,	A	3	248
1832.	do do clerk hire in his office,	S	1	10
1832.	do do disposition of the bank fund,	S	1	23
1832.	Report on petition of John and Matthew Pratt for the payment to them of certain surplus moneys obtained on the sale of certain land,	S	1	15
1832.	Report on bill respecting auctioneers in the city of New York,	S	1	44
1832.	Report relative to the accounts of the late clerk of the Auburn prison,	S	1	51
1832.	Report on petition of George Deming for the payment to him of certain surplus money received upon a resale of certain land,	S	1	53
1832.	Report of amount outstanding of the loans of 1786, 1792 and 1808, &c.,	S	1	25
1833.	Annual report of,	A	1	5
1833.	Report of expenditures on the canals,	A	1	16
1833.	Report relative to clerk hire in his office,	S	1	5
	PHILIP PHELPS, acting Comptroller:			
1833.	Report of, relative to the bank fund,	S	1	19
	A. C. FLAGG:			
1833.	Report of, on petition of Lucas Elmendorf for a law authorizing the comptroller to convey to him certain land, &c.,	A	1	27
1833.	Report of, on petition of David Clancy for the payment to him of certain surplus money received on the sale of certain land for taxes,	A	2	40
1833.	Report relative to the Economical School in New York,	A	3	232
1833.	Report relative to the situation and progress of the road from Cedar Point westward,	A	3	226
1833.	Report on petition of E. Cleavland and I. Whipple, commissioners of loans for Madison county,	A	3	156
1833.	Report of amount of money now on loan in the several counties under the acts of 1792 and 1808,	A	4	241
1833.	Report on petition of Perkins Nichols to extend the privilege allowing him to redeem certain land sold for taxes,	A	4	269
1833.	Report of amount of money, stock, and other property which the state has lost by banks,	A	4	283
1833.	Report on petition of Philip Church to suspend the sale of his lands,	A	4	289
1833.	Report relative to giving deeds for lands sold for taxes when the certificate is lost,	A	4	299
1833.	Report of amount expended for the improvement of Hudson river,	A	4	302
1833.	Report of amount received for fees, and amount paid to clerks of the supreme court under the law of 1810,	A	4	303
1834.	Annual report of,	A	1	5
1834.	Communication concerning his annual report,	A	1	25
1834.	Report of expenditures on the canals,	A	2	75
1834.	Report relative to clerk hire in his office,	S	1	21
1834.	Report giving the population of the state, valuation of real and personal estate, amount of auction duties, amount received for licenses for hawkers and pedlars, amount of incorporated bank capital, amount of tolls received on the canals from 1820 to 1834, &c.,	A	2	66

COMPTROLLER—*continued.*

		Doc.	Vol.	No.
1834.	Report on petition of Simeon Crane for a loan from the state,...	A	2	104
1834.	Report on petition of supervisors of Broome county relative to the payment of a loan,....	A	3	130
1834.	Report on petition of Herman Jenkins for the payment to him of certain surplus money received on the sale of certain land,...	A	3	174
1834.	Report of petition of Watson Dunham for extra allowance on a contract for making desks for the assembly chamber,........	A	3	203
1834.	Report on petition of John Denny for his portion of the money due 1st Christian party of Oneida Indians, &c.,............	S	1	37
1834.	Report relative to the bank fund,........	S	2	62
1835.	Annual report of,........	A	1	5
1835.	Report of expenditures on the canals,........	A	3	216
1835.	Report relative to clerk hire in his office,........	S	1	15
1835.	Report on petition of Maria Weaver and Henry Truax for remuneration for the sale of their land,........	S	1	23
1835.	Report on petition of Jacob I. Zimmerman,........	S	2	39
1835.	Report giving the taxable value of real and personal estate, a return of the capital stock of all corporations liable to taxation, the amount paid out of the general funds for the construction of the Erie and Champlain canals, and amount towards the bank fund,........	S	2	48
1835.	Report of amount paid for printing for the legislature for 1831, 1832, 1833 and 1834,........	S	2	67
1835.	Report on petition of Nehemiah Tower to be indemnified for costs and damages in consequence of the sale of his lands,........	S	2	57
1835.	Report on petition of Jabez Burrows, a canal contractor, to be released from a balance of errors charged against him,....	S	2	63
1835.	Report relative to the steam dredging machine belonging to the state,........	S	2	60
1835.	Report on petition of the supervisors of Herkimer county for a loan from the school fund,........	A	1	32
1835.	Report on petition of John B. Herrishoff and others to be relieved from the payment of interest on the taxes on their lands,.....	A	2	90
1835.	Report in relation to the payments to the court of errors,.......	A	2	125
1835.	Report on petition of John Hill, Jenny Hill and Anthony Otsequette, relative to their annuities,........	A	4	151
1835.	Report of amount of tolls paid on certain articles on the Chemung canal,........	A	2	159
1835.	Report on memorial of the St. Regis Indians, relative to the payment of their annuities,........	A	4	318
1835.	Report of, giving a statement of all the sales of lands for taxes (not heretofore reported), and the sales of lands for arrears of quit-rents in 1826,........	A	5	380
1835.	Report relative to the stock issued for the construction of the Chenango canal,........	A	5	381
1836.	Annual report of,........	A	1	5
1836.	Report of expenditures on the canals,........	A	4	211
1836.	Report of, relative to clerk hire in his office,........	A	2	67
1836.	Report of, relative to an execution issued by the attorney-general against Augustus Porter and Benjamin Barton,........	S	1	17
1836.	Report of, on petition for the extension of Spring street in the village of Sing Sing,........	S	1	51
1836.	Report of, relative to the revenues of the lateral canals,........	S	1	58
1836.	Report of amount of taxes paid by each county, from 1816 to 1826,........	S	2	67
1836.	Report of sales of land near the Oswego canal, and the contributions to and diversion from the Erie canal by the lateral canals,	S	2	73
1836.	Report on petition of Isaac Packard, for a law authorizing the commissioners of canal fund to redeem his canal stock, as proof that the certificate has been lost,........	A	2	48
1836.	Report giving statement of the incorporated bank capital in 1800, 1805, 1810, 1815, 1820, 1825, 1830 and 1835,........	A	2	102

COMPTROLLER—*continued.*

		Doc,	Vol.	No.
1836.	Report in relation to moneys paid by mariners and others, and the amount expended for the support of sick and disabled seamen, ...	A	3	152
1836.	Report of amount expended by the state for the benefit of the deaf and dumb, ...	A	3	172
1836.	Report on petition of Zebulon Douglass for a deed of certain land,	A	4	295
1837.	Annual report of, ...	A	1	4
1837.	Report of expenditures on the canals, ...	A	2	159
1837.	Report relative to clerk hire in his office, ...	S	1	14
1837.	Report of amount of appropriations made to academies and colleges, ...	S	1	32
1837.	Report of money loaned under the act of 1808, the amount now outstanding, and the amount supposed to be not collectable, ..	S	1	34
1837.	Report on application of the clerk of assembly for an advance of money to purchase copies of the Revised Statutes for the members of the legislature, ...	A	2	74
1837.	Report in relation to the steam dredging machine belonging to state, ...	A	3	155
1838.	Annual report of, ...	A	1	4
1838.	Report of expenditures on the canals, ...	A	1	5
1838.	Report relative to the clerk hire in his office, ...	S	2	76
1838.	Report of amount of moneys received, disbursed or invested by the commissioners of health, from 1834 to 1837, ...	S	1	17
1838.	Report giving abstracts of all returns in his office, in relation to incorporated companies, for the year 1837, ...	A	3	146
1839.	Annual report of, ...	A	1	4
1839.	Report of amount of expenditures on the canals, ...	A	1	16
1839.	Report relative to clerk hire in his office, ...	S	2	33
	BATES COOKE:			
1839.	Report of amount of salt and auction duties, received since the year 1812, ...	S	3	76
1839.	Report in relation to paying sheriff for conveying convicts to the Auburn prison, ...	S	3	100
1839.	Report relative to the interest on stock issued to railroads, ...	S	3	109
1839.	Report relative to the interest on stock issued to the Ithaca and Owego railroad, ...	S	3	111
1839.	Report in relation to the bank fund, ...	A	4	161
1839.	Communication from, relative to the appointment of a committee to examine the accounts of the commissioners of the canal fund and the accounts of the comptroller, in relation to the funds in his hands for the redemption of bank notes, ...	A	4	169
1839.	Report relative to the stock issued to the Catskill and Canajoharie Railroad Company, ...	A	5	314
1839.	Report on bill relative to the sale of land for arrears of taxes,	A	6	340
1838.	Report in relation to persons claiming pensions under acts of congress, ...	A	6	395
1839.	Report in relation to the application of certain moneys received for interest on the moneys received from the United States, &c.,	A	9	403
1840.	Annual report of, ...	A	1	10
1840.	Report relative to expenditures on the canals, ...	A	4	131
1840.	Report relative to clerk hire in his office, ...	S	2	47
1840.	Report in relation the valuation of real and personal estate, ...	S	1	11
1840.	Resolution relative to the payment of certain money by the, to canal contractors, ...	A	3	66
1840.	Report relative to paying the militia called out to assist the sheriff of Albany county, ...	S	3	67
1840.	Report relative to the investment of certain moneys received on account of the United States deposit fund, ...	S	4	122
1840.	Report relative to the contract for state printing, ...	A	2	47
1840.	Report relative to the issue of state stock to the New York and Erie Railroad Company, ...	A	4	127

COMPTROLLER—*continued.*

		Doc.	Vol.	No.
1840.	Report relative to the fees of clerks of the supreme court and of the register, assistant register and clerks in chancery, ...	A	3	77
1840.	Report transmitting reports relative to the investigation of the Seamen's Fund and Retreat, Marine hospital, City hospital and Bloomingdale asylum, ...	A	5	214
1840.	Report on petition of Sarah Herrishoff and others, to be relieved from certain taxes, ...	A	6	254
1840.	Report on petition of W. Hogan for same,........	A	6	256
1841.	Annual report of,............	A	1	13
1841.	Report relative to expenditures on the canals,................	A	3	51
1841.	Report relative to clerk hire in his office,....................			
1841.	Report giving the names of banking associations and individual bankers who have failed to redeem their notes on demand, ...	S	2	53
1841.	Report transmitting a report of the commissioners for building the State Lunatic Asylum,..................................	A	2	26
1841.	Report on petition of the Caughnawaga Indians relative to their annuity, ...	A	2	29
1841.	Report relative to stock issued to railroad companies, ...	A	3	70
1841.	Report on petition of Maria Weaver and Henry Truax for remuneration for sale of their lands,..............................	A	3	79
1841.	Communication from, in relation to an amendment to the general banking law,.....................	A	4	105
1841.	Report in relation to the issue of certificates of stock to the New New York and Erie Railroad Company, ...	A	4	113
1841.	Report relative to the loan commissioners of the United States deposit fund, ...	A	5	148
1841.	Report in relation to foreign insurance companies,..............	A	5	177
1841.	Report on bill relative to roads and bridges in the Buffalo creek reservation,..	A	6	198
1841.	Report relative to the amount of stock issued to railroad companies,..	A	7	273

AZARIAH C. FLAGG:

		Doc.	Vol.	No.
1842.	Report of, on a resolution of the senate relative to the canal revenue ,...	S	1	16
1842.	Report of, on a resolution of the senate relative to the fees of the clerks of the supreme court and court of chancery, ...	S	2	30
1842.	Report of, on a resolution of the senate relative to premiums paid on the stock of 1845 and loans of canal fund moneys to the banks, ...	S	3	62
1842.	Report of, on a resolution of the senate relative to the amount of premiums received on Chenango and Chemung canal stocks,..	S	4	87
1842.	Report of, on a resolution of the senate relative to the names of persons to whom interest was paid on the 1st of April, and also the names of the persons to whom interest was due, but not paid,.	S	4	98
1842.	Annual report of,..	A	1	15
1842.	Mr. Hoffman's resolution calling on, for statement of debt,......	A	2	23
1842.	Report (with commissioners of canal fund, &c.,) in compliance with Mr. H.'s resolution,................................	A	4	64
1842.	Communication from, in relation to the finances of the state, ...	A	4	61
1842.	Communication from, in relation to the new state hall,.........	A	7	134
1842.	Report of, transmitting correspondence of the Delaware and Hudson Canal Company and New York and Erie Railroad Company,	A	7	162
1843.	Report of, showing the sums paid for state printing, 1835 to 1842,	S	1	3
1843.	Report of the amount paid the state printer from 1823 to 1839,..	S	1	12
1843.	Report of the amount due on account of non-resident taxes,....	S	1	13
1843.	Report in relation to contracts on the enlarged Erie canal between Albany and Troy,..................................	S	1	15
1843.	Report of, in relation to the state debt,......................	S	1	18
1843.	Report of the amount of tolls on passengers on the Erie canal,..	S	1	21

COMPTROLLER—*continued.*

		Doc.	Vol.	No.
1843.	Report relative to the judge-advocate of the 3rd division of infantry,	S	1	29
1843.	Report relative to David Hamilton's connection with canal contracts, while acting as superintendent,	S	1	39
1843.	Report of the payment for services of non-acting canal commissioners,	S	1	45
1843.	Report relative to the services of non-acting canal commissioners and pay therefor,	S	3	80
1843.	Annual report of,	A	1	10
1843.	do relative to expenditures on the canals for 1842,	A	3	56
1843.	do relative to expenditures on the canals for 1841,	A	3	63
1843.	Report in answer to a resolution of the assembly respecting the amount of appropriation for internal improvements, and amount of stock issued, &c.,	A	3	65
1843.	Report in answer to a resolution of the assembly respecting the pledges of the proceeds of the mill tax,	A	3	66
1843.	Report in answer to a resolution of the assembly in relation to a call of twenty-five per cent of the United States deposit fund,	A	4	83
1843.	Report in answer to a resolution of the assembly of the 17th of February, 1843,	A	5	167
1844.	Report of, of the amount of printing done for his department,	S	3	94
1844.	Annual report of,	A	1	4
1844.	Report on the Genesee Wesleyan Seminary,	A	3	38
1844.	Report showing the real estate, capital, stock and taxes paid by incorporated companies,	A	3	98
1844.	Annual report of, relative to expenditures on the canals,	A	5	105
1844.	Report on reference from the assembly of the petition of Isaac Rowland,	A	5	110
1844.	Report on concurrent resolution directing the, to suspend the sale of the road of the Tioga Coal, Iron, Mining and Manufacturing Company,	A	6	152
1844.	Report of, on reference from the assembly of the petition of A. Seymour and others,	A	7	205
1845.	Report of, in answer to a resolution of the senate in relation to the mariner's fund,	S	1	29
1845.	Report of, in answer to a resolution of the senate in relation to clerks in the comptroller's office and canal department,	S	1	45
1845.	Report of, in answer to a resolution of the senate relative to the amount paid into the treasury; also amount charged and not paid in, for fees by the register, assistant register, &c., since September 30, 1844,	S	2	48
1845.	Report of, in relation to the pay, &c., of canal appraisers,	S	2	74
1845.	Annual report of,	A	1	25
1845.	Report of, in answer to a resolution of the assembly,	A	3	64
1845.	do relative to $84,000 received from U. S. government,	A	3	75
1845.	do relative to the expense of the Geological Survey,	A	5	153
1845.	do relative to the Delaware and Hudson Canal Company,	A	5	155
1845.	do in answer to a resolution of the assembly relative to the issue of registered notes to banks,	A	5	161
1845.	Annual report on expenditures on the canals,	A	5	162
1845.	Report of, in answer to a resolution of the assembly relative to the issue and redemption of canal stock,	A	5	175
1845.	Report of, relative to auction duties,	A	6	208
1845.	do do taxing, quarter sales, &c.,	A	6	228
1846.	do do moneys paid to the adjutant-general and attorney-general,	S	1	28
1846.	do do the expense of an extra session of the senate,	S	2	53
1846.	do do extra allowances made to the attorney-general,	S	2	63
1846.	do in answer to a resolution relating to payments to attorney-generals for extra services,	S	3	102

COMPTROLLER—*continued.*

Year		Doc.	Vol.	No.
1846.	Annual report of,	A	1	25
1846.	Report of, in answer to a resolution of the assembly,	A	2	31
1846.	Report of, relative to printing for executive departments,	A	3	75
1846.	Report of, on the claim of P. Dunham,	A	3	82
1846.	Annual report on canal expenditures,	A	4	90
1846.	Report of, in answer to a resolution relative to the public printing,	A	4	91
1846.	Annual report on canal expenditures, report of majority printing committee on,	A	4	94
1846.	Annual report on canal expenditures, report of minority printing committee on,	A	4	95
1846.	Report of, in answer to a resolution of the assembly relative to tolls on Erie canal, &c.,	A	4	113
1846.	do relative to expenses of canal commissioners,	A	4	118
1846.	do in answer to a resolution relative to purchasing assets of City Bank of Buffalo,	A	4	120
1846.	do on reference of petition of citizens of Erie county relative to Grand Island,	A	5	155
1846.	do relative to appropriations from the general fund,	A	5	178
1846.	do in answer to a resolution,	A	5	186
1846.	do relative to general fund,	A	5	193
1846.	do relative to state stock in trust for banks,	A	6	202
1847.	do relative to legal notices,	S	1	13
1847.	do on petition of George Murray,	S	1	17
1848.	do and governor relative to examination of Clinton prison,	S	1	18
1847.	do respecting commissioners of loans, of United States deposit fund,	S	1	32
1847.	do on petition of Amos S. Tryon,	S	1	35
1847.	do as to amount of tolls and amounts paid superintendents on canals,	S	1	40
1847.	do as to expenses of canals,	S	2	43
1847.	do relative to available and unavailable canal funds,	S	2	66
1847.	do relative to tolls of Palatine Bridge Company,	S	3	91
1847.	do on petition of Francis J. Stratton,	S	3	97
1847.	do as to claim of Isaac Denniston,	S	3	110
1847.	do relative to expenditures of salt works,	S	4	118
1847.	do relative to banks asking issues of bills,	S	4	123
1847.	do relative to sinking and general fund debt,	S	4	130
1847.	do relative to balance of canal fund,	S	4	132
1847.	do on petition of Central Bank for issue of bills,	S	4	141
1847.	do as to payments of banks to bank fund,	S	4	145
1847.	Annual report of,	A	1	5
1847.	Report of, relative to expenditures on the canals,	A	1	15
1847.	do in relation to expenditure of money in Columbia and Delaware counties,	A	2	99
1847.	do in answer to resolution relative to murder trials, &c.,	A	2	47
1847.	do giving list of newspapers that have published the new constitution and received payment therefor,	A	4	126
1847.	do as to expenses of canals for 1844, 1845, 1846, &c.,	A	4	129
1847.	do as to expense of public printing,	A	4	130
1847.	do as to payments made certain newspapers for publishing new constitution,	A	6	157
1847.	do relative to number and location of new banks,	A	7	199
1847.	do relative to removal of intruders on Indian lands,	A	7	207
1847.	do as to salaries due county superintendents of common schools,	A	8	245

MILLARD FILLMORE:

Year		Doc.	Vol.	No.
1848.	Report of, on petition of Elizabeth Gilchrist,	S	2	40
1848.	do on returns of insurance companies,	S	2	41

COMPTROLLER—*continued.*

		Doc.	Vol.	No.
1848.	Report of, in relation to the bank fund,	S	2	44
1848.	Annual report of,	A	1	4
1848.	Report of, as to expenses of government,	A	1	14
1848.	do as to expenditures on canals,	A	3	60
1848.	do on bill for lands, sale of, for taxes,	A	3	63
1848.	do relative to issues of banks,	A	3	91
1848.	do expenses of transportation of convicts,	A	3	124
1848.	do as to taxes unpaid in Cortland county,	A	5	136
1848.	do as to application of surplus revenues of canals,	A	5	137
1848.	do as to funds in deposit banks,	A	5	182
1849.	do in relation to expenses incurred in removing wrecks in Albany basin,	S	1	18
1849.	do of the amount of state stocks held by citizens of this country, and by citizens of foreign countries,	S	1	29
1849.	do of moneys paid by agents of foreign insurance companies,	S	2	36
1849.	do transmitting letter from commissioners of emigration,	S	2	39
1849.	do in relation to stocks issued to Delaware and Hudson Canal Company,	S	2	41
1849.	do of the amount on loan, &c., in charge of commissioners of loans,	S	2	47
1849.	do on the introduction of disease and pauperism,	S	3	76
1849.	Annual report of,	A	1	5
1849.	Report of, in answer to resolution for printing statement of lands sold for taxes, &c.,	A	1	8
1849.	do relative to extinguishing canal and general fund debts, &c., in answer to resolution of assembly,	A	1	13, 33
1849.	Communications from governor and, relative to funds for the support of fever and small pox hospitals at Quarantine,	A	1	39
1849.	Report of, in relation to money drawn by A. L. Robertson,	A	2	42
1849.	do in answer to resolution of assembly relative to expenses incurred under law appointing commissioners on practice and pleadings, and commissioners on the Code,	A	2	69
1849.	do relative to drafts paid by agents at Sing Sing prison to Wm. Radford,	A	2	92
1849.	do in answer to resolutions of assembly relative to bill to remunerate Jonathan W. Davis for losses from failure of title to certain lands,	A	2	98
1849.	do of all moneys drawn from state treasury by Chauncy Smith, late agent of the Sing Sing prison,	A	2	99
1849.	do in answer to resolutions of assembly respecting certain balances due United States deposit fund,	A	3	111
1849.	Communication from, respecting funds for support of marine hospital on Staten Island,	A	3	140
1849.	Communication from, respecting expiration of time for payment of loans of 1792 and 1808,	A	3	176
1849.	Communication from, and attorney-general, relative to marine hospital,	A	5	206

WASHINGTON HUNT:

		Doc.	Vol.	No.
1850.	Communication transmitting annual report of New York health officer,	S	1	11
1850.	Communication from, on cost of printing and binding reports of commissioners on practice and pleadings,	S	1	33
1850.	Communication from, in regard to public printing,	S	2	47
1850.	Communication from, relative to Hudson and Berkshire railroad,	A	1	6
1850.	Annual report of,	A	1	8
1850.	Report on non-resident lands,	A	3	39
1850.	Communication from, as to amount paid commissioners of the Code,	A	3	44

COMPTROLLER—*continued.*

Year	Subject	Doc.	Vol.	No
1850.	Communication from, in answer to a resolution in regard to annual report,	A	4	60
1850.	Report in relation to expenses of banking department,	A	5	85
1850.	Report in relation to erroneous payment of taxes,	A	5	120
1850.	Report relative to finance,	A	5	132
1850.	Majority report in answer to report of,	A	8	189
1850.	Minority report in answer to report of,	A	8	196
	PHILO C. FULLER:			
1851.	Report in answer to a resolution relative to Union College,	S	2	26
1851.	Report relative to counsel fees paid by the state,	S	2	33
1851.	Report in relation to the general fund,	S	2	48
1851.	Report on expenses for printing, binding, engraving, &c.,	S	2	56
1851.	Communication from,	S	3	83
1851.	Report in relation to the state finances,	S	3	91
1851.	Annual report,	A	1	9
1851.	Communication from, as to additional appropriation for expenses of government,	A	1	17
1851.	Report in relation to incorporated banks and other corporations,	A	3	87
1851.	Report in relation to destruction of bank notes,	A	5	136
	JOHN C. WRIGHT:			
1852.	Report of, relative to printing Documentary History,	S	1	5
1852.	Report of, relative to expenses of government,	S	1	31
1852.	Compensation paid clerks and other officers of legislature of 1851,	S	1	42
1852.	Report in relation to general fund state debt,	S	2	68
1852.	Minority report relative to the,	S	2	77
1852.	Report in regard to amount of state debt 1st of June, 1846,	S	2	87
1852.	Annual report of,	A	1	10
1852.	Report respecting receipts into the general fund and time of holding tax sale,	A	5	103
1852.	Report respecting unsold lands,	A	5	105
1852.	Report in answer to resolutions respecting his refusing to refund to the clerk amount advanced by him for postage stamps, &c.,	A	5	124
1852.	Report of commissioners appointed by, to inquire into and ascertain amount of unclaimed deposits and dividends,	A	7	127
1853.	Reply of, in answer to resolution of senate, January 17, 1853, in relation to the expenses of the Colonial History, &c.,	S	1	24
1853.	Reply of, in answer to resolution of senate in relation to clerks in his office,	S	2	36
1853.	Report of, in relation to unpaid taxes from certain counties,	S	2	49
1853.	Report of, on the resolution of the senate in relation to pay, &c., of officers and soldiers of the war of 1812,	S	2	52
1853.	Reply of. in answer to a resolution as to the expenses of state government, &c.,	S	2	76
1853.	Report of, relative to expenses of government,	S	3	76
1853.	Report of, in relation to unpaid taxes from certain counties,	S	3	78
1853.	Annual report of,	A	1	5
1853.	Report of, showing the state indebtedness from 1835 to 1852, and the number and amount of warrants, &c.,	A	2	24
1853.	Report of, in answer to a resolution of the assembly in relation to the amount of taxes due the treasury on land sold in December, 1852,	A	2	25
1853.	Report of, in reply to a resolution of W. W. Burroughs in relation to the time when the state tax would be available for the improvement of the canals,	A	3	61
1853.	Report of, in reply to a resolution of W. W. Burroughs in relation to the time when the state tax would be available for the improvement of the canals,	A	5	114
1853.	Communication from, in relation to the exhaustion of the annual appropriation of $75,000 for pay of members and officers of legislature,	A	5	128

COMPTROLLER—*continued.*

		Doc.	Vol.	No.
	JAMES M. COOK:			
1854.	Communication from, relative to moneys paid lieutenant-governor,	S	2	81
1854.	Communication relative to mileage,	S	2	93
1854.	Communication under resolution,	S	2	103
1854.	Annual report of,	A	1	5
1854.	Communication from, relative to stationery,	A	1	9
1854.	Communication from, relative to fire insurance companies,	A	3	95
1854.	Communication from, relative to non-resident lands,	A	3	101
1855.	Annual report of,	A	1	4
1855.	Report of condition of insurance companies,	A	4	115
	LORENZO BURROWS:			
1856.	Report of, relative to aid to colleges since 1840,	S	1	32
1856.	Report of, relative to Western House of Refuge,	S	2	54
1856.	Report of, in answer to a resolution,	S	2	84
1856.	Report in answer to resolutions relative to cost of printing,	A	3	33
1856.	Annual report of,	A	1	7
1857.	Report of, relative to moneys paid soldiers of 1812,	S	2	81
1857.	Annual report of the,	A	1	10
1857.	Report of, in reply to resolution relative to sales of Indian lands,	A	1	12
1857.	Report of, in reply to resolution relative to cost of Colonial and Documentary Histories,	A	2	81
1857.	Annual report of, on the condition of the several fire insurance companies doing business in this state,	A	2	135
	SANFORD E. CHURCH:			
1858.	Communication from, in reference to money paid judges in addition to their salaries,	S	2	51
1858.	Communication from, and attorney-general, relative to suit of Munson I. Lockwood,	S	2	85
1858.	Report of, relative to assessment laws,	S	2	95
1858.	Communication from, relative to assessment and taxation,	S	3	103
1858.	Report of, relative to the condition of the life insurance companies in this state,	S	3	131
1858.	Annual report of,	A	1	5
1858.	Communication from, relative to unpaid taxes due to the state from treasurer of Livingston county,	A	3	53
1858.	Report of, relative to the unpaid appropriations of last year,	A	4	91
1858.	Report of, relative to insurance companies,	A	4	100

COMPTROLLER'S OFFICE, BANKING DEPARTMENT OF, *see* Banking Department.

COMSTOCK, GEORGE F.

1850.	Answer to resolution of assembly,	A	5	96

COMSTOCK, RUSSELL.

1850.	Agricultural discoveries of,	A	3	23

CONCILIATION COURTS.

1847.	Memorial of Steen Bille relative to,	S	3	98

CONCORD, TOWN OF.

1831.	First Congregational Society, report on petition to sell real estate,	A	4	343
1833.	Report on petition to change the manner of voting for town officers. in,	A	4	251

CONESUS LAKE.

1850.	Report of canal board, relative to,	S	1	40

CONESUS OUTLET.

		Doc.	Vol.	No.
1838.	Feeder from, to the Genesee Valley canal, report in relation to,..	A	2	30

CONEWANGO CANAL, *see* Canals.

CONGRESS.

		Doc.	Vol.	No.
1842.	Resolutions of Georgia relative to provision of 27th at the extra session,	A	4	58
	MEMBERS OF LEGISLATURE ELECTED TO:			
1849.	Report of majority of judiciary committee on the subject of,.....	S	2	48
1849.	Report of minority on same,	S	2	49
	REPRESENTATIVES IN:			
1832.	Report relative to altering the time for electing,	S	2	105
1836.	Report relative to special elections for,....	A	2	77
1840.	Appointment to office of, resolution relative to the,	S	1	3
1840.	do do report on the subject,	S	1	29
1841.	do do resolution relative to the,	S	1	5
1842.	[Ex. Sess.] Act of, for the apportionment of representatives, &c.,	A	7	195
1842.	[Ex. Sess.] Resolutions protesting against action of congress on the subject of apportioning representatives, &c.,	A	7	196
	SENATOR IN:			
1839.	Report on bill and resolution of the assembly relative to the appointment of,	S	3	77
1839.	Report on the resolution of the senate relative to,	A	5	272
1839.	Report on bill to provide for the election of,	A	6	404
1845.	Communication from governor relative to,	A	1	8

CONGRESSIONAL DISTRICTS, *see* Apportionment.

		Doc.	Vol.	No.
1832.	Arrangement of, message from the governor relative to the,.....	A	4	330
1832.	Arrangement of, report of select committee,	A	4	336
1842.	Report on the organization of,	S	4	107
1842.	Report of the committee of conference on bill relative to,	S	4	109
1842.	[Ex. Sess.] Act to divide the state into congressional districts, report by the majority of select committee of sixteen,	A	7	196
1842.	[Ex. Sess.] Act for the same, report by the minority,	A	7	197
1842.	[Ex. Sess.] Report on senate bill to divide the state into,	A	7	198
1851.	Report of select committee on,	A	6	151
1851.	Minority report,	A	6	152, 153

CONGRESSIONAL DOCUMENTS.

		Doc.	Vol.	No.
1843.	Report of committee on colleges, academies and common schools, on a communication from secretary of state relative to,	A	2	31
1845.	Report of secretary of state relative to certain, in his office, &c.,..	S	2	71

CONHOCTON RIVER.

		Doc.	Vol.	No.
1834.	Dam across, report on petition of John Cooper, Jr., to build a,...	A	4	286

CONKLIN, VINCENT.

		Doc.	Vol.	No.
1834.	Report on petition of, for a lease of surplus water of the Chemung canal,	S	2	78
1835.	Report on petition of, for a lease of surplus water of the Chemung canal,	A	2	91

CONNECTICUT, STATE OF.

		Doc.	Vol.	No.
1831.	Resolution of the legislature of, relative to the election of president, &c.,	A	1	4

CONNECTICUT, STATE OF—*continued.*

		Doc.	Vol.	No.
1832.	Resolution of the legislature of, relative to the United States judicial department, &c.,	A	1	3
1834.	Resolution of the legislature of, relative to the tariff laws,	A	1	11
1839.	Resolution of the legislature of, relative to the public lands,	A	2	18
1839.	Resolution of the legislature of, relative to the increase of the executive patronage of the general government,	A	2	24
1841.	Resolution of the legislature of, relative to the protection of domestic industry,	A	1	14
1841.	Resolution of the legislature of, relative to the distribution of the proceeds of the public lands,	A	2	24
1834.	School fund, report relative to taxing debts due the,	A	3	137
1834.	School fund, report of committee on the judiciary,	A	3	148
1842.	Resolution of general assembly of, relative to tariff,	A	2	26
1842.	Resolution of general assembly of, relative to presidential term,	A	2	28
1843.	Resolution relative to the public lands, tariff, West Point Academy, transmitted by governor,	A	1	11
1844.	Communication from the governor transmitting resolution of legislature of, in relation to French spoliations, the military academy and the tariff,	A	1	7
1844.	Communication from the governor transferring resolution of legislature of, in relation to the franking privilege, &c.,	A	1	14
1851.	Report relative to boundary between, and New York,	S	4	165
1858.	Report of special committee on communication of commissioners to ascertain the boundary line between New York and,	A	4	132

CONRAD, I., AND I. MOORE.

		Doc.	Vol.	No.
1832.	Commissioners of highways of the town of Lansing report on petition of,	A	3	191

CONRO AND GREEN.

		Doc.	Vol.	No.
1857.	Report of committee on state prisons favorable on petition of, for payment for castings furnished Clinton state prison,	A	3	169

CONSIGNEES, AGENTS AND FACTORS.

		Doc.	Vol.	No.
1830.	Memorial of merchants of New York for a law to prevent abuses in the disposition of goods in the hands of,	S	1	46
1830.	Report of committee on the judiciary,	S	1	55
1830.	Remonstrance of merchants of Albany against the bill concerning,	S	2	105

CONSTABLES' FEES.

		Doc.	Vol.	No.
1836.	Report relative to, for serving subpœnas in criminal cases,	A	3	181
1838.	Report on petition to increase the,	A	5	220

CONSTITUTION OF 1821.

AMENDMENTS:

		Doc.	Vol.	No.
1842.	Report on proposed, in 1841,	A	5	120
1844.	Resolutions proposing,	S	1	11
1844.	do	S	1	13
1844.	do	S	1	15
1844.	do	S	1	16
1844.	do	S	1	17
1844.	do	S	1	22
1844.	do	S	1	29
1844.	Proposed, when in committee of the whole,	S	2	63
1844.	Proposed, by the committee on the judiciary,	S	2	90
1844.	Proposed, by Mr. Lester,	S	3	104
1844.	Report of the select committee on so much of governor's message as relates to,	A	6	150

CONSTITUTION OF 1821—*continued.*

		Doc.	Vol.	No.
1844.	Report of committees of conference on the proposed, ...	A	7	166
1844.	Report of committees of conference on the proposed, ...	A	7	178
1845.	Report of secretary of state relative to proposed, ...	A	1	7
1845.	Resolution of Mr. Worden relative to, ...	A	1	24
1845.	Report of select committee on, ...	A	3	43
	CANAL REVENUES:			
1832.	Resolution to amend the law relating to, ...	S	2	70
1832.	do do do	S	2	100
1834.	do do do	A	3	131
1835.	do do do	S	2	35
1836.	do do do	S	1	48
	COURTS:			
1844.	Amendments proposed by Le Grande Marvin relative to, ...	S	1	36
	ELECTORS:			
1837.	Resolutions to amend, so as to allow them to vote for president and vice-president, and for governor and lieutenant-governor, in any town or ward provided such elector is prevented by business from voting where he resides, ...	A	2	120
	GOVERNOR:			
1842.	Resolutions proposing to amend, as to qualifications for, ...	A	1	5
	MAYOR OF NEW YORK:			
1830.	Resolution to amend, so as to make him elective, ...	A	2	96
1833.	Report of secretary of state relative to the publication of the amendments to, relating to, ...	S	1	14
1833.	Report of the judiciary committee, on the report of the secretary of state, ...	S	1	45
	MAYORS:			
1836.	Resolution to amend, so as to make them elective, ...	A	2	75
1837.	Resolution to amend, so as to make them elective, ...	A	2	148
1838.	Communication from the secretary of state relative to the publication of said amendments, ...	A	2	28
1838.	Report of the committee on the judiciary on the report of the secretary of state, ...	A	3	110
1839.	Report of committee on the judiciary on the amendment, ...	A	3	96
1835.	Meeting of the legislature, resolution to amend, relative to the time of, ...	A	1	61
	SALT AND AUCTION DUTIES:			
1832.	To be applied to defraying the expenses of the government, resolution for the same, ...	S	2	70
1832.	To be applied to defraying the expenses of the government, resolution for the same, ...	S	3	100
1833.	Report of secretary of state relative to the publication of said amendments, ...	S	1	14
	SALT DUTIES:			
1831.	Resolution for the reduction of the, ...	S	1	67
1831.	Resolution for the reduction of the, ...	A	4	294
1833.	Report of secretary of state relative to the publication of said amendments, ...	S	1	14
1833.	Report of committee on judiciary on the same, ...	S	2	45
1834.	Resolution to restore the, to the general fund, ...	A	3	131
1835.	Report of the secretary of state relative to the publication of said amendments, ...	A	1	42
1835.	Report of committee on the judiciary on the same, ...	A	1	49
1835.	Resolution and recital on the same, ...	A	1	59

CONSTITUTION OF 1821—*continued.*

		Doc.	Vol.	No.
	STATE DEBT AND LIABILITY:			
1843.	Memorial of Herkimer county delegates asking for an amendment relative to the creation of,	A	4	90
1843.	Report of majority of select committee on same,	A	5	152
1843.	Minority report on same,	A	5	153
1844.	Report on so much of governor's message as relates to amendments to, &c.,	A	6	150

CONSTITUTION OF 1846.

		Doc.	Vol.	No.
1848.	Document containing,	A	1	7
1849.	Document containing, with index,	A	1	7
1858.	Opinion of attorney-general respecting a certain provision of,	A	1	22
1847.	Article three, section fifteen, report relative to,	S	1	15
1853.	Article seven, section three, report of select committee relative to,	S	2	42
1853.	Minority report on same subject,	S	2	46
1853.	Canals, majority and minority report of committee on, an amendment of, relative to completing,	A	4	98
1853.	Canals, majority and minority report of committee on, on the amendment of, relative to completing,	A	4	99
1857.	Court of appeals, report of committee on the judiciary on amending, relative to,	A	4	45
1853.	Elective franchise, report of the judiciary committee on the reference of the resolutions to amend relative to,	A	3	60
1847.	Index to,	S	1	16
1847.	Manufacturing corporations, report on so much as relative to,	S	2	53
1853.	New York Chamber of Commerce, memorial of,	A	4	100
1847.	Publishing, report of money paid for, by comptroller,	A	6	157
1847.	Publishing, report of list of papers,	A	4	126

CONSTITUTIONAL CONVENTION OF 1846.

		Doc.	Vol.	No.
1845.	Report of select committee on the bill from the assembly recommending,	S	3	107
1845.	Minority report of the same committee,	S	3	108
1845.	Report of select committee on the bill for,	A	6	211
1845.	Report of Mr. Comstock and others, on bill for,	A	6	231
1846.	Report of attorney-general in reply to a resolution relative to apportionment of members of,	A	4	122
1846.	Opinion of supreme court on apportionment of members of,	A	5	181

CONSTITUTIONAL REFORM.

		Doc.	Vol.	No.
1846.	Communication from governor transmitting proceedings of a public meeting in relation to,	A	1	32

CONSTITUTION OF THE UNITED STATES, *see* United States Constitution.

CONSUL OF THE UNITED STATES AT PARIS.

		Doc.	Vol.	No.
1843.	Communication from, transmitted by governor,	A	4	119

CONTRACT, DEBTS ON.

		Doc.	Vol.	No.
1842.	Report of the judiciary committee on the petition for repeal of laws for compulsory enforcement of,	A	7	178

CONTRACTS ON PERSONAL SECURITY.

		Doc.	Vol.	No.
1850.	Report on act in relation to,	S	1	30

CONTRIBUTIONS.

		Doc.	Vol.	No.
1833.	Of forwarding merchants on the Erie canal, report on petition of farmers and others of Western New York, in relation to,	A	4	320

CONVENTION OF THE STATES.

		Doc.	Vol.	No.
1833.	Resolution of the legislature of Georgia for a call for,........	A	2	39
1833.	do do South Carolina for a call for,....	A	2	39
1833.	do do Delaware against,..............	A	2	135
1833.	do do Ohio against, ...	A	3	139
1833.	do do Massachusetts against,.........	A	4	291
1833.	do do Mississippi against,...........	A	4	129
1833.	do do Alabama against,..............	A	4	244

CONVENTION, STATE.

1833.	At Poughkeepsie, in 1798, for the purpose of adopting the Constitution of United States, proceedings of, ...	A	1	11

CONVENTS, NUNNERIES, &c.

1838.	Report concerning,....................................	A	6	362

CONVICTIONS FOR CRIMINAL OFFENSES, *see* Criminal Offenses.

CONVICTS, *see* State Prisons.

COOK, ALLEN.

1858.	Report on claim of,....................................	S	2	65

COOK, C.

1854.	Report on petition of,...	A	3	115

COOK, J. J, AND J. T.

1844.	Report of canal commissioners on petition of,................	A	3	99

COOK, REBECCA.

1834.	Report on petition for certain relief,.........................	S	1	49

COOK, BATES, AND OTHERS.

	Report on petition relative to certain land in Lewiston,.........	A	1	28
1834.	do do do	A	1	49
1834.	do do do	A	4	281
1835.	do do do	A	3	228

COOL, KEYES P. AND HYMEN J.

1837.	Report on petition for compensation for damages on account of the loss of a boat on the Glens Falls feeder,.................	A	2	111

COOLEY, FITCH AND HUNT.

1855.	Memorial of,..	A	2	44
1855.	Report of select committee on bill for payment of judgment in favor of,.......................................	S	2	52, 54

COOPER, JOHN, Jr.

1834.	Report on petition to build a dam across Conhocton river,......	A	4	286

COPELAND, JOHN.

1849.	Report of committee on claims on petition of,.................	A	3	105

CORNELIUS, RACHEL, AND OTHERS.

1853.	Report of committee on Indian affairs on claim of, for relief,....	A	3	80

CORNELL, DANIEL, AND RANSON CLARK.

		Doc.	Vol.	No.
1849.	Report of committee on claims on petition of,.............. A	287	3	158
1850.	Report on claim of,..	S	3	110
1850.	Report of select committee on bill for relief of,................	A	3	26
1852.	Report on petition of,..	S	1	14

CORNELL, NATHAN.

1831.	Report on petition for interest on certain money,................	A	3	228

CORNELL, PERRY.

1841.	Report on petition for compensation for damages to property on his boat while passing one of the locks on the Erie canal,.....	A	4	135

CORNEY, PATRICK.

1846.	Report of committee on petition for relief of,...................	S	2	45

CORNWALL, AUGUSTUS.

1852.	Report on petition for relief,..................................	A	5	113

CORPORATIONS.

1832.	Assessment of taxes on, report of attorney-general relative to the,	S	2	103
1839.	Assessment of taxes on, report of attorney-general relative to the,	S	1	9
1833.	Exemption of real estate of, from taxation, report relative to the,	S	1	33
1833.	Charters, attorney-general's report on the subject of repealing by a two-thirds or a majority vote,.........................	S	1	8
1832.	Power of the legislature over, report of the attorney-general relative to the,..	S	1	8
1835.	Creation of, report of attorney-general on several questions relative to the,..	S	1	4
1838.	Abstract of returns of, in the comptroller's office for 1837,......	A	3	146
1835.	Capital stock of all the, liable to taxation, report of the,........	S	2	40
1837.	Power of the legislature to create or authorize, by one law, more than one corporation, report of attorney-general,............	A	4	303
1839.	Report of committee on the judiciary on the same,..............	A	5	277
1840.	Remonstrance against entrusting the taxes collected from the people to the custody of,..............................	A	8	362
1844.	Report of comptroller showing real estate, capital stock, &c., of,	A	3	98
1857.	Standing committee on finance, report relative to taxes on incorporated companies,..................................	S	2	55

CHARITABLE AND RELIGIOUS:

1836.	Report on bill concerning,......................................	A	3	111

MANUFACTURING:

1835.	Report of attorney-general on the bill to extend the provisions of the act of 1817, to the counties of Orange and Sullivan,......	S	1	4
1838.	Report of the committee on trade and manufactures on the bill to amend an act relative to,..............................	A	5	275
1838.	Report of majority of the committee on the judiciary on the same,	A	5	277
1837.	Revision of the laws relative to, report of the committee on manufactures recommending a,..............................	S	1	29
1835.	Taxation of, report on petition to amend the law relative to,....	A	3	212
1837.	Taxation of, exemption from, and from individual responsibility to their creditors, report on petition to repeal the laws,.......	A	3	182
1835.	Oppressive practices of, report on petition for relief from certain,	A	3	205
1836.	Education of children in, report on the expediency of providing by law for the proper education and government of,........	A	4	233
1845.	Report of attorney-general on the assembly bill to amend the act relative to, passed March 22, 1811,....................	S	2	59

	CORPORATIONS—*continued.*	Doc.	Vol.	No.
1846.	Report of committee on manufactures on petitions for incorporation of,	S	1	13
1846.	Report of committee on manufactures on petition of Seth C. Jones and others, for the same,	S	2	65
1847.	Report relative to,	S	2	53
1847.	Report relative to,	S	4	116
1847.	Report of committee of conference on bill for,	A	8	240
	MECHANICAL:			
1847.	Report on bill incorporating,	S	4	143
	CORRUPTION.			
1858.	Report of committee to investigate charges of,	A	4	114
	CORSS, GENERAL, AND OTHERS.			
1839.	Report on claim of, for services of certain field officers, called out to defend the northern frontier, &c.,	A	6	394
	CORTLAND COUNTY.			
1837.	Court of, report on petition to alter the time for holding,	A	1	14
1837.	Jail in, report on petition to raise money to build a,	A	1	49
1838.	Report on petition for a loan to complete the,	A	3	83
1839.	Report on petition for a loan to complete the,	A	2	52
1836.	Grand and petit jurors of, report on petition to authorize them to make their own certificates of attendance,	A	4	239
1848.	Report of comptroller as to taxes unpaid in,	A	5	136
	CORTLAND VILLAGE.			
1831.	Supreme court commissioner, report on bill to authorize the appointment of a,	A	1	44
	CORWIN, GERSHAM.			
1835.	Report on petition to sell certain land, &c.,	A	4	346
	CORYELL, C. AND W.			
1842.	Report on the petition of,	A	5	83
	CORYWELL, GEORGE.			
1835.	Report on petition for compensation for damages by the Chemung canal,	A	2	89
	COST, ELIAS.			
1847.	Report as to claim of,	S	2	57
	COSTS.			
1832.	Liability of the state for certain, under the excise law,	S	2	82
1840.	In cases of assault and battery, report on petition for a law requiring security for,	A	4	129
	For the foreclosure of mortgages, *see* Mortgages.			
	COTTON, GEORGE H., *see* W. Gibbs and others.			
	COTTON, HENRY G.			
1837.	Report on petition to confirm his official acts as a supreme court commissioner,	A	2	141

COULSON, NICHOLAS L.

		Doc.	Vol.	No.
1857.	Report of committee on state prisons favorable on petition of, for an appropriation,......	A	2	86

COUNSEL FEES.

1851.	Report of comptroller relative to, paid by the state,......	S	2	33

COUNTIES, NEW.

1839.	Report of attorney-general in relation to the erection of, from contiguous territory in different senate districts,......	A	4	227
1843.	Report of the committee on, relative to amending title five, part one, of the Revised Statutes, &c.,......	A	5	146
1843.	Minority report on same,......	A	5	164
1850.	Report of attorney-general on the division, alteration and erection of towns and counties,......	A	5	82

COUNTRYMAN, THOMAS.

1851.	Report on petition for canal damages,......	S	2	46
1852	Report on petition of, for relief,......	S	1	12
1856.	Report of committee on claims on petition of, for relief,......	S	1	34

COUNTY ACCOUNTS AND ABUSES.

1846.	Report of Mr. Barlow, from a select committee on a communication in relation to,......	S	3	76

COUNTY CHARGES.

1839.	Report of secretary of state in relation to,......	A	4	183

COUNTY CLERKS.

1845.	Report of secretary of state of the names of, who have not filed in his office a statement of their fees, &c., according to law,...	S	2	76
1847.	Report relative to fees of,......	S	2	58
1847.	Report of, in answer to a resolution,......	S	2	80
1847.	Petition of members of the New York Bar for reform in mode of payment of fees to,......	A	7	192
1849.	Report of secretary of state of the amount of fees of,......	S	3	77
1850.	List of, who have reported,......	A	6	152
1852.	Report of secretary of state respecting fees of,......	A	5	118

COUNTY COURTS.

1849.	Petition of E. F. Bullard and others, for restoration of jurisdiction of,......	A	3	142

COUNTY EXPENSES.

1847.	Report on petitions relative to town and,......	S	3	103

COUNTY JUDGES.

1833.	Report on petition to confer equity powers on, in causes upon sums less than $100,......	A	4	323
1837.	Report on bill authorizing them to inspect turnpikes, and to fix the location of gates on,......	S	2	67
1848.	Report of committee on roads and bridges as to powers of, to locate gates,......	A	5	134

COUNTY OFFICERS.

1837.	Report on petition to repeal the law associating county judges with supervisors in the appointment of,......	A	2	47

COUNTY POOR-HOUSES.

		Doc.	Vol.	No.
1838.	Abuses in, report concerning,	A	6	310
1838.	Abuses in, report concerning,	A	6	265
1840.	Poor-house system, report on petition to abolish the,	A	6	267
1841.	do do do	A	7	265
1831.	do do the subject, (Mr. Potter,)	A	4	305
1839.	Poor, report on petition to revive the distinction between town and county poor,	A	5	299
1832.	Report relative to the accounts of certain officers for supporting,	A	1	12
1832.	Report relative to the accounts of certain officers for supporting,	A	3	118

COUNTY PRISONS.

		Doc.	Vol.	No.
1835.	Report of select committee on altering the law relative to,	A	5	390
1847.	Report of committee on state prisons for regulation of state and,	A	8	241

COUNTY TREASURERS.

		Doc.	Vol.	No.
1830.	Balances due from comptroller's report relative to,	A	1	37
1838.	Compensation of, report relative to altering the law relative to,	A	3	130
1849.	Report of clerk of court of appeals relative to funds deposited with,	S	3	85

COURT OF APPEALS.

		Doc.	Vol.	No.
1849.	Report of clerk of, relative to progress made in execution of the provisions of the act respecting funds and securities in possession of, &c.,	A	3	110
1849.	Report of clerk of, in relation to funds and securities in his possession,	S	2	43
1849.	Report of clerk of, as to paying into state treasury the sum of $35,181.50,	S	2	44
1849.	Report of clerk relative to funds deposited with county treasurers,	S	3	85
1850.	Report of,	A	5	96
1855.	Report of clerk of, in answer to a resolution,	S	1	13
1857.	Report of judiciary committee on amending the constitution relative to,	A	1	45
1857.	Communication from the judges of, &c.,	A	1	45
1858.	Report of clerk of, in answer to a resolution of the senate,	S	2	36

COURT OF CHANCERY, *see* Chancery.

COURT OF ERRORS.

		Doc.	Vol.	No.
1835.	Report as to certain expenses of the,	A	2	125
1849.	Report of select committee on,	S	1	4
1847.	Report of select committee as to continuance of,	S	1	8
1847.	Report on continuance of,	S	1	9
1847.	Opinion of lieutenant-governor as to continuance of,	S	1	20

COURTS, ASSEMBLY DISTRICT.

		Doc.	Vol.	No.
1858.	Report on bill to establish,	A	4	110

COURTS OF JUSTICE.

		Doc.	Vol.	No.
1858.	Report of committee as to causes of delays in, of this state,	A	1	45

COURTS OF THE UNITED STATES, *see* United States Courts.

COURTS MARTIAL.

		Doc.	Vol.	No.
1839.	Report on petition to amend the law relative to,	A	6	398
1840.	In New York, report of amount of moneys received, &c.,	S	3	88

COURTS MARTIAL—*continued.*

		Doc.	Vol.	No.
1840.	Report on petition to amend the law, &c.,	S	4	108
1843.	Report of committee on the militia relative to abolishing brigade,	S	3	74

COVELL, LYMAN, *see* John Arnott.

COWASSELON AND NEW STOCKBRIDGE LANDS.

1830.	Report on petition of settlers on, for relief,	S	2	163

COWASSELON TRACT OF LAND.

1831.	Report of comptroller on petition of settlers on,	A	3	260
1831.	Report of committee on public lands, same,	A	4	336

COWEN, ESEK.

1832.	Report of amount of fees received by him as circuit judge,	A	2	147

COWEN, JUDGE.

1844.	Arrangements at funeral of,	S	2	54

COXE'S PATENT AT OSWEGO.

1830.	Report relative to the claim of the state to a portion of,	S	3	245

COX, J. & T.

1840.	Report on petition for compensation for damages to their mills by the erection of an aqueduct on the Genesee Valley canal,	A	3	100

COX, JAMES ISAAC.

1842.	Tupper, Mrs., report on petition of,	A	5	125
1842.	Report of committee on claims on petition of,	A	5	128

CRABB, ALANSING.

1833.	Report on petition to change his name,	A	3	230

CRABB, ISAAC.

1835.	Report on petition to change his name,	A	1	32

CRABTREE, W.

1834.	Memorial of, in relation to a state prison for female convicts,	S	2	86

CRAIN, PHILLIP.

1840.	Report on petition for a compensation for damages to his lands by the construction of the Chenango canal,	A	6	222

CRAMER, GEORGE, AND JAMES T. HAMILTON.

1857.	Report of committee on claims, favorable on petition of, for damages by diversion of water,	A	3	153

CRAMER, WILLIAM.

1847.	Report on petition of,	A	1	45

CRANDALL, CLARK.

1850.	Report on petition of,	A	6	148
1852.	Report on petition of, for relief,	A	5	106

CRANDALL, HENRY.

		Doc.	Vol.	No.
1849.	Report of committee on canals, on petition of,	A	3	150

CRANDALL, JUSTIN, AND OTHERS.

		Doc.	Vol.	No.
1847.	Report on petition of,	A	2	92

CRANDALL, LOUISA.

		Doc.	Vol.	No.
1836.	Report on petition for a divorce,	A	4	328

CRANE, SIMEON, AND OTHERS.

		Doc.	Vol.	No.
1833.	Report on petition for a loan to aid them in the discovery of salt in Delaware county,	A	4	276
1834.	Report of committee on the manufacture of salt,	A	1	45
1834.	Report of comptroller on the manufacture of salt,	A	2	104
1834.	Report of select committee on the manufacture of salt,	A	3	146

CRAVATH, EZEKIEL.

		Doc.	Vol.	No.
1831.	Report on petition for damages by the construction of a road in Genesee county,	A	1	25

CREDITORS OF THE STATE.

		Doc.	Vol.	No.
1858.	Report on bill for the relief of,	S	2	33

CRIMINAL CASES.

		Doc.	Vol.	No.
1848.	Report as to fees of witnesses in,	A	3	95

CRIMINAL COURT BILL.

		Doc.	Vol.	No.
1842.	Message from the governor returning the,	S	4	90

CRIMINAL LAW.

		Doc.	Vol.	No.
1838.	Digest of, report on petition of Dominick T. Blake for the purchase by the state of copies of his,	A	5	206

CRIMINAL OFFENSES, CONVICTIONS FOR.

		Doc.	Vol.	No.
1838.	Report of secretary of state giving abstracts of,	S	2	65
1839.	do do do do	S	2	35
1840.	do do do do	S	3	120
1841.	do do do do	S	3	67
1842.	Report of secretary of state relative to, &c.,	S	3	51
1843.	Annual report of secretary of state of abstracts of, and of return of sheriffs' reports of persons convicted,	A	4	110
1844.	Report of secretary of state of abstracts of,	S	2	92
1845.	Report of abstracts of, &c.,	S	2	54
1846.	Report of abstracts of, &c.,	S	3	98

CRIMINAL PROCEDURE, *see* Code of Criminal Procedure.

CRIMINALS, APPREHENSION OF.

		Doc.	Vol.	No.
1831.	Comptroller's report of items of charges for the, for the last two years,	A	4	339

CRIMINAL STATISTICS.

		Doc.	Vol.	No.
1847.	Report as to,	A	7	180
1848.	Report of secretary of state concerning,	A	6	193
1849.	Report of secretary of state respecting,	A	5	242
1850.	Annual report of, by secretary of state,	A	8	195

CRIMINAL STATISTICS—*continued.*

		Doc.	Vol.	No.
1851.	Annual report of secretary of state on,	A	5	140
1852.	Report of secretary of state relative to,	S	3	97
1853.	Report of secretary of state on,	S	3	77
1855.	Report of, by secretary of state,	S	3	79
1857.	Report relative to,	S	4	130
1858.	Annual report of secretary of state on,	A	6	168

CROOKED LAKE.

1835.	Outlet of, report on petition of owners of hydraulic works on the,	A	4	369
1855.	Report of state engineer and surveyor respecting improvement of,	A	5	117

CROOKED LAKE CANAL, *see* Canals.

CROSBY, EPENETUS.

1846.	Report of majority of committee on privileges and elections, relative to his claim to seat occupied by G. T. Peirce, from Dutchess county,	A	2	45
1846.	Report of minority committee on the same,	A	2	46

CROSS, JOSEPH R.

1847.	Report on petition of,	A	7	224

CROSSITT, W. L.

1836.	Canal contractors on the Chenango canal, report on petition for relief of,	A	4	317
1837.	Report of select committee on petition for relief of,	A	4	315
1837.	Report of canal commissioners on petition for relief of,	A	4	317
1838.	Report of committee on claims on petition for relief of,	A	4	177

CROSSITT, W. L., *see* John I. De Graff and others.

CROTON AQUEDUCT, *see* New York.

CROUSE, HENRY.

1851.	Report of committee on petition for canal damages,	A	2	38

CROW, T. J.

1832.	Report on petition to change his name,	A	2	129

CROWS, BOUNTY ON.

1830.	Report on petition for a,	A	5	222

CULVER, OLIVER.

1836.	Report on petition for compensation for damages by the Erie canal,	A	4	268
1841.	Report on petition for compensation for damages by the Erie canal,	A	4	163

CUNNINGHAM, JAMES, AND OTHERS.

1853.	Report of committee on claims on petition of,	A	2	45

CURRAN, JOHN W.

1851.	Report on petition of, for damages sustained in consequence of falling through canal bridge,	S	2	31

CURRENCY.

Year	Subject	Doc.	Vol.	No.
1843.	Communication from governor transmitting memorial of inhabitants of Oswego county on the subject of,	A	5	174

CURTIS, JUNIA.

Year	Subject	Doc.	Vol.	No.
1830.	Report on petition for pay for building new pump works at Salina,	A	3	271
1831.	Report on petition for pay for building new pump works at Salina,	A	4	320

CUYLER, WILLIAM T.

Year	Subject	Doc.	Vol.	No.
1858.	Report on claim of,	A	1	19

CYPRESS HILL AND WILLIAMSBURGH PLANKROAD COMPANY.

Year	Subject	Doc.	Vol.	No.
1854.	Petition for increase of stock,	S	1	14

CYPRESS HILL CEMETERY.

Year	Subject	Doc.	Vol.	No.
1850.	Report on petition of,	S	1	25
1850.	Report on petition of,	S	1	31

D.

DAILY, ABSALOM, AND HENRY FULLER.

Year	Subject	Doc.	Vol.	No.
1830.	Report on petition for compensation for damages to their lands,	A	4	357

DANA, AMASA, AND OTHERS.

Year	Subject	Doc.	Vol.	No.
1833.	Report on petition to construct and maintain a dam across Tioga river,	A	2	82

DANA, J., AND OTHERS.

Year	Subject	Doc.	Vol.	No.
1845.	Report of committee on grievances, on petition of,	A	3	77

DANSVILLE.

Year	Subject	Doc.	Vol.	No.
1839.	Report relative to a branch canal or side-cut from, to the Genesee Valley canal,	A	5	296
1834.	Report on petition for the division of,	A	2	35

DARBY, PLYNN.

Year	Subject	Doc.	Vol.	No.
1835.	Report on petition for extra allowance for work done on the Champlain canal, and for relief on account of the loss of his eyesight while blasting rocks,	A	2	118
1835.	Report of committee on grievances,	A	3	227
1837.	Report of committee on claims,	A	3	214
1838.	Report of canal board,	A	4	193
1839.	Report of committee on grievances,	A	5	293

DARIEN & PEMBROKE.

Year	Subject	Doc.	Vol.	No.
1838.	Report on petition for a classical school in,	A	1	118

D'AUTREMONT, LOUIS PAUL.

Year	Subject	Doc.	Vol.	No.
1833.	Report on petition to build a dam across the Genesee river,	S	2	58

DAVENPORT, TOWN OF.

Year	Subject	Doc.	Vol.	No.
1836.	Report on petition from, relative to taking fish in the Charlotte river,	A	6	340

DAVENPORT, TOWN OF,—*continued.*

		Doc.	Vol.	No.
1840.	Report of surveyor-general relative to the boundaries of, and Oneonta, ...	A	4	107
1840.	Report of surveyor-general relative to the boundaries of, and Oneonta, ...	A	4	124
1840.	Report of committee on towns and counties relative to the boundaries of, and Oneonta, ...	A	5	184

DAVIDSON, G. M., *see* Chancery, Clerks in.

DAVIDSON, J. M., *see* Chancery, Register in.

DAVIS, JONATHAN.

1849.	Report of committee on public lands, on petition of, ...	A	2	41
1849.	Report of comptroller in answer to a resolution of assembly, on bill to remunerate, for losses from failure of title to certain lands, ...	A	2	98

DAVIS, SOLOMON.

1835.	Report on petition for the conveyance to him of lot No. 31, in the "Two Mile tract,"	A	2	133

DAY, TOWN OF.

1849.	Report of attorney-general relative to bridge in, ...	A	3	181

DAYTON, JOHN A.

1858.	Report of committee appointed to investigate charges made by,..	A	4	115

DAYTON, JOHN H.

1845.	Report of committee on privileges, &c., on the case of, ...	A	1	12
1845.	Report of majority of committee on the judiciary, ...	A	1	19
1845.	Report of minority of committee on the judiciary, ...	A	1	20

DEAD, REMAINS OF THE.

1836.	Report on petition for a law to prevent the removal of, except in certain cases, ...	S	2	97

DEAF AND DUMB.

1832.	Annual report of superintendent of common schools relative to,...	S	2	106
1833.	do do do do ...	A	3	210
1834.	do do do do ...	S	1	41
1835.	do do do do ...	S	2	66
1836.	do do do do ...	S	1	47
1838.	do do do do ...	S	1	25
1839.	do do do do ...	S	2	31
1840.	do do do do ...	A	5	172
1834.	Report of select committee (Mr. Herttell), relative to the,........	A	3	163
1836.	Expenditures for the, report of comptroller giving the amount of, &c., ...	A	3	172
1836.	Establishment of an institution for, in the western part of the state, report of select committee on petition for,.....	A	3	199
1838.	Report on petition of Levi S. Backus to furnish each educated deaf mute with a copy of his newspaper at the expense of the state, ...	A	5	263
1839.	Report on petition of Levi S. Backus to furnish each educated deaf mute with a copy of his newspaper at the expense of the state, ...	A	3	160
1845.	Report of comptroller in relation to sums paid from treasury for,	S	2	52

CENTRAL ASYLUM, CANAJOHARIE:

1830.	Annual report of, ...	S	1	56

DEAF AND DUMB—*continued.*

		Doc.	Vol.	No.
1831.	Annual report of,	A	1	69
1832.	do	S	2	67
1833.	do	S	2	71
1833.	Report on petition for aid to,	S	2	62
1834.	Report on petition for aid to,	A	4	392
1834.	Annual report of,	A	4	278
1835.	Annual report of,	A	4	289
1835.	Report on petition for aid to,	A	4	302
1836.	Report on petition for aid to,	A	3	199
1836.	Annual report of,	S	1	49
1836.	Report of the amount of money paid by the state to,	A	3	172
1830.	Annual report of superintendent of common schools relative to,	S	3	235
1832.	do do do do	S	2	106
1834.	do do do do	S	1	41
1835.	do do do do	S	2	66
1836.	do do do do	S	1	47

New York Institution:

		Doc.	Vol.	No.
1830.	Annual report of the directors of,	S	2	131
1831.	do do and communication from the secretary of state,	A	2	95
1832.	do do	A	2	101
1833.	do do and communication from the secretary of state,	A	3	210
1834.	do do	A	3	108
1835.	do do	A	4	288
1836.	do do	A	3	125
1837.	do do	A	4	291
1838.	do do	A	2	31
1839.	do do	A	4	201
1840.	do do	A	5	179
1841.	do do and communication from the secretary of state,	A	5	157
1830.	Report on petition of the directors to increase the number of state pupils, &c.,	S	5	192
1833.	Memorial of the directors of, for aid,	S	2	61
1834.	do do for an annual appropriation of $5,000,	A	3	165
1834.	do do report of select committee on the same,	A	3	163
1836.	Report on petition to renew the charter of, &c.,	A	3	199
1836.	Comptroller's report of amount paid by the state to,	A	3	172
1838.	Report on petition to amend the law relative to the term of instruction,	A	2	52
1840.	Report on petition to continue the appropriation of 1834,	A	6	264
1841.	Communication from the principal of, to the governor,	S	1	2
1830.	Annual report of superintendent of common schools relative to,	S	3	235
1831.	do do do do	A	2	95
1832.	do do do do	S	2	106
1833.	do do do do	A	3	210
1834.	do do do do	S	1	41
1835.	do do do do	S	2	66
1836.	do do do do	S	1	47
1838.	do do do do	S	1	25
1839.	do do do do	S	2	31
1840.	do do do do	A	5	172
1841.	do do do do			
1832.	Report on petition of Erasmus Hall and other academies, to repeal the law authorizing the, to receive a share of the literature fund,	A	2	59

DEAF AND DUMB—*continued.*

		Doc.	Vol.	No.
1835.	Report on petition relative to their share of the income of the literature fund,........	A	3	263
1842.	Annual report of,........	A	4	57
1843.	Annual report relative to, transmitted by superintendent of common schools,........	A	4	74
1844.	Annual report relative to, transmitted by superintendent of common schools,........	A	1	26
1845.	Report of committee on charitable and religious societies, petition of,........	A	3	60
1846.	Report of printing committee, recommending the printing of extra numbers of annual report,........	A	4	114
1846.	Annual report of,........	A	5	140
1847.	do	A	2	51
1848.	do	A	2	49
1849.	Petition of the directors of, for an appropriation to extinguish their debt,........	A	1	38
1849.	Thirteenth annual report and documents of,........	A	2	89
1850.	Annual report of,........	A	4	67
1851.	Annual report of,........	A	2	22
1852.	Annual report and documents of,........	A	5	112
1853.	Annual report of,........	A	4	93
1854.	Annual report of,........	A	4	125
1854.	Communication of board of directors of,........	A	4	127
1855.	Memorial of board of directors of,........	A	2	57
1855.	Annual report of,........	A	3	80
1856.	Thirty-seventh annual report of,........	A	4	166
1857.	Memorial of, asking for aid, &c.,........	A	3	190
1857.	Annual report and documents of,........	A	3	199
1858.	Report of commissioners to examine the accounts and affairs of,	S	2	107
1858.	Annual report of,........	A	3	77

DEAN, T., AND SAMUEL DABAN.

		Doc.	Vol.	No.
1830.	Commissioners to settle the estate of Doxstader, an Indian woman, report on petition to confirm the conveyance of certain land,..	A	4	356

DEAN, THOMAS.

		Doc.	Vol.	No.
1840.	Report on petition for compensation for damages to his lands by the construction of the Chenango canal,........	A	4	125

DEATH PENALTY, *see* Capital Punishment.

DEATHS, REGISTRY OF, *see* Births, &c.

DEBT, IMPRISONMENT FOR, *see* Imprisonment for Debt.

DEBT OF THE STATE, *see* Finances, &c.

DEBTORS, Absconding, concealed and non-resident.

		Doc.	Vol.	No.
1834.	Report concerning attachments against,........	A	4	391
1839.	Report concerning attachments against,........	A	5	302
1835.	Declaration, service of, by other than executive officers, report relative to,........	A	2	146
1842.	Report of the judiciary committee relative to,........	S	2	42

DEBTORS, JOINT.

		Doc.	Vol.	No.
1849.	Report on bill to amend an act for relief of partners and,.......	A	3	112

DEBTS ON CONTRACT.

		Doc.	Vol.	No.
1842.	Report of judiciary committee on petitions for repeal of laws for the compulsory collection of,........	A	7	178

DE CASTERS, PIERRE, JOSEPH, AND OTHERS.

		Doc.	Vol.	No.
1833.	Report on petition of, to hold real estate, &c.,	A	3	212

DEEDS, COMMISSIONERS OF.

1832.	Report on petition for a law authorizing the election of,	A	1	35
1838.	Report on petition for a law authorizing the election of,	A	5	226
1840.	Report on governor's message relative to the election of,	A	2	46
1839.	Report on the propriety of abolishing the office of,	A	2	47

DEEDS FOR LAND SOLD FOR TAXES.

1833.	Report relative to granting new ones when the certificate is lost,	A	4	299

DEEDS OF CONVEYANCE, &c.

1840.	Letter from the United States consul at Paris, relative to, in foreign countries, touching property in this state,	A	4	132

DEER.

1830.	Report on the subject of hunting deer in Suffolk county,	S	4	394
1833.	Report on the subject of hunting deer in Schoharie county,	A	3	176

DEERFIELD, TOWN OF.

1832.	Report on bill to divide the,	S	1	46
1839.	McAdamized road from, to Utica, report on petition for a,	A	5	300
1840.	McAdamized road from, to Utica, report on petition to raise money to complete,	A	5	216

DEFENDORF, CHAS. AND DAVID.

1852.	Report on the petition of,	A	2	68

DE FERRIERE, POLLY.

1833.	Report on petition for compensation for damages to her lands by the Erie canal,	A	3	217
1834.	Report on petition for compensation for damages to her lands by the Erie canal,	A	2	87

DE GRAFF, JOHN I.

1840.	Report relative to his right to a seat as a member of assembly from Schenectady county,	A	7	291

DE GRAFF, JOHN I., AND OTHERS.

1837.	Report on petition for a law to settle claims for erecting bridges across the canals,	A	3	220

DE GRAFF, J. N.

1837.	Report on petition for extra allowance for building a bridge over the Erie canal,	A	3	179
1837.	Report of committee on claims,	A	3	204

DE GROVE, EDWARD W., AND QUINCEY.

1834.	Report on petition for certain escheated land in the city of New York,	A	3	177
1835.	Report of commissioners of the land office,	A	4	342
1835.	Report of committee on the judiciary,	A	4	371

DE HOMINE REPLEGIANDO.

		Doc.	Vol.	No.
1843.	Report of the minority of the judiciary committee on the subject of repealing all laws relative to the writ of, &c.,	A	5	141

DE KALB, TOWN OF.

1835.	Report relative to the school fund of the,	A	3	173

DE KAY, JAMES E., AND DANIEL FLEET.

1835.	Report on petition to erect a wharf, &c., in Oyster Bay, Queens county,	A	4	320

DELAMATER AND SHISLER.

1855.	Report of committee of ways and means on petition of,	A	2	39

DELAMATER, IRA W.

1847.	Report of commissioners of land office on petition of,	S	2	78

DELAVAN, DANIEL.

1830.	Report on petition for bounty lands for revolutionary services,	A	2	90

DELAWARE AND HUDSON CANAL COMPANY, *see* Canals.

DELAWARE, COUNTY OF.

1832.	Bank in, report on petition to incorporate,	A	2	126
1833.	Salt in, report on petition of S. Crane and others for aid from the state to aid them in the discovery of,	A	4	276
1834.	Report of committee on the manufacture of salt,	A	1	45
1834.	Report of select committee,	A	3	146
1840.	Report on petition for a new county from parts of Chenango, Otsego and, with the county seat at Unadilla,	A	6	242
1841.	Report on petition for a new county from parts of Greene, Schoharie and,	A	7	281
1846.	Report of comptroller relative to amount paid for men and horses used in enforcing the laws, &c., in,	S	1	37
1846.	Report of committee on division of counties, &c., relative to new county from parts of Greene, Schoharie and,	S	2	49
1846.	Report of committee on erection and division of towns and counties relative to new county from parts of Chemung, Otsego and,	A	4	97
1846.	Report of minority committee on erection and division of towns and counties relative to new county from parts of Chemung, Otsego and,	A	4	105
1847.	Comptroller's report of expenditures of money in, and Columbia counties,	A	2	99
1849.	Report of committee on erection and division of towns and counties on petitions and remonstrances relative to new county from parts of Greene, Schoharie and,	A	3	135
1850.	Report on petition of supervisors for expenses for public disturbance,	A	5	111

DELAWARE RIVER.

1832.	Toll bridge across at Deposit, report on petition for a,	A	1	46
1832.	Dam across, at Deposit, report on petition of Henry Peters and Newel Evans for a,	A	4	322
1838.	Fishing in, report relative to,	A	4	164

DELAWARE, STATE OF.

1830.	Resolution of the legislature of, relative to the tariff,	S	4	366
1832.	do do relative to the tariff and internal improvements,	A	1	3

DELAWARE, STATE OF—*continued.*

Year	Subject	Doc.	Vol.	No.
1832.	Resolution of the legislature of, relative to the surviving officers and soldiers of the revolution,	A	1	3
1832.	do do relative to the public lands,.....	A	1	3
1832.	do do relative to the mode of electing President of the United States,	A	1	3
1833.	do do for the re-organization of the militia, ...	A	3	211
1833.	do do relative to nullification,........	A	2	135
1841.	do do relative to the public lands,....	A	4	132
1841.	do do relative to the re-eligibility of the president,..................	A	5	149
1842.	Resolution of the general assembly of, relative to fugitives from justice, ...	A	2	27

DELHI, VILLAGE OF.

Year	Subject	Doc.	Vol.	No.
1832.	Bank at, report on petition to incorporate,....................	A	2	126
1841.	Charter of, report on petition to amend the, relative to roads and bridges,..	S	3	99

DELTA, VILLAGE OF.

Year	Subject	Doc.	Vol.	No.
1838.	Side-cut from the Black River canal to the, report relative to,...	A	3	91
1839.	Side-cut from the Black River canal to the, report relative to,...	A	2	68

DELURGEE, IRA.

Year	Subject	Doc.	Vol.	No.
1837.	Report on petition to change his name,.......................	A	3	275

DEMING, COL. ERIE.

Year	Subject	Doc.	Vol.	No.
1834.	Report on petition for payment of costs in defending a suit brought against him for destroying a gambling-table on parade ground, ...	A	4	364

DEMING, GEORGE.

Year	Subject	Doc.	Vol.	No.
1831.	Report on petition of, for the surplus moneys received on the re-sale of certain land,....................................	S	1	53

DEMISED PREMISES.

Year	Subject	Doc.	Vol.	No.
1840.	Report on bill declaratory of the provisions of law relative to summary proceedings to recover possession of,..............	S	3	65

DEMONT, JOSEPH, AND OTHERS.

Year	Subject	Doc.	Vol.	No.
1845.	Report of canal appraisers on petition of,.....................	A	3	46

DENINSTON, ISAAC.

Year	Subject	Doc.	Vol.	No.
1847.	Report as to claim of,..	S	3	110

DENNY, JOHN.

Year	Subject	Doc.	Vol.	No.
1834.	Report on petition for his share of the moneys due the first Christian party of Oneida Indians,..........................	S	1	37
1834.	Report on petition for his share of the moneys due the first Christian party of Oneida Indians,..........................	S	2	51

DENNY, MARTIN, AND OTHERS.

Year	Subject	Doc.	Vol.	No.
1830.	Report on petition of, relative to the annuities due the Oneida Indians, ...	A	4	432

DENSMORE, OBADIAH, *see* John Carr and others.

DENTAL SURGERY, N. Y. COLLEGE OF.

		Doc.	Vol.	No.
1854.	Report relative to,..	A	4	139

DEPARTMENTS OF STATE, *see* Executive Departments.

DE PEYSTER, TOWN OF.

1831.	State road between the, and the Ogdensburgh Turnpike, report relative to improving the,..............................	A	4	321

DEPOSIT BRIDGE COMPANY.

1832.	Report on petition to incorporate,...............................	A	1	46

DEPOSIT FUND OF THE UNITED STATES, *see* United States Deposit Fund.

DEPOSITS UNCLAIMED, *see* Banks.

DEPOSIT, VILLAGE OF.

1832.	Dam across the Delaware river at, report on petition for,.......	A	4	322
1832.	Toll bridge across the Delaware river at, report on petition for,	A	1	46
1855.	Memorial of citizens of, relative to bounds of,..................	S	2	36

DE RUYTER INSTITUTE, *see* Academies, &c.

DE ST. CROIX, B.

1832.	Report on petition to change his name,...........................	A	3	209

DESEAMUS, I. I.

1833.	Report on petition of, for a divorce,.............................	A	3	185

DE VEAUX, SAMUEL.

1839.	Report on petition to be repaid for provisions, &c., furnished the militia called out to defend the northern frontier,............	A	4	170

DEVENDORFF, SOLOMON.

1830.	Report on petition for remuneration for deficiency in certain land,	S	3	256

DEVOE, GILBERT.

1838.	Report on petition of the executor of the estate of,............	S	1	13

DEWEY, CHARLES.

1846.	Report on petition for relief of,................................	S	2	52

DE WOLF, JOHN, JR., AND OTHERS.

1844.	Heirs-at-law and legal representatives of Samuel Merry, Jr., report of commissioners of land office on petition of,..........	A	3	71

DEXTER COMPANY.

1837.	Report on petition of, relative to diverting the waters of Black river to supply the Black River canal, and Erie canal feeder,	A	3	205

DEXTER, H. S.

1840.	Communication from, relative to hydraulic cement,............	S	4	123

DEXTER S. NEWTON.

		Doc.	Vol.	No.
1835.	Report on petition for remuneration for deficiency in certain land,	A	2	134
1835.	Report on petition for remuneration for deficiency in certain land,	A	4	287

DEXTER, S. NEWTON, AND JAMES MERRIMAN.

1856.	Report of committee on claims on petition of, for relief,........	A	4	128

DE ZENG, W., AND OTHERS.

1841.	Report on petition for relief on account of injuries to their lands by the Erie canal,..	S	2	62

DE ZENG, WM. S.

1843.	Report of committee on claims on his petition,................	S	1	50
1855.	Report of committee on claims on petition of, ...	A	4	100

DICKINSON, H., AND SAMUEL ALEXANDER.

1843.	Report on commissioners of land office on petition of,..........	S	3	106

DICTIONARY, WEBSTER'S UNABRIDGED.

1851.	Report relative to,..	S	3	81
1851.	Report relative to,..	S	3	89

DIGEST OF CLAIMS, *see* Claims.

DIGEST OF PATENTS, *see* United States.

DILLON, GILBERT.

1830.	Report on petition for relief in consequence of wounds received while in performance of military duty,.....................	S	4	305
1831.	Report on petition for relief in consequence of wounds received while in performance of military duty, ...	S	1	69
1832.	Report on petition for relief in consequence of wounds received while in performance of military duty,.....................	A	3	178
1833.	Report on petition for relief in consequence of wounds received while in performance of military duty,.....................	S	2	65
1833.	Report on petition for relief in consequence of wounds received while in performance of military duty,.....................	S	2	101
1834.	Report on petition for relief in consequence of wounds received while in performance of military duty,.....................	S	1	24
1835.	Report on petition for relief in consequence of wounds received while in performance of military duty,.....................	A	2	127

DISBROW, JOHN Q. A.

1842.	Report of judiciary committee on petition of,..................	A	2	38

DISPENSARIES, *see* Brooklyn, Buffalo, New York.

DISTILLATION OF GRAIN, *see* Grain, &c.

DISTRICT ATTORNEYS.

1840.	Report of secretary of state respecting copies of bills and fees of, filed in his office,...	S	4	106
1841.	Report of secretary of state respecting copies of bills and fees of, filed in his office, ...	A	6	244
1842.	Report of secretary of state respecting copies of fee bills of, for 1841,..	A	5	89

Doc. Vol. No.

DISTRICTING THE STATE, *see* Apportionment, Congressional Districts.

DISTRICT OF COLUMBIA.

		Doc.	Vol.	No.
1837.	Slavery in, resolution of the Legislature of Vermont, relative to,	S	1	33
1841.	Remonstrance of citizens of, relative to the legislation of Congress over said district,..................................	A	1	7
1841.	Proceedings of a meeting of citizens of Georgetown, relative to the retrocession of that of the, to the State of Maryland,.....	A	2	25
1842.	Proceedings of Municipal Council of Alexandria in favor of retrocession of Alexandria to Virginia,........................	A	4	53

DISTRICT SCHOOLS, LIBRARIES, &c., *see* Common Schools.

DIVORCE.

		Doc.	Vol.	No.
1833.	Report on petition of Mary Seymour, for,........................	S	2	80
1833.	do do John Case, for,........................	A	2	49
1833.	do do J. J. Dereamus, for,........................	A	3	185
1833.	do do Levi Longwood, for,........................	A	2	47
1833.	do do M. Obrigon, for,........................	A	4	332
1833.	do do N. Winslow, for,........................	A	2	97
1836.	do do Sally Goff, for,........................	S	2	68
1836.	do do Louisa Crandall, for,........................	A	4	328
1838.	do do Daniel and Nancy Ellis,........................	A	2	41
1838.	do do Elias Hubbard, for,........................	A	4	176
1839.	do do David Frost and Eveline Willis,...........	A	2	21
1839.	do do do do	A	3	78
1840.	do do do do	A	8	324
1841.	do do do do	A	5	189
1841.	do do do do	A	6	202
1839.	Report of the Chancellor, on petition of H. Smiffen and wife, for,.	A	5	304
1840.	Report on petition of Jerome B. Ferrill,........................	A	8	323
1841.	do do Orcelia Minerva Gardner,................	S	3	85
1841.	do do Amanlis Lindsley,........................	A	4	143
1842.	Report relative to the petition of Nancy B. Thayer, for,........	S	2	103
1844.	Report on the memorial of Thomas Harttell, for a law making habitual drunkenness a good cause for,.....................	A	6	156
1844.	Report on the petition of Jacob Scramling and others, for,......	A	7	199
1845.	Report on the petition of Jacob Scramling, for,.................	A	4	139
1849.	Report of committee on judiciary, on petitions of John Black and W. H. Pillow, for, &c.,..................................	A	2	66
1850.	Report of select committee on,................................	A	4	72
1852.	Report on the subject of,....................................	A	2	73
1855.	Report of committee on the judiciary in relation to,............	A	5	119
1855.	Report of judiciary committee on petition of George Powsland for,	A	4	83
1855.	Report of judiciary committee on bill in reference to,..........	A	4	119
1856.	Report of judiciary committee on bill relative to,...............	S	2	49

DIXON, THOMAS H.

		Doc.	Vol.	No.
1851.	Report of the judiciary committee on petition of,..............	A	4	91

DOBBIN, JAMES.

		Doc.	Vol.	No.
1846.	Copy of last will and testament of,..................	A	3	80

DOCUMENTARY HISTORY.

		Doc.	Vol.	No.
1852.	Report of comptroller respecting expenses of printing,.........	S	1	5
1845.	Report of secretary of state relative to the general index to, and laws of the state, &c., in his office,......................	S	2	75
1854.	Communication from secretary of state respecting,............	A	4	136

DOCUMENTARY HISTORY—*continued.*

		Doc.	Vol.	No.
1857.	Report of comptroller relative to cost of,	A	1	10
1857.	Report of comptroller, in reply to resolution relative to cost of Colonial and,	A	2	81
1857.	Report of secretary of state, in reply to resolution relative to printing of Colonial and,	A	2	134

DOCUMENTS.

		Doc.	Vol.	No.
1833.	Report of committee appointed to inquire as to the security from fire of public papers and, in the state offices,	A	2	115
1847.	Report in regard to public, of the year 1845,	A	6	165
1849.	Report of committee on public printing respecting cause of delay in printing public,	A	5	228
1855.	Index to legislative, by W. H. Bogart,	S	1	33
1857	Report of clerk of assembly in reply to resolution relative to printing and distribution of,	A	2	115
1857.	Report of secretary of state in reply to resolution relative to contract for binding of legislative,	A	3	176
1858.	Report of library committee relative to books and, in the departments undisposed of,	S	2	52

DOCUMENTS, CONGRESSIONAL, *see* Congressional Documents.

DODD, ZACHARIAH.

		Doc.	Vol.	No.
1833.	A soldier of the revolution, report on petition for bounty lands,	A	2	102

DODGE, HORACE, AND OTHERS.

		Doc.	Vol.	No.
1846.	Report of committee on canals on the petition of,	A	4	123
1850.	Report on claim of,	A	5	108

DODGE, JOHN A.

		Doc.	Vol.	No.
1856.	Report on petition of,	A	4	154
1857.	Report of committee on claims favorable on petition of, as attorney of Silas Ball, for payment of interest on protested draft,	A	2	123

DODGE, ORIN.

		Doc.	Vol.	No.
1848.	Report of committee on canals on petition of,	A	3	147

DODGE, REUBEN D.

		Doc.	Vol.	No.
1834.	Letter from, relative to the Seventh Ward Bank, in New York,	S	2	80

DODGE'S CREEK.

		Doc.	Vol.	No.
1831.	Report relative to declaring it a public highway,	A	4	326

DOE, GERTRUDE.

		Doc.	Vol.	No.
1857.	Standing committee on expiring laws, report on an act for relief of,	S	2	65

DOE, NICHOLAS B.

		Doc.	Vol.	No.
1843.	Report of the commissioners of the land office on his petition,	A	5	158
1848.	Report of commissioners of land office on petition of,	S	2	32

DOGS.

		Doc.	Vol.	No.
1854.	Report of committee on internal affairs of towns and counties on,	A	1	4

DOGS, TAX ON.

		Doc.	Vol.	No.
1837.	Report on petition to amend the law in Columbia county,......	A	1	47
1837.	Report on petition from Yates, Wayne and Onondaga, to amend the law,..........	A	3	238
1839.	Report on petition from Dutchess and Columbia to repeal the law,	A	4	257

DOLAN, JAMES A.

1858.	Report of majority of committee on contested election on petition of, claiming seat of John G. Seeley,..........	A	4	95
1858.	Report of minority of committee on contested election on petition of, claiming seat of John G. Seeley,..........	A	4	97
1858.	Testimony taken on the same,..........	A	4	101

DOMESTIC DISTILLED SPIRITS, INSPECTION OF, *see* New York.

DOMESTIC INDUSTRY, *see* Tariff.

1841.	Resolution of the legislature of Connecticut relative to the protection of,..........	A	1	14
1841.	Resolution of the legislature of Alabama relative to the protection of,..........	A	3	57

DONNELLY, JOHN.

1848.	Report of committee on claims on petition of,..........	A	3	89
1848.	Report on petition of,..........	A	3	99

DOOLITTLE, URI, *see* Samuel Badger and Uri Doolittle.

DORR, THOMAS W.

1845.	Report on petition of two hundred democratic citizens of Madison county relative to,..........	A	7	248

DOTY, JOHN.

1856.	Report on petition of,..........	A	3	93

DOUGHTY, TIMOTHY.

1843.	Committee on claims, report on petition of,..........	S	2	54

DOUGLASS, ZEBULON.

1834.	Report on petition for extra allowance for work done on the Erie canal,..........	A	4	369
1835.	Report of committee on claims,..........	A	2	142
1835.	Report of canal board,..........	A	4	354
1836.	Report on petition for a law authorizing a deed for certain land to be executed and delivered to him,..........	A	4	295
1836.	Report of select committee,..........	A	4	298

DOVER AND UNION VALE TURNPIKE ROAD COMPANY.

1830.	Report on petition to amend the charter of the,..........	A	3	288

DOWER, RIGHT OF.

1841.	Report on bill to extend the, to widows,..........	A	4	89

DOWNEY, JOHN AND RICHARD, *see* Elizabeth Idley.

DOWNING, MARY E.

		Doc.	Vol.	No.
1856.	Report on petition of, in relation to escheated lands, ...	A	4	136
1858.	Report on petition of, for release of escheated lands,.............	A	1	32

DOXSTADER, MARY.

1830.	Report on petition of the commissioners to settle the estate of,...	A	4	356

DRAKE, JEREMIAH, AND OTHERS.

1837.	Report on petition for the pre-emptive right to certain lands on condition that they construct a railroad from the Erie canal to Piseco lake,..	A	3	267
1837.	Report of select committee,................................	A	3	279
1838.	Report on petition for the conveyance to them of certain lands,..	A	3	87
1838.	Report on petition for the conveyance to them of certain lands,..	A	5	203

DRAKE, JOHN, AND OTHERS.

1831.	Report on petition of, relative to the oyster-beds in Richmond county, ...	S	1	14

DRAKE, MOSES.

1839.	Report on petition for compensation for damages to his land by the Erie canal,..	A	6	368

DRED SCOTT.

1857.	Report of joint committee of senate and assembly on the decision of the Supreme Court of the United States in the case of,......	A	3	201

DRESDEN MANUFACTURING COMPANY.

1837.	Report on petition to incorporate,............................	S	1	22

DRESSER, ERASTUS.

1847.	Report on petition of,......................................	A	4	142

DRUM, JOHN, AND B. GLEASON.

1834.	Report on petition to be credited with certain money paid for land,..	A	4	254

DRUM, JOHN Z. AND JOHN W., *see* Aaron Parkhurst and others.

DRUNKENNESS, HABITUAL.

1844.	Report on the memorial of Thomas Harttell for a law making, a good cause for divorce,................................	A	6	156

DRUNKENNESS, SEWALL'S PATHOLOGY OF, *see* Pathology of Drunkenness.

DRYDEN, TOWN OF.

1831.	Report on petition for the division of the,.....................	A	3	258

DUANE, STEEL ORE AT.

1841.	Report of Professor Emmons, relative to,.....................	A	5	182

DUANESBURGH, TOWN OF.

1838.	Report on petition to extend the time for the collection of taxes in the,..	A	3	63

DUBOIS AND HUNT.

		Doc.	Vol.	No.
1844.	Report of commissioners of land office on petition of,	S	3	103

DUCKENFIELD, GEORGE (an alien).

1831.	Report on petition to take, hold and convey real estate,	S	1	59

DUCKMAN, ABRAHAM.

1830.	A soldier of the revolution, report on petition of the heirs of, for bounty lands,	A	4	418

DUDLEY, ABRAHAM.

1855.	Report of committee on erection and division of towns and counties on petition of,	A	2	30

DUDLEY, BLANDINA.

1847.	Report on petition of,	S	2	56

DUDLEY, E. E., *see* S. H. Addington.

DUELING.

1838.	Resolution requesting the members of congress from this state to use their exertions for the passage of a law to expel from congress all members engaged in,	A	5	230
1838.	Resolution requesting the members of congress from this state to use their exertions for the passage of a law to expel from congress all members engaged in,	A	5	229

DUELL, ABRAHAM.

1855.	Report of canal commissioners on petition of, and others,	S	2	37

DUNDEE SALT SPRINGS, *see* Salt, &c.

DUNHAM, ALBERT T., *see* Marlett & Dunham.

DUNHAM, CYRUS P., AND OTHERS.

1853.	Report of committee on claims in relation to the petition of, for relief,	S	2	55

DUNHAM, JEREMIAH.

1839.	Report on bill for the relief of,	A	6	385

DUNHAM, P.

1846.	Report of comptroller relative to claim of,	A	3	82

DUNHAM, SAGE AND WALRATH, *see* Sage, Walrath and Dunham.

DUNHAM, WATSON.

1834.	Report on petition for extra allowance for making desks for the Assembly Chamber,	A	3	203

DUNLAP, J.

1854.	Report of committee on grievances on petition of Francis Smith and heirs of,	A	2	67

DUNLAP, JANET.

1834.	Report on petition for escheated lands,	S	2	121

DUNLOP, JOHN, AND OTHERS.

		Doc.	Vol.	No.
1847.	Report of committee on public lands on petition of,........	A	4	141

DUNN, WILLIAM.

1844.	Report of commissioners of land office on petition of next of kin to, deceased,........	A	3	42

DUNNING, JONATHAN O.

1852.	Report on petition of,........	A	2	59

DURFEE & OGDEN.

1846.	Report on bill for the relief of,........	S	4	136

DURHAM AND WINDHAM TURNPIKE COMPANY.

1831.	Report on petition to abandon part of their road,........	A	2	113

DURHAM, CYRUS P., ROBERT L. MOORE, AND OTHERS.

1839.	Report on petition relative to the lease of certain surplus waters of the Erie canal,........	A	3	51

DURHAMVILLE AND WOOD CREEK PLANKROAD CO.

1856.	Report on claim of,........	A	4	152

DURLAND, DANIEL T., AND DANIEL FULLERTON.

1850.	Report of committee on elections on contested seat of,........	A	4	67

DURYEA, H. B., AND J. LOVERIDGE.

1855.	Report of judiciary committee on petition of,........	A	2	40

DUTCHESS COUNTY.

1830.	Game in, report on petition to prohibit the killing of certain kinds of,........	A	4	422
1834.	Court-house, report on petition to sell the present and to erect a new one,........	A	4	325
1835.	District-attorney, report on petition relative to the compensation of the,........	A	2	114
1839.	Dogs in, report on petition to repeal the law requiring a tax on,	A	4	257
1834.	Fish, report on petition for a law for the protection of, in certain waters in,........	A	2	58
1831.	Poor-house, report on petition to raise money by tax to erect a,..	A	3	204
1839.	Poor, superintendents of the, report on petition to require them to give them security, &c.,........	A	6	384
1834.	Turnpike company, report on bill granting further powers to,...	S	2	119
1834.	Turnpike company, report of committee of conference on the same,........	A	4	400
1836.	Road from the village of Fishkill to Croton river, and the bridge over said river, report on petition for aid to improve,........	A	4	277
1831.	Inspector of beef and pork, annual report of N. Concklin,.....	A	2	143
1842.	Report of committee on roads and bridges relative to a bridge across Wappinger's creek in,........	S	3	79
1846.	Report of majority of committee on privileges and elections, on contested seat from,........	A	2	45
1846.	Report of minority of committee on the same,........	A	2	46
1850.	Report on act to pay expenses for quelling riot,........	A	6	170

BANKS IN, *see* Banks, Dutchess county.

LANDS IN, claimed by John Jacob Astor, *see* J. J. Astor.

DUTCH RECORDS.

		Doc.	Vol.	No.
1840.	In the office of the secretary of state, communication relative to the translation of the,	A	8	350

DUTTON, JOHN E.

1847.	Report of committee on claims on petition of,	A	2	72

DUVAL, SALLY L.

1834.	Report on petition of, to change the name of her child,	A	1	47

DWIGHT, FRANCIS.

1843.	Report on a communication from,	S	1	34

DYGERT, HENRY.

1854.	Report on petition of,	A	1	26
1855.	Report of committee on claims on petition of,	A	2	26
1857.	Report of committee on claims adverse on petition of, for damages by burning of canal boat,	A	3	151

DYGERT, WARNER.

1840.	Report on petition for further allowance for work done on the Erie canal,	A	6	269

DYGERT, WILLIAM AND D. F.

1855.	Report of committee on claims on petition of,	A	2	29

DYGERT, WILLIAM W.

1841.	Report on petition for compensation for damages in consequence of a breach in the Erie canal,	A	5	175

E.

EARLL, D. & CO., *see* William Gibbs and others.

EARLL, DANIEL, *see* Dorastus Kellogg and others.

EARLL, JONAS, JR.

1844.	Statement of, relative to the claim of Amos B. and James H. King,	A	6	154

EAST HAMPTON.

1836.	Report on petition to levy a bounty on foxes in,	A	3	139

EASTKILL AND CAIRO TURNPIKE COMPANY.

1830.	Report on petition to renew the charter of,	A	2	134

EAST OSWEGO, *see* Oswego.

EAST RIVER.

1838.	Oysters in, report on petition to protect persons planting, &c.,	A	3	157
1857.	Report of committee on commerce and navigation on petition for a bridge over,	S	4	167
	Grants of land under water, *see* Brooklyn and Williamsburgh.			

EATON, AMOS.

1836.	Message from the governor on the memorial of,	A	4	327

EATON, E., AND OTHERS.

		Doc.	Vol.	No.
1847.	Report on petition of,	S	2	54

EATON, SAMUEL.

1834.	Report on petition for compensation for damages by the Erie canal,	A	3	212

EDDY, HARRIET.

1844.	Report of canal board on petition of,	S	1	43

EDDY, HARRIET AND OTIS.

1844.	Report of committee on claims on petition of,	S	3	109

EDDY, HIRAM.

1839.	Report on petition for pay for timber sold to William Van Nortwicke, former superintendent of repairs on the Champlain canal,	S	3	71
1839.	Report of the committee on claims,	A	4	252

EDDY, HIRAM AND ASA.

1839.	Report on petition for compensation for the damages to their boat and cargo,	A	5	297

EDDY, OTIS.

1843.	Report of committee on claims on petition of,	A	3	43

EDDY, OTIS, AND OTHERS.

1843.	Report of committee on claims on their petition,	S	2	58

EDDY, TIMOTHY.

1834.	Report on petition for compensation for damages to his lands by the erection of Fort Edward dam and feeder,	A	3	235
1844.	Report of the canal commissioners on petition of,	S	1	48
1844.	Report of committee on claims on petition of,	S	2	56
1845.	Report of canal board in relation to the claim of,	S	1	34
1845.	Report of committee on finance in relation to the claim of,	S	1	41

EDDYVILLE BRIDGE COMPANY.

1835.	Report on petition to revive an act to incorporate,	A	3	261
1840.	Report on petition to amend the charter of,	A	6	261
1841.	Report on petition to amend the charter of,	A	4	142

EDDYVILLE, VILLAGE OF.

1834.	Bridge over Rondout creek, report on petition to raise money by tax to build a,	A	3	217

EDGARTON, LEONARD I., *see* James M. Willard and L. I. Edgarton.

EDMONDS, JOHN W.

1836.	Report relative to his official conduct in the matter of the Commercial Bank,	S	2	104

EDMONDS, JOHN W., AND OTHERS.

1846.	Memorial of, relative to Aboriginal History of the State,	S	2	55

EDMONDS, J. W.

Year	Subject	Doc.	Vol.	No.
1858.	Communication of, relative to the sword of General Worth,.....	S	1	5

EDUCATION, *see* Common Schools, Colleges, Academies.

EDWARDS, HARVEY, AND OTHERS.

Year	Subject	Doc.	Vol.	No.
1833.	Report on petition to authorize the canal commissioners to take a grant of a canal constructed by them from the Limestone creek feeder to the Seneca turnpike,............................	S	2	73
1833.	Report of committee on canals,..............................	S	2	83
1834.	Report of canal commissioners,..............................	S	2	74

EDWARDS, MARY E.

Year	Subject	Doc.	Vol.	No.
1848.	Report on petition of,......................................	A	5	176
1849.	Report of commissioners of land office on petition of,..........	A	2	64
1850.	Report on petition of,......................................	A	3	46
1850.	Appendix to report of,......................................	A	4	61

EDWARDS, OGDEN.

Year	Subject	Doc.	Vol.	No.
1832.	Report of amount of fees received by him as circuit judge,.....	A	2	168

EGGLESTON AND SANFORD.

Year	Subject	Doc.	Vol.	No.
1844.	Report of canal board on petition of,.........................	A	3	69
1846.	Report of canal board on petition,...........................	A	3	78
1846.	Report of commissioners on claims on petition of,.............	A	4	99

EGGLESTON, DARIUS.

Year	Subject	Doc.	Vol.	No.
1831.	Report on petition for extra allowance for work done on the Erie canal,...	A	4	306

EGGLESTON, SILAS.

Year	Subject	Doc.	Vol.	No.
1846.	Report of canal board on petition of,.........................	A	5	147

EHLE, CHARLES.

Year	Subject	Doc.	Vol.	No.
1847.	Report on petition of,......................................	S	2	73
1847.	Report of canal commissioner on petition of,..................	S	2	76
1849.	Report of committee on canals, on petition of,................	A	3	161
1850.	Report on claim for canal damages,...........................	S	2	42
1851.	Report on claim of,...	A	3	48
1851.	Report of comptroller on claim of,...........................	S	3	94
1852.	Report on petition of, for relief,............................	S	1	44

EHLE JOHN A., AND JOHN SPENCER.

Year	Subject	Doc.	Vol.	No.
1837.	Report on petition for extra allowance for work done on the Chenango canal,...	S	1	36
1838.	Report of committee on claims on the same,....................	A	5	279

EHLE, JOHN A., AND OTHERS.

Year	Subject	Doc.	Vol.	No.
1838.	Report on petition for extra allowance for work done on the Erie canal,...	A	6	342

EINSTEIN, ELIZABETH.

Year	Subject	Doc.	Vol.	No.
1842.	Report of the commissioners of the land office on the petition and bill of, to convey certain lands to her,......................	S	2	22

ELBA, TOWN OF.

Year	Subject	Doc.	Vol.	No.
1832.	Report on petition for a new town from part of the,...........	A	2	57

ELECTION LAW OF 1842.

		Doc.	Vol.	No.
1847.	Report relative to,	S	2	55

ELECTION LAWS.

1856.	Report relative to publication of, &c.,	S	1	34

ELECTIONS.

1832.	For members of congress, report relative to altering the time for,	S	2	105
1836.	Special for members of congress, report relative to,	A	2	77
1839.	For senators in congress, report on bill to provide for the,	A	6	404
1839.	Betting on, report relative to,	A	5	286
1838.	Purity of, report on bill to preserve the, (Mr. Ogden,)	A	6	323
1841.	For election of president and vice-president to be held on the same day throughout the Union, resolution to amend the Constitution,	A	1	9
	And *see* President of the United States.			
1842.	Report of committee on privileges and elections, on numerous petitions in relation to general,	A	2	36
1857.	Report of committee on grievances, favorable on an act to prevent frauds at,	A	3	197
1858.	Majority report on act to prevent illegal voting at,	A	4	109

REGISTRY LAW, GENERAL, *see* Registry Law.

REGISTRY LAW IN NEW YORK, *see* New York.

ELECTIONS, ONE DAY.

1831.	Report on petition for (Mr. Van Buren),	A	4	359
1838.	do do (Mr. Ogden),	A	6	314
1840.	do do (Mr. Scott),	A	5	192

ELECTIVE FRANCHISE.

1840.	Report on petition of inhabitants of Verona for a law more effectually to secure the free exercise of,	A	5	185
1835.	Report on petition of inhabitants of Avon, for the same,	A	2	119
1841.	Report on petition to extend to colored persons,	A	5	183
1841.	Report on the resolutions proposed by Mr. Duer, for the same,	A	5	181
1842.	Report on petitions for extending to colored citizens,	A	7	155
1853.	Report of the committee on the judiciary, on the reference of the resolutions to amend the Constitution, relative to,	A	3	60

ELECTORS, QUALIFICATIONS OF.

1837.	Resolution to amend the Constitution, so as to allow electors to vote for president and vice-president, and governor and lieutenant-governor, in any town or ward, provided such elector is prevented by business from voting where he resides,	A	2	120
1841.	Report on a resolution to amend the Constitution relative to the,	A	5	181

ELGAR, JAMES (an alien).

1835.	Report on petition to hold real estate, &c.,	A	3	170

ELIZABETHTOWN.

1838.	Arsenal at, report relative to breaking open the,	A	5	217

ELLENBURGH, TOWN OF.

1846.	Report on bill to confirm the election and official acts of the officers of, &c.,	S	2	72

ELLICE, E.

		Doc.	Vol.	No.
1831.	Report relative to certain lands at Little Falls claimed by him, ..	S	1	35

ELLICOTT AND TONAWANDA CREEKS.

1830.	Report of canal commissioners relative to lands overflowed with water on the, ...	A	3	124

ELLICOTT CREEK.

1836.	Dam across, report on petition of Benjamin Herskey to build, ..	A	3	208
1847.	Report on petition for draining lands at, ...	A	7	198

ELLICOTT, TOWN OF.

1832.	Report on petition for the division of, ...	A	3	232
1839.	Report on petition to raise money to lease or purchase a town-house, ...	A	5	312

ELLIS, DANIEL AND NANCY.

1838.	Report on petition for a divorce, ...	A	2	41

ELLIS, JOHN.

1846.	Report of committee on claims on contract of, ...	A	3	81
1847.	Report on petition of, ...	A	2	53

ELLIS' REPEATING RIFLES.

1832.	Report on bill authorizing the commissary-general to receive, in lieu of the quota of arms, &c., due the state, ...	A	4	303

ELLSWORTH, SAMUEL S.

1842.	Report of committee on claims on petition of, ...	A	7	147

ELMENDORF, LUCAS.

1833.	Report on petition for the conveyance to him of certain land, ...	A	1	27
1833.	Report of attorney-general on the same, ...	A	3	191
1833.	Report of committee on claims on the same, ...	A	3	201
1834.	Report of committee on claims on the same, ...	A	1	30
1835.	Report on petition for a law authorizing the comptroller to execute deeds to him for two lots of land sold for taxes, ...	A	2	124
1835.	Report on petition for compensation for work done on the Neversink Turnpike Company, &c., ...	A	3	213
1835.	Report of majority of select committee on the same, ...	A	4	357
1835.	Report of minority of select committee on the same, ...	A	4	358
1843.	Report of committee on claims on petition of, ...	S	2	61

ELMIRA.

1835.	Report on petition of trustees of, relative to damages by the Chemung canal, ...	A	4	324
1835.	Report of committee on grievances on the same, ...	A	4	355
1835.	Survey of a route for a railroad from, to Williamsport, Pennsylvania, ...	A	4	351
1847.	Report on petition for bridge at, ...	A	6	152

ELMORE, A. L.

1831.	Report on petition for compensation for damages by the Erie canal, ...	A	4	337

ELMORE, JOB G.

1852.	Report on petition of, claiming seat held by Jacob Westbrook, Jr.,	A	2	28

ELMORE, JOB G.—*continued.*

		Doc.	Vol.	No.
1852.	Report on resolution to pay him while contesting seat of J. Westbrook, Jr.,	A	2	65

ELSWORTH, JOHN, AND OTHERS.

1834.	Report on petition to drain Flint creek and Nettle Valley swamp,	A	4	253

ELSWORTH, SAMUEL S., AND OTHERS.

1841.	Report on petition for compensation for the loss of a timber raft by a breach in the canal near Frankfort,	A	6	197

ELSWORTH, S. S., AND OTHERS.

1842.	Report of committee on claims on petition of,	A	7	147

ELWOOD, REUBEN, AND OTHERS.

1855.	Report of committee on claims on petition of,	A	2	49
1856.	Report on petition of, for relief,	A	3	42

ELY, HERVEY, AND OTHERS.

1839.	Report relative to the appraisal of their property taken for the enlarged Erie canal at Rochester,	A	5	283
1839.	Report of committee on canals,	S	3	108
1840.	Report of committee on canals,	A	4	140
1841.	Report of committee on claims,	A	2	45
1844.	Report of canal board on petition of,	S	2	65

EMIGRANT PASSENGERS.

1843.	Memorial of the mayor, &c., of New York, praying for the passage of an act for the relief of, with draft of an act therefor, ..	A	5	139

EMIGRANTS.

1847.	Report of committee of investigation relative to frauds on,	A	8	250
1848.	Report of committee of investigation of frauds on,	A	2	46
1851.	Report of select committee relative to and the public health,	A	6	155

EMIGRANT SOCIETY, IRISH.

1854.	Remonstrance against certain bill,	A	1	31

EMIGRATION AND AGRICULTURAL ASSOCIATION.

1852.	Memorial of the New York and Liberia, for an appropriation, ...	S	1	19

EMIGRATION, COMMISSIONERS OF.

1847.	Report of,	S	4	119
1848.	Memorial of, in relation to hospital fund,	S	2	46
1848.	Annual report of,	S	2	47
1849.	Report of comptroller transmitting letter from,	S	2	39
1849.	Annual report of,	A	2	50
1849.	Letter from, relative to quarantine establishment, &c.,	A	2	58
1849.	Communication from comptroller relative to letter of, &c.,	A	3	140
1849.	Report of, in answer to resolution of assembly,	A	5	214
1850.	Annual report,	A	4	52
1850.	Communication from, in relation to amendment of law,	A	5	99
1850.	Communication from, in regard to alien passengers,	S	2	71
1851.	Annual report,	A	2	37
1851.	Report of select committee on annual report,	A	4	92
1852.	Report of select committee to examine into the condition, &c., of the trusts under charge of,	A	2	34

EMIGRATION, COMMISSIONERS OF—*continued.*

		Doc.	Vol.	No.
1852.	Report of,	S	2	59
1853.	Annual report of,	S	2	37
1853.	Communication from, asking for legislative aid,	S	3	79
1854.	Annual report of,	A	3	97
1855.	Report of, in answer to resolution of senate,	S	1	32
1855.	Communication from, in answer to resolution of senate,	S	2	46
1856.	Report of, in answer to resolution,	S	2	62
1856.	Report of, as to embarrassments,	S	2	78
1856.	Report of, in answer to resolution as to sale of tickets, &c.,	S	2	87
1856.	Report of committee on finance on bill to pay money to,	S	2	94
1856.	Report of select committee to examine affairs of,	S	3	105
1856.	Report of committee on quarantine and,	A	4	109
1856.	Report relative to embarrassments and necessities of commission,	A	4	143
1857.	Preliminary report of,	S	2	59
1857.	Annual report of,	S	2	80
1858.	Annual report of,	A	3	83

EMIGRATION LAWS.

1849.	Report of select committee respecting,	A	5	219

EMMONS, EBENEZER.

1841.	Report in relation to the Duane steel ore,	A	5	182
1843.	Communication from,	S	2	60
1847.	Communication from,	A	7	211

EMPEY, RICHARD.

1851.	Report of committee on claim for canal damages,	A	3	84

ENDERS, JOHN.

1834.	Report on petition relative to the surplus waters of Schoharie creek,	A	3	237

ENDERS, PETER J.

1834.	Report on petition for compensation for damages to his lands by the dam across Schoharie creek,	A	4	328
1835.	Petition of,	A	4	322
1835.	Report of canal commissioners on petition of,	A	4	325
1836.	Report of canal commissioners on petition of,	A	4	229

ENDRESS, ISAAC I.

1843.	Report of finance committee on the petition of,	S	2	55

ENGLISHBEE, JAMES.

1841.	Report on petition for a release of escheated lands,	S	3	74

ENGLISHBEE, JAMES AND FRANCIS.

1841.	Report on petition for a release of escheated lands,	S	2	58

ENGRAVING, *see* Printing.

ENGRAVINGS.

1849.	Catalogue of, presented by Pope Pius IX.,	A	3	117

ENNIS, ELIJAH.

1852.	Claim reported on,	S	2	55

ENTERPRISE FERRY COMPANY.

		Doc.	Vol.	No.
1857.	Report on bill to incorporate,	S	4	168

ENTOMOLOGY.

1855.	Report of select committee on report of State Agricultural Society in reference to,	A	5	137
1855.	Report of Asa Fitch relative to,	A	5	151
1855.	Report of Asa Fitch respecting,	A	7	151
1856.	Communication from State Agricultural Society concerning,	A	5	207
1856.	Report of Asa Fitch, M. D., on the noxious and beneficial, and other insects of the State of New York,	A	6	215

EPHRATAH AND PALATINE.

1848.	Report of committee on roads and bridges relative to, &c.,	S	2	67
1848.	Minority report on same,	S	2	70

EQUITY AND JUDICIAL SYSTEM.

1838.	Report of commissioners appointed to digest and report an,	A	1	3
1838.	Report of committee on the judiciary on the same,	A	5	283

ERASMUS HALL ACADEMY, *see* Academies, &c.

ERIE CANAL, *see* Canals.

ERIE COUNTY.

1836.	Bridge over Cattaraugus creek at Zoar, report on petition to raise money by tax to build a,	A	4	241
1837.	Bridge over Buffalo creek, report on petition for a law directing the money raised to build a, to be expended in improving certain roads,	A	3	170
1831.	Jail in, report on petition to sell the old, and to raise money to build a new one,	A	1	45
1831.	Jail in, report on petition to sell the old, and to raise money to build a new one,	A	2	106
1833.	Jail in, report relative to the assessment of a tax for a,	A	2	44
1834.	Jail in, report on petition of the treasurer to raise money to pay for building,	A	3	120
1835.	Jail in, report on petition of the treasurer to raise money to pay for building,	A	2	136
1834.	Clerk's office, report on petition for a loan to build a,	A	3	120
1835.	Clerk's office, report on petition for a loan to build a,	A	2	136
1832.	Medical Society, report on petition of, for a law confirming the organization of the,	A	3	192
1836.	Poor-house, farm and lot, report on petition to sell the,	A	2	85
1835.	Road from, to Abbott's Corners, report on petition to raise money by tax to improve a,	A	4	313
1834.	Road across the Indian reservation, report on petition to raise money by tax to improve a,	A	3	218
1831.	Inspector of beef and pork, S. Russell, report of,	A	1	47
1832.	do beef and pork, S. Russell, report of,	A	2	153
1839.	do flour and meal, Foster Young, report of,	A	3	88
1840.	do flour and meal, Foster Young, report of,	A	1	11
1831.	do leather, John Dobson, report of,	A	1	7
1832.	do leather, N. Randall, report of,	A	2	117
1831.	do staves and heading, Sylvanus Russell, report of,	A	1	47
1842.	New county, report relative to the erection of, from parts of Chautauque, Cattaraugus and,	S	2	43
1842.	Excise, report on application of supervisors of, relative to,	A	2	46
1844.	Agricultural Society of, report of committee on agriculture on petition of,	A	7	198
1845.	New county, report of the committee on the division of towns and counties in relation to, to be formed from parts of Cattaraugus, Chautauque and,	S	1	30

ERIE COUNTY—*continued.*

		Doc.	Vol.	No.
1846.	Grand Island, report of comptroller on petition of citizens of, relative to,	A	5	155
1847.	Public lands, report relative to bill authorizing supervisors of, to take stone from,	A	1	44
1850.	Money, report on resolution of board of supervisors of, to refund,	A	5	93
1853.	New county, report of committee on erection and division of towns and counties on the erection of, from the counties of Chautauque, Cattaraugus and,	A	3	57

ERIE, TOWN OF.

1831.	Report on petition to change the name of the,	A	3	270

ERROR, WRITS OF, *see* Writs of Error.

ERWIN, ARTHUR.

1838.	Report on petition of, to build a dam across the Canisteo river,	A	6	327

ESCHEATED LANDS.

1857.	Report of committee on petition of aliens, relative to cases of,	A	2	62
1857.	do do do do do	A	2	83
1857.	do do do do do	A	3	146

ESCHEATS.

1833.	Bill concerning, proposed by the commissioners of the land office,	A	2	54
1833.	Report of select committee on the same,	A	4	326
1834.	Report of commissioners of the land office, giving a statement of all releases granted under the act concerning,	S	1	34
1835.	Report of commissioners of the land office, giving a statement of all releases granted under the act concerning,	A	1	67
1836.	Report of commissioners of the land office, giving a statement of all releases granted under the act concerning,	A	1	16
1837.	Report of commissioners of the land office, giving a statement of all releases granted under the act concerning,	S	2	72
1838.	Report of commissioners of the land office, giving a statement of all releases granted under the act concerning,	S	2	75
1839.	Report of commissioners of the land office, giving a statement of all releases granted under the act concerning,	S	1	16
1841.	Report of commissioners of the land office, giving a statement of all releases granted under the act concerning,	A	2	38
1844.	Report of commissioners of land office concerning,	S	1	12

ESOPUS CREEK.

1831.	Bridge over, report on petition of Henry Barclay to build a,	A	2	159
1832.	Bridge over, report on petition of Henry Barclay to build a,	A	1	25
1834.	Bridge over, report on petition of inhabitants of Marbletown to raise money by tax to build a,	A	3	215
1840.	Bridge over, report on petition of inhabitants of Saugerties to raise money to build a,	A	2	53
1832.	Channel of the, report on petition to incorporate a company for the purpose of improving the,	A	1	16
1834.	Pier at the mouth of, report on petition to incorporate a company to build a,	A	4	277

ESQUIROL, PETER, AND OTHERS.

1843.	Memorial of, remonstrance against any alteration in the inspection laws,	A	3	69

ESSEX COUNTY.

1838.	Academy, report on petition for aid,	A	5	269

ESSEX COUNTY—*continued.*

		Doc.	Vol.	No.
1832.	Clerk's office, report on petition to levy a tax to build a, ...	A	3	243
1840.	Poor-house system, report on petition to abolish the, ...	A	6	267
1841.	Poor-house system, report on petition to abolish the, ...	A	7	265
1832.	Road from Cedar Point westward, report of the comptroller and surveyor-general relative to the situation and progress of the,	A	3	226
1849.	Report on petition of sundry citizens of Clinton, Washington and, relative to road from Whitehall to Plattsburgh, ...	A	3	186
1851.	Report of select committee on petition of inhabitants of Franklin, Warren and, ...	A	4	94

BANKS, *see* Banks, Essex county.

EVANS, NEWAL.

1832.	Report on petition to erect a dam across the Delaware river at Deposit, ...	A	4	322

EVERETT, SAMUEL.

1843.	Report of committee on claims on petition of, ...	S	1	40

EWERS, HENRY W.

1838.	Report on petition for extra allowance for work done on the Chenango canal, ...	A	4	187
1839.	Report of committee on claims on the same, ...	A	3	114
1840.	Report of committee on claims on the same, ...	A	1	24

EXCHANGES, INTERNATIONAL, *see* International Exchanges.

EXCISE, COMMISSIONERS OF.

1834.	Report on bill to amend the law relative to, ...	A	3	122
1842.	Report on the application of the supervisors of Erie county, relative to, of the city of Buffalo, ...	A	2	46

EXCISE LAW, *see* Intoxicating Liquors.

1832.	Liability of the state for costs under the, ...	S	2	82
1834.	License to temperance taverns, report relative to granting without charge, ...	A	3	250
1834.	Report on petition from Seneca county to prevent tavern-keepers from retailing ardent spirits, ...	A	4	372
1835.	Report on petition from Franklin county to prohibit the sale of ardent spirits on Sundays, ...	A	3	191
1837.	Report on petition to amend the, for Monroe county, ...	A	1	40
1837.	Report on petition to amend the, for the city of Hudson, ...	A	4	308
1837.	Report on bill relative to licensing retailers of ardent spirits in Monroe county, ...	A	4	307
1837.	Report on petition to amend or repeal, (C. O. Shepard), ...	A	4	333
1838.	do do do (Mr. Garretson), ...	A	6	304
1839.	do do do (Mr. Hubbard), ...	A	4	249
1840.	do do do (Mr. Young), ...	S	3	73
1841.	Report relative to granting licenses for the sale of intoxicating liquors (Mr. Taylor), ...	S	2	41
1841.	Majority report on bill relative to licensing retailers of intoxicating liquors, ...	A	5	167
1841.	Minority report on the same, ...	A	7	294
1844.	Report of committee on internal affairs of towns and counties, on petitions on the subject of licenses, ...	A	3	83
1845.	Report of select committee on, ...	A	3	50
1850.	Report of majority of select committee, ...	A	5	119
1847.	Report of committee on poor laws relative to repeal of, ...	S	3	107
1847.	Report as to votes on, ...	A	1	40

EXCISE LAW—*continued.*

		Doc.	Vol.	No.
1847.	Majority report on petition relative to repeal of law of 1845,....	A	4	139
1847.	Minority report on petition relative to repeal of law of 1845,....	A	4	140
1851.	Report of select committee on,..................................	A	3	46
1851.	Report of the select committee,..........................	A	4	110
1851.	Report of the minority committee on the same subject,.........	A	4	111
1851.	Report of the select committee,..............................	A	4	118
1857.	Report of the majority of the select committee on the,..........	A	2	113

EXECUTION, OR DISTRESS FOR RENT.

1841.	Report on petition to extend the exemption of personal property from sale on,..	S	3	81

EXECUTIONS.

1850.	Report on the return of,..	A	4	62

EXECUTIVE DEPARTMENT.

1842.	Report of committee on expenditures of the, in relation to,......	A	7	184
1846.	Report of comptroller relative to printing for,..................	A	3	75
1846.	Report of committee on expenses of,...........................	A	5	143
1858.	Report of committee on judiciary relative to the powers and duties of the governor, and to fix compensation of officers in the,	S	2	72

EXECUTIVE MANSION.

1835.	Report of a committee relative to purchasing, ...	A	4	332
1836.	Report of a committee relative to purchasing,................	A	4	324
1838.	Report of trustees of the state hall relative to the purchase of,..	A	3	144
1838.	Report of select committee in relation to the purchase of,.......	A	6	363
1857.	Report relative to,..	S	3	83
1857.	Report of standing committee on incorporation of cities and villages relative to,..	S	3	89
1857.	Report of standing committee on finance relative to purchase of,	S	4	159

EXECUTORS OF WILLS.

1838.	Suits brought by, report in relation to,......................	A	5	261

EXEMPTION OF PROPERTY.

1842.	Report of judiciary committee relative to, from levy on sale,....	S	3	76

EXEMPTION, HOMESTEAD.

1847.	Majority report on memorials for limitation of land and,.......	A	7	203
1850.	Report of select committee on a,............................	A	5	123

EXEMPTION, HOUSEHOLD FURNITURE, IMPLEMENTS, &c.

1842.	Report on the bill for, from levy and sale on execution,.........	A	7	145
1843.	Report of committee on judiciary relative to the law exempting,	S	1	43

EXPENDITURES ON THE CANALS, *see* Canals.

EXPENSES OF STATE, *see* Government, State.

EXPUNGING RESOLUTION.

1835.	Resolution offered by Mr. Young instructing the senators from this state to use their efforts to cause to be expunged from the journal of the senate the resolution of the 28th March, 1834,	S	1	5
1836.	Resolution offered by Mr. Judd for the same,..................	A	2	74
1839.	Resolution of the legislature of North Carolina relative to the,	A	4	202

Doc. Vol. No.

EYE AND EAR INFIRMARY, NEW YORK, *see* New York.

EYE AND EAR INFIRMARY, WESTERN, *see* Syracuse.

F.

FACTORS, *see* Consignees, Agents and Factors.

FAILING, JACOB H.

1834. Report on petition for compensation for damages by the Erie canal, ... A 2 99

FAILING, JACOB H., AND JAMES AVERILL.

1835. Report on petition for compensation for damages by the Erie canal, ... A 2 94
1835. Report of committee on grievances on the same, ... A 4 365

FAILING, PETER, AND OTHERS.

1834. Report on petition for extra compensation for work done on the Oswego canal, ... S 1 26

FAIRBANK, DEXTER, AND OTHERS.

1852. Report of commissioners of land office respecting land under water at Westfield, ... A 5 121

FAIRFIELD ACADEMY, *see* Academies, &c.

FAIRFIELD, TOWN OF.

1841. Report on petition relative to the acts of inspectors of election in said town, ... A 7 304

FAIRPORT, VILLAGE OF.

1840. Report on petition to change the name of, to Horseheads, ... A 8 326

FAIRSERVICE, M. H.

1835. Report on petition for extra allowance for work done on the Erie canal, ... A 4 331

FALLEY, GEORGE F., AND OTHERS.

1847. Report of committee on claims on petition of, for relief, ... A 2 72

FANCHER, RICHARD.

1857. Report of committee on claims favorable on petition of, for damages by break in the Erie canal, ... A 2 61

FARLAND, DUDLEY, AND OTHERS, *see* Lake George.

FARMINGTON, TOWN OF.

1831. Report concerning the town-house of, ... A 3 255
1831. School district No. 11, report of superintendent of common schools on petition for a law authorizing a tax on, to indemnify the trustees for certain expenses incurred in a number of law-suits, &c., ... A 4 302
1831. Report of committee on colleges, &c., on the same, ... A 4 310
1832. Report of select committee on the same, ... A 2 103
1834. Report of committee on the judiciary on the same, ... A 3 314

FARWELL, GUSTAVUS AND E.

		Doc.	Vol.	No.
1831.	Report on petition to be released from a certain judgment,......	A	2	168

FARWELL, SAMUEL.

1835.	Report on petition for extra allowance for work done on the Erie canal,......	S	2	86
1835.	Report of canal board on the same,......	A	2	86
1835.	Report of committee on claims on the same,......	A	2	122

FARWELL, SAMUEL, AND OTHERS.

1839.	Report on petition for extra allowance for work done on the Chemung canal,......	A	3	110
1840.	Report of canal board for the same,......	S	4	100
1841.	Report on petition for compensation for building bridges over the Erie canal at Utica,......	A	5	194

FAVIE, ELIZABETH, AND OTHERS (aliens).

1835.	Report on petition for the release of the right of the state to certain lands,......	A	2	100

FAY, JOHN D.

1847.	Memorial of,......	S	3	93

FAY, JOHN WILLIAM, AND OTHERS, *see* New York Trinity Church.

FEDERAL GOVERNMENT, *see* General Government.

FELLOWS, J., *see* Pulteney estate.

FELT, NORMAN.

1857.	Report of committee on claims adverse on petition of, for damages by falling of bridge over the Chenango canal,......	A	3	150

FEMALE SEMINARIES, *see* Academies, &c.

FEME COVERT, *see* Women, Married.

FENCES, *see* Canal Fences.

1838.	Report on the subject of damages for not keeping up,......	A	5	227

FERDON, JOHN W.

1856.	Report relative to seat of,......	S	2	89

FERGUSON, JAMES G., *see* Thomas Geary and others.

FERGUSON, J. G.

1842.	Report of committee on claims on petition of,......	A	7	137

FERO, ROBERT.

1844.	Report of canal board in answer to a resolution of the assembly calling for testimony in the case of,......	A	6	153

FERRELL, JOHN A.

1833.	Report on petition to be released from a certain judgment and for a re-appraisal of certain land, &c.,......	A	3	184
1835.	Report of committee on public lands on the same,......	A	5	392

FERRIES, *see* New York Ferries.

Year	Subject	Doc.	Vol.	No.
1834.	Report of attorney-general relative to the power of the legislature to authorize and regulate,	A	2	61
1849.	Report of Commissioners of Code concerning,	A	1	12
1854.	Opinion of attorney-general relative to regulation of,	A	4	131
1855.	Report of committee on commerce and navigation relative to life-saving gates at,	S	2	41
1857.	Report of committee on judiciary on bill to incorporate Enterprise Ferry Company,	S	4	168
1857.	Report of committee on judiciary on bill to incorporate People's Steam Ferry Company,	S	4	169
1857.	Report of committee on commerce and navigation relative to Staten Island Railroad Company to have, own and run ferry boats, &c.,	A	2	64

FERRILL, TIMOTHY N.

Year	Subject	Doc.	Vol.	No.
1839.	Report on petition for extra allowance for work done on the Erie canal,	A	3	84
1839.	Report of the canal commissioners on the same,	A	3	142
1839.	Report of committee on claims on the same,	A	4	163
1840.	Report of committee on claims on the same,	A	1	29

FERRIS, JOHN.

Year	Subject	Doc.	Vol.	No.
1849.	Report of committee on claims on petition of,	A	2	57

FEUDAL TENURES, *see* Landlord and Tenant.

FIELD, D. D.

Year	Subject	Doc.	Vol.	No.
1842.	Proposed acts to simplify administration of justice,	A	5	81

FIERO & ANTHONY.

Year	Subject	Doc.	Vol.	No.
1850.	Report of canal board in relation to claim of,	A	3	33

FINANCES, STATE, *see* the respective Funds; Government, State; Loans; Retrenchment.

Year	Subject	Doc.	Vol.	No.
1830.	Report on the subject of (Mr. Todd),	A	3	205
1831.	do do (Mr. Selden),	A	3	224
1832.	do do (Mr. Bronson),	S	1	61
1833.	do do (Mr. Van Duzen),	A	4	245
1833.	do do (Mr. Bronson),	S	2	55
1834.	do do (Mr. Wheeler),	A	3	131
1835.	do do (Mr. Van Schaack),	S	2	38
1836.	do do (Mr. Van Schaack),	S	1	35
1835.	do do (Mr. Ruggles),	A	5	242
1839.	do do (Mr. Verplanck),	S	3	96
1839.	do do (Mr. Paige),	S	3	101
1839.	do do (Mr. Young),	A	3	103
1839.	do do (Mr. Davis),	A	6	388
1841.	do do (Mr. Verplanck),	S	2	51
1841.	do do (Mr. Holley),	A	7	266
1841.	do do (Mr. Loomis),	A	7	278
1842.	Communication from comptroller relative to,	A	4	61
1842.	Report of committee on ways and means on,	A	5	88
1842.	Report of minority on same,	A	7	166
1843.	Report of committee on finance on the subject of,	S	2	69
1844.	Report of Mr. Hoffman on so much of the governor's message as relates to,	A	7	185
1844.	Report of Mr. Davis on same subject,	A	7	186
1844.	Report of Mr. Bosworth on same subject,	A	7	188
1850.	Report of comptroller relative to,	A	5	132

FINANCES, STATE—*continued.*

		Doc.	Vol.	No.
1851.	Report of comptroller on,	S	3	91
1851.	Report of treasurer on,	S	3	93
1856.	Report on,	A	5	181

FINN, WILLIAM.

		Doc.	Vol.	No.
1839.	Report on petition for compensation for damages to his lands and fences,	A	6	358
1842.	Report of canal board on petition of,	A	5	100

FINNEY, JONATHAN.

		Doc.	Vol.	No.
1840.	Report on petition of, to be restored to the rights of citizenship,	S	2	55

FIRST CHRISTIAN PARTY ONEIDA INDIANS, *see* Indians—Oneidas.

FIRST GREAT SOUTHWESTERN TURNPIKE COMPANY.

		Doc.	Vol.	No.
1834.	Report on petition to amend the charter of,	A	3	188

FIRST GREAT WESTERN TURNPIKE COMPANY.

		Doc.	Vol.	No.
1831.	Report relative to a tax assessed on, in the city of Albany,	A	2	120

FISH.

		Doc.	Vol.	No.
1855.	Report of committee on agriculture in relation to breeding,	A	5	142

FISH, PAUL J., AND OTHERS.

		Doc.	Vol.	No.
1837.	Report on petition to erect docks, &c., adjacent to their lands on the East river, in the village of Williamsburgh,	A	4	287

FISHER, ALFRED, AND OTHERS.

		Doc.	Vol.	No.
1842.	Report of committee on claims on petition of,	S	3	73
1844.	Report of committee on claims on petition of,	S	1	41

FISHER, HANNAH.

		Doc.	Vol.	No.
1830.	Report relative to the proof of her will, &c.,	S	2	158

FISHERIES, SALMON.

		Doc.	Vol.	No.
1857.	Report of standing committee on agriculture, on petition relative to,	S	4	146

FISHKILL AND POUGHKEEPSIE, TOWNS OF.

		Doc.	Vol.	No.
1832.	Report on petition for a new town from parts of,	A	4	284
1832.	Report of committee on towns and counties (Mr. Tilford),	A	4	299
1840.	do do do (Mr. Hull),	S	3	91
1841.	do do do (Mr. Hull),	S	1	36

FISHKILL EDUCATION SOCIETY.

		Doc.	Vol.	No.
1835.	Report on petition to incorporate,	A	4	282

FISHKILL, TOWN OF.

		Doc.	Vol.	No.
1839.	Matteawan Company in the, report on petition to increase the capital of,	S	1	29
1839.	Rocky Glen Company in the, report on petition to increase the capital of,	S	1	29
1846.	Report on bill to authorize officers of, to appropriate certain moneys,	S	1	33

FISHKILL VILLAGE.

		Doc.	Vol.	No.
1836.	Road from, to the Croton river, report on petition for aid to improve,	A	4	277

FISK, THOMAS W.

1836.	Report on petition for compensation for the loss of a boat load of salt on the Erie canal,	A	4	244

FITCH, ABIJAH, AND OTHERS.

1851.	Report of judiciary committee, on bill for relief of,	A	3	76
1851.	Report of committee on claims,	A	4	96
1855.	Report of commissioners appointed to investigate affairs of state prisons relative to claim of,	S	1	22

FITCH, ASA, M. D., *see* Entomology.

FITCH, HUNT AND COOLEY.

1855.	Memorial of,	A	2	44
1855.	Report of select committee on bill for payment of judgment in favor of,	S	2	52
1855.	Report of select committee on bill for payment of judgment in favor of,	S	2	54

FITZBURGH, W., *see* Hervey Ely, and others.

FITZGERALD, DAVID.

1836.	Report on petition to be indemnified against a judgment for obstructing the waters of Mud creek, while repairing the Erie canal aqueduct,	A	3	122
1836.	Report of committee on the judiciary on petition to be indemnified against a judgment for obstructing the waters of Mud creek, while repairing the Erie canal aqueduct,	S	2	98
1836.	Report of committee on claims on petition to be indemnified against a judgment for obstructing the waters of Mud creek, while repairing the Erie canal aqueduct,	A	2	109
1838.	Report of committee on claims on petition to be indemnified against a judgment for obstructing the waters of Mud creek, while repairing the Erie canal aqueduct,	A	3	138
1839.	Report of canal commissioners on petition to be indemnified against a judgment for obstructing the waters of Mud creek, while repairing the Erie canal aqueduct,	A	5	173

FITZHUGH HENRY.

1853.	Communication from, in reply to the preamble and resolution offered in the assembly,	A	2	27
1853.	Report of select committee in the case of,	A	4	90

FITZSIMMONS, PATRICK, AND JAMES BRADY.

1841.	Report on petition for the payment of money due them on a contract for work on the Erie canal,	A	6	248
1842.	Report of canal board on petition of,	S	4	86
1843.	Report of the comptroller on the petition of,	S	1	16
1845.	Report of committee on grievances on petition of,	A	3	56
1846.	Report of committee on claims on petition of,	A	1	29
1847.	Report on petition of,	A	1	23
1850.	Report on petition of,	S	3	77
1851.	Report of committee on petition of, for canal damages,	S	2	47

FLEET, DANIEL, *see* James E. De Kay.

FLEMING, ROBERT.

		Doc.	Vol.	No.
1830.	Report on petition relative to certain land purchased of the State,	A	2	119

FLETCHER, NOAH T., AND OTHERS.

1853.	Report of committee on claims on petition of, for canal damages,	S	2	39

FLINT, ASHER.

1840.	Report on petition to authorize him to take the oath of office of commissioner of deeds,	A	8	328

FLINT CREEK AND NETTLE VALLEY SWAMP.

1834.	Report on petition to drain,	A	4	253

FLOUR INSPECTOR IN NEW YORK, *see* New York.

FLORENCE, TOWN OF.

1834.	Report on petition for a bounty on bears,	A	4	316
1835.	Report on petition for a bounty on bears,	A	1	43

FLORIDA BRIDGE.

1846.	Report of canal board relative to,	A	4	127

FLORIDA BRIDGE COMPANY.

1830.	Report on petition to collect toll on the tow-path bridge across Schoharie creek,	A	4	340
1850.	Report of committee on,	S	1	34

FLORIDA, STATE OF.

1851.	Resolutions of legislature of,	A	4	126

FLOYD, JOHN, *see* Leonard Hildreth, and others.

FLUSHING.

1832.	Fire company, report on petition to increase the number of members of,	A	6	318
1857.	Report of committee on roads, &c., on petition for road from Hunter's Point to Newtown and,	S	4	119

FLUSHING CREEK.

1841.	Report on petition of Benjamin W. Strong to rebuild a bridge over,	A	2	23

FLYNN, JOHN.

1854.	Report on petition of,	S	2	74

FOGARTY, DENNIS.

1848.	Report on petition of,	A	5	187

FOLTS, GEORGE.

1852.	Report on petition of,	A	2	37
1854.	Report on petition of,	A	2	53
1855.	Report of committee on claims on petition of,	A	3	69
1855.	Communication from canal appraisers in reference to claim of,	A	4	82
1856.	Report on petition of,	A	3	49

FOLTS, JAMES.

1847.	Report on petition of,	A	7	200

		Doc.	Vol.	No.
	FOLTS, JAMES—*continued.*			
1849.	Report of committee on canals on petition of,	A	3	119
	FOLTS, JAMES, AND OTHERS.			
1850.	Report on claim,	S	2	51
	FONDA, STAATS V. F.			
1850.	Report on claim,	A	4	65
	FOOT, STILMAN.			
1834.	Report on petition to be released from a certain judgment,	A	4	354
	FORBES, ISAAC J., *see* John Amphlett.			
	FORBUS, ALEXANDER, *see* Chancery, clerks in.			
	FORD, ASHER, Jr.			
1832.	Report on petition for bounty lands for revolutionary services,	A	4	289
	FORECLOSURES OF MORTGAGES, *see* Mortgages.			
	FOREIGN BANKS, NOTES OF, *see* Banks.			
	FOREIGN INSURANCE COMPANIES, *see* Insurance.			
	FOREIGN POOR, *see* Poor.			
	FOREIGN PRACTITIONERS, *see* Medicine.			
	FOREIGNERS.			
1845.	Report of committee on the judiciary on the petition of inhabitants of Sullivan county, in reference to the naturalization of,	A	7	245
	FOREMAN, WINFIELD S.			
1852.	Report on petition of, for damages,	A	2	80
	FORNCROOK, P., *see* D. Neff.			
	FORT ANN, TOWN OF.			
1838.	Report on petition to raise money for the support of roads and bridges,	A	5	264
1841.	Report on petition to raise money to cancel a certain debt for building bridges,	A	7	283
	FORT BREWERTON BRIDGE COMPANY.			
1847.	Report of, in answer to a resolution,	A	2	68
1857.	Report relative to charter of,	S	2	70
	FORT COVINGTON, TOWN OF.			
1832.	Report on petition for the division of the,	A	4	315
1832.	Academy in, report on petition for a grant of land to build an,	A	1	18
1832.	Report of committee on public lands do do	A	2	92
1833.	do do do do	A	1	29
1833.	Report of attorney-general, do do	A	2	41
1833.	Report of commissioners of the land office, do do	A	3	197
	FORT EDWARD.			
1837.	Report on petition to construct a dam at, between the state dam and the upper end of Rogers' island,	A	3	165

14

FORT EDWARD—*continued.*

		Doc.	Vol.	No.
1835.	Surplus water, report on petition for a grant of, at,	S	2	74

FORT HUNTER SUSPENSION BRIDGE.

1852.	Report in reference to the,	S	2	86

FORT MILLER DAM.

1830.	Report of canal commissioners relative to the,	A	2	86
1830.	Report of committee on canals relative to the,	A	3	226
1842.	Report of canal board on petition for, and remonstrance against removal of,	A	5	114
1849.	Report of canal board respecting,	A	3	125
1850.	Report on petition of John Davis and others,	S	2	66
1851.	Letters of secretary of war and brevet-colonel G. Wright relative to granting lands near,	S	3	82

FORT PLAIN.

1832.	Road from, to German Flats, report on petition to repeal the law to lay out a,	A	2	156
1833.	Report of committee on roads and bridges on the same,	A	3	165
1834.	Report of committee on roads and bridges on the same,	S	1	19

FORT SCHLOSSER, *see* Northern Frontier.

FORTIFICATIONS ON STATEN ISLAND.

1830.	Report relative to the sale of the, to the general government,	S	4	434

FOSTER AND FRAZEE, *see* Frazee and Foster.

FOSTER, HENRY A.

1845.	Memorial of, relative to the report of committee on claims of March 24, 1845, in regard to him as a former member of the senate,	S	3	90

FOSTER, JOHN C., AND OTHERS.

1857.	Report of committee on claims, favorable on petition of, for additional compensation,	A	2	122

FOWLER, DANIEL (a Stockbridge Indian).

1835.	Report on petition to sell certain lands,	A	4	299

FOWLER, J.

1845.	Report of secretary of state on the petition of,	A	5	183

FOX, LEANDER, AND OTHERS.

1849.	Report of committee on canals on petition of,	A	3	121

FOX, NORMAN.

1830.	Report on petition to vacate his seat as a member of assembly on account of his being a minister of the gospel,	A	4	376

FOXES, BOUNTY ON.

1836.	Report on petition for a bounty on, in East Hampton,	A	3	139
1838.	Report on petition for a bounty on, in Smithtown,	A	5	*222

FRANCE.

		Doc.	Vol.	No.
1836.	Demand of, for an apology for certain language used by the president, joint resolution relative to,	A	2	73
1838.	Indemnity of citizens of the United States against losses by the illegal conduct of, joint resolution relative to,	A	5	216
1844.	Resolution of Connecticut relative to spoliations by,	A	1	7
1844.	Report of select committee on same subject,	A	3	67
1850.	Letter of A. Vattemare relative to donations from,	A	8	192

FRANCHER, RICHARD.

		Doc.	Vol.	No.
1857.	Report of committee on claims, favorable on petition of, for damages by break in the Erie canal,	A	2	61

FRANCIS, JOHN BROWN, *see* John B. Herrishoff and others.

FRANCISCO, MICHAEL.

		Doc.	Vol.	No.
1841.	Report on petition for compensation for revolutionary services,	A	6	241
1842.	Report of committee on militia and public defense, on petition of,	A	2	16
1842.	Report of committee on militia on petition of,	A	2	19
1843.	Report of committee on claims on petition of,	A	5	124
1845.	Report of committee on the militia and public defense, on the petition of,	A	3	40

FRANKFORT, TOWN OF.

		Doc.	Vol.	No.
1844.	Report of canal appraisers on memorial of landowners in, on the subject of canal damages,	A	5	101
1847.	Report of canal board on petition of James Folts for a bridge at,	A	7	200

FRANKING PRIVILEGE.

		Doc.	Vol.	No.
1837.	Resolution of the legislature of Maryland to extend the, to governors of states and members and officers of the legislature of the several states,	A	2	146
1842.	Report of select committee on, and letter postage,	A	7	165
1843.	Resolutions of legislature of Vermont relative to, and postage,	A	2	15
1844.	Resolution of Connecticut relative to,	A	1	14

FRANKLIN COUNTY,

		Doc.	Vol.	No.
1831.	Claim of, to certain moneys of Clinton county, report relative to,	A	2	119
1835.	Arsenal lot, report on bill to provide for the redemption of a part of the,	A	4	366
1832.	Academy, report on petition to record the mortgages belonging to, in a separate book,	A	3	212
1840.	Poor-house system, report on petition to abolish the,	A	6	267
1841.	Poor-house system, report on petition to abolish the,	A	7	265
1841.	Spirituous liquors, report on petition to prohibit the sale of, in said county on Sundays,	A	3	191
1836.	Wolves, bounty on, report on petition for a,	A	1	39
1851.	Report of select committee on petition of inhabitants of Essex, Warren and,	A	4	94
	Military road in, *see* Clinton county.			

FRANKLIN, H. S., *see* Amos S. Tryon.

FRANKLINVILLE, TOWN OF.

		Doc.	Vol.	No.
1832.	Report on petition to extend the time for the collection of taxes in,	A	1	47
1836.	Fire company, report on petition to incorporate,	A	4	271

FRAZEE & FOSTER.

		Doc.	Vol.	No.
1845.	Report of committee on claims on the petition of, for relief,.....	S	2	77
1846.	Report of committee on claims in the case of,................	A	1	20
1847.	Report on petition of,..................................	S	2	74

FRAZEE, BENJAMIN.

		Doc.	Vol.	No.
1853.	Report of committee on claims on petition of, for relief,........	A	3	72
1854.	Report on petition of,..................................	A	2	64

FRAZEE, JAMES.

		Doc.	Vol.	No.
1858.	Report of majority of committee on contested seat, occupied by,	A	3	71
1858.	Report of minority of committee on the same,................	A	3	70

FRAZER, DONALD.

		Doc.	Vol.	No.
1832.	Report on petition for an extension of the lease of the Black Rock ferry,..	A	3	340

FRAZER, W.

		Doc.	Vol.	No.
1830.	Report on petition to be restored to the rights of citizenship,....	A	3	250

FRAZIER, JOHN.

		Doc.	Vol.	No.
1833.	Report on petition for compensation for damages to his lands by the construction of the Erie canal,......................	A	4	258

FREE ACADEMY OF NEW YORK, *see* Academies, &c.

FREEHOLD, VILLAGE OF.

		Doc.	Vol.	No.
1831.	Report on petition to incorporate a turnpike company from, to Leeds,..	A	4	345

FREEMAN, SAMUEL.

		Doc.	Vol.	No.
1838.	Report on petition of, relative to the practice of granting to high judicial officers passage on railroads free of charge,..........	A	6	337

FREEMASONS, *see* W. Morgan.

FREEMASONS' PATENT, *see* Lands, Freemasons' Patent.

FREE TRADE ASSOCIATION, *see* New York.

FRENCH BENEVOLENT SOCIETY, *see* New York.

FRÉNCH, LEMUEL, AND OTHERS.

		Doc.	Vol.	No.
1852.	Report on petition of, for relief,............................	S	1	25

FRENCH SPOLIATION, *see* France.

FRIDLEY, CATHARINE.

		Doc.	Vol.	No.
1837.	Report on petition for compensation for damages to her lands by the construction of the Chemung canal,...................	A	2	99
1837.	Report of committee on claims on the same,....	A	3	217

FRIENDSHIP.

		Doc.	Vol.	No.
1832.	Road from, to Olean, report on petition to appoint commissioners to lay out a,..	A	4	312

FRIENDS, SOCIETY OF.

		Doc.	Vol.	No.
1832.	Report on petition to allow their ministers to be taxed as other citizens,	S	1	20
1841.	Report on petition to repeal the law subjecting them to fine and imprisonment for the non-performance of militia duty,	A	5	170
1847.	Report of majority of committee of ways and means on memorial of,	A	7	190
1850.	Report of committee on charitable and religious societies on memorial of Genesee yearly meeting of,	A	5	117

FRITCHER AND WILES, *see* Wiles and Fritcher.

FROST, DAVID, AND EVELINE WILLIS.

1839.	Report on petition for a divorce,	A	2	21
1839.	Report of committee on grievances on the same,	A	3	78
1840.	do do do	A	8	324
1841.	do do do	A	5	189
1841.	Report of select committee on the same,	A	6	202

FROST, E., AND P. HARMAN.

1833.	Report on petition of, to erect a wharf at Williamsburgh,	A	4	311

FUGITIVES FROM JUSTICE, *see* Alabama, Virginia, Maine and Georgia.

1842.	Resolutions of Delaware relative to,	A	2	27
1843.	Communication from the governor in relation to,	A	5	140

FUGITIVES FROM LABOR OR SERVICE.

1843.	Report of committee on the judiciary respecting,	A	5	128

FUGITIVE SLAVES, *see* Slaves.

FULLER, ABIEL.

1835.	Report on petition for extra allowance for work done on the Erie canal,	A	5	388

FULLER, HENRY, *see* A. Dailey and H. Fuller.

FULLERTON, DANIEL, AND DANIEL T. DURLAND.

1850.	Report of committee on elections on contested seat of,	A	4	67

FULTON AND BLENHEIM, TOWNS OF.

1833.	Report on petition from, to prevent hunting deer with dogs,	A	3	176

FULTON COUNTY.

1840.	Report on petition from, for a division of the debts and assets of Montgomery county,	A	4	136
1856.	Report on petition of inhabitants of, for appropriation,	A	3	78
1849.	Report of committee on roads and bridges on petition of inhabitants of, and Montgomery county respecting bridge over the Mohawk at Fultonville,	A	2	73
1856.	Petition of inhabitants of, for appropriation,	A	3	78

FULTONVILLE.

1849.	Report of committee on roads and bridges on the petition of inhabitants of Fulton and Montgomery counties relative to erection of bridge over the Mohawk at,	A	2	73

		Doc.	Vol.	No.
	FUND, BANK, *see* Banks.			
	FUND, CANAL, *see* Canal Fund.			
	FUND, COMMON SCHOOL, *see* Common Schools.			
	FUND, GENERAL, *see* General Fund.			
	FUND, LITERATURE, *see* Literature Fund.			
	FUND, SAFETY, *see* Banks.			
	FUNDS INVESTED IN CHANCERY, *see* Chancery.			
	FUNDS OF THE STATE, *see* Finances; Government, State; Loans; Retrenchment.			
1844.	Report of Mr. Denniston on the subject of canals and,	S	3	98
1850.	Report on governor's message relating to certain,	S	2	70
	FURLONG, PATRICK (an alien).			
1831.	Report on petition concerning the estate of,	A	2	86
	FURMAN, JAMES, AND MEDAD ROGERS.			
1857.	Report of committee on claims, favorable on petition of, for damages by withdrawal of water from mill,	A	1	29

G.

		Doc.	Vol.	No.
	GAGE, SARAH, AND OTHERS.			
1841.	Report on petition of, relative to certain lands in Freemasons' patent,	A	4	130
	GAGE, S. G.			
1848.	Report of attorney-general as to claim of,	A	3	118
	GAGE, THOMAS, *see* Samuel Rider and others.			
	GALEN, TOWN OF.			
1841.	Report on petition to raise money by tax to build a bridge,	A	5	165
	GALL, WILLIAM.			
1847.	Report of committee on public lands, on petition of heirs of, deceased,	A	4	146
1849.	Report of committee on claims, on petition of heirs of,	A	1	25
	GAMAGE, GILBERT A.			
1830.	Report on petition for the settlement of a claim held by him against I. M'Lean, late a captain in the service of the state,	S	4	389
	GAME.			
1837.	Preservation of, in certain counties, report relative to the,	A	3	196
	GARDNER, ADDISON.			
1832.	Report of amounts of fees received by him as circuit judge,	A	2	132
	GARDNER, CHARLES.			
1832.	Report on petition to change his name,	A	3	237

GARDNER, GEORGE.

		Doc.	Vol.	No.
1844.	Report of the minority of the committee on claims on the petition of,	A	3	62
1847.	Report on petition of,	S	1	33

GARDNER, ORCELIA MINERVA.

		Doc.	Vol.	No.
1841.	Report on petition of, for a divorce,	S	3	85

GARRISON, BEVERLY.

		Doc.	Vol.	No.
1833.	Report on petition for a law vesting in him the title to certain land,	A	4	279

GATES.

		Doc.	Vol.	No.
1837.	Report on bill authorizing county judges to locate, on turnpikes,	S	2	67
1848.	Report as to power of county judges to locate,	A	5	134

GATES, JOHN.

		Doc.	Vol.	No.
1831.	A soldier of the revolution, report on petition of the heirs of, for bounty lands,	A	4	338
1835.	Gertrude, widow of, report on petition for bounty lands,	A	3	178

GATES, TOWN OF.

		Doc.	Vol.	No.
1834.	School district No. 3 in, report relative to,	A	2	52
1835.	Town meeting, report on petition for a law fixing the time and place for holding the next,	A	2	123

GATES, W., AND OTHERS.

		Doc.	Vol.	No.
1841.	Report on petition for relief on a contract on the enlarged Erie canal,	A	3	84

GAY, JUSTUS.

		Doc.	Vol.	No.
1833.	Report on petition of, in behalf of Mercy Shaw for bounty lands,	A	4	306
1834.	Report on petition of, in behalf of Mercy Shaw for bounty lands,	A	4	393

GAY, W., JR.

		Doc.	Vol.	No.
1840.	Report on petition of, for compensation for a mill site at Mount Morris,	A	1	30
1840.	Report of canal commissioners on the same,	A	2	37
1840.	Report of select committee on the same,	A	4	154
1841.	Report of committee on claims on the same,	A	4	123

GAZYNSKI, CAPT. TITUS FELIX.

		Doc.	Vol.	No.
1848.	Reports on petition of,	A	5	177
1848.	Reports on petition of,	A	5	178
1850.	Report on petition of,	A	5	94

GEARY, THOMAS, AND OTHERS.

		Doc.	Vol.	No.
1840.	Report on petition for compensation for services, and for materials furnished to Robert M'Bride, superintendent of repairs on the Erie canal,	A	3	95
1841.	Report of committee on claims on the same,	A	2	40

GEAUTEAU, A., AND OTHERS.

		Doc.	Vol.	No.
1846.	Committee on manufacture of salt, report on petition of a,	A	2	57

GEAUTEAU, C.

		Doc.	Vol.	No.
1846.	Report of committee on manufacture of salt, on petition of,......	A	2	57

GEDDES, JAMES, *see* Cayuga Marshes.

GEDDES, VILLAGE OF.

		Doc.	Vol.	No.
1831.	Report on petition to incorporate the,..........................	A	3	198
1833.	Report on petition relative to the streets in the,................	S	2	74
1850.	Report of canal board in relation to canal at,..................	A	5	103
1855.	Communication from canal commissioners respecting canal at,...	A	5	133
1856.	Report on the petition of owners of basin lots Nos. 9, 10 and 11, in village of,..	A	3	28

GEER & WEAVER.

		Doc.	Vol.	No.
1844.	Report of the canal board on the reference from the assembly of the petition of,..	A	1	23
1844.	Report of committee on claims on the petition of,..............	A	5	118
1845.	Report of committee on claims, on petition of,..................	A	3	32

GEER, D. S., AND SAMUEL P.

		Doc.	Vol.	No.
1847.	Report on petition of,..	A	1	32

GEER, KASSON & BREED.

		Doc.	Vol.	No.
1844.	Report of canal board on petition of,........................	S	4	133
1844.	Report of committee on claims on the petition of,...............	A	5	116
1844.	Report of the canal board on the reference from the assembly of, the petition of,..	A	3	58

GEERY, JAMES, *see* New York Second Associate Church.

GENERAL BANKING LAW, *see* Banks.

GENERAL FUND.

		Doc.	Vol.	No.
1846.	Report of comptroller relative to apportionments from,.........	A	5	178
1846.	Report of majority committee on ways and means on, canal and,	A	5	189
1846.	Minority report on same,..................................	A	5	190
1846.	Report of comptroller in answer to a resolution relative to,......	A	5	193
1847.	Report as to, and sinking,..................................	S	4	130
1849.	Report of comptroller as to time of extinguishing certain debts of canal and,..	A	1	13
1849.	Report of comptroller as to time of extinguishing certain debts of canal and,..	A	1	33
1851.	Report of comptroller relative to the receipts of,...............	S	2	48
1852.	Report of comptroller respecting debt of,.....................	S	2	68
1852.	Minority report relative to debt of,........................	S	2	77
1852.	Report of comptroller relative to receipts into,................	A	5	103

GENERAL GOVERNMENT, *see* Government, General.

GENESEE AND ALLEGANY.

		Doc.	Vol.	No.
1831.	Report on petition for a new county from parts of,.............	A	2	105
1839.	Report on petition for a new county from parts of,.............	A	6	393
1840.	Division of, report on petition for the,......................	A	7	292
1841.	Division of, report on petition for the, and for the location of the county buildings,..................................	A	6	210

GENESEE COUNTY.

		Doc.	Vol.	No.
1840.	Assessment rolls of the several towns in, report on petition to review and correct the equalization of,.....................	A	3	178

GENESEE COUNTY—*continued.*

		Doc.	Vol.	No.
1833.	Botanical Society, First Union, report on petition to incorporate,.	A	3	174
1834.	Botanical Society, First Union, report on petition to incorporate,.	A	3	236
1831.	Bridge over Tonawanda creek, report on petition to raise money to build,	A	4	358
1831.	High school, report on petition to incorporate,	A	4	319
1830.	Jail in, report on petition to raise money to build,	A	4	427
1831.	Jail in, report of select committee on the same,	A	1	67
1831.	Jail in, report of committee on towns and counties on the same, .	A	2	106
1835.	Lands in Batavia, report on petition for a law authorizing said company to relinquish certain lands to the Holland Land Company,	A	1	14
1838.	Poor-house, abuses in, report relative to,	A	6	310
1839.	Poor, town and county, report on petition to revive the distinction between, in said county,	A	5	299
1830.	Road in, report on petition to raise money by tax to improve,...	A	4	311
1830.	Sheriff of, report on petition of, for payment of board of persons imprisoned for non-payment of militia fines,	A	4	423
1834.	Wesleyan Seminary at Lima, members of the Genesee conference to incorporate,	A	1	50
1834.	Wesleyan Seminary, remonstrance against incorporating,	A	1	51
1834.	Wesleyan Seminary, memorial of citizens of Lima relative to,...	A	2	96
1839.	Wesleyan Seminary, report on petition for aid to,	A	4	179
1832.	Report of E. Higgins, inspector of sole leather,	A	2	140
1833.	R port of N. Bodwell, inspector of sole leather,	A	2	66
1834.	Report of H. G. Rice, inspector of sole leather,	A	1	38

BANKS IN, *see* Banks, Genesee County.

GENESEE RIVER.

		Doc.	Vol.	No.
1831.	Bridge across, report on petition of citizens of Allegany to raise money to build,	A	4	285
1832.	Bridge across, in the town of Hume, report on petition for,.....	A	4	256
1835.	Bridge across, report on petition to authorize the supervisors of Livingston county to raise money to build,	A	3	242
1840.	Bridge across, report on petition to loan money to the town of Chili, to build,	A	6	248
1839.	Bridge across, near the junction of the Honeoye creek, report on petition for,	A	6	346
1841.	Canal feeder dam, report on petition for the removal of,	A	6	250
1841.	Canal feeder dam, report of canal commissioners relative to,....	A	7	274
1833.	Dam acrosss, report on petition of Ira Bacon to build,	A	1	31
1833.	do do Louis Paul D'Autremont to build,	S	2	58
1832.	do do H. H. May to build,	A	3	219
1832.	do do Gardner Wells to build,	A	4	288
1835.	do do W. H. Spencer to build,	A	3	194
1835.	Dam and boat lock, report on petition of Felix Tracy to build,..	A	4	295
1833.	Boat lock, report on petition of Erastus Bailey to build,	A	2	88
1832.	Ferry across, report on petition for,	A	2	151
1830.	Report on petition of E. Bailey, to erect mills, &c., on,	A	4	375
1831.	Steamboat Company, report on petition to incorporate,	A	3	115
1846.	Report of committee on canals respecting water from,	A	6	204
1847.	Dam across, report on petition for,	A	7	182
1848.	Report relative to division of waters of,	A	5	172
1852.	Occupancy of waters of, at Rochester,	A	5	102
1853.	Report of committee on claims on memorial of owners of water of, at Rochester.	A	4	86
1856.	Report of committee on roads and bridges on petition and remonstrance for bridge over,	S	2	53

GENESEE SUSPENSION BRIDGE COMPANY.

		Doc.	Vol.	No.
1852.	Report on the bill entitled the,	A	2	45

GENESEE VALLEY CANAL, *see* Canals.

GENESEE WESLEYAN SEMINARY, *see* Academies, &c.

GENESEE YEARLY MEETING OF FRIENDS.

		Doc.	Vol.	No.
1850.	Report on memorial of,	A	5	117

GENESEO RIVER.

		Doc.	Vol.	No.
1839.	Side-cut from the Genesee Valley canal to the, report on petition for,	A	4	264

GENESEO, TOWN OF.

		Doc.	Vol.	No.
1835.	Bridge across the Genesee between York and, report on petition to build,	A	3	194.
1835.	Bridge across the Genesee river between York and, report on petition of supervisors of Livingston county to raise money by tax to build a,	A	3	242

GENET, EDMUND C.

		Doc.	Vol.	No.
1830.	Report on petition of, against usurped corporate privileges, &c.,	S	4	336
1831.	Memorial of, relative to the Astor claim,	S	1	29
1831.	do do	S	1	77
1832.	do do	S	1	59
1833.	And others, petition for a ship canal from Albany to New Baltimore,	S	1	24
1833.	Report on the same,	S	2	80

GENEVA, Supreme court clerk at, *see* Supreme Court.

GENEVA AND CANANDAIGUA RAILROAD, *see* Railroads.

GENEVA COLLEGE, *see* Colleges.

GENEVA, WESTERN HOSPITAL AT.

		Doc.	Vol.	No.
1839.	Report on petition to be incorporated, and for aid to the,	A	4	255
1840.	Report on petition for aid to the,	S	4	104

GEOGRAPHICAL SURVEY OF THE STATE.

		Doc.	Vol.	No.
1852.	Communication of governor respecting,	S	1	41

GEOLOGICAL CONTRACT.

		Doc.	Vol.	No.
1845	Message from governor transmitting Carroll & Cook's,	A	3	78

GEOLOGICAL SOCIETY, AMERICAN.

		Doc.	Vol.	No.
1857.	Memorial of, relative to improvement of Hudson river,	S	1	14

GEOLOGICAL SURVEY OF THE STATE.

		Doc.	Vol.	No.
1835.	Memorial of the American Institute for a,	A	4	374
1836.	Report of secretary of state in relation to a,	A	1	9
1836.	Report of a select committee on the subject,	A	2	77
1837.	Report of committee on colleges and academies on,	A	3	258
1837.	1st report of the,	A	2	161
1838.	2d do	A	4	200
1839.	3d do	A	6	406
1840.	4th do	A	2	50

GEOLOGICAL SURVEY OF THE STATE—*continued.*

Year	Subject	Doc.	Vol.	No.
1841.	5th report of the,	A	5	150
1840.	Report on petition for a law giving to each district school a copy of the,	A	7	290
1840.	Report on the continuation of the (Mr. Denniston),	A	8	338
1842.	Communication from governor relative to the progress of,	S	3	68
1843.	Communications from secretary of state in reference to act relative to,	S	2	67
1843.	Communication supplemental to the above,	S	3	72
1843.	Resolution relative to Samuel Young and his communication respecting,	S	3	91
1845.	Report of comptroller relative to expenses of,	A	5	153
1850.	Report on,	A	8	186
1851.	Report of James Hall on,	S	2	32

GEORGETOWN, DISTRICT OF COLUMBIA.

Year	Subject	Doc.	Vol.	No.
1841.	Proceedings of a meeting of citizens of, relative to the retrocession of said town to the State of Maryland,	A	2	25

GEORGIA AND MAINE, Controversy between, on account of the refusal of Maine to deliver certain fugitives from justice.

Year	Subject	Doc.	Vol.	No.
1839.	Resolution of the legislature of Georgia relative to,	A	2	45
1840.	do do South Carolina, relative to,	A	5	167
1841.	do do Alabama, relative to,	A	4	125

GEORGIA, STATE OF.

Year	Subject	Doc.	Vol.	No.
1830.	Resolution of the legislature of, relative to the American Colonization Society,	A	1	13
1830.	do do relative to the election of President of the United States,	A	2	123
1833.	do do relative to granting aid for works of internal improvements by the United States,	A	2	39
1834.	Communication from the executive in relation to the above resolution,	A	1	11
1834.	Resolution of the legislature of, relative to the public lands,	A	1	34
1836.	Resolution of the legislature of, relative to the abolitionists,	A	3	109
1842.	Resolution of the legislature of, relative to proceedings of 27th Congress at extra session,	A	4	58
1842.	Governor of, correspondence with governor of New York,	A	1	2
1842.	Report of judiciary committee on correspondence of governor with executive of,	A	7	185
1843.	Resolution of the legislature of,	A	3	51
1843.	do do	A	3	52
1844.	do do	A	7	195
1850.	do do on slavery,	A	8	176

GERE, NELSON, AND CHARLES W. STEVES.

Year	Subject	Doc.	Vol.	No.
1852.	Report relative to,	S	1	49

GERMAIN, JAMES.

Year	Subject	Doc.	Vol.	No.
1840.	Report on petition for compensation for work on the Erie canal,	A	8	327
1841.	Report of canal board on the same,	S	3	77
1841.	Report of committee on claims on the same,	A	2	20

GERMAN FLATS. Road from, to Fort Plain, *see* Fort Plain.

Year	Subject	Doc.	Vol.	No.
1844.	Report of canal appraisers on memorial of landowners in, relative to canal damages,	A	5	101

GERMAN, JAMES.

		Doc.	Vol.	No.
1839.	Report on petition for compensation for the loss of a saw-mill at the foot of Black Rock harbor,....	A	6	371
1840.	Report of committee on claims on the same,....	A	8	315
1841.	Report of committee on claims on the same,....	A	2	34

GERRY, TOWN OF.

1830.	Town officers, report on petition to confirm the election of,....	A	4	369

GIBBONSVILLE.

1831.	Report relative to that portion of the Erie canal which passes through the lands ceded to the United States at, and West Troy,	A	4	361
1831.	Report relative to the inspection of lumber at,....	A	2	114

GIBBS, W., AND D. EARLL.

1834.	Report on petition for compensation for damages by the Erie canal,....	A	4	353

GIBBS, W., ISAAC LEWIS, AND G. H. COTTON.

1836.	Report on petition for compensation for damages by the Erie canal,....	A	4	220
1838.	Report of committee on claims on the same,....	A	2	60

GIBSON, JOHN.

1847.	Report on petition of,....	A	7	195

GIBSON, WILLIAM H.

1842.	Report of canal board on petition of,....	A	5	102

GIHON, JOHN.

1857.	Report of committee on state prisons, on petition of, for damages,	A	2	74

GILBERT & SPRAGUE.

1837.	Report on petition for extra allowance for work done on the Chenango canal,....	A	1	44

GILBERT, JASPER W.

1844.	Report of attorney-general, on the petition of,....	S	1	40
1844.	Report on petition of....	S	2	71

GILBERT, THOMAS J.

1841.	Report on petition for extra allowance for work done on the Chenango canal,....	A	3	77
1841.	Report of committee on canals on the same,....	A	7	298

GILBERT, THOMAS J.

1845.	Report of committee on claims, on the petition of,....	S	2	64

GILBERT, WILLIAM J.

1851.	Report on claim of, to seat in senate,....	S	3	84

GILBOA.

1845.	Report of minority of committee on bill to erect the town of,....	A	6	234
1845.	Report of majority of committee on bill to erect the town of,....	A	7	241

GILCHRIST, A., *see* C. Baker and others.

		Doc.	Vol.	No.
	GILCHRIST, ARCHIBALD.			
1843.	Report of the committee on claims on his petition,............	A	4	120
	GILCHRIST, ELIZABETH.			
1841.	Heirs of, report of commissioners of the land office on petition of the,..	A	3	74
1842.	Report of committee on petition of legal representatives of,......	A	4	68
1848.	Report of comptroller on petition of,.........................	S	2	40
	GILCHRIST, ISABELLA.			
1849.	Report on bill to authorize her to hold and convey real estate,..	S	2	58
	GILES, JOHN AND SAMUEL.			
1843.	Report of the commissioners of the land office on the petition of,	A	1	7
	GILLET, JEREMIAH.			
1834.	Report on petition for compensation for damages by the Crooked Lake canal,..................................	A	4	351
	GILLET, Z. P.			
1837.	Report on petition for compensation for the failure of the title to certain land bought of the state,..........................	A	4	312
1838.	Report of commissioners of the land office on the same,.........	A	3	150
1840.	Report of committee on claims on the same,...................	A	6	226
	GILLETT, Z. P.			
1846.	Report of committee on canals on petition of,..................	A	3	124
	GILLETT, ZACHARIAH P.			
1847.	Report on petition of,.....................................	A	1	22
	GILLETT, ZACHEUS P.			
1849.	Report of committee on claims on petition of,..................	A	2	91
	GILLILAND, W.			
1834.	Report on petition of, for remuneration for costs and expenses incurred in the prosecution of an action of ejectment to recover possession of a lot of land bought of the state,...............	A	4	285
1838.	Report of committee on claims on the same,..................	A	6	345
	GILLILAND, WILLIAM.			
1844.	Report of committee on claims on the petition of,..............	A	5	117
	GILLITT, Z. P.			
1846.	Report of committee on claims on petition of,.................	A	4	124
	GILMAN, E. P.			
1842.	Report of committee on claims on petition of,.................	A	3	87
1857.	Report on petition of,......................................	S	2	61
	GILMAN, G. P.			
1844.	Report on petition of,.....................................	A	3	87

GILMAN, R. G., AND I. MYERS.

		Doc.	Vol.	No.
1833.	Report on petition of, to build a dam across the Canisteo river,..	A	2	50

GILMORE, JAMES.

1857.	Report of committee on claims, favorable on petition of, for damages by overflow of the Genesee Valley canal,.................	A	3	158

GLASS BALLOT BOXES.

1857.	Report of committee on grievances, in favor of,...............	A	3	197

GLEASON, B., AND JOHN DRUM.

1836.	Report on petition of, to be credited with certain moneys paid for land,..	A	4	254

GLEN COVE.

1838.	Fire engine company, report on petition to incorporate a,.......	A	5	257

GLEN'S FALLS, Improvement of the Hudson above, *see* Hudson River.

GLEN'S FALLS BRIDGE COMPANY.

1830.	Report on petition to renew the charter of,.....................	A	3	258

GLEN'S FALLS FEEDER DAM.

1835.	Surplus waters, report on a petition of B. J. Swartwout for a lease of,..	A	4	341
1837.	Surplus waters, report on a petition of Hiram Barber for a lease of,..	A	3	259
1840.	Surplus waters, report of canal commissioners relative to leasing the,..	S	4	114

GLEN'S FALLS FEEDER.

1841.	Improvement of, report on petition for the,.....................	A	4	166

GLENVILLE, TOWN OF.

1834.	Quit rents of, report on petition for a law authorizing the trustees of said town to receive commutation for,................	A	4	332

GOFF, SALLY.

1836.	Report on petition of, for a divorce,..........................	S	2	68

GOODMAN, DAVID.

1831.	A soldier of the revolution, report on petition for bounty lands,	S	1	54

GOODMAN, SAMUEL A., *see* Chancery, Clerks in.

GOODRICH, CALEB.

1851.	Report on claim for canal damages,............................	S	3	66
1856.	Report on petition for relief of,...............................	A	4	108

GOODSELL, THOMAS.

1851.	Report of committee on claims on petition of, for canal damages,	A	4	122
1852.	Report on petition of,......................................	A	2	51
1854.	Report of committee on petition of,...........................	A	1	19

GOODSELL, THOMAS P.

		Doc.	Vol.	No.
1851.	Report of committee on claims for canal damages,	A	4	122

GOODWIN, S. A.

1843.	Clerk in chancery, memorial of,	S	2	51

GORDON, ACKLIN.

1833.	Report on petition of, for the sale to him of a lot of land in Lewiston,	A	2	102

GORDON, THOMAS F.

1836.	Report on petition for the patronage of the state to a "Historical View and Gazette of the State,"	S	1	28

GORHAM, TOWN OF.

1840.	School district No. 1 in, report on petition for certain modifications in the district library regulations for the,	A	4	123

GORTON, D. & R.

1833.	Report on petitition for compensation for damages by the Chemung canal,	A	4	321

GOSHEN, TOWN OF.

1836.	Supreme court commissioner at, report on petition to enlarge the powers of the,	A	2	54
1837.	Bridge over the Walkill, report on petition to raise money to build a,	A	2	127

GOSKOFF, FREDERICK.

1854.	Report of committee on claims on petition of,	S	1	21

GOSLIN, J. E.

1854.	Report of committee on claims on petition of,	A	4	137

GOULD, IRA, AND OTHERS.

1842.	Report of canal commissioners on petition of,	S	4	84

GOULD, PHAREZ.

1841.	Report on petition for a release of such portion of the Nine Mile creek feeder as will not be wanted for public use,	S	2	60

GOUVERNEUR, F. P.

1830.	Report on petition to change his name,	A	3	247

GOVERNEUR HIGH SCHOOL.

1839.	Report on petition for a loan to the,	A	4	196
1839.	Report on petition for a loan to the,	A	4	253

GOUVERNMENT, GENERAL.

1839.	Executive patronage of the, resolution of the legislature of Connecticut relative to the,	A	2	24
1839.	Policy of the, resolution of the legislature of North Carolina disapproving of the,	A	4	202
1832.	Aid to works of internal improvement by the, resolution of the legislature of Maine and Delaware relative to,	A	1	3

GOVERNMENT, GENERAL—*continued.*

		Doc.	Vol.	No.
1832.	Aid to works of internal improvement by the, resolution of the legislature of Tennessee relative to,	A	3	183
1833.	Aid to works of internal improvement by the, resolution of the legislature of Georgia relative to,	A	2	39
1838.	Administration of the, resolution of the legislature of Kentucky relative to the,	S	2	58
1840.	Hostility of the, to the state institutions (Mr. Simmons), report relative to,	A	8	344
1843.	Resolution of the State of Georgia in relation to the assumption of state debts by the,	A	3	52

GOVERNMENT, STATE, *see* Finances, &c.

		Doc.	Vol.	No.
1842.	Amendments offered by Mr. Root to Mr. Sherwood's proposition relative to public faith and credit of the state,	S	2	23
1842.	Resolution of Mr. Hoffman calling for statement of debt, &c.,	A	2	23
1842.	Report of comptroller in compliance with above resolution,	A	4	64
1843.	Report of comptroller relative to debt of,	S	1	18
1843.	Resolution by Mr. Foster relative to faith of, in the discharge of its debts,	S	3	76
1843.	Substitute, by Mr. Rhoades, on the same subject,	S	3	76
1844.	Report relative to the debt and resources of the,	S	4	126
1844.	Act to provide for paying the debt and preserving the credit of the state, passed March 29, 1842,	A	5	103
1844.	Communication from the governor transmitting resolution of the legislature of Georgia in relation to the repudiation of the state debts,	A	7	195
1846.	Report of minority of committee on ways and means,	A	6	212
1848.	Report as to expenses of government,	A	1	14
1851.	Communication from comptroller as to additional appropriation for expenses of government,	A	1	17
1852.	Report of comptroller relative to expenses of,	S	1	31
1852.	Report in reference to that part of the debt falling due July 1st, 1852,	S	2	69
1852.	Report of comptroller in regard to debt of June 1, 1846,	S	2	87
1853.	Report of comptroller in relation to expenses of,	S	3	76
1853.	Report of comptroller in relation to the indebtedness of, from 1835 to 1852,	A	2	24
1853.	Report of committee on ways and means on bill to provide means to pay present claims upon the treasury, to carry on the public works and to support the,	A	2	48
1853.	Report of minority on same subject,	A	2	54
1855.	Report of committee on ways and means on bill for support of,	A	5	118
1856.	Report of committee on finance on act to renew appropriation,	S	1	11
1856.	Report of commissioners to supervise certain expenditures for,	S	3	114
1857.	Report of standing committee on finance on bill to pay for certain services for,	S	4	148
1857.	Report of committee on ways and means relative to bills making appropriations for expenses of, prior to the year 1857,	A	2	100
1857.	Report of committee on ways and means on bills making appropriations for expenses of, prior to the year 1857,	A	3	100
1858.	Report of committee on finance on bill for relief of creditors of,	S	2	33
1858.	Report of comptroller on unpaid appropriations of last year,	A	4	91

GOVERNOR, *see* Executive Mansion.

		Doc.	Vol.	No.
1842.	Resolution proposing to amend constitution as to qualifications for,	A	1	5
1845.	Report of secretary of state pursuant to resolution of senate of May 7, 1844, in relation to civil officers whose appointments are vested in, with the consent of the senate,	S	1	4
1847.	Majority report on power of, to appoint certain officers,	S	2	61
1847.	Minority report on same,	S	2	62

GOVERNOR—*continued.*

		Doc.	Vol.	No.
1858.	Report relative to powers and duties of, and to fix compensation of officers in the executive department,	S	2	72

GOVERNOR'S MESSAGES.

ENOS T. THROOP (acting governor):

		Doc.	Vol.	No.
1830.	Annual message of,	A	1	2
1830.	Documents accompanying communication from the attorney-general relative to the Astor trials and the New Jersey boundary line,	S	1	4
1830.	Documents accompanying communication from the attorney-general relative to the Astor trials and the New Jersey boundary line,	S	1	5
1830.	Message transmitting resolutions of the legislature of Missouri relative to the mode of electing president, and a report in relation to the American Colonization Society, and resolutions from Mississippi relative to the tariff,	A	1	13
1830.	Communication from the, relative to the cession of jurisdiction of certain lands at Watervliet to the United States,	A	1	53
1830.	Message transmitting the report of the special counsel on the subject of the Morgan trials,	A	1	67
1830.	do resolutions of Pennsylvania relative to the tariff,	A	2	120
1830.	do resolutions of Georgia relative to the election of president,	A	2	123
1830.	do resolutions of Vermont relative to the tariff, and the election of president,	A	2	123
1830.	do the annual report of the governors of the New York hospital,	A	2	145
1830.	Message relative to the conditions of the state prisons,	A	3	220
1830.	Message transmitting a report of the attorney-general relative to the trial of one of the causes on the Astor claims,	S	4	347
1830.	Message transmitting resolutions of Delaware and Ohio relative to the tariff,	S	4	366
1830.	Message transmitting resolutions of Vermont relative to fortifications on the northern frontier,	S	4	366
1831.	Annual message of,	A	1	2
1831.	Message transmitting resolutions of Vermont, Mississippi and Connecticut relative to the election of president, &c.,	A	1	4
1831.	do resolutions of Louisiana relative to the tariff,	A	1	4
1831.	do the report of the inspector-general of staves and heading for the city of New York,	A	1	9
1831.	do the adjutant-general's annual report,	A	1	16
1831.	do a communication from the special counsel in the Morgan trials,	A	1	39
1831.	do a communication from the special counsel in the Morgan trials,	A	4	353
1831.	do the commissary-general's annual report,	A	2	122
1831.	do a communication from Major Talcott relative to the surplus water of the canal at Watervliet,	A	3	207
1831.	do resolutions of Ohio relative to the American Colonization Society,	A	3	233
1831.	do resolutions of Massachusetts relative to the reorganization the militia,	A	3	281
1831.	do a letter from the attorney-general relative to the boundary line between this state and New Jersey,	A	1	3

GOVERNOR'S MESSAGES—*continued.*

		Doc.	Vol.	No.
1831.	Message relative to the boundary line between this state and New Jersey,	A	3	263
1831.	Message transmitting a communication from Smith Thompson relative to the Astor trials,	S	1	24
1831.	Message transmitting resolutions of Massachusetts relative to certain proceedings in Georgia,	S	1	64
1832.	Annual message of,	A	1	2
1832.	Documents accompanying resolutions of Connecticut, Maine, New Hampshire and Delaware on various subjects,	A	1	3
1832.	Message at the second meeting of the legislature,	A	4	330
1832.	Message transmitting the commissary-general's annual report,	A	2	58
1832.	do the adjutant-general's annual report,	A	2	60
1832.	do a communication from the attorney-general relative to the Astor trials,	A	2	149
1832.	do the report of the governors of the New York Hospital,	A	3	180
1832.	do the resolutions of Massachusetts, Tennessee and Indiana, on various subjects,	A	3	183
1832.	Message relative to the adulteration of potash,	A	3	260
1832.	Message transmitting the report of the secretary of state relative to maps and Revised Statutes sent to the different states,	A	4	305
	WILLIAM L. MARCY:			
1833.	Annual message of,	S	1	1
1833.	Documents accompanying, proceedings of South Carolina relative to nullification,	S	1	2
1833.	Message transmitting resolutions of Illinois on the subject of the militia,	S	1	34
1833.	Message transmitting resolutions of Pennsylvania, Georgia and South Carolina, on various subjects,	A	2	39
1833.	Message transmitting resolutions of Delaware in relation to nullification,	A	2	135
1833.	Message transmitting resolutions of Indiana, New Hampshire, North Carolina and Massachusetts, on various subjects,	A	2	115
1833.	Message transmitting the adjutant-general's annual report,	A	2	84
1833.	Message returning a bill relative to cullers of staves and heading in the county of Rensselaer, with objections,	A	4	329
1834.	Annual message of,	A	1	2
1834.	Documents accompanying, letter from the commissioners appointed to settle the boundary line between New York and New Jersey,	A	1	3
1834.	Message transmitting resolutions of New Hampshire, Georgia, Pennsylvania, Maryland and Connecticut, on various subjects,	A	1	11
1834.	Message transmitting resolutions of Georgia relative to the public lands,	A	1	34
1834.	Message transmitting a communication from the executive of Massachusetts relative to lotteries,	A	2	77
1834.	Message transmitting the commissary-general's annual report,	A	2	79
1834.	do the adjutant-general's annual report,	A	3	172
1834.	do resolutions of North Carolina on the militia and public defense,	A	4	109
1834.	Message recommending a state loan,	A	4	326
1835.	Annual message of,	S	1	1
1835.	Message transmitting resolutions of Maryland relative to the organization of the militia,	A	1	22
1835.	Message transmitting the commissary-general's annual report,	A	1	28
1835.	do the commissary-general's special report,	A	4	300
1835.	do the adjutant-general's annual report,	A	3	211
1835.	do a survey of a route for a railroad from Williamsport, Pennsylvania, to Elmira, New York,	A	4	351
1835.	Message returning a bill to regulate the weighing of merchandise in New York, with objections,	S	2	82

GOVERNOR'S MESSAGES—*continued.*

		Doc.	Vol.	No.
	Annual message of,	S	1	1
1836.	Special message relative to the great fire in New York,	S	1	2
1836.	Message transmitting resolutions of Michigan relative to slavery,	S	2	77
1836.	do do Kentucky,	S	2	79
1836.	do do Maine,	S	2	85
1836.	do do Ohio,	S	2	87
1836.	do do Pennsylvania relative to the public lands,	S	2	83
1836.	Message returning a bill relative to Geneva college,	S	2	110
1836.	Message transmitting the annual report of the commissary-general,	A	1	17
1836.	Message transmitting the annual report of the adjutant-general,	A	3	200
1836.	Message transmitting resolutions of North Carolina relative to the abolitionists,	A	1	22
1836.	Message transmitting resolutions of Georgia relative to the abolitionists,	A	3	109
1836.	Message transmitting resolutions of Alabama relative to the abolitionists,	A	3	209
1836.	Message transmitting resolutions of Virginia relative to slavery,	A	4	246
1836.	Message transmitting resolutions of Mississippi relative to the abolitionists,	A	4	301
1836.	Message transmitting resolutions of Maine relative to the election of president,	A	4	310
1836.	Message transmitting resolutions of Ohio relative to the election of president,	A	4	288
1836.	Message relative to the memorial of Amos Eaton,	A	4	327
1836.	Message returning the bill requiring railroad companies to carry the United States mail,	A	4	326
1837.	Annual message of,	S	1	1
1837.	Document accompanying, letter from the commissioners for the removal of the New York Indians,	S	1	1
1837.	Message transmitting resolutions of Vermont relative to the abolition of slavery in the District of Columbia, &c.,	S	1	33
1837.	Message returning the bill authorizing the suspension of specie payments by the banks,	S	2	71
1837.	Message transmitting the annual report of the adjutant-general,	A	1	12
1837.	Message transmitting the annual report of the commissary-general,	A	1	32
1837.	Message transmitting the annual report of the Geological Survey,	A	2	161
1837.	Message transmitting resolutions of Maryland, to extend the franking privilege,	A	2	146
1838.	Annual message of,	S	1	1
1838.	Documents accompanying, report of commissioners appointed to digest and report a judicial and equity system,	S	1	2
1838.	Message transmitting resolutions of Kentucky relative to the currency and the administration of the general government,	S	2	58
1838.	Message transmitting resolutions of Ohio against the annexation of Texas to the Union,	S	2	58
1838.	Message transmitting the commissary-general's annual report,	A	2	48
1838.	do adjutant-general's annual report,	A	2	50
1838.	do report of the Geological Survey,	A	4	200
1838.	Message in relation to the destruction of the steamboat Caroline,	S	1	4
1838.	Message transmitting information relative to the unlawful seizure and removal of ordnance, &c.,	A	5	217
1838.	Message in relation to the expenses attending the calling out of the militia for the defense of the frontier,	A	6	315
1838.	Message transmitting preamble and resolutions of Alabama relative to the annexation of Texas to the Union,	A	5	218
1838.	Message transmitting resolutions of Arkansas relative to the public lands,	A	6	365
1838.	Message in relation to the resumption of specie payments and recommending the issue of state stocks,	S	2	70

GOVERNOR'S MESSAGES—*continued.*

	W. H. Seward:	Doc.	Vol.	No.
1839.	Annual message of,	S	1	1
1839.	Documents accompanying communication from the commissioners for building the State Lunatic Asylum,	A	1	3
1839.	Message relative to the recent events on the northeastern frontier,	S	2	60
1839.	Message transmitting a communication from a committee of the senate of Pennsylvania relative to connecting the north branch division of the Pennsylvania canals with the Chemung and Chenango canals,	S	3	86
1839.	Message transmitting resolutions of Connecticut relative to the public lands,	A	2	18
1839.	Message transmitting resolutions of Connecticut relative to the increase of the executive patronage of the general government,	A	2	24
1839.	Message transmitting the annual report of the adjutant-general,	A	2	27
1839.	do the annual report of commissary-general,	A	2	40
1839.	do a report of the attorney-general relative to the reward for the arrest of Thomas Rector,	A	2	38
1839.	do resolutions of Georgia relative to the demand on the executive of Maine for the delivery of certain fugitives from justice,	A	2	45
1839.	do a circular from the American Antiquarian Society of Massachusetts,	A	3	118
1839.	do a memorial from the New York Historical Society for the appointment of an agent to transcribe certain documents,	A	3	153
1839.	do resolutions of North Carolina relative to the policy of the general government,	A	4	202
1839.	do the annual report of the governors of the New York hospital,	A	4	207
1839.	do resolutions of New Jersey relative to the public lands,	A	4	211
1839.	do resolutions of Indiana in relation to slavery,	A	5	282
1839.	do resolutions of Missouri relative to the public lands,	A	6	238
1839.	do the report of the Geological Survey,	A	5	275
1839.	do the report of the Geological Survey,	A	6	406
1839.	Communication from, in relation to the title papers of the Holland Land Company,	A	5	317
1839.	Message transmitting certain communications in relation to the recent events on the frontier of this state,	A	6	375
1839.	Message transmitting documents relative to the distubances on the northern frontier,	A	6	412
1839.	Message transmitting resolutions of Ohio relative to the northeastern boundary,	A	6	389
1840.	Annual message,	S	1	1
1840.	Documents accompanying correspondence between the governor of New York and the lieutenant-governor of Virginia,	S	1	1
1840.	History of the origin and progress of the New York University, &c.,	S	1	2
1840.	Message in relation to the difficulties in the manor of Rensselaerwick,	S	3	70
1840.	Message transmitting the proceedings of a public meeting in New York relative to a national bankrupt law,	S	3	78
1840.	Message returning, with objections, the bill for the protection of minors,	S	3	85
1840.	Message returning the bill to prevent illegal voting in the city of New York,	S	4	98
1840.	Message transmitting a communication from the executive of Virginia,	S	4	110
1840.	Message transmitting the commissary-general's annual report,	A	1	25

GOVERNOR'S MESSAGES—*continued.*

Year		Subject	Doc.	Vol.	No.
1840.	Message transmitting	the adjutant-general's report,	A	3	80
1840.	do	report of the Geological Survey,	A	2	50
1840.	do	resolutions of New Jersey relative to their members of congress,	A	3	70
1840.	do	resolution of Vermont relative to the public lands,	A	3	73
1840.	do	communication from the United States consul at Paris relative to acknowledgments of conveyances of real estate,	A	4	132
1840.	do	communication from the American Institute relative to the culture of silk and the manufacture of sugar from the beet root,	A	4	134
1840.	do	resolutions of Maine relative to the public lands,	A	4	139
1840.	do	resolutions of South Carolina relative to certain fugitives from justice,	A	5	167
1840.	do	resolutions of Missouri relative to slavery,	A	4	143
1840.	do	a communication from the secretary of war in relation to a wharf at Plattsburgh,	A	5	174
1840.	do	a communication from Hon. J. C. Kemble relative to the fort at Black Rock,	A	6	268
1840.	do	resolutions of Kentucky relative to the public lands,	A	7	285
1840.	do	resolutions of Maine relative to the north-eastern boundary,	A	7	305
1840.	do	resolutions of Indiana relative to same,	A	7	308
1840.	do	a communication from the governor of Virginia,	A	8	310
1841.	Annual message,		S	1	1
1841.	Message transmitting resolutions of Mississippi and other papers relative to the Virginia controversy,		S	2	56
1841.	Message transmitting report of commissioners of the land office concerning the Onondaga Indians,		S	2	63
1841.	Message transmitting a communication from the lieutenant-governor of Virginia, with a copy of his reply thereto,		S	3	71
1841.	Message announcing the death of the president of the United States,		S	3	70
1841.	Message transmitting	the proceedings on a complaint against the Madison county judges,	S	3	80
1841.	do	resolutions of Maryland relative to delivering up fugitives from justice,	S	3	88
1841.	do	resolution of Massachusetts relative to the public lands, revenue laws, &c.,	S	3	89
1841.	do	a memorial relative to mechanical labor in state prisons,	S	3	91
1841.	do	a communication from the lieutenant-governor of Virginia,	A	3	94
1841.	do	the remonstrance of citizens of the District of Columbia relative to the legislation Congress over said District,	A	1	7
1841.	do	the annual report of the commissary-general,	A	1	8
1841.	do	the annual report of the adjutant-general,	A	2	50
1841.	do	resolution of Connecticut relative to the protection of domestic industry,	A	1	14
1841.	do	resolution of Michigan relative to a ship canal around the Falls of St. Marie,	A	1	15
1841.	do	resolution of Connecticut relative to the public lands,	A	2	24
1841.	do	resolution of Vermont relative to amending the constitution in relation to the election of president,	A	2	27

GOVERNOR'S MESSAGES—*continued.*

Year	Subject	Doc.	Vol.	No.
1841.	Message transmitting proceedings of a meeting of citizens of Georgetown, District of Columbia, relative to the retrocession of, to the State of Maryland,	A	2	25
1841.	do do a letter from N. Garrow, United States marshal, relative to the census,	A	2	31
1841.	do do resolution of Alabama relative to the protection of domestic industry,	A	3	57
1841.	do do resolution of Indiana relative to the election of president of the United States,	A	3	78
1841.	do do resolution of Pennsylvania relative to the public lands,	A	4	109
1841.	do do resolution of Indiana relative to the election of president and vice-president,	A	4	120
1841.	do do resolutions of Alabama relative to the controversy between Maine and Georgia,	A	4	125
1841.	do do resolution of Delaware relative to the public lands,	A	4	132
1841.	do do a communication from the secretary of state of Alabama,	A	4	138
1841.	do do a communication from Nathan Burchard concerning his salary as attorney for the Oneida Indians,	A	4	139
1841.	do do resolution of Delaware and Kentucky relative to the eligibility of the president,	A	5	149
1841.	do do the annual report of the Geological Survey,	A	5	150
1841.	do do resolutions of Rhode Island relative to the public lands, sub-treasury and national bank,	A	4	158
1841.	do do resolution of Indiana relative to the public lands,	A	5	168
1841.	do do the resignation of Francis Granger as representative in Congress,	A	6	207
1841.	do do resolution of Maryland in relation to the northeastern boundary,	A	6	215
1841.	do do resolution of Mississippi in relation to the controversy between Virginia and New York,	A	6	230
1841.	do do resolution of Mississippi relative to the tariff,	A	6	235
1841.	do do a communication relative to the erection of the lunatic asylum,	A	7	280
1841.	do do correspondence relative to Alexander McLeod,	A	7	292

WILLIAM C. BOUCK:

Year	Subject	Doc.	Vol.	No.
1842.	Annual message,	S	1	1
1842.	Documents accompanying the same,	S	1	2
1842.	Message transmitting resolution of secretary of state,	S	1	11
1842.	Message transmitting resolution of the general assembly of Alabama relative to the national domain,	S	1	19
1842.	Resolution of Mr. Root relative to message of 22d of January,	S	2	21
1842.	Message transmitting resolution of general assembly of Alabama in favor of admitting the republic of Texas into the Union,	S	2	25
1842.	Message transmitting resolution of Kentucky relative to the soldiers of the revolution,	S	2	26
1842.	Message in relation to arms and other military stores,	S	2	27
1842.	Message transmitting a law, a report and resolution of the legislature of South Carolina relative to the Virginia controversy,	S	2	41
1842.	Communication relative to the Prison Discipline Society,	S	2	50
1842.	Communication transmitting resolution of the legislature of South Carolina relative to the public lands,	S	3	52

GOVERNOR'S MESSAGES—*continued.*

		Doc.	Vol.	No.
1842.	Communication transmitting resolution of the general assembly of Rhode Island relative to the election of president and vice-president,	S	3	54
1842.	Communication transmitting resolution of the council and general assembly of New Jersey relative to the tariff,	S	3	53
1842.	Communication relative to the progress of the Geological Survey,	S	3	68
1842.	Message returning the bill appointing bank commissioners,	S	4	83
1842.	Communication relative to the Colonial History of the State,	S	4	83
1842.	Communication transmitting correspondence from John R. Brodhead,	S	4	88
1842.	Message returning the criminal court bill,	S	4	90
1842.	Message relative to certain documents of Supreme Court of United States,	S	4	96
1842.	Message dissenting from the resolution of legislature relative to Virginia,	S	4	102
1842.	Message, at extra session,	S	4	106
1842.	Message transmitting correspondence from Holland relative to the annual reports of the regents of the University,	S	4	108
1842.	Annual message to the legislature,	A	1	1
1842.	Documents accompanying the same,	A	1	2
1342.	Letter to secretary of war,	A	1	2
1842.	Communication transmitting resolution of Vermont relative to time of holding election of President of United States,	A	1	14
1842.	Communication transmitting resolution of Connecticut in relation to the tariff,	A	2	26
1842.	Communication transmitting resolution relative to fugitives from justice,	A	2	27
1842.	Communication transmitting resolution of Connecticut and Maine, relative to one presidential term,	A	2	28
1842.	Message transmitting annual report of adjutant-general,	A	2	41
1842.	Communication transmitting resolution of Alabama in relation to national domain,	A	2	43
1842.	Communication transmitting resolution of Alabama relative to admitting Texas into the Union,	A	2	48
1842	Communication transmitting resolution of Kentucky relative to state debts,	A	3	51
1842.	Communication transmitting proceedings of municipal council of Alexandria in favor of retrogression to Virginia,	A	4	53
1842.	Communication transmitting resolution of Georgia relative to proceedings of 27th congress at the extra session,	A	4	58
1842.	Message transmitting a law and report and resolution of South Carolina in relation to controversy between Virginia and New York,	A	4	62
1842.	Message transmitting report of Mr. Casey relative to Ogdensburgh and Champlain Railroad,	A	4	70
1842.	Communication transmitting annual report of commissary-general,	A	5	80
1842.	Message in relation to New York City Registry Law,	A	5	87
1842.	Communication transmitting resolution of General Assembly of Kentucky, concerning the soldiers of the revolution,	A	5	96
1842.	Communication transmitting letter from New York and Erie Railroad Company	A	5	113
1842.	Communication transmitting resolution of general assembly of Maryland, concerning abolition of slavery,	A	7	149
1842.	Communication transmitting report from adjutant-general relative to appointment of officers in 29th division and 49th brigade,	A	7	157
1842.	Message returning the bill to provide for the public printing,	A	7	172
1842.	[Ex. Sess.] Message on opening of extra session,	A	7	195
1842.	[Ex. Sess.] Communication transmitting resolution of Mississippi relative to annexation of Texas to the United States,	A	7	199
1843.	Annual message to the legislature,	S	1	1

GOVERNOR'S MESSAGES—*continued.*

		Doc.	Vol.	No.
1843.	Documents accompanying the annual message to the legislature,	S	1	2
1843.	Message transmitting joint resolution of the legislature of New Jersey,....	S	3	86
1843.	Message transmitting joint resolution of the State of Maine,.....	S	3	87
1843.	Message transmitting joint resolution of the legislature of the Sta e of Alabama,....	S	3	88
1843.	Message relating to the Auburn state prison,....	S	3	97
1843.	Letter in relation to proceeds of sale of public lands of the United States,....	S	3	120
1843.	Annual message,....	A	1	2
1843.	Documents accompanying the annual message,....	A	1	3
1843.	Communication transmitting resolution of Connecticut relative to the public lands, tariffs, West Point academy, &c.,.....	A	1	11
1843.	Communication transmitting resolution of the legislature of Vermont relative to the franking privilege and postage,....	A	2	15
1843.	Message inclosing resolution from New Hampshire respecting po tage,....	A	2	19
1843.	Message inclosing a memorial from Free Trade Association of New York City,....	A	2	22
1843.	Communication transmitting the annual report of the adjutant-general,....	A	2	24
1843.	do do resolution of the legislature of Georgia,....	A	3	51
1843.	do do resolution of the legislature of Georgia,....	A	3	52
1843.	do do a memorial and resolution of legislature of State of Michigan,....	A	4	103
1843.	Message transmitting communication from the secretary of war,..	A	4	107
1843.	Communication transmitting resolution from legislature of State of Maine,....	A	4	115
1843.	Message transmitting communication from Charge d'Affaires and Consul of the United States, at Paris,....	A	4	119
1843.	Letter transmitting a communication of the New York State Mechanic Association in relation to a museum,....	A	5	137
1843.	Communication from, transmitting a resolution of the annual town meeting in Bainbridge, Chenango county, in relation to the United States deposit fund,....	A	5	138
1843.	Communication from, in relation to fugitives from justice,......	A	5	140
1843.	Communication from, transmitting a memorial of inhabitants of Oswego county on the subject of the currency,....	A	5	174
	Silas Wright:			
1844.	Annual message,....	S	1	2
1844.	Annual message,....	A	1	2
1844.	Communication transmitting resolution of legislature of Connecticut in relation to French spoliations, the Military Academy, and tariff,....	A	1	7
1844.	do do resolution of the State of Connecticut in relation to the franking privilege, &c.,....	A	1	14
1844.	do do resolution of the legislature of South Carolina,....	A	1	15
1844.	do do proceedings of a public meeting in relation to constitutional reform,	A	1	32
1844.	do do annual rep. of commissary-general,	A	3	50
1844.	do do resolution of the legislature of Massachusetts in relation to an amendment of the Constitution of the United States,....	A	3	52

GOVERNOR'S MESSAGES—*continued.*

Year	Title	Doc.	Vol.	No.
1844.	Communication transmitting resolution of the legislature of Massachusetts relative to Virginia,..	A	7	170
1844.	do do resolution of the legislature of Massachusetts relative to Texas,.....	A	7	175
1844.	do do resolution of the legislature of Massachusetts, &c., ...	A	7	184
1844.	do do resolution of the general assembly of Virginia in reply to resolution of the State of Massachusetts,...	A	7	190
1844.	do do resolution of the legislature of New Hampshire on the subject of Gen. Jackson's fine, ...	A	7	191
1844.	do do resolution of the legislature of Maryland relative to slavery,........	A	7	193
1844.	do do resolution of the legislature of the State of Kentucky,............	A	7	194
1844.	do do resolution of the legislature of Georgia in relation to the repudiation of state debts, ...	A	7	195
1844.	do do resolution of the general assembly of Rhode Island, ...	A	7	196
1844.	do do resolution of the legislature of Mississippi relative to Texas,.......	A	7	202
1845.	Message transmitting a memorial from the New York pilots,.....	S	1	25
1845.	Message transmitting the final report of the agent appointed "to procure and transcribe documents in Europe relative to the Colonial History of the State,"............................	S	1	47
1845.	Annual message, ...	A	1	2
1845.	Communication relative to United States Senators,.............	A	1	8
1845.	Resolution of Mr. T. R. Lee referring message,................	A	1	14
1845.	Communication transmitting annual report of commissary-general,	A	3	51
1845.	Message transmitting Carroll & Cook's Geological contract,......	A	3	78
1845.	Message in answer to a resolution of the assembly whether $10,-000 has been set apart from the United States land fund,.....	A	4	88
1845.	Message returning bill in relation to canals, with his objections,..	A	7	251
	JOHN YOUNG:			
1846.	Message relative to the Indians on the Allegany and Cattaraugus reservations, ...	S	2	57
1846.	Annual message, ...	A	1	3
1846.	Resolutions of Mr. Bailey referring message,..................	A	1	8
1846.	Communication relative to Geology of the state,................	A	2	41
1846.	do transmitting certain documents,..........	A	5	164
1846.	do transmitting memorial of Seneca Indians,......	A	5	197
1846.	do relative to petition of M. Aylesworth,..........	A	6	208
1847.	Report as to Clinton prison,..................................	S	1	18
1847.	Communication as to donations,.........	S	4	128
1847.	Annual message,..	A	1	3
1847.	Resolution offered by Mr. Wright as to reference of message,....	A	1	12
1847.	Message transmitting communication from secretary of the Navy of the United States,....................................	A	2	96
1847.	Communication transmitting annual report of commissary-general,	A	4	110
1847.	do do sundry resolutions of general assembly of Virginia,..................	A	4	111
1847.	do do a remonstrance from a portion of the Chiefs of the Onondaga Indians,..	A	4	124
1847.	do do joint resolutions of the legislature of Missouri relative to army of the United States,..................	A	6	164
1847.	do do letter from secretary of state as to districting Niagara county,......	A	6	170
1847.	do relative to international exchanges,............	A	8	244

GOVERNOR'S MESSAGES—*continued.*

HAMILTON FISH:

Year	Subject	Doc.	Vol.	No.
1848.	Communication transmitting letter of General Zachary Taylor,	A	6	212
1848.	Annual message,	A	1	3
1849.	Annual message,	A	1	2
1849.	Communication relative to the funds for the support of the fever and small pox hospitals at Quarantine,	A	1	39
1849.	Communication transmitting letter of commissioners of emigration,	A	2	58
1849.	Communication transmitting certain proceedings of Seneca tribe of Indians,	A	3	108
1849.	Communication inclosing letter from Bishop Hughes relative to interchange of donations between this state and the government of the Roman states, with catalogue of engravings presented by Pope Pius IX.,	A	3	117
1849.	Communication relative to completing the publication of Natural History of this state,	A	3	154
1849.	Message transmitting a report on the subject of international exchange, by Mons. Alexander Vattemare,	A	5	201
1849.	Message transmitting certain resolutions of the general assembly of Missouri on the subject of slavery,	A	5	229
1849.	Message transmitting annual report of Sailors' Snug Harbor,	A	5	233
1849.	Message transmitting communication from secretary of the Navy of the United States relative to purchase of land adjoining the Navy Yard in Brooklyn,	A	5	237
1849.	Message transmitting message of governor of Rhode Island relative to manuscript volume in secretary's office relative to boundaries of colony of, &c.,	A	5	239

WASHINGTON HUNT:

Year	Subject	Doc.	Vol.	No.
1850.	Message transmitting letter from clerk of Seneca Indians,	S	1	21
1850.	Answer in regard to Asiatic cholera,	S	1	36
1850.	Reply to resolution in relation to convictions for vagrancy,	S	2	43
1850.	Message transmitting papers in relation to Seneca Indians,	S	2	59
1850.	Annual message,	A	1	1
1850.	Message transmitting second annual report of A. Vattemare,	A	5	127
1850.	do do report of physicians to Marine hospital, New York,	A	6	154
1850.	do do report of secretary of the navy,	A	6	171
1850.	do do resolutions of State of Georgia on slavery,	A	8	176
1850.	do do correspondence in regard to London exhibition of works of industry,	A	8	177
1850.	do do resolutions of State of Mississippi on slavery,	A	8	179
1850.	do do resolutions of State of Rhode Island on agriculture,	A	8	180
1850.	do do resolutions of Rhode Island,	A	8	182
1850.	do do resolution of state of Vermont on slavery,	A	8	181
1850.	do do letter of governor of Mississippi in relation to volunteers in Mexican war,	A	8	188
1850.	do do letter of A. Vattemare in relation to donations from France,	A	8	192
1850.	do do resolutions of State of Texas on slavery,	A	8	193
1850.	do do resolutions of State of Maryland on slavery,	A	8	194
1851.	Communication transmitting letter of secretary of the interior relating to the census,	S	2	63
1851.	Message, extra session,	S	3	75
1851.	Communication from, transmitting letters of secretary of war and Brevet Colonel G. Wright relating to granting lands near Fort Ontario,	S	3	82
1851.	Annual message,	A	1	2
1851.	Communication in relation to the Colonial History,	A	3	66
1851.	Communication transmitting resolutions of the Canadian Parliament,	A	3	69

GOVERNOR'S MESSAGES—*continued.*

		Doc.	Vol.	No.
1851.	Communication transmitting resolutions of the Florida legislature,	A	4	126
1851.	Communication transmitting correspondence relative to the Washington Monument Association,	A	5	144
1851.	Communication relative to 7th census,	A	6	157
	HORATIO SEYMOUR:			
1852.	Communication transmitting memorial of American Association for the advancement of science respecting the geographical survey of the state,	S	1	41
1852.	Communication transmitting correspondence with Kossuth,	S	2	84
1852.	Communication transmitting resolutions of legislature of Indiana,	S	2	91
1852.	Annual message,	A	1	1
1853.	Message relative to making appropriations for the improvement of the Erie and Oswego canals,	S	2	67
1853.	Annual message,	A	1	1
1853.	Report to reprieves, pardons, commutations and restorations for 1852,	A	2	44
1853.	Message transmitting proceedings of a convention on the subject of erecting a monument in Independence square, Philadelphia,	A	4	89
1853.	Message relative to making appropriations for improving the Erie and Oswego canals,	A	4	91
1853.	Message, with objections to a bill in relation to banking privileges,	A	5	113
1853.	Communication in answer to resolution of assembly of June 1, 1853, relative to resistance of process,	A	5	119
	MYRON H. CLARK:			
1854.	Communication relative to harbor of New York,	S	1	8
1854.	Communication relative to industrial exhibition in London,	S	2	88
1854.	Special message relative to northern rivers,	S	2	91
1854.	Annual message,	A	1	3
1855.	Annual message,	A	1	3
1855.	Message relative to resolution of New Jersey legislature on New York harbor,	S	2	60
1855.	Annual message,	A	1	3
1855.	Special message relative to imposing canal tolls on railroads,	A	4	97
1855.	Message transmitting resolutions of New Jersey,	A	5	104
	JOHN A. KING:			
1856.	Annual message,	S	1	2
1856.	Annual message,	A	1	3
1856.	Communication accompanying a communication from Governor Robinson of Kansas,	S	3	52
1856.	Communication transmitting certain resolutions from State of Alabama,	A	4	117
1856.	Communication transmitting certain resolutions from State of Vermont,	A	4	124
1856.	Communication transmitting annual report of commissary-general,	A	4	141
1856.	Communication transmitting annual report of adjutant-general,	A	4	155
1857.	Communication transmitting communication from governor of New Jersey relative to quarantine,	S	1	16
1857.	Annual message,	A	1	1
1857.	Reply to resolution relative to abduction or enslavement of citizens of this state,	A	1	47
	E. D. MORGAN:			
1858.	Annual message,	S	1	3

GOWANUS BAY.

		Doc.	Vol.	No.
1857.	Report of harbor commissioners relative to,	S	4	126

GRAHAM, JOHN LORIMER, AND OTHERS.

		Doc.	Vol.	No.
1835.	Report on petition for a law granting them, respectively, lands and lands covered with water in the East river, &c.,	A	4	350

GRAIN, DISTILLATION OF, INTO ALCOHOL.

1837.	Report on the propriety of prohibiting the,	A	3	194

GRAIN, MEASURER-GENERAL OF, *see* New York.

GRAND CHAPTER OF FREEMASONS, *see* William Morgan.

GRAND ISLAND.

1846.	Report of comptroller on petition of citizens of Erie county relative to,	A	5	155

GRANGER, ELIZABETH S., AND WILLIAM CHAPIN.

1833.	Report on petition for compensation for damages by the Erie canal,	S	2	78
1834.	Report on petition for compensation for damages by the Erie canal,	S	1	27

GRANGER, ELIZABETH, AND OTHERS.

1849.	Report of committee on canals on petition of,	A	3	196
1850.	Report of committee on canals on petition of,	S	2	44
1850.	Report of canal board on petition of,	S	3	101

GRANGER, FRANCIS.

1841.	Resignation of, as a representative in Congress,	A	6	207

GRANGER, OSCAR, AND OTHERS.

1847.	Report of committee on claims on petition of,	A	2	76
1848.	Report on petition of,	A	5	127
1849	Report of committee on grievances on petition of,	A	2	93
1850.	Report on petition of,	S	2	73

GRANGER, WARREN.

1845.	Report of canal commissioners on petition of,	A	1	27

GRANT, ABRAHAM P., AND OTHERS.

1850.	Report of commissioners of the land office,	A	4	53

GRANT, RYAN AND TURNER.

1847.	Report as to moneys due,	A	7	212
1848.	Report on petition of,	A	2	42
1851.	Report of committee on canals,	A	3	78

GRANVILLE, TOWN OF.

1834.	Report on petition of commissioners of highways to raise money to repair bridges, &c.,	A	3	242
1835.	Report of select committee on the same,	A	7	41
1835.	do do do	A	4	290
1836.	do do do	A	4	217

GRAVE, *see* Cemeteries, &c.

1842.	Report of judiciary committee on petitions for law to protect the sanctity of,	A	7	186

GRAVES, GEORGE W., AND OTHERS.

		Doc.	Vol.	No.
1857.	Report of committee on claims favorable on petition of, for damages by break in the Erie canal,............................	A	2	119

GRAVES, JACOB.

1854.	Report of select committee relative to claims of,..............	A	3	104

GRAVES, JACOB, AND OTHERS.

1852.	Report on memorial relative to occupancy of waters of Genesee river at Rochester,..	A	5	102

GRAVESEND BRIDGE COMPANY.

1848.	Report of,..	A	5	180

GRAY, ISAAC, *see* Amos Dean and others.

GRAY, JEAN, AND OTHERS.

1834.	Report on petition for certain escheated lands,................	S	2	121

GRAY, MARY, alias Lupin.

1840.	Report on petition for a grant of a lot of land at Fort Covington,	A	8	319

GREAT BRITAIN.

1848.	Resolution relative to grants of land,........................	S	1	29
1848.	Resolution relative to grants of land,........................	S	2	31

GREAT VALLEY, TOWN OF.

1832.	Report on petition to declare Wright's creek a public highway,	A	1	27
1835.	Report on petition to extend the time for the collection of taxes in, ...	A	2	105

GREAT WESTERN TURNPIKE, FIRST COMPANY OF THE.

1831.	Report relative to a tax assessed on said company in the city of Albany,..	A	2	120
1834.	Report on petition to amend the charter,......................	A	3	188

GREECE, TOWN OF.

1834.	Report on petition of the board of health, relative to certain moneys expended by them in 1832,........................	A	4	319

GREEN AND CONRO.

1857.	Report of committee on state prisons favorable on petition of, for payment for castings furnished Clinton state prison,......	A	3	169

GREEN, BENJAMIN F.

1857.	Report on petition of,..	S	2	44

GREEN, D. S. & S. B.

1847.	Report of canal commissioners on petition of,.................	S	3	96
1847.	Report on petition of,..	S	3	99

GREEN, FRED., AND THEO. CATLIN.

1847.	Report of committee on canals on claims of,...................	A	4	108

GEEEN, FRED. AND THEO. CATLIN—*continued.*

		Doc.	Vol.	No.
1848.	Report of committee on claims on petition of,	A	3	114

GREEN, JOHN R.

1847.	Report on petition of,	S	3	87

GREEN, TERRY B., AND WIFE.

1844.	Report of committee on claims on petition of,	A	3	45
1849.	Report of committee on claims on petition of,	A	3	155

GREEN, TOWN OF.

1840.	Report relative to setting off part of the, to the town of Barker,	A	6	272

GREENBORO.

1847.	Report on petitions for annexation of, to Redfield,	A	8	262
1848.	Report on petition for annexation of, to Redfield,	A	3	94

GREENBUSH, VILLAGE OF.

1841.	Report on petition to amend the charter of,	S	3	98

GREENE COUNTY.

Banks in, *see* Banks, Greene county.

1831.	Highway labor in, report on petition of citizens of, to the exemption from,	A	4	332
1842.	Poor-house system, report on petition to abolish the,	A	6	267
1840.	Costs in criminal cases, report on petition of citizens of, for a law requiring security for	A	4	129
1834.	Surrogate of, report on bill in relation to the,	S	2	117
1831.	Inspector of beef and pork, reports of N. Wilson,	A	1	56
1832.	do do do	A	3	231
1833.	do do do	A	3	147
1834.	do do do	A	3	196
1834.	do do amended report of,	A	4	358
1835.	do do annual report of,	A	3	210
1836.	do do do	A	4	219
1839.	do do do	A	3	148
1840.	Inspector of sole leather, report of William Edwards,	S	1	34
1841.	Report on petition for a new county from parts of Delaware, Schoharie and,	A	7	281
1846.	Report on petition for a new county from parts of Delaware, Schoharie and,	S	2	49
1849.	Report on petitions and remonstrances for a new county from parts of Delaware, Schoharie and,	A	3	135
1849.	Remonstrance of inhabitants of, against the erection of the new county of Harrison, &c.,	A	3	172

GREENFIELD TURNPIKE ROAD.

1837.	Report on petition to abandon their road,	A	3	261

GREENSBURGH, TOWN OF.

1837.	Highway in the, report on petition to amend the law regulating,	A	3	215

GREENWOOD, OLIVER, Jr.

1834.	Report on petition for compensation for the loss of a horse on the canal,	S	1	35

Year	Subject	Doc.	Vol.	No.
	GREGG, JOHN.			
1831.	Report on bill directing the sale to him of certain lands,........	S	1	10
1833.	Report of commissioners of the land office on bill directing the sale to him of certain lands,........................	A	2	125
1836.	Report on petition for a grant of surplus waters at Elmira,......	A	3	108
1837.	Report of canal commissioners on petition for a grant of surplus water at Elmira,....................................	A	2	77
	GREGORY, HENRY, AND OTHERS.			
1853.	Report of committee on grievances on petition of, to amend seduction laws,..	A	2	51
1853.	Report on petition of, concerning same subject,.............	A	3	61
	GRIER, MARY ANN.			
1856.	Report on petition of,....................................	A	5	184
	GRIFFIN, HORATIO A.			
1857.	Report of committee on petitions of aliens favorable on petition of heirs of, for escheated lands,........................	A	3	146
	GRIFFIN, JONATHAN, *see* Joseph Russell and J. Griffin.			
	GRIFFIN, THOMAS, AND OTHERS.			
1847.	Report on petition of,....................................	S	1	14
	GRIFFIN, W., AND OTHERS.			
1838.	Report on petition to prohibit praying, &c., in academies and schools,...	A	2	55
	GRIFFITHS, JOHN M.			
1856.	Report on petition for relief,.............................	A	3	84
	GRIMES, W. HENRY.			
1839.	Report on petitions to change his name,.....	A	2	42
	GROSS, DANIEL, AND P. RICHARDSON.			
1848.	Report on petition of,....................................	A	5	154
1849.	Report of committee on claims on petition of,................	A	3	124
	GROSS, FRANCIS.			
1855.	Report of committee on public lands on petition of,...........	A	5	126
	GROSS, JOHN J.			
1848.	Report of committee on claims on petition of,................	A	3	120
	GROTON, TOWN OF.			
1831.	Report on petition for the division of,......................	A	2	166
	GROUND RENT, QUARTER SALES, &c., *see* Rensselaerwyck.			
1835.	Report on petition of citizens of Albany and Rensselaer on the subject of,..	A	2	83
	GROVE, TOWN OF.			
1839.	Town meeting in, report on petition to fix the time and place for holding,..	A	2	58

GROVER, L. C., AND B. H. MILLS.

		Doc.	Vol.	No.
1857.	Report of committee on claims, favorable on petition of, for damages by embankment and wall in front of building, ...	A	3	159

GRUNTHER, GEORGE.

1857.	Report on petition of, ...	S	2	42
1858.	Report relative to payment of moneys to,........	A	1	42

GUILFORD, TOWN OF.

1842.	Memorial of inhabitants of, for abolishing capital punishment,..	A	7	146
1844.	Report of committee on grievances on the petition of inhabitants of, for the removal of a turnpike gate,........	A	5	106

GUINNIP, GEORGE B.

1851.	Report on claim of, to seat in senate,........	S	3	84

GUMAER, ELIAS.

1838.	Report on petition for extra allowance for work done on the Erie canal,........	A	3	158

GUTHRIE, ABEL, AND OTHERS.

1831.	Heirs of Christian Guthrie a soldier of the revolution, report on petition of, for bounty lands, ...	A	1	13
1831.	Report of committee on two-third bills on bill for the relief of, ..	A	2	145
1831.	Report of committee on claims on bill for the relief of, ...	A	2	146

GYPSUM.

1836.	Toll on, report of canal board relative to, ...	A	4	294

H.

HACKNEY, JOSEPH.

1830.	A soldier of the revolution, report on petition of, for bounty lands,	A	3	264
1830.	Report of committee on claims on the same,........	A	4	309
1831.	Report of committee on claims on the same,........	A	2	79

HADCOCK, DANIEL.

1832.	Report on petition of, for remuneration for improvements on certain lands in the Oneida reservation,........	A	3	242
1833.	Report of committee on claims,........	A	3	178
1834.	do do do	A	2	64
1837.	do do do	A	3	168
1838.	do do do	A	3	119

HADCOCK, JOHN.

1834.	Report on petition for a grant of land,........	S	2	106
1839.	Report on petition for compensation for damages to his lands by the Erie canal,........	A	5	308
1841.	Report on the same,........	S	2	40

HAGAN, H.

1852.	Report of trustees of Sing Sing prison respecting an assault and battery on,........	S	3	95

HAIGHT, BLOOD AND CADY.

1846.	Report of committee on claims on petition of,........	A	4	107

		Doc.	Vol.	No.
	HAINES, DAVID.			
1832.	Report on petition for the conveyance to him of certain land,...	A	3	200
1832.	Report of committee on public lands on the same,............	A	3	263
1833.	Report on the same,..	A	3	166
	HALL, DANIEL, AND OTHERS, *see* Henry Price and others.			
	HALL, E. A., AND C. L. LILLIE.			
1846.	Report on bill for the relief of, ...	S	4	125
	HALL, HARRY.			
1854.	Communication from auditor relative to claim of,............	S	1	41
	HALL, JAMES.			
1843.	Communication from,..	S	2	59
1843.	Communication from,..	S	2	60
	HALL, MARIA S.			
1835.	Report on petition of, for a law vesting in her the right and title of the state to a lot of land in Schenectady,................	A	4	286
1836.	Report on the same,..	A	2	87
	HALL, NATHAN.			
1837.	Report on petition for compensation for damages to his lands by the construction of the Chemung canal,....................	A	2	147
	HALLETT, DEBORAH ANN.			
1845.	Report of commissioners of land office on petition of,..........	S	1	21
	HALLETT, W. P., *see* Supreme Court Clerks.			
	HAMBURGH AND BUFFALO TURNPIKE, *see* Buffalo.			
	HAMILTON ACADEMY, *see* Academies.			
	HAMILTON COLLEGE, *see* Colleges.			
	HAMILTON, DAVID.			
1843.	Report of the comptroller relative to,.......................	S	1	39
	HAMILTON, ELI, AND PETER D.			
1847.	Report on petition of,.......................................	A	1	36
	HAMILTON, GLOUDY, AND JAMES QUIGG.			
1837.	Report on petition of, for extra allowance for work done on the Chenango canal,..	A	2	88
1837.	Minutes of the canal board in the case of,...................	A	3	252
	HAMILTON, JAMES T.			
1857.	Report of committee on claims favorable on petition of George Cramer and, for damage by division of water,...............	A	3	153
	HAMILTON, JAMES W.			
1858.	Statement of, relative to his refusal to testify before investigating committee, ...	A	3	73

HAMILTON, ORRIS.

		Doc.	Vol.	No.
1844.	Report of attorney-general on a bill for the relief of,	S	1	14

HAMILTON, VILLAGE OF.

1832.	Water-Works Company, report on petition to incorporate,	A	3	215
1840.	Literary and Theological Institute, report on petition to incorporate,	A	7	209

MADISON UNIVERSITY, *see* Colleges, &c.

HAMILTON, W.

1840.	Report on petition of, relative to a lot of land claimed to be escheated,	S	2	60

HAMPTONBURGH, TOWN OF.

1830.	Report on petition for the erection of the,	A	2	113

HAND, HELENA.

1842.	Report of committee on aliens on petition of,	A	5	105

HARBORS.

1848.	Resolutions relating to,	S	1	4
1848.	Report on resolutions relating to rivers and,	A	3	70
1848.	Report on resolutions relative to improvement of rivers and,	A	3	71

HARBOR COMMISSIONERS.

1857.	Report relative to Gowanus bay,	S	4	126
1857.	Report of expenses of,	S	4	149

HARBOR MASTERS.

1857.	Report of standing committee on commerce and navigation relative to,	A	3	100

HARDEN, LYDIA.

1847.	Report relative to her rights,	A	7	189
1849.	Report on petition of,	S	2	66

HARLEM RIVER.

1838.	Report in relation to crossing the, with the Croton aqueduct,	A	6	319
1839.	Report in relation to the same,	A	4	190

HARMAN E., AND OTHERS

1848.	Report on petition of,	A	2	18

HARMON, P., *see* E. Frost.

HARNED, SAMUEL W.

1848.	Report on petition of,	A	2	21

HARON, J. W.

1849.	Report of committee on canals on petition of,	A	2	79

HAROUN, C.

1854.	Report on petition of,	A	2	60

HARPER, CHARLES CARROLL.

		Doc.	Vol.	No.
1839.	Report on petition of the trustees for the children of, to sell real estate,	A	2	64

HARPER, JOHN W.

1841.	Report on petition to extend an act authorizing him to erect a dam across the Susquehanna river,	A	7	287

HARRINGTON, JAMES.

1850.	Report on claim of,	A	5	95

HARRIS, CAMPBELL.

1849.	Report on petition of,	S	2	68

HARRIS, DAVID, AND OTHERS.

1837.	Sub-contractors on the Chenango canal, report on petition for extra allowance,	A	3	236

HARRIS, JOHN, AND OTHERS.

1850.	Report of canal board on petition of, in relation to Fort Miller dam,	S	2	66

HARRIS, W., DANIEL BURT AND GEORGE M. BURT.

1830.	Report on petition for compensation for damages to their lands by the erection of the Saratoga dam,	A	3	211
1831.	Report of committee on canals on the same,	A	2	187
1832.	do do do	A	2	148
1838.	do do do	A	3	64

HARRISON COUNTY.

1849.	Remonstrance of the inhabitants of Greene county against the erection of,	A	3	172
1849.	Report of majority of select committee on bill, &c., for erection of,	A	3	174
1849.	Report of minority of select committee on bill, &c., for erection of,	A	3	177

HARRISON, DENNIS.

1832.	Report on petition to authorize the commissioners of the land office to sell to him certain land in Lewiston,	S	1	29

HARRISON, WILLIAM HENRY, *see* President.

HARRISON, WILLIAM S., AND OTHERS.

1847.	Report of committee on claims on petition of, for remuneration for loss sustained on stock issued for Chemung canal loan of 1841,	A	2	54

HART, M., AND OTHERS.

1843.	Report of committee on claims on petition of,	A	4	78
1846.	Report of committee on claims on petition of,	S	1	19

HART, MARTIN, *see* Thomas Geary and others.

HART, SAMUEL, AND WILLIAM CANDE.

1842.	Report of committee on claims on petition of,	A	5	104
1845.	Report of canal board on petition of,	A	3	55

HARTER, HENRY, AND OTHERS.

		Doc.	Vol.	No.
1856.	Report on petition for relief,	A	3	73

HARTMAN, JOHN.

1852.	Report on petition of,	A	5	94

HARTNETT, DANIEL.

1856.	Report on petition for relief,	A	3	79

HARTLETT, THOS.

1844.	Report on the memorial of, for a law making habitual drunkenness a good cause for divorce,	A	6	156

HARTSTEIN, COMMANDER.

1858.	Communication from governor transmitting correspondence with, relative to gold medal ordered by the legislature,	A	4	139

HARWOOD, EMERSON B.

1848.	Report on petition of,	A	3	82

HASBROUCK, I., Jr., AND I. I. SCHOONMAKER, *see* Ulster County.

HASBROUCK, ISAAC L.

1847.	Report of committee on privileges and elections on petition of, to be admitted to seat occupied by John D. L. Montange,	A	1	16

HASBROUCK, PETER.

1843.	Report of commissioners of land office on his petition,	S	3	79

HASCALL, HIRAM, AND CHA'S. B. THOMPSON.

1857.	Report of committee on claims on petition of,	A	3	154

HASKINS, AMOS.

1831.	Report on petition for remuneration for deficiency in a lot of land bought of this state,	A	3	253
1831.	Report on petition for remuneration for deficiency in a lot of land bought of this state,	A	4	312

HASKINS AND ROSEBROOK.

1857.	Report of committee on claims adverse on petition of, to be released from contract,	A	3	181

HASTINGS, TOWN OF.

1847.	Report on petition of inhabitants of,	S	2	49

HATCH, J. M., AND OTHERS.

1846.	Report on petition for relief of,	S	1	11

HAVANA.

1848.	Report on petition of inhabitants of,	A	3	64

Canal from Seneca lake, *see* Chemung Canal.

HAWKERS AND PEDLARS.

		Doc.	Vol.	No.
1834.	Report of amount received for licenses to,	A	2	66
1837.	Report on petition to amend the law relative to,	A	3	260

HAWKES, RUTH.

1841.	Report on petition for compensation for damages to her lands by the enlargement of the Erie canal,	A	3	68

HAWKINS, GEORGE.

1851.	Report of committee on claims for canal damages,	A	4	117

HAWKINS, GEORGE, AND OTHERS.

1852.	Report on petition of,	S	2	52

HAWKINS, M. N.

1846.	Report of commissioners of land office on petition of,	A	5	183

HAWKINS, MALCOM N.

1847.	Report on petition of,	A	2	89

HAWLEY, ALPHEUS.

1832.	Report on petition to allow W. W. Hodges, of Pennsylvania, to take the acknowledgment of deeds and conveyances on the sale of certain land in Cattaragus county,	S	2	83

HAWLEY, JESSE.

1840.	Memorial of, against ceding to the United States the right to construct a ship canal around Niagara Falls,	S	4	108

HAWLEY, SETH C.

1850.	Answer to resolution of legislature,	A	5	137

HAY, JAMES.

1850.	Report on petition of,	A	5	87
1851.	Report of select committee on petition of,	A	4	101
1854.	Report on petition of,	A	3	93
1855.	Report of select committee on claim of,	A	2	31
1857.	Report on petition of,	S	2	67
1858.	Report of committee on claims on petition of,	A	4	131

HAY, JANET, or McAndrew, and others.

1841.	Report on petition of, for certain lands escheated to the state,	A	7	268

HAY, PRESSED.

1832.	Report on petition for a law to regulate the inspection of,	A	4	280
1835.	Report on petition to repeal the law requiring the inspection of,	A	4	265

HAYDEN, WILLIAM, AND OTHERS.

1848.	Report on petition of,	A	5	159

HAYES, PERKINS G.

1849.	Report of committee on claims on petition of,	A	2	77

HAYS, JOHN.

1840.	Report on petition for compensation on account of a wound received while in the service of the state on the Niagara frontier,	A	6	228

HAYWARD, JOHN R.

		Doc.	Vol.	No.
1847.	Report of committee on privileges and elections on petition that, of Westchester, be admitted to seat occupied by Jas. E. Beers,	A	1	29

HEADDING, HARLEY.

1839.	Report on petition of, to confirm his title to certain land,.......	A	2	30

HEALTH, COMMISSIONERS, *see* New York.

HEALTH, PUBLIC.

1846.	Report of select committee on bill to preserve,................	A	1	19
1850.	Report of attorney-general on law for the preservation of,......	A	5	126

HEATH, GEORGE.

1844.	Report of canal board on petition of,........................	A	3	91

HEATH, HENRY.

1841.	Report on petition for compensation for damages to his hydraulic works at Little Falls,....................................	A	6	229
1842.	Report of canal board on petition of,........................	A	7	150
1846.	Report of committee on claims on petition of,..........	A	3	62

HECKER, JOHN, AND OTHERS.

1842.	Memorial of,....................................	A	5	85

HECOX, SAMUEL, *see* Cady, Beaumont & Hecox.

HEISRADT, MARTIN, AND OTHERS.

1857.	Report of committee on claims favorable on petition of, for damages by break in the Erie canal,...........................	A	2	119

HELLGATE PILOTS.

1831.	Report on petition to repeal the law allowing them to receive half-pilotage in certain cases,...........................	A	2	193
1832.	Report on the same,....................................	A	2	138

HELMER, JOSEPH, AND R. ELWOOD.

1855.	Report of committee on claims in case of,..................	A	2	49

HEMP, CULTURE OF.

1830.	Report of committee on agriculture giving information relative to the,..	A	3	234

HEMPSTEAD, TOWN OF.

1838.	Report on petition to sell certain portions of the common lands belonging to the,..................................	A	4	169

HENDRICK, SUSA.

1846.	Report on petition for relief,........	S	4	127

HENDRICKS, JOEL.

1831.	Report on petition of, to convey to him a certain lot of land,....	A	2	117

HERKIMER COUNTY.

1833.	Jail in, report on petition for a new,..................... ..	A	2	100
1834.	Jail in, report on petition to raise money to build a,...........	A	2	59

HERKIMER COUNTY—*continued.*

Year	Subject	Doc.	Vol.	No.
1835.	Jail in, report on petition for a loan to pay for building,........	A	1	20
1835.	Report in relation to the same,..............................	A	1	33
1833.	Report on memorial from, in relation to leaks in the canal and the condition of fences and bridges,........................	A	4	272
1839.	Poor-house and farm, report on petition for authority to sell the,	A	6	337
1840.	Report on the same,....................................	A	5	163
1843.	Memorial of democratic delegates asking for an amendment to the constitution relative to the creation of a state debt, &c.,......	A	4	90
1843.	Report of majority of the select committee on the memorial,....	A	5	152
1843.	Report of minority on same,............................	A	5	153
1844.	Report of canal appraisers on memorial of landowners in, respecting canal damages,............................	A	5	101

Banks in, *see* Banks, Herkimer county.

HERKIMER, GENERAL JOHN.

Year	Subject	Doc.	Vol.	No.
1839.	Report relative to the erection of a monument to,..............	A	6	392

HERKIMER, JOHN.

Year	Subject	Doc.	Vol.	No.
1835.	Report on petition for compensation for damages to his lands by the Erie canal, ...	A	2	116
1835.	Report of committee on grievances on the same,..............	A	4	356

HERMANCE, WILLIAM J.

Year	Subject	Doc.	Vol.	No.
1847.	Report of majority of committee on colleges, &c., on the bill for relief of,...	A	7	201
1847.	Report of minority on same,............................	A	7	214

HERRESHOFF, JOHN B., AND OTHERS.

Year	Subject	Doc.	Vol.	No.
1835.	Report on petition to be relieved from the payment of interest on the taxes on their lands,..............................	A	2	90
1835.	Report of committee on claims on the same,................	A	2	154
1840.	Report on petition of, to be relieved from the payment of certain taxes,...	A	6	254

HERSKEY, BENJAMIN.

Year	Subject	Doc.	Vol.	No.
1836.	Report on petition to build a dam across Ellicott creek,.........	A	3	208

HERTTELL, THOMAS.

Year	Subject	Doc.	Vol.	No.
1844.	Report of judiciary committee on the memorial of, praying for a law making habitual drunkenness a good cause for divorce,...	A	6	156

HESS, MARIAH.

Year	Subject	Doc.	Vol.	No.
1842.	Report of select committee on petition of,....................	A	7	174

HETFIELD, SAMUEL A., AND OTHERS.

Year	Subject	Doc.	Vol.	No.
1857.	Report of committee on claims favorable on petition of, for additional compensation,..................................	A	2	122

HEWETT & BEACH.

Year	Subject	Doc.	Vol.	No.
1847.	Report relative to damages of,............................	S	4	150

HEWETT AND BUSH.

Year	Subject	Doc.	Vol.	No.
1847.	Report on petition of,....................................	A	8	230

HEWETT, JOSEPH P., & JNO. M. BUTTERLY.

		Doc.	Vol.	No.
1844.	Report of canal board on the petition of,	A	5	134

HIBERNIAN PROVIDENT SOCIETY, *see* New York.

HICKOX, L., AND M. SEYMOUR.

1831.	Report on petition of, to erect a wing dam on the Oneida river,	A	3	274

HICKS, JOHN G., JOHN SCHENCK AND JANE B. SMITH.

1835.	Report on petition of, for a grant of certain land under water, in front of the city of Brooklyn,	A	3	252

HICKS, J. L., AND OTHERS.

1835.	Report on petition for the use of surplus water of the Oswego canal, to raise salt water at Liverpool,	A	4	347

HIGBY, CHAS. G.

1851.	Communication from, relating to contested seat in 26th senate district,	S	3	92

HIGGINBOTTOM, JOHN.

1837.	Report of commissioners of the land office relative to the property escheated to the state on the death of,	S	1	21

HIGHLAND COUNTY.

1855.	Report of committee on erection of,	S	3	70
1858.	Report of a minority of the committee on the erection and division of towns and counties relative to the erection of,	S	2	73
1858.	Report of a majority of the committee relative to,	S	2	80

HIGHLAND GROVE GYMNASIUM ASSOCIATION.

1832.	Report on petition to incorporate,	A	3	199

HIGHLAND TURNPIKE COMPANY.

1831.	Report on petition for a law directing the repayment of certain taxes assessed on, in Westchester county,	A	1	23
1832.	Report on petition of inhabitants of Dutchess and Westchester counties to repeal certain sections of the laws relating to the,	A	3	179
1833.	Report on petition to repeal the charter,	S	2	54
1833.	Report of committee on two-third bills on bill to repeal the charter,	A	4	287

HIGHLANDS.

1835.	Road through the, report on petition for aid to improve a,	A	5	391

HIGHWAYS.

1830.	Assessment of taxes for making and repairing, report on petition to amend the law,	A	4	329
1832.	Report on the same,	S	2	84
1834.	Regulation of, report on petition to amend the laws in relation to the,	S	1	22
1834.	Regulation of, report on petition to amend the laws in relation to the,	A	4	385
1834.	Laying out, report on petition to amend the law in relation to,	S	2	122
1841.	Laying out, report on petition to amend the law in relation to,	A	5	179
1849.	Report of commissioners of Code concerning, and ferries, &c.,	A	1	12

HIGHWAYS—*continued.*

		Doc.	Vol.	No.
1851.	Report of committee on roads and bridges concerning, and work assessed thereon,..................	S	2	34
1851.	Report on bill for the enrollment of the militia, to abolish fines and exempt uniform companies from highway tax and jury duty, ...	A	4	113
1855.	Report of minority of select committee on bill to authorize additional sums to be raised for, and bridges,....................	A	2	48
1858.	Report of attorney-general relative to the constitutionality of laws making streams public highways,...........................	A	4	112

HIGHWAYS, COMMISSIONERS OF.

1832.	Report on bill to extend the powers of,........................	A	3	186
1834.	Report on petition for the election of, for three years,..........	A	4	385
1838.	do do do	A	6	337
1839.	do do do	A	3	79

HILDRETH, GEO. W.

1846.	Report of canal board on petition of,.........................	A	6	201
1846.	Report of committee on canals on petition of,.................	A	6	216

HILDRETH, LEONARD, AND OTHERS.

1842.	Report on petition of, relative to certain lands escheated to the state on the death of John G. Leake,........................	A	3	193

HILL, ANTHONY JOHN.

1842.	Report on petition of,.......................................	A	4	73
1842.	Report of committee on petition of aliens of,..................	A	4	75

HILL, C. J.

1845.	Report of canal commissioners on petition of,.................	A	6	209

HILL, HENRY, AND OTHERS.

1834.	Report of canal board relative to work done on the Oswego canal by, ...	S	2	102

HILL, JOHN AND JENNY, AND ANTHONY OTSEQUETTE.

1835.	Report on petition for the payment of the principal sum for which annuities are now paid them by the state,.............	A	2	151
1835.	Report on petition for the payment of the principal sum for which annuities are now paid them by the state,.............	A	3	257

HILL, NICHOLAS, Jr.

1847.	Communication from,...	A	7	197

HILL, WM. S., AND OTHERS.

1852.	*See* report of commissioners of land office respecting land under water at Westfield,....................................	A	5	121

HILLS, ALLEN.

1830.	Report on petition of, that the money paid by his father on certain lots in Oneida Castle, may be credited to him, &c.,.......	A	2	76
1830.	Report of comptroller on same,..............................	S	1	42
1830.	Report of committee on finance on same,.....................	S	2	162

HILLS, HUETT, *see* Allen Hills.

HILLS, ZIMRI.

		Doc.	Vol.	No.
1833.	Report on petition of, for the release of certain escheated land,..	A	1	25
1833.	Report of commissioners of the land office on the same,........	A	2	54

HILTON, CLARK.

1830.	Report on petition of, to build a dam and lock on the Tonawanda creek,........	A	4	293

HINDS, JACOB.

1850.	Charges against, as canal commissioner,........	A	5	84
1850.	Communication from,........	A	5	106
1850.	Communication from, in regard to alleged frauds,........	A	5	102

HINMAN, ELI.

1849.	Report of committee on public lands on petition of,........	A	1	23

HINMAN, J. E., AND H. W. SCHROEPPEL.

1830.	Report on petition of, to build a dam across Oneida river at Oak Orchard reef,........	S	2	37
1837.	Report on petition for compensation for damages to their lands by the erection of a dam across Oswego river,........	A	3	185

HINMAN, JOHN E., AND AARON BARNES.

1842.	Report of canal board on petition of,........	A	5	119
1845.	Report of canal board on petition of,........	A	3	73
1845.	Report of committee on claims on petition of,........	A	3	79

HISTORICAL AND ANTIQUARIAN COLLECTIONS, *see* Natural History, Regents of the University.

HISTORICAL SOCIETY, *see* New York.

HISTORIES.

1857.	Report of secretary of state in reply to resolution relative to printing of,........	A	2	134

HISTORY, ABORIGINAL, *see* Aboriginal History.

HISTORY, COLONIAL, *see* Colonial History.

HISTORY, DOCUMENTARY, *see* Documentary History.

HISTORY, NATURAL, *see* Natural History.

HITCHCOCK AND COLLINS.

1851.	Report of canal board on the petition of,........	S	1	18
1851.	Report of committee on canals on petition of,........	S	2	21

HITCHCOCK, LUTHER, *see* Granger, Oscar, and others.

HITCHINS, FRANCIS, AND OTHERS.

1847.	Report on petition of,........	A	4	143

HOAG, ESAIAS.

1858.	Report on claim of,........	A	4	127

HOAG, PETER, AND OTHERS.

		Doc.	Vol.	No.
1857.	Report of committee on claims on petition of, for damages by break in the Erie canal,	A	2	119

HOAR, DIX.

1835.	Report on petition to change the name of,	A	4	359

HOAR, LEONARD, AND OTHERS.

1833.	Report on petition to change the names of,	A	2	76

HOAR, MARTIN, AND OTHERS.

1832.	Report on petition to change the names of,	A	2	56

HODGMAN, LEONARD.

1856.	Report on petition of,	A	4	118

HOGAN, W.

1840.	Report on petition of, to be relieved from a tax unlawfully assessed,	A	6	256

HOLDEN, G. H., AND OTHERS, *see* Greece, town of.

HOLLAND.

1842.	Message of governor transmitting correspondence from, relative to the annual reports of the Regents of the University,	S	4	108

HOLLAND LAND COMPANY.

1830.	Report on petition of the agent of the, to allow them to purchase certain real estate,	A	2	69
1831.	Memorial of the agent of the, in relation to the taxation of land contracts, &c.,	A	4	282
1831.	Memorial of Adam Hoops, for relief, relative to certain contracts for land bought of the, *see* Adam Hoops.			
1833.	Memorial of the agent of, relative to the taxation of land contracts, &c.,	A	3	235
1839.	Title papers of, governor's message relative to the preservation of the,	A	5	317
1839.	Report of select committee on the same,	A	5	318
1840.	Communication from the secretary of state relative to,	A	3	350
1835.	Report on petition of supervisors of Genesee county to relinquish certain lands in Batavia to the,	A	1	14
1837.	Title of the, majority report concerning the,	A	3	224
1837.	Title of the, minority report concerning the,	A	3	222

HOLLAND, MARY.

1857.	Report of committee on claims favorable on petition of, for damages to house, &c., by enlargement of the Erie canal,	A	1	42

HOLLAND, TOWN OF.

1830.	Report on petition of the supervisor of the, relative to certain moneys,	A	3	249

HOLLISTER, I. & S.

1831.	Report on petition of, for compensation for damages by the construction of the Erie canal,	S	1	58
1833.	Report of committee on claims on the same,	A	3	202
1834.	Report of committee on claims on the same,	A	4	303

HOLLISTER, JESSE.

		Doc.	Vol.	No.
1849.	Report of committee on canals on petition of,	A	2	62

HOLLISTER, JOHN.

1846.	Report of canal board on petition of,	A	5	152

HOLLISTER, NATHAN S.

1840.	Report on petition of, for compensation for damages to his house and lands by the enlargement of the Erie canal,	A	3	35
1841.	Report on petition of, for compensation for damages to his house and lands by the enlargement of the Erie canal,	A	3	67

HOLLISTER, N. S.

1845.	Report of committee on claims on petition of,	A	5	178
1846.	Report of canal commissioners on petition of,	S	1	15
1846.	Report on petition for relief of,	S	4	128

HOMEOPATHY, &c.

1846.	Report of committee on medical societies and colleges concerning,	A	4	125

HOMEOPATHIC COLLEGE.

1846.	Report relative to,	S	4	108

HOMER, TOWN OF.

1830.	Report on petition to repeal an act for the division of the,	A	4	315

HOMER, VILLAGE OF.

1837.	Report on petition relative to the charter of,	A	4	283

HOMESTEAD EXEMPTION, *see* Exemption.

HONEOYE, LAKE.

1850.	Report of canal board in relation to,	S	1	40

HONYOST, SALLY, AND OTHERS.

1853.	Report of committee on Indian affairs on claim of, for relief,	A	3	80

HOOD, JACOB.

1857.	Report of committee on claims adverse on petition of, for extra compensation,	A	2	65

HORKER, JAS. H.

1848.	Report on petition of,	A	5	152
1849.	Report on petition of,	S	2	32
1849.	Report of committee on claims on petition of,	A	1	16
1850.	Report on canal claim,	A	5	118

HOOKER, J. H., AND T. P. WATERS.

1857.	Report on petition of,	S	2	57

HOOSICK FALLS, VILLAGE OF.

1839.	Report on petition to repeal the charter of,	A	4	208

HOOSICK, TOWN OF.

		Doc.	Vol.	No.
1837.	Report on petition to raise money by tax on, to build a bridge over Hoosick Falls,	A	4	334

HOOP, ANN, AND OTHERS (aliens).

		Doc.	Vol.	No.
1835.	Report on petition of, to hold real estate,	A	1	45

HOOPER, SANFORD A.

		Doc.	Vol.	No.
1843.	Report of committee on claims on petition of,	A	5	125
1843.	Report of committee on claims on a bill for his relief,	S	3	111
1844.	Report of committee on claims on petition of,	A	3	39

HOOPER, SANFORD A., AND OTHERS.

		Doc.	Vol.	No.
1853.	Report of attorney-general in relation to a certain note,	A	4	85

HOOPS, ADAM.

		Doc.	Vol.	No.
1832.	Memorial of, for relief in relation to injuries sustained under certain contracts for lands purchased of the Holland Land Company,	S	2	110
1833.	Report of select committee on the same,	S	2	118
1835.	Report of select committee on the same,	S	2	86
1837.	Report of committee on claims,	S	1	25

HOPE, JAMES, AND N. JOHNSON.

		Doc.	Vol.	No.
1842.	Report of committee on militia on petition of,	A	2	39

HOPE, TOWN OF.

		Doc.	Vol.	No.
1838.	Report relative to tax list of non-resident lands in the,	A	5	208

HOP LAW.

		Doc.	Vol.	No.
1846.	Report of committee on trade and manufactures relative to,	A	4	92

HOPS, INSPECTOR OF, *see* Albany, New York.

HOPKINS, GILBERT.

		Doc.	Vol.	No.
1850.	Report on petition of,	S	1	39
1850.	Report on petition of,	S	3	39

HOPKINS, S. M., *see* State Prison at Mount Pleasant.

HOPKINTON AND PORT KENT ROAD, *see* Port Kent and Hopkinton.

HOPKINTON, TOWN OF.

		Doc.	Vol.	No.
1841.	Report on petition to raise money by tax to repair the town-house,	A	6	227

HORNBY ESTATE.

		Doc.	Vol.	No.
1848.	Report of finance committee relative to,	S	2	60

HORNELLSVILLE, TOWN OF.

		Doc.	Vol.	No.
1838.	Report relative to taxes on non-resident lands in,	A	6	361

HORSE ARTILLERY, FIRST REGIMENT OF.

		Doc.	Vol.	No.
1835.	Report on petition to exempt them from jury duty after serving seven years,	A	2	112

HORSE RACING.

		Doc.	Vol.	No.
1831.	Report relative to extending the privilege of, throughout the state,	A	4	351
1830.	Report on petition to extend the law relative to, to Cayuga county,	A	3	236
1830.	Report on petition to extend the law relative to, to Saratoga county,	A	4	294
1838.	Report on petition to extend the law relative to, to Livingston county,	A	4	198
1845.	Report on bill to prevent, on Albany and Troy road, &c.,	S	3	88

HORSE-SHOE DAM.

		Doc.	Vol.	No.
1842.	Report of canal commissioners relative to,	A	7	167
1843.	Report of canal commissioners respecting the removal of,	A	4	93

HORTON, ALLEN W.

		Doc.	Vol.	No.
1852.	Report on petition of,	A	2	31
1854.	Report on petition of,	A	1	28
1855.	Report of committee on claims on petition of,	A	2	38

HORTON, GEO. W.

		Doc.	Vol.	No.
1844.	Report of canal board on petition of,	A	3	68

HOSICK AND WHITE CREEK BRIDGE COMPANY.

		Doc.	Vol.	No.
1833.	Report on petition to amend the charter of,	A	3	164

HOSMER, W. H. C.

		Doc.	Vol.	No.
1850.	Report on claim of,	A	5	89

HOSPITAL, ALBANY, *see* Albany.

HOSPITAL, MARINE, *see* New York, Sandy Hook.

HOSPITAL, NEW YORK, *see* New York.

HOSPITAL, STATE, *see* New York.

HOTCHKISS AND SMITH.

		Doc.	Vol.	No.
1849.	Petition of, for appointment of commissioners to examine and liquidate claims of, against agent of state prison at Sing Sing,	A	2	85
1851.	Report of committee on claims on petition of Abijah Fitch relative to claim of,	A	4	96

HOTCHKISS, CALVIN.

		Doc.	Vol.	No.
1834.	Report on petition of, for a re-appraisement of certain land in Lewiston,	S	2	68

HOTCHKISS, W. & CALVIN.

		Doc.	Vol.	No.
1832.	Report on petition of, to authorize the commissioners of the land office to sell to them certain land in Lewiston,	S	1	29

HOUGH, FRANKLIN B.

		Doc.	Vol.	No.
1854.	Report on petition of,	A	3	111

HOUNSFIELD AND BROWNSVILLE, TOWNS OF.

		Doc.	Vol.	No.
1836.	Report concerning highways in the,	A	4	276

HOUNSFIELD, TOWN OF.

		Doc.	Vol.	No.
1830.	Report relative to certain notes held by the overseers of the poor of said town,	A	4	372

HOUSE, A., *see* M. Hart and others.

HOUSE, ALANSON, *see* Thomas Geary and others.

HOUSE, F., AND OTHERS.

		Doc.	Vol.	No.
1844.	Report of committee on canals respecting application of, to connect a slip and basin with the Dansville branch of the Genesee Valley canal,	A	7	164

HOUSEAUR, MICHAEL.

		Doc.	Vol.	No.
1852.	Report on petition of for relief,	A	5	98

HOUSEHOLD FURNITURE, EXEMPTION OF, *see* Exemption.

HOUSE OF REFUGE, *see* Juvenile Delinquents.

HOWARD, DEAN S.

		Doc.	Vol.	No.
1851.	Report of committee on claim for canal damages,	A	4	115

HOWARD, NATHANIEL S.

		Doc.	Vol.	No.
1840.	Report on petition of, for compensation for damages to his mills, &c., by the construction of the Chenango canal,	A	4	128
1841.	Report of committee on claims on the same,	A	3	82

HOWE, ELIJAH.

		Doc.	Vol.	No.
1856.	Report on petition for relief,	A	4	164

HOWE, JOSHUA.

		Doc.	Vol.	No.
1830.	Report on petition for compensation for damages by the erection of the Minden dam,	A	2	109

HOWELL, GILBERT.

		Doc.	Vol.	No.
1840.	Report on petition for compensation for damages by the construction of certain feeders to the Erie canal,	A	6	259
1841.	Report of committee on claims on the same,	A	3	65

HOWELL, HEZEKIAH, *see* S. Barnum.

HOWLAND, HUMPHREY.

		Doc.	Vol.	No.
1842.	Report of committee on grievances on petition of,	A	2	17

HOYLE, HENRY (an alien).

		Doc.	Vol.	No.
1836.	Report on petition of, to hold real estate,	A	2	100

HOYT, JOHN C., *see* James Nichols and J. C. Hoyt.

HUBBARD, ALEXANDER.

		Doc.	Vol.	No.
1850.	Report on petition of,	S	2	52

HUBBARD, ELIAS.

		Doc.	Vol.	No.
1838.	Report on petition for a divorce,	A	4	176

HUBBARD, I. H., *see* Supreme Court Clerks.

	HUBBARD, JOSEPH.	Doc.	Vol.	No.
1830.	A soldier of the revolution, report on bill for the relief of the heir of,....	A	2	126
1830.	Report in relation to the same,....	A	1	45
1831.	Report on the same,....	A	2	171

HUDSON AND BERKSHIRE RAILROAD, *see* Railroads.

HUDSON AND DELAWARE CANAL, *see* Delaware and Hudson.

HUDSON, CITY OF.

		Doc.	Vol.	No.
1836.	Aqueduct Company, report on petition to increase the capital stock of the,....	A	4	248
1837.	Report relative to the same,....	A	1	19
1837.	Academy in, report on petition to be relieved from a mortgage held by the state,....	A	5	260
1836.	City Hall in, report on petition to raise money to convert the present jail into a,....	A	4	287
1837.	City Hall in, report on petition to raise money to build a,....	A	3	186
1837.	Corporation of, report on petition of, to borrow money to aid in the construction of the Hudson and Berkshire railroad,....	A	3	264
1838.	do report on bill to vest in, the title to certain lands under water,....	A	4	318
1839.	do report on the same,....	A	6	373
1837.	Excise law, report on petition to amend the, for the city of,....	A	4	308
1839.	Fires by steamboats, report on petition for the prevention of,....	A	5	301
1831.	Fires in,....	A	2	76
1838.	Highways, report on petition for a law sentencing convicts to labor on the,....	A	6	330
1845.	Jail, report of committee on the militia on the bill entitled "An act to pay the guard of one hundred enlisted men for protection of,"....	S	1	42
1835.	Lancaster School, report on petition to raise money by tax for the support of the,....	A	5	384
1835.	Public Square, report on petition for a,....	A	4	378
1830.	Towboat Company, report on petition to resume and continue their limited partnership,....	A	1	57
1830.	Towboat Company, report of committee on two-third bills on the bill relative to the,....	A	2	177
1845.	Troops at, communication from adjutant-general relative to,....	A	1	16
1845.	Report of committee on the militia, &c., on bill to pay,....	A	4	86
1845.	Report of commissary-general relative to expenses of,....	A	4	87
1840.	Whaling Company, report on bill to repeal the charter of,....	S	3	93

BANKS IN, *see* Banks, Columbia county.

INSPECTORS' REPORTS, *see* Columbia county.

LUNATIC ASYLUM, *see* Samuel White.

HUDSON, RICHARD.

		Doc.	Vol.	No.
1848.	Report on petition of,....	A	5	128

HUDSON RIVER.

		Doc.	Vol.	No.
1850.	Aqueduct across, report of committee on canals on,....	A	6	144
1855.	Beacon lights on, statement of United States attorney-general relative to,....	S	1	6
1831.	Bridge across at Troy, report on petition to construct,....	A	1	29
1841.	do at Troy, report on petition for the removal of,....	A	7	299

HUDSON RIVER—*continued.*

		Doc.	Vol.	No.
1841.	Bridge across at Troy, report on petition for the removal of,.....	A	7	300
1841.	do *see* Athol and Warrensburgh.			
1830.	do report on petition of citizens of Johnsburgh for aid to build,..	A	3	268
1837.	do at Schuylerville, report on petition for,...........	S	1	12
1854.	Bridge over, report of committee on,..........................	S	2	97
1856.	do report of committee on roads and bridges relative to,..	S	2	70
1858.	Channel of, near West Troy, report in relation to,..............	S	2	82
1837.	Dam across, at Fort Edward, report on petition for,.............	A	3	165
1835.	Ferry across, between Caldwell's and Peekskill, report on petition for,..	A	4	313
	Ship canal from, *see* Ship Canal.			
1834.	State road from, to Owego and Cherry Valley, report on petition for,..	A	4	363
1845.	Steamboat Swallow, report of the select committee of the senate appointed to investigate "the cause of the late disaster to,"....	S	3	102
1834.	Surplus waters of the, report of canal commissioners relative to,	A	4	359
1831.	Report on bill to provide for the survey of the middle branch of,	A	3	248
1840.	Survey of the several branches, report of the canal board in relation to,..	S	2	61
1840.	Continuation of the survey of the northern branches of the, report of the canal board relative to,.........................	A	7	275
	And *see* Sacandaga canal.			

BRIDGE ACROSS, AT ALBANY:

		Doc.	Vol.	No.
1835.	Report on petition for,...	A	4	363
1841.	Majority report (Mr. Strong),......................................	A	6	200
1841.	Minority report (Mr. Brodhead),....................................	A	6	253
1845.	Memorial of corporation of Troy concerning,........................	A	3	72
1845.	Report of majority of committee on roads and bridges against,..	A	6	198
1845.	Minority report in favor of,.......................................	A	6	199
1848.	Report of committee on roads and bridges on bill to authorize,..	A	5	149
1852.	Report on,..	A	5	114
1856.	Testimony relative to,...	A	5	196
1856.	Testimony relative to,...	A	5	206
1856.	Report relative to,..	S	2	56
1857.	Report of committee on roads and bridges relative to,...........	A	3	203
1857.	Testimony relative to,...	A	3	203

IMPROVEMENT OF:

		Doc.	Vol.	No.
1830.	Report relative to the use of the steam dredging machine for,...	A	4	335
1833.	Report of amount of appropriations and expenditures for the,...	A	4	302
1838.	Report on petition for, above Glen's Falls, for the survey of a canal route from the head waters of, to the Champlain canal feeder,...	A	5	238
1839.	Report on petition for, of the several branches of,..............	A	3	117
1840.	Letter from George E. Hoffman relative to,.......................	S	1	2
1849.	Report of select committee on bill to provide for improving upper waters of,..	A	5	203
1853.	Report of state engineer and surveyor in relation to removing obstructions of channel of,..................................	S	1	23
1854.	Communication relative to,.......................................	S	1	31
1855.	Report of committee on commerce and navigation on resolution relative to,..	S	1	23
1857.	Memorial of American Geological Society, relative to...........	S	1	14
1857.	Report of standing committee on finance on petition to improve west branch of,...	S	4	118

HUGHES, COLLINS AND WOOLSTON.

		Doc.	Vol.	No.
1843.	Report on petition,..	A	5	174

HUGHES, FREEMAN.

		Doc.	Vol.	No.
1855.	Report of committee on ways and means on petition of,	A	3	79
1856.	Report on claim of,	S	1	22

HUGHES, RICHARD.

		Doc.	Vol.	No.
1850.	Report on petition,	S	1	18

HUGHES, RT. REV. BISHOP.

		Doc.	Vol.	No.
1849.	Letter from, relative to interchange of donations with Roman states, &c.,	A	3	117

HUGHES, VOLNEY, AND C. W. WOOLSTON.

		Doc.	Vol.	No.
1851.	Report of committee on claims,	A	3	47
1852.	Report on petition of, for relief,	S	1	38

HUGHSTON, JONAS A.

		Doc.	Vol.	No.
1846.	Report of committee on claims on the petition of,	A	2	50
1847.	Report on petition of,	A	2	52

HULBERT AND VROOMAN.

		Doc.	Vol.	No.
1853.	Report of committee on claims on petition of,	S	1	19
1855.	Communication from auditor respecting award to,	A	5	138
1856	Report of judiciary committee on bill to pay,	S	1	30

HULBERT, GURDON.

		Doc.	Vol.	No.
1856.	Report on petition of,	A	4	101
1857.	Report of committee on claims favorable on petition of, for payment of balance of an award,	A	2	69

HULBERT, HORACE, AND D. PORTER.

		Doc.	Vol.	No.
1834.	Report on petition for extra allowance for work done on the Chemung canal,	A	4	315

HULBURT, LEVI.

		Doc.	Vol.	No.
1852.	Report on petition of,	A	2	58

HULETT, CHAS.

		Doc.	Vol.	No.
1847.	Report on petition of,	A	1	18

HULL & SHIPMAN.

		Doc.	Vol.	No.
1857.	Report on petition of,	S	2	91
1857.	Report on petition of standing committee on judiciary,	S	3	91

HULSE, DAVID.

		Doc.	Vol.	No.
1852.	Report on petition of,	A	2	59

HUME, TOWN OF.

		Doc.	Vol.	No.
1833.	Bridge over the Genesee at, report on petition for a,	A	4	256

HUMPHREY, EBENEZER.

		Doc.	Vol.	No.
1851.	Report of committee on claims for canal damages,	A	1	19

HUMPHRIES, ELLEN, *see* Laura Jones and others.

HUNT, ABIJAH.

		Doc.	Vol.	No.
1831.	Report on petition of, for the release of the title of the state to certain lands,	A	4	300
1831.	Report of committee on claims on the same,	A	4	346
1841.	Report on petition of, relative to certain funds deposited in the court of chancery,	S	1	33

HUNT & DUBOIS.

1844.	Report of commissioners of land office on petition of,	S	3	103

HUNT, FITCH AND COOLEY.

1855.	Memorial of,	A	2	44
1855.	Report of select committee on bill for payment of judgment in favor of,	S	2	52, 54

HUNT, RUSSELL AND OTHERS.

1857.	Report of committee on claims on petition of, for damages by break in the Erie canal,	A	2	119

HUNT, SETH.

1854.	Report on petition of,	A	3	90

HUNTER'S POINT.

1857.	Report relative to road from Newtown and Flushing,	S	4	119

HUNTER, WARD.

1835.	Report on petition of, to maintain a ferry across the Hudson, between Peekskill and Caldwell's Landing,	A	4	313

HUNTINGTON, MATTHEW.

1844.	Report of committee on claims on petition of,	A	3	65
1850.	Report on canal claim of,	A	3	34
1852.	Report on petition of, for relief,	S	1	47

HUNTINGTON, TOWN OF.

1830.	Report of attorney-general on the bill to divide the,	A	4	392

HUNTLEY, W., AND OTHERS.

1838.	Report on petition to construct a tunnel under the Erie canal for the purpose of draining a certain swamp,	S	2	59

HURD, DAVIS.

1837.	Report on petition of, to be admitted to a seat as a member of assembly in place of Reuben H. Boughton,	A	2	61

HUTCHINSON, HOLMES, *see* Jacob Trumpbour.

1832.	Report of canal board on memorial of, relative to the survey of the canals,	A	3	188
1832.	Report of the select committee on the same,	A	4	334
1832.	Documents accompanying,	A	4	335
1834.	Report on petition for compensation for services in examining the inclined planes of the Morris canal, &c.,	A	2	62
1834.	Resolution offered by Mr. Bagley in relation to the memorials of Jacob Trumpbour and Holmes Hutchinson,	A	4	268
1835.	Report on petition of, for compensation for making a survey of the canals,	A	2	140

HUTCHINSON, HOLMES—*continued.*

		Doc.	Vol.	No.
1835.	Report of committee on canals on the same,	A	3	197
1836.	Report of committee on canals on the same,	A	2	61
1841.	Report on petition of, to be repaid certain moneys advanced by him to Jacob Trumpbour,	A	2	33
1847.	Memorial of, as to report of select committee for investigating canal frauds,	A	7	218

HUTCHINSON, J.

1857.	Report on petition of,	S	3	106

HUTCHINSON, JOHN.

1858.	Report of committee on claims on petition of,	S	3	119

HYAT, JOHN C., *see* Robert Land and others.

HYDE, WILKES AND OTHERS.

1831.	Report on petition to be exempted from highway labor,			

HYDRAULIC CEMENT.

1840.	Company at Lawrensville, report on petition to incorporate,	A	3	94
1840.	Communication from H. S. Dexter, civil engineer, relative to,	S	4	123
1840.	Report on petition of E. C. Warner relative to his,	A	7	297

HYDROSTATIC SCALE, AMSDEN'S, *see* Canals.

HYNEY, JOHN, AND OTHERS.

1839.	Report on petition to build a dam, &c., on Flat brook,	A	5	289

I.

IDIOTS.

1846.	Report on that portion of the census relating to,	S	1	23

IDIOT ASYLUM, STATE.

1847.	Report on bill for,	S	2	44
1852.	Report of trustees of,	S	1	30
1853.	Report of committee on state charitable institutions in favor of an appropriation for,	A	2	68
1853.	Report of the committee on state charitable institutions in favor of an appropriation for,	A	3	68
1854.	Annual report of,	A	2	54
1855.	Annual report of,	A	2	33
1855.	Report of committee on state charitable institutions on completion of buildings for,	A	2	36
1856.	Report of the trustees of,	A	3	99
1857.	Sixth annual report of the trustees of,	A	2	90
1858.	Annual report of,	A	1	33

IDLEY, ELIZABETH.

1832.	Report on bill vesting the title to certain lands in,	A	1	57

ILLEGAL VOTING.

1858.	Report of majority on act to prevent,	A	4	109

ILLINOIS, STATE OF.

		Doc.	Vol.	No.
1833.	Resolution of the legislature of, relative to the reorganization of the militia,......	A	1	34

IMPEACHMENT.

		Doc.	Vol.	No.
1853.	*See* state officers, report of judiciary committee relative to power of,......	A	5	123

IMPLEMENTS, EXEMPTION OF, *see* Exemption.

IMPRISONMENT FOR DEBT.

		Doc.	Vol.	No.
1830.	Resolution offered by Mr. Stilwell, to amend the law in relation to,......	A	2	132
1830.	Abolishment of, report of a select committee in relation to the,..	A	4	409
1830.	Abolishment of, in certain cases, report on petition of Elihu Clark and others, to amend the law for the,......	A	4	425
1830.	Exemption of officers and soldiers of the revolution from, report on the subject,......	A	4	388
1831.	Abolishment of, report on petition for the (Mr. Stilwell),......	A	2	190
1831.	Abolishment of, report on petition for the (Mr. Stilwell),......	A	4	284
1833.	Abolishment of, report on petition to repeal the law (Mr. Hertell,)..	A	3	216
1834.	do do do (Mr. Grinnell),	A	3	222
1835.	do do do (Mr. Wilkinson),	A	3	183
1836.	do do do (Mr. Eno),.....	A	3	119

INCORPORATIONS, *see* Corporations.

INDEPENDENCE, AMERICAN, *see* American Independence.

INDEPENDENCE SQUARE, PHILADELPHIA.

		Doc.	Vol.	No.
1853.	Proceedings of a convention on the subject of erecting a monument in,......	A	4	89

INDEPENDENT TREASURY, STATE.

		Doc.	Vol.	No.
1840.	Report on petition for (Mr. Roosevelt),......	A	2	58
1842.	Memorial for adopting,......	A	5	86

INDEPENDENT TREASURY SYSTEM.

		Doc.	Vol.	No.
1838.	Report and resolution offered by Mr. Holly in relation to the,....	A	3	95
1839.	Resolution of the legislature of North Carolina protesting against,	A	4	202
1840.	Resolution offered by Mr. King protesting against,......	A	1	27
1841.	Resolution of the general assembly of Rhode Island, for the repeal of,......	A	5	158

INDIANA, STATE OF.

		Doc.	Vol.	No.
1832.	Resolution of the legislature of, relative to revolutionary pensioners and the militia,....	A	3	183
1833.	do do relative to nullification in South Carolina,......	A	2	115
1839.	do do relative to slavery,......	A	5	282
1840.	do do relative to the northeastern boundary,......	A	7	308
1841.	do do relative to the re-eligibility of the president,......	A	3	78
1841.	do do relative to holding elections for electors of president and vice-president on the same day throughout the United States,......	A	4	120
1841.	do do relative to the public lands,..	A	5	168
1852.	do do respecting the slave trade,....	S	2	91

INDIAN AGENT.

		Doc.	Vol.	No.
1834.	John Sergeant, report on petition of, for compensation for services as,	A	3	182
1838.	John Sergeant, report on petition of, for compensation for services as,	A	4	162

INDIANS.

		Doc.	Vol.	No.
1842.	Affairs of, report on so much of governor's message as relates to,	S	4	95
1842.	Affairs of, report of committee on, on so much of the governor's message as relates to that subject,	S	5	95
1850.	Affairs of, report from commissioners of land office,	A	5	130
1846.	Affairs of, on Allegany and Cattaraugus reservations, governor's message relative to,	S	2	57
1850.	Boarding schools, report of select committee on,	A	5	136
1845.	Census, report of committee on Indian affairs on resolution of senate relative to,	S	2	84
1846.	Census of, Schoolcraft's report relative to,	S	1	24
1854.	Claims, majority and minority report relative to certain,	A	3	106
1846.	Collins, Mr., resolution offered by, relative to,	A	3	63
1845.	Lands purchased by Wm. Smith, Jr., report of secretary of state relative to,	A	6	212
1847.	Lands, report as to intruders on,	A	7	207
1847.	Lands in Broome and Chenango counties, report on petition of Indians relative to,	A	7	215
1847.	Lands, report of Jacob Powless and others relative to, at Wood creek,	A	7	216
1854.	Lands, report of committee on, on claims to certain,	A	2	49
1857.	Lands, report of comptroller in reply to resolution relative to sales of,	A	1	12
1855.	Schools and asylums on reservations, report of committee on Indian affairs on petitions for,	A	2	43
1842.	Tribes of, report of committee on Indian affairs relative to certain,	S	4	92

BROTHERTOWN:

		Doc.	Vol.	No.
1830.	Report on petition of inhabitants of the towns of Marshall and Kirkland relative to the survey of the lands set apart for the,	A	4	367
1835.	Report on petition to amend the law relative to the,	A	4	301

CAUGHNAWAGAS:

		Doc.	Vol.	No.
1841.	Report of comptroller in relation to their annuity,	A	2	29

CAYUGAS:

		Doc.	Vol.	No.
1848.	Report as to treaties with,	A	3	61
1849.	Report on petition of Peter Wilson, chief of,	S	2	64
1849.	Report of commissioners of land office in answer to a resolution of the assembly relative to distribution of annuities of,	A	3	165
1850.	Memorial of Peter Wilson, chief of,	A	6	164
1851.	Petition of in relation to annuities,	A	3	83
1853.	Report of committee on Indian affairs on petition to pay an annuity to,	A	2	26
1853.	Memorial of Peter Wilson, chief of,	S	2	56
1853.	Report of committee on Indian affairs on petition of Peter Wilson, chief of,	S	3	81
1853.	Report of committee on Indian affairs on petition of Peter Wilson for adjustment of claims of,	S	4	81

IROQUOIS, OR SIX NATIONS:

		Doc.	Vol.	No.
1842.	Petition of,	A	1	2
1847.	Report of committee on Indian affairs relative to,	S	2	70

INDIANS—*continued.*

Year	Subject	Doc.	Vol.	No.
	MOHAWKS:			
1853.	Report of select committee on petition of the Stockbridge Indians and part of the branch of Mohawks,	A	3	79
	OCHQUAGAS:			
1834.	Report on the claim of the, to certain lands,	S	2	126
	ONEIDAS:			
1841.	Report of commissioners of the land office respecting their proceedings under the act relating to the,	S	1	14
1841.	Attorney for the, communication from Nathan Burchard concerning his salary,	A	4	139
1830.	Annuities of the, report on petition of Martin Denny in relation to the,	A	4	432
1848.	Report of attorney-general in relation to,	S	2	35
1852.	Report on claims of purchasers of lands from,	A	2	61
1857.	Report of committee on public lands favorable on petition of purchasers of certain land from,	A	3	211
	ONEIDAS, FIRST CHRISTIAN PARTY OF:			
1830.	Report on petition of Baptist Paulus, and others, chief of the, relative to the sale of their lands to the state,	A	4	296
1831.	Comptroller's report of items constituting the payment of moneys for the lands of the,	A	4	339
1833.	Residing at Green Bay, report on petition of the chiefs of the, for an investigation of their accounts with the state,	A	4	315
1834.	Report on petition of John Denny for his portion of the money due the,	S	1	37
1834.	Report of committee on Indian affairs on the same,	S	2	51
1834.	Report on petition of the remnant of the, desirous to remain in the state,	S	2	74
1835.	Report on petition of the, for additional compensation for their lands,	A	3	260
1838.	Residing at Duck creek, Wisconsin, report on petition of the chiefs of the, relative to their annuities,	S	2	51
1832.	Report on petition of Peter Augustine to sell real estate,	A	2	150
1849.	Report on petition of chiefs, &c., of,	S	2	46
	ONEIDAS, ORCHARD PARTY OF:			
1834.	Report on petition for compensation for improvements on their lands,	S	2	88
1834.	Report of committee on Indian affairs on the same,	S	2	98
1835.	Report on petition of W. Page in relation to a contract between him and the,	S	2	29
1838.	Residing at Green Bay, majority report on petition of Henry Jourdon in behalf of the, for additional compensation for their lands,	A	5	287
1838.	Minority report on the same,	A	5	289
1838.	Report of committee on Indian affairs on the same,	A	6	350
1849.	Report of commissioners of land office relative to lands ceded to state by,	A	3	103
	ONONDAGAS:			
1841.	Annuities, report of commissioners of the land office relative to their,	S	2	63
1835.	Lands, road through the, report on petition for a grant from the state of $2,000 to improve,	A	3	222
1847.	Remonstrance of chiefs of,	A	4	124
	ST. REGIS:			
1833.	Report on petition of the, to amend the law to prevent trespasses on their lands,	A	4	281

INDIANS—*continued.*

Year	Entry	Doc.	Vol.	No.
1835.	Report of comptroller on petition of the, relative to the payment of their annuities,..	A	4	318
1838.	Report of W. Quaw to lease certain lands of the,..............	A	5	280
1841.	Lands of the, report of surveyor-general on petition relative to the,..	A	4	131
1842.	Communication to the governor,......................................	A	1	2
1843.	Report of the commissioners of the land office on the petition of the trustees of, in relation to certain islands in the river St. Lawrence,..	A	5	136
1850.	Communication from secretary of state relative to,..............	A	3	27
1851.	Communication from the commissioners of the land office relative to,..	A	2	32
1853.	Report of committee in relation to compensation for certain islands in the St. Lawrence river,....................................	A	2	39
1854.	Report on petition of,..	A	1	27
1855.	Memorial relative to,...	S	2	43
1856.	Report on petition of,..	A	3	34
1856.	Report on petition of,..	A	3	34
	SENECAS:			
1834.	Report on petition to prevent the sale of ardent spirits to,.......	A	4	365
1836.	Report on bill for the extinguishment of the claim of,...........	A	2	82
1836.	Report on petition of Governor Blackmake, and other chiefs of, to confirm certain contracts,..	A	3	168
1841.	Treaty with the United States, report on a resolution of the assembly relative to,...	A	4	88
1843.	Report of committee on Indian affairs relative to,................	S	3	84
1845.	Report of committee on Indian affairs on bill from assembly in relation to,...	S	3	93
1845.	Remonstrance from R. L. Tillotson against the last mentioned bill,	S	3	94
1845.	Remonstrance of Governor Jennison and others, against the same,	S	3	104
1846.	Message from governor transmitting memorial of,..............	A	5	197
1849.	Communication from governor transmitting certain proceedings of,..	A	3	108
1849.	Report of minority of committee on Indian affairs on,...........	A	3	189
1849.	Report of majority of committee on Indian affairs on,...........	A	3	190
1849.	Letter from secretary of war relative to payment of annuities of,	A	5	205
1850.	Message from governor transmitting letter from clerk of,........	S	1	21
1850.	Governor's message and papers,....................................	S	2	59
1850.	Report of committee on Indian affairs on memorial of,..........	S	3	108
1850.	Report on memorial of warriors of,..................................	S	5	108
1857.	Report of committee on judiciary on memorial of, for relief,.....	S	1	23
1857.	Report on memorial for relief,..	S	1	28
1857.	Communication from governor relative to sale of lands belonging to,..	A	1	17
	SIX NATIONS, *see* Iroquois.			
	STOCKBRIDGE:			
1834.	Report on petition for the payment of the principal sum due the,	A	4	343
1838.	Report on petition relative to the annuities due the,............	A	3	173
1846.	Report of commissioners of the land office on petition of,........	A	5	158
1848.	Petition for relief,...	A	3	81
1848.	Report as to lands sold by, to the state,..........................	A	2	53
1853.	Report of select committee on petitions of, and a branch of the Mohawks,..	A	3	79
1855.	Report of committee on Indian affairs on bill for relief of,.......	S	2	66
1855.	Report of majority and minority of committee on same subject,..	A	4	103
1856.	Minority report on petition of,.......................................	A	5	205
1857.	Report of committee on Indian affairs on petition and papers of,	A	1	46
1857.	Report of committee on Indian affairs on petition of Stockbridge Indians, for distribution of their funds,............................	S	2	72

INDIANS—*continued.*

		Doc.	Vol.	No.
	TUSCARORAS:			
1850.	Memorial of chiefs of,	S	2	65

INDUSTRIAL ASSOCIATIONS.

1844.	Report of judiciary committee on petition for protection of,	A	6	162

INDUSTRIAL EXHIBITION, LONDON.

1850.	Correspondence in regard to,	A	8	177
1854.	Special message relative to,	S	2	88

INEBRIATE ASYLUM, STATE.

1856.	Memorial of residents of Geneva, for an,	A	3	55
1856.	Report on petition for an,	A	4	135
1857.	Report of directors of,	S	1	33
1857.	Report of committee on medical societies and colleges favorable to the establishment of a "home for inebriates,"	A	2	78
1858.	Memorial of trustees of,	S	2	58

INFANTRY, THIRD DIVISION.

1848.	Report of comptroller relative to the judge-advocate of,	S	1	28

INFANT SCHOOLS.

1832.	Report on petition for a general law to incorporate,	A	4	327

INGERSOLL, FREDERICK W.

1848.	Report of committee on grievances on petition of,	A	2	51
1848.	Report on petition of,	A	5	161

INGLIS, WILLIAM.

1840.	Report on petition of John A. Barry for the impeachment of,	A	8	348

INGRAHAM, J.

1845.	Report of canal board on petition of,	A	6	218

INGRAHAM, JONAS.

1846.	Report of committee on claims on petition of,	A	2	47
1848.	Report relating to,	S	1	13
1850.	Charges against canal commissioner Hinds,	A	5	84

INGRAHAM, JONAS, AND OTHERS.

1843.	Report of canal commissioners on petition of,	S	1	11
1843.	Report of judiciary committee on petition of,	S	1	19

INGRAHAM, SILAS, AND OTHERS.

1844.	Report of the canal commissioners on petition of,	S	2	74

INGRAIN CARPETING.

1844.	Report of attorney-general in reply to a resolution of the assembly of February 10, relative to the manufacture of,	A	3	75

INSANE ASYLUM, *see* Lunatic Asylum.

INSECTS, NOXIOUS, BENEFICIAL, &c., *see* Entomology.

INSOLVENT NOTICES IN NEW YORK.

		Doc.	Vol.	No.
1830.	Report relative to the publication of, in one newspaper,........	A	1	17

INSPECTION LAWS.

		Doc.	Vol.	No.
1841.	Memorial of New York Chamber of Commerce, relative to the,..	S	3	78
1843.	Memorial of Peter Esquirol and others against any alteration in,	A	3	69
1843.	Report of select committee relative to,......................	A	5	142

INSPECTORS.

		Doc.	Vol.	No.
1845.	Report of committee on manufactures on bill concerning,.......	S	2	69

INSPECTORS OF COMMON SCHOOLS, *see* Common Schools.

INSPECTORS OF PROVISION, MERCHANDISE, &c.

		Doc.	Vol.	No.
1834.	Report of committee appointed to examine the reports of,......	A	3	162
1834.	Report relative to the same,................................	A	4	297
1837.	Report of secretary of state giving a list of,.................	A	3	226
1841.	Abstracts of returns of, report of secretary of state transmitting,	A	7	259
1842.	Abstract of returns from,..................................	A	7	139
1843.	Abstracts of the returns of, for 1842, transmitted by the secretary of state,..	A	5	131
1844.	Report of, by secretary of state,............................	S	2	81
1845.	Abstracts of returns of, for 1844,..........................	S	2	56
1846.	Abstract of returns of, for 1845,...........................	S	3	82

INSPECTOR-GENERAL.

		Doc.	Vol.	No.
1852.	Annual report of,...	A	1	8
1853.	Annual report of,...	A	2	19
1854.	Annual report of,...	A	2	55
1855.	Annual report of,...	A	1	16
1856.	Annual report of,...	A	3	63
1857.	Annual report of,...	A	2	140
1858.	Annual report of,...	A	3	56

INSTITUTES, *see* Academies, &c.

INSURANCE COMPANIES.

		Doc.	Vol.	No.
1830.	Amount of taxes paid by, on their capital stock, in the years 1826 and 1827,..	A	1	32
1834.	Reports of unclaimed dividends in, ...	A	1	42
1834.	do do do	A	2	103
1834.	do do do	A	3	207
1845.	Report of committee on banks and insurance companies relative to,..	S	3	97
1848.	Report of committee on, in relation to governor's message relating to,..	S	1	27
1848.	Report of comptroller on,..................................	S	2	41
1850.	Report of committee on,...................................	S	1	25
1850.	Report of majority on,....................................	S	2	53
1850.	Report of minority on,....................................	S	2	54
1854.	Communication from secretary of state relative to,............	S	1	23
1854.	Communication from comptroller relative to,..................	S	1	19
1855.	Report of committee on report of, by comptroller, in relation to,	A	4	93
1855.	Report of comptroller in reference to condition of,............	A	4	115

FIRE:

		Doc.	Vol.	No.
1854.	Communication from comptroller relative to,..................	A	3	95
1856.	Annual report of comptroller on,............................	A	5	208
1857.	Annual report of comptroller relative to condition of, doing business in this state,...	A	2	135
1858.	Report of comptroller relative to,...........................	A	4	100

INSURANCE COMPANIES—*continued.*

		Doc.	Vol.	No.
	FOREIGN:			
1837.	Report on bill to reduce the taxes on,........................	A	3	177
1839.	Report on petition to repeal the law of 1837 relative to,........	A	6	380
1841.	Report of comptroller of returns made to him by the agents of, &c.,......	A	5	177
1841.	Report on petition for a further tax on,........................	A	6	221
1845.	Report of minority of committee on banks, &c., relative to,.....	A	4	105
1847.	Report relative to taxing,.....................................	A	8	251
1849.	Report of moneys paid by agents of,...........................	S	2	36
	LIFE:			
1852.	Report on petitions and memorials in reference to business of,...	A	5	111
1853.	Petition of Edmund Blunt relative to,..........................	A	5	121
1857.	Report of secretary of state concerning,........	S	4	166
1858.	Report of comptroller on condition of, in this state,............	S	3	131
	MUTUAL:			
1836.	Report on petition for a general law for,......................	S	1	25
	NEW YORK AND BROOKLYN:			
1839.	Report on petition of receivers of certain, for further time to close up their affairs,.............	A	3	99
1841.	Report on memorial of the, for a further tax on foreign insurance companies, ...	A	6	221
1845.	Report of committee on banks, &c., on memorial of,...........	A	3	80
1857.	Report of commissioners on,.......	S	4	172
	ÆTNA FIRE:			
1845.	Report of, in answer to a resolution,.........................	A	4	124
	AMERICAN LIFE INSURANCE AND TRUST COMPANY:			
1833.	Report on petition to incorporate,............................	A	3	209
1834.	Report on petition to incorporate,............	A	1	40
	ASSURANCE:			
1833.	Report on petition to incorporate the, ...	A	2	133
	BOWERY FIRE:			
1845.	Report of the, in answer to a resolution,......................	A	4	82
	BROOKLYN FIRE:			
1845.	Report of, in answer to a resolution,..........................	A	4	142
	BUFFALO FIRE AND MARINE:			
1830.	Report on petition to incorporate,............................	S	2	161
	CHAUTAUQUE COMPANY, MUTUAL:			
1854.	Report of committee on petition of,....................	S	1	20
	CITY FIRE:			
1845.	Report of, in answer to a resolution of the assembly,............	A	4	115
	COLUMBIA LIFE INSURANCE AND TRUST COMPANY:			
1834.	Report on petition to incorporate,............................	A	1	40
	CONTRIBUTIONSHIP:			
1845.	Report of, in answer to a resolution of the assembly,...........	A	4	98
	EAGLE:			
1845.	Report of, in answer to a resolution of the assembly,...........	A	4	120
	EAST RIVER MUTUAL:			
1845.	Report of, in answer to a resolution of the assembly,...........	A	4	123

INSURANCE COMPANIES—*continued.*

		Doc.	Vol.	No.
	FARMERS' FIRE INSURANCE AND LOAN COMPANY:			
1834.	Report on petition to amend the charter of,....................	A	1	40
1836.	Report of attorney-general on bill to alter the name of, &c.,......	A	4	311
	FARMERS' FIRE MUTUAL, UTICA:			
1832.	Report on petition to incorporate,..........................	S	1	41
	FIRE:			
1845.	Report of, in answer to a resolution of the assembly,...........	A	4	127
	FIREMEN'S:			
1845.	Report of, in answer to a resolution of the assembly,...........	A	4	111
	FULTON:			
1839.	Report on petition to incorporate,..........................	A	2	39
	GOOD HOPE:			
1832.	Report on petition to incorporate,..........................	A	1	32
	GREENWICH:			
1845.	Report of, in answer to a resolution of the assembly,...........	A	4	106
	GUARDIAN:			
1845.	Report of, in answer to a resolution of the assembly,...........	A	4	119
1845.	Second report of, in answer to a resolution of the assembly,.....	A	4	128
	HOWARD:			
1845.	Report of, in answer to a resolution of the assembly,...........	A	4	112
	INCOME:			
1858.	Report on bill to incorporate the,...........................	A	3	84
	JEFFERSON:			
1845.	Report of, in answer to a resolution of the assembly,...........	A	4	100
	LONG ISLAND:			
1845.	Report of,..	A	4	144
	MANHATTAN FIRE:			
1845.	Report of,..	A	4	116
	MERCHANTS' FIRE:			
1845.	Report of,..	A	4	143
	MUTUAL SAFETY:			
1849.	Answer of,..	S	1	25
	NATIONAL FIRE:			
1845.	Report of, in answer to a resolution of the assembly,...........	A	4	137
	NAUTILUS:			
1849.	Report of committee on banks and insurance companies on the subject of,..	S	2	53
	NEW YORK LIFE INSURANCE AND TRUST COMPANY:			
1830.	Report on petition to incorporate,..........................	A	2	84
1831.	Report of the bank committee on a resolution of the assembly relative to the,..	A	4	331
1832.	Communication from the chancellor relative to the,............	S	2	112
1833.	Report of a select committee on the bill to restrain the powers of the,..	A	4	285

INSURANCE COMPANIES—*continued.*

Year	Subject	Doc.	Vol.	No.
1834.	Names of agents and stockholders of the,	A	4	279
1834.	Memorial of persons having, as trustees or agents, placed within the, various sums of money, &c., against an alteration of the charter of said company,	S	2	66
1834.	Memorial of the trustees of, against proposed alteration in their charter,	S	2	67
1834.	Communication from the chancellor relative to the,	S	2	59
1835.	do do do	A	4	284
1836.	do do do	A	3	143
1837.	do do do	A	3	257
1838.	do do do	A	6	353
1839.	do do do	S	3	70
1840.	do do do	A	8	253
1843.	do do do	A	2	37
1843.	Annual report of, to the chancellor,	A	3	53
	NORTH AMERICAN FIRE:			
1845.	Report of, in answer to a resolution of the assembly,	A	4	138
1846.	Report of committee on grievances on petition of,	S	1	21
	NORTH RIVER:			
1845.	Report of,	A	4	108
	OCEAN:			
1839.	Report on petition to amend the charter of,	A	3	104
	PROTECTION FIRE:			
1832.	Memorial for a dissolution of said company,	A	3	264
	SARATOGA MUTUAL:			
1840.	Report on petition to amend the charter of,	A	6	265
	TRUST FIRE:			
1845.	Report of, in answer to a resolution of the assembly,	A	4	114
	UNITED STATES FIRE:			
1845.	Report of, in answer to a resolution of the assembly,	A	4	89
1845.	Report of, relative to premiums and taxes,	A	4	89
	WASHINGTON:			
1838.	Report on petition of receivers of, to extend the time for making a final dividend of the assets of said company,	A	2	41

INSURANCE DEPARTMENT.

Year	Subject	Doc.	Vol.	No.
1856.	Act to regulate business of insurance,	S	1	39
1857.	Report of committee on insurance companies on bill relative to,	S	3	94

INSURANCE LAW, GENERAL.

Year	Subject	Doc.	Vol.	No.
1852.	Report on the act to amend the, of 1849,	A	5	99

INTEREST, RATE OF, *see* Usury.

Year	Subject	Doc.	Vol.	No.
1831.	Report of committee on finance on bill to reduce the,	S	1	78
1832.	do do do	S	2	109
1833.	do do do	S	2	106
1833.	Remonstrance of citizens of Albany against the bill to return the,	S	2	76
1851.	Report of select committee on the laws regulating,	A	3	86

INTERMURAL INTERMENTS.

Year	Subject	Doc.	Vol.	No.
1850.	Report of committee on cities and villages in relation to,	S	3	81

INTERNAL AFFAIRS.

		Doc.	Vol.	No.
1850.	Report of committee on,	S	1	19

INTERNAL IMPROVEMENTS.

		Doc.	Vol.	No.
1832.	Aid to works of, by the United States, resolution of the legislature of Maine relative to.	A	1	3
1832.	do by the United States, resolution of the legislature of Tennessee relative to,	A	3	183
1833.	do by the United States, resolution of the legislature of Georgia relative to.	A	2	39
1834.	do communication from the executive of Georgia relative to a resolution of the legislature in relation to,	A	1	11

INTERNAL IMPROVEMENTS OF THIS STATE.

		Doc.	Vol.	No.
1831.	Report on the subjects of (N. P. Tallmadge),	S	1	32
1833.	do do (S. M. Stilwell),	A	4	268
1834.	do do (Mr. Hubbard),	S	2	55
1840.	do do (Mr. Lay),	A	7	227
1838.	do do (Mr. Ruggles),	A	5	242
1841.	Report of committee on railroads on the bill to provide means for the construction of works of,	A	7	289
1843.	Report of the comptroller in answer to a resolution of the assembly respecting the amount of appropriations for, and amount of stocks issued, &c.,	A	3	65
1846.	Report of committee on ways and means on prosecution of,	A	5	187

INTERNATIONAL BRIDGE COMPANY.

		Doc.	Vol.	No.
1857.	Report on bill to incorporate,	S	3	99
1857.	Report of committee on roads and bridges on bill to incorporate,	S	4	124
1857.	Testimony relative to,	A	3	200

INTERNATIONAL EXCHANGES.

		Doc.	Vol.	No.
1845.	Communication from A. Vattemare relative to,	A	5	185
1847.	Report of trustees of state library relative to,	S	4	129
1847.	Report relative to,	A	7	226
1847.	Communication from governor relative to,	A	8	244
1849.	Message from governor transmitting a report on, by Mons. Alexander Vattemare,	A	5	201
1849.	Communication from same respecting,	A	5	208
1850.	Second annual report of A. Vattemare,	A	5	127
1850.	Letter of same relative to donations from France,	A	8	192

INTOXICATING LIQUORS, *see* Excise Law.

		Doc.	Vol.	No.
1848.	Remonstrance against legalizing sale of,	A	5	169
1849.	Report of select committee on petitions for a law prohibiting the sale of,	A	5	230
1849.	Report on petitions for a law prohibiting sale of,	A	5	220
1850.	Report of select committee on petition for a law prohibiting sale of,	A	5	121
1852.	Report on petition to prohibit the traffic in,	S	1	26
1852.	Report relative to the adoption of stringent measures for the suppression of intemperate use of,	A	2	88
1853.	Report of minority on petition for a law prohibiting the sale of, as a beverage,	A	3	66
1854.	Reports of majority and minority of select committee on message relative to intemperance,	A	1	20
1854.	Reports of majority and minority of select committee on senate bill for the suppression of intemperance,	A	3	112, 118

INTOXICATING LIQUORS—*continued.*

Year	Subject	Doc.	Vol.	No.
1854.	Report of committee of conference on senate bill for the suppression of intemperance,	A	4	126
1854.	Report of select committee on,	S	1	37
1855.	Reports of majority and minority of select committee on intemperance, accompanied by bill to suppress,	A	1	13
1856.	Reports of majority and minority committees relative to the repeal of the act on intemperance, pauperism and crime,	A	4	137
1857.	Report of select committee on memorial in relation to bill to regulate sale of,	S	4	139
1857.	Answer of attorney-general to resolution inquiring what statutes are in force regulating the sale of,	A	1	39

IRISH EMIGRANT SOCIETY, *see* New York.

IRON, *see* State Prison, Clinton.

IRVIN, RICHARD.

Year	Subject	Doc.	Vol.	No.
1840.	Report on petition of, for the release of certain lands escheated to the state,	S	2	54

IRVING, WASHINGTON.

Year	Subject	Doc.	Vol.	No.
1833.	Life of Columbus, report relative to the introduction of, into the common schools,	A	4	333

IRWIN, WM. M., AND ASA A. LYMAN.

Year	Subject	Doc.	Vol.	No.
1855.	Report of committee on claims in case of,	A	4	88

ITHACA AND OWEGO RAILROAD, *see* Railroads.

ITHACA INLET, *see* Cayuga Inlet.

ITHACA, TOWN OF.

Year	Subject	Doc.	Vol.	No.
1831.	Report on petition to increase the number of constables in,	A	4	340

IVANS, AUGUSTUS H.

Year	Subject	Doc.	Vol.	No.
1855.	Report of committee on privileges and elections on contested seat of,	A	2	46

IVES, JOHN B., (a canal contractor).

Year	Subject	Doc.	Vol.	No.
1839.	Report on petition for extra allowance,	A	3	95
1839.	Report of canal board on the same,	A	6	352
1844.	Report of canal board on petition of,	A	3	85
1848.	Report on petition of,	A	3	119

J.

JACKSON, ANDREW, *see* President of the United States.

Year	Subject	Doc.	Vol.	No.
1843.	Report of committee on the subject of the fine imposed on him,	S	2	56
1843.	Report of select committee on so much of governor's message as relates to fine upon,	A	5	171
1844.	Report of a select committee on the subject of the fine of,	S	1	9
1844.	Communication from governor transmitting resolution of the legislature of New Hampshire on the subject of fine imposed on,	A	7	191

JACKSON, ISAAC.

		Doc.	Vol.	No.
1833.	Sheriff of Montgomery county, report on petition of, for pay for transporting convicts to the Mount Pleasant prison,..........	S	1	31
1846.	Report of committee on claims on petition of,................	A	3	69
1846.	Report of canal commissioners on the bill for the relief of,......	S	4	133

JACKSON, JAMES.

1854.	Report on petition of,..	A	2	42

JACKSON, OBADIAH.

1835.	Report on petition of, for a grant of certain lands for the purpose of docking in the East river at Brooklyn,..................	A	3	235
1836.	Report of select committee on the same,......................	A	1	29

JACKSON, TRUEMAN.

1837.	Report on petition for compensation for damages by the Erie canal,	A	2	149
1839.	Report of canal commissioners on the same,..................	A	4	263

JACKSON, W.

1834.	Report on petition for compensation for damages by the Erie canal,..	A	4	271

JACKWAY, W.

1840.	Report on petition for compensation for damages by the Erie canal,..	S	1	26

JACOBS, OZIAS.

1847.	Report on petition of,...	A	4	107
1847.	Report of committee on public lands on petition of,............	A	4	141

JACOBS, URIAH.

1835.	Report on petition of, for compensation for revolutionary services,	A	3	224

JAILS.

1855.	Report relative to commission to examine, and workhouses, &c.,	S	1	27
1857.	Report of visitation of, and poor-houses, &c.,.................	S	1	8

JAMAICA AND MYRTLE AVENUE PLANKROAD.

1853.	Report of committee in relation to increase of capital of the,....	A	4	96

JAMES, HENRY, AND OTHERS.

1835.	Report on petition of, for compensation for damages to their lands by the sloop lock dam at Troy,..............................	A	4	247

JAMESPORT, SUFFOLK COUNTY.

1834.	Wharf and Ways Company, report on petition to incorporate,..	A	3	231

JAMES, WM. AND JOHN.

1847.	Report on petition of,..	S	4	140

JAMIESON, DAVID.

1847.	Report on petition of,..	A	8	257

JAQUES, MOSES, AND LEVI D. SLAMM.

1837.	Report of a select committee on the petition of,................	A	3	198

JAQUES, MOSES, AND LEVI D. SLAMM—*continued.*

		Doc.	Vol.	No.
1837.	Report of a select committee on the petition of,	A	3	225
1837.	Report of a select committee on same,	A	4	325
1837.	Report of committee on the judiciary on petition relative to the proceedings of the assembly in the case of,	A	4	327

JAQUET, HECTOR.

1843.	A silk manufacturer, petition of,	S	3	82

JAY, PETER A., AND OTHERS.

1842.	Report of select committee on memorial of, concerning assessments in New York, with accompanying documents,	S	4	100

JAYNE, SAMUEL.

1851.	Report of committee on contested seat,	A	3	55

JEFFERSON ACADEMY, SCHOHARIE COUNTY, *see* Academies, &c.

JEFFERSON AND ONEIDA TURNPIKE COMPANY.

1839.	Report on petition to incorporate the, and for aid from the state,	A	4	232

JEFFERSON AND ST. LAWRENCE.

1836.	Road in, report on petition of the commissioners to lay out a,..	A	3	203
1838.	Report on the same,	A	4	195

JEFFERSON COUNTY.

1830.	Carlton island, report on petition of settlers on, for relief,	A	2	92
1831.	Clerk's office, report on petition to raise money by tax to build a,	A	1	19
1835.	Fish, inspection of, in, report on petition to repeal the law relative to the,	A	2	92
1830.	Race-course, report on petition for the establishment of,	A	4	308
1837.	Poor, report on petition for a loan for the support of,	A	4	295
1833.	Poor-house, report on petition to sell and convey the,	A	2	104
1844.	Report of attorney-general on a petition to sell "Centre lot" in,	S	3	115
1849.	Report of superintendent of poor of,	A	5	240

JEFFERSON, ONEIDA AND OSWEGO.

1830.	Road through, report on petition for aid to improve a,	A	4	350

JENKINS, HERMAN.

1834.	Report on petition for the payment of certain surplus money received on the sale of his land,	A	3	174
1836.	Report in relation to the same,	A	4	201

JENNINGS, PHILIP, *see* David Barnes.

JEROME, W., Engineer on the Oswego canal.

1840.	Report on petition of, to be repaid costs and expenses in certain suits brought against him by James Lyon, and by Ichabod Bracket,	A	5	209

JEROME, WILLIAM.

1842.	Report of committee on claims on petition of,	S	3	59

18

JEWELL, GUSTAVUS.

		Doc.	Vol.	No.
1830.	Report on petition of, for compensation for the destruction of a dam at the Caughenay reef,	S	2	137

JOHNSBURGH, TOWN OF.

1830.	Report on petition from, for aid to build a bridge across the Hudson river,	A	3	263

JOHNSON & LEONARD.

1846.	Report of canal board on petition of,	A	5	154

JOHNSON, EDWIN F.

1835.	Report of, relative to a steamboat or ship canal from Lake Ontario to the Hudson river,	A	3	195
1838.	Report of, on railroads,	A	4	171
1840.	Report on petition of, for pay for services for surveying a route for a railroad from Ogdensburgh to Lake Champlain,	S	1	27

JOHNSON, EVAN M., AND OTHERS.

1835.	Report on petition of, relative to unpaid taxes in Brooklyn,	A	4	375

JOHNSON, HEZEKIAH.

1847.	Report on petition of,	A	4	112

JOHNSON, JOHN.

1852.	Report on petition of,	S	2	80

JOHNSON, JOHN H.

1831.	Report on petition of, relative to the sale of certain land,	A	1	46
1831.	Report of committee on ways and means on the same,	A	2	130

JOHNSON, MARIAH, AND OTHERS.

1842.	Heirs of Wm. Gall, report on petition of,	A	4	66
1849.	Heirs of Wm. Gall, report of committee on claims on petition of,	A	1	25

JOHNSON, MORGAN.

1846.	Report on petition of, for seat in assembly,	A	5	147

JOHNSON, N., AND JAMES HOPE.

1842.	Report on petition of,	A	2	39

JOHNSON, STEPHEN H.

1851.	Senator, report in relation to charges,	S	2	60

JOHNSON, STILES, AND NORMAN BUTLER.

1850.	Report on claim of,	S	3	109
1850.	Report of committee on claims on claim of,	A	5	101
1851.	Majority report of committee on grievances on claim of, for canal damages,	S	2	61
1851.	Report of committee on claims for canal damages,	A	2	24

JOHNSON, W.

1838.	Report on petition of, to legalize the acknowledgment of a certain deed,	A	2	37

JOHNSTON, MARY (an alien).

		Doc.	Vol.	No.
1835.	Report on petition of, for the release of the right of the state to certain lands,......	A	2	99

JOHNSTOWN.

1833.	Supreme court commissioner, report on petition for,......	S	1	40
1836.	Taxes in, report on petition to extend the time for collection of,..	A	3	137
1837.	do do do do ..	A	2	55
1838.	do do do do ..	A	3	67
1842.	Report of the judiciary committee relative to reducing the number of assessors in,......	S	2	44
1842.	Report relative to reducing number of assessors in,......	S	2	45

JONES, ABIGAIL, AND W. D., *see* Jones' Fund.

1838.	Jones' fund for the support of the poor in Oyster Bay and North Hempstead, report on petition for the appointment of trustees of the,......	A	5	228

JONES, CHAS. A.

1852.	Report on petition of,......	S	2	72
1852.	Report on recommittal of the petition of,......	S	2	73

JONES, DAVID.

1853.	Report of attorney-general in reference to claim of,......	A	5	118

JONES, DAVID S., AND GERRIT SMITH.

1835.	Report on petition of, for a grant of land for a basin in the village of Oswego,......	S	2	69
1836.	Report on petition of the trustees of the village of Oswego relative to said basin,......	A	3	153
1836.	Resort on petition of, relative to the extension of said basin, ...	A	4	266

JONES, H. F.

1830.	Report on petition of, to be admitted to a seat as member of assembly from Queens county in the place of T. Tredwell,....	A	1	51

JONES, JOHN H.

1840.	Report on petition of, to erect a wharf at Cold Spring harbor,...	A	7	283

JONES, JOHN M.

1844.	Report of canal commissioners on petition of,......	S	3	99

JONES, LAURA (an alien).

1840.	Report on petition of, for the release of certain escheated lands,	A	2	51
1840.	Report on petition of, for the release of certain escheated lands,..	A	7	296

JONES, SETH C., AND OTHERS.

1846.	Report of committee on manufactures on petition of, for incorporation of manufacturing companies,......	S	2	65

JONES' WOOD PARK ACT.

1854.	Report of select committee on bill repealing,......	A	1	18

JOSLIN, JOSIAH E.

1855.	Report of committee on claims on petition of,......	A	4	111

JOSLYN, J. E.

		Doc.	Vol.	No.
1854.	Report on petition of,	A	4	137

JOURDAN, HENRY, *see* Oneida Indians.

JUDD, BETHEL.

		Doc.	Vol.	No.
1854.	Report on petition of,	S	1	33

JUDGE-ADVOCATE-GENERAL.

		Doc.	Vol.	No.
1834.	Report of amount of his official business,	A	4	272

JUDGES.

		Doc.	Vol.	No.
1858.	Report of comptroller relative to money paid in addition to salaries,	S	2	51

JUDGES, CIRCUIT, *see* Circuit Judges.

JUDGES, COUNTY, *see* County Judges.

JUDGES, SUPREME COURT, *see* Supreme Court.

JUDGMENTS, PLAINTIFFS IN (in United States Courts).

		Doc.	Vol.	No.
1839.	Resolution relative to,	A	1	10
1834.	Report concerning the canceling and discharging of,	A	3	248
1840.	Number of, docketed in the offices of the supreme court clerks, *see* Supreme Court Clerks.			

JUDICIAL AND EQUITY SYSTEM.

		Doc.	Vol.	No.
1838.	Report of commissioners appointed to digest and report a,	A	1	3
1838.	Report of committee on the judiciary thereon,	A	5	283

JUDICIAL DISTRICTS.

		Doc.	Vol.	No.
1847.	Committees, select, report of conferees, on the part of the senate on the act to divide the state into,	S	2	71
1847.	Report of conferees on same subject,	S	3	86
1847.	Report of conferees on same subject,	S	3	99
1847.	Report relative to bill on,	S	3	106
1857.	Report of committee of conference, on bill to divide the state into,	A	4	117
1847.	Report of committee of conference on bill to divide the state into,	A	4	138
1856.	Report of committee on,	S	2	92

JUDICIAL DISTRICT, THIRD.

		Doc.	Vol.	No.
1849.	Report on certain matters touching the official integrity of one or more judicial officers of,	A	5	221
1857.	Report of committee on the judiciary on failure to hold courts in,	A	3	188

JUDICIAL OFFICERS.

		Doc.	Vol.	No.
1838.	Report relative to granting free tickets on railroads to,	A	6	337
1856.	Minority report relative to change of mode of choice of,	A	4	158

JUDICIAL SYSTEM.

		Doc.	Vol.	No.
1834.	Report of committee on the judiciary relative to reorganizing the court of chancery and the supreme court,	S	2	107
1835.	Resolution offered by Mr. Livingston to increase the number of justices of the supreme court, for the abolishment of the office of circuit judge and the creation of a supreme court, &c.,	A	3	193

JUDICIAL SYSTEM—*continued.*

		Doc.	Vol.	No.
1835.	Resolution to abolish the office of circuit judge, to increase the number of justices of the supreme court, and for the creation of a superior court of common pleas, &c.,	A	4	337
1835.	Resolution to abolish the office of circuit judge, to increase the number of justices of the supreme court, and for the creation of a superior court of common pleas, &c.,	A	4	338
1835.	Report of select committee on the same,	A	4	370
1836.	Resolution offered by Mr. Gansevoort to increase the number of justices of the supreme court, and for the creation of a superior court,	S	1	22
1836.	Resolution offered by Mr. Powers to reorganize the court of chancery, to increase the number of justices of the supreme court, to abolish the office of circuit judge and for the creation of a superior court,	S	1	26
1836.	Report and resolution offered by Mr. Edwards to increase the number of justices of the supreme court, and to organize a superior court,	S	2	66
1836.	Resolution reported by the committee on judiciary to reorganize the court of chancery, to appoint two additional justices of the supreme court, and to organize a superior court of common pleas,	A	4	265
1837.	Resolution offered by Mr. Bradish, to increase the number of justices of the supreme court, to reorganize the court of chancery, &c.,	A	3	173
1837.	Resolution offered by Mr. Edwards for the same,	S	1	13
1838.	Resolution offered by Mr. Patterson, to reorganize the court of chancery, to organize a superior court of common pleas, to increase the number of justices of the supreme court, and to abolish the office of circuit judge, &c.,	A	1	24
1838.	Resolution proposed by Mr. Ogden, to organize a superior court of common pleas, to reorganize the court of chancery, to increase the number of justices of the supreme court, and to abolish the office of circuit judge,	A	5	267
1839.	Report and resolution by Mr. Edwards, to reorganize the court of chancery, and to increase the number of justices of the supreme court,	S	1	28
1839.	Resolution proposed by Mr. Verplanck, to reorganize the court of chancery, to abolish the office of circuit judge, to increase the number of justices of the supreme court, to organize a superior court of common pleas, and to erect a court of probates, &c.,	S	2	50
1839.	Resolution offered by Mr. Taylor, to reorganize the court of chancery, to abolish the office of circuit judge, to organize a superior court of common pleas, and to increase the number of justices of the supreme court,	A	1	15
1839.	Report of committee on the judiciary on the same,	A	3	93
1840.	Resolution offered by Mr. Verplanck, to vest the judicial power in the court for the correction of errors, and in such subordinate courts of law and equity as the legislature shall from time to time create and establish, &c.,	S	1	13
1840.	Memorial of the New York bar for a reform in the,	S	1	16
1840.	Resolution offered by Mr. Taylor, to reorganize the court of chancery, to vest equity courts in any of the courts of common law, &c.,	A	3	61
1840.	Resolution offered by Mr. Taylor, to increase the number of the justices of the supreme court, to organize a superior court of common pleas, to abolish the office of circuit judge, &c.,	A	6	270
1841.	Report and resolution by Mr. Simmons on so much of the governor's message as relates to the,	A	4	136
1841.	Report of select committee (Mr. Simmons) on the same,	A	7	288
1847.	Memorial on legal reform,	A	2	48
1842.	Letter of D. D. Field, on law reform,	A	5	81

JUDICIAL SYSTEM—*continued.*

		Doc.	Vol.	No.
1845.	Report on lawyers' fees,	A	6	227
1851.	Report of select committee on bill to stay proceedings in certain cases,	S	1	9
1842.	Report, in part, on so much of governor's message as relates to the administration of justice,	A	5	81
1842.	Further report on same subject,	A	5	94
1852.	Report on the administration of justice,	A	5	97

JUNCTION CANAL, *see* Canals.

JURORS, FEES OF.

		Doc.	Vol.	No.
1833.	Report relative to increasing the compensation of,	A	3	180
1836.	Report relative to increasing the compensation of,	A	4	263

JURY DUTY.

		Doc.	Vol.	No.
1851.	Report on bill for enrollment of the militia, to abolish fines and exempt uniformed companies from highway tax and,	A	4	113

JURY, TRIALS BY.

		Doc.	Vol.	No.
1834.	Report on bill providing that on the trial of all civil causes, if three-fourths of the jury agree upon a verdict the court shall render a judgment upon said verdict accordingly,	A	4	376
1843.	Remonstrance of numerous citizens of the village of Salina, in the county of Onondaga, against the repeal of the law for the extension of,	A	3	60
1843.	Report of the minority of the judiciary committee on the subject of repealing the law extending the right of, passed May 6, 1840, &c.,	A	5	141

JUSTICES' COURTS.

		Doc.	Vol.	No.
1834.	Certiorari and appeals from, report of a select committee on a resolution to inquire whether any alterations are required in the law relative to,	A	4	273
1833.	Witnesses and jurors in, report relative to increasing the pay of,	A	3	180

JUSTICES OF THE PEACE.

		Doc.	Vol.	No.
1830.	Elections of, report on the constitutionality of the law of 1829 relative to the,	A	2	70
1830.	Elections of, to fill vacancies occasioned by death or otherwise, &c., report on bill relative to the,	A	3	270
1833.	Election and classification of, report of attorney-general relative to the,	S	1	10
1833.	Elections of, report on petition of Jeffrey Chipman for an act explanatory of the act of 1832, relative to the,	A	1	35
1833.	Report of attorney-general on the same,	A	2	99
1838.	Fees of, report on petition to increase the,	A	5	220
1832.	Oath of office of, report on bill relative to the,	A	4	287
1833.	Official acts of, in certain cases, report on bill to confirm the,	A	2	62
1830.	Report on petition to prohibit, from being keepers of jails,	A	6	384
1833.	Report on bill to allow those who have removed from the places for which they were elected to issue executions,	A	3	179
1833.	Vacancies in the office of, report of attorney-general concerning the power of the legislature in providing for,	A	4	300
1835.	Vacancies in the office of, report of committee on privileges and elections on the same,	A	1	39

JUVENILE DELINQUENTS.

House of Refuge for, New York:

Year	Title	Doc.	Vol.	No.
1830.	Report on petition to repeal part of an act to create a fund in aid of the, &c.,	A	3	273
1830.	Report of amount of moneys paid to the, from 1826 to 1829,	A	3	252
1831.	Report on petition against appropriating the moneys received from seamen and passengers to the support of the,	A	2	204
1838.	Report on petition to amend the law to create a fund in aid of,	A	6	300
1838.	Report on petition to amend the law to create a fund in aid of,	A	6	314
1840.	Report of president of, giving certain information relative to,	S	1	2

House of Refuge for, Western:

Year	Title	Doc.	Vol.	No.
1838.	Report on petition for,	A	4	181
1839.	do	A	5	323
1840.	do	A	8	360
1842.	do	A	7	182
1846.	Report of select committee relative to,	A	4	93
1846.	Report of select committee on,	A	5	160
1850.	First annual report of managers,	A	3	42
1850.	Memorial respecting,	A	5	115
1851.	Annual report of managers,	S	1	8
1852.	Annual report of,	S	1	45
1853.	Annual report of managers of,	A	2	31
1853.	Report of committee on charitable and religious societies in relation to the introduction of water and building of a kitchen,	A	2	49
1853.	Report in relation to appropriation for,	A	2	50
1854.	Report on,	S	2	107
1855.	Annual report of,	A	2	25
1856.	Annual report of,	S	1	10
1856.	Report of committee on finance on management of,	S	1	38
1856.	Report of comptroller relative to,	S	2	54
1856.	Report of, as to appropriation of certain moneys,	S	2	73
1857.	Report of managers,	S	1	9
1858.	Annual report of managers of,	S	1	10

Society for the Reformation of, New York:

Year	Title	Doc.	Vol.	No.
1847.	Report of,	A	4	120
1848.	Report of,	A	5	190
1849.	Twenty-fourth annual report of,	A	5	224
1850.	Memorial of,	S	1	17
1850.	Annual report of managers,	A	6	172
1855.	Memorial of,	A	3	77
1858.	Annual report of managers of,	A	5	156

K.

KADER, JOAN CAR S.

Year	Title	Doc.	Vol.	No.
1835.	Report on petition for compensation for damages to his lands by the Erie canal,	A	3	169

KANE, JOHN.

Year	Title	Doc.	Vol.	No.
1830.	Heir of Henry Kane, a soldier of the revolution, report on petition of, for bounty lands,	A	4	318
1833.	Heir of Henry Kane, a soldier of the revolution, report on petition of, for bounty lands,	A	3	237

KANSAS TERRITORY.

Year	Title	Doc.	Vol.	No.
1856.	Report of select committee on message relative to, and Nebraska,	S	2	91
1856.	Communication from Governor Robinson, of,	A	3	52
1857.	Report of select committee on message relating to,	S	4	164

KASSON & CO., *see* Geer, Kasson & Breed.

KASSON, JOHN M., AND HENRY CADY.

		Doc.	Vol.	No.
1843.	Report of committee on claims on their petition,...............	S	1	36
1848.	Report on petition of,..	A	3	117

KEARNEY, HELENA R.

1849.	Report on petition of,..	S	3	75

KEELER, J. R., & CO.

1832.	Report on petition of, relative to the assessment on personal property in the town of Mina,..................................	A	2	142

KEISLER & BABCOCK.

1851.	Report on claim for canal damages,..........................	S	3	65
1854.	Report of committee on claims on petition of,.................	A	3	79
1855.	Report of committee on claims in case of,....................	A	3	75

KELLOGG & OSGOOD.

1844.	Report of canal board on petition of,........................	S	2	59

KELLOGG, DORASTUS, DANIEL EARLL AND JOHN KELLOGG.

1840.	Report on petition for damages on account of the drawing off the waters of the Skaneateles lake to supply the Erie canal,.......	A	5	202

KELLOGG, JOSIAH S.

1850.	Report on canal damages,....................................	A	5	97
1851.	Report of committee on claims for canal damages,..............	A	1	11
1851.	Report of minority of committee on claims for canal damages,...	S	2	23

KELLOGG, S.

1848.	Report on petition of,..	A	2	33

KELLY, JOHN.

1840.	Report on petition of, for relief,.............................	S	1	20

KELLY, SAMUEL, AND OTHERS.

1835.	Defendants in the suit brought by J. J. Astor, report on petition of, for pay as witnesses,.................................	A	3	234

KELSEY, E. N., & H. TUPPER.

1855.	Report of committee on claims in reference to petition of,.......	A	3	62
1856.	Report on petition of, for relief,............................	A	3	68
1857.	Report of committee on claims on petition of,.................	A	1	32

KEMBLE, JOHN C.

1836.	Report relative to the official conduct of, in the matter of the Commercial Bank of Albany,..................................	S	2	94

KEMPSHALL, THOMAS, *see* Hervey Ely, and others.

KENDALL, DAVID, AND OTHERS, *see* New Stockbridge school lot.

KENNEDY, JOHN.

1856.	Report on petition of, for relief,............................	A	3	50

	KENNEY, ELLEN.	Doc.	Vol.	No.
1854.	Report on petition of,......................................	A	3	84
	KENT COUNTY.			
1856.	Report of committee on erection and division of towns and counties, as to erection of,......................................	S	2	76
	KENTUCKY AND VIRGINIA.			
1833.	Resolutions of the legislatures of, on the alien and sedition laws,	S	2	41
	KENTUCKY, STATE OF.			
1836.	Resolutions of the legislature of, relative to slavery,...........	S	2	79
1838.	do do relative to the currency and the administration of the general government,................	S	2	58
1840.	do do relative to the public lands,....	A	7	285
1841.	do do relative to the re-eligibility of the president,..............	A	5	149
1842.	Resolution of general assembly of, relative to state debts,.........	A	3	51
1842.	Resolution of general assembly of, relative to soldiers of the revolution,......................................	A	5	96
1842.	Message of governor transmitting resolution of general assembly of, relative to the soldiers of the revolution,..................	S	2	26
1844.	Resolution of the legislature of,..............................	A	7	194
	KETCHUM, JARED.			
1832.	Report on petition to erect a dam across the Canisteo river,.....	A	2	87
	KETCHUM, ZEBULON.			
1839.	Report on petition for allowance for a deficiency in the quantity of certain land,......................................	S	3	75
	KEYSER, ABRAHAM, *see* Treasurer.			
	KIDDER, LEVI.			
1834.	Letter from, in relation to the Seventh Ward Bank investigation,	S	2	89
	KIDNAPPING.			
1840.	Of free colored persons, report on petition to prevent,...........	A	8	341
1857.	Citizens of this state, reply of the governor to resolution relative to,......................................	A	1	47
	KIMBALL, WOODMAN, AND J. C. SHIPPEY.			
1846.	Report on petition for relief of,..............................	S	1	40
1846.	Report of committee on claims on petition of,..................	S	2	60
1848.	Report on petition of,......................................	A	5	151
	KINDERHOOK CREEK, BRIDGE OVER.			
1841.	Report on petition of inhabitants of Stuyvesant, to be relieved from paying one-half the expense of maintaining the,........	S	2	64
	KING, AMOS B. & JAMES H.			
1844.	Report of canal board on the petition of,......................	A	1	28
1844.	Report of committee on claims on the petition of,..............	A	6	141
1844.	Statement of Jonas Earll, Jr., in relation to the claim of,........	A	6	154
1848.	Report on petition of,......................................	A	3	112
1849.	Report of committee on claims on petition of,..................	A	2	75

KING, DAVID (an alien).

		Doc.	Vol.	No.
1833.	Report on petition to hold real estate,........................	A	2	55

KING, DAVID B., AND FRANKLIN LIVINGSTON.

1838.	Report on petition for compensation for the violation of their patent right to a wicket and paddle gate,.....................	A	2	45
1841.	Report of canal commissioners on the same,....................	A	6	221
1841.	Report of the commissioners of the canal fund on the same,.....	A	6	228

KING, DEXTER S., AND OTHERS.

1852.	Report of commissioners of land office respecting the granting of land under water at Westfield,..........................	A	5	121

KING, JOHN.

1848.	Report on petition of,..	A	5	166

KING, JOHN F.

1831.	Report on petition of, for the use of the water of the Champlain canal,..	S	1	53

KING, SAMUEL.

1833.	Report on petition of, to be relieved from a certain judgment,...	S	2	90

KING, SAMUEL (an alien).

1835.	Report on petition to hold real estate,.......	A	4	300

KINGSBURY, JOHN.

1839.	Report on petition of, for damages to his saw mill, by the change of the site of a lock on the Chemung canal,..................	A	4	286
1840.	Report on the same,..	A	4	122

KINGS, COUNTY OF.

1833.	Assessors, board of, report on petition for a,.................	A	2	124
1835.	Clerk's office in, report on petition to raise money to build a,....	A	1	13
1838.	Cemetery, Greenwood, report on petition to incorporate,........	A	6	334
1833.	Court-house, report on bill for the erection of a,...............	S	2	86
1831.	Jail limits, report on petition to extend the,..................	A	2	173
1835.	Jail in, report on petition to raise money to build a,............	A	1	13
1837.	do do do to complete the,.......	A	4	289
1838.	do do do do	A	2	38
1837.	Game, preservation of, report on petition to amend the law for the,..	A	3	196
1838.	Highways and bridges, report on bill to amend the law of 1830, relating to,..	A	3	80
1833.	Mechanics' and Manufacturers' Society, report on petition to amend their charter,......................................	A	4	319
1834.	Memorial from several towns in, relative to incorporating the city of Brooklyn, &c.,..	A	3	183
1830.	Poor, foreign, report on petition to be released from the support of,..	A	2	112
1838.	Poor, superintendents and overseers of the, report on bill relative to,..	A	4	179
1831.	Race course, report on petition for a law to regulate the,........	A	2	87
1838.	Taxes unpaid, report on petition of the board of supervisors relative to,..	A	6	326
1832.	Taxes, report on bill to extend the time for the collection of,....	A	4	279
1834.	Wharf at the Narrows in, report on petition to rebuild,.........	A	3	179
1834.	Wharf at the Narrows in, report on petition to rebuild,.........	A	3	238

KINGS, COUNTY OF—*continued.*

		Doc.	Vol.	No.
1830.	Inspector of lumber, report of E. Smith,	A	2	146
1839.	do do Benjamin Meeker,	A	4	212
1840.	do do do	A	5	210
1853.	Report of committee on roads and bridges on petition of sundry inhabitants of, relative to toll on plankroads,	A	4	88
1858.	Petition of board of supervisors of, for the repeal of the Metropolitan Police Law,	S	2	66

BANKS IN, *see* Banks—Kings county.

INSPECTOR OF FLOUR, *see* New York inspector of flour.

POLICE, *see* Metropolitan Police.

KINGSLAND, N. B., AND LEWIS BASTIDO.

1846.	Report on petition for relief of,	S	4	129

KINGSLEY, A., AND OTHERS.

1844.	Report of committee on claims on the petition of,	A	7	201

KINGSLEY, AVERY L.

1849.	Report of committee on claims on petition of,	A	1	17

KINGSTON AND MIDDLETOWN PLANKROAD.

1850.	Report of,	S	1	20

KINGSTON, TOWN OF.

1839.	Report on petition from the, to borrow money to rebuild a bridge over Esopus creek,	A	6	386

KINGSTON, VILLAGE OF.

1845.	Report on bill from the assembly providing for the appointment of a police justice in the,	S	3	117

KINNEY, ELLEN.

1854.	Committee on grievances, report on petition of,	A	3	84

KINSELLA, GEORGE.

1831.	Report on petition for compensation for his lands taken for the Erie canal,	S	1	52
1832.	Report of committee on claims on the same,	S	2	88
1834.	Report by same committee on the same,	A	3	144
1835.	Report of committee on grievances on the same,	A	3	223
1836.	Report by same committee on the same,	A	4	251
1837.	Report of committee on canals on the same,	S	1	7
1838.	Report of committee on grievances on the same,	A	3	81
1848.	Report on petition of,	A	5	158
1852.	Report on claim of,	S	2	56

KIRK, WM. R.

1854.	Report on petition of,	A	2	60

KIRKLAND AND MARSHALL, TOWNS OF.

1830.	Report on petition of inhabitants of, relative to the survey of a tract of land set apart for the Brothertown Indians,	A	4	367

KNAPP, AARON.

		Doc.	Vol.	No.
1847.	Report on petition of,	A	8	260
1849.	Report of committee on claims on petition of,	S	3	72
1849.	Report by same committee on same,	A	2	68
1852.	Reappraisement of damages to,	S	2	76
1852.	Report on petition of,	A	2	32

KNAPP, ABRAHAM.

1831.	Report on petition of, for compensation for damages by the Erie canal,	S	1	38

KNIGHT, DANIEL.

1846.	Report on petition of, for relief,	S	4	132
1846.	Report of committee on petitions of aliens on petition of,	A	2	56

KNIGHT, JAMES.

1842.	Report on petition of,	A	5	82

KNIGHT, JAMES, Jr.

1840.	Report on petition of, for compensation for damages to his lands by the Erie canal,	A	6	221

KNOWER, EDWARD.

1838.	Report on petition of, for a grant of land under water adjoining his land in West Oswego,	A	4	183
1838.	Report on the same,	A	5	214

KOSSUTH.

1852.	Communication from the governor transmitting correspondence with,	S	2	84

KRAICK, GOTLEIB.

1830.	A soldier of the revolution, report on petition of, for bounty lands,	A	3	269

L.

LACEY, WILLIAM.

1835.	Report on petition to build a bridge across Niagara river at Black Rock,	A	4	333

LADD, BRADLEY.

1834.	Report on petition to change his name,	A	1	17

LADD, JOHN AND NANCY, *see* Daniel Cameron.

LAFAYETTE, COUNTY OF.

1846.	Report of committee adverse to the proposed,	A	4	109

LA FOY & CLEMENS.

1845.	Report of canal commissioners on petition of,	A	4	132
1850.	Report on canal claim,	A	3	31
1855.	Report of committee on claims on petition of,	A	1	21

LA FOY, JOHN.

1852.	Report on petition of,	A	2	54

LAING, HUGH.

		Doc.	Vol.	No.
1832.	Report on petition of, to erect a dock in Westchester county,....	A	2	130

LAING, PAISLEY.

		Doc.	Vol.	No.
1830.	Report on petition for compensation for damages by the erection of the Saratoga dam,....................................	A	3	280
1831.	Report of committee on canals on the same,....................	A	1	50
1834.	Report of committee on claims on petition of,....................	A	3	127
1835.	Report relative to same,..	A	2	141
1836.	Report of committee on grievances on the same,................	A	2	101

LAKE CHAMPLAIN.

		Doc.	Vol.	No.
1831.	Ferry across, report on petition of Nicholas Allen relative to,....	A	3	220
1846.	Communication from surveyor-general relative to road from Clinton prison to,..	A	2	55
1849.	Report on bill to allow the Northern railroad to construct a draw-bridge across (majority),....................................	S	1	24
1849.	Committee, select, report on same (minority),..................	S	2	56
1849.	Report of select committee on bill to allow the construction of a draw-bridge by the Northern railroad across the outlet of, at Rouse's Point,..	A	1	24
1850.	Testimony relative to bridging,..................................	S	3	87
1851.	Report on subject of bridging, at Rouse's Point,................	S	1	20
1855.	Report of select committee in relation to obstructions to navigation in,..	A	4	84

LAKE CHAMPLAIN AND OGDENSBURGH RAILROAD, *see* Railroads.

LAKE ERIE AND BATH TURNPIKE, *see* Bath, &c.

LAKE GEORGE.

		Doc.	Vol.	No.
1830.	Road from, to Warrensburgh, report on petition of Dudley Fairland and others for aid to improve a,........................	A	3	283

LAKE ONTARIO.

		Doc.	Vol.	No.
1838.	Steamboat Company, report on petition to incorporate the,......	A	5	235
	SHIP CANAL FROM, to the Hudson river, *see* Ship Canal.			

LAMB, JOSEPH.

		Doc.	Vol.	No.
1831.	Report on petition for bounty lands,..............................	A	3	216
1832.	Report on same,..	A	1	43

LANDHOLDERS.

		Doc.	Vol.	No.
1846.	Report relative to the tax of the interests of,..................	S	4	135

LANDLORD AND TENANT, *see* Albany County—Manor of Rensselaerwyck.

		Doc.	Vol.	No.
1844.	Report on the petition of sundry inhabitants of the Manor of Rensselaerwyck praying for certain modifications of the law respecting the rights of, &c.,.............................	A	7	183
1844.	Report of select committee on above petition,.................	A	7	189
1845.	Report of majority of select committee on,......................	A	6	222
1845.	Report of minority of select committee on,.....................	A	7	247
1846.	Report of Mr. Spencer, from the select committee, on so much of governor's message as relates to leasehold estates, &c.,.......	S	3	92
1846.	Report relative to tax of leasehold estates,.....................	S	4	107
1846.	Report on so much of governor's message as relates to taxation of leasehold estates,..	S	4	115

LANDLORD AND TENANT—*continued.*

		Doc.	Vol.	No.
1846.	Resolutions of Mr. Perkins relative to leases,	A	1	12
1846.	Report relative to anti-rent petitions, &c.,	A	5	156
1846.	Concurrent resolutions concerning anti-rent prisoners,	A	5	159
1847.	Report on leasehold estates, and difficulties between,	A	6	162
1847.	Report respecting,	A	8	261
1847.	Report on a bill relative to,	A	8	263
1848.	Report of majority of, on petitions relative to,	A	4	125
1848.	Report of minority of, on the same,	A	5	126
1851.	Report of minority of judiciary committee on feudal tenures,	S	3	96
1851.	Report of majority of select committee on petition to stay proceedings against,	A	5	139

LAND OFFICE, COMMISSIONERS OF.

		Doc.	Vol.	No.
1830.	Report of the repayment, in certain cases, of moneys paid for taxes,	S	4	413
1832.	do do do do do	S	2	107
1834.	do do do do do	S	2	125
1835.	do do do do do	S	2	89
1836.	do do do do do	S	6	109
1837.	do do do do do	S	2	72
1838.	do do do do do	S	2	74
1840.	do do do do do	S	4	126
1841.	do do do do do	A	7	305
1834.	Report giving a statement of all releases granted under the "Act concerning escheats,"	S	1	34
1835.	Report on the same,	A	1	67
1836.	do	A	1	16
1837.	do	S	2	72
1838.	do	S	2	75
1839.	do	S	1	16
1841.	do	A	2	38
1830.	Report on petition of the heirs of Joseph Hubbard, for bounty lands,	A	2	126
1830.	Report on petition of Justus Burt to be repaid certain money paid for land,	S	2	156
1830.	Report of the quantity of land belonging to each fund which has been sold within the last five years, and the aggregate of such sales, &c.,	S	3	279
1830.	Report relative to the re-appraisement of lot No. 14, Oneida creek tract, in New Stockbridge,	A	4	349
1830.	Report on petition of T. Dean and S. Dakin (commissioners to settle the estate of Mary Doxstader, an Indian woman), to confirm certain conveyances of land,	A	4	356
1830.	Communication from, relative to certain property in Albany mortgaged to the state by John Van Ness Yates, &c.,	A	4	368
1831.	Report on petition of settlers on the school lot in New Stockbridge for relief,	A	1	11
1831.	Report on bill directing the sale to John Gregg of 250 acres of land in the New Stockbridge reservation,	S	1	10
1831.	Report on petition of Polly Risley for pay for certain improvements on land in New Stockbridge,	S	1	5
1831.	do John C. McLean, to be repaid certain moneys paid for land,	A	2	72
1831.	do Esther Chase, for remuneration for a lot of land sold by mistake,	A	2	78
1831.	do John McCrea, for the pre-emptive right to a lot of land,	A	2	150
1831.	do John Moore and Catharine McLaughlin, for an extension of their lease for a lot of land,	A	2	150
1831.	Report relative to an opening in the Albany pier,	A	2	94

LAND OFFICE, COMMISSIONERS OF—*continued.*

		Doc.	Vol.	No.
1831.	Report on petition of Amos Haskens for compensation for a deficiency in a lot of land bought of the state,	A	3	253
1831.	do John Shaw and others, for the remission of interest due on certain land,	A	3	265
1831.	do the trustees of the village of Oswego for land to erect a marine railway,	A	4	289
1831.	Report on claim of Gideon Castle to certain land,	A	4	303
1832.	Report on petition of the trustees of Fort Covington Academy for liberty to erect a building on the public square in Fort Covington,	A	1	18
1832.	do David Haines relative to the title of lands in the Minisink and Hardenburgh patents,	A	3	200
1832.	do inhabitants of Oswego for the sale or lease of certain land described as "Fish Market lot,"	A	3	227
1832.	Report on bill for a re-appraisement of certain lands in Oneida Castle,	A	3	238
1832.	Report on petition of William Long for damages in consequence of being kept out of possession of certain land,	S	1	37
1832.	do the heirs, devisees and grantees of John Thurman,	S	1	48
1832.	do John J. Campbell relative to the sale of his land by the surveyor-general,	S	2	97
1832.	do John C. McLean for indemnity in consequence of the sale of his land,	S	2	98
1832.	Report relative to improved lands belonging to the state, showing which are rented, their location, quantity, &c.,	S	2	102
1833.	Report relative to unpatented lots in township No. 3, Old Military tract, Clinton county,	S	2	98
1833.	Report on bill authorizing them to sell the missionary lot in Westmoreland,	A	2	42
1833.	Report on petition of Zimri Hills for escheated lands,	A	2	54
1833.	do John Gregg for a grant of certain land,	A	2	125
1833.	do trustees of Fort Covington Academy for a grant of land,	A	3	197
1833.	do James Wickham for remuneration for a deficiency in certain land,	A	3	236
1833.	Report on bill to vest in the city of Hudson certain lands under water,	A	4	318
1834.	Report relative to the survey of lots in Lewiston,	A	4	308
1834.	Report relative to lands in Salina set apart for the manufacture of coarse salt,	A	4	292
1834.	Report on petition of Richard Pennell for a grant of land under water,	A	3	179
1834.	do Anthony Rhodes and others for remuneration for improvements on lots 28 and 64, Freemasons' patent,	A	3	199
1834.	do John Dunn and Barnes Gleason to be credited with certain moneys paid for land,	A	4	254
1834.	do Phineas Waller and others relative to certain land in Garnsey's tract,	A	4	264
1834.	do Joseph Carter and others to be released from a certain mortgage,	A	4	386
1834.	do Justus Gay, in behalf of Mary Shaw, for remuneration of certain land escheated to the state,	A	4	313
1834.	do Franklin Rose for remuneration for deficiency in certain land,	A	4	394
1834.	do T. W. & Daniel Newcomb, relative to the location of certain land,	A	4	397

LAND OFFICE, COMMISSIONERS OF—*continued.*

Year	Subject	Doc.	Vol.	No.
1834.	Report on petition of John H. Lathrop, for a grant of a gore of land in the village of Lodi,	S	2	95
1834	do John Hadcock for a grant of land,	S	2	106
1835.	do David S. Jones and Gerrit Smith for a grant of land in the village of Oswego,	S	2	69
1835.	do Samuel L. Lush for remuneration for deficiency in certain land,	A	1	26
1835.	do Curtis Peck for a grant of land under water,	A	1	51
1835.	do S. Newton Dexter for remuneration for deficiency in the quantity of certain land,	A	2	134
1835.	do Charles McLain to be released from further payments on a lot of land,	A	2	152
1835.	do John S. Quackenboss and others for bounty land or an equivalent in money,	A	3	236
1835.	do John Ridden and Catharine, his wife, in relation to certain escheated land in New York,	A	4	349
1835.	do Edward W. De Grove for certain escheated land in New York,	A	4	342
1835.	do the bill to provide for the redemption of a part of arsenal lot in Franklin county,	A	4	366
1836.	Report relative to the estate of the late Dennis McCarthy,	S	1	16
1836.	Report relative to the lands now owned by the state,	S	1	29
1836.	Report on petition of Jesse Porter and others for a grant of land,	S	2	82
1836.	Report relative to lands escheated to the state on the death of John G. Leake,	S	2	86
1836.	Report in relation to the Freemasons' patent,	S	2	91
1836.	Report in relation to lots 28 and 64 in Freemasons' patent,	S	2	92
1836.	Report on petition of the Auburn and Syracuse Railroad Company for a grant of land on which to terminate their road,	S	2	103
1836.	Report relative to a grant of land made to D. S. Jones and Gerrit Smith, in Oswego,	A	3	153
1836.	Report on petition of Leonard Hildreth and others for escheated lands,	A	3	193
1836.	Report on the claim of Abraham Van Horne and Jane his wife,	A	4	262
1836.	Report on petition of Gerrit Smith and D. S. Jones relative to a grant of land made to them,	A	4	266
1836.	Report relative to the school lots in East Oswego,	A	4	267
1836.	Report on petition of Aaron B. Mack to be refunded the amount of principal and interest paid for a lot of land,	A	4	292
1836.	Report on petition of the common council of Buffalo relative to certain lands sold to the trustees of the Buffalo Marine Hospital,	A	4	319
1836.	Report on petition of W. Cochran and others relative to the title of the Trinity church to certain lands, &c.,	A	4	321
1837.	Report on petition of John I. Palmer relative to certain escheated lands.	S	2	57
1837.	Report on petition of the Auburn and Syracuse Railroad Company for a grant of land at Syracuse,	S	2	56
1837.	Report relative to certain property escheated to the State on the death of John Higginbottom,	S	1	21
1837.	Report on petition of W. Russell,	A	2	79
1837.	do John I. Campbell relative to the sale of his land by the surveyor-general,	A	2	156
1837.	do the trustees of the First Presbyterian Society of Lewistown, for certain land,	A	3	210
1837.	do C. J. Burckle for a conveyance to him of certain land,	A	3	216
1837.	do I Drake and others for the pre-emptive right to certain land,	A	3	267
1837.	do Z. P. Gillett for compensation for failure of the title to a lot of land,	A	4	312

LAND OFFICE, COMMISSIONERS OF—*continued.*

		Doc.	Vol.	No.
1837.	Report relative to the cemetery in East Oswego,	A	3	239
1837.	Report relative to the cemetery in East Oswego,	A	3	277
1838.	Report on petition of Samuel Rider relative to certain lands in the Freemasons' patent,	S	2	61
1838.	do Z. P. Gillett for compensation for failure of the title to a lot of land,	A	3	150
1838.	do John H. Minse and others for a grant of land under water,	A	6	322
1838.	do John R. Stephens and others relative to the assessment roll of the town of Hornellsville,	A	6	36
1838.	do Edward Knower for a grant of land under water,	A	4	183
1838.	Report in relation to the lands escheated to the State on the death of John G. Leake,	A	2	54
1839.	Communication from, in relation to their duties,	S	3	78
1839.	Report on petition of John Purmort and others to be released from a certain mortgage,	S	3	104
1839.	Report on petition of Franklin Rose for a remuneration for deficiency in a lot of land,	A	3	75
1839.	Report relative to the Lewiston cemetery,	A	6	332
1839.	Report relative to the grant of certain lands under water to the city of Hudson,	A	6	373
1840.	Report on claim of Samuel Rider to certain lands in the Freemasons' patent,	S	2	41
1840.	Report on claim of Anson Rider for same,	S	2	42
1840.	Report on petition of Richard Irvin for lands escheated to the state,	S	2	54
1840.	do S. A. Rich and wife for lands escheated to the state,	S	2	57
1840.	do W. Hamilton relative to certain lands claimed to be escheated to the state,	S	2	60
1840.	do Archibald Campbell relative to certain lands claimed to be escheated to the state,	S	4	69
1840.	do Elijah Burmingham and others to confirm their title to certain land,	S	3	66
1840.	do Elijah Burmingham and others to confirm their title to certain land,	S	4	124
1840.	do Harman W. Van Buren to purchase a portion of the salt lands,	A	7	284
1840.	do Mary Gray *alias* Lupin for a grant of land,	A	8	319
1840.	Report relative to granting lands in Syracuse for a cemetery,	S	2	59
1840.	do removing the coarse salt vats in Syracuse,	A	8	351
1841.	do the salt lands in Salina,	S	2	45
1841.	Report of proceedings under the act relative to the Oneida Indians,	S	1	14
1841.	Report concerning the Onondaga Indians,	S	2	63
1841.	Report on bill relative to the Onondaga salt springs,	A	3	83
1841.	Report on petition of Thomas Plumer Smith, I. & F. Englishbee, S. A. Rich and wife, and John Miller, relative to escheated lands,	S	2	58
1841.	Report on petition of James Englishbee relative to escheated lands,	S	3	74
1841.	Report on petition of Stephen S. Wilson,	A	4	134
1841.	Report on petition of Theron Roblee and others, and the heirs of Elizabeth Gilchrist	A	3	74
1842.	Report of, on bill to convey certain lands to Elizabeth Einstein, in obedience to resolution of senate, May 25 1841,	S	2	22
1842.	Report on petition of representatives of E. Gilchrist and C. West, and others,	A	4	68
1842.	Report on bill for relief of children of David Roberts,	A	7	180
1842.	Report relative to the repayment of money paid for taxes,	A	7	183
1843.	Communication in relation to over payment of money for taxes,	S	1	8

LAND OFFICE, COMMISSIONERS OF—*continued.*

		Doc.	Vol.	No.
1843.	Communication in relation to the claim of Manuel Myers,.......	S	3	78
1843.	Report on the petition of Peter Hasbrouck,..................	S	3	79
1843.	Report on the bill for the relief of Samuel Alexander and H. Dickinson,.....	S	3	106
1843.	Report on the petition of John Giles and Samuel Giles,..........	A	1	7
1843.	Communication from, relative to the Onondaga salt springs reservation,........	A	2	39
1843.	Report of, on the resolution of the assembly relative to the Oneida creek feeder,........	A	2	45
1843.	Report on the petition of the trustees of the St. Regis Indians in relation to certain islands in the river St. Lawrence,..........	A	5	136
1843.	Report in relation to the bill entitled "An act to extend the manufacture of coarse salt in town of Salina," and the remonstrance of the Syracuse C. Salt Company,..................	A	5	150
1843.	Report on the petition of Nicholas B. Doe,..................	A	5	158
1843.	Report in obedience to a resolution of the assembly in relation to the north gore, lying between townships No. 12 and 14, in Totten and Crossfield's purchase,........................	A	5	161
1843.	Report on the documents referred to them by the assembly in relation to ceding certain lands at the village of Black Rock, to the United States for military works,..................	A	5	162
1843.	Report on the petition of the associated mechanics in the county of Ontario,........	A	5	163
1844.	Report of, concerning escheats,........................	S	1	12
1844.	Report on the petition of James Wrigglesworth and others, next of kin to Wm. Dunn, deceased,........................	A	3	42
1844.	Report of, on petition of owners of Old Fortification Block No. 2, West Oswego,.....	A	3	59
1844.	Report of, on petition of John De Wolf, Jr., and others, heirs-at-law and legal representatives of Samuel Merry, Jr., deceased,..	A	3	71
1844.	Report of, on the petition of Alvin Bronson and others, relative to Old Fortification Block No. 2, West Oswego,..............	A	5	111
1844.	Report of, on the petition of Thomas Ball and Mary his wife, and their infant son William Ball,........................	A	5	112
1844.	Report on the bill relative to the exchange of certain lands set apart for the manufacture of salt in the county of Onondaga,..	A	6	155
1845.	Report of, on the petition of Eleazer Williams, a St. Regis Indian,	S	1	7
1845.	do do Deborah Ann Hallett,.............	S	1	21
1845.	do in relation to recording patents for lands in certain cases,........................	S	1	22
1845.	do on the petition of Peter Bain and others,............	A	1	18
1846.	do on the petition of John H. Vedder and others, for relief,........................	S	1	7
1846.	do on the bill for the relief of certain purchasers of land in the Oneida Reservation, in 1840 and 1841,....	S	1	9
1846.	do relative to certain Oneida purchasers,..............	A	2	34
1846.	do on petition of Asa Baxter,........................	A	3	85
1846.	do on reference of the petition of Stockbridge Indians,..	A	5	158
1846.	do relative to Sing Sing guard,........................	A	5	163
1846.	do on reference of the petition of M. N. Hawkins,.......	A	5	183
1846.	do on reference of the petition of S. Ableman,..........	A	5	191
1847.	do in answer to a resolution of February 17, 1847,......	S	2	48
1847.	Report on petition of E. Eaton and others,...................	S	2	54
1847.	Communication from, as to Elias Cost.....................	S	2	57
1847.	Report of, on petition of David A. Leighton and Ira W. Delamater,	S	2	78
1847.	Report on petition of John H. Green,......................	S	3	87
1847.	Report relative to land contiguous to salt springs,..............	S	3	108
1847.	do Asa Baxter's claim,......................	S	4	117
1847.	do Montezuma salt springs,....................	S	4	121
1847.	Report of, in answer to a resolution,........................	A	7	191
1847.	do on petition of John L. Stevenson for relief,....... ...	A	2	65
1847.	do on petition of Ozias Jacobs for relief,...............	A	4	107

LAND OFFICE, COMMISSIONERS OF—*continued.*

		Doc.	Vol.	No.
1847.	Report of, on petitions of purchasers of land in Oneida purchase of 1834,	A	1	43
1847.	do on petition of Wm. Cramer and others, for relief,	A	1	45
1847.	do do James F. Whitney,	A	7	186
1847.	do do Zachariah P. Gillett, under resolution of the assembly,	A	1	22
1847.	do to permit board of supervisors of Erie county to take stone from public lands in Black Rock,	A	1	44
1847.	do on petition of Samuel Poole and Wm. Poole,	A	2	70
1847.	do do Malcom N. Hawkins,	A	2	89
1847.	do do Oneida and Onondaga Indians, relative to land in Broome and Chenango,	A	7	215
1847.	do do Jacob Powless and others (Indians),	A	7	216
1847.	Communication from, as to Lydia Harden's right,	A	7	189
1848.	Report of, on petition of N. B. Doe,	S	2	32
1848.	do on bill to cede lands to village of Oswego,	S	2	37
1848.	do as to cost of completing New York arsenal,	S	2	54
1848.	do in answer to resolutions relating to,	S	2	55
1848.	do on petition of E. Harman and others,	A	1	18
1848.	do do Asa Baxter,	A	2	41
1848.	do do A Bronson and others,	A	3	121
1848.	do do John Cammerdon,	A	5	143
1849.	Communication from, transmitting report of commissioners to superintend the erection of the new state arsenal,	A	1	29
1849.	Report of, on petition of Mary E. Edwards,	A	2	64
1849.	do do Harriet R. Burt,	A	3	102
1848.	do relative to land ceded to state by the Orchard party of Oneida Indians,	A	3	103
1849.	do secretary of state relative to resolution on the petition of Ben. Bursdell and others,	A	3	162
1849.	do in answer to resolution of assembly relative to the distribution of the annuities of the Cayuga Indians,	A	3	165
1850.	Report on escheated lands of J. G. Leake,	A	3	22
1850.	Report on petition of Abraham P. Grand and others,	A	4	53
1850.	Report on Indian affairs,	A	5	130
1851.	Communication in relation to the St Regis Indians,	A	2	32
1851.	Report on petition of Wm. E., and Morgan L. Worden,	A	3	53
1852.	Report relative to hospital at Sandy Hook,	S	3	96
1852.	Report respecting an act granting land under water in the town of Westfield,	A	5	121
1853.	Report of the, relative to the marine hospital at Sandy Hook,	S	2	57
1853.	Report of, on resolution referring the matter of Jacob Barnhart and others to,	A	2	34
1854.	Communication from,	S	1	46
1854.	do under resolution,	A	2	59
1854.	do on old state hall,	A	3	89
1855.	Report of, relative to lands conveyed to Sacketts Harbor and Saratoga Railroad Company,	A	4	96
1855.	Report in relation to lands granted to John Thurman,	A	5	140
1857.	Report of, in reply to resolution relative to claim of Submit Baxter and the children and heirs-at-law of Asa Baxter, deceased,	A	3	182

LAND, ROBERT, AND OTHERS.

		Doc.	Vol.	No.
1841.	Report on petition of, for a re-assessment for damages to their mills, &c.,	A	4	141
1841.	Report of canal commissioners on the same,	A	5	191

LANDS.

		Doc.	Vol.	No.
1838.	Overflowed by water on the Tonawanda and Ellicott creeks, report of survey of the,	A	3	124

LANDS—*continued.*

		Doc.	Vol.	No
1841.	Ceded to the United States, report of attorney-general relative to assessing,	A	5	145
1845.	Report of commissioners of land office in relation to recording patents for lands in certain cases,	S	1	22
1847.	Report of commissioners of land office respecting, contiguous to salt springs,	S	3	108
1848.	Montauk, report on petitions of owners of,	A	1	12
1852.	Unsold, report of comptroller relative to,	A	5	105
	In Cowasselon and New Stockbridge, *see* Cowasselon and New Stockbridge.			
	In Oneida Castle, *see* Oneida Castle.			

LIMITATION OF :

		Doc.	Vol.	No
1847.	Minority report as to, &c.,	A	8	233
1848.	Report relative to petitions for,	A	3	78
1851.	Report of committee on public lands,	A	4	130
1858.	Report relative to,	A	3	78

NON-RESIDENT :

		Doc.	Vol.	No
1834.	Report on bill to amend the law relative to the survey of, by supervisors, &c.,	A	2	86
1838.	In Hornellsville, report relative to taxes on,	A	6	361
1843.	Report of the comptroller of the amount due on account of taxes on,	S	1	13
1850.	Report of attorney-general and comptroller relative to,	A	3	39
1854.	Communication from comptroller relative to,	A	3	101

SALE OF, FOR TAXES :

		Doc.	Vol.	No
1830.	Report of the comptroller on the bill concerning,	A	3	239
1831.	do comptroller giving the expense of the last sale of,	A	3	264
1835.	do comptroller relative to and quit-rents, in obedience to a resolution of assembly,	A	5	380
1839.	do comptroller on bill relative to,	A	6	340
1849.	do select committee on so much of governor's message as relates to, in the counties where such lands lie,	A	3	107
1856.	do committee on ways and means relative to,	A	3	92

SOLD FOR TAXES :

		Doc.	Vol.	No
1830.	Report of committee on the judiciary relative to the redemption of,	A	3	237
1832.	do comptroller on petition to amend the law relative to the redemption of,	A	1	37
1833.	Report relative to giving deeds for, when the certificate is lost,	A	4	299
1848.	Report of comptroller on bill relative to	A	3	63
1849.	Report of comptroller relative to printing certain statements of,	A	1	8
1849.	Report relative to execution of deeds of, sold in the name of the people,	A	3	160
1853.	Report of comptroller relative to the amount of taxes due the treasury on lands sold in December, 1852,	A	2	25

FREEMASONS' PATENT :

		Doc.	Vol.	No
1836.	Report of commissioners of the land office in relation to,	S	2	91
1836.	Report of commissioners of the land office in relation to,	S	2	92
	Applications for remuneration for improvements on, *see* Moses Brockway, Samuel Rider, Anthony Rhodes and others, Nathan Bumpus and others, Sarah Gage and others, Anson Rider and Nathan Underwood.			

OLD MILITARY TRACT :

		Doc.	Vol.	No
1831.	Report on petition of owners of township No. 11 for a new survey of said township,	S	1	31
1833.	Reports relative to patents for reserved and escheated lots in the,	S	2	87

LANDS—*continued.*

		Doc.	Vol.	No.
1833.	Report relative to unpatented lots in township No. 3, Clinton county,..	S	2	98

LANDS, INDIAN, *see* Indians.

LANDS, MILITARY BOUNTY.

		Doc.	Vol.	No.
1830.	Report of surveyor-general on a resolution to report whether any lands remain unappropriated, and if none remain unsold, then the price for which the last were sold,......................	S	2	82
	Reports on applications for, *see* Henry Becker, David Carman, Joseph Carley, Daniel Delevan, Z. Dodd, A. Dyckman, Asher Ford, Michael Francisco, John Gates, L. Rackney, Christian Guthrie, Joseph Hubbard, John Kane, Gotleib Kraick, Joseph Lamb, Jacob Lawson, Tousant Levernway, Francis Mayotte, Joseph Minard, Thomas Mott, Basil Nadeau, John Odell, Isaac Satterly, David Schauber, Jacob Shew, Henry Smith, Aaron Smith, Orson Smith, Trueman Spencer, Ashbel W. Treat, Solomon Utter, B. E. Vrooman, Major Watson, John Watson.			

LANDS, PUBLIC, OF THE UNITED STATES, *see* United States.

LANDS, PUBLIC, OF THIS STATE.

		Doc.	Vol.	No.
1830.	Quantity of land belonging to each fund sold within the last five years, and the product in the aggregate of such sales, &c.,....	S	3	279
1836.	Report of amount of lands now owned by the state, designating the quantity in each county, with the estimated value, and designating also those belonging to the different funds,.........	S	1	29
1838.	Statement of unimproved lands, the number of acres of said lands, with the counties in which they are located,.....	S	2	63
1837.	Quantity of land now owned by the state in Hamilton, Essex, Clinton, Franklin and St. Lawrence counties, distinguishing in each county the lands that may have heretofore been sold, and the right thereof again reverted to the state, &c.,............	A	6	382
1840.	Quantity of lands now owned by the state in Essex and Hamilton, &c ,..	A	4	153
1832.	Statement showing the improved lands, which have been leased, and on which leases there are rents in arrear,...............	S	2	102
1848.	Report of state engineer of amount of,.........................	A	3	104
1849.	Report of state engineer and surveyor on,....................	S	1	27
1850.	Report of state engineer and surveyor respecting,..............	A	5	88
1851.	Report by same officers relative to,....................	S	1	19
	In the Village of Oswego, *see* Oswego, Village of.			

WOOD CREEK TRACT:

		Doc.	Vol.	No.
1831.	Surveyor-general, report relative to,........................	S	1	19
1832.	Surveyor-general, report relative to,........................	S	1	12
1832.	Report of committee on finance relative to the same,...........	S	1	27

ST. REGIS RESERVATION:

		Doc.	Vol.	No.
1831.	Communication from the surveyor-general relative to the,.......	S	1	19
1832.	Communication from same source relative to the,...........	S	1	12
1832.	Report of committee on finance on the same,....	S	1	27
1836.	Near the Oswego canal, report of comptroller relative to sales of, &c.,....	S	2	73
1841.	Report of committee on public lands on amending the Revised Statutes relative to,..	A	3	60

LANDS UNDER WATER, GRANTS OF.

		Doc.	Vol.	No.
1832.	Report of attorney-general relative to,........................	S	1	45

LANDS UNDER WATER, &c.—*continued.*

		Doc.	Vol.	No.
1838.	Directions to applicants for,	A	4	322
1854.	Opinion of attorney-general relative to,	A	3	105

At Hudson, *see* Hudson.
At Brooklyn, *see* Brooklyn.
At Williamsburgh, *see* Williamsburgh.
At Shelter island, *see* S. B. Nicoll.
At the Narrows, Kings county, *see* R. Pennell.
At West Oswego, *see* E. Knower.
At Oyster Bay, *see* James De Kay and others.
At Rye, Westchester county, *see* John H. Minuse and others.
At Rye, Westchester county, *see* Curtis Peck.
At Sag Harbor, *see* Marcus B. Osborn.
At New York, *see* New York.

LANGLEY, MARGARET, AND OTHERS.

1833.	Report on petition of, to enlarge the power of the executors of the last will, &c., of James Langley, deceased,	S	2	94

LANNIER, D., AND J. LOCKENTELLY.

1854.	Report of committee on grievances on petition of,	A	1	33

LANSING, ABRAHAM Y.

1857.	Report of committee on claims favorable on petition of, for re-hearing of claim by canal board,	A	3	164

LANSING, TOWN OF.

1832.	Report on petition of commissioners of highways of, for the payment of costs in a certain suit,	A	3	191
1835.	Report on petition for a special law for the election of a justice of the peace to fill a vacancy,	A	1	39

LANSINGBURGH AND TROY MACADAM ROAD.

1832.	Report on petition to incorporate,	A	1	34

LANSINGBURGH, VILLAGE OF.

1852.	Report on petition of corporate authorities of, for a toll bridge,	A	2	77

LAPHAM, JOHN.

1855.	Report of committee on claims in case of,	A	4	109
1855.	Report by same committee on petition of,	A	5	109
1856.	Report on petition of,	A	4	139

LARABEE, MAJOR CHARLES.

1841.	Report on petition of,	A	3	86

LARZELERE, HARVEY W.

1856.	Report for relief,	A	5	198

LASHER, G. J. E.

1846.	Report on petition for relief of,	S	2	51

LATHAM, E. & E.

1856.	Report on claim of,	S	2	57

		Doc.	Vol.	No
	LATHAM, E. S. & O.			
1857.	Report on petition of,	S	1	22
	LATHROP, JEDEDIAH H., AND OTHERS.			
1841.	Report on petition of, for an investigation into their acts and proceedings as directors of the City Bank of Buffalo,	A	7	290
	LATHROP, JOHN N.			
1834.	Report on petition of, for a grant of land in the village of Lodi,	S	2	65
1834.	Report of select committee on the same,	S	2	81
	LAWRENCEVILLE, VILLAGE OF.			
1840.	Report on petition to incorporate a Hydraulic Cement Company at,	A	3	94
	LAW REPORTS, Exchange of, with the different states, *see* Supreme Court Decisions.			
	LAWS OF THE STATE.			
1845.	Report of the secretary of state respecting general index to, and documents in his office,	S	2	71
1848.	Report of select committee on codification of,	S	2	69
	LAWSON, JACOB.			
1841.	A soldier of the revolution, report on petition of, for bounty lands,	A	6	242
1843.	Report of committee on the militia and public defense on petition of,	A	4	114
1843.	Report of committee on claims on a bill for his relief,	S	3	115
1844.	Report of committee on the militia and public defense on the petition of,	A	3	35
	LAWSON, JAMES.			
1843.	Report of committee on claims on bill for the relief of,	S	3	115
	LAWYERS' FEES.			
1845.	Report of select committee on,	A	6	227
	LEAD.			
1840.	Report relative to reducing the canal tolls on,	A	8	343
	LEAKE AND WATTS ORPHAN HOUSE, *see* New York.			
	LEAKE, JOHN G.			
1830.	Report on petition of Z. Barker and others in relation to certain lands escheated to the state on the death of,	A	2	73
1831.	Report on petition of the trustees of the Leake and Watts Orphan House to vest in them the right and title of the state to said lands,	S	2	71
1833.	Report on petition of the trustees of the Leake and Watts Orphan House to vest in them the right and title of the state to said lands,	S	2	100
1834.	Report on petition of the trustees of the Leake and Watts Orphan House, and the petition of Jean Gray, Janet Dunlop and others for the same,	S	2	121
1835.	Report on memorial of the Leake and Watts Orphan House, and also of the next of kin of J. G. Leake for the same,	S	2	80

LEAKE, JOHN G.—*continued.*

		Doc.	Vol.	No.
1836.	Report of commissioners of the land office relative to the sale of the lands escheated to the state on the death of,......	S	2	86
1836.	Report of commissioners of the land office on petition of Leonard Hildreth and others in relation to the same,................	A	3	193
1838.	Report of commissioners of the land office relative to the sale of said lands,..	A	2	54
1838.	Report on petition of the trustees of the Leake and Watts Orphan House for the release to them of the said lands,.............	A	2	24
1839.	Report on petition of the trustees of the Leake and Watts Orphan House for the release to them of said lands,................	A	2	28
1840.	Report of committee on finance on the memorial of Janet McAndrew and the petition of the trustees of the Leake and Watts Orphan House,....................................	S	4	117
1841.	Report of the attorney-general on petition of Janet Hay, or McAndrew, Alexander Leck and James Thompson relative to the same,..	A	7	268
1844.	Report of select committee on the escheated lands of deceased,..	A	3	74
1844.	Report of committee on charitable and religious societies on same,	A	5	126
1845.	Report of committee on aliens concerning the Leake and Watts estate,...	A	6	210
1845.	Minority report of committee on aliens concerning the Leake and Watts estate,..	A	6	215
1845.	Minority report on the Leake and Watts estate,................	A	6	233
1850.	Report of commissioners of land office on escheated lands of,....	A	3	22
1850.	Report of select committee on petition of Jas. Hay, relative to escheated lands of,....................................	A	5	87
1851.	Report on petition of Jas. Hay in relation to,.................	A	4	101

LEARNED AND JOHNSON.

1846.	Report of canal board on petition of,........................	A	5	154

LEASES, *see* Landlord and Tenant.

LEAVENWORTH, E. W.

1848.	Report on memorial of,......................................	A	5	160
1848.	Report of canal board on memorial of,........................	A	5	171

LEAVITT, JOSHUA.

1841.	Memorial of, relative to the importance of an equitable and adequate market for American wheat,........................	A	7	295

LEBANON, TOWN OF.

1838.	First Congregational Society of, report on petition to confirm the acts of the trustees of, ...	A	5	266

LECK, ALEXANDER, *see* Janet Hay or McAndrew and others.

LEDYARD, ISAAC, AND JOHN P. MATTHEWS.

1845.	Report of canal board on petition of,.........................	A	6	201
1845.	Report of committee on claims on petition of,.................	A	6	226
1847.	Report on petition of, ...	A	6	159
1848.	Report on petition of, ...	A	3	110

LEE, BENJAMIN, AND OTHERS, *see* Henry Price and others.

LEEDS, VILLAGE OF.

1831.	Turnpike from, to Freehold, report on petition to incorporate, ..	A	4	345

LEGAL NOTICES.

Year	Subject	Doc.	Vol.	No.
1833.	Report of state printer of amount received for bankrupt and,...	S	1	14
1846.	Report relative to publication of,........................	S	4	113
1847.	Report relative to,..	S	1	13

LEGGETT, ABRAHAM.

Year	Subject	Doc.	Vol.	No.
1857.	Report of committee on state prisons favorable on petition of, for payment for goods furnished Sing Sing State Prison,.........	A	3	168

LEGISLATIVE DOCUMENTS, *see* Documents.

LEGISLATURE, *see* Assembly, Senate.

Year	Subject	Doc.	Vol.	No.
1832.	Chaplains, report on the subject of dispensing with the,........	A	4	298
1833.	Report relative to the payment of the, ...	S	1	28
1838.	Communication from the clergy of Albany accepting the invitation to officiate as,........	S	1	6
1833.	Members of the, report relative to the eligibility of, as senators in congress, ...	S	1	18
1834.	Report relative to the payment of postage on letters received by,	A	3	164
1835.	Compensation of, report relative to the,................	A	1	54
1835.	Annual meeting of, report relative to changing the time for the,..	A	1	61
1835.	Printing for the, amount paid for, in the years 1831, 1832, 1833 and 1834.	S	2	67
1836.	do of bills, report recommending the,............	A	4	289
1838.	do report of select committee on the subject of,....	A	6	346
1838.	do communication from the state printer (E. Croswell), relative to the above report, ...	A	6	348
1840.	do report of the comptroller and secretary of state relative to the contract with Thurlow Weed for the, ...	A	2	47
1840.	do communication from Thurlow Weed, state printer, in answer to a resolution of assembly requesting him to report the expense of, during the present session,......................	S	4	125
1841.	do communication from Thurlow Weed, state printer, in answer to a resolution of assembly requesting him to report the expense of, during the present session,......................	A	7	276
1845.	Titles of acts,..	A	7	250
1847.	Titles of acts,..	A	8	264
1858.	Titles of acts passed 1848, ...	A	5	189
1849.	Titles of acts passed 1849,..................................	A	5	215
1849.	Majority report on resolution relative to members of, elected to congress,..	S	2	48
1849.	Minority report on resolution relative to members of, elected to congress,..	S	2	49
1850.	Joint rules of,..	S	1	32
1850.	Joint rules of,..	A	3	38
1851.	Report of committee of conference on joint rules of,............	S	2	36
1852.	Joint rules and orders of,...................................	S	1	4
1852.	Joint rules, report relative to,.............................	S	1	10
1852.	Joint rules of,..	A	2	36
1853.	Report of committee on public expenditures on contingent expenses of,..	S	1	26
1853.	Joint rules of, as amended by the senate, ...	A	2	17
1853.	Joint rules of, adopted January 25, 1853,..	S	1	15
1853.	Communication from the comptroller relative to the exhaustion of the annual appropriation of $75,000 for pay of members and officers of,..	A	5	128
1854.	Joint rules proposed,................	A	1	11

LEGISLATURE—*continued.*

		Doc.	Vol.	No.
1855.	Joint rules of,..	S	1	26
1856.	Report of committee respecting the printing of journals,........	A	1	10
1856.	Report of committee on revision of joint rules,................	A	1	11
1856.	Joint rules of,..	A	3	24
1857.	Joint rules of,..	S	1	35
1857.	Joint rules and orders of,..............................	A	1	34
1858,	Joint rules, as adopted February 17, 1858,....................	A	1	35
	Power of the, over corporations, &c., *see* Corporations.			

LEICESTER, TOWN OF.

1832.	Boundary line of, report relative to the,......................	A	2	172
1835.	Dam and boat lock on the Genesee river, report on petition of Felix Tracy to build a,....................................	A	4	295

LEIGHTON, DAVID, AND IRA W. DELAMATER.

1847.	Report on petition of,....................................	S	2	78

LENOX, TOWN OF.

1846.	Report of committee on canals on petition of,..................	A	4	130
1847.	Report on petition of, relative to surplus water on Rome level,..	A	4	109

LENOX, AND SULLIVAN, TOWNS OF.

1838.	Swamp lands in, report relative to an amendment of the law for draining the,..	S	1	15
1840.	Report on petition to change the place of meeting of the proprietors of the,..	A	5	203

LENT, DE HURON.

1853.	Report of committee on claims on petition of,..................	S	2	48

LE RAY, TOWN OF.

1840.	Report on petition for a loan to build bridges across Black river,	A	8	336

LE ROY, HERMAN, Jr.

1834.	Report on petition of, to construct a dam across a creek in the town of Pelham,..	A	3	157

LE ROY, TOWN OF.

1844.	Report on the petition of inhabitants of,.....................	S	4	122

LESTER, FRANKLIN.

1857.	Report on award to,..	S	4	111

LESTER, M. W.

1854.	Report on petition of,......................................	A	1	30

LETTER POSTAGE, *see* Postage.

LE VALLEY AND MORRELL.

1852.	Report on their petition,....................................	S	2	53

LE VALLEY, F. J.

1854.	Report on petition of,......................................	A	3	100

LE VALLEY, FRANKLIN.

1852.	Report on petition of,......................................	A	1	18

LEVERIDGE, J., AND H. B. DURYEA.

		Doc.	Vol.	No.
1855.	Report of committee on judiciary on petition of,	A	2	40

LEVERNWAY, TOUSANT.

1833.	Heir-at-law of Francis Levernway, a Canadian refugee, report on petion for bounty lands,	A	4	296

LEVY, HARMAN AND CATHARINE B.

1835.	Report on petition to change the names of,	A	1	24

LEWIS COUNTY.

1831.	Road in, report on petition to raise money by tax to construct a,	A	3	212
1832.	Road district, through the towns of Leyden, West Turin, Turin and Martinsburgh, report on petition for a,	S	2	79
1838.	Bounty on wolves, report on petition to raise the,	A	6	325

LEWIS, ISAAC, *see* W. Gibbs, and others.

LEWIS, ISAIAH.

1846.	Report relative to certain costs, &c., of school district No. 11, Otselic, Chenango county, in suit with,	S	4	110

LEWIS, LEONARD.

1854.	Report on petition of,	A	2	41
1856.	Report on petition of, for relief,	A	3	41

LEWISTON AND PORTER, TOWNS OF.

1833.	Baptist church and society of the, report on the petition of the trustees of, to sell their real estate,	A	2	101

LEWISTON, VILLAGE OF.

1834.	Report on petition for a re-survey of the plot of the,	A	4	308
1837.	First Presbyterian Society, report on petition for the conveyance of certain land,	A	3	210
1839.	Cemetery, &c., report in relation to,	A	6	332

LIBBY, JAS. S., AND OTHERS.

1852.	Report of commissioners of land office respecting the granting of land under water at Westfield,	A	5	121

LIBERIA EMIGRATION AND AGRICULTURAL ASSOCIATION.

1852.	Memorial of, for an appropriation,	S	1	19

LIBERTY, PERSONAL.

1848.	Report of judiciary committee on bill for the protection of,	S	1	14

LIBRARIES, DISTRICT, *see* Common Schools.

LIBRARY, ASSEMBLY, *see* Assembly.

LIBRARY, ASTOR, *see* New York.

LIBRARY, OSWEGO CITY, *see* Oswego City.

LIBRARY, SENATE, *see* Senate.

		Doc.	Vol.	No.
	LIBRARY, STATE, *see* State Library.			
	LICENSE LAW, *see* Excise.			
	LICENTIOUSNESS.			
1842.	Report of committee on petition for laws to punish,............	A	7	159
1844.	Report of committee on the judiciary on petition for the suppression of,..	A	3	63
1845.	Report of select committee on,..........	A	1	23
	LIEN LAW.			
1830.	Report on petition for a law giving mechanics a lien upon buildings erected by them for labor and materials furnished,......	A	1	24
1830.	Report of select committee on the same,......................	S	3	231
1831.	do do do	A	4	286
1841.	do do do	A	5	161
	LIEUTENANT-GOVERNOR.			
1847.	Opinion of, as to court of errors,............	S	1	20
1847.	Report on election of,..	S	4	115
1851.	Communication in relation to the commissioners of the canal fund,...................	A	2	30
1854.	Communication from comptroller relative to moneys paid, &c.,..	S	2	81
1854.	Communication from comptroller relative to moneys paid, &c.,..	S	2	93
	LIFE BOAT ASSOCIATION, *see* Rockaway.			
	LILLIE, C. L, & E. A. HALL.			
1846.	Report on bill for relief of,................	S	4	125
	LIMA, TOWN OF.			
1830.	Fire engine company in, report on petition for a,.............	A	3	290
	SEMINARY IN, *see* Genesee and Wesleyan Seminary.			
	LIMESTONE CREEK.			
1836.	Report of canal commissioners relative to the waters of,........	S	2	80
	LIMESTONE CREEK FEEDER.			
	Canal from the, to the Seneca road, *see* H. Edwards and others.			
	LIMITED PARTNERSHIPS.			
1837.	Report of attorney-general on bill,..........................	A	4	304
	LINDSLEY, AMANLIS.			
1841.	Report on petition of, for a divorce,........................	A	4	143
	LITERATURE FUND.			
1830.	Distribution of the income of, report of Regents of the University relative to the best method for the,.............	S	4	400
1830.	Distribution of the income of, report on petition of trustees of Hamilton Academy for an equal,........................	S	4	304
1830.	Distribution of the income of, report of Regents of the University relative to the exclusion of Red Hook and Union Hall Academies, and the Union Literary Society, from the,.............	A	4	320
1830.	And canal funds, report of Regents of the University on bill relative to,.....	S	4	371
1831.	Increase of the, report of the Regents on bill to provide for the application of the,......................................	S	1	74

LITERATURE FUND—*continued.*

		Doc.	Vol.	No.
1832.	Income of the, report on petition of Erasmus Hall, Oyster Bay, Clinton and Union Hall Academies, to repeal the law authorizing the New York Institution for the Deaf and Dumb to receive a distributive share of the,....	A	2	59
1830.	Income of the, report of Regents of amount distributed by them from 1832 to 1830,....	S	3	218
1835.	Distribution of the income of the, report on the propriety of amending the law relative to,....	A	3	263
1839.	Distribution of the income of the, report on petition to change the present mode,....	A	3	76
1841.	Distribution of the income of the, report on petition to change the present mode,....	A	6	256
1839.	Distribution of the income of the, report of Regents of the University relative to altering the present mode,....	A	3	141
1836.	Income of the, report on petition of Greenbush and Schodack Academy for a portion of the,....	A	4	218
1844.	Report of committee on colleges, &c., in regard to distribution of,	A	5	135

LITTLE FALLS.

		Doc.	Vol.	No.
1831.	Bank at, report on petition to incorporate,....	S	1	16
1837.	School district No. 1,....	A	2	113
1839.	Road district from, to Salisbury, report on petition for a,....	A	2	49
1839.	Road district from, to Salisbury, report on petition to amend the law relative to a,....	A	6	342
1839.	Market, &c., report on petition to raise money by tax to build a,	A	6	350
1843.	Report of canal commissioners relative to bridges lying between Utica and,....	S	3	105
1844.	Report of canal board on petition of citizens of, for finishing a bridge,....	A	6	157
1845.	Report on bill to authorize inhabitants of, to borrow money,....	S	3	114
1848.	Report on changing name of,....	S	3	74

LITTLEFIELD, LYMAN, *see* I. Campbell.

LITTLE VALLEY, TOWN OF.

		Doc.	Vol.	No.
1839.	Report on petition to extend the time for the collection of taxes in the,....	A	1	9

LIVERPOOL, VILLAGE OF.

		Doc.	Vol.	No.
1835.	Report of canal commissioners on petition for the use of the surplus waters of the Oswego canal to raise salt water at,....	A	4	347
1837.	Report by same committee relative to the same,....	A	2	93
1845.	Report of canal board relative to side-cut canals in,....	S	3	99

LIVINGSTON COUNTY.

		Doc.	Vol.	No.
1835.	Bridge over Genesee river, report on petition to raise money by tax to build a,....	A	3	242
1836.	Clerk's office, report on petition to raise money by tax to build a,	A	4	213
1838.	Clerk's office, report on petition to raise money by tax to build a,	A	1	19
1832.	Commissioners of deeds, report on petition to authorize the election of,....	A	1	35
1838.	Race-course, report on petition for a law to establish a,....	A	4	198
1835.	Surrogate of, report on petition to confirm his official acts,....	A	1	47
1839.	Treasurer of, report relative to the appointment of,....	A	2	43
1857.	Minority report on annexation of Ossian to,....	S	4	116
1858.	Communication relative to unpaid taxes due the state from the treasurer of,....	A	3	53

BANKS IN, *see* Banks—Livingston County.

LIVINGSTON, FRANKLIN, *see* D. B. King and F. Livingston.

Doc. Vol. No.

LIVINGSTON, R. M., *see* Daniel Stevenson.

LIVINGSTON, THOMAS.

1834. Report on petition for compensation for damages to his boat on the canal, ... A 3 125

LLOYD, JOHN.

1832. Report on petition of, for the appointment of commissioners to settle his accounts for building the Allegany county poor-house, A 3 241

LOAN, STATE.

1834. Message from the governor recommending a (W. L. Marcy),..... A 4 320
1834. Report of joint committee on the governor's message,.......... A 4 350
1835. Report of commissioners under the act authorizing a,.......... S 1 25
1835. Report on the same,........ A 2 144
1838. Message from the governor recommending a,........ S 2 70

LOANS BY THE STATE.

1832. Loans of 1786, 1792 and 1808, report of comptroller of amount outstanding, &c.,........ S 1 25
1832. Report of committee on finance on the report of the comptroller,........ S 2 69
1833. Loans of 1792 and 1808, report of comptroller of amount now on loan in the several counties,........ A 4 241
1839. Report on the propriety of extending the time for the payment of,........ A 5 270
1849. Communication from comptroller relative to expiration of time for payment of,........ A 3 176
1837. Loan of 1808, report of comptroller of amount outstanding, and the amount supposed to be not collectable, ... S 1 34
1850. Loans of 1849, report of committee on ways and means on governor's message relative to premiums on,........ A 5 133
1830. Loan of the principal of the school and literature funds, resolution offered by Mr. McMartin relative to a,........ S 4 398
1850. Report on governor's message relating to premiums on,..... S 2 68
1856. Report of committee on finances on act to authorize loan of certain moneys,........ S 1 12

LOANS, COMMISSIONERS OF.

1847. Report as to, of United States deposit fund,........ S 1 32
1849. Amount of money on loan, &c., in charge of,........ S 2 49
1857. Communication from the attorney-general relative to suits against, A 1 19
1858. Report of proceedings of supervisors of county of New York relative to,........ A 3 72

LOANS, COMMISSIONER OF, AND SUPERVISOR.

1838. Report on resolution to inquire whether the offices of, ought to be vested in one person,........ A 3 75

LOBAN, DAVID, *see* Martin Bettinger.

LOCKENTELLY, JOHN, AND DAVID LEMONNIER.

1854. Report on petition of,........ A 1 33

LOCKPORT, VILLAGE OF.

1839. Canal bridge at, report on petition for,........ S 3 88
1841. Firemen in, report on petition to amend the act relative to the,.. S 3 79
1843. Locks at, report of canal commissioners relative to combined, .. S 3 98

LOCKPORT, VILLAGE OF—*continued.*

Year	Subject	Doc.	Vol.	No.
1844.	Locks at, report of canal board relative to the five combined,....	S	4	130
1844.	do do canal commissioners having charge of western division of Erie canal in relation to combined,	A	5	131
1846.	Materials at, report of committee on canals relative to,..........	A	5	185
1831.	Surplus waters of the canal at, memorial of Lyman A. Spalding relative to the,..............	A	1	55
1831.	do do memorial of inhabitants of Niagara county relative to the,...	A	1	61
1831.	do do remonstrance of Lot Clark against the memorial of L. A. Spalding relative to the,...........	A	2	91
1831.	do do communication from Henry Seymour requesting the appointment of a committee to investigate the charges against him,	A	2	121
1831.	do do report of committee on canals relative to the,................	A	4	280
1831.	do do report of amount paid for investigating the charges against the canal commissioners relative to the,..........	A	4	339

BANK, *see* Banks—Niagara County.

RACEWAY around the locks at, *see* W. Buel.

LOCKPORT AND NIAGARA FALLS RAILROAD, *see* Railroads.

LOCKVILLE, VILLAGE OF.

Year	Subject	Doc.	Vol.	No.
1834.	Surplus canal water at, report concerning,....................	A	4	287

LOCKWOOD, MUNSON I.

Year	Subject	Doc.	Vol.	No.
1858.	Communication from comptroller and attorney-general relative to suit of,..	S	2	85
1858.	Late agent of Sing Sing prison, report of referees in case of,.....	S	2	106

LOGAN, WM., AND CO.

Year	Subject	Doc.	Vol.	No.
1850.	Report on petition of,..........	S	2	67

LOGAN, WM., AND OTHERS.

Year	Subject	Doc.	Vol.	No.
1849.	Report of select committee on petition of,....................	A	3	133

LONGBY, LYMAN.

Year	Subject	Doc.	Vol.	No.
1833.	Report on petition to confirm his title to certain lands,..........	A	2	60

LONG ISLAND.

Year	Subject	Doc.	Vol.	No.
1831.	Canal company, report on petition to confer banking powers on the,..	S	1	60
1835.	Ferries between New York and, report on petition for the establishment of additional, ...	A	2	138
1836.	do do report on bill to establish and regulate,.	A	4	258
1836.	do do minority report,.............	A	4	259
1840.	Game, preservation of, report on petition to repeal the law for the, so far as relates to Huntington, Islip and Brookhaven,....	A	3	83
1834.	Life Insurance and Trust Company, report on petition to incorporate,......................................	A	1	40
1832.	Trout, preservation of, in certain waters of,....................	A	4	337
1833.	Trout, preservation of, in certain waters of,....................	A	2	65

Year	Subject	Doc.	Vol.	No.
	LONG ISLAND—*continued.*			
1832.	Wreck masters, report on petition to amend the law relative to,	A	4	276
1830.	Sound Harbor Company, report on petition to incorporate,......	S	3	265
1838.	Sound oysters, report relative to planting,......................	A	3	157
	LONG ISLAND RAILROAD, *see* Railroads.			
	LONG, JOSEPH.			
1841.	Report on petition for compensation for damages by the construction of the Chenango canal,..............................	A	6	254
	LONGSTREET, C. P., AND OTHERS.			
1853.	Report of committee on grievances on petition of, to amend seduction laws,..	A	3	57
1853.	Report of committee on grievances on petition of, to amend seduction laws,..	A	3	61
	LONG, W.			
1832.	Report on petition of, for remuneration for damages in consequence of his being kept out of possession of certain land bought of the state,..	S	1	37
1834.	Report on petition of, for remuneration for damages in consequence of his being kept out of possession of certain land bought of the state,..	A	4	374
	LONGWOOD, LEVI.			
1833.	Report on petition for a divorce,..............................	A	2	47
	LOTTERIES.			
1832.	Report of attorney-general relative to,........................	A	4	292
1833.	Petition of Palmer Canfield relative to,........................	S	2	108
1833.	Petition of Yates & McIntyre relative to,.....................	S	2	119
1833.	Report of attorney-general relative to,........................	A	1	13
1833.	Report of select committee (Mr. Herttell) relative to,............	A	2	98
1834.	Resolutions of the legislature of Pennsylvania in relation to,.....	A	1	11
1834.	Resolutions of the legislature of Massachusetts in relation to,....	A	2	76
1834.	Foreign, tickets of, report relative to the sale of,..............	S	2	52
	LOUISIANA, STATE OF.			
1831.	Resolution of the legislature of, relative to the tariff law of 1828,	A	1	4
	LOVERIDGE, J., AND H. B. DURYEA.			
1855.	Report of judiciary committee on petition of,..................	A	2	40
	LOWELL, WILLIAM.			
1833.	Report on petition of D. Neff and P. Fancrook relative to the last will, &c., of,..	S	2	93
	LOWER REDHOOK LANDING.			
1840.	Report on petition for a law to protect, from damages by fire from steamboats,..	A	5	164
	LOWRIE, JAMES, AND OTHERS, *see* Northern Turnpike.			
	LOZIER, JAMES, AND OTHERS.			
1845.	Report on the petition of James Lozier and others, for a reduction of fees of county clerk of New York,....................	S	3	126
	LUDDINGTON, PHILIP.			
1832.	Report on petition of, for a bridge across the Erie canal,........	S	2	75

LUCE, HERVEY.

		Doc.	Vol.	No.
1841.	Report on petition of, for compensation for damages by the Chemung canal,	S	3	84

LUMBARD, JAMES, AND OTHERS.

1849.	Report on petition of,	S	2	70

LUMBERLAND TURNPIKE, *see* Mount Hope.

LUNATIC ASYLUMS.

1855.	Report relative to commission to examine into, and workhouses, jails, &c.,	S	1	27

Hudson, *see* White, Samuel.
New York, *see* New York Bloomingdale Asylum.

LUNATIC ASYLUM, STATE.

1830.	Report on the subject of building a,	A	4	408
1831.	Report on the same (Mr. Potter),	S	2	84
1831.	Report of a select committee on the same,	A	2	263
1832.	Report on the same (Mr. Kemble),	A	2	174
1834.	do (A. J. Parker),	A	4	347
1835.	do (Mr Herttell,)	A	3	167
1836.	Memorial of New York State Medical Society for the erection of a,	S	1	38
1837.	Report of commissioners appointed to locate the,	S	1	39
1839.	Statement of the commissioners to the governor,	S	1	2
1839.	Annual report of commissioners to build,	S	1	22
1839.	Report of select committee relative to the (Mr. Paige,)	S	2	39
1839.	Communication from F. E. Spinner relative to,	S	2	57
1840.	Annual report of commissioners,	S	1	2
1840.	Report of select committee relative to the (Mr. Herttell),	A	4	105
1841.	Letter from the commissioners to the governor,	S	1	2
1841.	Communication from the commissioners,	S	2	52
1841.	Annual report of commissioners,	A	2	26
1841.	Report of select committee relative to the,	A	3	61
1841.	Report of select committee relative to the (Mr. Pierpont),	A	7	262
1841.	Message from the governor transmitting a communication from one of the commissioners,	A	7	280
1842.	Report of, the commissioners of, to the governor,	A	1	2
1842.	Report of the trustees of, and documents accompanying same,	S	1	20
1843.	Report of the managers of,	A	3	50
1844.	Report of committee on medical societies, &c., on the bill relative to the,	S	4	127
1844.	Report of committee on medical societies, &c., on the bill relative to the,	S	4	128
1844.	Annual report of managers of,	A	1	21
1844.	Report of majority of select committee on so much of governor's message as relates to,	A	3	95
1844.	Report of minority of select committee on so much of governor's message as relates to,	A	3	94
1845.	Annual report of managers of,	A	1	29
1846.	Report of managers of,	S	1	25
1846.	Report of committee on medical societies, &c., relative to,	S	1	12
1846.	Report of committee on medical societies, &c., relative to,	S	2	58
1846.	Report of comptroller relative to payments from treasury on account of the,	S	2	61
1847.	Annual report of superintendent of,	S	1	30
1848.	Report of,	S	1	20
1849.	Report, sixth annual, of managers of State Lunatic Asylum,	A	2	90
1850.	Annual report of managers,	S	2	57
1851.	Managers' annual report,	S	2	42
1852.	Managers' report,	S	1	46

LUNATIC ASYLUM, STATE—*continued.*

		Doc.	Vol.	No.
1853.	Report of managers of,	S	1	27
1854.	Annual report of managers,	A	3	76
1854.	Report on part of message relative to,	S	2	84
1855.	Annual report of,	S	1	14
1855.	Report of committee on medical societies relative to commission to examine into, &c.,	S	1	27
1855.	Report of committee on state charitable institutions in reference to bill to establish a second,	A	4	91
1856.	Thirteenth annual report of trustees of,	A	4	120
1856.	Report on locating,	A	3	71
1857.	Fourteenth annual report of managers of,	A	1	15
1858.	Report on so much of governor's message as relates to the,	S	2	26
1858.	Fifteenth annual report of managers of,	S	2	55

LUNATICS IN STATE PRISONS, *see* State Prisons.

LUPIN, MARY, *see* Mary Gray.

LUSH, MICHAEL.

1833.	Report on petition for bounty lands,	A	4	278

LUSH, SAMUEL S.

1835.	Report on petition of, for remuneration for deficiency in the quantity of certain lands,	A	1	26
1835.	Report of committee on claims on the same,	S	2	33

LYMAN, ASA A., AND WILLIAM M. IRWIN.

1855.	Report of committee on claims on petition of,	A	4	88

LYME, TOWN OF.

1832.	Election of justices of the peace in, report relative to the,	A	4	291

LYNCH, MARGARET.

1857.	Report of committee on claims, adverse on petition of, for damages by overflow of Cornelius creek,	A	2	108

LYNDS, ELAM, *see* State Prison at Mount Pleasant.

1844.	Members of, relative to his removal, &c.,	S	2	91
1844.	Report of select committee thereon,	S	5	135
1844.	Report of select committee on the petition of,	S	4	135

LYON, JAMES.

1840.	Report on petition for compensation for stone taken from his quarry for the Oswego canal and for the payment of certain costs, &c.,	A	5	209

LYON, REUBEN.

1851.	Report of Committee on petition for canal damages,	A	2	35

LYSANDER TOWN OF.

1839.	School district No. 25 in, report concerning,	A	6	385
1832.	School district No. 25 in, report concerning,	S	3	89
1831.	Lot No. 75 in the township of, report relative to the sale of for non-payment of taxes,	S	1	46

M.

McANDREW, JANET.

		Doc.	Vol.	No.
1840.	Report on petition for certain land escheated to the state on the death of John G. Leake,........	S	4	117
1841.	Report on the same,..	A	7	268

McBRIDE, JAMES, Jr.

		Doc.	Vol.	No.
1856.	Report on petition of,.................	A	4	105

McBRIDE, JAMES, Jr., AND AARON VANDERPOOL. Executors.

		Doc.	Vol.	No.
1857.	Report of committee on claims adverse on petition of, for reappraisement of canal damages to lot,........................	A	1	44

McBRIDE, R., late superintendent on the Erie canal, *see* S. Mattison, Asa Campbell, J. Rogers.

McBRIDE, ROBERT.

		Doc.	Vol.	No.
1848.	Report on petition of,..	A	6	215
1849.	Report of select committee on petition, &c., of,................	A	3	193
1850.	Report on claim,..	A	4	64

McCABE, JAMES.

		Doc.	Vol.	No.
1850.	Report on petition,..	S	2	60
1851.	Report of committee on claim for canal damages,.............	A	1	15

McCARTHY, DENNIS.

		Doc.	Vol.	No.
1836.	Report of commissioners of the land office, on petition of Eliza McCarthy and Joanna Bant, for the release of the right of the state to the lands of,..................................	S	1	16
1836.	Report of majority of committee on the judiciary on the same,...	A	3	154
1836.	Report of minority,...	A	3	155

McCLENAHAN, WM.

		Doc.	Vol.	No.
1857.	Report of committee on claims favorable on petition of, for damages to house by water from the Erie canal,.............	A	1	36

McCLURE, GEORGE, *see* B. S. Brundage.

		Doc.	Vol.	No.
1830.	Report of comptroller on the petition of, relative to a mortgage executed to the people of the state by Benjamin S. Brundage,	S	1	19
1830.	Report of committee on finance on the same,..................	S	1	33

McCOMB, WILLIAM (an alien).

		Doc.	Vol.	No.
1839.	Report on petition to confirm the last will of William Boyes,....	A	3	81

McCONNELL AND WESTLAKE.

		Doc.	Vol.	No.
1836.	Report on petition of, for extra allowance for work done on the Chemung canal,..	A	4	280

McCRACKEN, WILLIAM.

		Doc.	Vol.	No.
1850.	Report on petition,..	S	2	62

McCREA, JAMES, *see* John Purmort and others.

McCREA, JOHN.

		Doc.	Vol.	No.
1831.	Report on petition of, for the pre-emptive right to a lot of land in Fort Covington,........	A	2	150
1831.	Report on the same,..	A	3	235

McCULLOCH, WILLIAM.

1834.	Report on petition of, for the release of certain escheated land,...	S	1	16

McDONALD, A. P. AND OTHERS.

1852.	Report on petition of, for relief,............................	S	1	36
1852.	Report on petition of,....................................	S	2	51

McDONALD, MERRILL AND BARNUM.

1842.	Report of committee on claims on petition of,................	A	5	111

McDONOUGH, TOWN OF.

1839.	Report on petition to incorporate a company to buy and sell articles of merchandize,.......	A	6	345

MACEDON, TOWN OF.

1831.	Road in, report on petition for the appointment of commissioners to lay out a,.....................................	S	1	34
1834.	First Baptist Society of, report on petition to sell certain real estate,...........	A	3	176

McGHEE, ALEXANDER.

1852.	Report on petition of, for relief,............................	S	1	22

McGUIRE, P. H.

1854.	Report on petition of,....................................	A	2	51

McHUGH, PETER TYLER.

1836.	Report on petition to change his name,......................	A	4	283

McINROY, DANIEL.

1830.	Report on petition for extra allowance for work done on the Champlain canal,.......................................	A	2	104
1840.	Report of committee on claims on the same,.................	A	6	220
1840.	Report of canal commissioners on the same,.................	A	8	279
1840.	Report of committee on grievances on the same,..............	A	7	295

McINTYRE, JOHN.

1858.	Report on bill directing payment of moneys to,...............	S	3	137

McINTYRE, JOHN, AND OTHERS.

1835.	Report on petition for a grant of surplus water in the Fort Edward feeder,..	S	2	74

McINTYRE, JOHN J., *see* Charles Baker, and others.

MACK, AARON B.

1836.	Report on petition for a law to refund to him the amount of principal and interest paid for certain land,................	A	4	292

McKINSTRE, SARAH, AND OTHERS.

1844.	Report of committee on claims on the petition of,.............	A	3	45
1849.	Report of committee on claims on petition of,................	A	3	155

McKINSTRY, JOHN.

		Doc.	Vol.	No.
1838.	Report on petition for the repayment of certain money paid for taxes, ...	A	2	36

McKINSTRY, SAMUEL.

1837.	Report on petition to change his name, ...	A	3	229

McKNIGHT, CHAS., deceased.

1845.	Report of attorney-general on petition of heirs of, for relief, ...	S	2	63
1845.	Report of committee on claims on same, ...	S	2	79

McLACHLIN, THOMAS.

1844.	Report of canal board on petition of, ...	A	5	109

McLACHLIN, WM.

1844.	Report of the canal board on the petition of, ...	A	5	109
1845.	Report of committee on claims relative to claim for relief of, ...	S	1	12
1845.	Report of committee on claims on the petition of, ...	S	1	26

McLAIN, CHARLES.

1835.	Report on petition of, to be released from further payments on a lot of land, ...	A	2	152
1835.	Report of committee on public lands on the same, ...	A	3	239

McLEAN, JOHN C.

1830.	Report on petition of, for relief in consequence of the sale of his land by mistake, ...	S	2	77
1831.	Report of commissioners of the land office on the same, ...	S	2	72
1832.	Report of the committee on claims on the same, ...	S	1	47
1832.	Report of the committee on claims on the same, ...	S	2	73
1832.	Report of the commissioners of the land office on the same, ...	S	2	98

McLENAHAN, WM.

1856.	Report on petition of, for relief, ...	A	3	83

McLEOD, ALEXANDER.

1841.	Correspondence between the authorities of this state and of the United States concerning, ...	A	7	292
1842.	Correspondence of the governor on the subject of, ...	A	1	2

McLOUGHLIN, CATHARINE.

1831.	Report on petition for an extension of a lease of certain land, ...	A	2	150

McLOUTH, WILLIAM W. AND C. OSGOOD, *see* Farmington School District.

McMAHAN, JAMES.

1830.	Report on petition for compensation for services, &c., in the last war, ...	A	4	393
1831.	Report of committee on claims on the same, ...	A	2	71

McMASTER AND MERRIT.

1844.	Report of committee on claims on petition of, ...	S	1	46
1853.	Report of committee on claims on petition of, ...	S	2	45
1854.	Report of judiciary committee on petition of, ...	S	1	15
1854.	Report of same on appeal from judgment of, ...	S	1	42

McNAIR, H. T.

		Doc.	Vol.	No.
1854.	Report on petition of,	A	3	107

McNAIR, JAMES.

1847.	Report on petition of,	A	8	253

MADISON COUNTY.

1833.	Commissioners of loans of, report on petition of,	A	3	156
1833.	First judge of, report on petition to confer on the equity powers upon sums less than $100,	A	4	323
1841.	Judges, governor's message in relation to proceedings on a complaint against the,	S	3	80
1837.	New county from part of, report on petition for a,	A	2	131
1833.	Sheriff of, report on petition for pay for transporting convicts, ..	A	2	85
1845.	Report of select committee on petition of two hundred democrats of, relative to Thos. W. Dorr,	A	7	248

REPORTS OF INSPECTORS OF BEEF AND PORK:

1830.	Annual report of J. Ingersoll,	A	2	142
1831.	do do	A	2	138
1832.	do do	A	2	100
1833.	do do	A	2	71
1834.	do do	A	3	195
1835.	do do	A	2	72
1836.	do do	A	2	94
1838.	Annual report of Henry Shapley,	A	3	116
1839.	do do	A	3	122
1840.	do do	A	4	111

MADISON, VILLAGE OF.

1831.	Report relative to highway labor in,	A	2	167

MAIL STEAMSHIP COMPANY, UNITED STATES.

1850.	Majority and minority reports concerning,	S	3	79

MAINE LAW, *see* Intoxicating Liquors.

MAINE, PAUL P.

1843.	Report of the attorney-general on the petition of,	A	3	58

MAINE, STATE OF.

1832.	Resolutions of the legislature of, relative to the tariff and internal improvements,	A	1	3
1833.	do do relative to nullification in South Carolina,	A	4	277
1836.	do do relative to slavery,	S	3	85
1836.	do do relative to the election of president, &c.,	A	4	310
1840.	do do relative to the public lands, ..	A	4	139
1840.	do do relative to the northeastern boundary,	A	7	305
1839.	Controversy between Maine and Georgia, resolution of the legislature of Georgia relative to the,	A	2	45
1840.	Resolution of the legislature of South Carolina relative to the, ..	A	5	167
1841.	Resolution of the legislature of Alabama relative to the,	A	4	125
1842.	Resolution of general assembly of, relative to one presidential term,	A	2	28
1843.	Joint resolution of legislature of,	S	3	87
1843.	Resolution of the legislature of,	A	4	115

Boundary line between Maine and New Brunswick, *see* Northeastern Boundary.

MALLORY, JAMES H., AND OTHERS.

		Doc.	Vol.	No.
1840.	Report on petition for extra allowance for work done on the enlarged Erie canal,........	A	3	87

MALLORY, OGDEN.

1833.	Report on petition for extra allowance for building locks on the Oswego canal,........	S	1	25
1833.	Report of committee on canals on the same,........	S	1	35
1833.	do do	S	2	84
1834.	do do	S	1	25
1839.	Report of committee on claims on the same,........	A	5	292

MALONE, TOWN OF.

1831.	Arsenal at, report as to its occupation as a school house,........	A	3	231
1832.	Fire company, report on petition to incorporate,........	A	3	204
1851.	Report on sale of arsenal lot,........	S	1	14

MANCHESTER, GEO. W.

1849.	Report of committee on canals on petition of,........	A	2	52

MANDEVILLE, JANE.

1849.	Report of committee on claims on petition of,........	A	3	187

MANG, JOHN JACOB.

1851.	Report of committee on bill for relief,........	A	2	28

MANHEIM, TOWN OF.

1837.	Report on petition relative to the support of the poor in the, ...	A	3	271
1839.	Road district, report on petition for a,........	A	2	49
1840.	Road from, to Cherry Valley, report on petition to repeal the law to lay out a,........	A	8	357

MANLIUS, TOWN OF.

1838.	Report on petition for a law to drain a swamp in the,........	S	2	59

MANLY. JAMES R.

1833.	Memorial of, in relation to the public health,........	S	2	121

MANN, G.

1854.	Report on petition of,........	A	4	140

MANN, GERRITT.

1855.	Report of committee on claims on petition of,........	A	4	113

MANOR OF RENSSELAERWYCK, *see* Albany county.

MANUFACTURING.

1848.	General law in relation to,........	S	1	28

MANUFACTURING CORPORATIONS, *see* Corporations.

MAP AND ATLAS OF THE STATE.

1830.	Report of surveyor-general relative to the publication of a, ...	A	2	189
1857.	Report of state engineer and surveyor in reply to resolution relative to the,........	A	2	114

MAPES, WM.

		Doc.	Vol.	No.
1854.	Report on petition of,	A	2	66

MAPS AND REVISED STATUTES.

1832.	Sent to the governors of the several states, report of secretary of state relative to,	A	4	305
1833.	Sent to the governors of the several states, report of secretary of state relative to,	A	1	19

MARBLETOWN, TOWN OF.

1834.	Bridge over Esopus creek at, report on petition to raise money by tax to build a,	A	3	215
1840.	Bridge over Rondout creek, report on petition to raise money to complete,	A	4	137

MARCELLUS, ALBERT.

1848.	Report on petition of,	A	3	123
1848.	Report of committee on claims on petition of,	A	5	153
1856.	Report on petition of,	S	2	83
1856.	Report on petition of,	A	3	27

MARCY, HENRY.

1848.	Report of canal board on petition of,	A	5	179

MARCY, W. L., *see* Governor.

1841.	Receiver of the City Bank of Buffalo, communication from in answer to a resolution of assembly,	A	4	144
1841.	Receiver of the City Bank of Buffalo, communication from in answer to a resolution of assembly,	A	5	159

MARINE HOSPITAL, *see* New York, Sandy Hook, &c.

MARKHAM, CHAUNCEY W., AND WIFE.

1839.	Report on petition for compensation for a house destroyed during the last war,	A	4	204
1840.	Report on petition for compensation for a house destroyed during the last war,	A	2	48

MARKS, SILAS H.

1848.	Report on petition of,	A	5	156

MARKS, SILAS H., AND OTHERS.

1848.	Report of committee on claims on petition of,	A	5	157
1847.	Report on petition of,	A	7	181

MARLETT AND DUNHAM.

1839.	Contractors for building certain locks on the Erie canal, report on petition of, for relief,	S	3	73
1839.	Report of canal board on the same,	A	2	31
1839.	Report of committee on claims on the same,	A	2	63
1839.	Report of canal commissioners on the same,	A	3	72
1844.	Report of committee on claims on the petition of,	A	3	97
1844.	Report of canal board on the petition of,	A	3	56

MARRIAGE.

1830.	Report of committee on the judiciary on the law concerning and the solemnization thereof,	A	4	361

MARRIAGE CONTRACT, *see* Divorce.

MARRIAGES, REGISTRY OF, *see* Births, &c.

MARRIED WOMEN, *see* Women, Married.

MARSELES, CORNELIA.

		Doc.	Vol.	No.
1833.	Report on petition for compensation for damages by the Erie canal,	S	2	92

MARSH, C. C., AND C. L. MORGAN, *see* W. L. Morgan.

MARSHALL AND KIRKLAND, TOWNS OF.

1830.	Report on petition from, relative to the survey of the tract set apart for the Brothertown Indians,	A	4	367

MARSHALL, JOHN.

1833.	Report on petition for compensation for the loss of his canal boat on the Mohawk river,	A	4	295

MARSHAL OF THE NORTHERN DISTRICT OF NEW YORK.

1841.	Communication from, relative to the census of the state,	A	2	31

MARTIN, AGNES.

1845.	Report of committee on claims on petition of,	A	5	172

MARTIN, MOSES L.

1850.	Report on bill for relief of,	A	5	124

MARVIN, LE GRAND.

1844.	Petition of, proposing amendments to the constitution,	S	1	36

MARVIN, THOMAS.

1850.	Report on petition of,	S	2	58

MARYLAND, STATE OF.

1834.	Resolutions of the legislature of,		relative to the tariff and the South Carolina ordinance,	A	1	11
1835.	do	do	for a reorganization of the militia,	A	1	22
1841.	do	do	and report on the subject of surrendering fugitives from justice,	S	3	88
1837.	do	do	to extend the franking privilege,	A	2	146
1841.	do	do	relative to the northeastern boundary,	A	6	215
1842.	do	do	concerning abolishing slavery,	A	7	140
1844.	do	do	respecting slavery,	A	7	193
1850.	do	do	relative to slavery,	A	8	194

MARYLAND, TOWN OF.

1838.	Report on petition to extend the time for the collection of taxes in,	A	3	159
1840.	Road from Benedict's mills in the, to the Erie canal, report concerning a,	S	3	77

MASON, ARNOLD, AND FREDERICK PRATT.

1837.	Report on petition for extra allowance for work done on the Chenango canal,	A	3	219

MASQUERADES, *see* New York.

MASSACHUSETTS, STATE OF.

Year	Subject	Doc.	Vol.	No.
1831.	Resolution of the legislature of, relative to certain late proceedings in Georgia,	S	1	64
1832.	do do relative to the northeastern boundary,	A	3	183
1832.	do do for a reorganization of the militia,	A	3	281
1833.	do do relative to nullification in South Carolina,	A	4	259
1833.	do do relative to the tariff, &c.,	A	2	115
1833.	do do relative to the public lands,	A	4	327
1833.	do do relative to a call for a convention of the states,	A	4	291
1834.	do do relative to lotteries,	A	2	77
1841.	do do relative to the public lands, the revenue laws, the re-eligibility of the president, and the north-eastern boundary,	S	3	89
1844.	do do relative to an amendment of the United States Constitution,	A	3	52
1844.	do do relative to Virginia,	A	7	170
1844.	do do relative to Texas,	A	7	175
1844.	Resolution of legislature of, &c.,	A	7	184
1844.	Resolution of general assembly of Virginia in reply to resolution of legislature of,	A	7	190
1845.	Concurrent resolution, offered by Mr. Van Schoonhoven, relative to South Carolina and,	A	1	26
1849.	Communication from secretary of state transmitting petition of inhabitants of the district of Boston Corner in, to be annexed to State of New York,	A	2	54
1849.	Report on annexation of Boston Corner in, to state of New York,	A	3	194

MASSACHUSETTS ANTIQUARIAN SOCIETY.

Year	Subject	Doc.	Vol.	No.
1839.	Circular from,	A	3	118

MASSENA, TOWN OF.

Year	Subject	Doc.	Vol.	No.
1837.	Report on petition to raise money by tax on the, to build a bridge across Grass river,	A	3	274

MASTERS, N., AND I. WEBB.

Year	Subject	Doc.	Vol.	No.
1832.	Report on petition for remuneration for deficiency in the quantity of certain land bought of the state,	A	3	177

MATHER, ELIHU.

Year	Subject	Doc.	Vol.	No.
1830.	Report of judge of the 8th circuit relative to the trial of, for the abduction of W. Morgan,	S	2	186

MATHER, JOHN C.

Year	Subject	Doc.	Vol.	No.
1853.	Communication from, in answer to a report and resolution of impeachment of the select committee of the assembly,	A	4	11

MATTEAWAN COMPANY, *see* Fishkill.

MATTEMERE, JOHN, AND WM. H. GIBSON.

Year	Subject	Doc.	Vol.	No.
1842.	Report of canal board on petition of,	A	5	102

MATTHEWS, JOHN P., AND ISAAC LEDYARD.

		Doc.	Vol.	No.
1845.	Report of canal board on petition of,	A	6	201
1847.	Report of committee on canals on petition of,	A	6	159
1845.	Report of committee on claims on petition of,	A	6	226
1848.	Report on petition of,	A	3	110

MATTHEWS, SAMUEL R.

1835.	Report on petition for relief for damages sustained by the seizure of his horse, sleigh, &c., for an evasion of the salt duties,	A	4	367

MATTISON, SIMON.

1835.	Report on petition for pay for lumber furnished by him for the Erie canal,	A	2	101
1835.	Report of committee on claims on the same,	A	3	221
1836.	Report of majority of committee on the same,	A	3	131
1836.	Report of minority of committee on the same,	A	3	132
1837.	Report by same committee on the same,	S	2	65

MATTISON, SIMON, AND OTHERS.

1843.	Report of committee on claims on petition of,	A	5	127
1849.	Report of canal appraisers on petition of,	A	3	145

MAY, HARVEY H., AND OTHERS.

1832.	Report on petition to erect a dam across Genesee river,	A	3	219

MAY, W., AND OTHERS.

1846.	Report on petition for relief of,	S	1	20

MAYFIELD, TOWN OF.

1849.	Report on petition to annex part of the, to the town of Perth,	A	6	246

MAYORS OF CITIES, *see* Cities, Mayors of.

MAYOTTE, FRANCIS, AND OTHERS.

1833.	Report on petition for bounty lands,	A	4	334

MEAD, JOHN.

1847.	Report of committee on claims on petition of,	A	2	83

MEARS, JAS. R. AND WM.

1852.	Report on petition of,	A	1	24

MEASURES AND WEIGHTS, *see* Weights and Measures.

MEASURE, STANDARD, for Bran and Shorts.

1839.	Report on petition to repeal a law requiring a,	A	6	366

MECHANICAL CORPORATIONS, *see* Corporations.

MECHANICS' ASSOCIATION, STATE.

1843.	Communication from, relative to a museum,	A	5	137

MECHANICS' LIEN LAW, *see* Lien Law.

MEDBURY, ALFRED, AND BYRON POOLE.

1853.	Report of committee on claims on petition of, for relief,	S	1	33

MEDICAL COLLEGES.

		Doc.	Vol.	No.
	ALBANY:			
1833.	Report of Regents of the university on petition to incorporate,...	A	4	288
1837.	Minority report on petition to incorporate,....................	A	3	172
1838.	Majority do do	A	3	149
1838.	Minority do do	A	5	253
1839.	Mr. Hull's report on petition to incorporate,..................	S	1	19
1839.	Mr. Pratt's report on petition to incorporate,.................	A	2	29
1840.	Majority report (Mr. Hull), on petition for aid,................	S	4	118
1840.	Minority report (Mr. Peck), on petition for aid,................	S	4	119
1840.	Report on bill to aid (Mr. King),..............................	A	3	91
1840.	Report on bill to aid (Mr. Trowbridge),........................	A	4	155
1841.	Report on petition for aid (Mr. Emmons),.......................	A	3	56
1844.	Report of the committee on colleges, academies and common schools, on the petition of the trustees of,....................	A	5	136
	BUFFALO:			
1850.	Report of committee on medical societies,......................	A	4	94
	DISPENSARIES, *see* Brooklyn, Buffalo, New York.			
	ECLECTIC CENTRAL NEW YORK:			
1852.	Report on petition and bill to incorporate the,................	A	5	108
	GENEVA, MEDICAL DEPARTMENT OF:			
1835.	Report on petition for power to confer the degree of Doctor of Medicine,..	A	3	182
1841.	Report on petition for aid to,.................................	A	3	62
	HOMŒOPATHIC:			
1846.	Report relative to the establishment of,.......................	S	4	108
	MANHATTAN:			
1830.	Memorial of Rutgers' Medical Faculty to incorporate the,........	S	2	74
1830.	Memorial of the students of Rutgers' Medical Faculty for the same,..	A	2	75
1830.	Memorial of the trustees of the College of Physicians and Surgeons against the said incorporation,......................	S	3	241
1830.	Memorial of Rutgers' Medical Faculty against the memorial of the College of Physicians and Surgeons,........................	S	4	297
	METROPOLITAN:			
1856.	Report of committee on medical colleges, &c., relative to,.......	S	2	82
	NEW YORK UNIVERSITY, MEDICAL FACULTY OF:			
1842.	Report of committee on medical colleges, &c., on petition of,....	A	5	125
	PHARMACY:			
1838.	Report on petition to amend the charter of the,................	A	3	101
1842.	Committee on medical colleges and societies, report on the petition of,..	S	3	71
1845.	Report of committee on medical societies and medical colleges on the petition of,..	S	1	32
1852.	Appropriation to,..	S	2	67
	PHYSICIANS AND SURGEONS, NATIONAL:			
1853.	Report of committee on medical societies against incorporating the,..	A	3	65
	PHYSICIANS AND SURGEONS, NEW YORK:			
1830.	Remonstrance of, against the establishment of a second medical school in the city of New York,............................	A	3	124
1830.	Memorial of, against the establishment of another medical college in New York,..	S	3	241

MEDICAL COLLEGES—*continued.*

		Doc.	Vol.	No.
1839.	Report on petition for aid to,	S	3	89
1845.	Report of committee on medical societies, &c., on aid to,	A	3	76
1846.	Report of committee on medical societies, &c., relative to,	A	2	44
	RUTGERS' MEDICAL FACULTY:			
1830.	Memorial of, for an act of incorporation by the name of "Manhattan College,"	S	2	74
1830.	Memorial of students of, for the same,	S	2	75
1830.	Memorial of professors of, in refutation of an attack on them by the College of Physicians and Surgeons,	S	4	297
	MEDICAL EDUCATION.			
1832.	General report of the committee on medical societies and colleges on the subject of (Mr. Milledoler),	A	2	171
1832.	Memorial of the Medical Society of New York for an alteration of the law regulating,	A	3	249
	MEDICAL PRACTICE.			
1843.	Report of select committee on petitions praying for the repeal of laws restricting,	A	3	62
1844.	Report of committee on public printing on the subject of printing the report of the select committee on repealing the laws restricting,	S	1	30
1844.	Report of select committee for a repeal of the laws restricting,	S	1	31
1844.	Report of select committee on petitions, praying for the repeal of laws restricting,	A	3	60
1846.	Report of committee on medical societies, &c., on Homœopathy, &c.,	A	4	125
1851.	Report of committee on medical societies and colleges, on petition of Dr. Wm. Turner, for penal enactment against bleeding,	A	5	148
	MEDICAL SCHOOLS.			
1831.	Report on petition for legal provision for supplying, with subjects for the study of practical anatomy,	A	3	246
1830.	Remonstrance of the State Medical Society against increasing the number of,	A	2	182
	NEW YORK:			
1840.	Report on petition of S. W. Frisbee and others, to incorporate a,	S	4	113
	MEDICAL SOCIETIES.			
1842.	Report of committee of,	S	4	105
1843.	Report of committee on, &c., relative to a society for the relief of widows and orphans of medical men,	S	2	53
1844.	Report of committee on, &c., on the petition of physicians of Tompkins county,	A	3	76
1846.	Report of committee on,	A	6	217
1850.	Report on,	A	8	188
	COUNTY:			
1839.	Report relative to the right of, to impose a tax on the admission of members, &c.,	A	2	199
	NEW YORK:			
1831.	Report on petition of the, for a law authorizing the said society to appoint a board of examiners, to be styled "The Faculty of Medicine and Surgery," with power to confer the degree of Doctor of Medicine and Surgery,	A	3	223
1831.	Remonstrance of the, against said report,	A	4	292

MEDICAL SOCIETIES—*continued.*

		Doc.	Vol.	No.
1832.	Report of Mr. Milledoler, introducing a bill authorizing the New York Medical Society to appoint a board of examiners to examine candidates for the degree of Doctor of Medicine, &c.,...	A	2	171
1832.	Remonstrance of the State Medical Society against said bill,.....	A	3	185
1832.	Memorial of the Medical Society of New York relative to said bill,	A	3	244
1832.	Remonstrance of 76 practitioners against the same,.............	A	3	246
1832.	Remonstrance of I. A. Smith and others, against the same,......	A	3	250
1832.	Memorial of the College of Physicians and Surgeons in favor of the same,..........	A	3	261
1832.	Remonstrance of I. M. Smith and others, against the same,......	A	3	262
1832.	Remonstrance of T. R. Beck and J. McNaughton against the same,	A	3	372
1832.	Report of committee on medical societies against the same,.... .	A	3	251
1832.	Memorial of, to amend the law regulating medical education, ...	A	3	249

STATE:

		Doc.	Vol.	No.
1830.	Memorial of, against increasing the number of medical schools, and relative to the botanic practice,..........	A	2	182
1832.	Remonstrance of, against the passage of the bill to regulate the practice of physic and surgery,..........	A	3	185
1832.	Memorial of the New York Medical Society against said remonstrance,..........	A	3	244
1836.	Memorial of the, recommending the erection of an asylum for the insane,..........	S	1	38
1844.	Memorial of,..........	S	2	55
1850.	Memorial of,..........	A	8	173
1850.	Transactions of,..........	A	8	174
1850.	Communication in regard to vital statistics,..........	S	3	80
1851.	Annual report of transactions,..........	A	4	125
1852.	Transactions of,..........	A	2	85
1853.	do	A	3	67
1854.	do	A	4	133
1855.	Annual report of,..........	A	5	135
1856.	Transactions of,..........	A	4	138
1857.	Annual report of,..........	S	2	77
1858.	Transactions of,..........	A	3	85

MEDICINE AND SURGERY.

1830.	Report on petition to repeal the laws regulating the practice of,..	A	3	217

MEDICINE, PRACTITIONERS OF.

1842.	Report of committee on medical colleges and societies on bill from assembly, to enable certain, to recover pay for their services,..........	S	4	105

FOREIGN:

1840.	Report on petition to repeal the law requiring them to undergo an examination before the Censors of the State Medical Society,	A	6	266
1841.	Report on petition of the Monroe County Medical Society to repeal or modify the law of 1836 relative to,..........	A	2	47

UNLICENSED:

1840.	Report on petition for a law more effectually restraining,........	A	8	346

MEDICINES AND MEDICAL COMPOUNDS.

1848.	Report relative to sale of,..........	A	2	20
1849.	Report of committee on medical societies and colleges on bill to prevent frauds in the manufacture and sale of patent medicines, nostrums, &c.,..........	A	3	184

MELICK, JOHN.

		Doc.	Vol.	No.
1834,	Report on petition to refund to him certain money paid for a pedlar's license,..	A	4	312

MEMBERS OF ASSEMBLY, *see* Assembly.

MEMBERS OF CONGRESS, *see* Congress.

MEMBERS OF LEGISLATURE, *see* Legislature.

MEMBERS OF SENATE, *see* Senate.

MENTZ, TOWN OF.

1830.	Report on petition of inhabitants of, relative to the Cayuga marshes,..	A	2	178

MERCHANDISE.

1839.	Report on petition to incorporate a company to buy and sell,....	A	6	345

MERCHANDISE, INSPECTION OF, *see* Inspectors, &c.

MERCHANDISE, WEIGHING OF, *see* New York.

MERCHANT, HORATIO, late Clerk of the Assembly.

1838.	Report on petition for certain relief,..............................	A	5	284
1841.	Report of committee on grievances on the same,...............	A	4	91

MERRIAM, ELA, AND JAMES WARD.

1857.	Report of committee on claims favorable on petition of, for damages by leakage of the Black River canal, &c.,................	A	2	96

MERRIAM, ELA N.

1857.	Report of committee on ways and means favorable on petition of, for payment of a canal draft,..................................	A	1	50

MERRIAM, J., AND OTHERS.

1844.	Report of canal board on the petition of,.......................	A	5	138

MERRIAM, JOHN.

1845.	Report of committee on claims on petition of,.................	A	3	74

MERRIAM, JOHN, AND OTHERS.

1838.	Report on petition of, for extra allowance for work on the Champlain canal,..	A	3	79
1839.	Report of committee on claims on the same,....................	A	3	87
1841.	Report of committee on claims on the same,....................	A	3	75
1846.	Report of committee on claims on petition of,.................	A	2	38

MERRIAM, W. S.

1841.	Report on petition of, for indemnification for liabilities and expenses incurred in protecting the state arsenal at Elizabethtown,	A	7	291

MERRILL, JOHN.

1852.	Report on petition of,..	A	2	66

MERRILL, JOHN—*continued.*

		Doc.	Vol.	No.
1853.	Report of committee on claims against further allowance to, for erroneous sale of lot,	A	2	53

MERRILL, McDONALD AND BARNUM.

1842.	Report of committee on claims on petition of,	A	5	111

MERRIMAN, JAMES.

1856.	Report on petition of,	A	4	128

MERRITT, ANDREW, AND ELIAS STONE.

1832.	Report on petition of, for a ferry across the Allegany river,	A	2	151

MERRITT & McMASTER.

1844.	Report of committee on claims on petition of,	S	1	46
1853.	Report of committee on claims on petition of,	S	2	45
1854.	Report of judiciary committee on petition of,	S	1	15
1854.	Report of same committee on appeal from judgment,	S	1	42

MERRY, SAMUEL, Jr.

1844.	Report of commissioners of land office on petition of John De Wolf, Jr., and others, heirs-at-law and legal representatives of,	A	3	71

MERSEREAU, DAVID.

1834.	Report on petition of, to maintain a dam across the Susquehanna river,	A	2	97

METEOROLOGICAL OBSERVATIONS.

1854.	Report of Regents of the University relative to,	A	2	72

METOXEN, JOHN, AND OTHERS.

1848.	Petition of, for relief,	A	3	81
1849.	Report on petition of,	S	2	45

METROPOLITAN POLICE.

1858.	Communication from attorney-general in reference to appointment of,	S	2	41

METROPOLITAN POLICE COMMISSIONERS.

1858.	Report of the,	A	3	80

METROPOLITAN POLICE DEPARTMENT.

1857.	Report of the majority of the committee on incorporation of cities and villages relative to the,	A	2	127
1857.	Report of minority of committee on same subject,	A	3	149

METROPOLITAN POLICE LAW.

1858.	Report relative to the,	A	1	40
1858.	Report of majority of committee on bill to repeal,	S	2	48
1858.	Report of minority of committee on same,	S	2	46
1858.	Petition for repeal of, by board of supervisors of Kings county,	S	2	66
1858.	Memorial of the mayor, aldermen and commonalty of the city of New York for the repeal of the,	S	2	74

MEXICAN WAR.

1848.	Resolution relating to,	S	1	3
1848.	Majority and minority reports on,	S	1	19

NEW YORK VOLUNTEERS IN.

		Doc.	Vol.	No.
1847.	Report on outfit of, in the service of the United States,	A	1	13
1847.	Report of adjutant-general as to organization of,	A	2	80
1847.	Report of adjutant-general relative to vacancies in office of volunteer regiments in Mexico,	A	6	151
1847.	Report relative to removal of remains of,	A	8	238
1848.	Report relative to,	A	3	93
1850.	Letter of governor of Mississippi relative to,	A	4	74
1850.	Report of select committee on,	A	6	163
1851.	Report of select committee on bill for relief of survivors of first regiment of,	A	3	58
1852.	Report on the act relative to,	S	1	48
1855.	Petition of, for relief,	A	1	14
1857.	Report of committee on militia and public defense in reply to resolution relative to, who were in actual service in,	A	2	133

MEXICO ACADEMY, *see* Academies, &c.

MICHIGAN, STATE OF.

1836.	Resolutions of the legislature of, relative to slavery,	S	2	77
1841.	Resolutions of same relative to a ship canal around the falls of St. Marie,	A	1	15
1843.	Communication from the governor transmitting a memorial, &c., of the legislature of,	A	4	103

MIDDLEBURGH BRIDGE COMPANY.

1831.	Report on petition to amend the charter of the,	S	1	39

MIDDLEBURY ACADEMY, *see* Academies.

MIDDLETOWN AND KINGSTON TURNPIKE ROAD.

1850.	Report relative to,	S	1	20

MIDLER, COLUMBUS C.

1858.	Report on claim of, for relief,	S	2	86

MILITARY ACADEMY AT WEST POINT.

1832.	Report on petition to prohibit the sale of wine and liquors to the students and soldiers at the,	A	3	228
1843.	Resolution of Connecticut relative to,	A	1	11
1844.	Resolution of Connecticut relative to,	A	1	7

MILITARY ASSOCIATIONS.

1839.	Report on petition of several, for acts of incorporation,	A	6	409

MILITARY CONVENTION, PROCEEDINGS OF.

1843.	Held 25th day of January, 1843,	A	3	46
1843.	Report of the joint committee on their communication,	S	3	114

MILITARY STORES.

1842.	Message of governor relative to arms and other,	S	2	27

MILITARY SYSTEM OF THE UNITED STATES.

1831.	Re-organization of the, resolutions of the legislature of Massachusetts for a,	A	3	281
1832.	do do resolutions of the legislature of Indiana for a,	A	3	183

MILITARY SYSTEM OF THE UNITED STATES—*continued.*

Year	Subject	Doc.	Vol.	No.
1833.	Re-organization of the, resolutions of the legislature of Illinois for a,	A	1	34
1833.	do do resolutions of the legislature of Delaware for a,	A	3	211
1833.	do do report of committee on the militia on the same,	A	2	80
1834.	do do resolutions of the legislature of New Hampshire for a,	A	1	11
1834.	do do resolutions of the legislature of North Carolina for a,	A	3	109
1835.	do do resolutions of the legislature of Maryland for a,	A	1	22
1836.	do do resolutions offered by Mr. Viele for the,	A	4	240
1837.	Resolutions offered by Mr. Willis to amend the law so as to exempt all persons under 21 and over 40 years of age,	A	3	246
1837.	Report on the same,	A	4	288

MILITIA.

Year	Subject	Doc.	Vol.	No.
1839.	Courts-martial, report on petition of officers of the 43d regiment to amend the law relative to,	A	6	398
1843.	Report of the committee on the, relative to brigade courts-martial,	S	3	74
1832.	Officers of, report on the subject of electing or appointing to office,	A	3	222
1832.	do minority report on the same,	A	3	223
1834.	do rendezvous by brigades of the, report on bill to provide for a, &c.,	A	4	370
1830.	Parades of, report on petition to reduce the number of,	A	2	179
1830.	do report on petition to reduce the number of,	S	3	206
1831.	do memorial against reducing the number of,	S	1	40
1832.	do report of adjutant-general on bill to reduce the number of,	S	1	4
1842.	Report of committee on militia and public defense in relation to the improvement of,	A	5	97
1846.	Memorial of Major D. S. Holcomb, and others, relative to,	S	2	67
1846.	Concurrent resolution offered by Mr Sherwood relative to,	A	1	13
1846.	Bill, report of minority of select committee on,	A	6	211
1846.	Report of committee on, respecting petition of inhabitants of Rensselaer county,	A	4	108
1846.	Minority of report on bills relative to,	A	6	211
1848.	Report of committee on, in relation to the organization of the 12th regiment of the 1st division of New York militia,	S	2	52
1849.	Report of adjutant-general in answer to resolution of assembly relative to non-commissioned officers and privates of uniform companies in 1st division of, &c.,	A	2	45
1851.	Report of committee on, and public defense on the governor's message,	A	3	54
1838.	Governor's message in relation to the expenses of the, called out to defend the frontier,	A	6	315
1838.	Report of committee on ways and means on the same,	A	6	348
1840.	Report on bill for the payment of the, called into the service of the state in December, 1839,	A	5	175
1838.	Organization of to suppress insurrection, &c., report relative to the,	A	6	324

MILITIA FINES.

Year	Subject	Doc.	Vol.	No.
1830.	Report on petition of P. Adams, sheriff of Genesee county, for the payment for board for persons imprisoned for the non-payment of,	A	4	423
1841.	Report on petition of the Society of Friends to be relieved from the payment of,	A	5	170
1830.	Report on petition to abolish imprisonment for non-payment of,	A	2	179

MILITIA FINES—*continued.*

		Doc.	Vol.	No.
1834.	Report on bill to exempt persons employed in nail factories, &c., from,	A	3	190
1847.	Report as to,	A	7	219
1851.	Report on bill for enrollment of the militia, to abolish fines and exempt uniform companies from highway tax and jury duty,	A	4	113
1853.	Report of Major-General Charles W. Sandford relative to moneys collected for, in New York,	A	2	30

MILITIA LAWS.

1843.	Report of committee on militia and public defense on petitions praying for amendments to,	A	3	42
1843.	Report of the minority of committee on same,	A	3	54
1843.	Report of the select committee on petitions for the repeal of,	A	5	172
1845.	Report of majority of committee on public defense on a modification of,	A	4	110
1845.	Report of minority of committee on public defense on a modification of,	A	4	109
1853.	Report of commissioners and adjutant-general in relation to codifying,	S	2	66

MILITIA SYSTEM.

1839.	Report on petition of several conventions of militia officers for a reform of the present (I. Armstrong),	A	6	410
1841.	Report of petition for a reform in the present (Mr. Hubbell),	A	6	223
1840.	Report on same (Mr. Lasak),	A	5	200
1844.	Report of committee on militia, &c., on the bill to improve the,	A	3	64
1851.	Report of adjutant-general as to its cost,	S	2	28

MILLARD, C. AND C.

1842.	Report of committee on claims on petition of,	A	5	112

MILL CREEK.

1843.	Report of canal commissioners relative to the plan to construct a reservoir on,	S	2	75

MILLER, ABSALOM C.

1841.	Report relative to the right of, to a seat as a member of assembly from the city of New York,	A	2	17

MILLER, JOHN.

1841.	Report on petition of, to confirm his title to certain land,	S	2	58

MILLER, JULIUS F. H.

1852.	Report on petition of, to change his name,	S	1	24

MILLER, MARIAH.

1851.	Report of committee on claims,	A	4	95

MILLER, RUTGER B.

1858.	Memorial of, relative to the regulation of the currency,	S	2	71

MILLER, S., Jr.

1834.	Report on petition of, relative to the mode of settling disputes in school districts,	S	1	43

MILLIGAN, FREDERICK (a slave sold by the commissioners of sequestration).

		Doc.	Vol.	No.
1832.	Report on petition of, for the payment to him of the amount for which he was sold,	A	3	213

MILLINER, J. D.

1854.	Report on petition of,	A	3	81
1858.	Report on claim of,	A	4	87

MILLINER, JOHN D.

1857.	Report of committee on claims favorable on petition of, for damages by sinking of a canal boat,	A	1	23
1857.	Report of committee on claims adverse on petition of, for damages by sinking of a canal boat,	A	2	98

MILLS, B. H., AND L. C. GROVER.

1857.	Report of committee on claims favorable on petition of, for damages by construction of embankment and wall in front of their building,	A	3	159

MILLS, COL. JOHN.

1843.	Report on the petition of the officers and members of the Albany Republican Artillery Company for leave to erect a monument in Capitol Park to the memory of the late,	A	5	145

MILLS, DAVID S.

1855.	Report of committee on privileges and elections on petition of,..	A	2	46

MILLS, WARREN.

1847.	Report on petition of,	A	7	204

MILLS, WARREN, AND OTHERS.

1848.	Report of committee on claims on petition of,	A	5	150
1849.	Report of committee on claims on petition of,	A	2	59
1850.	Report of committee on grievances on petition of,	S	2	45

MILLS, WM. A.

1847.	Report on petition of,	A	4	112

MILTON, TOWN OF.

1832.	Report on petition to raise money by tax for the support of bridges in,	A	4	290

MINA, TOWN OF.

1832.	Report on petition for the division of the,	S	2	91
1832.	Report on petition of J. R. Keeler & Co. relative to the assessment of personal property in the,	A	2	142

MINARD, JOSEPH.

1831.	Son of a Canadian refugee, report on petition for bounty lands,..	A	2	181
1833.	Report of committee on claims on the same,	A	3	182
1835.	Report of committee on claims on the same,	A	3	231

MINDON, TOWN OF.

1848.	Report on annexation of Canajoharie to,	A	3	96
1848.	Report on petition of,	A	3	100

MINING COMPANY, NORTH AMERICAN.

		Doc.	Vol.	No.
1832.	Report on petition to incorporate,	A	1	40
1832.	Report on petition to incorporate,	A	2	72

MINISINK, TOWN OF.

1839.	Report on petition to extend the time for the collection of taxes in the,	A	5	288
1837.	Report on petition to raise money to build a bridge over the Wal-kill,	A	2	127

MINISTERS OF THE GOSPEL.

1830.	Report on petition to vacate the seat of Hon. W. Fox, a member of assembly, on account of his being a,	A	4	376
1838.	Report on petition to repeal the laws exempting them from taxation, to prohibit them from acting as inspectors of common schools, &c.,	A	5	262
1839.	Report on petition to repeal the laws exempting them from taxation,	A	4	180
1840.	Report of committee on ways and means on the same,	A	5	182
1841.	Report of committee on judiciary on the same,	A	6	226
1850.	Report on exemption from taxation,	A	5	117

MINORS.

1840.	Message from the governor returning, with objections, the bill for the protection of,	S	3	85

MINUSE, JOHN.

1838.	Report on petition of, for a water grant to build a wharf in the town of Rye,	A	6	312
1838.	Report of commissioners of the land office on the same,	A	6	322

MISSIONARY CONVENTION, STATE BAPTIST, *see* Baptist Missionary Convention.

MISSIONARY LOT IN WESTMORELAND, *see* Westmoreland.

MISSISSIPPI, STATE OF.

1830.	Resolutions of the legislature of, for a revision of the tariff laws,	A	1	13
1831.	do do relative to the election of president,	A	1	4
1833.	do do relative to the nullification in South Carolina,	A	4	259
1833.	do do on the call for a convention of the states,	A	4	291
1836.	do do relative to the abolitionists,	A	4	301
1841.	do do relative to the controversy between Virginia and New York,	S	2	56
1841.	do do relative to the policy of a protective tariff,	A	6	235
1842.	Resolution of, relative to the annexation of Texas to the United States,	A	7	199
1844.	Resolution of the legislature of,	A	7	202
1850.	Letter of governor of, respecting Mexican volunteers,	A	4	74
1850.	Resolutions of, on slavery,	A	8	179
1850.	Letter of governor of, relative to volunteers in Mexican war,	A	8	188

MISSOURI, STATE OF.

1830.	Resolutions of the legislature of, relative to the election of president and vice-president, and relative to the power of congress to appropriate money to aid the colonization society,	A	1	13

MISSOURI, STATE OF—*continued.*

		Doc.	Vol.	No.
1839.	Resolutions of the legislature of, relative to the public lands,....	A	6	328
1840.	Resolutions of the legislature of, relative to slavery,............	A	4	143
1847.	Resolution of legislature respecting the federal army,..........	A	6	164
1849.	Resolutions of general assembly of, respecting slavery,.........	A	5	229

MITCHELL, AGNES.

1842.	Report of committee on claims on petition of,..................	A	2	21
1842.	Report of committee on claims on petition of,,................	A	2	22
1843.	Report of the committee on claims on the petition of,..........	S	1	26

MITCHELL, JAMES.

1835.	Report on petition for relief, on account of the loss of his eyesight by the blasting of rocks at Lockport,..................	A	1	153

MITCHELL, T., & T. J. BROWN.

1855.	Report of committee on claims on petition of,..................	A	2	51

MOBS.

1838.	Property destroyed by, report relative to,....................	A	5	240

MOGER, HULDAH, *see* Joseph Hubbard.

MOHAWK AND HUDSON RAILROAD, *see* Railroads.

MOHAWK AND ST. LAWRENCE RAILROAD, *see* Railroads.

MOHAWK BRIDGE COMPANY.

1835.	Report on memorial of, relative to the location of the eastern section of the Utica and Schenectady railroad, &c.,............	A	4	303
1835.	Report on petition for a law requiring the, to remove certain obstructions or reduce the rates of toll,......................	A	5	396
1836.	Report on petition of the, to prevent the Utica and Schenectady Railroad Company from building a bridge over the Mohawk at Schenectady,....................................	A	4	232
1837.	Report on petition of, for legislative construction of the act incorporating, &c.,....................................	S	2	54

MOHAWK INDIANS, *see* Indians, Mohawk.

MOHAWK RIVER.

1830.	Report on petition to annex two certain islands lying in the north forks of the, to Rensselaer county,.......................	A	4	346
1834.	Surplus waters of, report of canal commissioners relative to the,	A	4	359
1835.	Towing-path bridge on the, report of canal board relative to the,	A	4	364
1841.	Bridge over, near the lower aqueduct, report of canal board relative to a,..	A	6	233
1846.	Petition for extension of Troy and Schenectady Railroad on south side of,..	A	2	36
1848.	Bridge over, at Fultonville, report of committee on petition of inhabitants of Fulton and Montgomery counties respecting erection of,..	A	2	73

MONELL, JOSEPH D., AND OTHERS.

1853.	Resolution of Mr. Beekman on petition of,..................	S	2	68

MONELL, ROBERT.

		Doc.	Vol.	No.
1832.	Report of amount of fees received by him as circuit judge,......	A	2	135

MONGIN, F. A.

1845.	Report of committee on aliens for relief of,....................	A	5	169

MONROE COUNTY.

1840.	Bridge across the Genesee, in the town of Chili, report on petition to raise money by tax to build a,.....................	A	6	248
1833.	Clerk's office, report on petition to raise money to build a,......	A	1	20
1836.	Clerk's office, report on petition to raise money to build a,......	A	4	286
1840.	Clerk of, report on petition to require him to perform certain duties without compensation,..................................	A	1	21
1847.	Dam across Genesee river, report of committee on canals on petition of citizens of, relative to,..........................	A	7	182
1840.	District attorney, report on petition to make the office of, a salary office,..	A	1	21
1837.	Excise laws, report on petition relative to licensing retailers of ardent spirits,..	A	1	40
1837.	Report of committee on two-third bills on bill relative to the same,	A	4	807
1831.	Inspectors of beef and pork, annual report of John Brace,.......	A	2	154
1832.	do do do	A	2	111
1833.	do do do	A	3	172
1834.	do do do	A	3	184
1835.	do do do	A	3	207
1836.	do do do	A	3	123
1837.	do do do	A	2	106
1832.	do do do M. G. Woodbury,..	A	2	105
1833.	do do do	A	3	234
1830.	Inspector of flour, annual report of John Brace,................	A	2	103
1830.	Inspector of lumber, annual report of A. Hubbard,..............	A	1	29
1831.	Inspector of lumber, annual report of A. Hubbard,..............	A	4	341
1830.	Inspectors of sole leather, annual report of Isaac Leonard,.......	A	2	117
1831.	do do do	A	2	125
1832.	do do do	A	2	152
1833.	do do do	A	2	91
1834.	do do do	A	3	138
1835.	do do do	A	3	184
1836.	do do do	A	3	179
1837.	do do do	A	2	144
1839.	do do do	A	4	230
1840.	do do do	A	3	89
1831.	do do do E. Higgins,..........	A	2	163
1840.	do do do Waterman Davis.....,	A	4	157
1831.	Jail in, report on petition to raise money to build a,............	A	1	18
1832.	Jail in, report on petition to raise money to build a,............	A	1	13
1841.	Medical society of, report on petition to repeal or modify the law of 1836 relative to foreign practitioners,....................	A	2	47
1837.	Poor-house and farm, report on petition to sell the,............	A	2	76
1837.	Report on petition of the board of health, in the town of Greece, for the payment of certain moneys expended in 1832,........	A	4	319

BANKS in, *see* Banks—Monroe County.

CANAL FEEDER DAM, *see* Genesee River.

MONTANYE, ISAAC L.

1847.	Report on petition of Isaac L. Hasbrouck to be admitted to seat occupied by,..	A	1	16

MONTAUK LANDS.

1848.	Report of select committee relative to,.......................	A	1	12

MONTEZUMA SALT SPRINGS, *see* Salt.

MONTEZUMA, VILLAGE OF.

		Doc.	Vol.	No.
1834.	Turnpike and Bridge Company, report of attorney-general on petition to repeal the charter of,	A	4	342
1850.	Report of canal commissioners as to supply of water between Tonawanda and,	S	2	41

MONTGOMERY AND NEW YORK MINING COMPANY.

1851.	Report respecting,	A	3	79

MONTGOMERY, COUNTY OF.

1833.	Criminal expenditures of, report on bill in relation to,	A	4	246
1833	Sheriff of, report on petition of, for pay for transporting convicts,	S	1	31
1833.	Supreme court commissioner at Johnstown, report on petition for a,	S	1	40
1837.	Poor-house, report in relation to the sale of the,	A	2	121
1838.	Poor-house, abuses in the, report relative to,	A	6	360
1840.	Debts and assets of, report on petition for a division of the,	A	4	136
1849.	Report of committee on roads and bridges on petition of citizens of Fulton and, relative to the erection of a bridge over the Mohawk at Fultonville,	A	2	73

COUNTY BUILDINGS :

1836.	Report on bill to remove the, to the village of Fonda,	A	2	93
1836.	Majority report on the same,	A	2	104
1836.	Minority report on the same,	A	3	123
1837.	Report on bill to authorize the sale of the,	A	1	37
1837.	Report on petition to raise money to complete the,	A	1	48
1838.	Report on petition for a loan to complete the,	A	4	180

DEAF AND DUMB INSTITUTION IN, *see* Deaf and Dumb.

MONTGOMERY, VILLAGE OF, ORANGE COUNTY.

1840.	Report on bill erecting a road district in,	S	3	93

MONUMENT.

1839.	To De Witt Clinton, report relative to the erection of a,	A	4	215
1839.	To George Clinton, D. D. Tompkins and General Herkimer, report relative to the erection of,	A	6	392
1839.	Report on petition for the appropriation of certain funds for the same,	A	5	321
1840.	Report in relation to the same,	A	3	101
1839.	Over the remains of the crew and passengers of the ships Bristol and Mexico, report on bill for the erection of a,	A	6	341
1839.	Minority report on the same,	A	6	349
1843.	To Colonel John Mills, report on petition of the Albany Republican Artillery Company for leave to erect, in the Capitol park,	A	5	145
1848.	To David Williams, report on bill to erect,	A	3	76
1852.	In Independence Square, Philadelphia, resolutions of common council of Philadelphia relative to erecting,	S	1	6
1853.	Proceedings of a convention respecting same,	A	4	89
1853.	Report of select committee on governor's message respecting the same,	A	4	102

MONUMENT ASSOCIATION, *see* Newburgh.

MOODY, SIMEON D.

1857.	Report of committee on state prisons favorable on petition of, for payment for goods furnished to Sing Sing State Prison,	A	2	99

Year	Entry	Doc.	Vol.	No.
	MOOERS, BENJAMIN.			
1833.	Report on petition of, for the re-payment of certain money paid into the treasury by mistake,	A	2	73
	MOOERS, TOWN OF.			
1830.	Report concerning the poor moneys of the,	A	4	313
	MOON, JOHN.			
1831.	Report on petition of, for an extension of his lease of certain land,	A	3	254
	MOORE, JOHN.			
1831.	Report on petition of, for an extension of his lease of certain land,	A	3	150
	MOORE, JONAH, *see* J. Conrad.			
	MOORE, ROBERT L., *see* Cyrus P. Dunham and others.			
	MOORE, ZEBULON.			
1849.	Report on petition of,	S	1	12
1850.	Report on petition,	A	4	73
	MOOSE AND RAQUETTE RIVERS.			
1850.	Report of select committee on,	A	4	68
	MOOT, JOHN.			
1846.	Report of commissioners of land office on petition of, for relief,	S	1	8
	MORAN, PATRICK.			
1856.	Report on petition for relief,	A	3	51
	MORGAN, JONATHAN, *see* S. Stillman.			
	MORGAN, WILLIAM.			
1830.	Abduction of, report of special counsel (J. C. Spencer), on the subject of the,	S	1	67
1830.	do report of judge of the eighth circuit relative to the trial of Elihu Mather for the,	S	2	185
1830.	do report of attorney-general relative to the charges against the Grand Chapter of Freemasons relative to the,	A	4	417
1830.	do report of amount paid to the special counsel,	S	3	254
1831.	do a letter from the special counsel (V. Birdseye) to the governor relative to the trials for the,	A	1	3
1831.	do letter from the same concerning the special circuit court and court of oyer and terminer in Niagara county,	A	1	39
1831.	do letter from the same,	A	1	39
1831.	do report of select committee on the same,	A	1	54
1831.	do report of special counsel in relation to the trials for the,	A	4	353
	MORGAN, WILLIAM L.			
1834.	Report on petition of the executor and executrix of the last will, &c., of,	S	2	75
	MORIN, JOHN, AND OTHERS.			
1845.	Report of attorney-general on petition of, heirs of C. McKnight,	S	2	63
1845.	Report of committee on claims on same,	S	2	79

MORRELL & LE VALLEY.

		Doc.	Vol.	No.
1852.	Report on petition of,....	S	2	53

MORRIS MINING COMPANY.

1839.	Report on petition to incorporate,....	A	6	338

MORTGAGES.

1838.	Of personal property, report on bill requiring them to be filed in town clerks' and other offices,....	A	3	193
1838.	Of personal property, report on a resolution relative to (Mr. Ogden),....	A	3	111
1852.	Report on taxation of real estate and,....	S	1	28
1855.	Report of committee on banks in reference to, as a basis for banking,....	A	3	70

MORTGAGES, FORECLOSURE OF.

1834.	By advertisements, report on bill to amend the Revised Statutes relative to the,....	A	3	247
1839.	Report concerning the (Mr. Edwards),....	S	1	28
1839.	Report concerning the (Mr. Healy),....	A	6	407
1840.	Report of the number of bills filed for the, *see* Chancery, clerks in.			
1843.	Report of committee on judiciary on the subject of,....	A	4	89

MOSELEY, DANIEL.

1832.	Report of amount of fees received by him as circuit judge,....	A	2	134

MOSHER & VAN ALSTYNE.

1854.	Report of committee on claims on petition of,....	A	3	98

MOSHER, DIGHTON.

1849.	Report on petition of,....	A	6	166

MOSHIER, DAVIDSON.

1849.	Report of committee on claims on petition of,....	A	3	113

MOSS, J. B.

1847.	Report on petition of,....	A	7	185

MOSS, JARED B.

1850.	Report on petition,....	S	3	86

MOSS, SOLOMON.

1848.	Report as to claim of seat in assembly,....	A	5	147

MOTT, S. M.

1833.	Sheriff of Oneida county, report on petition for pay for transporting convicts,....	A	2	85

MOTT, THOMAS.

1841.	A soldier of the revolution, report on petition of the heirs of, for bounty lands,....	A	6	240
1843.	Report of committee on claims on petition of,....	A	4	79
1843.	Report of same committee on a bill for the relief of his heirs,....	S	3	107

MOTT, THOMAS—*continued.*

		Doc.	Vol.	No.
1843.	Report of committee on claims on bill for relief of the heirs of,..	S	3	117
1844.	Report of committee on claims on the petition of children of,...	A	3	79
1847.	Report of committee on claims on petition of John M. Still and wife for relief to heirs of,....	A	1	33
1848.	Report relating to claim of, ...	S	2	38

MOTT, TIMOTHY.

		Doc.	Vol.	No.
1849.	Report on petition of,....	S	1	17

MOUNT HOPE AND LUMBERLAND TURNPIKE COMPANY.

		Doc.	Vol.	No.
1832.	Report on petition of the, to sell certain lands,....	A	3	214
1833.	Report on petition to levy a tax on the present stock of said company to pay a certain debt, ...	A	4	316
1834.	Report on petition to amend the charter of,....	A	3	219

MOUNT MORRIS DAM.

		Doc.	Vol.	No.
1839.	Report on petition of the proprietors of, to have a certain bond canceled,....	S	3	95
1840.	Report on petition of the proprietors of, to have a certain bond canceled,....	S	3	81

MOUNT PLEASANT ACADEMY, *see* Academies.

MOUNT PLEASANT PRISON, *see* State Prisons.

MOWREY, WASHINGTON JEFFERSON.

		Doc.	Vol.	No.
1844.	Report of canal board on the petition of,....	A	3	49

MUGGLEWORTH, JANE.

		Doc.	Vol.	No.
1844.	Report of commissioners of the land office on the petition of,...	A	3	42

MULBERRY TREE.

		Doc.	Vol.	No.
1832.	Report on bill to encourage the propagation of the,....	S	2	101
1832.	Report relative to giving a bounty upon the cultivation of the, ..	A	3	176

MUMFORD, JOHN I.

		Doc.	Vol.	No.
1836.	Communication from, relative to Commercial Bank investigation,	S	2	107

MUNSON, A., & CO., *see* Thomas Geary and others.

MUNSON, ALFRED.

		Doc.	Vol.	No.
1844.	Report of committee on claims on petition of,....	S	1	24

MUNSON & HART, AND OTHERS.

		Doc.	Vol.	No.
1843.	Report of committee on claims on the petition of, ...	A	3	78
1846.	Report on petition for relief of,....	S	1	19

MUNSON, MERRITT.

		Doc.	Vol.	No.
1838.	Report on petition of, to confirm his official acts as a justice of the peace, ...	S	1	16

MURDER.

		Doc.	Vol.	No.
1847.	Trials for, report relative to,....	A	2	47

Punishment by death for, *see* Capital Punishment.

MURDOCK, E.

		Doc.	Vol.	No.
1846.	Report on petition for relief of,	S	3	77

MURDOCK, EBENEZER.

1853.	Report of committee on claims on petition of, for relief,	S	2	62

MURPHY, JACOB AND PETER.

1834.	Report on petition of, to allow them to repair a mill-dam across the Schoharie creek,	A	4	321

MURRAY, DAUPHIN.

1843.	Report of committee on claims on petition of,	S	2	65

MURRAY, DAVID.

1843.	Report of the canal board on the petition of,	S	1	28
1843.	Report of committee on claims on the petition of,	S	2	64

MURRAY, EDWARD.

1853.	Report of committee on claims on petition of, for relief,	S	1	32
1853.	Report of committee on claims on petition of, for relief,	S	2	35
1854.	Communication from auditor of canal department relative to,	A	2	70

MURRAY, GEORGE.

1847.	Report of comptroller on petition of,	S	1	17

MURRAY, GEORGE W.

1846.	Report on petition for relief of,	S	1	22
1847.	Report on petition of,	S	3	88
1848.	Report in relation to petition of,	S	1	26
1849.	Report on petition of,	S	1	13

MURRAY, MARY, *see* Susan Ogden.

MURRAY, MARY, AND OTHERS.

1844.	Report of the canal board on the petition of,	A	1	22
1844.	Report of committee on claims on the petition of,	A	3	51
1845.	Report of committee on claims on petition of,	A	4	147
1849.	Report of committee on claims on petition of,	A	3	128
1855.	Report of committee on ways and means on petition of,	A	1	22
1855.	Report of committee on ways and means on petition of,	A	3	67

MUTUAL INSURANCE, *see* Insurance.

MUZZY, AMOS W.

1847.	Report on petition of,	S	1	36
1848.	Report on petition of,	A	3	62

MYERS, I., *see* R. G. Gilman.

MYERS, JOHN.

1842.	Report of committee on canals on petition of,	A	7	179
1843.	Report of the committee on claims on the petitions of,	S	1	27

MYERS, MANUEL.

1842.	Report of committee on petition of representatives of,	A	5	115
1842.	Report on petition of representatives of,	A	5	117
1843.	Report of commissioners of land office relative to his claim,	S	3	78

MYERS, M. S.

		Doc.	Vol.	No.
1848.	Report of committee on judiciary on petition of, ...	S	1	25

MYGATT, AUSTIN.

1840.	Report on bill for the relief of, ...	S	3	82

MYNDERSE, EDWARD, AND OTHERS.

1845.	Report of canal appraisers on petition of,....................	A	3	46

MYRTLE AVENUE AND JAMAICA PLANKROAD.

1853.	Report in relation to increase of capital,.....................	A	4	96

N.

NADEAU, BASIL, a Canadian refugee.

1833.	Report on petition of, for bounty lands,......................	A	2	52

NATIONAL BANK, *see* United States Bank.

NATIONAL DOMAIN, *see* United States Public Lands, &c.

NATIONAL REVENUE, *see* United States.

NATURAL HISTORY, STATE.

1843.	Report of the select committee on an act in relation to the,......	A	4	82
1844.	Report of secretary of state in relation to,......................	A	3	87
1845.	do do in relation to the bill respecting, passed May 3d, 1844,...............	S	1	6
1845.	do do in relation to the books of,.........	S	1	43
1845.	do select committee in relation to,.....................	S	3	123
1845.	do minority of same select committee,.....................	S	3	124
1845.	do judiciary committee in relation to,....................	S	3	125
1846.	do Regents of the University on the condition of the cabinets of,...............................	S	3	91
1846.	do governor and secretary of state relative to,............	A	2	41
1846.	do select committee on,................................	A	5	172
1849.	Communication from governor in relation to completing publication of,..	A	3	154
1849.	Report of select committee on so much of governor's message as relates to the publication of,.................................	A	3	179
1850.	Report of select committee on,.................................	A	1	9
1851.	Geological report of committee appointed to take charge of publication of,..	A	4	124
1852.	Report of commissioners to superintend the completion of the printing of the,...	A	1	23
1853.	Report of the commissioners appointed to superintend the publication of,..	A	3	74
1854.	Report of commissioners of publication of,.....................	A	2	71
1855.	do do to superintend publication of,.........	A	2	53
1856.	do do appointed to superintend the completion of,..........................	A	4	150
1856.	do select committee,..	A	5	211
1857.	Annual report of the commissioners appointed to superintend the publication of, in reply to resolution relative to cost of,.......	A	2	117
1857.	Annual report of commissioners appointed to superintend the publication of the,.......................................	A	2	120
1858.	Report of commissioners to complete the,......................	A	4	120

NATURAL HISTORY, STATE CABINET OF.

		Doc.	Vol.	No.
1849.	Annual report of the Regents of the University on the condition of,........	S	1	20
1850.	Report of the Regents of the University respecting,.............	S	2	75
1851.	Annual report of the Regents of the University on,.............	S	2	30
1852.	Annual report of the Regents of the University concerning,.....	A	5	122
1853.	Sixth annual report of the Regents on the condition of, and the historical and antiquarian collections annexed thereto,.......	S	1	16
1854.	Report of Regents relative to,..............................	S	1	50
1855.	Annual report of Regents on,................................	S	2	40
1856.	Report of Regents relative to,..............................	S	3	112
1857.	Annual report of Regents on,................................	S	3	109
1858.	Report of Regents relative to,..............................	A	6	163

NATURALIZATION OF FOREIGNERS.

1845.	Report of committee on the judiciary on petition of inhabitants of Sullivan county in reference to,......................	A	7	245

NAVY, SECRETARY OF, *see* United States.

NAVY YARD, *see* Brooklyn.

NEBRASKA AND KANSAS TERRITORIES.

1856.	Report of select committee on message relative to,.............	S	2	91

NEELYTOWN.

1832.	Associate Reformed Congregation in, report on petition to change the name of,...............................	A	4	282

NEFF, DERICK, AND P. FORNCROOK, *see* W. Lowell.

NELLIS, ABRAHAM, AND OTHERS.

1857.	Report on petition of,....................................	S	3	88

NELSON & PHILLIPS, *see* Phillips & Nelson.

NEVERSINK NAVIGATION COMPANY.

1830.	Loan to the, report of comptroller relative to the,.............	A	1	49
1830.	do report on memorial of the president for a further loan,.....................................	S	4	358
1833.	do report of attorney-general on petition to be released from the payment of the,....................	A	4	262
1836.	do report on bill to provide for the liquidation of the stock loaned to the,........................	S	1	60

NEVERSINK RIVER.

1847.	Report relative to bridge over, and bill for same,...............	A	2	67

NEWARK, TOWN OF.

1836.	School district No. 7, report concerning,......................	A	4	216

NEWARK, VILLAGE OF.

1853.	Report on petition of inhabitants of, praying for the removal of the county buildings to Newark,..........................	A	2	53

NEW BERLIN.

1841.	School district No. 16 in, report on petition of the trustees of,...	A	5	188
1841.	School district No. 16 in, report on petition of the trustees of,...	A	7	275

NEWBURGH.

		Doc.	Vol.	No.
1833.	North River Whaling Company, report on bill to incorporate,...	A	4	313
1838.	Washington Monument Association, report on petition to incorporate the,......	A	6	320
1839.	Washington Monument Association, report on petition to incorporate the,......	A	6	356
1840.	Report on petition to extend the time to organize the same,.....	A	8	349
1851.	Correspondence concerning same,......	A	5	144
1850.	Washington's head-quarters, report of select committee concerning,......	A	5	122
1851.	Washington's head-quarters, report respecting,......	A	3	57
	BANK, *see* Banks—Orange County.			

NEWCOMB, THOMAS W. AND D.

		Doc.	Vol.	No.
1833.	Report on petition of, relative to certain lands,......	A	4	307
1835.	Report of the commissioners of the land office on the same,.....	A	4	397
1835.	Report of the surveyor-general on the same,......	A	3	257

NEWCOMB, TOWN OF.

		Doc.	Vol.	No.
1831.	Report on petition to increase the fees of collectors in the,......	A	1	63

NEWELL, GEORGE W.

		Doc.	Vol.	No.
1833.	Report of commissioners of the canal fund in relation to certain moneys paid to him,......	A	4	271
1855.	Communication from attorney-general in relation to suit against,	A	5	122

NEWELL, ISAAC.

		Doc.	Vol.	No.
1840.	Report on petition to be restored to the rights of citizenship,....	A	4	130

NEWELL, SAMUEL H.

		Doc.	Vol.	No.
1835.	Report on petition to change his name,......	A	1	23

NEWFIELD, TOWN OF.

		Doc.	Vol.	No.
1833.	Highway labor in, report concerning,......	A	4	254

NEW GRENADA.

		Doc.	Vol.	No.
1855.	Report relative to improvement of roads in,......	S	2	64

NEW GRENADA CANAL AND STEAM NAVIGATION CO.

		Doc.	Vol.	No.
1855.	Report of committee on commerce and navigation on bill relative to,......	S	2	49

NEW HAMBURGH AND BUFFALO TURNPIKE ROAD CO.

		Doc.	Vol.	No.
1830.	Report on petition to incorporate,......	S	1	16
1832.	Report on the same,......	A	3	216

NEW HAMBURGH TURNPIKE.

		Doc.	Vol.	No.
1830.	Report on bill declaring it a public highway,......	A	4	313

NEW HAMPSHIRE, STATE OF.

		Doc.	Vol.	No.
1832.	Resolution of the legislature of, for a re-organization of the militia,	A	1	3
1833.	do do against re-chartering the United States Bank,......	A	2	115
1834.	do do for a re-organization of the militia,	A	1	11
1843.	Message from the governor transmitting resolution of the legislature of,......	A	2	19
1844.	Resolution of the legislature of, on the subject of Gen. Jackson's fine,......	A	7	191

NEW JERSEY, STATE OF.

		Doc.	Vol.	No.
1833.	Resolutions of the legislature of, relative to nullification in South Carolina,	A	3	211
1839.	Resolutions by the same relative to the public lands,	A	3	211
1840.	Members of congress of, resolutions of the legislature of, relative to the,	A	3	70
1840.	do do preamble and resolutions offered by Mr. Taylor relative to the,	A	5	171
1840.	do do report of the committee on the judiciary on the same,	A	5	173
1842.	Resolution of the council and general assembly of, respecting the tariff,	S	3	53
1843	Joint resolution of the legislature of,	S	3	86
1855.	Resolutions by the same,	A	4	104
1855.	Resolutions of, relative to New York harbor,	A	5	104
1855.	Governor's message on same,	S	2	60
1857.	Communication from governor of, relative to Quarantine,	S	1	16

BOUNDARY LINE BETWEEN, AND NEW YORK:

		Doc.	Vol.	No.
1830.	Communication from the attorney-general in relation to the suit brought before the supreme court of the United States by New Jersey against the State of New York,	S	1	4
1831.	Communication from same relative to same,	A	1	3
1831.	Communication from the governor, and a report of the attorney-general on the same,	A	3	268
1831.	Report of majority of a select committee relative to the,	A	3	314
1831.	Report of minority of a select committee relative to the,	A	3	316
1833.	Report of joint committee in relation to the,	S	1	17
1834.	Report of commissioners appointed to settle the,	S	1	2

NEWLAND, EPHRAIM, AND T. WOODWORTH.

		Doc.	Vol.	No.
1856.	Report on petition of, for relief,	A	4	177
1857.	Report of committee on claims adverse on petition of, for damages by falling of bridge over the Champlain canal,	A	2	105

NEW MEXICO AND CALIFORNIA.

		Doc.	Vol.	No.
1849.	Report of select committee on so much of governor's message as relates to the introduction of slavery into,	A	3	139

NEW PALTZ, TOWN OF.

		Doc.	Vol.	No.
1852.	Report on petition of inhabitants of, for the erection of a new town,	A	5	107

NEW STOCKBRIDGE LANDS, *see* John Gregg.

		Doc.	Vol.	No.
1830.	Report on petition of settlers on the, for a re-appraisal of said lands, &c.,	S	2	163
1831.	School lot, report on petition of settlers on the, for relief,	A	1	11

NEWTON, WILLIAM.

		Doc.	Vol.	No.
1830.	Report on petition for extra allowance for work done on the Chenango canal,	A	3	242
1838.	Report of committee on claims on the same,	A	5	286
1839.	do do do	A	3	102
1840.	do do do	A	3	92
1841.	do do do	A	2	44
1841.	Report of canal board on the same,	A	7	270
1841.	Report of canal commissioners on the same,	A	3	81

NEWTON.

		Doc.	Vol.	No.
1857.	Report of standing committee on roads and bridges on petition for road from Hunter's Point to, and Flushing,	S	4	119

Year	Subject	Doc.	Vol.	No.
	NEW WINDSOR, TOWN OF.			
1838.	Report on petition to raise money to build a bridge across Murderer's creek,	A	6	331
	NEW YORK.			
1845.	Report of committee on privileges and elections on petition of citizens of,	A	3	71
1851.	Report on union with Brooklyn and Williamsburgh,	S	3	74
1851.	Report of select committee of the members from, on bills to raise money in,	A	4	123
1858.	Memorial from the mayor, aldermen and commonalty of,	A	4	141
	ACADEMY OF INVENTIONS AND ARTS:			
1833.	Report on petition to incorporate, A 2	64,	3	228
	AGRICULTURAL SCHOOL:			
1833.	Report on petition for the establishment of an,	S	2	79
	ALIEN PASSENGERS:			
1845.	Report of select committee on memorial of citizens of, relative to,	A	6	216
	ALMS-HOUSE:			
1845.	Memorial of the commissioners of, for amendments of the law relating to,	S	2	57
1853.	Report of board of ten governors of, relative to corruption, &c.,	A	2	35
1855.	Communication from governors of, transmitting resolution,	S	2	63
1856.	Report of governors of,	S	2	77
1856.	Communication from governors of,	S	2	79
1857.	Memorial of governors of,	S	2	60
	ALMS-HOUSE FARM:			
1832.	In Queens county, report on petition of the common council relative to the,	A	4	304
	ALMS-HOUSE SCHOOL:			
1835.	Report on petition for a portion of the school moneys,	A	3	174
	AMERICAN ART UNION:			
1853.	Report of select committee on the affairs of the,	A	5	115
	AMERICAN ASSOCIATION FOR THE ADVANCEMENT OF SCIENCE:			
1852.	Communication from governor transmitting memorial of, respecting geographical survey,	S	1	41
	AMERICAN GEOGRAPHICAL AND STATISTICAL SOCIETY:			
1854.	Memorial of,	A	3	96
	AMERICAN INSTITUTE:			
1835.	Report on memorial of the, relative to a geological survey of the state,	A	4	374
1838.	Report on memorial of, for aid,	A	6	309
1839.	do do	S	1	8
1840.	do do	S	3	90
1841.	Report of a committee on a communication from, on the subject of agriculture,	A	6	218
1842.	Report of, on agriculture,	S	4	101
1843.	Second annual report of,	S	3	108
1844.	Annual report of,	S	4	124
1846.	Annual report of,	S	4	105
1846.	Report of committee on agriculture recommending the printing of annual report of,	A	6	200
1847.	Annual report of,	A	6	151

22

NEW YORK—*continued.*

		Doc.	Vol.	No.
1848.	Annual report of,	A	7	216
1849.	Annual report of managers of,	A	7	244
1850.	Annual report of,	A	9	199
1851.	Transactions of,	A	5	149
1852.	Transactions of.	A	7	129
1853.	Transactions of,	A	5	133
1854.	Annual report of,	A	5	150
1855.	Annual report of,	A	5	144
1856.	Transactions of,	A	6	216
1857.	Annual report of,	A	4	171
1858.	Transactions of,	A	6	164
	AMERICAN SEAMEN'S FRIEND SOCIETY:			
1840.	Report on petition of, for a loan out of the "passengers' fund,"	A	7	300
	ARSENAL IN, *see* Arsenal, State.			
	ARTILLERY, HORSE:			
1835.	Report on petition to be exempt from jury duty,	A	2	112
1839.	9th Brigade, report on petition to be exempt from certain taxes and to reduce the number of parades,	A	2	182
	ASSESSORS, BOARD OF:			
1854.	Report of select committee on,	A	3	117
	ASSESSMENTS:			
1830.	Report on petition of common council to postpone the sale of lands advertised to be sold for,	A	4	295
1830.	Report on petition of common council for a law to equalize,	A	4	364
1839.	For laying out streets, &c., report on petition for a revision and amendment of the laws relative to,	A	5	313
1842.	Report of a select committee on the memorial of Peter A. Jay and others relative to, and accompanying documents,	S	4	100
1850.	Report of select committee on,	A	5	100
	ASSOCIATE CHURCH, SECOND:			
1834.	Report on petition to amend the charter of the,	S	2	112
	ASTOR LIBRARY:			
1849.	Report on petition to incorporate,	A	1	10
1850.	Annual report of trustees of,	A	3	43
1851.	do do	A	2	36
1852.	do do	S	1	20
1854.	do do	A	2	56
1855.	do do	A	5	130
1856.	do do	S	2	41
1857.	do do	A	1	57
1858.	do do	A	1	12
	ASTRONOMICAL OBSERVATORY:			
1847.	Report on,	S	2	45
	AUCTIONEERS:			
1830.	Report on bill respecting sales by,	A	4	381
1832.	Report of comptroller on a bill respecting.			
	AUCTIONS:			
1831.	Retail, report on petition for a law to prevent frauds and abuses arising from sales at,	A	1	53
	AVENUE C:			
1835.	Report on petition of the common council to widen,	A	3	163

NEW YORK—*continued.*

Year	Entry	Doc.	Vol.	No.
	BANKS, *see* Banks.			
	BAPTIST CHURCH, FIRST:			
1835.	Report on petition to sell certain real estate,	S	2	75
	BAR:			
1839.	Memorial of members of the, for the appointment of commissioners for the dispatch of the arrears of equity business,	S	2	36
1840.	Memorial of, for a reform in the judicial system,	S	1	16
1847.	Memorial of members of, relative to legal reform,	A	2	48
1847.	Petition of members of, for reform in mode of payment of fees to county clerks,	A	7	192
	BEEF AND PORK, INSPECTORS OF:			
1830.	Annual report of H. Howard,	A	2	73
1831.	do do	A	2	97
1832.	do do	A	2	65
1833.	do do	A	3	139
1834.	do do	A	3	230
1830.	Annual report of Philo Lewis,	A	2	169
1831.	do do	A	2	101
1832.	do do	A	2	99
1833.	do do	A	3	161
1834.	do do	A	3	213
1835.	do do	A	2	155
1836.	do do	A	3	176
1837.	do do	A	2	137
1838.	do do	A	3	120
1839.	do do	A	3	138
1840.	do do	A	4	114
1830.	Annual report of J. Lowerre,	A	2	95
1831.	do do	A	2	139
1832.	do do	A	2	61
1833.	do do	A	3	146
1835.	do do	S	1	19
1836.	do do	A	3	189
1837.	do do	A	2	118
1838.	do do	A	3	108
1839.	do do	A	4	173
1835.	Annual report of Thomas Gardner,	S	2	51
1836.	do do	A	4	227
1837.	do do	A	2	57
1838.	do do	A	4	167
1839.	do do	A	5	310
1840.	do do	A	4	113
1839.	Annual report of James Gardner,	A	5	309
1840.	Annual report of James Gardner,	A	4	112
1833.	Annual report of T Moor,	A	3	190
1840.	Annual report of Columbus Seguine,	A	2	57
1830.	Annual report of J. Shumway,	A	2	122
1831.	do do	A	2	126
1832.	do do	A	2	97
1833.	do do	A	2	132
1834.	do do	A	3	142
1835.	do do	A	3	181
1836.	do do	A	3	175
1837.	do do	A	2	136
1835.	Annual report of R. Usher,	A	3	188
1836.	do do	A	4	257
1837.	do do	A	3	233
1831.	Annual report of A. Wilson,	A	2	183
1832.	do do	A	2	158

NEW YORK—*continued.*

Year	Subject	Doc.	Vol.	No.
1833.	Annual report of A. Wilson,	A	3	188
1834.	do do	A	3	223
1834.	do do	A	4	355
1835.	do do	A	3	165
1836.	do do	A	3	174
1837.	do do	A	2	81
1838.	do do	S	2	48
1839.	do do	A	4	229
1840.	do do	A	5	197
1830.	Annual report of A. W. Youle,	A	2	159
1831.	do do	A	2	157
	Benevolent Society:			
1830.	Report on petition of, to admit members of said society as witnesses in certain suits,	A	4	391
	Blind, Institution for, *see* Blind.			
	Bloomingdale Asylum, *see* New York Hospital.			
1830.	Report concerning and resolution to appoint a committee to investigate the affairs of the,	A	4	308
1831.	Report of committee appointed to investigate, &c., the affairs of the,	A	3	263
1831.	Report of amount paid commissioners to investigate, &c.,	A	4	339
1840.	Report of committee appointed to investigate the affairs of the,	A	5	214
	Bloomingdale Road:			
1849.	Answer of comptroller of New York city to resolution of assembly relative to opening of,	A	5	216
	Board of Assessors:			
1854.	Report of select committee relative to, &c., in city of,	A	3	117
	Board of Brokers:			
1834.	Report of a select committee appointed to inquire into the expediency of a law to regulate the sale of stocks and bills of exchange by,	A	4	339
1836.	Memorial of the, against the bill to regulate the sale of stocks and bills of exchange,	A	4	291
	Board of Education, *see* New York Common Schools.			
	Board of Supervisors, County:			
1857.	Report of committee on incorporation of cities and villages, relative to the,	A	2	132
	Broadway:			
1856.	Report of majority and minority of committee on railroads in relation to one in,	A	4	168
	Building Associations:			
1856.	Report of legislative committee on,	A	3	46
	Butchers' Benevolent Society:			
1831.	Report on petition to renew the charter of,	A	4	298
	Cemetery, Greenwood:			
1838.	Report on petition to incorporate the proprietors of the,	A	6	334
	Cemetery, Marble:			
1832.	Report on petition to incorporate the proprietors of the,	A	3	184

NEW YORK—*continued.*

		Doc.	Vol.	No.
	CENSUS MARSHALS:			
1856.	Report of committee on petition of,	A	3	21
	CENTRAL PARK:			
1857.	Report of committee on incorporation of cities and villages relative to,	A	2	131
	CENTRE MARKET:			
1835.	Report relative to the enlargement of,	A	2	145
	CHAMBER OF COMMERCE:			
1835.	Memorial of, relative to the weighing of merchandise,	S	2	65
1837.	Memorial of, against the bill to prevent usury,	S	2	62
1841.	Memerial of, relative to the inspection laws,	S	3	78
1845.	Memorial of, in opposition to increase of tolls on Oswego canal,	S	2	61
1849.	Resolution of, against change of quarantine establishment,	S	2	40
1853.	Memorial of, relative to the enlargement of Erie canal,	A	4	100
1857.	Memorial of, relative to quarantine,	S	2	68
	CHARITABLE INSTITUTIONS:			
1841.	Report of commissioners on the condition of the,	A	1	4
1848.	Report as to expenses, &c., of,	A	5	139
1850.	Report of commissioners on,	A	5	138
1851.	Report of commissioners to supervise expenditures of,	A	4	121
1852.	Report relative to certain,	S	2	89
1855.	Report of commissioners to supervise expenditures of	A	4	112
1858.	Report of commissioners appointed to supervise receipts and expenditures of certain,	A	5	162
	CHARTER OF:			
1830.	Report of select committee on a bill to amend the,	A	4	322
1853.	Report of select committee on reference of bills and petition in regard to amendment of,	A	4	82
1857.	Report of committee on incorporation of cities and villages relative to, and municipal affairs of,	A	2	125
1857.	Minority report on same,	A	2	126
	CHEMICAL MANUFACTURING COMPANY, *see* Banks.			
	CITY COAL AND TRANSPORTATION COMPANY:			
1833.	Report on petition to incorporate,	A	2	37
	CITY COAL ASSOCIATION:			
1830.	Report on petition to incorporate,	A	2	155
	CITY HALL:			
1831.	Report relative to the judicial extension of the,	A	3	257
	CITY HALL, NEW:			
1857.	Majority report of committee on incorporation of cities and villages relative to the,	A	2	130
1857.	Minority report on same,	A	3	163
	CLERK AND REGISTER:			
1849.	Report of, in answer to resolution of assembly respecting amount of fees,	A	2	86
	COAL COMPANY:			
1832.	Report on petition to renew the charter of the,	A	3	203
	COLLECTORS OF TAXES:			
1831.	Report relative to the appointment of,	A	1	40
1838.	Bonds of, report concerning,	A	4	168

NEW YORK—*continued.*

College of Pharmacy, *see* Medical Colleges.

College of Physicians and Surgeons, *see* Medical Colleges.

College of Dental Surgery:

		Doc.	Vol.	No.
1854.	Report relative to,	A	4	139

Colored Home:

1845.	Report on the memorial of,	S	3	112

Colored Orphans' Asylum, New York:

1851.	Report of committee on charitable and religious societies relative to,	A	2	43

Commercial affairs:

1842.	Proceedings of a public meeting relative to,	S	3	82

Commissioners of Health, *see* Health Department.

Commissioners of Records:

1857.	Report of, in reply to resolution,	A	3	147
1858.	Report of,	S	3	121
1858.	Report of,	S	4	121

Common Council:

1830.	Memorial of the, relative to the support of foreign poor,	A	3	260
1831.	Memorial of the, relative to the tax on the seamen,	S	1	72
1834.	Remonstrance against incorporating the city of Brooklyn,	A	3	175
1836.	Memorial of, to authorize them to raise moneys on loan, and for other purposes,	A	1	8
1835.	Report on petition of the, to vest in them the title to certain land,	A	3	251
1839.	Resolutions of, relative to the New York and Albany railroad,	S	1	20
1840.	Resolutions of the, relative to the re-organization of the criminal courts,	S	1	35
1840.	Communication from, relative to the sale of the water stock,	A	7	304
1841.	Preamble and resolutions of, relative to the defense of the coast, harbor and frontier,	S	2	44
1835.	Ordinances of the, report on petition to repeal the law limiting the duration of the,	A	3	258

Common Pleas:

1835.	Report relative to the docket book of judgments for the court of,	A	2	77

Common Schools:

1831.	Report on petition for an additional tax for the support of,	A	3	244
1831.	Report on bill for the same,	A	4	288
1835.	Moneys, report on petition of the alms-house school for a portion of the,	A	3	174
1841.	Moneys, report of secretary of state relative to the distribution of of the,	S	3	86
1841.	Education, report on bill to extend the benefits of (Mr. O'Sullivan)	A	8	296
1841.	Public School Society, report of secretary of state giving copies of certain reports relative to the schools of the, and other schools,	S	3	90
1841.	Public School Society, memorial and remonstrance of the trustees of,	S	3	97
1832.	Corporate rights of, report of the committee on the judiciary relative to the,	S	2	93
1842.	Report on so much of governor's message as relates to,	A	4	60
1851.	Report on memorial of board of education,	S	2	53
1853.	Board of education, *see* annual report of state superintendent of common schools,	A	1	4

NEW YORK—*continued.*

		Doc.	Vol.	No.
1853.	Report of state superintendent of common schools in relation to moneys due from,	A	3	63
	Common School System:			
1858.	Report in relation to,	A	2	50
	Counsel:			
1854.	Petition of taxpayers against allowance of costs to city,	S	1	18
	Coroners:			
1848.	Statement of fees received by,	A	2	36
	Courts-Martial:			
1840.	Report of amount received by the president of, for fines, &c.,	S	3	88
1840.	Report on petition to substitute regimental courts-martial in the place of brigade courts-martial for the 1st and 6th brigades,	S	4	103
	Criminal Courts:			
1840.	Report and resolution of the common council relative to re-organization of,	S	1	35
1840.	Report of committee on the judiciary on the bill for same,	A	3	98
1842.	Message from governor returning bill relative to,	S	4	90
1842.	Report on memorial and bill respecting,	A	2	30
	Croton Aqueduct:			
1842.	[Ex. Sess.] Scientific description of,	A	7	195
	Croton Aqueduct Department:			
1858.	Report of committee on claims on petition of, for payment for water furnished the state prison in 1857,	A	3	66
	County Clerk:			
1845.	Report on petition for a reduction of the fees of,	S	3	126
	Deaf and Dumb Institution, *see* Deaf and Dumb.			
	Dental Surgery, College of:			
1854.	Report of committee on colleges, academies and common schools, on petition of,	A	4	139
	Dispensaries:			
1845.	Report of committee on medical societies, &c., on petitions of citizens for aid for,	A	4	140
	Dispensary:			
1831.	Report on petition for aid,	A	2	153
1837.	Report on petition for the release of a lot of ground in the 6th ward to the,	A	3	249
1842.	Annual report of trustees of,	S	3	64
1842.	do do	A	5	99
1844.	do do	A	7	169
1846.	do do	A	6	207
1848.	do do	S	3	76
1850.	Report of trustees,	S	3	103
1850.	Annual report of trustees,	S	3	107
1853.	Annual report,	S	2	65
1854.	Report of,	S	2	105
1857.	Report of,	S	2	64
1858.	Petition of president of,	S	1	6
1858.	Report on petition of, and annual report of the,	A	3	68
	Dispensary, Demilt:			
1853.	Annual report,	S	1	6

NEW YORK—*continued.*

		Doc.	Vol.	No.
1853.	First annual report of the,	S	2	60
1858.	Petition of president of,	S	1	6
	DISPENSARY, EASTERN:			
1842.	Annual report of the,	S	3	80
1843.	Report of,	S	1	47
1844.	Annual report of,	A	7	174
1847.	Report of,	A	4	113
1848.	Report of,	A	6	197
1849.	Annual report of,	A	5	234
1851.	Annual report of,	A	4	119
1858.	Petition of president of,	S	1	6
	DISPENSARY, NORTHERN:			
1842.	Annual report of the trustees of the,	S	3	61
1843.	Report of,	S	1	33
1843.	Annual report of,	A	3	61
1844.	Annual report of,	A	6	163
1844.	Annual report of trustees of,	A	7	169
1845.	Report of,	S	1	37
1845.	Annual report of,	A	5	160
1846.	Report of,	S	4	145
1847.	Report of,	S	1	29
1849.	Annual report of,	S	3	82
1851.	Annual report of trustees of,	S	2	51
1851.	Annual report of,	S	2	52
1851.	Report of trustees of, for 1851,	S	1	11
1854.	Report of,	S	1	40
1855.	Annual report of,	S	1	19
1858.	Petition of president of,	S	1	6
1858.	Report of,	A	1	7
	DISPENSARY, NORTHWESTERN:			
1858.	Petition of president of,	S	1	6
	DISTRICT COURTS:			
1855.	Minority report of committee on bill relative to clerks in,	S	2	68
	DOMESTIC DISTILLED SPIRITS:			
1831.	Inspection of, report on petition of distillers and others of the counties of Oneida, Yates and Chenango, to amend the law relative to the,	A	1	33
1832.	Inspector-general, report on petition to abolish the office of,	A	2	114
1830.	A. Dalley, annual report of,	S	1	41
1831.	do do	A	2	99
1832.	do do	A	2	11
1832.	do do	A	2	102
1833.	do do	A	2	100
1834.	do do	A	2	94
1835.	do do	A	3	204
1838.	John Cooper, annual report of,	A	3	125
1839.	do do	A	3	129
1840.	do do	S	2	53
	DRY DOCK COMPANY, *see* Banks.			
	DYEING AND PRINTING ESTABLISHMENT:			
1843.	Report of committee on manufactures, on petition of,	S	2	62
	EAST RIVER:			
1857.	Bridge over,	S	4	167

NEW YORK—*continued.*

		Doc.	Vol.	No.
	ECONOMICAL SCHOOL:			
1833.	Comptroller's report of amount of moneys paid to the, &c.,....	A	3	232
	EDUCATION, BOARD OF, *see* New York Common Schools.			
	ELECTORS:			
1831.	Qualifications of, report on memorial of the common council relative to the, ...	A	3	243
	And *see* Registry Law.			
	ELEVENTH WARD:			
1833.	Public square in, report concerning the,......	A	2	90
1833.	Fire limits in the, report on petition to extend the,......	A	4	324
	ESSEX MARKET:			
1835.	Report relative to the enlargement of,......	A	3	251
	EMIGRANT PASSENGERS:			
1843.	Memorial of the mayor, aldermen and commonalty of, praying for the passage of an act for the relief of, with draft of an act therefor,......	A	5	139
	EXCAVATIONS:			
1855.	Report on petitions relative to,......	S	2	50
	EYE AND EAR INFIRMARY:			
1845.	Report of committee on charitable and religious societies, on petition for the relief of,......	A	4	146
	EYE INFIRMARY:			
1830.	Annual report of, and memorial for aid,......	S	2	184
1832.	Report and memorial for aid,......	A	1	19
1834.	Memorial of, for aid,......	A	1	29
1836.	Annual report of,......	S	2	100
1837.	Memorial of, for aid,......	A	2	87
1839.	Annual report of,......	A	6	396
1842.	Report of committee on medical colleges, &c., on petition of,...	A	5	98
1846.	Annual report of, ...	A	5	180
1849.	Annual report of the surgeon of......	A	5	236
1853.	Report of commissioners to inquire as to condition of,......	A	4	92
1854.	Report of,......	S	2	104
1855.	Annual report of,......	S	2	56
1857.	Annual report of directors of,......	S	2	47
	FAMILY INDUSTRIAL SOCIETY, MARINERS:			
1854.	Memorial of,......	S	2	73
	FEMALE ASSOCIATION:			
1830.	Memorial of, for aid,......	A	3	266
	FERRIES BETWEEN, AND LONG ISLAND:			
1835.	Report on petition for additional ones,......	A	2	138
1836.	Majority report on bill to establish and regulate,......	A	4	258
1836.	Minority report on same subject,......	A	4	259
1837.	Report of committee on commerce and navigation adverse to an act in relation to,......	A	3	210
1858.	Report on petitions, and an act in relation to,......	A	4	102
1858.	Minority report on, and rates of ferriage between New York and Long Island,......	A	4	130
	FIRE DEPARTMENT:			
1849.	Memorial of,......	S	1	9

NEW YORK—*continued.*

Year	Subject	Doc.	Vol.	No.
	FIRE, GREAT, in December, 1835, *see* Insurance Companies.			
1836.	Message from the governor relative to the,	S	1	2
1836.	Report of joint committee on the same,	S	1	4
1836.	Memorial of mayor, &c., of, to raise money on loan, &c.,	A	1	8
	FIRE LIMITS:			
1831.	Report on petition for the extension of the,	A	3	250
1832.	do do do	A	4	317
1833.	do do do	A	4	324
	FIREMEN:			
1831.	Report on bill to abridge the term of service of, &c.,	A	1	62
1840.	Memorial of, for re-organization of the fire department,	S	3	68
	FISH, INSPECTOR OF:			
1830.	Annual report of Hiram Scofield,	A	2	197
1831.	do do	A	2	96
1832.	do do	A	2	96
1833.	do do	A	3	189
1835.	do do	A	2	157
1836.	do do	S	1	55
1837.	do do	A	3	212
1837.	do do	A	4	301
1831.	Annual report of John Betts,	A	3	239
1832.	do do	A	2	144
1831.	Annual report of Thomas Moore,	A	3	240
1832.	do do	A	2	143
1835.	do do	A	3	201
1831.	Annual report of D. B. Young,	S	1	23
1832.	do do	S	1	34
1836.	do do	A	4	260
	FLAX SEED, INSPECTOR OF:			
1830.	Annual report of I. K. Townsend,	A	2	143
1831.	do do	A	2	89
1832.	do do	A	2	146
1832.	Annual report of R. B. Fosdick,	A	2	64
1833.	do do	A	2	123
1834.	do do	A	4	261
1835.	do do	A	1	57
1836.	do do	A	4	253
1837.	do do	A	2	51
1838.	do do	S	1	21
1840.	do do	A	4	103
	FLOUR, INSPECTION OF:			
1830.	Report on the expediency of dividing the duties of the inspector of,	A	3	289
1831.	Majority report on petition to amend the law relative to,	A	2	188
1831.	Minority report on same subject,	A	2	194
1832.	Majority report on bill to amend the law relative to the,	A	3	197
1832.	Minority report on same subject,	A	3	198
	FLOUR, INSPECTOR OF:			
1830.	Report on petition to increase the number of,	S	4	341
1830.	Remonstrance of millers and others against increasing the number of,	S	4	342
1831.	Report of committee appointed to examine the report of the,	A	2	178
1830.	Annual report of Richard McCarty,	S	2	79
1831.	do do	A	2	88
1831.	do do	A	3	211
1832.	do do	A	2	83

NEW YORK—*continued.*

		Doc.	Vol.	No.
1833.	Annual report of Richard McCarty,	A	3	138
1834.	do do	A	3	111
1835.	do do	A	2	156
1835.	Annual report of John Lane,	A	2	128
1835.	Annual report of C. P. Tappan,	A	2	129
1836.	do do	A	3	161
1838.	do do	A	3	114
1839.	do do	A	3	119
1840.	Annual report of John Gray,	A	1	13
1836.	Annual report of Frederick Tarr,	A	3	180
1837.	Annual report of Frederick Tarr,	A	2	123
	FORECLOSURE OF MORTGAGES:			
1849.	Report of sheriff of, in answer to resolution of assembly, relative to amount of sales under, made by him, amount of money received, &c.,	A	2	56
	FOREIGN POOR:			
1830.	Memorial of common council relative to the support of,	A	3	260
1842.	Report of committee on internal affairs of towns, &c, on support of,	A	5	129
	FREE ACADEMY, *see* Academies, &c.			
	FREE TRADE ASSOCIATION:			
1843.	Memorial from,	A	2	22
	FRENCH BENEVOLENT SOCIETY:			
1843.	Report of Mr. Daly on the memorial of,	A	5	181
	GAS LIGHT COMPANY, MANHATTAN:			
1855.	Communication from, in answer to resolution of assembly,	A	5	123
	GAS LIGHT COMPANY, METROPOLITAN:			
1856.	Report on petition to repeal act,	A	4	145
	GAME IN:			
1837.	Report relative to the preservation of,	A	3	196
	GERMAN SOCIETY:			
1848.	Memorial of,	A	5	165
	GRAIN, MEASURER GENERAL OF:			
1831.	Report on petition for the appointment of a,	A	3	252
1832.	do do do	S	1	30
1832.	do do do	S	2	93
1833.	Annual report of Samuel Satterlee, Jr.,	A	3	149
1834.	do do	A	3	181
1835.	do do	A	3	237
1836.	do do	A	3	163
1837.	do do	A	2	110
1837.	Report of committee appointed to examine the annual report of,	A	3	183
1837.	Report of, in answer to a resolution of the assembly,	A	3	221
1838.	Annual report of,	A	3	142
1839.	do	S	1	41
1840.	do	A	5	198
	GRAND JURY:			
1837.	Presentment of, relative to the pilot system,	A	2	160
	GREEN HIDES AND SKINS:			
1832.	Annual report of Robert Dingee,	A	2	79
1833.	do do	A	2	87

NEW YORK—*continued.*

Year		Doc.	Vol.	No.
1834.	Annual report of Robert Dingee, ...	A	2	90
1835.	do do	A	1	52
1836.	do do	A	3	117
1837.	do do	A	1	25
1838.	do do	A	2	43
1839.	do do	A	2	60
1840.	do do	A	2	33
	HARBOR, *see* Port Wardens:			
1854.	Communication relative to,....	S	1	8
1854.	Report of committee on commerce and navigation relative to,...	S	1	49
1854.	Report relative to grants of land under water in,.... S	1	12,	34
1854.	Report of committee on commerce and navigation relative to,...	S	1	49
1855.	New Jersey resolutions respecting,....	A	5	104
1855.	Governor's message on same,....	S	2	60
1856.	Report in reference to payment of expenses connected with,....	A	3	61
1856.	Report of commissioners relative to encroachments on,....	S	1	3
1856.	Report, second,....	S	1	25
1856.	Report of committee on commerce and navigation on water lines of,....	S	2	85
1856.	Report of commissioners relative to encroachments and preservation of,....	A	1	8
1856.	Report on payment of expenses connected with,....	A	3	61
1857.	Report of commissioners relative to encroachments in	S	1	40
1857.	Report of committee on commerce and navigation relative to encroachments on,....	A	3	206
	HARBOR COAST SURVEY:			
1858.	Report of Professor A. D. Bache relative to,....	S	2	16
	HARBOR MASTERS:			
1857.	Report relative to,....	S	3	100
	HAY, PRESSED:			
1832.	Inspection of, report on petition for a law requiring the,....	A	4	280
1855.	Report on petition to repeal the law requiring the,....	A	4	265
	HEALTH DEPARTMENT, *see* Marine Hospital.			
1830.	Comptroller's report of amount of receipts and expenditures of the, with a statement of balances in the hands of the commissioners annually from 1823 to 1829, &c.,....	A	3	252
1831.	Comptroller's report of amount of receipts and expenditures for 1830, ...	A	2	127
1838.	Comptroller's report relative to same for 1835, 1836 and 1837,...	S	1	17
1840.	Board of commissioners of health, report of investigation of the affairs of the,....	A	5	214
1843.	Report of committee on executive expenditures on the bill entitled "An act to reduce the fees of the health officer, and the amount of hospital moneys, and for other purposes,"....	A	4	104
1847.	Memorial of commissioners of health,....	A	7	196
1850.	Annual report of health officer,....	S	1	11
1855.	Report of fees received by health officer,....	A	5	121
1857.	Report of select committee relative to health and sanitary police,	S	4	115
1858.	Report of health officer relative to the ventilating of vessels undergoing quarantine,....	S	3	127
	HEALTH, PUBLIC:			
1833.	Memorial of I. K. Manley, resident physician, relative to the,...	S	2	121
	HELL-GATE PILOTS:			
1831.	Report on petition to repeal the law authorizing them to receive half-pilotage in certain cases, ...	A	2	193
1832.	Report relative to the same,....	A	2	138

NEW YORK—*continued.*

		Doc.	Vol.	No.
	HIBERNIAN PROVIDENT SOCIETY:			
1836.	Report on petition to incorporate,	S	1	14
1837.	Report on bill to incorporate,	A	3	111
	HISTORICAL SOCIETY:			
1839.	Memorial of, for an agent to transcribe documents relative to the Colonial History of the state,	A	3	153
1839.	Report of select committee on the same,	A	4	231
1849.	Report of committee on colleges, &c., on application of, for an appropriation for the erection of a fire-proof building,	A	2	95
1850.	Memorial of,	S	1	15
	HOPS:			
1830.	Annual report of Robert Barnes, an inspector of,	S	1	18
1831.	do do do	S	1	17
1832.	do do do	S	1	35
1833.	do do do	S	1	37
1834.	do do do	S	1	46
1835.	do do do	A	1	10
1836.	do Cornelius Higgins, do	S	1	13
1837.	do do do	A	2	85
1838.	do do do	A	2	51
1839.	do do do	A	3	113
1840.	do John F. Raymond, do	A	4	110
	HOSPITAL, STATE, *see* Bloomingdale Asylum.			
1830.	Annual report of the governors of the,	A	2	145
1831.	do do	A	3	200
1832.	do do	A	3	180
1833.	do do	A	3	181
1834.	do do	A	3	239
1835.	do do	A	4	291
1836.	do do	A	4	275
1837.	do do	A	3	266
1838.	do do	A	5	250
1839.	do do	A	4	207
1840.	do do	S	2	52
1841.	do do	S	1	35
1830.	Report of the governors of, in answer to a resolution of the assembly giving the denomination and amount of pay of the officers attached to the institution, &c.,	A	4	324
1830.	Report of a select committee relative to the, with a resolution to appoint a committee to investigate the affairs of the,	A	4	408
1831.	Report of committee appointed to investigate the affairs of the,	A	3	263
1831.	Report of committee on the report of the committee to investigate, &c.,	A	4	305
1831.	Report of amount paid the committee appointed to investigate, &c.,	A	4	339
1840.	Report of committee appointed to investigate, &c,	A	5	214
1840.	Report of committee on petition to amend the charter of the, and for aid to,	A	6	223
1842.	Annual report of governors of the,	S	3	60
1842.	Report of governors of,	A	5	95
1843.	Report of governors of,	S	1	41
1843.	Annual report of governors of,	A	5	147
1844	Report of governors of,	S	2	86
1844.	Annual report of governors of,	A	3	81
1845.	Annual report of governors of,	S	1	41
1845.	Report on the memorials, &c., relative to,	S	3	112
1845.	Annual report of governors of,	A	5	176
1846.	Report of governors of,	S	2	62
1846.	Annual report of governors of,	A	4	121

NEW YORK—*continued.*

		Doc.	Vol.	No.
1847.	Report of,	A	1	13
1847.	Report of governors of,	A	2	73
1848.	Annual report of,	S	3	77
1848.	Report of governors of,	A	6	194
1849.	Annual report of governors of,	S	3	80
1849.	Annual report of governors of,	A	5	226
1850.	Report of officers,	S	3	106
1850.	Report of committee on charitable and religious societies on,	A	1	15
1850.	Report of president, secretary and governors,	A	8	178
1853.	Annual report of governors of,	S	2	58
1853.	Report of commissioners to examine condition of,	A	4	92
1857.	Report of governors of,	S	4	128
1858.	Annual report of governors of,	A	5	159
	HOSPITAL MONEYS, *see* Marine Hospital.			
	HOUSE OF REFUGE, *see* Juvenile Delinquents.			
	HYDROSTATIC DOCK COMPANY:			
1831.	Report on petition to incorporate the,	A	3	276
	INFIRMARY FOR INDIGENT WOMEN AND CHILDREN:			
1858.	Report on petition of,	A	3	65
	INSOLVENT NOTICES:			
1830.	Report relative to the publication of, in one or more papers,	A	1	17
	INSTITUTION FOR THE DEAF AND DUMB, *see* Deaf and Dumb.			
	INSURANCE COMPANIES, *see* Insurance Companies.			
	INSURANCE COMPANIES, affected by the great fire:			
1836.	Memorial of the mayor, &c., of, for a law to authorize the mayor, &c., to purchase certain bonds belonging to the,	A	1	8
1836.	Communications from the, in answer to a resolution of assembly calling for certain information,	A	2	103
1836.	Communications from the, in answer to a resolution of assembly calling for certain information,	A	3	113
1836.	Communications from the, in answer to a resolution of assembly calling for certain information,	A	4	236
	IRISH EMIGRANT SOCIETY:			
1854.	Remonstrance of, against certain bill,	A	1	31
	ITALIAN OPERA ASSOCIATION:			
1833.	Report on petition to incorporate,	A	4	263
	JAIL LIMITS:			
1830.	Report on petition for an extension of the,	A	2	138
	JEWISH CHARITABLE SOCIETY:			
1831.	Report on petition to incorporate,	A	3	201
	JURORS:			
1848.	Statement of fees for summoning, by sheriff,	A	2	35
	JUDGES, PER DIEM, COMPENSATION TO:			
1830.	Report on petition for a,	A	2	135
1832.	do do	A	1	64
1836.	do do	A	4	263
1837.	Majority report on the same,	A	3	234
1837.	Minority report on the same,	A	3	251
1839.	Report on the same,	A	6	399

NEW YORK—*continued.*

		Doc.	Vol.	No.
	JUSTICES, SPECIAL OR POLICE:			
1832.	Report on petition for an additional one,	A	4	326
1835.	Report on petition for an additional one,	A	3	167
	JUSTICE:			
1852.	Report on the administration of,	A	5	97
	JUVENILE ASYLUM:			
1850.	Report of committee on charitable and religious societies on incorporation of,	A	5	78
1858.	Annual report of,	A	5	160
	JUVENILE DELINQUENTS, SOCIETY FOR THE REFORMATION OF, *see* Juvenile Delinquents.			
	LANDS:			
1854.	Report of committee on judiciary relative to certain,	S	2	67
	LEAKE AND WATTS' ORPHAN HOUSE:			
1831.	Report on petition of the trustees of, to vest in them the right of the state to certain lands, escheated on the death of John G. Leake,	S	1	71
1833.	Report on petition of the trustees of, to vest in them the right of the state to certain lands, escheated on the death of John G. Leake,	S	2	100
1834.	Report on petition of the trustees of, to vest in them the right of the state to certain lands escheated on the death of John G. Leake,	S	2	121
1835.	Report on petition of the trustees of, to vest in them the right of the state to certain lands, escheated on the death of John G. Leake,	S	2	80
1838.	Report on petition of the trustees of, to vest in them the right of the state to certain lands, escheated on the death of John G. Leake,	A	2	24
1839.	Report on petition of the trustees of, to vest in them the right of the state to certain lands, escheated on the death of John G. Leake,	A	2	28
1840.	Report on petition of the trustees of, to vest in them the right of the state to certain lands, escheated on the death of John G. Leake,	S	4	117
1842.	Report of committee on petition of aliens respecting,	A	2	37
1842.	Bill for relief of,	A	2	37
1845.	Report of minority of committee on,	A	6	23
1845.	Report of minority of committee on,	A	6	233
1855.	Memorial of,	S	2	65
	LIEN LAW:			
1830.	Report on petition of mechanics and others, for a,	A	1	24
1830.	do do do	A	3	231
1831.	do do do	A	4	286
	LIVER OIL, INSPECTOR OF:			
1831.	Annual report of Robert C. Theall,	A	2	100
1832.	do do	A	2	95
1833.	do do	A	2	119
1834.	do do	A	2	91
1834.	do do	A	4	280
1835.	do do	A	1	46
1837.	do do	A	1	30
1838.	do do	A	3	143
1839.	do do	A	2	66
1840.	do do	A	2	40
	LOAN:			
1836.	Memorial of the mayor, &c, for a law authorizing a, to purchase bonds of insurance companies affected by the great fire,	A	1	3
	LOAN COMMISSIONERS:			
1840.	Report on petition of citizens for an extension of the, for the payment of the interest due the,	A	3	82

NEW YORK—*continued.*

		Doc.	Vol.	No.
1858.	Report of proceedings of supervisors relative to,	A	3	72
	LOAN, WATER, *see* Water.			
	LUMBER, INSPECTORS OF:			
1839.	Annual report of Samuel Bowelle,	A	3	127
1830.	do Peter Conroy,	A	2	94
1831.	do do	A	2	84
1832.	do do	A	2	80
1833.	do do	A	2	92
1834.	do do	A	3	194
1835.	do do	A	1	70
1836.	do do	A	3	204
1837.	do do	A	2	80
1838.	do do	A	3	74
1839.	do do	A	3	136
1831.	Annual report of Alexander Denniston,	A	2	110
1832.	do do	A	2	88
1833.	do do	A	2	122
1834.	do do	A	3	119
1835.	do do	A	3	171
1836.	do do	A	3	188
1837.	do do	A	2	140
1838.	do do	A	2	57
1839.	do do	A	4	228
1840.	do do	A	5	188
1837.	Annual report of William Green,	A	2	84
1838.	do do	S	2	57
1839.	do do	A	4	245
1840.	do do	A	2	43
1838.	Annual report of Smith Hicks,	A	6	343
1832.	do S. Howell,	A	2	98
1833.	do do	A	2	109
1834.	do do	A	4	307
1835.	do do	A	4	274
1836.	do do	A	4	250
1837.	do do	A	2	135
1840.	do do	A	1	15
1831.	Annual report of Edward G. Fuller,	A	2	75
1830.	do Jeffrey Hand,	A	2	128
1831.	do do	A	2	137
1832.	do do	A	2	109
1833.	do do	A	2	106
1834.	do do	A	3	218
1835.	do do	A	4	268
1836.	do do	A	4	309
1830.	Annual report of Jacob Lockman,	A	2	91
1831.	do do	A	1	68
1832.	do do	A	1	49
1833.	do do	A	2	77
1834.	do do	A	3	170
1835.	do do	A	1	40
1836.	do do	A	2	106
1837.	do do	A	2	66
1838.	do do	A	3	97
1839.	do do	A	3	112
1840.	do do	A	3	67
1832.	Annual report of John J. Morris,	A	2	63
1833.	do do	A	2	112
1834.	do do	A	3	197
1835.	do do	A	1	69
1836.	do do	A	3	186

NEW YORK—*continued.*

		Doc.	Vol.	No.
1837.	Annual report of John J. Morris,	A	2	97
1838.	do do	A	3	85
1839.	do do	A	3	191
1840.	do do	A	2	38
1830.	Annual report of J. M. Nelson,	A	2	116
1831.	do do	A	2	83
1832.	do do	A	2	62
1833.	do do	A	2	116
1834.	do do	A	3	234
1835.	do do	A	3	187
1836.	do do	A	3	205
1837.	do do	A	2	72
1838.	do do	A	4	166
1839.	do do	A	4	214
1836.	Annual report of George W. Noble,	A	3	185
1831.	do N. Roberts,	A	1	36
1832.	do do	A	2	90
1833.	do do	A	2	86
1834.	do do	A	3	124
1835.	do do	A	1	56
1836.	do do	A	3	118
1838.	do do	A	1	17
1839.	do do	A	4	174
1840.	do do	A	1	26
1838.	Annual report of W. M. Shepard,	A	3	133
1839.	do do	A	4	221
1840.	do do	A	5	192
1831.	Annual report of A. A. Slover,	A	2	82
1832.	do do	A	2	164
1833.	do do	A	2	95
1834.	do do	A	3	224
1835.	do do	A	1	27
1836.	do do	A	3	187
1837.	do do	A	2	133
1838.	do do	A	3	76
1839.	do do	A	4	172
1830.	Annual report of Caleb Smith,	A	2	125
1831.	do do	A	2	96
1832.	do do	A	2	67
1833.	do do	A	2	81
1834.	do do	A	3	221
1835.	do do	A	3	172

LUNATIC ASYLUM, *see* Bloomingdale Asylum.

MANHATTAN MEDICAL COLLEGE, *see* Medical Colleges.

MAP AND PLAN OF THE CITY:

1832.	Report of petition to alter the, by laying out a new street in the 12th ward,	A	3	239
1832.	Enlargement of Union Place, report relative to the,	A	2	115
1835.	Between Thirteenth and Twenty-third streets, the 1st Avenue and the East river, report on petition to alter, &c.,	A	4	376

MARBLE CEMETERY:

1832.	Report on petition to incorporate the proprietors of,	A	3	184

MARINE COURT:

1849.	Report of clerk of, in reply to resolution of the assembly,	A	3	183

MARINE DRY DOCK COMPANY:

1834.	Report on petition to incorporate,	A	4	275

NEW YORK—*continued.*

		Doc.	Vol.	No.
	MARINERS' FAMILY INDUSTRIAL SOCIETY:			
1854.	Memorial of,	S	2	73
	MARINE HOSPITAL:			
1839.	Investigation of the, report of committee appointed for an,	A	6	408
1840.	Investigation of the, report of committee appointed for an,	A	5	214
1841.	Communication from A. S. Doane in relation to the,	S	1	2
1831.	Expenditure of the, report on bill relative to the,	S	1	68
1850.	Message of governor and report of physician,	A	6	154
1850.	Remonstrance of physicians,	A	6	168
1853.	Report of commissioners,	A	4	92
1856.	Report of physician of,	S	3	104
1857.	Annual report of,	S	3	105
	MARINE HOSPITAL MONEYS:			
1830.	Report of balance of, in the hands of the health commissioners from 1823 to 1829, &c.,	A	3	252
1831.	Report of amount received in 1830,	A	2	127
1834.	Report on petition relative to the payment of, for passengers on steamboats plying between New York and Charleston,	S	2	96
1836.	Report on petition of American seamen to be relieved from the payment of,	A	4	247
1839.	Report on petition of American seamen to be relieved from the payment of,	A	6	387
1843.	Report of committee on executive expenditure on act to reduce fees of health officer and the amount of, and for other purposes,	A	4	104
1849.	Communication from commissioner of emigration respecting,	A	3	140
1849.	Communication from comptroller and attorney-general concerning,	A	5	206
	MARINERS' FUND:			
1845.	Report of Comptroller in answer to a resolution of the senate relative to,	S	1	29
	MARKETS:			
1835.	Centre, report relative to the enlargement of,	A	2	145
1835.	Essex, report relative to the enlargement of,	A	3	251
1839.	In the 12th ward, report on petition to vest in the corporation the title to certain lands for a,	A	4	203
	MARRIAGES:			
1854.	Communication from city inspector relative to registry of,	A	3	123
	MARSHALS.			
1833.	Report on petition to increase the number of,	A	2	118
	MASONIC HALL ASSOCIATION:			
1835.	Report on petition to authorize the dissolution of,	A	4	377
	MASQUERADES:			
1830.	Report on petition for a law to prevent,	A	4	354
	MAYOR OF:			
1830.	Proposition to amend the Constitution so as to make him elective,	A	2	96
1833.	Report of secretary of state relative to the publication of said amendment,	S	1	14
1833.	Report of committee on the judiciary on the same,	S	2	45
	MECHANICS:			
1830.	Memorial of, against the bill to repeal the law imposing a tax on bank stock,	A	3	272
1840.	Report of a committee appointed at a public meeting of, relative to teaching trades to state prison convicts,	A	7	276

NEW YORK—*continued.*

		Doc.	Vol.	No.
	MECHANICS' INSTITUTE:			
1854.	Petition of,	S	2	94
	MEDICAL SCHOOL, *see* Medical Schools.			
	MEDICAL SOCIETY, *see* Medical Societies.			
	MERCHANDISE, WEIGHER GENERAL OF:			
1836.	Annual report of John I. Bedinet,	A	3	129
1837.	Annual report of John I. Bedinet,	S	2	63
1838.	Annual report of George R. Hebberd,	S	1	24
1839.	Annual report of George R. Hebberd,	S	1	42
1840.	Annual report of D. D. Crane,	A	2	54
	MERCHANDISE, WEIGHING OF:			
1835.	Report on petition for a law to regulate the,	S	2	54
1835.	Memorial of the chamber of commerce against the bill to regulate the,	S	2	65
1835.	Objections of governor to the bill to regulate the,	S	2	82
1836.	Report on petition to amend the law to regulate the,	A	2	81
1838.	Report on bill to repeal the law regulating the,	S	2	56
1844.	Report of committee on trade and manufactures on the subject of,	A	3	36
	METHODIST EPISCOPAL CHURCH:			
1836.	Report on bill to increase the number of trustees of the, of the East circuit in,	A	3	111
	METROPOLITAN MEDICAL COLLEGE, *see* Medical Colleges.			
	METROPOLITAN POLICE LAW, *see* Metropolitan Police.			
1858.	Memorial of mayor, &c., for the repeal of,	S	2	74
	MILITARY FINES:			
1853.	Report of Major-General Chas. W. Sanford in answer to a resolution of the assembly, of the 13th January, 1853, in relation to moneys collected for,	A	2	30
	MILK:			
1854.	Report relative to sale of,	S	2	100
1854.	Report relative to sale of impure,	S	2	102
	MINING COMPANY:			
1832.	Report on petition to incorporate,	A	2	72
	MINING COMPANY, NORTH AMERICAN:			
1832.	Report on petition to incorporate,	A	1	40
	MORAL AND EQUITABLE ASSOCIATION:			
1836.	Report on petition of the, relative to the removal of the remains of the dead, &c.,	S	2	97
	MORTGAGES, FORECLOSURE OF:			
1849.	Report of sheriff in answer to resolution of assembly relative to amount of sales, &c., under, &c.,	A	2	56
	MUSEUM:			
1839.	Report on petition of Reuben Peale and others to incorporate a,	A	3	71
	NEW YORK AND BOSTON STEAMBOAT COMPANY:			
1830.	Report on petition to amend the charter of the,	A	4	345
	NEW YORK AND BROOKLYN COAL COMPANY:			
1837.	Report on petition to incorporate,	A	3	174

NEW YORK—*continued.*

		Doc.	Vol.	No.
	NEW YORK AND MONTGOMERY MINING COMPANY:			
1851.	Report of committee,	A	3	79
	NINETEENTH WARD:			
1854.	Report of select committee relative to park in,	A	1	21
	NINTH WARD:			
1832.	Report on petition to divide the,	A	4	296
	NORTH AMERICAN MINING COMPANY:			
1832.	Report on petition to incorporate the,	A	1	40
	NOTARIES PUBLIC:			
1838.	Report on petition to increase the fees of,	A	2	34
	ORDINANCES OF THE COMMON COUNCIL:			
1835.	Report on petition to repeal the law limiting the duration of the,	A	3	258
	ORPHAN ASYLUM:			
1834.	Prince street, report on petition for aid to the,	A	2	105
1847.	Report relative to,	A	7	217
1847.	do	A	8	259
1847.	do	A	8	234
	See Leake and Watts.			
	OPHTHALMIC DISPENSARY:			
1838.	Report on petition for aid to the,	A	5	274
	OPHTHALMIC HOSPITAL:			
1858.	Report on petition of the,	A	3	62
	PAUPERS AND VAGRANTS:			
1831.	Report on petition of the common council for a law relative to,	A	3	259
	PHARMACY, COLLEGE OF, *see* Medical Colleges.			
	PHYSICIANS AND SURGEONS, COLLEGE OF, *see* Medical Colleges.			
	PILOTS:			
1831.	Hell-Gate, report on petition to repeal the law authorizing them to receive half pilotage in certain cases,	A	2	193
1832.	Hell-Gate, report on petition to repeal the law authorizing them to recieve half pilotage in certain cases,	A	2	138
1836.	Sandy Hook, report on petition to increase the number of deputy pilots,	A	4	237
1836.	Sandy Hook, report of the wardens of the port relative to increasing the number of,	A	4	272
1838.	Sandy Hook, report on memorial of the commissioners of pilots to amend the law relative to the,	A	4	174
1845.	Governor's message transmitting a memorial from,	S	1	25
1845.	Report of committee on commerce and navigation on the message from the governor and the memorial of the,	S	1	40
1845.	Report of committee on judiciary on the laws respecting,	A	5	186
1846.	Report of select committee on,	A	4	104
1848.	Report of committee on commerce and navigation on resolutions relative to pilots,	A	2	27
1858.	Report of commissioners of,	S	1	13
	PILOT SYSTEM:			
1837.	Presentment of the, by the grand jury,	A	2	160
	PLAN OR MAP OF THE CITY, *see* Map, &c.			

NEW YORK—*continued.*

POLICE COURT:

		Doc.	Vol.	No.
1855.	Minority report of committee on bill relative to, clerks,	S	2	68

POLICE DEPARTMENT:

		Doc.	Vol.	No.
1833.	Report on petition of the common council for a law relative to the,	A	1	24
1846.	Report of minority of select committee on police bill,	A	5	174
1846.	Report of majority of select committee on police bill,	A	5	174
1856.	Report relative to,	S	2	97
1858.	Memorial of mayor, &c., for the repeal of the metropolitan police law,	S	2	74

See Metropolitan Police.

POLICE JUSTICE:

		Doc.	Vol.	No.
1832.	Report on petition for an additional one,	A	4	326
1835.	Report on petition for an additional one,	A	3	176

PORT WARDENS:

		Doc.	Vol.	No.
1836.	Report of the, relative to increasing the number of pilots by the way of Sandy Hook,	A	4	272
1844.	Petition of master and,	S	2	64
1847.	Report of master,	S	1	38
1856.	Report on reorganization of office of,	A	5	182
1857.	Report of committee on commerce and navigation relative to bill to reorganize the office of,	A	2	67

POT AND PEARL ASHES, INSPECTORS OF:

		Doc.	Vol.	No.
1830.	Annual report of J. J. Bogart,	A	1	47
1830.	Annual report of S. Cooper,	A	1	54
1830.	Annual report of R. Snow,	A	2	88
1831.	Annual report of R. Snow,	A	2	136
1831.	Annual report of George Seaman,	A	2	111
1832.	do do	A	2	75
1833.	do do	S	1	39
1834.	do do	A	2	65
1835.	do do	S	2	44
1835.	Annual report of William Dumont,	S	1	16
1836.	do do	S	1	34
1837.	do do	A	2	69
1838.	do do	S	1	22
1839.	do do	S	1	18
1838.	Annual report of Nathan H. Jewett,	S	1	21
1839.	Annual report of Nathan H. Jewett,	S	2	39
1845.	Report of inspectors of,	S	2	65

POUDRETTE COMPANY:

		Doc.	Vol.	No.
1839.	Report on petition to incorporate,	A	5	279

PRINCE STREET ORPHAN ASYLUM:

		Doc.	Vol.	No.
1834.	Report on petition for aid to,	A	2	105

PRISON ASSOCIATION:

		Doc.	Vol.	No.
1845.	Report of committee on charitable and religious societies on petition of,	A	4	96
1847.	Report of committee on state prisons on petition of,	A	7	222
1847.	Report of,	A	8	255
1847.	Memorial of,	A	8	256
1849.	Report of,	A	6	243
1850.	Annual report of,	A	8	198
1851.	do	A	4	120
1852.	do	A	5	123

NEW YORK—*continued.*

		Doc.	Vol.	No.
1854.	Annual report of,	A	4	143
1855.	do	A	7	149
1857.	do	S	4	145
	PROTESTANT EPISCOPAL PUBLIC SCHOOL:			
1845.	Report of committee on charitable and religious societies on the petition of the trustees of,	S	1	46
	PUBLIC PARK:			
1853.	Report of select committee on bill relative to,	S	3	82
1853.	Report of minority,	S	3	83
	PUBLIC SCHOOL SOCIETY, *see* New York Common Schools.			
	PUBLIC SQUARE:			
1833.	In the 11th ward, report on petition for a law to establish a,	A	2	90
1833.	In the 12th ward, report on petition for a law to establish a, &c.,	A	4	297
1833.	In the 12th ward, report on petition to repeal part of an act relative to the,	A	4	205
	QUARANTINE ESTABLISHMENT, *see* Marine Hospital and Health Department:			
1831.	Report on bill relative to the expenditures of the, and the compensation of the officers thereof,	S	1	68
1849.	Letter from commissioners of emigration relative to,	A	2	58
1849.	Report of select committee relative to removal of,	A	2	60
1849.	Remonstrance of William B. Townsend respecting,	A	3	144
1849.	Communication from Dr. A. H. Stevens relative to removal of,	A	3	146
1849.	Memorial of A. B. Whiting relative to difficulty of enforcing the health laws at, and asking an amendment of the law,	A	3	191
1849.	Resolution of New York Chamber of Commerce against changing location of,	S	2	40
1849.	Report of committee on grievances on petition relative to, and to the bill on that subject (1848, majority report),	S	2	51
1849.	Report on petitions relative to same (1848, minority report),	S	2	57
1856.	Report relative to wharves, &c., at,	S	3	100
1856.	Report of committee on,	A	4	109
1857.	Communication from governor of New Jersey relative to,	S	1	16
1857.	Report and memorial of Chamber of Commerce relative to,	S	2	68
1857.	Report of committee on commerce and navigation relative to petitions for the removal of,	A	2	72
1858.	Report of health officer relative to ventilating vessels at,	S	3	127
1858.	Report of commissioners for the removal of,	A	1	30
1858.	Report of commissioners for the removal of,	A	3	69
	QUARANTINE HOSPITALS:			
1848.	Report of majority of committee on grievances in relation to,	S	2	61
1848.	Minority report on same,	S	2	62
1849.	Communication from governor and comptroller relative to the funds for the support of the fever and small pox,	A	1	39
1849.	Communication from governor and comptroller relative to the funds for the support of fever and small pox,	A	2	39
1849.	Letter from commissioners of emigration relative to,	A	2	58
1858.	Annual report of physicians of marine,	S	2	94
	QUARANTINE REGULATIONS:			
1830.	Report on petition of the common council to amend the law,	A	4	351
1845.	Report relative to,	A	7	243
1845.	Report of judiciary committee on,	A	7	243
1845.	Report of committee on the judiciary,	A	7	243
1846.	Report of select committee, appointed at last session of the legislature, relative to,	A	3	60

NEW YORK—*continued.*

		Doc.	Vol.	No.
	RAILROADS:			
1835.	Report of attorney-general, relative to granting the privilege of collecting tolls on railroads in the public streets, &c.,	A	4	329
	New York and Harlem Railroad, *see* Railroads.			
	New York and Erie Railroad, *see* Railroads.			
	New York and Albany Railroad, *see* Railroads.			
	REGISTER AND CLERK:			
1849.	Report of, in answer to resolution of the assembly, respecting fees,	A	2	86
	REGISTRY LAW:			
1838.	Report on petition of the Native American Association for a,	S	2	62
1839.	Report on petition for a (Mr. Powers),	S	3	107
1840.	Report of the judiciary committee on the bill to provide for a,	A	6	262
1840.	Report of select committee on the same,	A	6	273
1840.	Message from the governor returning the bill to provide for a,	S	4	98
1841.	Report of majority of select committee on petition to repeal the,	A	6	243
1841.	Report of minority on same subject,	A	6	237
1842.	Report of select committee on,	A	1	13
1842.	Message of governor in relation to,	A	5	87
	RETREAT, *see* Seamen's Fund and Retreat.			
	RIOTS OF 1834:			
1835.	Special report of the commissary-general relative to the issue of arms for the use of the troops called out to suppress the,	A	2	200
	ROADS AND LANES:			
1833.	Report on petition to amend the law relative to closing of, &c.,	A	3	151
	ROMAN CATHOLIC BENEVOLENT SOCIETY:			
1833.	Report on petition for aid to the,	A	3	225
1835.	Report on petition for aid to the, and to change the name and renew the charter of,	A	4	353
	ROMAN CATHOLICS:			
1853.	Report of committee on colleges, &c., on petition of certain, relative to instruction of their children,	A	4	97
	RUTGER'S MEDICAL FACULTY, *see* Medical Colleges.			
	SACRED MUSIC SOCIETY:			
1834.	Report on petition to amend the charter of the,	A	1	21
	SAILORS' SNUG HARBOR:			
1830.	Annual report of the trustee of the,	S	2	81
1831.	do do	S	1	30
1832.	do do	S	1	26
1833.	do do	S	2	52
1834.	do do	S	2	58
1835.	do do	S	2	53
1836.	do do	S	1	52
1837.	do do	S	1	19
1838.	do do	S	2	72
1839.	do do	S	3	85
1840.	do do	S	3	83
1841.	do do	S	1	31
1842.	Annual report of treasurer of the,	S	2	32
1844.	Report of trustees of,	S	1	47
1845.	Annual report of,	A	4	91
1847.	Report of,	S	1	39
1848.	Report of treasurer of,	A	6	195

NEW YORK—*continued.*

		Doc.	Vol.	No.
1849.	Annual report of trustees of,	A	5	233
1850.	Report of trustees,	S	3	104
1851.	Annual report of treasurer,	S	3	67
1858.	Annual report of trustees of,	A	5	157
	St. George's Society:			
1851.	Report of committee on commerce and navigation on petition of,	S	2	24
	Schools and School Moneys, *see* Common Schools.			
	Scott Life Guard:			
1858.	Report on bill to organize the,	S	2	53
	Seamen, Asylum for Destitute Children of:			
1855	Memorial of,	A	2	56
1858.	Report on the petition of,	A	4	99
	Seamen's Fund and Retreat:			
1831.	Report on bill to provide for the erection of a,	S	1	68
1832.	Report on petition of the trustees of the, for aid,	A	3	199
1833.	Report on petition of the trustees of the, for aid,	S	2	77
1836.	Report on petition of the trustees of the, to borrow money to complete the new hospital,	S	1	20
1837.	Report on petition of the trustees of the, to borrow money to complete the new hospital,	S	1	23
1836.	Statement of amount of receipts and expenditures from 1831 to 1835,	A	3	152
1839.	Report of committee appointed to examine the reports, vouchers and affairs of the,	A	6	408
1840.	Memorial and remonstrance of the trustees of the, against any alteration in the law in relation to said institution,	S	4	111
1840.	Report of investigation of the affairs of the,	A	5	214
1845.	Report of, for 1844,	S	1	28
1846.	Annual report of trustees of,	A	5	182
1847.	Report of physician of,	S	1	34
1853.	Report of commissioners to investigate affairs of,	A	4	92
	Second Associate Church:			
1834.	Report on petition to amend the charter of,	S	2	112
	Sheriff:			
1848.	Statement of fees received by, for summoning jurors,	A	2	35
1849.	Report of, in answer to resolution of assembly respecting amount of sales under foreclosure of mortgages, amount of money received, &c.,	A	2	56
	Society for the Reformation of Juvenile Delinquents, *see* Juvenile Delinquents.			
	Sole Leather:			
1840.	Report on bill to increase the number of inspectors of,	S	2	56
	Sole Leather, Inspectors of:			
1839.	Annual report of Benjamin Brady,	A	3	109
1840.	Annual report of Benjamin Brady,	A	1	22
1834.	Annual report of Benjamin Cooper,	A	3	145
1835.	do do	A	2	76
1836.	do do	A	3	156
1837.	do do	A	2	105
1838.	do do	A	3	151
1839.	do do	A	3	140
1840.	do do	A	5	194

NEW YORK—*continued.*

		Doc.	Vol.	No.
1834.	Annual report of Daniel Dietrich,	A	3	226
1835.	do do	A	2	81
1836.	do do	A	3	195
1834.	Annual report of Daniel Gordon,	A	3	214
1835.	do do	A	4	273
1836.	do do	A	3	165
1837.	do do	A	2	154
1838.	do do	A	3	117
1839.	do do	A	3	90
1840.	do do	A	5	218
1830.	Annual report of J. P. Haff,	A	2	130
1831.	do do	A	2	123
1832.	do do	A	2	163
1833.	do do	A	2	108
1834.	do do	A	3	145
1835.	do do	A	2	76
1836.	do do	A	3	156
1837.	do do	A	2	105
1838.	do do	A	3	151
1830.	Annual report of H. Leek,	A	2	130
1831.	do do	A	2	132
1832.	do do	A	2	163
1833.	do do	A	2	108
1837.	Annual report of Evert Marsh,	A	2	134
1838.	do do	A	3	140
1839.	do do	A	3	130
1840.	do do	A	2	55
1830.	Annual report of Othameir Osborn,	A	2	130
1832.	Annual report of Othamier Osborn,	A	2	110
1839.	Annual report of James Robinson,	A	3	90
1831.	Annual report of Isaac Sherwood,	A	2	147
1832.	do do	A	2	163
1833.	do do	A	2	108
1834.	do do	A	3	141
1835.	do do	A	2	79
1836.	do do	A	3	178
1837.	do do	A	2	98
1838.	do do	A	3	141
1839.	do do	A	3	121
1840.	do do	A	4	108
1831.	Annual report of Howard A. Simons,	A	3	214
1832.	do do	A	2	110
1834.	do do	A	3	214
1835.	do do	A	4	273
1836.	do do	A	3	165
1837.	do do	A	2	154
1838.	do do	A	3	117
1839.	do do	A	3	90
1840.	do do	A	5	218
1835.	Annual report of Oliver H. Taylor,	A	4	319
1836.	do do	A	4	224
1837.	do do	A	2	86
1838.	do do	A	3	152
1840.	Annual report of Zenas Wheeler,	A	4	151

STAVES AND HEADING:

		Doc.	Vol.	No.
1830.	Annual report of Francis Peckwell, inspector-general,	A	1	66
1831.	do do do	A	1	9
1832.	do do do	A	1	52
1833.	do do do	A	1	30
1833.	do do do	A	2	93

NEW YORK—*continued.*

		Doc.	Vol.	No.
1834.	Annual report of Francis Peckwell, inspector-general,..........	A	4	276
1835.	do do do	A	1	36
1836.	do do do	A	3	147
1837.	do do do	A	2	52
1838.	do do do	A	3	102
1839.	do do do	A	3	83
1839.	do John Hunt, do	A	3	77
1840.	do Francis O'Brien, an inspector of,.............	A	4	115
1831.	Communication from F. Peckwell recommending certain modifications in the law relative to the inspection of,..............	A	1	9
	STEAMBOAT COMPANY:			
1832.	Report on petition of Daniel Richards and others to incorporate a,	S	1	58
	STREETS:			
1830.	Stuyvesant street, report on petition to have the same declared a public street,..	A	4	298
1833.	Report on petition to amend the law relative to the closing of roads and lanes,..	A	3	151
1833.	Report on petition to extend Amos street and to discontinue part of 9th and 10th streets,..................................	A	3	136
1839.	Report on petition to amend the laws by which the mayor, &c., are authorized to lay out streets, &c.,........................	A	5	313
1838.	Report on petition to lay out a new street in the 12th ward,.....	A	4	164
	SUFFRAGE:			
1845.	Report of select committee on right of,........................	A	3	69
	SUPERIOR COURT OF LAW:			
1843.	Report of committee on judiciary on the bill to amend the act to establish a,......................................	A	5	130
	SUPERVISORS:			
1857.	Report of committee on act relating to the,...................	A	2	132
1858.	Report of proceedings of, relative to commissioners of loans,...	A	3	72
	TAX, ANNUAL:			
1830.	Report on petition to levy,.................................	A	4	343
1831.	do do	A	3	242
1838.	do do	A	4	170
1839.	do do	A	3	149
1831.	For the support of common schools, report on petition for an additional tax of three-eighths of a mill,.....................	A	3	244
1831.	Report on bill for the same,.................................	A	4	288
	TAXES:			
1830.	Report on petition of the common council to equalize the assessment of,..	A	4	364
1835.	Unpaid, report relative to adding a per centage to,.............	A	3	208
1840.	Remonstrance of citizens against intrusting the custody of the, to corporations, &c.,......................................	A	8	362
1831.	Collectors of, report relative to the appointment of,............	A	1	40
1838.	Collectors of, bonds of, report concerning the,................	A	4	168
1839.	Collection of, report on petition to amend the law for the,......	A	6	347
1842.	Collection of, report on the memorial of the mayor, aldermen and commonalty relative to,...................................	S	3	77
1854.	Receiver of, communication from,.............................	A	3	103
1856.	Majority and minority report on tax bill relative to,............	A	5	193
	TENEMENT HOUSES:			
1856.	Report on,...	A	5	199
1857.	Report of select committee to examine,........................	A	3	205

NEW YORK—*continued.*

		Doc.	Vol.	No.
	TOBACCO, INSPECTION OF:			
1834.	Communication from the State of Ohio relative to the,	A	1	46
1839.	Remonstrance against repealing the law for the,	S	3	63
1841.	Memorial of Chamber of Commerce relative to the,	S	3	78
1841.	Remonstrance of Egbert Benson against any alteration in the law for the,	S	3	82
1841.	Remonstrance of sundry merchants against any alteration in the law for the,	S	3	83
1841.	Memorial of merchants and dealers in tobacco for a repeal of all compulsory inspection, &c.,	S	3	87
	TOBACCO, INSPECTOR OF:			
1835.	Annual report of J. D. Stevenson,	S	2	43
1836.	do do	A	2	84
1837.	do do	A	3	247
1837.	do do	A	3	278
1838.	do do	S	1	12
1839.	do do	S	2	55
1840.	do do	S	1	14
	TRINITY CHURCH:			
1836.	Report on memorial of W. Cockran and others relative to,	A	4	321
1846.	Report of rector, wardens and vestrymen of, answer to a resolution relative to their real and personal property,	S	3	86
1846.	Report of Mr. Clarke relative to,	S	4	117
1846.	Report of Mr. Emmons from a majority of committee on same subject,	S	4	118
1847.	Report on petition for change of title of corporation of,	A	4	114
1853.	Memorial of rector, &c., of,	S	2	63
1854.	Communication from vestry, &c., under resolution,	A	4	130
1856.	Report of vestry of, to resolution,	S	2	45
1857.	Report of select committee relative to report of,	S	2	46
1857.	Report and testimony relative to report of,	S	3	95
1857.	Report of select committee on memorial of G. M. Ogden,	S	4	134
1857.	Memorial and protest of rector, &c., of,	S	4	136
1857.	Memorial of J. C. Ray and others relative to, and law of 1814,	S	4	143
	TWELFTH WARD:			
1833.	Public place in the, report on petition for a law to establish a,	A	4	297
1838.	New street in the, report on petition to lay out a,	A	4	164
1839.	Public square in the, report on petition to repeal part of an act to establish a,	A	4	205
1839.	Public market, report on petition to vest in the common council certain lands for a,	A	4	203
	UNION PLACE:			
1831.	Report relative to opening,	A	4	296
	UNION RIFLEMEN:			
1842.	Report of committee on petition of,	A	7	169
	UNIVERSITY, *see* Colleges, &c.			
	VOLUNTEERS, *see* Mexican War.			
	WASHINGTON MONUMENT ASSOCIATION:			
1833.	Report on petition to incorporate the,	A	3	144
	WATER:			
1831.	Boring for, report on petition for a law to authorize the expense of, to be assessed on the inhabitants,	A	3	247

NEW YORK—*continued.*

		Doc.	Vol.	No.
1832.	Report on the petition of the common council to procure a supply of pure and wholesome,	A	2	166
1834.	Report of the commissioners under the act relative to supplying the city with,	A	1	15
1840.	do do in pursuance of a resolution of the assembly,	A	7	289
1841.	do do relative to the progress of the work, &c.,	S	2	43
1838.	Report relative to crossing the Harlem river with the Croton aqueduct,	A	6	319
1839.	Report relative to the same,	A	4	190
1838.	Loan, report on petition to raise money by loan,	A	6	299
1840.	Stock, report on petition to raise money by loan by the creation of a fund to be denominated the,	A	2	52
1840.	Stock, communication from the common council relative to the sale of the,	A	7	304

WEIGHER GENERAL, *see* Merchandise, &c.

WESTCHESTER COUNTY, ROADS IN:

1837.	Report relative to the alteration of such roads as may be necessary by the plan adopted for supplying the city with,	A	3	175

WHARFAGE:

1850.	Report on,	A	6	162
1851.	Report of committee on commerce and navigation on the subject of,	A	4	112

WHARVES, PIERS AND SLIPS:

1830.	Report on petition for the better regulation of the,	A	4	314

WITNESSES:

1836.	Report relative to granting additional compensation to,	A	4	263

WOMAN'S HOSPITAL:

1856.	Report on memorial of trustees of,	S	2	52

WOOSTER STREET:

1833.	Report relative to the extension of, to Union Place,	A	2	56

NIAGARA COUNTY.

1833.	Poor-house, report on petition for a loan to build,	A	2	59
1842.	Memorial of citizens of, asking the incorporation of a company to complete canals,	A	7	160
1842.	Report on proceedings of a meeting of citizens of, on subject of letter postage and the franking privilege,	A	7	165
1847.	Communication relative to districting,	A	6	170

NIAGARA FALLS.

1850.	Report of committee on canals against mill race around,	A	6	157

NIAGARA FALLS MANUFACTURING COMPANY.

1832.	Report on petition to incorporate the,	A	2	113

NIAGARA RIVER.

1836.	Ferry across, at Youngstown, majority report on petition for,	A	2	62
1836.	Ferry across, at Youngstown, minority report on petition for,	A	2	63
1831.	Ferry at Squaw island, report relative to the,	A	2	192

NIAGARA RIVER HYDRAULIC COMPANY.

		Doc.	Vol.	No.
1846.	Report relative to,	S	1	30

NIAGARA SUSPENSION BRIDGE COMPANY.

		Doc.	Vol.	No.
1837.	Report concerning the,	A	4	331
1855.	Petition of,	S	2	59

NIAGARA SHIP CANAL.

		Doc.	Vol.	No.
1834.	Preamble and resolution relative to the construction of a,	A	3	166
1839.	Report on bill to authorize the United States to construct a,	S	1	23
1840.	Memorial of Jesse Hawley against the construction of the, by the United States,	S	4	108
1853.	Minority report of committee on canals on petition for,	A	3	76
1853.	Minority report,	A	3	77

NICHOLLS, SAMUEL B.

		Doc.	Vol.	No.
1836.	Report on petition of, for a grant of land under water in the town of Shelter island,	S	1	44

NICHOLS, JAMES.

		Doc.	Vol.	No.
1856.	Report on claim of,	S	2	61
1857.	Report on petition of,	S	1	15

NICHOLS, JAMES, AND JOHN C. HOYT.

		Doc.	Vol.	No.
1840.	Report on petition for compensation for damages to their mills on the Chemung river,	A	7	298
1841.	Report on petition for compensation for damages to their mills on the Chemung river,	A	6	208
1848.	Report on petition of,	A	5	170
1854.	Report on petition of,	S	2	78
1855.	Report of petition of,	S	1	29

NICHOLS, PERKINS.

		Doc.	Vol.	No.
1833.	Report on petition of, relative to the redemption of his land sold for taxes,	A	4	269

NICHOLS, SAMUEL.

		Doc.	Vol.	No.
1833.	Report on petition of, to erect a wharf in the town of Flushing,	A	4	257

NICHOLSON, NICHOLAS.

		Doc.	Vol.	No.
1843.	Report of canal commissioners on petition of,	S	3	71

NICKERSON, N.

		Doc.	Vol.	No.
1846.	Report on petition for the relief of,	S	3	94

NICKLES, WILEY.

		Doc.	Vol.	No.
1834.	Report on petition of, for a single horse pedler's license,	A	2	60
1834.	Report on petition of, for a single horse pedler's license,	S	2	90

NILES, JOHN.

		Doc.	Vol.	No.
1847.	Report on petition of,	A	1	31
1849.	Report of committee on claims on petition of,	A	1	36

NILES, RICHARD.

		Doc.	Vol.	No.
1853.	Report of committee on claims on petition of, for relief,........	A	5	124
1854.	Report on petition of,....................................	S	1	22

NILES, W. W.

1848.	Report relative to petition of,..............................	A	2	19
1848.	do do	A	5	161
1848.	do do	A	5	164
1848.	do do	A	5	186
1849.	Report on claim of,...	S	2	31
1850.	Report of attorney-general on claim for destruction of property,	S	2	61
1850.	Report of select committee,................................	S	3	82
1852.	Report on petition of, for relief,..........................	S	1	32
1854.	Report on petition of,......................................	S	2	86

NON-RESIDENT DEBTORS.

1839.	Remonstrance against repealing the law for the imprisonment of,	S	3	65
1839.	Attachment against, report concerning,......................	A	5	302

NON-RESIDENTS.

1834.	Lands of, report on petition to amend the law relative to the survey of, &c.,..	A	2	87
1838.	Lands in Hornellsville, report relative to taxes on,............	A	6	361
1850.	Lands, report of attorney-general and comptroller respecting,...	A	3	39
1854.	Lands, communication from comptroller, relative to,...........	A	3	101
1831.	Tax on debts due, petition for a law requiring a,..............	A	3	208
1831.	do memorial of the agent of the Holland Land Company against the same,...............	A	4	282
1833.	do report on petition for a law requiring a,......	A	3	162
1833.	do memorial of the agent of the Holland Land Company against the same, ...	A	3	235
1835.	do report on petition to amend the law, ...	A	2	87
1836.	do memorial of a committee of citizens of New York for the repeal of the law,...........	A	1	8
1836.	do report on petition to repeal the law, ...	S	1	30
1834.	Taxation of debts owing to the Connecticut School Fund, report relative to the, ...	A	3	148
1834.	Taxation of debts owing to the Connecticut School Fund, report of attorney-general on the same, ...	A	3	137
1843.	Report of the comptroller of the amount due on account of taxes,	S	1	13
1846.	Report of committee on finance, relative to tax of personal property of, ...	S	4	109

NORMAL SCHOOL, *see* Common Schools.

NORMAN, HENRY H.

1856.	Report on petition for relief, ...	A	4	161

NORMAN, I. E., AND I. RUSSELL.

1834.	Report on petition of, to construct a dam across Schroon river,..	A	4	373

NORTH AMERICAN MINING COMPANY.

1832.	Report on petition to incorporate,...........................	A	1	40
1832.	Report on petition to incorporate,...........................	A	2	72

NORTH CAROLINA, STATE OF.

1833.	Resolution of the Legislature of, relative to nullification in South Carolina,..	A	1	115

NORTH CAROLINA, STATE OF—*continued.*

Year	Subject	Doc.	Vol.	No.
1834.	Resolution of the Legislature of, relative to the militia and the public defence,	A	3	109
1836.	Resolution of the Legislature of, relative to the abolitionists,	A	1	22
1839.	Resolution of the Legislature of, relative to the policy of the General Government,	A	4	202

NORTHEASTERN BOUNDARY LINE.

Year	Subject	Doc.	Vol.	No.
1833.	Resolution of the Legislature of Massachusetts, concerning the,	A	3	183
1839.	Resolut on of the Legislatute of Ohio, relative to the course of the General Government in relation to the,	A	6	389
1839.	Message from the Governor, relative to the recent events on the frontier,	S	2	60
1839.	Report of select committee on the same,	S	3	68
1839.	Report of select committee on the same,	A	5	324
1839.	Communication from M. Van Buren, President of the United States, acknowledging the receipt of certain resolutions of the Legislature of New York,	S	3	79
1840.	Resolution of the Legislature of Maine, relative to the,	A	7	305
1840.	do do Indiana, relative to the,	A	7	308
1841.	do do Massachusetts, relative to the,	S	3	89
1841.	do do Maryland, relative to the,	A	6	215

NORTHERN FRONTIER.

Year	Subject	Doc.	Vol.	No.
1830.	Resolution of the Legislatnre of Vermont, relative to fortifications on the,	S	4	366
1838.	Message from the Governor in relation to the destruction of the steamboat Caroline,	S	1	4
1838.	Report of joint committee, on the same,	S	1	7
1838.	Message of the Governor, relative to the seizure of State ordnance, &c.,	A	5	217
1838.	Report on the same,	A	5	241
1838.	Report of the commissary-general, relative to the arms and ordnance taken from the State arsenals,	A	6	308
1838.	Message from the Governor, relative to the expense of calling out the militia for the defence of the,	A	6	315
1838.	Report on the same,	A	6	348
1839.	Message from the Governor, transmitting certain communications in relation to the recent events on the,	A	6	375
1839.	Message from the Governor, transmitting documents relative to the disturbances on the,	A	6	412
1839.	Report on petition of General Corss and others, for compensation for services, &c., in the defence of the,	A	6	394

NORTHERN NEW YORK.

Year	Subject	Doc.	Vol.	No.
1843.	Remonstrance of inhabitants of,	A	5	129

NORTHERN RIVERS.

Year	Subject	Doc.	Vol.	No.
1854.	Report relative to improvement of,	S	2	91

NORTHERN TURNPIKE ROAD.

Year	Subject	Doc.	Vol.	No.
1830.	Report on petition of James Lowrie and others, concerning the,	A	2	154

NORTH GORE.

Year	Subject	Doc.	Vol.	No.
1843.	Report of the commissioners of the land office in relation to, lying between townships Nos. 10 and 12 in Totten and Crossfield's purchase,	A	5	161

NORTH HEMPSTEAD, TOWN OF.

		Doc.	Vol.	No.
1835.	Wharf at, report on petition of R. Udall and J. B. Cheeseman to build a,	A	4	305
1838.	Jones' fund for the support of the poor of, report on petition for the appointment of trustees of the,	A	5	228

NORTHROP, NORMAN.

1850.	Report on claims for canal damages,	A	5	91
1857.	Report of committee on claims, adverse on petition of for damages to clay bed, and by overflow of the Erie canal,	A	2	106

NORTON, HARVEY, AND C. C. CHURCH.

1842.	Report on petition of,	A	2	44

NORTON, J. A.

1833.	Report on petition for compensation for services in apprehending certain fugitives from justice,	A	2	126
1835.	Report on the same,	A	2	66

NORTON, P., AND J. G. FERGUSON.

1842.	Report of committee on claims on petition of,	A	7	137

NORTON, PATRICK, *see* Thomas Geary and others.

NORTON, WARREN.

1852.	Claim of, and J. C. Smith,	S	2	57

NOTARIES PUBLIC.

1838.	In New York, report on petition to increase the fees of,	A	2	34
1840.	Report on bill in relation to,	S	2	51

NUGENT, JANE, *see* C. Strong.

NULLIFICATION.

1833.	Proceedings of South Carolina in relation to,	S	1	2
1833.	Proclamation of President Jackson, relative to,	S	1	4
1833.	Message of the President to Congress,	S	1	23
1833.	Report of joint committee, relative to,	S	1	34
1833.	Resolutions offered by Mr. Hubbard, relative to,	S	2	48
1833.	Concurrent resolutions in relation to,	A	3	163
1833.	Resolution of Pennsylvania, in relation to,	A	2	31
1833.	Resolution of Indiana, North Carolina and Massachusetts, relative to,	A	2	115
1833.	Resolution of Delaware, relative to,	A	2	135
1833.	do Virginia and New Jersey, relative to,	A	3	211
1833.	do Ohio, relative to,	A	3	239
1833.	do Massachusetts and Mississippi, relative to,	A	4	259
1833.	do Alabama, relative to,	A	4	274
1833.	do Maine, relative to,	A	4	277
1833.	do Maryland, relative to,	A	1	11

See Convention of the States.

NUNNERIES, CONVENTS, &c.

1838.	Report on petition concerning,	A	6	362

O.

OAK ORCHARD CREEK.

Doc. Vol. No.

1833. Dam across, report on petition of Alexis Ward, to build a,..... A 4 253

O'BRIEN, JEREMIAH.

1856. Report on petitiou of,.................................... A 4 122
1857. Report of committee on claims favorable on petition of, for additional compensation,.................................... A 1 28

O'BRIEN, JERRY.

1857. Report of standing committee on claims on petition of,.......... S 3 113
1857. Report on petition of,.................................... S 4 113

O'BRIEN, JOHN.

1854. Report on petition of,.............................. A 1 39, 2 44

OBRIGON, MARGARETTA.

1833. Report on petition for a divorce,.............................. A 4 332

OCHQUAGA INDIANS, *see* Indians—Ochquagas.

ODELL, JOHN.

1830. Report on petition of, for bounty lands,...................... A 4 418

OGDEN AND DURFEE.

1846. Report on bill for the relief of,.............................. S 4 136

OGDEN, G. M.

1857. Report of select committee on memorial of, relative to Trinity Church,.................................... S 4 134

OGDEN, SUSAN, AND MARY MURRAY.

1839. Proprietors of the dam at Mount Morris, report on petition of, to have a certain bond canceled,.............................. S 3 95
1840. Report of the canal commissioners on the same,............... S 3 81

OGDENSBURGH.

1831. Memorial from, for a law to regulate auction sales,.............. A 1 12

OGDENSBURGH ACADEMY, *see* Academies, &c.

OGDENSBURGH AND CANTON ROAD.

1850. Report on bill authorizing it to borrow money,.................. S 1 13

OGDENSBURGH AND LAKE CHAMPLAIN RAILROAD, *see* Railroads.

OGDEN, TOWN OF.

1836. First Baptist Society in the, report on petition to sell certain land, A 3 184

OHIO, STATE OF.

1830. Resolution of the legislature of, relative to the tariff,........... S 4 336

OHIO, STATE OF—*continued.*

Year	Subject	Doc.	Vol.	No.
1831.	Resolution of the legislature of, relative to the American Colonization Society,..............	A	3	233
1833.	do do relative to nullification in South Carolina,...................	A	3	239
1836.	do do relative to the abolition of slavery,	S	2	87
1836.	do do relative to the election of president, &c.,.................	A	4	288
1838.	do do against the annexation of Texas to the Union,...............	S	2	58
1839.	do do relative to the course of the general government in relation to the northeastern frontier,..	A	6	389

OHLL, GEORGE.

Year	Subject	Doc.	Vol.	No.
1834.	Report on petition to change the name of himself and family,....	A	4	384
1835.	Report on petition to change the name of himself and family,...	A	2	102

OILS.

Year	Subject	Doc.	Vol.	No.
1849.	Report of committee on commerce and navigation on an act to repeal an act for the prevention of frauds in the sale of,......	S	2	34

OIL, SPERM.

Year	Subject	Doc.	Vol.	No.
1838.	Report on petition for the repeal of the law making the oleometer a test of,..	A	6	365

OLDENBARNEVELD MANUFACTURING COMPANY.

Year	Subject	Doc.	Vol.	No.
1831.	Report of the comptroller relative to the loan to the,......	A	4	290

OLD MILITARY TRACT, *see* Lands.

OLEAN.

Year	Subject	Doc.	Vol.	No.
1832.	Road from to Friendship, report on petition for a,.............	A	4	312
1836.	Bridges in the town of, report on petition to raise money to build,	A	4	274
	Canal from, to Rochester, *see* Canals.			

OLEOMETERS.

Year	Subject	Doc.	Vol.	No.
1837.	Distribution of, to the several counties, report of secretary of state relative to the,...........	A	1	7
1839.	Report on petition to repeal the law making oleometers a test of sperm oil,..	A	6	365

OLIVER, JANE.

Year	Subject	Doc.	Vol.	No.
1844.	Report of committee on the petitions of aliens on the petition of,	A	3	47

OLIVER, WILLIAM M.

Year	Subject	Doc.	Vol.	No.
1832.	Report of amount of fees received by him as clerk of the supreme court,.......................................	A	3	270

ONEIDA CASTLETON, VILLAGE OF.

Year	Subject	Doc.	Vol.	No.
1830.	Report on petition for a re-appraisal of certain lands in,...	A	4	339
1832.	do do do	A	1	21
1832.	do do do	A	3	238
1833.	do do do	S	2	82
1836.	do do do	A	3	138

ONEIDA, COUNTY OF.

Year	Subject	Doc.	Vol.	No.
1830.	Beef and pork, inspector of, report of William Barber,..........	A	2	148

ONEIDA, COUNTY OF—*continued.*

Year	Subject	Doc.	Vol	No.
1831.	Beef and pork, inspector of, report of William Barber,..........	A	2	133
1833.	do do do	A	2	111
1834.	do do do	A	3	229
1835.	do do do	A	3	198
1836.	do do do	A	1	56
1837.	do do do	A	3	171
1838.	do do do	A	4	199
1839.	do do do	A	4	193
1832.	Beef and pork, inspector of, report of E. Robbins,..............	A	2	106
1833.	do do do	A	2	105
1834.	do do do	A	3	233
1835.	do do do	A	4	323
1836.	do do do	A	3	198
1837.	do do do	A	2	48
1833.	Common pleas, report on petition for an additional term,........	A	1	14
1837.	County courts and jails in, report on bill relative to the,.........	A	4	314
1839.	do do report on petition of the board of supervisors relative to the,..........	A	3	98
1839.	do do report on bill relative to the,........	A	6	348
	Lumber, inspectors of, annual report of W. Sheffield,............	A	2	147
1837.	Memorial from, against the enlargement of the Erie canal and for the construction of a ship canal from Oswego to Utica,........	A	2	132
1840.	Division of, report on petition for,..........................	A	3	76
1835.	Manufacturing corporations in, report relative to oppressive practices of,.....	A	3	205
1833.	Sheriff of, report on petition of, for pay for transporting convicts,	A	2	85
1832.	Salmon trout in certain waters of, report on petition for a law for the protection of,..	A	2	116
1839.	Oneida and Jefferson Turnpike Company, report on petition to incorporate, and for aid to,..................................	A	4	232

Oneida, road through, *see* Jefferson county.

ONEIDA CREEK FEEDER.

Year	Subject	Doc.	Vol	No.
1843.	Report of the commissioners of the land office on the resolution of the assembly in relation to,........................	A	2	45

ONEIDA INDIANS, *see* Indians—Oneidas.

ONEIDA LAKE.

Year	Subject	Doc.	Vol	No.
1830.	Report of canal commissioners relative to lowering the waters of,	A	1	68
1830.	Report of committee on canals on the same,.....................	A	3	225
1858.	Communication of state engineer in reference to petition of inhabitants living in vicinity of,............................	A	4	121

ONEIDA LAKE AND RIVER.

Year	Subject	Doc.	Vol	No.
1838.	Steam navigation of, report concerning,........................	A	5	202

ONEIDA LAKE CANAL, *see* Canals.

ONEIDA PURCHASE OR RESERVATION.

Year	Subject	Doc.	Vol	No.
1845.	Report on bill from the assembly for relief of purchasers of land in, in 1840 and 1841, ...	S	2	58
1846.	Report on bill for relief of purchasers in the, in 1840 and 1841,.	S	1	9
1846.	Report of commissioners of land office relative to purchasers in,	A	2	34
1847.	Report on petitions of purchasers of land in,.................	A	1	43
1847.	Report of committee on public lands on petition of purchasers in, purchase of 1830, ...	A	4	144
1849.	Report of committee on public lands on petition of certain purchasers of land on,................................	A	2	76
1850.	Report of committee on public lands,......................	A	3	32

ONEIDA RIVER.

		Doc.	Vol.	No.
1830.	Dam across, at Oak Orchard reef, report on petition for a, ...	S	2	137
1831.	Wing dam, report on petition to erect a, ...	A	3	274
1836.	Navigation of, report on petition for the improvement of the, ...	A	4	264
1837.	Survey of the, report of canal commissioners relative to the, ...	A	2	90
1838.	Navigation of, by steam power, report in relation to the, ...	A	5	202
1838.	do do do	A	5	232
1839.	do do do	A	4	182
1839.	Report of the engineer appointed to survey the, ...	A	2	59
1850.	Report on drawbridge, ...	A	3	49

O'NEIL, MARY E. (Executrix).

		Doc.	Vol.	No.
1842.	Report of the judiciary committee upon the petition of, and Andrew Parsons and John G. Blauvelt, executors of the last will and testament of John O'Neil, deceased, ...	S	3	72

ONEONTA AND DAVENPORT, TOWNS OF.

		Doc.	Vol.	No.
1840.	Report of surveyor-general relative to the boundaries of the, ...	A	4	107
1840.	Report of surveyor-general relative to the boundaries of the, ...	A	4	124
1840.	Report of committee on towns and counties relative to the boundaries of the, ...	A	5	184

ONONDAGA COUNTY.

		Doc.	Vol.	No.
1834.	Beef and pork, inspector of, annual report of S. E. Maltby, ...	A	3	244
1835.	do do do	A	3	207
1836.	do do do	A	3	194
1838.	do do do	A	4	190
1831.	Beef and pork, inspector of, annual report of Israel Sloan, Jr., ...	A	3	241
1832.	do do do ...	A	4	311
1833.	do do do ...	A	3	223
1834.	do do do ...	A	3	129
1835.	do do do ...	A	4	276
1836.	do do do ...	A	4	249
1836.	Jails in, report on petition to raise money for removing and improving the, ...	A	1	11
1836.	Jail in, report on petition to raise money to build a wall around the, ...	A	3	192
1836.	Accounts, report relative to auditing town accounts, ...	A	4	160
1837.	Dogs, tax on, report on petition to amend the law, ...	A	3	238
1831.	Common pleas, report on petition for an additional term, ...	A	3	272
1834.	First judge, report relative to the salary of the, ...	A	4	301
1836.	Stone quarries in, report relative to the quality of the stone in the,	A	4	261
1836.	Taxes in, report on petition to extend the time for the collection of, ...	A	3	142
1841.	Tax, report on petition to raise money by tax to build a bridge over Seneca river at Jack's reefs, ...	A	5	180
1836.	Tax, report on petition to raise money by tax to build a bridge over Seneca river, at Baldwinsville, ...	A	3	149
1840.	Overseers of the poor and commissioners of schools, report on petition for a law requiring them to give security for the public moneys in their hands, &c., ...	A	2	41
1830.	Public buildings, report on petition of Zebulon Rust for compensation for loss sustained by him by the change of the location of the, ...	A	1	34
1840.	Treasurer of, report on petition of Daniel Reynolds for a law requiring the, to refund certain money, ...	A	6	241
1844.	Report of canal board on petition of a number of residents of, ..	A	5	114
1850.	Report of committee on canals on petition of inhabitants of Otsego and, ...	A	3	49
1850.	Petition of inhabitants of, for repeal of free school law, ...	A	6	166

ONONDAGA COUNTY—*continued.*

Year	Subject	Doc.	Vol.	No.
1851.	Minority report on petition to discharge sureties of C. M. Brosnan, treasurer of,	A	3	51
1851.	Majority report on same subject,	A	3	51
	BANKS IN, *see* Banks.			

ONONDAGA COUNTY INSTITUTE, *see* Academies, &c.

ONONDAGA INDIANS, *see* Indians—Onondagas.

ONONDAGA SALT SPRINGS, *see* Salt.

ONTARIO AND HUDSON STEAMBOAT OR SHIP CANAL.

Year	Subject	Doc.	Vol.	No.
1834.	Petition for a survey of a,	A	4	367
1834.	Report of select committee on the same,	A	4	380
1835.	Report of E. F. Johnson relative to a,	A	3	195
1835.	Report of canal board relative to a,	A	4	334
1835.	Proceedings of a meeting of citizens of Utica relative to a,	A	2	158

ONTARIO, COUNTY OF.

Year	Subject	Doc.	Vol.	No.
1836.	Jail, report on petition to raise money by tax to repair the,	A	1	11
1833.	Justices of the peace, report relative to the election of the,	A	1	35
1833.	Justices of the peace, report relative to the election of the,	A	2	99
1832.	Race-course, report on petition for a,	A	4	285
1834.	Race-course, report on petition for a,	A	4	304
1831.	Surrogate's office, report on petition for the erection of a,	A	4	327
1830.	New county from part of, report on petition for a,	A	4	378
1843.	Report of commissioners of land office on the petition of the Associated Mechanics of,	A	5	163
	BANKS IN, *see* Banks.			

OPPENHEIM, TOWN OF.

Year	Subject	Doc.	Vol.	No.
1849.	Report of judiciary committee on petition of inhabitants of, for annexation of part of, to St. Johnsville, &c.,	A	3	138

OPP, HENRY B.

Year	Subject	Doc.	Vol.	No.
1848.	Report on petition of,	A	2	48

OPHTHALMIC DISPENSARY, *see* New York.

ORANGE COUNTY.

Year	Subject	Doc.	Vol.	No.
1831.	Bridges, report on petition to make certain bridges by a county tax,	S	1	37
1832.	Game, report on petition for the preservation of,	A	2	73
8838.	Game, report on petition for the preservation of,	A	4	192
1830.	Marsh lands in, report relative to draining certain,	A	4	430
1830.	Poor-house, report on petition to raise money to complete,	A	3	215
1840.	New county from part of, report on petition for a,	A	8	312
1830.	New town from parts of Walkill, Goshen and others, report on petition for a,	A	2	113
1842.	Report of the committee on railroads on the remonstrance of Sullivan, Ulster and, relative to the New York and Erie railroad,	S	3	74
	BANKS IN, *see* Banks.			

ORCHARD PARTY ONEIDA INDIANS, *see* Indians—Oneidas.

OREGON TERRITORY.

Year	Subject	Doc.	Vol.	No.
1844.	Joint resolution on the occupation of,	S	1	39
1846.	Concurrent resolutions relative to,	A	1	24

ORISKANY.

		Doc.	Vol.	No.
1838.	Erie canal at, report on petition against changing the route of the,........	A	5	225
1839.	Erie canal at, report on petition against changing the route of the,........	A	4	261

ORISKANY FALLS, VILLAGE OF.

		Doc.	Vol.	No.
1842.	Report of committee on canals, on petition of inhabitants of,....	A	4	69
1843.	Report of committee on canals, on the petition of inhabitants of, and vicinity, in relation to moneys paid by them on account of locating the Chenango canal through said village, ...	A	4	105
1844.	Report of committee on claims, on petition of the inhabitants of,	A	3	77
1844.	Report of the minority of committee on claims, on petition of the inhabitants of,........	A	3	82

ORLEANS, COUNTY OF.

		Doc.	Vol.	No.
1832.	Bridge over Oak Orchard creek, report on petition for an appropriation to build a,........	A	1	30
1836.	Clerk's office, report on petition to raise money to build a,......	A	3	207
1834.	Hydraulic Company, report on petition to incorporate, ...	S	2	111
1839.	Jail, report on petition for a loan to complete the, ...	A	1	13
1839.	Jail, report on petition for a loan to complete the, ...	A	2	35
1833.	Sole leather, inspector of, annual report of I. Bagley, ...	A	3	145
1831.	do do Lewis Warner,......	S	1	13
1832.	do do Lewis Warner,......	A	1	41

ORPHAN ASYLUMS, *see* Albany, New York, &c.

		Doc.	Vol.	No.
1847.	Report of majority of committee on colleges, &c., on bill to provide for instruction in,........	A	8	234

ORWAN, CHARLES.

		Doc.	Vol.	No.
1836.	Report on petition of, for the use of the surplus water at Elmira,	A	2	107

OSBORN, ABIJAH.

		Doc.	Vol.	No.
1847.	Report of canal board relative to bill for relief of, ...	A	7	209
1847.	Report of committee on claims on petition of, for compensation for building locks on Erie canal enlargement, ...	A	2	64
1851.	Report of committee on claims for canal damages,............	A	4	108
1852.	Report on petition of, for relief,........	S	1	16
1856.	Report on petition of,........	A	3	35

OSBORN, MARCUS B.

		Doc.	Vol.	No.
1835.	Report on petition of, to construct a wharf at Sag Harbor,......	A	3	180

OSGOOD & KELLOGG.

		Doc.	Vol.	No.
1844.	Report of canal board on petition of, ...	S	2	59

OSGOOD, CALVIN, *see* W. W. McLouth and others.

OSGOOD, J. C.

		Doc.	Vol.	No.
1844.	Report of canal board on petition of,........	S	2	58

OSSIAN, TOWN OF.

		Doc.	Vol.	No.
1857.	Report of minority of standing committee on erection and division of towns and counties on annexation of, to Livingston county,	S	4	116

OSSINSING, TOWN OF.

		Doc.	Vol.	No.
1846.	Report on bill to confirm the erection and official acts of the officers of, &c.,	S	3	90

OSTRANDER, WILHELMUS A.

1837.	Report on petition to change his name,	A	3	188

OSTRANDER, WILLIAM.

1834.	Report on petition for bounty lands for revolutionary services, ..	A	2	57

OSWEGATCHIE NAVIGATION COMPANY.

1836.	Report on petition to revive an act to incorporate the,	A	4	314
1837.	Report on petition to increase the capital stock of the,	A	3	228

OSWEGATCHIE RIVER.

1852.	Report on bill for an appropriation to improve the,	A	5	93

OSWEGATCHIE, TOWN OF.

1836.	Roads and bridges in, report on petition to raise money by tax for the support of,	A	4	304
1837.	Roads and bridges in, report on petition to raise money by tax for the support of,	A	4	321
1837.	Roads and bridges in, report on petition to raise money by tax for the support of,	A	4	323
1833.	Town-house, report on petition for a,	A	4	249

OSWEGO AND UTICA RAILROAD, *see* Railroads.

OSWEGO BRIDGE.

1848.	Report of committee on roads and bridges in relation to,	S	2	36

OSWEGO, CITY OF.

1848.	Report of commissioners of land office relative to petition to cede lands to,	S	2	39

OSWEGO CITY LIBRARY.

1857.	Report of trustees of,	A	2	85
1858.	Annual report of,	S	2	27

OSWEGO, COUNTY OF.

1837.	County courts of the, report on petition to change the time of holding,	A	3	227
1833.	Sole leather, report of L. Warner, an inspector of,	S	2	50
1833.	Fishing in the, report on petition for the repeal of the act relative to the,	A	4	242
1830.	Road through, report on petition for aid to improve a,	A	4	350
1842.	Report of canal commissioners on petition of inhabitants of, relative to dam at Oswego Falls,	A	7	167
1843.	Communication from Governor transmitting a memorial of inhabitants of, on the subject of the currency,	A	5	174
1844.	Report of canal board on petition of a number of residents of,..	A	5	114

OSWEGO FALLS.

1842.	Dam at, report of canal committee relative to,	A	7	167
1843.	Report of the canal commissioners in answer to a resolution of the assembly in relation to the removal of, and Horse Shoe dam,	A	4	93

OSWEGO, VILLAGE OF.

Year	Subject	Doc.	Vol.	No.
1839.	Oswego Guards, report on petition to incorporate the, ...	A	6	409
1837.	Weigh-lock at, report of canal board on petition for a,.........	A	3	231
1836.	Wet Dock and Bridge Company, report on petition to incorporate,	A	4	290
1834.	Ship canal from, to Albany, petition for a survey of a,........	A	4	367
1834.	do report on the same, ...	A	4	380
1835.	do proceedings of a meeting of citizens of Utica in relation to a, ...	A	2	158
1835.	do report of a survey of a route for a,.	A	3	195
1835.	do report of canal board relative to a, .	A	4	334
1834.	Ship canal from, to Utica, memorial of inhabitants of Utica for a, ...	S	2	104
1837.	Ship canal from, to Utica, memorial of inhabitants of Oneida for a, ...	A	2	132
1831.	Canal company, report on petition of the, for extra allowance, ..	A	4	309
1831.	do memorial of Alvin Bronson, president of the,...	A	4	348
1831.	do report of committee on canals on the same,.....	A	4	362
1843.	Property shipped and left at, report of canal board relative to, ..	A	5	148
1845.	Remonstrance of inhabitants of, against proposed discriminating duties on Erie canal,....................................	A	4	85
1846.	Police justice, report relative to,..........................	S	3	93

OSWEGO, EAST.

Year	Subject	Doc.	Vol.	No.
1830.	Public lands in, report on petition relative to certain, ...	S	2	78
1830.	Public lands in, report of committee on two-third bills on the bill relative to,..	A	3	278
1835.	Public lands in, report on petition of Jones & Smith for a grant of a portion of the,..................................	S	2	69
1836.	Public lands in, report on petition of the president, &c., of Oswego, relative to a grant of land made to Jones & Smith,...	A	3	153
1836.	Public lands in, report on petition of Jones & Smith relative to the same,..	A	4	266
1836.	School lots in, report concerning the,........................	A	4	267
1837.	Cemetery in, report concerning the,..........................	A	3	239
1837.	Cemetery in, report concerning the,.........	A	3	277

OSWEGO, WEST.

Year	Subject	Doc.	Vol.	No.
1832.	Fish market lot, report on petition to authorize the sale of the,..	A	3	227
1831.	Marine railway, report on petition for land to erect a,..........	A	4	289
1831.	do report of select committee on the same, ...	A	4	329
1834.	do report on petition of A. Varick and others concerning the, ...	A	3	201
1839.	do report on petition of A. Varick and others concerning the, ...	A	4	181

OLD FORTIFICATION BLOCK, No. 2:

Year	Subject	Doc.	Vol.	No.
1838.	Report concerning, ...	A	4	183
1838.	Report concerning, ...	A	5	214
1843.	Report of the committee on ways and means on the petition of the owners of, for relief,..................................	A	4	101
1844.	Report of commissioners of land office on the petition of the owners of,...	A	3	59
1844.	Report of commissioners of land office on petition of Alvin Bronson and others relative to,............................	A	5	111
1848.	Report of committee on claims on petition of purchasers of,....	A	3	107

OTIS, O. G.

Year	Subject	Doc.	Vol.	No.
1832.	Oration of, delivered on the centennial anniversary of Washington's birthday,...	A	4	306

OTSEGO AND SCHOHARIE RAILROAD, *see* Railroads.

OTSEGO, COUNTY OF.

		Doc.	Vol.	No.
1841.	County buildings, report on bill to provide for the location and erection of the,........	S	3	69
1841.	County buildings, minority report on the same,........	A	5	164
1834.	Jail, report on petition to erect a,........	A	3	200
1838.	Jail limits, report on petition to enlarge the,........	A	3	131
1837.	New county from part of, report on petition for a,........	A	2	131
1840.	New county from part of, report on petition for a,........	A	6	242
1846.	Report of committee on erecting a new county from Delaware, Chemung and,........	A	4	97
1846.	Report of minority of committee on same,........	A	4	105
1850.	Report of committee on lands on petition of inhabitants of Onondaga and,........	A	3	49

OTSEGO LAKE.

1830.	Report relative to connecting Otsego lake with the Erie canal by canal or railroad,........	A	1	63

OTSELIC, TOWN OF.

1846.	Report relative to certain costs, &c., of school district No. 11, in a suit with Isaiah Lewis,........	S	4	110

OTSEQUETTE, ANTHONY, *see* John and Jenny Hill.

OTSQUAGO CREEK.

1841.	Report of canal board on petition for a bridge over,........	A	6	225

OTT, JAS. C.

1846.	Report of canal board on petition of,........	A	5	151
1846.	Report of committee on claims on petition of,........	A	5	169

OVID, TOWN OF.

1831.	Wharf and harbor near Sheldrake point, report on petition to construct a,........	A	4	342

OVID, VILLAGE OF.

1841.	Report on petition for a new act of incorporation,........	S	1	37

OWASCO LAKE.

1830.	Report relative to the erection of a gate at the foot of,........	A	4	399

OWASCO LAKE IMPROVEMENT.

1855.	Report of commissioners of,........	A	2	35

OWASCO OUTLET.

1847.	Report of committee on state prisons on bill to improve,........	A	8	231

OWEGO AND UTICA RAILROAD, *see* Railroads.

OWEGO, VILLAGE OF.

1830.	Coxe's patent at, report relative to the claim of the state to a portion of,........	S	3	245
1834.	State road from, to Hudson's river, report on petition for a,........	A	4	363
1835.	Macadam road from, to Albany, report on petition for a,........	A	5	387

OXFORD, VILLAGE OF.

		Doc.	Vol.	No.
1835.	Report on petition for a lock to connect the canal with the river at,	S	2	64

OYSTER BAY.

1832.	Academy, report on petition of, relative to the distribution of the literature fund,	A	2	59
1838.	Poor of, report on petition to appoint trustees of the "Jones fund" for the support of the poor,	A	5	228
1835.	Wharf at, report on petition of J. E. De Kay and Daniel Fleet to erect a,	A	4	320

OYSTER BEDS.

1830.	In Staten Island Sound, report concerning,	A	3	242
1831.	On the shores of Westfield and Southfield, report relative to,	S	1	14

OYSTERPOND, VILLAGE OF.

1835.	Wharf at, report on petition of Joseph Terry to erect a,	A	4	352

OYSTERS.

1838.	In the East river, report on petition to protect persons planting,	A	3	157

P.

PACAMA FLY AND BEAVERKILL SWAMPS.

1848.	Report as to draining,	A	2	34

PACKARD, ISAAC.

1836.	Report on petition of, for the redemption of the canal stock held by him on proof that the certificate is lost,	A	2	48

PACKARD, JOHN F.

1855.	Report of committee on claims on petition of,	A	4	110
1856.	Report on petition of,			

PACKARD, S. S.

1856.	Report on petition of, with others,	A	3	40

PACKET BOATS, *see* Canals.

PADDOCK, HENRY, AND OTHERS.

1840.	Report on petition of, for compensation for damages to their lands by the Oswego canal,	A	4	158

PADDOCK, NATHAN.

1835.	Report on petition of, for compensation for damages by the Erie canal,	A	4	344
1835.	Report of committee on grievances on the same,	A	5	389
1836.	Report of committee on canals relative to same,	A	4	296
1839.	Report of committee on claims relative to same,	A	3	80

PAGE, DORCAS.

1851.	Report of committee on claims of,	A	3	60

PAGE, KELLOG, SAGE & CO.

		Doc.	Vol.	No.
1838.	Report on petition for extra allowance for work done on the Glens Falls feeder,	A	3	99
1838.	Report of select committee on the same,	A	5	215
1839.	Report of canal commissioners on the same,	A	2	69
1839.	Report of committee on claims,	A	4	165

PAGE, WILLIAM.

		Doc.	Vol.	No.
1835.	Report on petition of, to confirm a contract between him and the Orchard party of Oneida Indians,	S	2	29
1835.	Report in relation to the same,	A	4	280

PAIGE, H. C., *see* Claims, Digest of.

PAIGE, JOHN KEYS, *see* Supreme Court clerks.

PAIGE, WM.

		Doc.	Vol.	No.
1842.	Report of canal board on petition of,	A	7	164
1843.	Report of committee on claims on a bill for relief of,	S	3	121
1843.	Report by same committee on petition of,	A	5	123
1844.	Report by same committee on petition of,	S	1	25

PAINE, ABIAL.

		Doc.	Vol.	No.
1843.	Report of committee on claims on petition of,	A	4	99
1843.	Report of committee on grievances on petition of,	A	5	160
1844.	Report of committee on claims on petition of,	A	3	37

PALATINE AND EPHRATAH, &c.

		Doc.	Vol.	No.
1848.	Report of committee on roads and bridges relative to,	S	2	67
1848.	Minority report on same,	S	2	70

PALATINE BRIDGE COMPANY.

		Doc.	Vol.	No.
1847.	Report of comptroller relative to tolls of,	S	3	91

PALMER, I. L., *see* S. M. Mott.

PALMER, JOHN J.

		Doc.	Vol.	No.
1837.	Report on petition of, relative to certain land,	S	2	57

PALMER, NOAH.

		Doc.	Vol.	No.
1854.	Report on petition of,	A	2	57
1856.	Report on petition of,	S	2	66

PALMYRA, TOWN OF.

		Doc.	Vol.	No.
1849.	Proceedings of a meeting of citizens of, relative to Rochester and Syracuse railroad, &c.,	A	3	122

PAMELIA, TOWN OF.

		Doc.	Vol.	No.
1834.	Report on petition to borrow money to rebuild bridges over Black river,	A	2	63
1840.	Report on petition for a loan to build bridges across Black river,	A	8	336

PAPER MONEY, *see* Banks.

		Doc.	Vol.	No.
1837.	Report relative to reducing the amount of, in circulation, and increasing the proportion of metallic currency,	A	4	302

PAPINEAU, LOUIS JOSEPH AMEDEE.

		Doc.	Vol.	No.
1841.	Report on petition to allow him to practice as an attorney at law,	A	2	22

PARDEE, LUTHER, AND OTHERS.

1833.	Report on petition of, for compensation for damages by the dam across East Canada creek,	A	4	322
1835.	Report of canal commissioners on the same,	A	4	361
1835.	Report of committee on grievances on the same,	A	5	393
1836.	Report of canal commissioners relative to same,	S	1	93
1841.	do do relative to same,	A	5	155
1842.	do do on petition of,	A	5	101
1843.	Report of committee on claims on petition of,	A	5	123
1843.	Report by same committee on petition of,	A	5	132

PARDONS, REPRIEVES, &c., *see* Governor, Secretary of State.

PARIS, CITY OF.

1843.	Communication from charge d'affaires and consul of the United States at,	A	4	119

PARIS, TOWN OF.

1840.	Report on petition to authorize Asher Flint to take the oath of commissioner of deeds,	A	8	328

PARISH, WM.

1841.	Report on petition of, for compensation for damages by the construction of a lock at Fort Ann,	A	4	133

PARK, JONES' WOOD.

1854.	Report relative to,	A	1	18

PARKER, R. L., AND OTHERS, *see* Daniel Cameron.

PARKHURST, AARON.

1834.	A sub-contractor on the Erie canal, report on petition of, for pay for labor, &c.,	A	4	329

PARKHURST, AARON, AND JOHN Z. DUNN.

1838.	Report on petition of, for a grant of surplus water of the Erie canal,	A	4	197
1840.	Report relative to same,	A	3	99

PARKHURST, THOMPSON.

1841.	Report on petition for pay for certain land taken for the enlarged Erie canal,	A	6	220

PARKINS, JOSEPH W. (an alien).

1831.	Report on petition of, to hold real estate,	A	2	169

PARMA, TOWN OF.

1830.	First Methodist church in, report relative to the incorporation of the,	A	4	390

PARMALEE, SOLOMON, AND OTHERS.

1851.	Report of committee on petition for damages for salt lands,	S	2	43

PARMELE, HORACE.

		Doc.	Vol.	No.
1844.	Report of canal board on petition of,	A	3	44

PARSONS, ANDREW, *see* Mary O'Neil.

PARSONS, DANIEL B.

1840.	Report on petition of, for pay for damages to his lands by the Chemung canal,	S	3	36
1841.	Report on petition of, for pay for damages to his lands by the Chemung canal,	A	4	115

PARSONS, HIRAM, AND OTHERS.

1841.	Report on petition of, relative to certain lands bought of the State,	A	7	263

PARTNERS AND JOINT DEBTORS.

1849.	Report of select committee on bill to amend act for relief of,	A	3	112

PATHOLOGY OF DRUNKENNESS, DR. SEWALL'S (with Plates).

1843.	Report on the, on the subject of distributing,	S	3	116
1843.	Report of select committee on the petition of citizens of New York relative to,	A	2	33
1844.	Report of select committee, to whom was referred a bill for the distribution of plates,	A	5	102

PATENTS, DIGEST OF.

1842.	Communication from secretary of state relative to, issued by the United States,	A	5	123

PATENT, WOODWORTH'S.

1852.	Extension of,	A	2	64

PATTEN, A. AND F. G.

1851.	Report of committee on canal damages,	A	4	100

PATTEN, ALBERT & CO.

1854.	Report on petition of,	S	2	76

PATTEN, HENRY N.

1834.	Report on petition for compensation for damages by the Erie canal,	A	4	267

PATTEN, JAMES W., AND RICHARD NILES.

1853.	Report of committee on claims, on petition of, for relief,	A	5	124

PATTERSON, COUNTY OF.

1849.	Report of attorney-general on the constitutionality of erecting, from parts of different senate and assembly districts,	A	3	123
1849.	Report of committee on erection and division of towns, &c., on petition for erection of,	A	3	152

PAUPERS, *see* Poor.

PAWLING AND BEEKMAN TURNPIKE COMPANY.

1830.	Report on petition to amend the charter of the,	A	4	416

PAYN, BENJAMIN H.

Year	Entry	Doc.	Vol.	No.
1830.	Report on petition of, for compensation for damages by the Champlain canal,	A	4	328
1831.	Report on petition of, for compensation for damages by the Champlain canal,	A	2	80

PAYNE, ABIAL.

Year	Entry	Doc.	Vol.	No.
1846.	Report of committee on claims, on petition of,	A	1	26
1847.	Report of committee on claims, on petition of,	A	1	14

PAY, THOMAS.

Year	Entry	Doc.	Vol.	No.
1834.	A resident alien, report on petition of, to hold real estate,	A	4	382

PEAKE, JOHN L.

Year	Entry	Doc.	Vol.	No.
1848.	Report on petition of,	A	2	40

PEALE, RUBENS, AND OTHERS, *see* New York Museum.

PEARSONS, IRA.

Year	Entry	Doc.	Vol.	No.
1845.	Report of committee on claims on the act for the relief of, &c ,	A	3	52

PEARSON, SAMUEL.

Year	Entry	Doc.	Vol.	No.
1836.	Report on petition of, for compensation for damages to his lands by the Champlain canal,	A	3	110
1837.	Report of committee on claims on the same,	A	3	230
1838.	Report of committee on grievances on the same,	A	3	78
1841.	Report of committee on grievances on the same,	A	4	110

PECK, CURTISS.

Year	Entry	Doc.	Vol.	No.
1834.	Report on petition of, to construct a wharf in the town of Rye,	A	3	210
1835.	Report of commissioners of the land office on the same,	A	1	51
1835.	Report of select committee on the same,	A	2	103

PECK, ISAAC AND ELIJAH.

Year	Entry	Doc.	Vol.	No.
1835.	Report on petition of, to erect a dock at Flushing,	A	2	111

PECK, JAMES L.

Year	Entry	Doc.	Vol.	No.
1856.	Report on petition of,	A	4	167

PECKHAM, LUCIEN T.

Year	Entry	Doc.	Vol.	No.
1853.	Report of committee on claims, on petition of,	S	2	50

PEEBLES, GERRIT, AND R. VANDEKAR.

Year	Entry	Doc.	Vol.	No.
1830.	Report on petition of, to annex two islands in the Mohawk river to the county of Rensselaer,	A	4	346

PEEKSKILL VILLAGE.

Year	Entry	Doc.	Vol.	No.
1835.	Ferries between and Caldwell's, report concerning,	A	4	313
1839.	Report on petition for a new act of incorporation,	A	4	162

PEIRCE, J., AND OTHERS.

Year	Entry	Doc.	Vol.	No.
1843.	Report of committee on manufactures, on the petition of,	S	3	75

PEKIN, VILLAGE OF.

		Doc.	Vol.	No.
1841.	Arsenal at, report on petition for an,	A	6	196

PELHAM, TOWN OF.

1834.	Report on petition to authorize George Rapelje to build a bridge across Eastchester creek,	S	2	116

PELL, R. L.

1857.	Report on petition of, relative to salmon fisheries,	S	4	146

PEMBROKE, TOWN OF.

1834.	Bridges in, report on petition relative to the support of,	S	1	18
1831.	Division of the, report on petition for the,	A	2	107
1832.	Division of the, report on petition for the,	A	2	54
1838.	Classical school, report on petition for a,	A	1	18

PENFIELD, HENRY F.

1831.	Report on petition of, relative to the ferry at Squaw Island, Niagara river,	A	2	192

PENITENTIARY, ALBANY, *see* Albany City.

PENNELL, RICHARD.

1834.	Report on petition of, to rebuild a wharf at the Narrows, in Kings county,	A	3	179
1834.	Report on petition of, to rebuild a wharf at the Narrows, in Kings county,	A	3	238

PENNSYLVANIA, STATE OF.

1830.	Resolutions of the Legislature of, relative to the tariff,	A	2	120
1833.	Resolutions of the Legislature of, relative to nullification in South Carolina,	A	2	39
1834.	Resolutions of the Legislature of, relative to lotteries,	A	1	11
1836.	do do relative to the public lands,	S	2	83
1841.	do do relative to the public lands,	A	4	109
1839.	North Branch canal, governor's message relative to the connection of the, with the Chemung or Chenango canals,	S	3	86
1839.	Report of a joint select committee on the same,	S	3	112
1839.	Report on petition to connect the Chenango canal with the,	A	4	195

MORRISON, WM.

1845.	Resolution of, authorizing the New York and Erie railroad to run into,	A	4	133
1846.	Act relative to the New York and Erie railroad,	A	5	170

PENSIONS, *see* Revolution.

1839.	Report of comptroller relative to persons claiming pensions under acts of Congress,	A	6	395

PEOPLE'S STEAM FERRY COMPANY.

1857.	Report on bill to incorporate,	S	4	169

PERCE, W. L.

1830.	A debtor imprisoned in Cayuga county jail, report of attorney-general concerning,	A	2	193

PERCH RIVER.

		Doc.	Vol.	No.
1830.	Report on petition of inhabitants of Jefferson county, to remove obstructions in,....	A	4	379

PERKINS, JAMES.

1834.	Communication from, relative to the Seventh Ward Bank,......	S	2	94

PERRINE, JOSEPH, AND OTHERS.

1848.	Report on petition of,....	A	5	156

PERRY, A. H.

1832.	Report on petition to change his name,....	A	4	294

PERRY, GEORGE T. AND HENRY.

1835.	Report on petition for compensation for damages by the Erie canal,....	A	3	226
1841.	Report on petition for compensation for damages by the Erie canal,....	A	6	238

PERRY, TOWN OF.

1832.	Boundary line of, report concerning the,....	A	2	172
1856.	Report of judiciary committee on petition of, ...	S	1	21

PERSONAL ESTATE, VALUATION OF, *see* Real and Personal Estate.

PERSONAL LIBERTY.

1848.	Report of committee on judiciary on bill for the protection of,...	S	1	14

PERSONAL PROPERTY.

1841.	Report on petition to extend the exemption of, from sale on execution or distress for rent,....	S	3	81
1837.	Mortgages of, report on bill requiring them to be filed in the town clerk's and other offices,....	A	3	193
1838.	Mortgages of, report concerning,....	A	3	111

PERSONS.

1830.	That abandon their families; report relative to amending the Revised Statutes, so as to give relief to the wives and children of,	A	3	214

PERSONS, CHAUNCEY.

1835.	One of the guard of the Auburn prison, wounded in the discharge of his duty, report on petition of, for relief,....	A	2	104

PERTH, TOWN OF.

1840.	Report on petition to annex parts of Mayfield and Broadalbin to the,....	A	6	246
1842.	Report of the committee on towns, &c., relative to enlargement of the,....	S	2	34

PETERS, HENRY.

1832.	Report on petition of, to erect a dam at Deposit, ...	A	4	322

PETERS, HENRY T.

1850.	Report on petition,....	S	1	18

PETERSBURGH, TOWN OF.

Year	Subject	Doc.	Vol.	No.
1832.	First and Seventh Day Baptist, societies of, report on petition of, to alter their charters,	A	4	324

PETITION, RIGHT OF.

Year	Subject	Doc.	Vol.	No.
1838.	Resolution protesting against a resolution of the house of representatives, in relation to the,	A	5	270
1839.	Report of Mr. Young, on the resolutions from the assembly, relative to the same,	S	2	53
1839.	Resolution protesting against the Atherton resolutions,	A	3	91
1840.	Resolution protesting against the Atherton resolutions,	A	3	86

PHARES, ANDREW.

Year	Subject	Doc.	Vol.	No.
1830.	Report on petition of, relative to the salt lands at Geddes,	S	3	219

PHELPS, HORACE G., *see* Robert Land and others.

PHELPS, TOWN OF.

Year	Subject	Doc.	Vol.	No.
1830.	Leather manufacturing company in the, report on petition to incorporate,	A	4	403
1831.	Bridges in the, report on petition to raise money for the support of,	A	4	301
1846.	Report of committee on colleges, on petition of the inhabitants of,	A	5	176

PHELPS, WALTER, JR.

Year	Subject	Doc.	Vol.	No.
1856.	Report on petition of,	A	3	53

PHILADELPHIA.

Year	Subject	Doc.	Vol.	No.
1852.	Resolutions of common council of, in relation to the erection of a monument in,	S	1	6
1853.	Message from governor, transmitting proceedings of a convention on the subject of erecting a monument in Independence square,	A	4	89
1853.	Select committee, report of, on reference of governor's message, in relation to monument in Independence square,	A	4	102

PHILIPS, JOHN C.

Year	Subject	Doc.	Vol.	No.
1852.	Report on petition of,	A	2	47

PHILIPS AND NELSON.

Year	Subject	Doc.	Vol.	No.
1842.	Report of canal board on petition of,	A	5	107
1844.	Report of canal board on petition of,	A	1	17
1844.	Report of committee on claims on petition of,	S	1	26, 27
1844.	Report of the committee on finance on the petition of,	S	1	44
1844.	Report of canal board on petition of,	A	3	86
1844.	Report of committee on claims on the petition of,	A	5	107
1844.	Report of committee on claims on the petition of,	A	6	142
1851.	Report of committee on canal damages,	S	2	35
1851.	Report on petition of, for canal damages,	S	2	37
1851.	Report of committee on grievances on petition of, for canal damages,	A	4	103

PHILLIPS, JOHN, AND JOHN BEACH.

Year	Subject	Doc.	Vol.	No.
1836.	Majority report on petition of, for a grant of the ferry across the Niagara river at Youngstown,	A	2	63
1836.	Minority report on the same,	A	2	62

PIERCE, G. T.

Year	Subject	Doc.	Vol.	No.
1846.	Majority report relative to claim of Epenetus Crosby to seat occupied by,	A	2	45

PIERCE, G. T.—*continued.*

		Doc.	Vol.	No.
1846.	Minority report on same subject,........................	A	2	46

PIERSON, EDWARD.

1847.	Report on petition of,........................	A	2	63

PIKE, SAMUEL.

1840.	Report on bill for the relief of the widow and heirs of,..........	S	1	25

PILLOW, WM. H., AND JOHN BLACK.

1849.	Report of committee on judiciary on petition of, for divorce, &c.,	A	2	66

PILOT AND PILOT SYSTEM, *see* New York.

PINE, C. M.

1833.	Report on petition of, for the repayment of money paid by him for a pedler's license,........................	S	2	96
1833.	Report on the same,........................	A	2	152

PINE PLAINS.

1836.	Road from, to Poughkeepsie, report on petition to repeal the law to lay out a,........................	A	2	97

PITCHER, MATTHEW C.

1847.	Report on petition of,........................	S	4	124

PITCHER, MATTHEW L.

1849.	Report of committee on claims on petition of,..................	A	2	70

PITTSFORD, TOWN OF.

1835.	Surplus canal water at, report concerning,....................	A	2	83

PITTSFORD, VILLAGE OF.

1856.	Report on petition of inhabitants of,........................	A	4	163

PITTSTOWN, TOWN OF.

1834.	Memorial of inhabitants of, relative to the Troy Turnpike and Railroad Company,........................	A	3	204

PIUS IX, POPE.

1849.	Catalogue of engravings presented by, &c.,....................	A	3	117

PLANKROADS.

1844.	Report of committee on roads and bridges relative to,...........	A	7	197
1847.	Report on general law for,........................	S	2	50
1848.	Report on petition of, for alterations in law relative to,.........	A	5	163
1850.	Report of secretary of state,........................	S	2	74
1853.	Report of committee on roads and bridges on petition of inhabitants of Kings county relative to toll on,..................	A	4	88

PLANTOU, A.

1835.	Report on petition of, relative to an improvement in steam navigation,........................	A	5	385
1837.	Report on petition for an appropriation for building a canal steamboat,........................	A	2	100

PLATO, TOWN OF.

		Doc.	Vol.	No.
1832.	Report on petition to change the name of the,	A	3	201

PLATTSBURGH.

1840.	Wharf at, communication from the secretary of war in relation to a,	A	5	174
1843.	Resolution of public meeting in, recommending the employment of convicts in mining and manufacturing of iron,	A	5	157

PLATTSBURGH AND WHITEHALL ROAD.

1849.	Report of committee on roads, &c., on petition of sundry citizens of Washington, Essex and Clinton, in relation to,	A	3	186

POLLEY, JONATHAN.

1856.	Report on petition for relief,	A	3	85

POMEROY, MEDAD.

1843.	Report of committee on claims on petition of,	S	3	89
1843.	Report of the canal board on petition of,	S	3	90
1852.	Report on petition of, for relief,	S	1	29

POMFRET, TOWN OF.

1839.	Report on petition relative to the school moneys of the,	A	5	305

POOLE, BYRON, AND OTHERS.

1853.	Report of committee on claims on petition of, for relief,	S	1	33

POOLE, OLIVER.

1852.	Report on petition of, for relief,	A	2	84

POOLE, SAMUEL AND WILLIAM.

1847.	Report on petitions of,	A	2	70

POOR, COUNTY.

1832.	Accounts of certain officers for the support of, report relative to,	A	1	12
1832.	Accounts of certain officers for the support of, report relative to,	A	2	118

POOR, COUNTY AND TOWN.

1839.	Report on petition to revive the distinction between,	A	5	299

POOR, FOREIGN.

1850.	Memorial of the New York Common Council against the bill for the relief of the several counties in this state, from the support of,	A	3	260
1830.	Report on petition of supervisors of Washington county for a revision of the law relative to the importation of,	A	4	330
1830.	Report on petition of supervisors of Kings county to be relieved from the support of,	A	2	112
1838.	Funeral, inquests and expenses of, report on petition of Queens county relative to the,	A	5	282
1842.	Report of committee relative to support, in New York,	A	5	129
1849.	Communication from attorney-general recommending measures respecting the introduction of disease and,	S	3	76
1855.	Report of select committee on resolution of legislature of Rhode Island in relation to,	A	5	134

POOR-HOUSE SYSTEM.

		Doc.	Vol.	No.
1831.	Report in relation to the,	A	4	305
1840.	Report on petition to abolish the, in certain counties,	A	6	267
1841.	Report on petition to abolish the, in certain counties,	A	7	265

POOR-HOUSES, COUNTY.

1838.	Abuses in, report in relation to,	A	6	310
1838.	Abuses in, report in relation to,	A	6	360
1857.	Report of select committee relative to visitation of jails, &c.,	S	1	8

POOR LAWS.

1832.	Report as to publishing them in pamphlet form,	A	3	189
1837.	Report on petition to amend the law granting temporary relief,	A	1	41
1853.	Communication from secretary of state in answer to a resolution of the assembly relative to,	A	1	14

POOR STATISTICS.

1846.	Annual report of secretary of state relative to,	A	5	199
1847.	Annual report of,	S	3	100
1849.	Report of secretary of state respecting,	S	3	83
1850.	Report of secretary of state,	A	6	169
1851.	Report of secretary of state concerning,	A	5	147
1853.	Report of secretary of state of, for 1851 and 1852,	A	5	120
1854.	Report relative to,	A	4	144
1855.	Report of secretary of state of,	S	3	72
1856.	Annual report of, by secretary of state,	A	5	214
1857.	Report of,	S	4	131
1858.	Annual report on,	A	1	10

POOR, SUPERINTENDENTS OF.

1831.	Abstract of reports of,	A	1	66
1832.	do do	A	1	33
1833.	do do	A	2	38
1834.	do do	A	3	173
1835.	do do	A	3	185
1836.	do do	A	2	72
1837.	do do	A	3	270
1838.	do do	A	6	311
1839.	do do	A	3	146
1840.	do do	A	3	332
1841.	do do	A	7	277
1838.	To make additional returns, resolution for the same,	A	6	360
1839.	Report on petition to require them to give security, &c.,	A	6	384
1842.	Abstract of returns of,	A	5	121
1843.	Annual report of secretary of state transmitting abstracts of the returns for the year 1842,	A	2	38
1844.	Report of secretary of state with abstracts from reports of,	S	2	73
1856.	Memorial of, relative to pauperism and crime,	S	1	17

POPE PIUS IX.

1849.	Catalogue of engravings presented by, &c.,	A	3	117

PORT BAY, TOWN OF.

1834.	Report on petition to change the name of the,	S	1	40

PORT BYRON.

1855.	Communication from canal board in relation to line of canal at,	A	3	74
1857.	Report of state engineer and surveyor in reply to resolution relative to enlargement of the Erie canal at,	A	2	88

PORT CHESTER, VILLAGE OF.

		Doc.	Vol.	No.
1838.	Report on petition to change the name of, to Sawpit,..........	A	5	221
1841.	Report relative to same,..................................	S	1	23

PORTER, AUGUSTUS, AND OTHERS.

1832.	Report on petition of, to incorporate the Niagara Manufacturing Company, and to construct a canal from Niagara Falls to the Erie canal,..........	A	2	113
1833.	Report on petition of, relative to the said canal,..........	S	1	29

PORTER, AUGUSTUS, AND BENJAMIN BARTON.

1836.	Report relative to an execution issued against,..........	S	1	17

PORTER, DAVID, *see* H. Hulbert.

PORTER, JAMES, *see* Chancery, Register in.

PORTER, JESSE, AND OTHERS.

1836.	Report on petition for a grant of certain lands at their appraised value,..........	S	2	82

PORTER, RICHARD W.

1847.	Petition of,..........	A	2	79

PORTER, TOWN OF.

1831.	Report on petition to legalize a town meeting of the,..........	A	3	219

PORT HENRY, VILLAGE OF.

1835.	Report of commissioners appointed to survey a road from, to Whitehall,..........	S	1	14

PORT KENT, VILLAGE OF.

1831.	Road from, to Hopkinton, communication from the comptroller in relation to the,..........	S	1	62
1835.	Road from, to Hopkinton, report on petition to erect two half toll gates in lieu of the one now established by law,..........	S	1	12
1846.	Report of the surveyor-general answering a resolution relative to state lands lying near the proposed railroad and slack-water navigation from, to Boonville,..........	S	3	88

PORT SCHUYLER, Road through, *see* Watervliet.

1843.	Resolution of Mr Dickinson for the appointment of a select committee to inquire relative to the village lots of, &c.,..........	S	1	24

POSTAGE.

1834.	Report relative to paying the, on letters of the members of the legislature out of the contingent fund,..........	A	3	164
1842.	Report on proceedings of a meeting of citizens of Niagara county on subject of, and the franking privilege,..........	A	7	165
1843.	Resolution of the legislature of Vermont relative to the franking privilege and,..........	A	2	15
1843.	Message from the governor inclosing resolutions from New Hampshire relative to,..........	A	2	19
1844.	Joint resolution in relation to the reduction of,..........	S	1	3
1850.	Report of literature committee,..........	S	2	55

POSTAGE STAMPS.

		Doc.	Vol.	No.
1852.	Reports of comptroller in answer to resolution of assembly in regard to the amount advanced by the clerk for,	A	5	124

POST NOTES.

1837.	Petition from Albany to allow banks to issue,	A	4	294
1837.	Petition from Troy relative to same,	A	3	293
1837.	Report on the same,	A	4	309

POTASH.

1832.	Adulteration of, governor's message in relation to the,	A	3	260
1832.	Adulteration of, report of committee on the subject,	A	4	307
1833.	Inspection of, report in relation to the,	A	4	298
1834.	Improvement in the manufacture of, report of the secretary of state relative to an,	A	2	54

POTSDAM, VILLAGE OF.

1831.	Report on petition to incorporate the,	A	1	26

POTTER, CLARK S.

1855.	Report of committee on claims on petition of,	S	1	18
1855.	Report of committee on claims in case of,	A	3	73

POTTER, JOHN T.

1839.	Report on petition of, for compensation for damages by the Erie canal,	A	5	283

POTTERSVILLE AND CHESTER.

1856.	Report on petition of inhabitants of,	A	3	64

POUGHKEEPSIE, VILLAGE OF.

1836.	Clock Manufacturing Company, report on petition to incorporate,	S	2	88
1839.	Firemen, report on petition of the, for certain exemptions,	A	4	259
1839.	Fires by steamboats, report on petition for a law for the prevention of,	A	5	301
1839.	Guards, report on petition to incorporate the,	A	6	409
1836.	Mechanics' Association, report on petition to incorporate,	S	1	37
1839.	New town from parts of, and Fishkill, report on petition for a,	A	4	299
1840.	Report relative to same,	S	3	91
1841.	Report relative to same,	S	1	36
1836.	Road from, to Pine Plains, report on petition to repeal the act to lay out a,	A	2	97

BANKS IN, *see* Banks—Dutchess County.

POUNDRIDGE, VILLAGE OF.

1834.	Presbyterian church at, report on petition of, to sell real estate,	A	3	147

POWEL, W. R., AND OTHERS.

1858.	Report on claim for relief of,	S	2	62

POWERS AND TRUSTS.

1836.	Report relative to amending the Revised Statutes in relation to,	S	2	89

POWLES, HENRY, AND OTHERS, *see* Oneida Indians.

POWLESS, JACOB, AND OTHERS.

1847.	Report of commissioners of land office on petition of,	A	7	215

POWSLAND, GEO.

		Doc.	Vol.	No.
1855.	Report of committee on judiciary on petition of, for divorce,....	A	4	83

PRACTICE AND PLEADINGS, *see* Code of Practice and Pleadings.

PRATT, FREDERICK, *see* Arnold Mason.

PRATT, HIRAM, *see* Erie county, treasurer of.

PRATT, JOHN.

1844.	Report of commissioners of land office on petition of,..........	S	3	105

PRATT, JOHN AND MATTHEW.

1832.	Report on petition of, for certain moneys in the treasury obtained on the sale of their lands,..................................	S	1	24
1832.	Report on petition of, for certain moneys in the treasury obtained on the sale of their lands,..............................	S	1	15
1833.	Report on petition of, for certain moneys in the treasury obtained on the sale of their lands,..............................	S	2	59
1834.	Report on petition of, for certain moneys in the treasury obtained on the sale of their lands,..............................	S	2	113

PRATT, WATSON & CO.

1837.	Canal contractors, report on memorial of,....................	S	2	47

PRAY, S., and others, *see* Cowasselon Tract.

PRESCOTT, EBENEZER.

1852.	Report on petition of,..	A	2	39
1854.	Report on petition of,..	A	1	36
1855.	Report on committee on claims on petition of,.................	A	1	23

PRESIDENT AND VICE-PRESIDENT.

1831.	Election of, without the intervention of electors, resolutions of Missouri to provide for the,..............................	A	1	13
1831.	Resolutions of Georgia and Connecticut on the same,...........	A	2	123
1831.	Resolutions of Connecticut, Vermont and Mississippi on the same,	A	1	4
1832.	Resolutions of Delaware on the same,..........................	A	1	3
1832.	Resolution to extend the term of office to six years and to make the president ineligible,..................................	A	1	3
1840.	Resolutions proposed by Mr. Root for the same,................	S	1	3
1840.	Report of joint committee on the same,........................	S	1	29
1841.	Resolutions proposed by Mr. Root for the same,................	S	1	5
1841.	Resolutions of the Legislature of Vermont to restrict the eligibility of the president to a single term,....................	A	2	27
1841.	Resolutions of the Legislature of Indiana for the same,.........	A	3	78
1841.	Resolutions of the Legislatures of Delaware and Kentucky for the same,..	A	5	149
1841.	Resolutions of the Legislature of Massachusetts for the same,....	S	3	89
1841.	Election of, to be held on the same day throughout the Union, resolutions of Indiana for the same,......................	A	4	120
1841.	Resolutions proposed by Mr. Swackhamer for the same,........	A	1	9
1841.	Resolutions of the Legislature of Massachusetts for the same,...	S	3	89
1842.	Resolution of general assembly of Rhode Island respecting electors of,..	S	3	54
1842.	Resolution of Vermont relative to time of holding election of,..	A	1	14
1842.	Resolutions of Connecticut and Maine relative to one term,......	A	2	28

PRESIDENT OF THE UNITED STATES.

		Doc.	Vol.	No.
	ANDREW JACKSON:			
1833.	Proclamation of, in relation to nullification,	S	1	4
1833.	Message to congress on the same,	S	1	23
1834.	Communication made by him to his cabinet in relation to the removal of the public deposits,	S	1	7
1834.	Message of, returning the bill for distribution of the proceeds of the public lands,	S	2	109
	Fine upon, *see* Andrew Jackson.			
	MARTIN VAN BUREN:			
1839.	Communication from, acknowledging the receipt of certain resolutions relative to the northeastern boundary,	S	3	79
	WILLIAM HENRY HARRISON:			
1841.	Message from the governor announcing the death of,	S	3	70
1841.	Report of joint committee on the same,	S	3	68
1841.	Report of joint committee on the same,	S	3	75

PRESTON, JOHN, AND OTHERS.

1835.	Petition of, relative to an improved manner of teaching schools,	A	1	34
1835.	Report on the same,	A	1	63

PRICE, HENRY, AND OTHERS.

1834.	Report on petition of, relative to certain land in the Oneida reservation,	A	2	76
1834.	Report on petition of, relative to certain land in the Oneida reservation,	A	3	112

PRINTING FOR THE LEGISLATURE, *see* Legislature, State Printing.

PRISON ASSOCIATION, *see* New York.

PRISON DISCIPLINE SOCIETY.

1842.	Communication from governor relative to the,	S	2	59

PRISONS, *see* State Prisons.

PROCEDURE, CIVIL, *see* Code of Civil Procedure.

PROCEDURE, CRIMINAL, *see* Code of Criminal Procedure.

PROCESS, RESISTANCE OF.

1853.	Communication from the governor in relation to,	A	5	119

PRODUCE, PROVISIONS, &c., INSPECTORS OF, *see* Inspectors, &c.

PROHIBITORY LAW, *see* Intoxicating Liquors.

PROSSER, JOHN B., *see* Warren County poor-house farm.

PROUGE, PIERRE JEAN.

1830.	Report on petition of, to hold real estate,	A	2	114

PROVIDENT SOCIETY, HIBERNIAN, *see* New York.

PUBLIC DEPOSITS, REMOVAL OF.

1834.	Resolutions approving of the,	A	1	8
1834	The president's and secretary's reasons for the same,	S	1	7

PUBLIC DOCUMENTS, *see* Documents.

		Doc.	Vol.	No.
	PUBLIC EXECUTIONS.			
1835.	Report on the propriety of abolishing, ...	S	2	79
	PUBLIC HEALTH.			
1846.	Report of select committee on bill for preservation of, ...	A	1	19
1850.	Report of attorney-general on law for preservation of, ...	A	5	126
	PUBLIC INSTRUCTION, *see* Common Schools.			
	PUBLIC LANDS OF THIS STATE, *see* Lands.			
	PUBLIC LANDS OF THE UNITED STATES, *see* United States.			
	PUBLIC WORKS, *see* Canals.			
	PULASKI, VILLAGE OF.			
1833.	Report on bill to elect constables in the, ...	S	2	88
1838.	Paper Manufacturing Company, report on petition to incorporate,	A	3	107
	PULTENEY ESTATE.			
1831.	Memorial of the agent of the, relative to the taxation of land contracts, &c., ...	A	4	282
1833.	Memorial of the agent of the, relative to the taxation of land contracts, &c., ...	A	3	235
1840.	Report on petition for an investigation of the title of trustees of, to certain lands in Allegany county, ...	A	6	232
1840.	Report of attorney-general on same, ...	A	9	342
1844.	Report of attorney-general relative to the commencement of a suit against some person holding land by deed or contract from the heirs or trustees of, ...	A	6	145
1847.	Report on petition of citizens of Steuben county relative to, ...	A	4	121
1848.	Report in relation to, and Hornby estate, ...	S	2	60
1850.	Report relative to, ...	A	8	197
	PULTENEY, TOWN OF.			
1830.	First Presbyterian Union Society in the, report on petition of, to exchange real estate, ...	A	4	353
1857.	Report relative to annexation of, ...	S	1	29
	PUNISHMENT, CAPITAL, *see* Capital Punishment.			
	PURMORT, JOHN, AND OTHERS.			
1838.	Report on petition to be released from a certain mortgage, ...	A	6	366
1839.	Report of commissioners of the land office on the same, ...	S	3	104
1839.	Report of committee on the judiciary on the same, ...	A	6	364
1840.	Report of committee on the judiciary on the same, ...	A	5	168
	PUTNAM, ABM. V.			
1847.	Report as to allowance to, ...	A	2	98
	PUTNAM, COUNTY OF.			
1832.	North boundary line of, report relative to the, ...	A	3	245
1840.	Report on petition to annex part of Westchester county to the, ..	A	7	294
1836.	Highway in, from Fishkill to Croton river, report on petition for aid to improve a, ...	A	4	277
	Lands, claimed by J. J. Astor, *see* J. J. Astor.			

Q.

QUACKENBUSH, ISAAC J., AND OTHERS.

		Doc.	Vol.	No.
1853.	Report of committee on claims on petition of, for canal damages,	S	2	39

QUACKINBUSH, GERRIT.

1833.	Report on petition of, relative to a lot of land sold for taxes,....	A	4	294

QUACKINBUSH, JOHN S., AND OTHERS.

1835.	Report on petition of, for bounty lands,....................	A	3	236

QUAKERS, *see* Friends.

QUARANTINE, *see* New York.

QUAW, WILLIAM.

1838.	Report on petition of, relative to certain lands belonging to the St. Regis Indians,..................................	A	5	280

QUEENS-COUNTY.

1833.	Clerk's office in, report on petition to raise money to complete,..	A	3	206
1835.	Court-house and jail, report on petition to raise money to build,	A	2	131
1832.	Fish, preservation of, report concerning,..................	A	4	337
1838.	Foreign poor, report relative to the funeral inquests and expenses of,..................................	A	5	282
1837.	Game in, report relative to the preservation of,...............	A	3	196
1838.	Highways and bridges in, report on bill in relation to,..........	A	3	80
1839.	Monument over the remains of the crew and passengers of the ships Bristol and Mexico, report on petition for the erection of a,..................................	A	5	321
1839.	Majority report on the bill for the erection of,................	A	6	341
1839.	Minority report on the same,............................	A	6	349
1840.	Report of select committee on the same,....................	A	3	101
1838.	Uniform companies, report on petition of, for certain exemptions and privileges,..................................	A	5	205
1832.	Wreckmasters in, report relative to coroners and sheriffs acting as,..................................	A	4	276
1855.	Judiciary, report of committee in reference to cost of general sessions in Queens county,..........................	A	4	102

QUIGE, JAMES, *see* Gloudy Hamilton.

QUIGG, BEN. D.

1848.	Report on petition of,..................................	A	1	13

QUIGG, DANIEL M., AND OTHERS.

1857.	Report of committee on claims, favorable on petition of, for additional compensation,..................................	A	2	122

QUIT-RENTS IN GLENNVILLE, *see* Glennville.

1835.	Sales of lands for arrears of, report relative to the,...........	A	5	380

R.

RACE-COURSES.

		Doc.	Vol.	No.
1831.	Report relative to extending the privilege of, to all the counties of the state, ...	A	4	351

RACKETT RIVER.

1854.	Report of select committee on improvement of,......	S	1	24

RADFORD, WM.

1849.	Report of comptroller relative to draft paid by the agents of Sing Sing prison to,......	A	2	92

RAILROADS.

1841.	Assumption of, by the state, report on a resolution to inquire and report which of the railroad companies contain in their charters a provision authorizing to assume the same, &c.,......	A	7	264
1835.	And canals, relative cost of, ...	A	4	296
1832.	Mr. Stillwell's report on the subject of,......	A	2	68
1838.	Mr. E. F. Johnson's report on the same,......	A	4	171
1839.	State stock issued to, comptroller's report relative to the interest on,......	S	3	100
1830.	do amount of, liabilities incurred and amount paid for surveys, &c., ...	A	6	388
1841.	do comptroller's report in relation to,......	A	3	70
1841.	do comptroller's report in relation to,......	A	7	273
1841.	Statistical information relative to railroads in the different states, by E. H. Brodhead,......	A	6	218
1836.	Transportation of the United States mail on, report relative to requiring the, ...	A	4	302
1836.	Governor's message returning the bill for the same,......	A	4	326
1839.	Report on bill to aid in the construction of several,......	A	6	353
1836.	List of applications for, ...	A	2	91
1839.	List of bills before the legislature, proposing to loan the credit of the state to,......	S	3	110
1835.	Report of a survey of the route from Williamsport, Pennsylvania, to Elmira, New York,......	A	4	351
1843.	Report of select committee on petitions for a law to prevent combinations between, and for other purposes,......	A	4	85
1843.	Remonstrance of the several companies on the line from Buffalo to Schenectady, against the bill entitled "An act in relation to railroad companies, and to protect passengers and others from imposition and annoyance,"......	A	4	106
1845.	Report of committee on, on petition of Saul Alley and others to construct a, from Albany to New York, ...	S	2	73
1845.	Report on petition for a, from head of Seneca lake to the New York and Erie,......	S	3	91
1845.	Memorial of, companies from Albany to Attica, ...	A	5	194
1846.	Report of committee on, on sundry petitions, &c.,......	A	2	51
1846.	Report of secretary of state, in answer to a resolution relative to,	A	3	66
1846.	Report of secretary of state transmitting annual reports of,......	A	3	80
1846.	Report of committee on, on resolutions referred to them,......	A	4	89
1849.	Report of state engineer and surveyor concerning,......	S	3	84
1849.	Proceeding of citizens of Palmyra relative to bills for, &c.,......	A	3	122
1850.	Annual report relative to, ...	A	5	92
1851.	Annual report of state engineer and surveyor, ...	S	1	12
1851.	Report of committee on, relative to a draw-bridge over the Big Chazy river, ...	A	5	145
1852.	Annual report of state engineer and surveyor, ...	A	1	27

RAILROADS—*continued.*

		Doc.	Vol.	No.
1853.	Report of state engineer and surveyor respecting turnouts, switches, &c., on,	S	1	31
1854.	Report of committee on, relative to subscriptions to certain,	A	3	80
1855.	Report of committee on, on subject of canal revenues,	S	3	74
1855.	Report of select committee in relation to passage of bill in reference to, in cities,	A	5	136
1858.	Report of railroad companies relative to the assessment laws,	S	2	68
1858.	Report of state engineer and surveyor on,	A	4	89
	ACCIDENTS:			
1852.	Report relative to,	A	2	82
1853.	Report of the select committee appointed by the senate, April 15, 1852, to examine and report the causes of, the means of preventing their occurrence, &c.,	S	1	13
1853.	Report of committee to inquire into the causes of,	A	5	117
	COMMISSIONERS:			
1856.	Report of committee on bill relative to,	S	2	96
1856.	Annual report of,	A	2	12
1856.	Report on petition of state engineer and surveyor to repeal the act creating office of,	A	4	123
1857.	Annual report of,	A	4	212
1857.	Report of, in answer to resolution,	S	4	156
1858.	Communication of state engineer relative to,	S	1	9
	FARE, REDUCTION OF:			
1845.	Report of committee on, relative to,	A	6	224
1849.	Report of committee on, relative to,	A	3	166
1851.	Report of committee on, on petition for,	A	3	88
	FREE TICKETS:			
1838.	Report relative to granting, to judicial officers,	A	6	337
1851.	Report on bill to prohibit,	A	4	98
1858.	Report of majority of committee on bill to prevent public officers from accepting or using,	A	4	149
	FREIGHT:			
1839.	Report relative to allowing companies parallel with the Erie canal to transport passengers, furniture, &c., free of toll,	A	6	355
1845.	Report of committee on canals on the petitions for the repeal of act allowing companies to carry,	A	6	236
1846.	Report of commissioners of canal fund answering a resolution relative to, carried by,	S	3	78
1846.	Report of the commissioners of canal fund on the omission of certain, to pay, &c.,	S	4	106
1846.	Report of committee in regard to tolls on,	A	5	192
1850.	Report in regard to tolls on,	A	5	131
1850.	Report of committee on finance on tolls on,	S	3	95
1851.	Report of select committee respecting canal tolls on,	S	2	38
1851.	Report on tolls on,	S	3	86
1853.	Report of state engineer and surveyor in reply to a resolution of the senate, 10th January, 1853, relating to,	S	2	59
1853.	Report relative to,	S	3	59
1855.	Special message of governor in relation to imposition of canal tolls on,	A	4	97
1855.	Report of majority of committee on ways and means on imposing tolls on,	A	4	107
1855.	Report of minority on same,	A	5	143
	GENERAL LAW:			
1847.	Report of committee on railroads relative to,	S	2	64
1848.	Report of railroad committee relative to, &c.,	S	2	33

RAILROADS—*continued.*

		Doc.	Vol.	No.
1848.	Minority report by Mr. Geddes,...........................	S	2	34
1848.	Report of select committee on,...........................	A	3	105
1849.	Report of select committee on bill to repeal section 30 of the act authorizing the formation of railroad companies,...........	A	5	207
	PASSES, *see* Free Tickets.			
	STATISTICS:			
1840.	Report of receipts and expenses of, for the last year,..........	A	8	314
1844.	Report of secretary of state relative to,....................	A	5	123
1845.	Report of secretary of state relative to,....................	A	4	129
1847.	Annual report of secretary of state relative to,...............	A	4	102
1848.	Report of, by secretary of state,..........................	A	5	132
1848.	Annual report of secretary of state of,......................	A	6	193
1849.	Report of state engineer and surveyor relative to,..............	S	3	84
1849.	Report of secretary of state respecting,.....................	A	3	182
1853.	Report of state engineer and surveyor on,...................	A	1	10
1854.	Report of,...	A	3	120
1855.	Report of,...	S	2	35
	TOLLS, *see* Freight.			
	ALBANY AND COHOES:			
1848.	Report of committee on, in relation to petition for,...........	S	1	15
1848.	Report of committee on, in relation to a law for incorporating companies, and on,.................................	S	2	33
1848.	Minority report of Mr. Geddes,............................	S	2	34
	ALBANY AND GOSHEN:			
1842.	Report of engineer relative to,............................	A	5	108
	ALBANY AND SCHENECTADY:			
1847.	Report of,...	S	4	138
1848.	Report of, as to agreement for use of cars for transportation,.....	A	3	68
1849.	Report of, in answer to a resolution of assembly respecting the transportation of emigrant passengers over road of,..........	A	3	143
1849.	Report of committee on railroads on bill to preserve fair competition between, and Troy and Schenectady Railroad Company,	A	3	159
	ALBANY AND SUSQUEHANNA:			
1858.	Report of majority of committee on railroads on petitions to extend the time for completing, and authorizing subscriptions to capital stock of,.....................................	S	2	87
1858.	Report of minority of committee on same subject,.............	S	2	88
	ALBANY AND WEST STOCKBRIDGE:			
1837.	Report on petition of the common council of Albany to borrow money to aid in the construction of,.......................	A	3	256
1837.	Report on petition of the common council of Albany to borrow money to aid in the construction of,.......................	A	3	155
1839.	Report on petition of the common council of Albany to borrow money to aid in the construction of,.......................	A	4	189
1838.	Report on petition for aid to,.............................	A	6	367
1841.	Abstract from the contract between the Western Railroad Corporation and the Albany and West Stockbridge Railroad,.......	A	5	169
1841.	Copy of agreement with the Western Railroad Company,.......	A	5	171
1841.	Report relative to the contracts between the Hudson and Berkshire Railroad Company and the Albany and West Stockbridge Company,..	A	6	212
1842.	Report of,...	A	5	86
1847.	Report on an investigation of,............................	A	4	103
	ATTICA AND BUFFALO:			
1836.	Bill to incorporate the,..................................	A	4	318

RAILROADS—*continued.*

		Doc.	Vol.	No.
1839.	Report on petition for aid to the,	A	4	243
1841.	Report of a committee appointed to inquire if the requisitions of the law to provide for the construction of the, &c., have been complied with,	S	3	92
1841.	Report on petition for aid to,	A	7	303
1842.	Report of committee on bill relative to organization of,	A	4	67
1843.	Remonstrance of the common council of the city of Buffalo, against granting further powers to,	A	3	44
1847.	Report of,	S	4	135
1850.	Report on,	A	4	58
	AUBURN AND BINGHAMTON:			
1849.	Majority report on a bill to declare the public utility of,	S	2	54
	AUBURN AND CANANDAIGUA:			
1835.	Memorial of the Seneca Turnpike Company relative to the,	A	2	148
	AUBURN AND ROCHESTER:			
1838.	Report on petition to modify the charter of the,	A	4	178
1838.	Report on petition for aid to,	A	6	367
1839.	Report on petition for aid to,	A	3	144
1839.	Report on petition of Titus Goodman, and others, to amend the charter of the,	A	2	34
1842.	Reports of,	A	7	191, 194
1846.	Report of names of stockholders of, &c.,	S	2	64
1847.	Report of,	S	4	147
1847.	Report of,	S	4	136
1848.	Report of committee of last senate relative to,	S	2	42
1848.	Report as to use of cars, &c.,	A	3	73
1849.	Report of, in answer to resolution of the assembly,	A	3	149
1850.	Memorial of,	A	1	13
1850.	Report concerning,	A	3	37
	AUBURN AND SYRACUSE:			
1836.	Report on petition for a grant of land on which to terminate their road,	S	2	103
1837.	Report of commissioners of the land office on the same,	S	2	56
1838.	Report on petition for a loan of the credit of the state,	A	5	239
1847.	Report of,	S	4	139
1848.	Report of, as to use of cars,	A	3	79
1849.	Report of, in answer to resolution of the assembly,	A	3	118
1849.	Report on the same,	A	3	149
1850.	Memorial of,	A	1	13
1850.	Report respecting,	A	3	37
	BATH AND CROOKED LAKE:			
1831.	Report on petition to incorporate the,	S	1	33
	BLACK ROCK AND NIAGARA FALLS:			
1833.	Report on petition to incorporate the,	A	3	132
	BROADWAY, NEW YORK:			
1856.	Report of one for,	A	4	168
	BROOKLYN AND JAMAICA:			
1831.	Report on petition to incorporate the,	S	1	63
	BUFFALO AND BATAVIA:			
1838.	Report on petition to incorporate the,	A	3	132
1841.	Resolution offered by Mr. Scott, in relation to the application of the said company for an act of incorporation,	A	7	293
1842.	Report of Mr. Lott on petition to incorporate,	A	7	156

RAILROADS—*continued.*

Year	Subject	Doc.	Vol.	No.
	Buffalo and Black Rock:			
1834.	Report on petition of the, to construct part of their road on lands belonging to the state,	A	2	84
1834.	Report on petition of the, to construct part of their road on lands belonging to the state,	A	3	134
1851.	Report of committee on canals, on petition of Buffalo and Black Rock railroad company,	A	3	59
	Buffalo and Hornellsville:			
1849.	Report of committee on, on petitions for, &c.,	A	3	101
	Buffalo and Niagara Falls:			
1834.	Report on petition to incorporate the,	A	3	132
1837.	Report on petition to increase the capital stock of the,	A	2	56
	Canada:			
1850.	Report on petition of,	A	5	98
	Canajoharie and Catskill:			
1830.	Report on petition to incorporate,	S	2	180
1837.	do do for a loan of $400,000,	S	2	59
1838.	do do for aid,	A	4	165
1839.	do do for aid,	A	4	199
1839.	Investigation of the, report of,	S	3	106
1839.	Report on petition to amend the act of 1838, relative to the,	A	3	147
1839.	Report of comptroller relative to the stock issued to the,	A	5	314
1840.	Report on petition for the construction of the, by the state,	S	2	49
1842.	Report of,	A	5	118
	Canandaigua and Corning:			
1850.	Report on,	S	1	37
	Canandaigua and Geneva:			
1831.	Report on petition to increase the capital stock of the,	A	4	325
	Cayuga and Susquehanna:			
1847.	Report of,	A	2	86
	Central:			
1847.	Report of committee on railroads to consolidation of between Albany and Buffalo,	S	4	149
1847.	Report of committee on railroads as to union between Albany and Buffalo,	S	3	104
1856.	Report of committee of investigation, appertaining to the consolidation of,	A	5	210
1858.	Report of minority of committee on an act in relation to the payment of fare on,	S	3	111
	Division Avenue, Kings Co.:			
1853.	Report of railroad committee with reference to,	A	3	62
	Hudson and Berkshire:			
1837.	Report on petition to authorize the common council of Hudson to borrow money to aid in the construction of the,	A	3	264
1839.	Report on petition for aid,	A	4	243
1839.	Report relative to granting certain lands under water to the,	A	6	373
1840.	Report on petition for aid,	S	1	33
1841.	Remonstrance of the, against increasing the capital stock of the Albany and West Stockbridge company,	A	6	212
1842.	Company, report of,	A	5	109
1847.	Report on petition of.	A	4	116
1850.	Communication from comptroller relative to,	A	1	6

RAILROADS—*continued.*

		Doc.	Vol.	No.
	HUDSON RIVER:			
1843.	Report of committee on, on the bill to incorporate, ...	S	3	104
1846.	Report of minority committee on, on petitions for,.....	A	2	53
1848.	Communication from attorney-general relative to location of, through state lands at Sing Sing, ...	S	2	64
1850.	Report on petitions,....................................	A	1	11
1854.	Communication under resolution,.........................	S	1	27
	ITHACA AND OWEGO:			
1832.	Report on petition to extend the time for the completion of,.....	A	1	45
1838.	Report on petition for a loan of the credit of the state, ...	A	5	237
1839.	Report of comptroller relative to the interest on the stock issued to the, ...	S	3	111
1842.	Report of, ...	A	7	138
1842.	Report of, ...	A	7	114
	LOCKPORT AND NIAGARA FALLS:			
1834.	Report on petition to incorporate,..........................	A	3	118
1850.	Report relative to, ...	A	3	48
	LONG ISLAND:			
1838.	Report on petition for aid to the, ...	A	6	367
1839.	Petition of the common council of Brooklyn, for aid to the,....	S	3	67
1839.	Report on petition for aid, ...	A	4	243
1840.	Report on petition for aid, ...	S	4	99
1841.	Communication from the president of the, in relation to the affairs, &c., of the,.............	S	1	2
1842.	Committee, report of, ...	A	7	163
1845.	Report of minority committee on two-third bills, relative to,....	A	7	242
1845.	Answer of, in reply to certain interrogatories,................	A	6	203
1847.	Report on petition of E. H. Wells, asking relief against oppression of,..	A	4	123
	MAYSVILLE AND PORTLAND:			
1834.	Report on petition to amend the charter of the, ...	A	3	126
	MOHAWK AND HUDSON:			
1832.	Report on petition of the, for authority to construct a branch road to the Albany basin, ...	A	1	36
1832.	Report of the president of the, in answer to a resolution of the assembly, ...	A	2	78
1834.	Report on petition of the, for an explanatory act,..............	S	2	99
1835.	Report on petition to build a basin between the Erie canal and their road in Schenectady,.....	S	2	31
1835.	Report of superintendent, of amount received for the transportation of produce, &c., ...	S	2	56
1835.	Report of the secretary of, of the quantity of land purchased for the, the amount of moneys received for the transportation of passengers and property, &c.,.........................	S	2	73
1839.	Report on petition for aid,................................	A	5	274
1841.	Report of secretary of the, of the number of passengers transported over said road, from 1832 to 1840,..................	A	7	285
1842.	Report of,..	A	7	192
1847.	Report of,..	S	3	82
	MOHAWK AND ST. LAWRENCE:			
1839.	Report on petition for a survey of a route,....................	A	4	262
	NEW YORK AND ALBANY:			
1833.	Report on bill to amend the charter of the, ...	S	2	95
1834.	Report on petition to extend the time for the completion of the,	S	2	115
1839.	Resolutions of the common council of New York, for aid to,....	S	1	20

RAILROADS—*continued.*

Year	Title	Doc.	Vol.	No.
1839.	Report on petition for aid to (Mr. Scoles),	A	4	171
1840.	Report on petition for aid to (Mr. Furman),	S	4	99
1842.	Annual report of,	S	2	35
1842.	Report of the president of, in pursuance of a resolution of senate,	S	2	28
1843.	Resolution by Mr. Denniston relative to,	S	3	73
1843.	Report of,	S	3	110
1843.	Memorial of the president of, transmitting the statement of E. F. Johnson, relative to the comparative merits of their route and the river route,	A	4	89
	NEW YORK AND ERIE:			
1833.	Memorial for a subscription to the stock of said company by the state, of $5,500,000,	S	2	107
1833.	Report on petition for aid to the,	S	2	110
1834.	Petition and memorial for aid to,	A	1	11
1834.	Petition for a survey of the, by the state,	A	3	113
1834.	Report on bill to authorize the survey of the,	A	4	387
1834.	Majority report on petition for aid,	A	4	336
1834.	Minority report on petition for aid,	A	4	337
1835.	Petition from the southern tier of counties, for aid to.	S	2	30
1835.	Communication from the president of the, to the governor,	S	1	1
1835.	Communication from the secretary of state, transmitting a report of a survey of the,	A	2	107
1836.	Report on bill authorizing a loan of the credit of the state to the,	S	1	62
1836.	Names of the stockholders, &c.,	S	2	71
1837.	Report on petition to amend the act to expedite the construction of the,	S	2	69
1837.	Annual report of the, for 1836,	A	3	190
1838.	Annual report of the, for 1837,	A	2	27
1838.	Report on petition for aid, with Mr. E. F. Johnson's report on railroads,	A	4	171
1839.	Memorial of the, for aid,	S	2	37
1839.	Report on petition for the immediate construction of the said road by the state,	S	2	38
1839.	Report on petition for aid to the (Mr. Scoles),	A	2	67
1839.	Resolutions and memorial of the board of directors for aid,	A	4	200
1839.	Names of the stockholders, &c.,	A	5	271
1839.	Report on bill in relation to the loan to the,	A	6	405
1840.	Report on petition for the construction of, by the state,	S	2	45
1840.	Comptroller's report in relation to the issue of stock to the,	A	4	127
1840.	Report of secretary of state, transmitting copies of all reports in his office, of the proceedings and expenditures of the, for 1835, '36, '37, and '38,	A	4	159
1840.	Report on the same, for 1839,	A	5	176
1840.	Resolution requiring the, to report the names of stockholders, their residence, the number of shares held by each, &c.,	A	5	190
1840.	Report in answer to the above,	A	6	260
1840.	Report on petition for the construction of the, by the state,	A	5	215
1841.	Communication from the president to the governor,	S	1	2
1841.	Comptroller's report in relation to the issue of stock to the,	A	4	113
1841.	Report of secretary of state, on a resolution calling for a copy of the annual report of the,	A	4	116
1841.	Report of the secretary of state, transmitting the annual report,	A	4	128
1841.	Report of committee appointed to investigate the affairs and condition of the,	A	7	284
1841.	Report on petition for the speedy completion of the,	A	7	397
1842.	Petition of, for aid,	S	1	19
1842.	Petition of, relative to the survey in Broome and Sullivan counties for location of road,	S	3	58
1842.	Report of committee on, on remonstrance of above counties relative to,	S	3	74

RAILROADS—*continued.*

Year	Subject	Doc.	Vol.	No.
1842.	Report to the governor,	A	1	2
1842.	Report of committee to investigate affairs of,	A	2	44
1842.	Report of select committee appointed by the assembly in 1840, to investigate the affairs of,	A	3	50
1842.	Petition of, relative to different routes surveyed,	A	5	92
1842.	Letter from president of, to governor, March 12, stating that the means of the company were exhausted,	A	5	113
1842.	Report of, complying with resolution of February 3,.	A	7	141
1842.	Letter of president of, to comptroller, relative to payment of interest on state stocks loaned to it,.	A	7	162
1842.	Letter of president of, to comptroller relative to payment of interest on state loan,	A	7	169
1843.	Report of,	S	1	38
1843.	Petition of directors of, praying for aid from the state in the construction of,	A	1	12
1843.	Report of, in answer to a resolution of the assembly of January 27, 1843,.	A	4	76
1844.	Report of railroad commissioner relative to,	A	1	6
1844.	Resolution of the directors of,	A	1	31
1845.	Report in relation to the construction of,	S	3	109
1845.	Report of committee on railroads relative to,	A	3	31
1845.	Report of committee to whom was referred the resolution in regard to,	A	3	58
1845.	Annual report of railroad commissioners relative to,	A	3	63
1845.	Joint resolution authorizing change of route of,	A	4	122
1845.	do do do	A	4	123
1845.	do do do	A	4	149
1845.	Resolution, by Mr. Morrison, authorizing to run into Pennsylvania,.	A	4	133
1845.	Memorial against altering charter of,	A	5	182
1845.	Report of the attorney-general concerning,	A	6	204
1846.	Report of committee concerning,	A	5	142
1846.	Report of the minority of committee on, respecting,.	A	5	157
1846.	Pennsylvania act relative to,	A	5	170
1847.	Majority report of commissioners to determine location of,	A	1	25
1847.	Minority report on same,	A	2	46
1847.	Report of majority in relation to the location of the,	A	4	118
1847.	Minority report on same,	A	4	119
1847.	Majority report on bill relative to location and construction of,..	A	4	122
1851.	Report relative to,	A	4	131
1853.	Report in answer to a resolution of 5th of March,.	A	4	83
	New York and Harlem:			
1835.	Report on petition to extend the time for the completion of, and to increase the capital stock,	A	3	162
1835.	Report of attorney-general relative to the power of the legislature to grant the privilege of collecting tolls in the public streets of New York,	A	4	329
1835.	Report of the names of the stockholders, the amount expended during the year, &c.,	A	4	360
1839.	Report on petition for aid,	A	4	243
1840.	Report on petition to extend their road, and to increase their capital stock,	S	1	28
1840.	Report on petition for aid,	S	4	99
1841.	Communication from the president to the governor,	S	1	2
1841.	Report on petition for aid,	S	2	46
1841.	Report on petition to connect with the New York and Erie railroad,	S	2	59
1842.	Report of,	A	7	193
1845.	Report of committee on the petition of,	A	3	44
1854.	Communication from,	S	1	26

RAILROADS—*continued.*

		Doc.	Vol.	No.
	NEW YORK AND NEW HAVEN:			
1858.	Report on petition of citizens of Westchester county living on line of,......	A	5	158
	NORTHERN:			
1847.	Report as to change of location,......	S	4	144
1849.	Majority report on allowing the, to construct a bridge across Lake Champlain,......	S	1	24
1849.	Minority report on same,......	S	2	56
1849.	Report on bill to allow, to construct a draw-bridge, &c.,......	A	1	24
1849.	Report on petitions to authorize the, to construct a draw-bridge, &c.,......	A	2	94
1850.	Testimony relative to bridging Lake Champlain,......	S	3	87
1851.	Report on subject of bridging Lake Champlain at Rouse's point,.	S	1	20
1851.	Report on allowing the, to extend its pier at Rouse's point,......	S	3	90
	OGDENSBURGH AND CANTON:			
1850.	Report of committee on finance on,......	S	1	13
	OGDENSBURGH AND LAKE CHAMPLAIN:			
1839.	Report of a survey of a route,......	A	3	133
1839.	Report on petition for the construction of the, by the state,......	A	4	233
1840.	Report on petition for the construction of the, by the state,......			
1840.	Report on petition for a survey of a southern route,......	A	6	240
1841.	Report of the commissioners appointed under the act to provide for a survey of the several routes,......	S	1	2
1841.	Report on the same,......	A	2	43
1841.	Report on the same,......	A	7	279
1841.	Memorial adopted by a convention of citizens of St. Lawrence, Franklin and Clinton counties, for the construction of said road as a state work,......	A	2	32
1841.	Report on petition for the construction of the, by the state,......	A	4	107
1842.	Report of committee on railroads on petitions for,......	A	5	127
1842.	Report of engineer in relation to,......	A	4	70
	OSWEGO AND UTICA:			
1838.	Report on petition to amend the charter of the,......	A	2	25
1838.	Report on petition for aid to the,......	A	6	367
1839.	Report on petition for aid to the,......	A	6	351
	OTSEGO AND SCHOHARIE:			
1832.	Report of Ephraim Beack as to practicability of a railroad from the Canajoharie and Catskill road to the Susquehanna river,..	A	2	102
	PANAMA:			
1849.	Report of committee on bill to incorporate,......	A	1	35
1855.	Report of committee on commerce and navigation on,......	S	1	9
	POTSDAM AND WATERTOWN:			
1852.	Report on petition of citizens of St. Lawrence county respecting,	S	2	63
	RENSSELAER AND SARATOGA:			
1842.	Report of,......	A	5	117
1846.	Report of, answering a resolution relative to names and residences of their stockholders,......	S	2	43
	SACKETTS HARBOR AND SARATOGA:			
1848.	Report of committee on,......	S	2	39
1851.	Report of committee,......	A	4	93
1854.	Report on the memorial of,......	A	3	88
1855.	Report of commissioners of land office in relation to lands conveyed,......	A	4	96
1855.	Report relative to improvement of rivers in Northern New York,	S	1	8

RAILROADS—*continued.*

Year	Title	Doc.	Vol.	No.
1855.	Report of committee on memorial of,	S	1	31
1855.	Report of committee on memorial of,	S	2	53
1856.	Report of committee on roads and bridges on petition of,	S	2	93
1857.	Report of committee on ways and means favorable on petition of, to release lands from taxation,	A	1	53
	Saratoga and Schenectady:			
1834.	Remonstrance of, against incorporating the Saratoga and Washington Railroad Company,	A	4	331
1842.	Report of,	A	5	130
	Saratoga and Washington:			
1833.	Report on bill to incorporate,	S	2	123
1834.	Remonstrance of the Saratoga and Schenectady Railroad Company against incorporating the,	A	4	331
1838.	Report on petition for aid to the,	A	6	367
1839.	do do	A	4	166
1840.	do do	A	8	311
1841.	do do	A	5	185
1847.	Report as to repeal of its charter,	S	4	152
	Saratoga and Whitehall:			
1833.	Report on bill to incorporate the,	S	2	91
1833.	Report relative to same,	S	2	123
	Schenectady and Troy:			
1837.	Report on petition of the corporation of Troy to borrow money to aid in the construction of the,	A	2	75
1838.	Report on petition for aid to,	A	6	367
1839.	Report relative to same,	A	4	258
1841.	Communication from, to the governor relative to the affairs, &c., of the,	S	1	2
1846.	Report of committee on finance relative to stock in,	S	3	74
1846.	Report of Mr. Williams, from committee on railroads, on bill to allow the, to extend their road to Utica,	S	4	122
1846.	Report of Mr. Beekman, from same committee,	S	4	123
1846.	Petition for the extension of, on south side of the Mohawk,	A	2	36
1847.	Report of,	S	3	84
1849.	Report of committee on railroads on bill to preserve a fair competition between, and Albany and Schenectady Railroad Co.,	A	3	159
1850.	Report of committee on,	A	8	191
	Staten Island:			
1857.	Report of committee on commerce and navigation favorable on an act to enable the, to have, own and run ferry boats, &c.,	A	2	64
1858.	Report on act to enable the county of Richmond to make a loan to aid in the completion of,	A	4	123
	Syracuse and Rochester:			
1849.	Report of committee respecting,	A	2	81
1849.	Report of committee on bill for, &c.,	A	2	82
1850.	Memorial relative to, direct,	A	1	14
	Tonawanda:			
1840.	Report on petition for a loan of the credit of the state,	A	7	288
1841.	Resolutions offered by Mr. Scott concerning the,	A	7	293
1842.	Report of,	A	7	152
1842.	Report of,	A	7	161
1846.	Report of committee on railroads concerning reduction of freight on,	A	2	58
1847.	Report of,	S	4	133
1848.	Report as to use of cars, &c.,	A	3	77

RAILROADS —*continued.*

		Doc.	Vol.	No.
	TORONTO, SIMCOE AND HURON:			
1850.	Report of judiciary committee on,	A	5	98
	TROY AND GREENBUSH ASSOCIATION:			
1845.	Report of, in answer to Mr. Harris' resolution,	A	3	68
1845.	Testimony before railroad committee in the matter of,	A	4	118
1845.	Report of committee on b ll to incorporate,	S	3	86
	TROY AND RUTLAND:			
1849.	Memorial of citizens of Washington and Rensselaer counties relative to,	A	3	151
	UTICA AND SCHENECTADY:			
1833.	Report on bill to incorporate the,	A	2	53
1836.	Report on petition of the Mohawk Bridge Company to prohibit the Utica and Schenectady Railroad Company from building a bridge across the Mohawk at Schenectady,	A	4	232
1838.	Report on petition of inhabitants of Montgomery county in relation to the,	S	2	73
1841.	Report of cost of road, amount of capital stock paid in, amount of dividends, amount received for carrying passengers, number of passengers, &c.,	A	5	147
1841.	Report of receipts and expenditures,	A	6	219
1842.	Report of,	A	4	76
1847.	Report of,	S	3	83
1847.	Report of,	S	4	134
	SCHENECTADY AND UTICA RAILROAD COMPANY:			
1848.	Answer of, as to acts of George R. Baker,	A	3	74
1848.	As to use of cars for transportation,	A	3	80
1848.	Report of, in answer to resolution of assembly relative to transportation of emigrant passengers over road of,	A	3	143
	UNADILLA AND SCHOHARIE:			
1838.	Report on petition for aid to,	A	6	367
	UTICA AND SYRACUSE:			
1835.	Memorial of the Seneca Turnpike Company in relation to the,	A	2	148
1841.	Report on petition to increase the capital stock of the,	A	2	39
1842.	Report of,	A	4	78
1846.	Report of John Wilkinson, president of, in answer to a resolution of the senate,	S	3	103
1847.	Report of,	S	4	137
1847.	Report of in answer to a resolution,	S	4	154
1848.	Report of expense of road,	A	5	144
1848.	Remonstrance against reducing fare,	A	3	69
1848.	Report of, as to use of cars,	A	3	92

RANDALL, HULDAH.

1833.	Report on petition for relief,	A	3	183

RANDALL, JOHN.

1848.	Report of committee on claims, on petition of,	A	5	181

RANDEL, JOHN, JR.

1849.	Report of state engineer and surveyor, on petition of,	A	5	209

RANSOM, JEROME R.

1850.	Report of committee on petition,	S	2	46

RANSOM, LEWIS.

		Doc.	Vol.	No.
1852.	Report on petition of,	A	2	47

RANSON, PRINTICE, *see* Tioga County Sheriff.

RAPELJE, GEORGE.

1834.	Report on petition of, to build a bridge across East Chester creek, in the town of Pelham,	S	2	116
1841.	Report on petition of devisees of,	A	6	224

RATHBONE, JAMES H.

1834.	Report on petition of, for compensation for damages by the Erie canal,	A	4	294

RATHBUN, SOLOMON, AND OTHERS.

1858.	Report on claim of,	A	3	60

RAQUETTE RIVER.

1850.	Report of select committee on,	A	4	68

RAUB, HARMAN C.

1839.	Report on petition of, to be refunded interest overpaid on a mortgage executed to the loan commissioners of New York,	A	6	331
1840.	Report on petition of, to be refunded interest overpaid on a mortgage executed to the loan commissioners of New York,	A	3	84
1841.	Report on petition of, to be refunded interest overpaid on a mortgage executed to the loan commissioners of New York,	A	4	119

RAWSON, JOSIAH, AND ROBERT TOAN.

1835.	Report on petition of, relative to certain lands bought by them of the Oneida Indians,	A	3	218

RAY, J. E., AND OTHERS.

1857.	Memorial of, relative to Trinity church and law of 1814,	S	4	143

REAL ESTATE.

1852.	Report on taxation of,	S	1	28

REAL AND PERSONAL ESTATE.

1834.	Valuation of, report of comptroller relative to the,	A	2	66
1835.	do do do	S	2	40
1840.	do do do	S	1	11

RECTOR, HENRY.

1844.	Report of committee on claims on the petition of,	A	5	119
1844.	Report of the minority of committee on claims on the petition of,	A	6	143
1845.	Report of committee on claims on petition of,	A	4	97
1847.	Report relative to claim,	A	7	188
1848.	Report of committee on petition of,	S	1	16
1849.	Report of committee on claims on petition of,	A	2	71
1851.	Report on petition,	A	3	72
1852.	Report on the petition of,	A	2	53
1854.	Report on petition of,	A	3	102
1857.	Report of committee on claims, on petition of, for additional compensation,	A	2	75

RECTOR, THOMAS.

Year	Subject	Doc.	Vol.	No.
1839.	Report of attorney-general in relation to the reward for the arrest of,	A	2	38
1840.	Report on petition of supervisors of Saratoga county for indemnity for expenses incurred on the trial of,	A	4	121

REDEMPTION OF LAND SOLD FOR TAXES, *see* Lands.

REDFIELD, TOWN OF.

Year	Subject	Doc.	Vol.	No.
1834.	Report on petition from, relative to the bounty on wolves,	A	4	378
1847.	Report on petitions for annexation of Greenboro to,	A	8	262
1848.	Report of committee on erection and division of towns and counties, on annexation of Greenboro to,	A	3	94

REDHOOK ACADEMY, *see* Academies, &c.

REDHOOK AND SAUGERTIES.

Year	Subject	Doc.	Vol.	No.
1831.	Ferry between, report on petition to extend the charter of,	A	3	217

RED JACKET, TOWN OF.

Year	Subject	Doc.	Vol.	No.
1850.	Report of committee on towns and counties, on the erection of,	A	6	167

REED, JOSHUA.

Year	Subject	Doc.	Vol.	No.
1845.	Report of canal board on petition of,	A	5	156

REES, JAMES R.

Year	Subject	Doc.	Vol.	No.
1850.	Report on petition,	A	6	159

REFUGE, HOUSE OF, *see* Juvenile Delinquents.

REGENTS OF THE UNIVERSITY.

Year	Subject	Doc.	Vol.	No.
1830.	Annual report of the,	A	3	216
1831.	do do	S	1	50
1832.	do do	S	2	72
1833.	do do	S	2	70
1834.	do do	S	2	83
1835.	do do	S	2	70
1836.	do do	S	1	65
1837.	do do	S	1	45
1838.	do do	S	2	52
1839.	do do	S	2	56
1840.	do do	S	3	64
1841.	do do	S	2	39
1830.	Report of amount of money belonging to the literature fund, distributed by them from, from 1823 to 1830, inclusive, distinguishing the amount paid to each senate district,	S	3	218
1830.	Report of, relative to the exclusion of the Redhook and Union Hall academies, and the Union Literary Society, from the distribution of the income of the literature fund,	A	4	320
1830.	Report of, on bill concerning the literature fund and the Oswego canal fund, and the Erie and Champlain canal fund,	S	4	371
1830.	Report of, concerning Hamilton College,	A	4	373
1830.	Report of, relative to the best mode of distributing the income of the literature fund,	S	4	400
1831.	Report of, on the "Act to provide for the application of the income of the literature fund,"	S	1	74
1831.	Report transmitting the reports of the Columbia and Hamilton colleges, and from the college of physicians and surgeons,	S	1	73
1833.	Report of, on bill to incorporate the Albany Medical College,	A	4	288

REGENTS OF THE UNIVERSITY—*continued.*

		Doc.	Vol.	No.
1834.	Report of, relative to the purchase of books, &c., for the use of academies and schools under their charge,..................	S	1	44
1839.	Report relative to the distribution of the income of the literature fund, ...	A	3	141
1840.	Report of, relative to the New York University,....	S	1	10
1840.	Report of, on petition of the trustees of Hamilton Academy,....	S	2	58
1842.	Report of the, and accompanying documents,................	S	3	55
1842.	Report relative to the centigrade thermometer,...............	S	4	94
1843.	Report of,...	S	2	57
1844.	Report of,...	S	2	78
1844.	Report of, secretary of,.................................	S	3	113
1844.	Report of, ...	S	4	131
1845.	Annual report of,......................................	S	2	51
1845.	Report of, concerning St. Lawrence Academy,................	A	5	158
1845.	Communication from Martin Van Buren, declining the appointment of,...	A	5	196
1846.	Annual report of,......................................	S	2	71
1846.	Report of, on the condition of the cabinets of natural history,..	S	3	91
1846.	Report of, relative to Union Hall Academy,.................	A	5	141
1847.	Report of, on petition of George Wood, ...	S	3	89
1847.	Annual report of,......................................	S	3	101
1847.	Communication from,..................................	A	1	35
1848.	Annual report of,......................................	S	3	71
1848.	Report on the state cabinet of curiosities,..................	S	3	72
1849.	Report of, on the condition of the state cabinet of natural history,	S	1	20
1849.	Annual report of,......................................	S	3	78
1849.	Report of, on the historical and other papers and parchments received from secretary's office, for deposit in the state library,	A	3	148
1850.	Report of, on state cabinet of natural history, ...	S	2	75
1851.	Report on the state cabinet of natural history, ...	S	2	30
1851.	Annual report of,......................................	S	3	72
1852.	Annual report of,......................................	S	2	92
1852.	Annual report of, respecting natural history,.................	A	5	122
1853.	Sixth annual report of the regents of the university on condition of state cabinet of natural history, &c., ...	S	1	16
1853.	Sixth annual report of,..................................	S	2	70
1853.	Report of, in answer to a resolution of the assembly of March 27, 1852, ...	A	2	22
1854.	Report of, relative to cabinet of natural history,......	S	1	50
1854.	Annual report of, ...	S	2	77
1854.	Report relative to meteorological observations, ...	A	2	72
1855.	Annual report of, on state cabinet of natural history,..........	S	2	40
1855.	Annual report of,......................................	S	3	78
1856.	Annual report of,......................................	S	1	20
1856.	Report of, relative to state cabinet of natural history,..........	S	3	112
1857.	Annual report of,......................................	S	2	82
1857.	Report relative to cabinet of natural history,.................	S	3	109
1857.	Report relative to certain papers,..........................	S	4	156
1858.	Annual report of,......................................	S	3	130
1858.	Report of, on state cabinet of natural history,................	A	6	163

REGISTER IN CHANCERY, *see* Chancery.

REGISTRY LAW IN NEW YORK, *see* New York.

REGISTRY LAW, GENERAL.

		Doc.	Vol.	No.
1841.	Report on petition for a (Mr. Scott),.......................	A	5	192
1841.	Report on petition for a (Mr. Scott),.......................	A	6	243
1841.	Minority report on the same, ...	A	6	237
1857.	Report of standing committee on incorporation of cities and villages relative to,.......................................	S	2	69
1858.	Report of minority of select committee on,..................	S	3	126

REGISTRY OF BIRTHS, MARRIAGES AND DEATHS, *see* Births, &c.

REID, JANE (an alien).

		Doc.	Vol.	No.
1839.	Report on petition to confirm the title of her son to certain land,	A	3	74

RELIGIOUS CORPORATIONS, *see* Corporations.

REMINGTON, E., AND OTHERS.

		Doc.	Vol.	No.
1844.	Report of canal commissioners on the petition of, ...	A	5	132

REMOVAL OF THE SEAT OF GOVERNMENT, *see* Capitol.

REMSEN, VILLAGE OF.

		Doc.	Vol.	No.
1841.	Report on petition to incorporate the, ...	S	3	96

RENSSELAER, COUNTY OF.

		Doc.	Vol.	No.
1830.	Bridge company, report on petition to renew the charter of the,	A	1	106
1832.	Court-house, report on petition for an additional tax to complete the, ...	A	2	127
1838.	District attorney, report in relation to the fees of the, ...	A	1	22
1833.	Glass manufacturing company, report on petition to incorporate,	A	3	204
1832.	Infant schools, report on petition for a general act to incorporate,	A	4	327
1832.	Staves and heading, message from the governor returning a bill relative to the inspection of, with objections, ...	A	4	329
1834.	Society for the apprehension of horse thieves, report on petition to incorporate, ...	A	4	269
1834.	Society for the apprehension of horse thieves, report on petition to incorporate, ...	S	2	120
1831.	Beef and pork, annual report of H. Turner, inspector of, ...	A	1	65
1832.	do do do	A	2	91
1833.	do do do	A	3	205
1834.	do do do	A	3	153
1835.	do do do	A	3	206
1836.	do do do	A	3	157
1831.	Beef and pork, annual report of Dennis Belding, inspector of, ..	A	2	160
1832.	do do do do ..	A	3	257
1833.	do do do do ..	A	3	194
1834.	do do do do ..	A	3	228
1831.	Beef and pork, annual report of E. L. Boynton, inspector of, ..	A	2	164
1832.	do do do do ..	A	2	157
1833.	do do do do ..	A	3	193
1834.	do do do do ..	A	3	243
1835.	do do do do ..	A	4	270
1836.	do do do do ..	A	4	216
1834.	Beef and pork, annual report of B. Heartt, inspector of, ...	A	3	128
1838.	Beef and pork, annual report of Underhill Boynton, inspector of,	A	3	77
1839.	Beef and pork, annual report of Underhill Boynton, inspector of,	S	2	59
1837.	Beef and pork, annual report of William Gary, inspector of, ...	A	1	38
1838.	do do do do	A	3	104
1839.	do do do do	A	5	268
1840.	do do do do	S	2	40
1830.	Beef and Pork, annual report of George Smith, inspector of, ...	A	2	165
1831.	do do do do	A	2	165
1832.	do do do do	A	3	256
1837.	Beef and pork, annual report of Charles H. Turner, inspector of,	A	3	273
1831.	Flour, annual report of J. Greenman, inspector of, ...	A	4	360
1833.	Green hides and skins, annual report of E. Platt, inspector of, ...	A	3	142
1834.	Green hides and skins, annual report of E. Platt, inspector of, ...	A	2	69
1836.	Green hides and skins, annual report of E. Wilmarth, inspector of, ...	A	3	171

RENSSELAER, COUNTY OF—*continued.*

Year	Subject	Doc.	Vol.	No.
1837.	Green hides and skins, annual report of E. Wilmarth, inspector of,	A	3	272
1833.	Leather, annual report of E. Platt, inspector of,	A	3	142
1834.	Leather, annual report of E. Platt, inspector of,	A	2	80
1835.	Leather, annual report of James Holliday, inspector of,	S	2	49
1836.	do do do	A	3	169
1837.	do do do	A	2	83
1838.	do do do	A	3	126
1839.	do do do	A	4	213
1832.	Leather, annual report of B. Heartt, inspector of,	A	2	82
1833.	do do do	A	3	140
1835.	do do do	A	2	88
1836.	do do do	A	3	151
1838.	Lumber, annual report of E. S. Fuller, inspector of,	A	1	30
1832.	do do do	A	1	48
1833.	do do do	A	1	21
1834.	do do do	A	2	71
1834.	Lumber, amended report of E. Fuller, inspector of,	A	4	256
1835.	Lumber, annual report of E. Fuller, inspector of,	S	1	47
1836.	do do do	A	1	13
1838.	do do do	A	2	59
1839.	do do do	S	1	12
1840.	do do do	S	1	36
1835.	Lumber, annual report of Robert Christie, inspector of,	A	1	35
1836.	do do do	A	2	52
1837.	do do do	A	2	117
1838.	do do do	A	3	88
1839.	do do do	A	2	55
1840.	do do do	S	3	75
1830.	Lumber, annnal report of N. Challes, inspector of,	A	2	127
1831.	do do do	A	2	144
1832.	do do do	A	2	53
1833.	do do do	A	3	158
1834.	do do do	A	1	14
1834.	do do do	A	4	257
1835.	do do do	S	1	45
1836.	do do do	S	1	26
1837.	do do do	A	2	137
1838.	do do do	A	3	103
1839.	do do do	A	4	192
1840.	do do do	A	2	42
1837.	Lumber, annual report of John Burlison, inspector of,	A	2	107
1838.	Lumber, annual report of John Burlison, inspector of,	A	2	58
1839.	Lumber, annual report of John C. Bostwick, inspector of,	A	3	105
1831.	Lumber, annual report of Elias Disbrow, inspector of,	A	2	90
1832.	Lumber, annual report of Elias Disbrow, inspector of,	A	2	81
1833.	Lumber, annual report of D. H. Fuller, inspector of,	A	1	21
1834.	do do do	A	2	68
1834.	do do do	A	4	255
1835.	do do do	S	1	28
1836.	do do do	A	1	41
1837.	do do do	A	2	115
1833.	Lumber, annual report of, T. L. Ostrom, inspector of,	A	1	32
1834.	Lumber, annual report of T. L. Ostrom, inspector of,	A	2	78
1834.	Lumber, amended report of T. L. Ostrom, inspector of,	A	4	260
1835.	Lumber, annual report of T. L. Ostrom, inspector of,	S	1	41
1836.	do do do	A	1	14
1837.	do do do	A	2	108
1835.	Lumber, annual report of Moses J. Winne, inspector of,	S	2	46
1837.	do do do	A	2	116
1838.	do do do	A	3	115
1839.	do do do	A	3	94

RENSSELAER, COUNTY OF—*continued.*

		Doc.	Vol.	No.
1830.	Lumber, annual report of Charles Lemon, inspector of, ...	A	2	153
1839.	Lumber, annual report of Jacob Heermance, inspector of,.......	S	3	72
1846.	Report of committee on militia, &c., on petition of citizens of,..	A	4	108
1849.	Memorial of citizens of Washington and, on the Troy and Rutland railroad, ...	A	3	151
1853.	Report of agricultural committee authorizing the Agricultural Society to hold and convey real estate,..............	S	1	4
	BANKS IN, *see* Banks.			

RENSSELAER INSTITUTE, *see* Academies, &c.

RENSSELAERWYCK, *see* Albany County.

RENT.

1842.	Report relative to exemption of property from levy or sale on execution or distress for, ...	S	3	76
1846.	Report of select committee on a bill in regard to rent charges,...	A	6	223
1851.	Majority report of select committee on petitions praying for a stay of the collection of,.......................................	A	5	132
1851.	Minority report on the same,................................	A	5	133
1855.	Report of judiciary committee on bill to repeal act to abolish distress for, ...	A	4	87

RENWAY, PETER (a Canadian refugee).

1830.	Report on petition of, for bounty lands,......................	A	3	285

RENWICK, ROBERT, JR.

1844.	Report of committee on claims on the petition of,.............	A	6	160

RENWICK, ROBERT, JR., AND HENRY TRAY.

1848.	Report on petition of,.......................................	A	5	179

REPORTS OF INSPECTORS OF MERCHANDISE, &c., *see* Inspectors, &c.

REPRESENTATIVES IN CONGRESS, *see* Congress.

RESTRAINING LAWS.

1837.	Report on petition to repeal the,............................	S	1	10
1838.	do do (Mr. Young), ...	S	2	42
1838.	do do (Mr. Young), ...	S	2	68
1838.	do do (Mr. Pattison),...............	A	3	122

RETRENCHMENT.

1843.	Report of committee on,.....................................	A	4	113
1846.	Report of committee on, on bill to reduce salaries of officers of state, ...	S	3	79
1846.	Report of committee on,.....................................	A	6	205
1846.	do	A	6	206
1846.	do	A	4	134

REVENUE LAWS, *see* United States.

REVENUES, NATIONAL, *see* United States.

REVISED STATUTES.

1831.	Report of secretary of state relative to the sale and distribution of the,....................	S	1	22

REVISED STATUTES—*continued.*

Year	Subject	Doc.	Vol.	No.
1832.	Report of secretary of state relative to the sale and distribution of the,	S	2	68
1833.	do relative to same,	S	1	15
1833.	do relative to the distribution of the,	A	3	158
1839.	do relative to the sale and distribution of the,	A	3	158
1837.	Report of select committee on bill to furnish the legislature with the,	A	2	129
1837.	Report of comptroller relative to drawing money from the treasury on a resolution of the assembly for the purchase of copies of the, for the members of the legislature,	A	2	74
1833.	Report on petition from Westchester county relative to the,	A	2	48
1842.	Report of committee on the judiciary relative to amending, concerning absconding, concealed and non-resident debtors,	S	2	42
1843.	Report of committee on the erection and division of towns and counties on the bill to amend title five, part one of, &c.,	A	5	146
1843.	Report of the minority on same,	A	5	164
1846.	Report of committee on the judiciary on bill to amend, relative to judges and their law partners,	S	1	17
1851.	Report of committee on expenditures in relation to,	A	1	16
1856.	Report on bill to amend,	A	3	77
1857.	Report of librarian of assembly library in reply to resolution relative to copies of, in library,	A	1	33

REVISED STATUTES AND MAPS.

Year	Subject	Doc.	Vol.	No.
1832.	Sent to the governors of the different states, report of secretary of state relative to the,	A	4	305
1833.	Report of secretary of state relative to the,	A	1	19

REVISERS OF THE LAWS.

Year	Subject	Doc.	Vol.	No.
1830.	Report of the, in obedience to a joint resolution,	S	4	404

REVOLUTION.

Year	Subject	Doc.	Vol.	No.
1832.	Officers and soldiers of the, resolutions of the legislature of Delaware relative to compensating them,	A	1	3
1832.	Officers and soldiers of the, resolutions from Indiana,	A	3	183
1832.	do do report on the same,	A	1	44
1830.	do do report relative to exempting them from imprisonment for debt,	A	4	388
1835.	do do report relative to granting relief to,	A	5	386
1842.	Resolution of general assembly of Kentucky concerning soldiers of,	S	2	26
1842.	Resolutions of Kentucky concerning the soldiers of,	A	5	96
1856.	Resolution relative to martyrs who died in Wallabout bay,	A	4	111

REXFORD, JEMIMA.

Year	Subject	Doc.	Vol.	No.
1840.	Report on petition for a portion of the bed of the Erie canal,	S	3	87

REXFORD, JEMIMA, AND CYRUS W.

Year	Subject	Doc.	Vol.	No.
1843.	Report of judiciary committee on petition of,	S	1	17

REYNOLDS, DANIEL.

Year	Subject	Doc.	Vol.	No.
1840.	Report on petition of, for a law requiring the treasurer of Onondaga county to refund certain money,	A	6	241

REYNOLDS, ELISHA, AND ROBERT.

Year	Subject	Doc.	Vol.	No.
1836.	Report on petition of, to be repaid certain moneys,	A	4	313

REYNOLDS, JOHN.

		Doc.	Vol.	No.
1843.	Report of committee on claims on petition of,	A	5	126
1846.	Report of committee on claims on petition of,	A	4	96
1846.	Report of committee on claims on petition of,	A	4	103
1847.	Report on petition of,	A	1	24

RHINELANDER AND DE KAY, DOCTORS.

1832.	Communication from, relative to diseased emigrants,	A	4	388

RHOADES, JOHN, AND OTHERS.

1831.	Report on petition of, in relation to lot No. 75, in the township of Lysander,	S	1	46

RHOADES, RICHARD D.

1849.	Report of committee on canals on petition of,	A	3	175

RHODE ISLAND, STATE OF.

1841.	Resolutions of the general assembly of, in relation to the public domain, the sub-treasury and a national bank,	A	5	158
1842.	Communication from governor transmitting resolution of general assembly of, relative to electors of president and vice-president,	S	3	54
1844.	Resolution of the general assembly of,	A	7	196
1849.	Message of governor of, relative to manuscript volumes in secretary's office respecting boundaries of colony of, &c.,	A	5	239
1849.	Report and resolution of joint library committee relative to application from, for a volume of manuscript records,	A	3	132
1850.	Resolutions of, on agriculture,	A	8	180
1850.	Resolutions of, on book presented,	A	8	182
1855.	Resolution of legislature of, in relation to foreign papers,	A	5	134

RHODES, ANTHONY, AND OTHERS.

1834.	Report on petition of, for remuneration for improvements on certain lands in Freemasons' patent,	A	3	199
1834.	Report on petition of, relative to same,	A	4	302

RHODES, ELIAKIM, Jr.

1836.	Report on petition to change his name,	A	3	182

RHODES, R. D.

1849.	Report of committee on canals on petition of,	A	3	175

RICE, DAVID.

1851.	Report of committee on grievances,	A	3	61

RICE, HENRY, AND OTHERS, *see* Henry Price and others.

RICE, JAMES J.

1838.	Report on petition of, for compensation for the use of a gravel pump at the salt works,	A	5	290
1839.	Report on petition of the administratrix of, for the same,	A	4	187

RICE, R.

1845.	Report of committee on canals on petition of,	A	5	152

RICH, J. B.

		Doc.	Vol.	No.
1850.	Report on memorial of,	S	3	99

RICH, LYMAN.

1850.	Report of committee on canals on petition of,	A	3	25

RICHARDSON & GROSS.

1848.	Report on petition of,	A	5	154
1849.	Report of committee on claims on petition of,	A	3	124

RICHARDSON, BENJ., Jr.

1851.	Report on petition for canal damages,	S	1	16

RICHARDSON, CALVIN P., AND OTHERS.

1846.	Report of canal board on petition of,	A	4	103
1847.	Report on petition of,	A	2	74
1849.	Report of committee on claims on petition of,	A	3	134

RICHARDSON, D. H.

1834.	Report on petition of, for a lease of the surplus waters of the Erie canal at Macedon,	A	4	298

RICHARDSON, RICHARD.

1853.	Report of committee on claims of, for canal damages,	A	4	101

RICHMOND, ALVAN, AND LEVI CASLER.

1857.	Report of committee on claims favorable on petition of, to be released as sureties for John Uhle,	A	1	49

RICHMOND, BARZILLA.

1839.	Report on petition of, for a bridge over the canal on his farm,	A	3	137

RICHMOND, COUNTY OF.

1837.	County buildings, report on petition to raise money to build,	A	2	119
1837.	Game, report on petition for the preservation of,	A	3	196
1832.	Grant of lands under water around, opinion of the attorney-general relative to,	S	1	45
1833.	Highway laws, report on petition to amend the,	S	2	53
1830.	Oyster beds in Staten Island Sound, report relative to the rights of the citizens of Richmond to the same,	A	2	242
1831.	Oyster beds in the towns of Southfield and Westfield, report concerning the,	S	1	14
1832.	Poor of, report on petition of the superintendents of the,	S	2	66
1837.	Road in, from the village of Richmond to Mersereau's ferry, report concerning,	A	2	128
1832.	St. Andrew's church in, report on petition of, to apply certain money toward the erection of an academy,	S	2	87
1834.	St. Andrew's and St. Paul's churches in, report on petition of, to apply certain money toward the erection of a church in the village of Tompkinsville,	S	1	20
1831.	Act concerning, report as to the operation of an,	A	3	225
1831.	Act concerning, report as to the operation of an,	A	3	261
1843.	Memorial of the ship masters, owners and others of, in relation to the Virginia suspension law,	A	2	26
1851.	Report of committee on roads and bridges on the memorial of inhabitants of,	A	4	99

RICHMOND COUNTY—*continued.*

		Doc.	Vol.	No.
1858.	Report on an act to enable the, to make a loan to aid in the completion of the Staten Island railroad,	A	4	123

POLICE, *see* Metropolitan Police.

RICHMOND GRANITE COMPANY.

		Doc.	Vol.	No.
1841.	Report on petition to incorporate the,	A	4	106

RICHMOND, TOWN OF.

		Doc.	Vol.	No.
1834.	Report on petition to annex a part of the town of Canadice to the,	A	4	334

RICH, STEPHEN A. AND JANE.

		Doc.	Vol.	No.
1840.	Report on petition of, for the release of certain escheated land,	S	2	57
1841.	Report on petition of, for the release of certain escheated land,	S	2	58

RIDDEN, JOHN, AND CATHARINE.

		Doc.	Vol.	No.
1835.	Report on petition of, relative to certain escheated lands in New York,	A	4	349

RIDDLE, SAMUEL.

		Doc.	Vol.	No.
1843.	Report of the committee on claims on his petition,	S	3	109

RIDDLE, S. S., AND OTHERS.

		Doc.	Vol.	No.
1844.	Report of committee on claims on petition of,	S	3	95
1845.	Report of canal commissioners on petition of,	S	2	49
1845.	Report of committee on claims on petition of,	S	2	67

RIDER, ANSON.

		Doc.	Vol.	No.
1840.	Report of the commissioners of the land office on the claim of, to certain land in Freemasons' patent,	S	2	42

RIDER, SAMUEL.

		Doc.	Vol.	No.
1837.	Report on petition of, to be repaid certain moneys paid to the state for land in Freemasons' patent,	A	3	244
1838.	Report of commissioners of the land office on the same,	S	2	61
1839.	Majority report on the same,	A	3	124
1839.	Minority report on the same,	A	3	125
1840.	Report of the commissioners of the land office on the same,	S	2	41

RIFLEMEN.

		Doc.	Vol.	No.
1842.	Report of S. E. Church on petition to incorporate a company of,	A	7	169

RIFLES, ELLIS'S REPEATING.

		Doc.	Vol.	No.
1832.	Report on bill authorizing the commissary-general to receive from the ordnance department a certain number of,	A	4	303

RIGGS, LEWIS.

		Doc.	Vol.	No.
1836.	Report on petition of, to be admitted to a seat in the house of assembly in place of Chauncey Keep,	A	1	15

RIGHTS OF WOMEN, *see* Woman's Rights.

RILEY, WM. S.

		Doc.	Vol.	No.
1844.	Report of committee on claims on the petition of,	A	3	72

RIOTS AND MOBS.

		Doc.	Vol.	No.
1838.	Report in relation to the destruction of property by,............	A	5	240

RISLEY, POLLY.

1831.	Report on petition of, for remuneration for improvements on certain land in New Stockbridge,............................	S	1	5

RIVERS, *see* Harbors.

ROADS, *see* Highways.

ROBBINSON, J., AND OTHERS.

1842.	Report of committee on claims on petition of,..................	A	7	147

ROBB, JAMES.

1857.	Report of committee on petition of aliens favorable on petition of, for power to hold land,....................................	A	2	84

ROBERTS, BENJAMIN S.

1843.	Report of the committee on claims on the petition of,...........	A	5	122

ROBERTS, DANIEL.

1842.	Report of commissioners of land office on bill for relief of children of,...	A	7	180

ROBERTSON, A. L.

1849.	Report of comptroller relative to moneys drawn by, as one of the commissioners of the Code,..............................	A	2	42
1849.	Communication from, respecting, &c.,........................	A	2	46
1849.	Communication from, resigning his office as one of the commissioners of the Code,....................................	A	5	223

ROBINSON, B.

1848.	Report of committee on judiciary on petition of,..............	S	2	53

ROBINSON, CHAS. D.

1851.	Senator, report in relation to charges,.......................	S	2	60

ROBINSON, JABEZ.

1842.	Report of committee on claims on petition of,.................	A	5	124
1842.	Report on petition of,..	A	5	127

ROBINSON, PETER.

1847.	Report on petition of,......................................	A	2	57

ROBLEE, THERON, AND OTHERS, Heirs of Elizabeth Gilchrist.

1841.	Report on petition of, relative to certain land,.................	A	3	74

ROCHESTER AND AUBURN RAILROAD, *see* Railroads.

ROCHESTER, CITY OF.

1831.	Auctions, retail, report concerning,.........................	A	2	151
1834.	Aqueduct at, report as to rebuilding the,....................	A	2	88
1839.	And Buffalo Packet Boat Company, report on petition of the, to be refunded certain moneys paid for canal tolls,..............	A	3	132

ROCHESTER, CITY OF—*continued.*

		Doc.	Vol.	No.
1830.	And Buffalo Packet Boat Company, report on petition of the, to be refunded certain moneys paid for canal tolls, ...	A	4	210
1840.	Corporation of, report on petition of F. Stanley to authorize the, to pay him certain money,....................................	A	3	71
1839.	Canal at, report relative to the location of the,................	A	5	287
	Appraisal of property taken for the, *see* Harvey Ely and others.			
1839.	Child's slip, report on petition of the proprietors of, for relief from a resolution of the canal commissioners closing said slip,	A	3	120
1830.	Common schools, memorial of citizens relative to,..............	A	4	387
1831.	Firemen of, report on petition to increase the number of,.......	A	3	209
1830.	Incorporation of, report on petition for the,.................	A	4	414
1832.	Incorporation of, report of committee on conference on bill for the,	S	2	113
1832.	School for people of color, report in relation to a,............	A	2	77
1835.	School district No. 2, report relative to the boundaries of,......	A	2	117
1835.	School district No. 10, report on petition to sell part of the school lot,..	A	4	327
1835.	Water Works Company, report on petition to incorporate the,..	A	3	233
1832.	Wood measurer, report on petition for the appointment of a, ...	A	1	23
1838.	Supreme court commissioner, report on petition for a,..........	A	5	295
1839.	"Williams' Light Infantry," report on petition to incorporate,..	A	6	409
1846.	Memorial of citizens of, relative to education,.................	A	4	101
1847.	Memorial of citizens of, relative to Erie canal,.............. ...	A	7	183
1847.	Report of canal commissioners on petition of H. B. Smith and others, for bridge in,..................................	A	7	221
1852.	Report on petition of citizens of, in relation to canal feeder,.....	A	5	109
1853.	Report of committee on claims in relation to reconstruction of Platt street sewer in,...........	A	2	43
1853.	Report of committee on claims in relation to the Platt street sewer,...	A	2	33
1853.	Report of committee on claims on the memorial of owners of the water of the Genesee river at,...........................	A	4	86
1854.	Report relative to claims of mill-owners at,..........	A	2	63
1856.	Report of committee on bill relative to claims of mill-owners,...	S	3	103
1857.	Communication from canal board relative to mill-owners at,.....	S	1	12
1857.	Report of committee on finance relative to Rochester mill-owners' claims,...	S	2	79
	BANKS, *see* Banks—Monroe County.			
	ELECTIC MEDICAL COLLEGE, *see* Medical Colleges.			
	INSPECTORS' REPORTS, *see* Monroe County.			

ROCHESTER, TOWN OF.

		Doc.	Vol.	No.
1850.	Report on petition of inhabitants of, for the erection of a new town,..	A	5	107

ROCKAWAY, VILLAGE OF.

		Doc.	Vol.	No.
1840.	Marine Pavillion and Life Boat Association, report on petition to incorporate the,....................................	A	8	337

ROCKLAND, COUNTY OF.

		Doc.	Vol.	No.
1830.	Commissioner of deeds, report on petition of I. I. Cole to confirm his official acts as a,..............................	A	4	363
1835.	Ferries between, and Westchester county, report in relation to,..	A	4	313
1834.	Highways, regulation of, to report on petition to amend the law relative to the,...............................	S	1	22
1839.	School moneys, report concerning the,......................	A	4	184
1840.	Road from Rockland lake to Slaughter's Landing, report on petition for a toll gate on a,............................	A	5	205
1835.	Report on petition to inclose a tract of woodland in,...........	A	4	294

ROCKWELL, A.

		Doc.	Vol.	No.
1846.	Report in relation to claim of,.............................	S	4	134

ROCKWELL, ANDREW.

		Doc.	Vol.	No.
1847.	Report on petition of,.............	A	2	55
1848.	Report on petition of,.............	A	2	38
1851.	Report of committee on grievances,.............	A	3	70

ROCKWELL, ANDREW, & CO.

1852.	Report on petition of, for a law authorizing the canal board to hear and determine their claim,.............	A	2	72

ROCKY GLEN COMPANY.

1839.	Report on petition to increase the capital stock of the,.............	S	1	29

ROGERS, DAVID.

1852.	Report on petition of,.............	S	1	13
1855.	Report of committee on ways and means on petition of,.............	A	2	41

ROGERS, ISAIAH.

1837.	Report on petition for compensation for the loss of two horses, drowned in the Erie canal,.............	A	3	254

ROGERS, J. & J., AND OTHERS.

1857.	Report of committee on claims favorable on petition of, for compensation for loss, by the giving way of the dam across the Ausable river,.............	A	3	167

ROGERS, J. B. R.

1844.	Report of commissioners of land office on the petition of executors of,.............	S	1	49

ROGERS, JUNIUS.

1835.	Report on petition for payment for work done on the Erie canal under the superintendence of Robert McBride,.............	A	2	121
1836.	Report of committee on claims on the same,.............	A	3	132
1839.	Report of committee on claims on the same,.............	A	3	145

ROGERS, MEDAD, AND JAMES FURMAN.

1857.	Report of committee on claims favorable on petition of,.............	A	1	29

ROGERS, PATRICK.

1851.	Report of committee on claims on petition of, for canal damages,	A	3	52

ROGERS, S.

1846.	Report of committee on claims on petition of,.............	A	1	27

ROGERS, SIMEON.

1842.	Report of the committee on claims on the petition of,.............	S	3	66

ROGGEN, EDWARD.

1858.	Report relative to claim of,.............	A	4	152

ROLLO, MORRISON, AND OTHERS.

1848.	Report of committee on canals on petition of,.............	A	3	90

ROMAN CATHOLICS.

1853.	Report on petition of certain, relative to the instruction of their children,.............	A	4	97

ROMAN STATES.

		Doc.	Vol.	No.
1849.	Communication from governor, inclosing letter from Bishop Hughes relative to interchange of donations between this state and the government of, with catalogue of engravings presented by Pope Pius IX,....	A	3	119

ROME, VILLAGE OF.

1841.	State road from, to Sacketts Harbor, report on petition of the towns of Rome, Annsville, Florence and Redfield, for a loan on the credit of said towns to improve the,....	A	4	97
1844.	Report of committee on canals on the petitions relative to new line of canal at,....	A	5	125
1845.	Report of canal commissioners in answer to a resolution of the senate relative to new line of canal through, &c.,....	S	2	70
	CANAL FROM, to the High Falls on Black river, *see* Black River Canal.			

ROOF, JOHN.

1845.	Report of committee on grievances on the petition of,....	A	6	239
1845.	Report of attorney-general in reply to a resolution referring petition of,....	A	7	240
1846.	Report of committee on grievances on petition of heirs of,....	A	6	218

ROONEY, PATRICK (an alien).

1835.	Report on petition of, for the release of the right of the state to certain land,....	A	2	130

ROOT, O. P., AND OTHERS.

1843.	Report of committee on ways and means on the petition of,....	A	4	81

ROOT, TOWN OF.

1843.	Report of committee on canals on the petition of inhabitants of,..	S	3	103

ROSEBROOK & HASKINS.

1857.	Report of committee on claims on petition of,....	A	3	181

ROSE, FRANKLIN.

1834.	Report on petition of, for compensation for a deficiency in the quantity of a lot of land,....	A	4	394
1839.	Report of the commissioners of the land office on the same,....	A	3	75
1839.	Report of committee on public lands on the same,....	A	2	241

ROSE, THOS., AND JOHN FLINT.

1844.	Report of the canal board on the petition of,....	A	3	93

ROSS, GEORGE P., AND OTHERS.

1852.	Report on petition of, for aid in testing the value and availability of the Dundee salt springs,....	A	5	91

ROSSIE, TOWN OF.

1837.	Lead and Galena Companies in, report on petition to incorporate the,....	A	3	263

ROSS, JOHN J.

1847.	Report on petition of,....	S	4	148
1847.	do	A	6	163
1848.	do	A	3	120

ROSS, JOSEPH (an alien).

		Doc.	Vol.	No.
1831.	Report on petition of, to hold and convey real estate,..........	S	1	59

ROSS, MAHLON L.

1852.	Report on petition of, for relief,...........................	A	5	101
1854.	Report on petition of,....................................	A	3	77
1855.	Report on petition of,....................................	S	1	34

ROTTERDAM, TOWN OF.

1831.	Report on petition to loan out the town moneys of the, ...	A	4	324
1832.	Town property of the, report concerning, ...	A	2	167
1832.	Report on petition to require applicants for private roads to pay the expense of such applications, ...	A	3	234

RONDOUT RIVER.

1831.	Bridge over, report on petition to incorporate a company to build a,..	A	4	205

ROUSE'S POINT.

1849.	Report of select committee on bill to allow the construction of a draw-bridge, by Northern railroad, across the outlet of Lake Champlain at,..	A	1	24
1851.	Report on subject of bridging Lake Champlain at,..............	S	1	20
1851.	Report on allowing the Northern railroad to extend its pier at,..	S	3	90
1851.	Report of select committee on bridge at,....................	A	5	134

ROWE, MATTHEW.

1857.	Report on committee on claims on petition of, ...	A	3	166

ROWLAND, CHARLOTTE, AND OTHERS.

1844.	Report of committee on the petitions of aliens on the petition of,	A	1	33

ROWLAND, ISAAC.

1844.	Report of comptroller on the petition of, ...	A	5	110

ROWLAND, JOHN.

1844.	Report on a bill to confirm lands in the heirs of,...............	S	2	85

ROYALTON CENTRE.

1839.	Academy at, report on petition to incorporate, and for a loan to,.	A	3	115

RUDO, ELIAS.

1830.	Report on petition for the re-appraisement of certain land,......	S	4	349

RUGGLES, C. H.

1832.	Report of amount of fees received by him as circuit judge,.....	A	3	193

RUSH, M.

1854.	Report of committee on claims on petition of,.................	A	1	37

RUSSELL, DAVID.

1834.	Communication from, relative to Seventh Ward Bank investigation,..	S	2	64

RUSSELL, JAMES, Jr. (an alien).

		Doc.	Vol.	No.
1834.	Report on petition of, to hold real estate,	A	4	295

RUSSELL, JOSEPH, AND J. GRIFFIN.

1840.	Report on petition to construct a dam across the Schroon river,	A	5	180

RUSSELL, JOSEPH, AND JOHN E. NORMAN.

1834.	Report on petition of, to construct a dam across the Schroon river,	A	4	373

RUSSELL, WILLIAM.

1837.	Report on petition of, for compensation for a defective title to a lot of land bought of the state,	A	2	79
1837.	Report on the same,	A	3	166
1838.	do	A	3	147
1839.	do	A	2	36

RUST, ZEBULON.

1830.	Report on petition of, for the loss sustained by him, in consequence of the change of the location of the public buildings in Onondaga county,	A	1	34

RUTGERS' FEMALE INSTITUTE, *see* Academies, &c.

RUTGERS' MEDICAL FACULTY, *see* Medical Colleges.

RUTHERFORD, JOHN, *see* Virginia.

RYAN, GRANT & TURNER.

1847.	Report of canal commissioners respecting moneys due,	A	7	212
1848.	Report of committee on claims on petition of,	A	2	42
1851.	Report of committee on canals on petition of,	A	3	78

RYAN, JOHN.

1852.	Report on bill for relief of,	S	2	90

RYAN, JOHN, AND OTHERS.

1843.	Report of committee on claims on petition of,	S	1	37
1855.	Report of committee on claims on petition of,	A	1	18

RYAN, WILLIAM H.

1841.	Report on petition of, relative to the cure of the insane,	S	2	49

RYE, TOWN OF.

1834.	Wharf at, report on petition of Curtiss Peck, to erect a,	A	3	210
1835.	do do do	A	1	51
1835.	do do do	A	2	103
1838.	Wharf at, report on petition of John Minuse and others, for a grant of land to build a,	A	6	312
1838.	Report on the same,	A	6	322
1834.	Public lands in, report on petition of the trustees of the,	A	4	309

S.

SABBATH.

		Doc.	Vol.	No.
1838.	Report on petition to repeal the laws for the observance of,.....	A	5	262
1844.	Report of committee on canals on the subject of closing the locks on, &c.,.....	S	4	119
1845.	Report of committee on canals relative to closing locks on,.....	A	4	148
1847.	Report relative to observance of,.....	S	4	131
1849.	Report on subject of closing locks on the canals of this state on,	S	2	61
1858.	Report of committee on canals relative to closing locks on,.....	S	2	77
1858.	Report of minority of committee on same, ...	S	2	91
1858.	Majority report on closing locks on the canals on,.....	A	4	134
1858.	Minority report on same,.....	A	4	137

SACANDAGA CANAL, *see* Canals.

SACANDAGA RIVER.

1831.	Report on bill to provide for the survey of the,.....	A	3	248
1857.	Report of committee on roads and bridges, favorable on petitions for an appropriation to repair the state bridge over the,.....	A	3	161

SACKETT, GARY V., *see* Supreme Court Clerks.

SACKETTS HARBOR, VILLAGE OF.

1841.	Road from, to Rome, report on petition for a loan from the school fund to improve a, ...	A	4	97
	BANKS, *see* Banks—Jefferson County.			
	CANAL FROM, to Carthage, *see* Black River Canal.			

SAFETY FUND, *see* Banks.

SAGE, BENJAMIN H.

1844.	Report of canal board on petition of,.....	A	5	121

SAGE, CASLER & CO.

1840.	Report on petition of, for extra compensation for work done on the Erie canal, ...	A	8	320
1842.	Report of committee on canals on petition of,.....	A	7	176
1843.	Report of the committee on canals on the petition of,.....	A	4	80

SAGE, HEZEKIAH.

1851.	Report of committee on grievances,.....	A	3	77
1852.	Report on petition of,.....	A	2	69

SAGE, WALRATH & DUNHAM.

1844.	Report of canal board on petition of,.....	S	2	52
1844.	Report of committee on claims on petition of,.....	S	3	84
1845.	Report of committee on claims on claim of,.....	A	4	126
1845.	Report of canal commissioners relative to,.....	A	4	135
1847.	Report on petition of, ...	A	8	237
1848.	Report on petition of, ...	A	3	88
1850.	Report on claim, ...	A	6	155
1851.	Report of committee on petition for canal damages, ...	S	2	64

SAG HARBOR, VILLAGE OF,

1831.	State pier at, report on petition to repair the,.....	S	1	44
1835.	Wharf at, report on petition of M. B. Osborn to construct a,....	A	3	180

SAILORS' SNUG HARBOR, *see* New York.

ST. CLAIR, C. N. AND JAMES.

		Doc.	Vol.	No.
1847.	Report on petition of,	S	2	75

ST. JOHNSVILLE, TOWN OF.

		Doc.	Vol.	No.
1849.	Report of judiciary committee on petition of inhabitants of town of Oppenheim, for the annexation of a part of that town to,	A	3	138

ST. LAWRENCE ACADEMY, *see* Academies, &c.

ST. LAWRENCE AND MOHAWK RAILROAD, *see* Railroads.

ST. LAWRENCE COUNTY.

		Doc.	Vol.	No.
1832.	Literary association, report on petition to incorporate,	A	4	313
1832.	Turnpike, report on petition for a tax to improve the,	A	2	94
1832.	Turnpike, report on petition for a tax to improve the,	S	2	85
1836.	Records, report in relation to the,	A	2	70
1835.	Poor laws, report on petition for an alteration of the,	A	4	285
1836.	Roads in, report on petition to lay out and open certain,	A	3	203
1838.	Roads in, report on petition to extend an act to lay out,	A	4	195
1833.	Sole leather, annual report of N. Parmenter, an inspector of,	A	3	168
1834.	do do do	A	4	258
1837.	do do do	S	1	46
1843.	Report of the committee on roads and bridges, on the petition of the inhabitants of, and Clinton, for a wagon road,	A	4	84
1847.	Report of majority committee on grievances, relative to rivers in,	A	7	223
	BANKS, *see* Banks—St. Lawrence county.			

ST. LAWRENCE RIVER.

		Doc.	Vol.	No.
1843.	Report of commissioners of the land office on petition of trustees of St. Regis Indians, relative to certain islands,	A	5	136
1853.	Report of committee on internal affairs of towns and counties, in relation to compensating the St. Regis Indians for certain islands in,	A	2	39

ST. REGIS INDIANS, *see* Indians, St. Regis.

ST. REGIS RESERVATION.

		Doc.	Vol.	No.
1830.	Road through, report on petition for aid to construct a,	A	3	223
1831.	Public lands in the, report of the surveyor-general relative to the,	S	1	19
1832.	Public lands in the, report of the surveyor-general relative to the,	S	1	12
1832.	Public lands in the, report of the committee on finance, on the report of the surveyor-general,	S	1	27
1845.	Report of committee on public lands, on bill to lease lots,	A	5	168

ST. REGIS RIVER.

		Doc.	Vol.	No.
1856.	Report on improvements of,	A	4	112

SALEM, TOWN OF.

		Doc.	Vol.	No.
1831.	Report on petition of the supervisors of, to credit the treasurer of Washington county for certain compound interest,	A	1	51
1831.	Report on the same,	A	2	129
1831.	Report on petition of Moses Cleaveland, to compel the town of, to remunerate him for expenses incurred as commissioner of highways,	A	4	313

SALINA, TOWN OF.

		Doc.	Vol.	No
1836.	Census of the, report of secretary of state relative to the, ...	A	3	162
1836.	Census of the, report of select committee on the same, ...	A	3	166
1833.	School district No. 4, report on petition of trustees of, ...	S	2	103
1833.	School district No. 4, report of surveyor-general on petition of trustees of, ...	S	2	97
1842.	Remonstrance of inhabitants of, against abolishing capital punishment, ...	A	7	133
1843.	Remonstrance of numerous citizens of the village of, against the repeal of "the extension of the trial by jury law,"	A	3	60
1843.	Petition of manufacturers of salt, and of inhabitants of, for increasing the revenue of state by extending the market for salt, ...	A	5	133
	BANK, *see* Banks—Onondaga County.			
	SALT, *see* Salt Springs, Salina.			

SALISBURY CENTRE, VILLAGE OF.

1840.	Road from, to Racket lake, report of surveyor-general relative to a, ...	A	4	153

SALISBURY, VILLAGE OF.

1839.	Road district from, to Little Falls, report in relation to a, ...	A	2	49
1839.	Road district from, to Little Falls, report on petition to amend an act in relation to a, ...	A	6	343
1839.	Road from, to Boonville, report on petition for a, ...	A	5	325

SALMON FISHERIES.

1857.	Report on petition relative to, ...	S	4	146

SALMON, GEORGE, AND OTHERS.

1847.	Report of committee on claims on petition of, ...	A	2	72

SALMON RIVER.

1857.	Report of select committee favorable on petitions for the improvement of, ...	A	1	37

SALT.

1833.	Report on petition of Simeon Crane and others, for a loan to aid them in the discovery of salt in Herkimer county, ...	A	4	276
1834.	Report on the same, ...	A	1	45
1834.	Report on the same, ...	A	3	146
1843.	Report of the committee on the manufacture of, ...	A	4	111
1843.	Petition of manufacturers of and inhabitants of town of Salina, for increasing the revenue of the state by extending the market for, ...	A	5	133
1846.	Report on bill to repeal the act giving bounty on, &c., ...	S	2	47
1847.	Report on expenditures of works, ...	S	4	118
1849.	Report of committee on finance, on bill to sell certain lands in Syracuse, ...	S	3	81
1849.	Report of state engineer and surveyor, relative to sale of certain lands covered with coarse salt vats in Syracuse, ...	A	3	130
1854.	Report of committee on, relative to certain laws concerning manufacture of, ...	A	4	132

SALT COMPANY, SYRACUSE.

1850.	Report of committee on claims on bill in relation to, ...	S	3	76

SALT DUTIES.

		Doc.	Vol.	No.
1830.	Report of attorney-general as to the constitutionality of increasing,	S	4	344
1831.	Reduction of the, memorial of manufacturers for the,	S	1	25
1831.	do report on the same,	S	1	56
1831.	do resolution for the same,	S	1	67
1831.	do resolution for the same,	A	4	294
1832.	To be applied to defraying the expenses of the government, resolution for,	S	2	70
1832.	Report on the same,	S	2	100
1833.	Report of secretary of state, relative to the publication of amendments to the Constitution relative to the same,	S	1	14
1833.	Report of committee on the judiciary, on the same,	S	2	45
1834.	To be restored to the general fund, resolution for the,	A	3	131
1835.	Report of secretary of state, relative to the publication of amendments to the Constitution, relative thereto,	A	1	42
1835.	Report of committee on the judiciary, on the same,	A	1	49
1835.	Resolution and recital relative to the same,	A	1	59
1834.	Report on petition for the reduction of the,	A	1	23
1834.	Report on petition for the reduction of the,	S	1	31
1833.	Duty of two mills per bushel, for pumping salt water, report on petition to repeal said law,	A	3	231
1835.	Report on the same,	A	3	164
1839.	do	A	6	327
1840.	do	A	6	255
1839.	Amount of, received from 1812 to 1838, with the number of bushels manufactured in each year,	S	3	76
1831.	Revenue at Salina, report relative to frauds on the,	S	1	18
1850.	Report on,	A	6	165
1850.	Report of committee on manufacture of salt, on petition to reduce duty of foreign salt,	A	8	148

SALT SPRINGS.

		Doc.	Vol.	No.
1847.	Report relative to land near,	S	3	108

SALT SPRINGS, DUNDEE.

		Doc.	Vol.	No.
1852.	Report on petition of G. P. Ross and others, in relation to testing the,	A	5	91

SALT SPRINGS, MONTEZUMA.

		Doc.	Vol.	No.
1838.	Report on petition for the construction of salt wells, &c.,	A	4	172
1839.	do do do	A	6	327
1839.	do do do	S	2	58
1842.	Report of committee on manufactures, relative to,	S	4	91
1846.	Report in relation to,	S	2	70
1847.	Report relative to,	S	4	121
1847.	Report of committee on manufacture of salt, on petition of inhabitants of Montezuma, for appropriation to rebuild salt reservoir,	A	2	56
	SUPERINTENDENT OF:			
1841.	Report of Solomon P. Jacobs,	S	1	18
1842.	Report of,	S	2	49
1842.	Extra session, communication to governor from,	A	7	195
1844.	Report of superintendent of,	S	1	19
1845.	Report of,	S	1	11
1846.	Report of,	S	2	41

SALT SPRINGS, ONONDAGA.

		Doc.	Vol.	No.
1838.	Diving or gravel pump, used at the, report on petition for compensation for the,	A	5	290

SALT SPRINGS, ONONDAGA—*continued.*

		Doc.	Vol.	No.
1839.	Diving or gravel pump, used at the, report on petition for compensation for the,	A	4	187
1839.	Report of the superintendent and inspector, relative to the cost of reservoirs, &c., to carry out the plan of freeing the brine from impurities, &c.,	A	3	108
1839.	Report on petition for the construction of reservoirs, &c.,	A	6	327
1841.	Report of the commissioners of the land office on the bill relative to the,	A	3	83
1831.	Memorial of manufacturers in relation to the salt duties,	S	1	25
1831.	Report of the select committee on the same,	S	1	56
1838.	Report of the committee on the manufacture of salt (Mr. Lawrence),	A	6	306
1841.	Memorial of manufacturers of salt in Salina, relative to the bill in relation to the,	A	4	127
1844.	Report of commissioners of land office on bill relative to the exchange of certain lands set apart for the manufacture of salt in the county of Onondaga,	A	6	155
1843.	Reservation, communication from the commissioners of the land office relative to,	A	2	39
	SUPERINTENDENT OF :			
1830.	Annual report of,	A	2	144
1831.	do	A	2	118
1832.	do	A	1	24
1833.	do	S	1	16
1834.	do	A	1	22
1834.	Report of relative to their compensation, &c.,	A	4	290
1834.	Report of relative to their compensation, &c.,	A	4	293
1835.	Annual report of,	S	1	6
1836.	do	S	1	10
1837.	do	A	1	36
1838.	do	S	1	14
1838.	Monthly account of,	A	5	209
1839.	Annual report of,	S	1	9
1840.	do	S	1	12
1841.	do	S	1	19
1842.	Report of the,	S	1	8
1842.	Communication to the governor,	A	1	2
1842.	Annual report of,	A	1	11
1842.	do	A	5	130
1843.	do	S	1	7
1843.	do	A	1	6
1844.	do	A	1	13
1845.	Report of,	S	1	39
1845.	Annual report of,	A	1	10
1846.	Annual report of,	A	1	9
1846.	Report of committee on manufacture of salt relative to,	A	3	79
1847.	Annual report of,	A	1	11
1848.	Report of,	A	2	23
1849.	Annual report of,	A	1	19
1850.	Report of,	A	3	36
1851.	Annual report of,	A	2	25
1852.	do	A	2	43
1853.	do	A	3	76
1854.	do	A	2	50
1855.	do	A	1	20
1856.	do	A	3	75
1857.	do	A	1	30
1858.	do	A	3	55

SALT SPRINGS, SALINA.

		Doc.	Vol.	No.
1830.	Pump works at, report on petition of Junia Curtiss, for pay for building,	A	3	271

SALT SPRINGS, SALINA—*continued.*

Year	Subject	Doc.	Vol.	No.
1831.	Pump works at, report on petition of Junia Curtiss, for pay for building,	A	4	320
1833.	Rock salt at, report on petition of B. Byington, for a loan to aid him in the discovery of,	A	4	314
1831.	Salt revenues, report relative to frauds on the,	S	1	18
1834.	Lands set apart for the manufacture of coarse salt, report of the commissioners of the land office concerning,	A	4	292
1836.	Report on petition for the sale of a part of the,	A	4	329
1840.	Report on petition of H. W. Van Buren, to purchase a portion of the,	A	7	284
1840.	Report on petition and bill relating to the,	A	8	351
1841.	Report of the commissioners of the land office, giving the names of individuals and companies to whom land has been set apart, &c.,	S	2	45
1833.	Report on petition of manufacturers of salt in, to repeal the law imposing a tax for pumping brine,	A	3	231
1840.	Report on petition of citizens of, to abolish the office of inspector of salt, and that one be appointed for each village, and for the repeal of the tax for raising the water, &c.,	A	6	255
1841.	Memorial of manufacturers of salt, for amendments to the bill in relation to the Onondaga salt springs,	A	4	127
1843.	Report of commissioners of land office on the act to extend the manufacture of salt at,	A	5	150

SAMSONDALE, VILLAGE OF.

Year	Subject	Doc.	Vol.	No.
1835.	Fire company, reeport on petition to incorporate,	A	4	336

SANDERS, THEODORE W.

Year	Subject	Doc.	Vol.	No.
1840.	Report on petition to vacate his seat as a member of assembly from Schenectady county,	A	7	291

SANDFORD, LEVI, AND OTHERS.

Year	Subject	Doc.	Vol.	No.
1847.	Report of committee on claims on petition of,	A	2	92

SAND LAKE, TOWN OF.

Year	Subject	Doc.	Vol.	No.
1836.	Report on petition to extend the time for the collection of taxes in the,	A	2	102

SANDY HILL, VILLAGE OF.

Year	Subject	Doc.	Vol.	No.
1833.	Firemen, report on petition to incorporate the,	A	2	113

SANDY HOOK.

Year	Subject	Doc.	Vol.	No.
1852.	Report of commissioners of land office relative to a hospital at,	S	3	96
1853.	Report of commmissioners of land office in relation to marine hospital at,	S	2	57

SANDY HOOK PILOTS.

Year	Subject	Doc.	Vol.	No.
1836.	Report on petition to increase the number of,	A	4	237
1836.	Report of wardens of the port of New York, relative to increasing the number of,	A	4	272
1838.	Report on petition of commissioners of pilots to amend the law in relation to the,	A	4	174

SANFORD & EGLESTON.

Year	Subject	Doc.	Vol.	No.
1844.	Report of the canal board on the petition of,	A	3	69
1846.	Report of canal board on petition of,	A	3	78
1846.	Report of committee on claims on petition of,	A	4	99

SANFORD, CHARLES W.

Year	Subject	Doc.	Vol.	No.
1853.	Major-general, report of, in answer to a resolution in relation to moneys collected for military fines in the city of New York,..	A	2	30

SANFORD, ROLLO & WIBERT.

Year	Subject	Doc.	Vol.	No.
1848.	Report of committee on canals on petition of,................	A	3	90

SANGERSFIELD, TOWN OF.

Year	Subject	Doc.	Vol.	No.
1833.	Justices of the peace in, report on petition to legalize the acts of,	A	2	114
1844.	Report of the committee on charitable and religious societies on the petition of the Presbyterian church in, ...	S	1	38

SARATOGA AND WASHINGTON RAILROAD, *see* Railroads.

SARATOGA COUNTY.

Year	Subject	Doc.	Vol.	No.
1830.	Beef and pork, annual report of J. Bliven, an inspector of,......	A	2	100
1832.	Highway labor in, report in relation to, ...	A	3	258
1834.	Courts of oyer and terminer, report on memorial of the judges of the court of common pleas, for a law declaratory of the manner of proceedings in,..................................	A	4	399
1840.	Report on petition for indemnity for expenses incurred on the trial of Thomas Rector, ...	A	4	121
1830.	Race-course in, report on petition for the establishment of a,....	A	4	294
1836.	Suit against the treasurer of, report concerning a,.............	A	4	223
1833.	Turnpike company, report on petition to incorporate,..........	A	3	219
1840.	Lumber inspector, annual report of Thomas McGiness,.........	S	2	50
1838.	Wood and timber, report of J. Bliven, a measurer of,...........	S	2	36
1839.	do do do	S	1	30
1840.	do do do	A	4	109
1838.	Wood and timber, report on petition for an additional inspector of,..	A	6	303
	BANKS, *see* Banks—Saratoga County.			

SARATOGA SPRINGS, VILLAGE OF.

Year	Subject	Doc.	Vol.	No.
1832.	Report on petition to amend the charter of,..................	A	2	159
1834.	Report on petition to raise money to repair roads and bridges,...	A	3	187

SATTERLEY, ISAAC (heir of Henry Satterley).

Year	Subject	Doc.	Vol.	No.
1834.	Report on petition of, for bounty lands, ...	A	3	111
1835.	Report on petition of, for bounty lands,......................	A	3	253

SATTERLY, ISAAC.

Year	Subject	Doc.	Vol.	No.
1849.	Report of committee on claims on petition of,..................	A	1	15
1854.	Report on petition of,..	A	3	116
1856.	Report on petition of,..	A	3	86

SAUGERTIES, TOWN OF.

Year	Subject	Doc.	Vol.	No.
1831.	Ferry between, and Red Hook, report in relation to the,........	A	3	217
1840.	Bridge over Esopus creek, report on petition of citizens to raise money by tax to build a,................................	A	2	53

SAUQUOIT, VILLAGE OF.

Year	Subject	Doc.	Vol.	No.
1836.	Fire company, report on petition to incorporate a,.............	A	4	242

SAXTON & CO., C. M.

Year	Subject	Doc.	Vol.	No.
1857.	Report of committee on agriculture, favorable on petition of, to furnish a library of agricultural books to each school district,	A	3	173

SAYRE & HOUSE, AND OTHERS.

		Doc	Vol.	No.
1846.	Report on petition of,	S	1	19

SAYRE, JAMES, *see* M. Hart and others.

SAYRE, JOHN.

1830.	A commissioner for loaning money for the county of Seneca, report on petition of,	S	1	23

SAYRE, M.

1848.	Report on petition of,	A	3	103

SAYRE, MATTHEW.

1844.	Report of the committee on claims on the petition of,	A	3	66
1849.	Report of committee on claims on petition of,	A	1	26

SAYRE, WILLIS B.

1857.	Report of committee on claims, adverse on petition of, for damages by overflow of the Chemung canal and feeder,	A	2	107

SCADDEN, JOHN.

1835.	Report on petition of, for compensation for damages by the Erie canal,	A	3	169

SCAJOCKETY CREEK.

1840.	Report in relation to lands overflowed adjacent to,	S	3	92

SCHAUBER, DAVID.

1841.	Report on petition of, for bounty lands,	A	6	209

SCHENANDO COTTON MANUFACTORY.

1830.	Report on petition to sell their real estate,	S	4	327

SCHENCK, JAMES W.

1856.	Report on petition of,	A	3	53

SCHENCK, JOHN, *see* John G. Hicks and others.

SCHENECTADY AND ALBANY TURNPIKE COMPANY, *see* Albany and Schenectady Turnpike Company.

SCHENECTADY AND TROY RAILROAD, *see* Railroads.

SCHENECTADY AND UTICA RAILROAD, *see* Railroads.

SCHENECTADY, CITY OF.

1835.	Bridge across the Mohawk at, report in relation to a,	A	5	396
1839.	Report on petition to borrow money to aid in the construction of the Coxsackie and Schenectady railroad,	A	5	322
1840.	Alleged election frauds in, report and documents concerning the,	A	7	291
1830.	Jail limits, report on petition for an extension of the,	A	4	419
1833.	Canal bridges at, report on petition for repairs to the,	A	4	317
1832.	Water, report relative to supplying the city with,	A	4	301
1835.	Water, report relative to supplying the city with,	A	4	345

BANKS, *see* Banks—Schenectady County.

SCHENECTADY, COUNTY OF.

		Doc.	Vol.	No.
1834.	Court-house, report on petition to raise money to build a, ...	A	4	356
1838.	Taxes in, report on petition to extend the time for collecting, ...	A	3	109

QUIT-RENTS IN, *see* Glenville.

SCHERMERHORN, LAWRENCE.

1834.	Report on petition of, for compensation for damages by the Erie canal, ...	A	3	296
1835.	Report on petition of, for compensation for damages by the Erie canal, ...	A	3	175

SCHLOSSER, Attack at, *see* Northern Frontier.

SCHMIDT & BALCHER.

1851.	Report of committee on claims, ...	A	4	97

SCHOHARIE AND OTSEGO RAILROAD, *see* Railroads.

SCHOHARIE AND UNADILLA RAILROAD, *see* Railroads.

SCHOHARIE, COUNTY OF.

1833.	Jefferson Academy in, report on petition for aid to, ...	A	3	260
1834.	Fishing in certain waters of, report on petition relative to, ...	A	4	317
1841.	New county from part of, report on petition for a, ...	A	7	281
1842.	Report of minority in relation to titles to certain lands in Albany and, ...	A	7	177
1842.	Report of majority on same subject, ...	A	7	181
1846.	Report of the committee on division of towns and counties, relative to new county from parts of Delaware, Greene and, ...	S	2	49
1846.	Report of committee on internal affairs of towns and counties relative to court-house, ...	A	3	65
1849.	Report of committee on erection and division of towns and counties, on petitions and remonstrances relative to a new county from parts of Greene, Delaware and, ...	A	3	135

SCHOHARIE CREEK.

1838.	Report relative to obstructing, by throwing tan bark in, ...	A	4	191
1832.	Ferry across, report on petition of I. Bradway to continue a, ...	A	4	277
1834.	Mill dam across, report on petition of I. & P. Murphy to repair a,	A	4	321
1843.	Report relative to the aqueduct across, ...	S	1	44
1843.	Report of canal commissioners relative to aqueduct across, &c., .	S	3	94

SCHOHARIE TURNPIKE.

1843.	Report of the select committee in relation to western branch of the, ...	S	2	65
1846.	Report of select committee to examine gates on, ...	A	2	37
1848.	Report as to gates, ...	A	3	106
1848.	Western branch, report of treasurer, ...	A	3	58
1848.	Western branch, report of treasurer as to penalties, ...	A	3	113

SCHOLEFIELD, CHAS. M.

1857.	Report of committee on claims, favorable on petition of, for damages by leakage of the Erie canal, &c., ...	A	2	109

SCHOOLS, SCHOOL MONEYS, SCHOOL DISTRICTS, &c., *see* Common Schools.

SCHOONMAKER, I. I., *see* J. Hasbrouck, Jr.

		Doc.	Vol.	No.
	SCHOONMAKER, MARIUS.			
1851.	Report of secretary of state in relation to,	S	2	62
	SCHROEPPEL, HENRY W., *see* John E. Hinman.			
	SCHROON RIVER.			
1831.	Survey of, report on bill to provide for the,	A	3	248
1834.	Dam across, report on petition of I. Russell and I. E. Norman to build a,	A	4	373
1840.	Dam across, report on petition of I. Russell and I. Griffin to build a,	A	5	180
	SCHUYLER, AARON.			
1857.	Report of committee on claims, favorable on petition of, for the release of his bail,	A	2	66
	SCHUYLER, COUNTY OF.			
1845.	Report of attorney-general on bill entitled an act to erect, &c.,	S	2	66
1856.	Communication from county judge,	A	4	175
1856.	Report of the majority committee on the location of the site of,	A	4	110
1856.	Report of the minority on same subject,	A	4	104
1857.	Report of committee on internal affairs of towns and counties, relative to location of buildings,	A	2	76
1858.	Report of minority of committee on petition and papers relating to county buildings in,	A	4	86
	SCHUYLER, LIVINGSTON.			
1846.	Report on bill for the relief of,	S	4	130
	SCHUYLER, NICHOLAS.			
1846.	Report of committee on claims on petition of,	A	4	98
1849.	Report of committee on claims on petition of,	A	3	168
	SCHUYLER, PHILIP, AND OTHERS.			
1835.	Report on petition of, for remuneration of expenses in maintaining fences along the Champlain canal,	S	2	55
1836.	Report of canal board on the same,	A	4	234
1836.	Report of the committee on grievances on the same,	A	4	252
1836.	Report on petition of, to erect a toll bridge across Hudson river at Schuylerville,	S	1	12
	SCHUYLERVILLE, VILLAGE OF.			
1832.	Report relative to highway labor in,	A	3	258
	SCOTT, DRED.			
1857.	Report of joint committee of senate and assembly, on the decision of the supreme court of the United States, in case of,	A	3	201
	SCOTT, ELIZABETH.			
1834.	Report on petition of, for compensation for damages by the erection of the Troy dam,	A	3	180
	SCOTTSVILLE CANAL ASSOCIATION.			
1841.	Report on bill for the relief of the,	S	3	72

SCRAMBLING, J.

		Doc.	Vol.	No.
1844.	Report on petition of, for divorce,	A	7	199
1845.	Report of committee on the judiciary on the petition of, for a divorce,	A	4	139

SCRIVEN, AMOS W.

1844.	Report of canal board on petition of,	A	1	29

SEAMEN.

1831.	Tax on, resolutions of the common council of New York in relation to the,	S	1	72
1836.	Report of amount of moneys received from, from 1831 to 1835,	A	3	152
1836.	American, report on petition to be released from the payment of hospital moneys,	A	4	247
1839.	American, report on petition to be released from the payment of hospital moneys,	A	6	387

SEAMEN'S FRIEND SOCIETY, AMERICAN.

1840.	Report on petition of the, for a loan from the passengers' fund,	A	7	300

SEAMEN'S FUND AND RETREAT, *see* New York.

SEARS, ELIPHALET, AND HORACE ADAMS.

1852.	Report on the petition of,	A	2	29
1853.	Report of committee on claims, on petition of, for relief,	S	2	44
1857.	Report of committee on claims, on petition of,	A	2	112

SEAVERSON, JOHN A.

1835.	Report on petition of, to erect a dam across Susquehanna river,	A	3	159

SECRETARY OF NAVY, *see* United States.

SECRETARY OF STATE, *see* Common Schools, Superintendents of; Poor, Superintendents of.

AZARIAH C. FLAGG:

1830.	Report of, relative to furnishing counties with standard weights and measures,	A	2	188
1831.	Report on the same,	A	1	5
1831.	Report of the, relative to the distribution and sale of the Revised Statutes,	S	1	22
1832.	Report of the same,	S	2	68
1839.	Report on the same,	A	3	158
1832.	Report of the, in relation to the archives of the assembly chamber,	A	4	302
1832.	Report of the, giving the census of the several congressional districts, &c.,	S	1	65
1833.	Report of the, relative to the distribution of the Revised Statutes,	A	4	304
1833.	Report of the, relative to the distribution of the Revised Statutes,	S	1	15
1833.	Report of the, relative to the maps and Revised Statutes sent to the governors of the several states,	A	4	305
1833.	Report on the same,	S	1	19
1833.	Report of the, relative to the publication of certain amendments to the constitution,	S	1	14
1835.	Report on the same,	S	1	42
1838.	Report on the same,	A	2	18
1834.	Report of the, relative to an improvement in the manufacture of potash,	A	2	54

SECRETARY OF STATE—*continued.*

Year	Entry	Doc.	Vol.	No.
1835.	Report of the, transmitting the report of a survey of a route for the New York and Erie railroad,	A	2	107
1835.	Report of the, in relation to the census of the state,	A	3	114
1835.	Report of the, on petition of inhabitants of the town of Salina, relative to the census of said town,	A	3	162
	John A. Dix:			
1836.	Report of the, relative to the geological survey of the state,	A	1	9
1837.	Report of the, relative to the distribution of oleometers to the several counties,	A	1	7
1837.	Report of the, transmitting a list of inspectors of provisions, produce, &c.,	A	3	226
1837.	Report of the, transmitting the report of New York and Erie railroad company, for 1836,	A	3	190
1838.	Report of the, transmitting the report of New York and Erie railroad company, for 1837,	A	2	27
1840.	Report of the, transmitting the report of New York and Erie railroad company, for 1835, '36, '37, and '38,	A	4	159
1840.	Report of the, transmitting the report of New York and Erie railroad company, for 1839,	A	5	176
1838.	Report of the, transmitting abstracts of convictions for criminal offenses,	S	2	65
1839.	Report of the, &c., concerning the same,	S	2	35
1840.	Report of the, &c., concerning the same,	S	4	120
1841.	Report of the, &c., concerning the same,	S	3	67
	John C. Spencer:			
1839.	Communication transmitting the report of a survey of the Ogdensburgh and Lake Champlain railroad,	A	3	133
1839.	Communication from the, as state sealer of weights and measures,	A	3	151
1839.	Report of the, in relation to town and county charges,	A	4	183
1840.	Report relative to the contract for the state printing,	A	1	47
1840.	Communication in relation to the title papers of the Holland Land Company, and the translation of certain Dutch records,	A	8	350
1840.	Report of the, respecting copies of bills and fees of district attorneys, filed in his office,	S	4	106
1841.	Report on the same,	A	6	244
1841.	Report of the, in answer to a resolution calling for the annual report of the New York and Erie Railroad Company,	A	4	116
1841.	Report of the, transmitting said annual report,	A	4	128
1841.	Report of the, transmitting abstracts of returns of inspectors of provisions, produce and merchandise,	A	7	259
	Samuel Young:			
1842.	Report of the acting, relative to the printed laws of the state in pamphlet form,	S	1	9
1842.	Resolution of (John C. Spencer), transmitted by governor,	S	1	11
1842.	Report of, relative to convictions for criminal offenses and of returns of sheriffs respecting persons convicted in 1841,	S	3	51
1842.	Communication from, relative to publishing Session Laws,	S	3	81
1842.	Report respecting copies of fee bills of district attorneys for 1841,	A	5	89
1842.	Report transmitting abstracts of returns of superintendents of the poor,	A	5	121
1842.	Communication relative to digest of patents issued by the United States,	A	5	123
1842.	Communication transmitting transactions of New York State Agricultural Society,	A	6	131
1842.	Report transmitting abstracts of returns of inspectors and measurers of merchandise, produce, &c.,	A	7	139
1843.	Communication from, relative to the act in relation to the geological survey of the state, passed April 9, 1842,	S	2	67

SECRETARY OF STATE—*continued.*

		Doc.	Vol.	No.
1843.	Supplemental communication from, on the same subject, ...	S	3	72
1843.	Resolution of Mr. Foster relative to, ...	S	3	76
1843.	do Mr. Rhoades relative to, ...	S	3	76
1843.	do relative to, ...	S	3	91
1843.	Annual report of, transmitting abstracts of returns of superintendents of the poor, ...	A	2	38
1843.	Communication from, transmitting the annual report of the New York Institution for the Blind, ...	A	4	88
1843.	Report of, transmitting abstracts of convictions for criminal offenses, and of returns of sheriffs respecting the persons convicted, ...	A	4	110
1843.	Report of, transmitting correspondence in relation to the public lands, ...	A	4	116
1843.	Report of, of abstracts of returns of inspectors and measurers of merchandise, provisions and produce for the year 1842, ...	A	5	131
1844.	Report of, concerning paupers, ...	S	2	73
1844.	Report of, of the printing done for his office, ...	S	2	79
1844.	Report of, with abstracts from returns of inspectors, weighers and measurers of merchandise, &c., ...	S	2	81
1844.	Communication from, transmitting annual report of New York Blind Institute, ...	A	3	57
1844.	Report of, in relation to the Natural History of the State, ...	A	3	87
1844.	Report of, relative to railroad statistics, ...	A	5	123

NATHANIEL S. BENTON:

		Doc.	Vol.	No.
1845.	Report of, in relation to bill entitled an act in relation to the Natural History of New York, passed May 3, 1844, ...	S	1	6
1845.	do in relation to clerk hire, ...	S	1	33
1845.	do in relation to books of the Natural History of the State,	S	1	43
1845.	do relative to the report of inspectors of certain cities and counties, ...	S	2	53
1845.	do of abstracts of convictions for criminal offenses, and of returns of sheriffs respecting the persons convicted,	S	2	54
1845.	do of abstracts of the returns of the inspectors, measurers and weighers of merchandise, &c., for 1844, ...	S	2	56
1845.	do in relation to certain congressional documents, and the general index to the documents and laws of the state in his office, ...	S	2	71
1845.	do of the names of county clerks who have not, as required by law, filed in his office a statement of their fees, &c., ...	S	2	76
1845.	do of the names of surrogates who have not made reports of their fees and disbursements as required by law,	S	2	78
1845.	do relative to proposed amendments to the constitution,	A	1	7
1845.	do relative to weights and measures, ...	A	1	22
1845.	Annual report of, of railroad statistics, ...	A	4	129
1845.	Annual report of, relative to the poor, ...	A	3	197
1845.	Report of, relative to lands of Indians purchased by Wm. Smith, Jr., ...	A	6	212
1846.	do transmitting report of Mr. Schoolcraft relative to census of the Indians, ...	S	1	24
1846.	do and chancellor of university, transmitting report of the executive committee of the State Normal school, ..	S	1	32
1846.	do of abstracts of returns of inspectors of weights and measures of merchandise, &c., for 1845, ...	S	3	82
1846.	do of abstracts of convictions for criminal offences and of the returns of sheriffs respecting persons convicted,	S	3	98
1846.	do transmitting New York State census, ...	A	1	5
1846.	do in answer to a resolution of the assembly, ...	A	1	23
1846.	do and governor, relative to Natural History of New York,	A	2	41
1846.	do in answer to a resolution in relation to railroads, ...	A	3	66

SECRETARY OF STATE—*continued.*

		Doc.	Vol.	No.
1846.	Report of, transmitting annual railroad reports,	A	3	80
1846.	Communication from, relative to claim of Conrad Brown and others,	A	4	132
1846.	Report of, transmitting annual report of New York Institution for the Blind,	A	5	140
1846.	do relative to lands purchased by Wm. Smith,	A	5	149
1846.	do in answer to a resolution of the assembly,	A	5	188
1846.	do in answer to a resolution respecting prisoners pardoned,	A	5	198
1846.	do transmitting annual report of pauper statistics,	A	5	199
1847.	do relative to fees and county clerks,	S	2	58
1847.	do relative to statistics of the poor,	S	3	100
1847.	do relative to elections on the subject of licensing the sale of intoxicating liquors (in answer to resolution),	A	1	40
1847.	Letter from, as to districting Niagara county,	A	6	170
	CHRISTOPHER MORGAN:			
1848.	Report of, in relation to pardons granted since 1825,	S	2	66
1848.	Report of, in relation to births, marriages and deaths,	S	3	73
1848.	Statement by, of lands sold Stockbridge Indians,	A	2	53
1848.	Report of, as to surrogates reporting fees received by them,	A	3	57
1848.	Report of, as to treaties between State of New York and Cayuga Indians,	A	3	61
1848.	Report of, on petition of Francis Seger,	A	3	98
1848.	Report of, as to school laws under resolution,	A	3	115
1848.	Report of, as to railroad statistics,	A	5	132
1848.	Report of, as to criminal statistics,	A	6	193
1849.	Communication from, transmitting the contracts for the public printing,	S	1	15
1849.	Report of the amount of fees of county clerks,	S	3	77
1849.	Report relative to the poor,	S	3	53
1849.	Report relative to births, marriages and deaths,	S	3	86
1849.	Communication from, transmitting petition of inhabitants of Boston Corner, Massachusetts, to be annexed to the State of New York,	A	2	54
1849.	Report of, in answer to resolution of assembly respecting appointment of trustees for New York Institution for the Blind,	A	3	109
1849.	Communication from, transmitting report of state engineer and surveyor relative to sale of certain salt lots in Syracuse,	A	3	130
1849.	Report of Regents of the University on the historical and other papers and parchments received from office of, for deposit in state library,	A	3	148
1849.	Report of, respecting resolution on the petition of Ben Burdsall and others,	A	3	162
1849.	Report of, relative to railroad statistics,	A	3	182
1849.	Communication from, relative to manuscript documents concerning Colonial History of the State, and recommending their publication,	A	3	188
1849.	Communication from, transmitting report on weights and measures, by W. H. Clark of the State Normal School,	A	5	241
1849.	Annual report of, respecting criminal statistics,	A	5	242
1850.	Report of, on plankroads,	S	2	74
1850.	Communication from, in relation to St. Regis Indians,	A	3	27
1850.	Report of, on non-resident lands,	A	3	39
1850.	Report of, in answer to resolution relative to chap. 438, Laws of 1849,	A	4	59
1850.	Report of, in relation to county clerks,	A	6	152
1850.	Annual report of pauperism,	A	6	169
1850.	Annual report of criminal statistics,	A	8	195
1851.	Communication from, in relation to the Colonial History,	A	3	66
1851.	Report of, on criminal statistics,	A	5	140

SECRETARY OF STATE—*continued.*

Year		Doc.	Vol.	No.
1851.	Report of, on the poor,	A	5	147
1851.	Report of, in relation to Marius Schoonmaker,	S	2	62
	HENRY S. RANDALL:			
1852.	Report about births, marriages and deaths,	S	1	50
1852.	Annual report of criminal statistics,	S	3	97
1852.	Report of, in reference to Session Laws,	A	1	11
1852.	Report of, respecting fees of county clerks,	A	5	118
1852.	Report of, respecting books purchased by the attorney-general,	A	5	120
1853.	Report of, in answer to resolutions in relation to the Colonial History,	S	2	43
1853.	Report of, respecting clerical force in his office,	S	2	53
1853.	Annual report of, on criminal statistics of the state for 1852,	S	3	78
1853.	Communication from, in answer to resolutions relative to the poor laws,	A	1	14
1853.	Report of, of the statistics relative to the poor for 1851 and 1852,	A	5	120
	ELIAS W. LEAVENWORTH:			
1854.	Communication from, relative to insurance companies,	S	1	23
1854.	Report of, relative to state prisons,	S	1	54
1854.	Report of criminal statistics,	S	2	111
1854.	Communication from, transmitting certificate of state canvassers,	A	3	85
1854.	Communication from, relative to Documentary History,	A	4	136
1854.	Report of statistics of poor,	A	4	144
1855.	Report of statistics of poor,	S	3	72
1855.	Annual report of criminal statistics,	S	3	79
	JOEL T. HEADLEY:			
1856.	Report of, relative to printing election laws,	S	1	34
1856.	Report of, answering resolution in reference to savings banks,	A	3	60
1856.	Annual report relative to the poor,	A	5	214
1857.	Report of criminal statistics,	S	4	130
1857.	Report of poor statistics,	S	4	131
1857.	Report of life insurance companies,	S	4	166
1857.	Report of, in reply to resolutions relative to Colonial History,	A	2	70
1857.	Report of, in reply to resolutions relative to printing Colonial and Documentary Histories,	A	2	134
1857.	Report of, in reply to resolution relative to the contract for binding documents,	A	3	176
	GIDEON J. TUCKER:			
1858.	Reply of, relative to census report,	S	2	45
1858.	Annual report of, on statistics of the poor,	A	1	10
1858.	Annual report of, on criminal statistics,	A	6	168

SECRETARY OF WAR, *see* United States.

SEDGWICK, C. F., *see* Richard Swan.

SEDUCTION AND ADULTERY.

Year		Doc.	Vol.	No.
1840.	Report on petition for a law for the punishment of,	A	3	68
1840.	Report on petition for a law for the punishment of,	A	8	333
1842.	Report of committee on petitions for law to punish,	A	7	159
1843.	Report of select committee on petitions for a law more effectually to punish,	A	5	134
1844.	Report of committee on the judiciary on the petition for the suppression of,	A	3	63
1847.	Reports on petition relative to,	S	2	68

SEDUCTION LAWS.

Year		Doc.	Vol.	No.
1853.	Report of committee on grievances on petition of Oliver Teal and others to amend,	A	2	51

SECRETARY OF STATE—*continued.*

		Doc.	Vol.	No.
1853.	Report of committee on grievances on petition to amend,	A	3	57
1853.	Report of committee on grievances on petition to amend,	A	3	61

SEEBER, JOHN A. (a commissioner of deeds).

1837.	Report on petition to confirm his official acts,	A	1	50

SEELEY, EBENEZER.

1858.	Report on claim of,	A	1	31

SEELEY, JOHN G.

1858.	Report of majority of committee on contested elections on petition of James A. Dolan claiming seat of,	A	4	95
1858.	Minority report on same subject,	A	4	97
1858.	Testimony taken in same case,	A	4	101

SEGER, DAVID G.

1835.	Report on petition of, to take his seat as member of assembly in the place of Henry G. Wheaton,	A	1	11

SEGER, FRANCIS.

1848.	Report of secretary of state on petition of,	A	3	98

SELDEN, JACOB S.

1855.	Report of majority and minority of committee on privileges and elections in reference to contested seat of,	A	2	37
1855.	Report of majority and minority of committee on privileges and elections in reference to contested seat of,	A	2	47
1855.	Report of majority and minority of committee on privileges and elections in reference to contested seat of,	A	2	59

SELDEN, SAMUEL L., *see* Chancery, Clerks in.

SEMINARIES, *see* Academies, &c.

SEMPRONIUS, TOWN OF.

1840.	First Congregational Church, report on petition to change the name of, to increase the number of trustees, &c.,	A	8	334

SENATE.

1835.	Report of committee appointed to revise the rules and orders,	S	1	9
1835.	Rules and orders of the,	S	1	11
1837.	Additional rule,	S	1	20
1840.	Journal of the, report of a committee appointed to inquire into the correctness of the, relative to the passage of the resolutions for a general bankrupt law,	S	4	127
1842.	List of senators with nearest post-office, &c.,	S	1	3
1842.	List of senators and place of residence in Albany,	S	1	4
1842.	List of standing committees of, and on governor's message,	S	1	5
1842.	Report of the sergeant-at-arms in pursuance of resolution of 1841,	S	2	24
1842.	General orders,	S	4	89
1843.	List of standing committees,	S	1	4
1843.	List of senators with classes, district and residence,	S	1	5
1843.	List of senators with classes and nearest post-office,	S	1	6
1843.	General orders of,	S	2	68
1843.	General orders of,	S	3	93
1844.	List of standing committees,	S	1	6
1844.	List of senators, with residences, &c.,	S	1	1

SENATE—*continued.*

		Doc.	Vol.	No.
1844.	List of senators and officers, with residence in Albany, ...	S	1	7
1844.	General orders of, ...	S	4	120
1845.	List of senators, with residences, &c., ...	S	1	1
1855.	Calendar of business of, ...	S	1	17
1855.	do	S	1	25
1855.	do	S	1	30
1855.	do	S	2	39
1855.	do	S	2	42
1855.	do	S	2	44
1855.	do	S	2	48
1855.	do	S	2	51
1855.	do	S	2	62
1845.	List of general orders and unfinished business, ...	S	2	80
1845.	List of general orders and unfinished business, ...	S	3	95
1846.	List of senators, &c., ...	S	1	1
1846.	List of standing committees, ...	S	1	5
1846.	List of senators, &c., ...	S	1	1
1846.	List of senators, &c., ...	S	1	3
1846.	Report of comptroller relative to expense of an extra session of,	S	2	53
1847.	Official list of senators, ...	S	1	1
1847.	Official list of senators, with residences, &c., ...	S	1	6
1847.	Rules and orders of, ...	S	1	25
1847.	Rules and orders of, as corrected, ...	S	1	26
1847.	General orders, ...	S	2	69
1847.	General orders, ...	S	4	111
1848.	Rules and orders of, ...	S	1	1
1848.	Standing committees of, ...	S	1	7
1848.	Members, officers, &c., of, ...	S	1	8
1848.	Members, officers, &c., of, ...	S	1	9
1848.	Amendments to rules and orders of, offered by Mr. Cornwell, ...	S	1	10
1848.	General orders of unfinished business, ...	S	2	68
1849.	Rules and orders of, ...	S	1	1
1849.	Members and officers of, ...	S	1	3
1849.	Committees of, ...	S	1	4
1848.	Report of joint select committee on library, ...	A	3	131
1850.	Standing committees, ...	S	1	5
1850.	Members of, &c., ...	S	1	1
1850.	Members of, with place of birth, &c., ...	S	2	72
1851.	Members and officers of, &c., ...	S	1	1
1851.	Rules and orders of last, ...	S	1	3
1851.	Rules and orders of, adopted, ...	S	1	6
1851.	Rules of, report of the minority of the committee, ...	S	1	7
1851.	Members and officers of, with post-office address, &c., ...	S	1	10
1851.	Standing committees of, ...	S	1	11
1851.	Official list of members, ...	S	3	76
1851.	Calendar of business at regular session, ...	S	3	77
1851.	Standing committees of, ...	S	3	78
1851.	Rules and orders of, adopted, ...	S	3	79
1851.	Members and officers, &c., ...	S	3	80
1851.	Standing committees of, ...	A	1	11
1852.	Standing committees of, ...	S	1	3
1852.	Report relative to adopting the rules, ...	S	1	7
1852.	Members and officers of, ...	S	1	9
1853.	Standing committees of, ...	S	1	3
1853.	Rules and orders of the, adopted January 11, 1853, ...	S	1	2
1853.	Report of select committees to revise rules of, ...	S	1	5
1853.	Clerk of, *see* Digest of Claims, ...	S	1	6
1853.	Members and officers of, with post office, residence, &c., ...	S	1	8
1854.	Rules and orders of, ...	S	1, 2	11
1854.	Members and officers of, ...	S	1	6
1854.	Standing committees of, ...	S	1	7

SENATE—*continued.*

Year	Subject	Doc.	Vol.	No.
1855.	List of senators,....................................	S	1	1
1855.	Rules and orders of,....................................	S	1	2
1855.	Standing committees of,....................................	S	1, 5,	7
1855.	Report of select committee on rules and orders of,............	S	1	10
1855.	Rules and orders of,....................................	S	1	12
1855.	Members and officers of,....................................	S	1	24
1856.	List of senators,....................................	S	1	1
1856.	Standing committees of,....................................	S	1	6
1856.	Rules and orders of,....................................	S	1	7
1856.	Rules and orders of, adopted January 25th,.................	S	1	18
1856.	List of senators, with residence, &c.,....................	S	1	28
1856.	List of general orders,....................................	S	2, 75,	86
1857.	List of senators,....................................	S	1, 2,	5
1857.	Standing committees of,....................................	S	1	4
1857.	Rules and orders of,....................................	S	1, 11,	21
1857.	List of senators, with post-office, residence, &c.,...............	S	1	18
1858.	List of senators,....................................	S	1	2
1858.	Members and officers of, with residence, &c.,...............	S	2, 21,	42
1858.	Rules and orders of,....................................	S	2	25
1858.	Rules and orders of, as adopted February 9, 1858,.............	S	2	32
1858.	Report relative to library,....................................	S	2	60

FOR JOINT RULES OF, AND ASSEMBLY, *see* Legislature.

SENATE DISTRICTS.

Year	Subject	Doc.	Vol.	No.
1856.	And representation, report relative to,.........................	S	3	102

SENATORS, UNITED STATES.

Year	Subject	Doc.	Vol.	No.
1839.	Report on bill and resolutions from the assembly for the appointment of a,....................................	S	3	77
1839.	Report on the resolutions of the senate for the appointment of a,	A	5	272
1839.	Report on bill to provide for the election of,.................	A	6	404
1845.	Communication from the governor relative to,................	A	1	8

SENECA, COUNTY OF.

Year	Subject	Doc.	Vol.	No.
1833.	Beef and pork, annual report of H. Halsey, an inspector of,....	S	2	68
1834.	Beef and pork, annual report of H. Halsey, an inspector of,....	S	2	62
1830.	Commissioner of loans, report on petition of John Sayre, a,....	S	1	23
1834.	Ardent spirits, report on petition to prevent tavern keepers from retailing,....................................	A	4	372
1830.	New county from part of, report on petition for a,............	A	4	378
1832.	Race-course in, report on petition for a,......................	A	4	385
1835.	Tax to repair the free bridge over Genesee river, report on petition for a,....................................	A	5	383
1834.	Road Company, memorial of, relative to the application for the Utica and Schenectady railroad,	A	1	48
1835.	do do relative to same,................	A	2	148
1839.	do report on petition to abandon their road,.......	A	2	48
1830.	Division of, report on petition for the,....................	A	4	378

BANKS, *see* Banks—Seneca County.

SENECA FALLS, VILLAGE OF.

Year	Subject	Doc.	Vol.	No.
1832.	Report on bill to revive an act to incorporate the,...............	S	2	90

SENECA INDIANS, *see* Indians—Senecas.

SENECA LAKE.

Year	Subject	Doc.	Vol.	No.
1830.	Report relative to the discharge of water at the foot of,.........	A	4	374

SENECA LAKE—*continued.*

		Doc.	Vol.	No.
1831.	Wharf and harbor on, near Sheldrake Point, report on petition to construct a,	A	4	342
1841.	Canal from, to Havana, report relative to the cost of a,	S	2	90
1843.	Report of canal commissioners relative to the outlet of,	A	4	102
1846.	Report of canal board in regard to weirs at,	A	5	166
1846.	Report of committee on canals respecting outlet of,	A	5	179
1856.	Remonstrance relative to bill for damming,	S	2	90
1856.	Report of state engineer and surveyor relative to,	S	2	81

SENECA RIVER.

1835.	Free bridge across, report on petition to raise money by tax for the support of the,	A	5	383
1836.	Bridge across, at Baldwinsville, report on petition to raise money to build,	A	3	149
1836.	Wing dam, report on petition of Porter Wethey to build a,	A	1	31
1841.	Bridge over, at Jack's reef, report on petition to raise money on the towns of Elbridge, Lysander and Van Buren to build a,	A	5	180
1836.	Towing path on the, report on petition for a,	A	3	127
1837.	do report on petition for a,	A	2	114
1841.	do report of canal board concerning the,	S	3	76
1839.	do report on petition for a fence along the,	A	4	242
1836.	And Oneida river, report on bill to improve the navigation of,	A	4	264
1837.	And Oneida river, report of canal commissioners relative to the survey of the,	A	2	90
1837.	Report on petition to amend the act to improve the,	A	4	306
1846.	Report of canal board relative to water power along,	A	5	144
1850.	Report of canal board in relation to improvement of, at Baldwinsville,	S	5	94

SERGEANT, AARON.

1833.	Report on petition of, for new certificates on the sale of certain land for taxes, in lieu of the original ones, which are lost,	A	3	214

SERGEANT, JOHN—INDIAN AGENT.

1832.	Report on petition of, for compensation for services,	S	1	17
1834.	do do do do	A	3	182
1838.	do do do do	A	1	162

SERLES, JACOB, *see* John Carr and others.

SESSION LAWS.

1842.	Report of secretary of state relative to the printed laws of this state in pamphlet form,	S	1	9
1842.	Communication from secretary of state relative to publishing,	S	3	81
1844.	Report of committee on public printing on petitions in relation to publishing,	A	5	124
1852.	Report of secretary of state in relation to,	A	1	11

SEWALL'S (Dr.) PATHOLOGY OF DRUNKENNESS.

1843.	Report of finance committee on the subject of the distribution of, with plates, &c.,	S	3	116
1843.	Report on petition of citizens of New York relative to,	A	2	33
1844.	Report on a bill for the distribution of plates,	A	5	102

SEVENTH DAY BAPTISTS.

1839.	Report on petition of, for certain exemptions,	A	6	333

SEWARD, TOWN OF.

1849.	Report on petition of inhabitants of, relative to place of holding their next annual town meeting,	A	2	40

SEXTON, HENRY, AND ANSON GIBBS.

		Doc	Vol.	No.
1832.	Report on petition for a ferry across the Allegany river,........	A	2	151

SEYMOUR, A., & CO.

1852.	Report on the petition of,..........................	A	2	41

SEYMOUR, A., AND OTHERS.

1844.	Report of comptroller on the petition of,....................	A	7	205

SEYMOUR, ASAPH, AND OTHERS.

1845.	Report of committee on canals on the petition of,..............	A	4	121
1846.	Minority report of committee on claims on petition of,..........	A	4	126
1847.	Report on petitions of, ...	A	2	54

SEYMOUR, DANIEL L.

1840.	Report on petition of, for the lease or sale of a lot of land in Fort Covington,..	A	3	64

SEYMOUR, HENRY (a Canal Commissioner).

1831.	Communication from, in relation to the memorial of Lyman Spalding, relative to the surplus waters, at Lockport,........	A	2	121
1831.	Memorial of Gerrit Smith, specifying his charges against, and praying for his removal from office,...........	A	3	236
1831.	Communication from, relative to the memorial of Gerrit Smith,.	A	3	234
1831.	Report of committee on canals on petition for the removal of,...	A	3	237
1831.	Report of committee on canals on petition for the removal of,...	A	4	356
1831.	Testimony taken before the committee,........................	A	4	354

SEYMOUR, JAMES.

1843.	Report of the committee on claims on the petition of,..........	A	2	21

SEYMOUR, LAUREN.

1854.	Report on petition of,...................................	S	1	38

SEYMOUR, LAUREN, AND MOREHOUSE HICKOX.

1831.	Report on petition of, to erect a wing dam on the Oneida river,..	A	3	274

SEYMOUR, LAWRENCE, AND OTHERS.

1853.	Report of committee on claims on petition of, for relief,........	A	2	40
1853.	Report of committee on claims on petition of, for relief,........	A	2	49

SEYMOUR, LORENZO.

1857.	Report of standing committee on finance on petition of,........	S	4	117

SEYMOUR, MARY.

1830.	Report on petition for a divorce, ...	S	2	80
1834.	Report on petition for a divorce,..........................	A	3	215

SHAKERS.

1830.	Remonstrance of the society called, against the passage of a certain law, ...	A	4	300
1849.	Report of select committee relative to certain trusts held by, &c.,	A	3	198
1850.	Report of trustees of society at New Lebanon,................	S	3	89

SHAWANGUNK COMPANY.

		Doc.	Vol.	No.
1839.	Report on petition to incorporate the,	A	4	218

SHAWANGUNK, TOWN OF.

1852.	Report on petition of inhabitants for a new town,	A	5	107

SHAW, JOHN, AND OTHERS.

1831.	Report on petition of, for the remission of interest due on certaln land,	A	3	265

SHAW, MERCY, *see* J. Gay.

SHEARER, URIAH.

1833.	Report on the claims of, for compensation for damages by the Saratoga dam,	A	3	238
1834.	Report on the same,	A	3	58
1839.	Report on the same,	A	3	150

SHEPARD, JOHN D.

1857.	Report of majority of committee, favorable on bill entitled an act for the relief of,	A	3	179
1857.	Report of minority of committee on same subject,	A	3	186

SHEPHERD, CHARLES, AND OTHERS.

1845.	Report of committee on canals, on the petition of, relative to Dansville side-cut,	A	4	117

SHEPHERD, FITCH, *see* Z. Hills.

SHEPHERD, WILLIAM.

1842.	Report on petition of,	A	7	171

SHEPPARD, C. O., *see* Hamilton College.

SHEPPARD, MORRIS F.

1836.	Report on petition of, for compensation for damages by the Crooked Lake canal,	A	4	299

SHEPPARD, WILLIAM.

1841.	Report on petition of, to purchase a part of the bed of the Erie canal,	A	5	187

SHERBURNE, TOWN OF.

1830.	Town-house, report on petition to raise money by tax to build,	A	4	321
1835.	Room for the transaction of town business, report relative to a,	A	4	379
1838.	Room for the transaction of town business, report on petition to raise money to pay for finishing a,	A	5	254
1837.	Liabilities of the, to the state, report on petition to be released from,	A	3	211
1839.	Liabilities of the, to the state, report on petition to be released from,	A	3	139
1839.	Liabilities of the, to the state, report on petition to be released from,	A	4	217

SHERBURNE UNION ACADEMY, *see* Academies, &c.

SHERBURNE, VILLAGE OF.

1832.	Report on petition to amend the charter of the,	A	4	266

SHERBURNE, VILLAGE OF—*continued.*

		Doc.	Vol.	No.
1830.	Road from, to Utica, report on petition to appoint commissioners to lay out a,	S	3	253
1831.	Road from, to Utica, report on petition to repeal the same,	S	1	41

SHERIFFS.

		Doc.	Vol.	No.
1831.	Fees of, report of comptroller relative to the payment of,	A	4	339
1832.	Fees of, and the manner of serving process, report in relation to,	A	3	259
1833.	Fees of, for the transportation of convicts, report in relation to the,	A	2	84
1833.	Fees of, for the transportation of convicts, report in relation to the,	S	1	31
1839.	Fees of, for the transportation of convicts, report in relation to the,	A	5	319
1839.	Report of comptroller on the same,	S	3	100
1840.	Report of comptroller on the same,	A	3	75
1850.	Report of select committee on petition in relation to fees of, and return of executions,	A	4	62

SHERMAN, GEORGE W., AND OTHERS.

		Doc.	Vol.	No.
1857.	Report of committee on claims adverse on petition of,	A	2	103

SHERMAN, WASHINGTON, AND OTHERS.

		Doc.	Vol.	No.
1848.	Report of committee on claims on petition of,	A	5	150
1849.	Report of committee on claims on petition of,	A	2	59
1850.	Report of committee on grievances on petition of,	S	2	45

SHERMAN, WILLIAM AND URIAL.

		Doc.	Vol.	No.
1849.	Report of committee on claims on petition of,	A	1	22
1850.	Report on petition of,	A	6	142

SHERRILL, JAMES H.

		Doc.	Vol.	No.
1847.	Report on petition of,	S	2	72
1856.	Report on petition of,	A	3	93

SHERWIN, JOSHUA.

		Doc.	Vol.	No.
1830.	Report on petition for a grant of certain land at its appraised value,	S	1	58

SHEW, JACOB.

		Doc.	Vol.	No.
1833.	Report on petition of, for bounty lands for revolutionary services,	S	2	49
1833.	Report on petition of, for bounty lands for revolutionary services,	S	1	26

SHILAND, JOHN.

		Doc.	Vol.	No.
1830.	Report on petition of, to be reimbursed for a lot of land sold for taxes,	A	2	165
1831.	Report of committee on claims for the same,	A	2	170
1832.	do do	A	3	181
1834.	do do	A	4	362
1835.	do do	A	3	214
1838.	Report of attorney-general on the same,	A	5	272
1841.	Report of committee on grievances on the same,	A	4	111

SHIP CANAL AROUND NIAGARA FALLS.

		Doc.	Vol.	No.
1834.	Preamble and resolution relative to the construction of the,	A	3	166
1839.	Report on bill to authorize the United States to construct a,	S	1	23
1840.	Memorial of Jesse Hawley against ceding to the United States the right to construct a,	S	4	108

SHIP CANAL AROUND NIAGARA FALLS—*continued.*

		Doc.	Vol.	No.
1853.	Minority report of committee on canals in relation to a,...	A	3	76
1853.	Majority report on same subject, ...	A	3	77

SHIP CANAL AROUND THE FALLS OF ST. MARIE.

1841.	Resolutions of the legislature of Michigan relative to a,.........	A	1	15

SHIP CANAL FROM ALBANY TO NEW BALTIMORE.

1833.	Petition for the construction of a,..........................	S	1	24
1833.	Report of committee on canals on petition for a, ...	S	2	80

SHIP CANAL FROM OSWEGO TO UTICA.

1834.	Memorial of inhabitants of Utica for the construction of a,......	S	2	104
1837.	Petition from Oneida county for the construction of a,.........	A	2	132

SHIPMAN & HULL.

1857.	Report on petition of,......................................	S	2	91
1857.	Report of judiciary committee on petition of, ...	S	3	91

SHIPPEY, J. C., AND W. KIMBALL.

1846.	Reports on petition for the relief of, ...	S	1	40
1846.	Report of committee on claims on petition of, ...	S	2	60
1848.	Report of committee on claims on petition of, ...	A	5	151

SHIPS AND VESSELS.

1847.	Report as to collection of demands against, ...	A	2	77

SHIP STEAMBOAT CANAL from Lake Ontario to Albany.

1834.	Petition for a survey of a route for a, ...	A	4	367
1834.	Report of select committee on the same,......................	A	4	380
1835.	Proceedings of a meeting of citizens of Utica in relation to a, ...	A	2	158
1835.	Report of a survey of a route for a, ...	A	3	195
1835.	Report of canal board relative to the construction of a,.........	A	4	334

SHOWDY, HENRY.

1852.	Report on petition of, for payment of interest, ...	A	2	86

SHULER, WM. S., & A. H. DELAMATER.

1855.	Report of committee of ways and means on petition of,........	A	2	39

SIBBERAD, LEWIS, AND OTHERS.

1846.	Report on petition of, relative to taxation of personal property of non-residents,....................................	S	4	109

SICKLES, D. E.

1857.	Report on contested seat of,................................	S	1	25

SILK.

1832.	Report on the propriety of introducing the manufacture of,.....	A	3	176
1832.	Report on bill to encourage the culture of, &c., ...	S	2	101
1838.	Report on petition to encourage the growth and manufacture of,.	A	3	135
1839.	Petition and bill for the same,..............................	A	6	329
1840.	Communication from the American Institute relative to the culture of, ...	A	4	134
1841.	Report on bill to encourage the growth and manufacture of,.....	A	4	140

SILK—*continued.*

		Doc.	Vol.	No.
1842.	Report to the governor respecting the manufacture of, in Auburn prison,	A	1	2
1843.	Report of the inspectors of Auburn state prison relative to manufacture,	S	1	23

SIMMONS, GEO. A., AND OTHERS.

		Doc.	Vol.	No.
1846.	Memorial of,	S	3	73

SIMPSON, EDWARD.

		Doc.	Vol.	No.
1830.	Remonstrance of, against the payment of the annual tax of $500 on each theatre in the city of New York,	A	3	263
1831.	Remonstrance of, against the payment of the annual tax of $500 on each theatre in the city of New York,	A	2	85

SIMSON, JOHN.

		Doc.	Vol.	No.
1844.	Report of the canal board on the petition of,	A	6	151

SING SING, VILLAGE OF.

		Doc.	Vol.	No.
1836.	Report on petition for the extension of Spring street,	S	1	51
1840.	St. Paul's church at, report on petition of the trustees of, to be released from a debt due the state prison,	A	5	183
1846.	Report of commissioners of land office concerning guards,	A	5	163
1848.	Report of attorney-general in relation to Hudson River railroad at,	S	2	64

SINKING FUND, *see* General Fund.

SKAJAQUADA CREEK.

		Doc.	Vol.	No.
1847.	Report relative to,	A	1	27

SKANEATELES, TOWN OF.

		Doc.	Vol.	No.
1835.	School district No. 7, report on petition to sell the school house and lot,	A	2	113
1836.	Report relative to a re-survey and recording of roads in,	A	1	34

SKANEATELES, VILLAGE OF.

		Doc.	Vol.	No.
1836.	Bank at, report on petition for a,	A	3	136

SKENANDOAH, CHRISTINE, AND OTHERS.

		Doc.	Vol.	No.
1853.	Report of committee on Indian affairs, on claim of, for relief,	A	3	80
1857.	Report of committee on petition of,	A	3	198

SKINNER, BENJAMIN AND SARAH.

		Doc.	Vol.	No.
1841.	Report on petition of, for compensation for damages to their property by the construction of the Chenango canal,	A	6	251

SLACK, WILLARD.

		Doc.	Vol.	No.
1841.	Report on petition of, for compensation for damages by the construction of the Chenango canal,	A	3	69

SLAM, LEVI D., *see* Moses Jaques.

SLAVERY, *see* Abolitionists' Petition.

		Doc.	Vol.	No.
1836.	Abolition of, resolutions of the legislature of Michigan relative to the,	S	2	77

SLAVERY—*continued.*

		Doc.	Vol.	No.
1836.	Abolition of, resolutions of the legislature of Kentucky relative to the,	S	2	79
1836.	Abolition of, resolutions of the legislature of Maine relative to the,	S	2	85
1836.	Abolition of, resolutions of the legislature of Ohio relative to the,	S	2	87
1836.	Report of a joint committee on the subject of the,	S	2	106
1838.	And the slave trade, report of a majority of the committee on the judiciary on the subject of,	A	6	359
1839.	Resolutions of the legislature of Indiana on the subject of,	A	5	282
1840.	Resolutions of the legislature of Missouri on the subject of,	A	4	143
1840.	Report on petition for a law for the rescue of free colored persons reduced to,	A	8	341
1842.	Resolutions of Maryland, concerning abolition of,	A	7	149
1843.	Report of the minority of the judiciary committee on the subject of repealing the law extending the right of trial by jury, passed May 6, 1840, and also on the subject of repealing all laws relative to the writ *de homine replegiando*,	A	5	141
1844.	Communication from the governor transmitting resolutions of the legislature of the general assembly of Maryland, relative to,	A	7	193
1846.	Concurrent resolutions offered by Mr. Worden, relative to,	A	5	162
1848.	Resolutions relative to the extension of,	S	1	5
1849.	Report of select committee on so much of governor's message as relates to the introduction of, into New Mexico and California,	A	3	139
1849.	Message from the governor transmitting resolutions of general assembly of Missouri, respecting,	A	5	229
1850.	Report of minority of select committee relative to,	A	3	29
1850.	Resolutions of Georgia concerning,	A	8	176
1850.	do Mississippi in respect to,	A	8	179
1850.	do Vermont respecting,	A	8	181
1850.	do Texas concerning,	A	8	193
1850.	do Maryland relative to,	A	8	194
1850.	Report of select committee on governor's message concerning,	S	1	8

SLAVES.

		Doc.	Vol.	No.
1841.	Report on petition to repeal the law allowing them to be held in this state,	A	5	183
1841.	Report on petition to repeal the law allowing them to be held in this state,	A	6	239
1832.	Report on petition of F. Milligan, a slave, sold by the commissioners of sequestration, for the payment of the amount for which he was sold,	A	3	213

SLAVES, FUGITIVE, *see* Georgia, Virginia.

		Doc.	Vol.	No.
1847.	Report on subject of arrest of,	A	6	168

SLAVE TRADE.

		Doc.	Vol.	No.
1852.	Resolutions of legislature of Indiana,	S	2	91

SLEEPER, JAS.

		Doc.	Vol.	No.
1850.	Report on canal damages,	A	5	95

SLOCUM, PELEG, AND OTHERS.

		Doc.	Vol.	No.
1851.	Report on petition for canal damages,	S	2	55

SMALL BILLS, *see* Banks.

SMALLDEN, ANN, AND MARY THOMAS.

		Doc.	Vol.	No.
1850.	Report on petition of,	S	1	23

SMALLEY, DAVID P.

		Doc.	Vol.	No.
1846.	Report on petition of,	S	3	97

SMALL POX.

1833.	Report on petition for a law for the prevention of the,	A	2	68
1839.	Report on petition for a law for the prevention of the,	S	3	80

SMITH & CO. (Of Canajoharie).

1852.	Report on petition of for relief,	A	5	104

SMITH & HOTCHKISS.

1849.	Petition of, for appointment of commissioners to examine and liquidate claims of, against agent of state prison at Sing Sing,	A	2	85
1851.	Report of committee on claims on petition of Abijah Fitch, in relation to claim of,	A	4	96

SMITH & STILLWELL.

1853.	Report of committee on claims on petition of, for relief,	S	1	22

SMITH, A. J.

1847.	Report of committee of five Smiths on petition of,	A	8	252

SMITH, ASA P.

1846.	Report of committee on claims on petition of,	S	3	83

SMITH, ASA T.

1840.	Report on petition of, for extra compensation for work done on the Erie canal,	A	4	156
1841.	Report on petition of, for extra compensation for work done on the Erie canal,	A	4	241
1842.	Report of canal board on the petition of,	S	2	31
1842.	Report of committee on claims on the petition of,	S	3	70
1843.	Report of the canal board on the petition of,	A	4	108
1843.	Report of committee on canals on the petition of,	A	4	118
1844.	Report of committee on claims on petition of,	S	1	28
1845.	Report of committee on claims on petitition of,	A	4	95
1846.	Report on petition of,	S	3	83
1846.	Report of canal board on petition of,	A	2	49
1847.	Report on petition of,	A	2	69

SMITH, BENJAMIN.

1856.	Report on petition of,	A	3	26

SMITH, CHAUNCEY.

1849.	Report of comptroller of all moneys drawn from state treasury by, late agent of Sing Sing state prison,	A	2	99
1851.	Remonstrance of inspectors of Sing Sing prison against releasing,	S	2	57
1851.	Agent Sing Sing, report of committee on claims on petition of,	A	4	105

SMITH, DAVID.

1830.	Report on petition of the heirs of, for bounty lands,	S	1	43
1831.	do do do	A	1	21
1833.	do do do	A	3	224

SMITH, DAVID, AND OTHERS.

1847.	Report of committee on claims on petition of,	A	2	92

SMITH, DAVID W.

		Doc.	Vol.	No.
1836.	Report on petition of, for a loan to aid the Hudson River Scientific and Agricultural Seminary,........................	S	1	19

SMITH, E. G. R.

1846.	Report on bill of,.....	S	4	114

SMITH, FRANCIS.

1854.	Report on petition of, and heirs of J. Dunlap,..................	A	2	67

SMITH, HENRY.

1841.	Report on petition of, for bounty lands,........................	A	7	282

SMITH, GERRIT, *see* D. S. Jones and G. Smith.

1831.	Memorial of, specifying his charges against Henry Seymour, and praying for his removal,.....	A	3	236
1831.	Report of committee on canals on the same,...................	A	3	237
1831.	Report of committee on canals on the same,...................	A	4	356
1831.	Testimony taken before said committee,........................	A	4	354
1831.	Memorial of Henry Seymour in relation to the memorial of,.....	A	3	234
1850.	Report on granting assembly chamber to,.....................	A	5	112

SMITH, H. B., AND OTHERS.

1847.	Report on petitions of,....	A	8	221

SMITH, JAMES.

1855.	Report of committee on claims on petition of,.................	A	3	63
1858.	Report on claim of,..	A	4	94

SMITH, JANE B., *see* John G. Hicks and others.

SMITH, JOHN B., AND OTHERS.

1837.	Report on petition of, for extra allowance for work done on the Chenango canal,..	A	3	202
1839.	Report of canal commissioners on the same,..................	A	3	72
1839.	Report of committee on claims on the same,..................	A	4	247

SMITH, JOHN C.

1852.	Claim of, report on,..	S	2	57

SMITH, JOHN H.

1839.	Report on petition of, to change his name,...................	A	5	306

SMITH, JOHN H. T.

1845.	Report of the attorney-general on the petition of,.............	S	1	20

SMITH, JOHN P.

1852.	Report on petition of, for relief,..............................	S	1	18

SMITH, JOSEPH E., & CO.

1834.	Report on petition for extra allowance for work done on the Oswego canal,..	A	3	209
1834.	Report of the committee on claims on the same,...............	A	4	363
1835.	Report of canal commissioners on the same,...................	A	2	109

SMITH, JOSEPH E., & CO.—*continued.*

Year	Subject	Doc.	Vol.	No.
1835.	Report of committee on grievances on the same,	A	3	177
1836.	do canal commissioners do	A	3	128
1836.	do committee on claims do	A	4	322

SMITH, JUSTIN.

Year	Subject	Doc.	Vol.	No.
1832.	Report on petition of, relative to supplying Whitehall with water,	A	1	17
1834.	do do do	A	2	74
1835.	do do do	A	1	16

SMITH, LYMAN B., AND OTHERS.

Year	Subject	Doc.	Vol.	No.
1858.	Report on claim of,	A	4	122

SMITH, NATHANIEL.

Year	Subject	Doc.	Vol.	No.
1834.	Report on petition of, to change his name,	A	2	100

SMITH, NOAH.

Year	Subject	Doc.	Vol.	No.
1850.	Majority report on claim,	S	2	50

SMITH, OTIS.

Year	Subject	Doc.	Vol.	No.
1854.	Report on petition of,	A	1	35
1855.	Report of committee on claims on petition of,	A	4	86
1856.	Report on petition of,	A	3	59
1857.	Report of committee on claims on petition of,	A	2	73

SMITH, RUSSELL.

Year	Subject	Doc.	Vol.	No.
1852.	Minority report in relation to his seat,	A	2	46

SMITH, THOMAS, *see* Jacob Bergen.

SMITH, THOMAS PLUMER.

Year	Subject	Doc.	Vol.	No.
1841.	Report on petition of, to confirm his title to certain land,	S	2	58

SMITHTOWN, TOWN OF.

Year	Subject	Doc.	Vol.	No.
1838.	Report on petition for a bounty on foxes and crows in the,	A	5	222

SMITH, WILLIAM.

Year	Subject	Doc.	Vol.	No.
1840.	Report on petition to change his name,	A	1	4
1845.	Report of committee on grievances on the petition of,	A	7	244
1846.	Report of secretary of state relative to lands purchased by,	A	5	149
1848.	Report on petition of,	A	3	85

SMITH, WM., JR.

Year	Subject	Doc.	Vol.	No.
1845.	Report of secretary of state respecting Indian lands purchased by,	A	6	212

SNIFFIN, H., AND WIFE.

Year	Subject	Doc.	Vol.	No.
1839.	Report on petition for a divorce,	A	5	304

SOAP, JOHN.

Year	Subject	Doc.	Vol.	No.
1836.	Report on petition of, relative to certain land,	A	4	285

SODUS BAY BRIDGE COMPANY.

Year	Subject	Doc.	Vol.	No.
1832.	Report on petition to extend the charter of the,	S	1	11

SODUS, TOWN OF.

		Doc.	Vol.	No.
1830.	Report relative to the sale of a lot of land in, by the trustees of the First Presbyterian Society,..........	S	1	60
1838.	Report on petition to extend the time for the collection of taxes in,..	A	6	329
1850.	Report of canal board respecting canal at,....................	A	6	151

SOLDIERS AND OFFICERS OF THE REVOLUTION, *see* Revolution.

SOLDIERS AND OFFICERS OF WAR OF 1812, *see* War of 1812.

SOMERSET, TOWN OF.

		Doc.	Vol.	No.
1832.	Report on petition from the, relative to fishing in Golden Hill creek,...	A	2	173

SONS OF TEMPERANCE.

		Doc.	Vol.	No.
1852.	Report on petition of the, ...	A	2	50

SOULE, NATHAN, AND OTHERS.

		Doc.	Vol.	No.
1838.	Report on petition for extra allowance for work done on the Erie canal,.....................	A	5	219

SOUTH BAY.

		Doc.	Vol.	No.
1858.	Report of commissioners relative to bridge across, in Washington county, ...	A	6	167

SOUTH BAY TRACT.

		Doc.	Vol.	No.
1831.	Report on petition of E. Chapman and others, relative to the,...	A	3	230
1832.	Report on petition of D. Allen and others, relative to the, ...	A	3	195
1832.	Report on petition of D. Allen and others, relative to the, ...	A	3	235

SOUTH CAROLINA, STATE OF, *see* Nullification.

		Doc.	Vol.	No.
1833.	Ordinance of, to nullify certain acts of Congress, ...	S	1	2
1833.	Resolutions of the Legislature of, recommending a convention of the states,..	A	2	39
1840.	Report and resolutions of the legislature of, relative to the controversy between Maine and Georgia,......................	A	5	167
1842.	Message from governor, transmitting a law, a report and resolution of the legislature of, relative to the Virginia controversy,	S	2	41
1842.	Message from governor, transmitting resolution of the legislature of, relative to the public lands,..........................	S	3	52
1842.	Law and resolution of, in relation to controversy between New York and Virginia, ...	A	4	62
1842.	Report of judiciary committee on the correspondence of governor with executive of, ...	A	7	185
1844.	Resolution of the legislature of, in relation to state debts and the annexation of Texas to the Union,......................	A	1	5
1844.	Communication from governor, transmitting resolution of the legislature of,...	A	1	15
1845.	Concurrent resolution by Mr. Van Schoonhoven, relative to South Carolina and Massachusetts,..........................	A	1	26

SOUTH EAST.

		Doc.	Vol.	No.
1852.	Report on petition of Sons of Temperance in,................	A	2	51

SOUTHFIELD, TOWN OF.

		Doc.	Vol.	No.
1846.	Report relative to town election, &c., in,	S	4	112

SOUTHAMPTON, TOWN OF.

1833.	Report on petition of, for a law to inclose the common lands of,	S	2	113

SOUTH MIDDLETOWN.

1832.	Fire engine company, report on petition to incorporate,	A	3	275

SOUTHPORT.

1850.	Report on petition of inhabitants,	A	6	161

SPAFFORD, TILLOTSON, AND OTHERS.

1858.	Report of committee on petition of, for the repayment of moneys illegally collected,	S	3	115

SPAFFORD, TOWN OF.

1834.	Report on petition for the division of the,	A	4	282
1843.	Report of the committee on grievances, on the petition of the town auditors and overseers of the poor of,	A	5	165

SPALDING, EMERY D.

1833.	Report on petition of, for a pension, on account of injuries received while in the discharge of military duty,	A	3	200

SPALDING, F. A., AND OTHERS.

1847.	Report on petition of,	S	3	85

SPALDING, LYMAN A., *see* Lockport surplus waters.

SPAULDING, HARRISON.

1853.	Report of committee on claims, on petition of,	A	4	84

SPENCER, AMBROSE.

1848.	Report relative to obsequies of,	A	5	131

SPENCER, JOHN, AND JOHN A. EHLE.

1837.	Report on petition of, for extra allowance for work done on the Chenango canal,	S	1	36
1838.	Report on petition of, for extra allowance for work done on the Chenango canal,	A	5	279

SPENCER, JOHN, AND OTHERS.

1840.	Report on petition of, for extra allowance for work done on the Genesee Valley canal,	A	6	258
1840.	Report on petition of, for extra allowance for work done on the Genesee Valley canal,	A	7	278

SPENCER, JOHN, AND L. SPRAKER.

1834.	Report on petition of, for compensation for the loss of a lot of timber by the breaking away of a dam on the Mohawk river,	A	4	345
1838.	Report on petition of, for extra allowance for work done on the Erie canal,	A	6	342

SPENCER, JOHN C., *see* W. Morgan.

SPENCERPORT.

		Doc.	Vol.	No.
1850.	Report relative to nuisance,...............................	A	5	139

SPENCER, SAMUEL W., *see* Livingston County Surrogate.

SPENCER, THOMAS, *see* Huet Hills.

SPENCER, TRUMAN.

1833. Report on petition of, for bounty lands,.......................... A 3 186

SPENCER, WILLIAM H.

1835. Report on petition of, to build a bridge over Genesee river,..... A 3 194

SPINNER, F. E.

1839. Communication from, in relation to State Lunatic Asylum,...... S 2 57

SPIRITUOUS LIQUORS, *see* Excise, Intoxicating Liquors.

SPOOR, ROBERT.

1844. Report of canal board on petition of,........................ A 5 128

SPRAGUE, CHARLES.

1831. Report on petition of, to maintain a dam across a branch of the Chenango river,.. A 3 232

SPRAKER, JAMES.

1845. Report of canal commissioners, on the petition of, ... A 3 42

SPRAKER, JOSEPH AND JAMES.

1852. Report on claims of, ... S 2 65

SPRAKER, LIVINGSTON, AND JOHN SPENCER.

1834. Report on petition of, for compensation for the loss of a lot of timber by the breaking away of a dam on the Mohawk,....... A 4 345

SPRAKER, LIVINGSTON, AND OTHERS.

1838. Report on petition for extra allowance for blasting rock at Little Falls, ... A 8 342
1839. Report on bill for the same,................................ S 3 91

SPRINGSTEEN, JOHN AND ELIZABETH.

1834. Report on petition of, for the release of certain escheated lands, A 3 177

SQUAW ISLAND.

1848. Report of canal board, relative to improvements at,............ S 3 57

SQUAW ISLAND FERRY, *see* H. F. Penfield.

STAFFORD, MARY.

1848. Report on petition of,...................................... A 2 32

STAHL, WILLIAM.

1855. Report of committee on claims, on petition of,................ A 2 52
1856. Report on petition of,...................................... A 3 82
1857. Report of committee on claims, favorable on petition of,........ A 3 183

STANLEY, FREDERICK.

		Doc.	Vol.	No.
1830.	Report on petition of, to purchase a lot of land in West Oswego,	A	2	99
1830.	Report on petition of, to purchase a lot of land in West Oswego,	S	2	115

G. W. STANTON, AND OTHERS.

1845.	Report of the canal board on the petition of, in relation to excavating Albany basin,	S	4	83

STANTON, HENRY B.

1851.	Report as to right of, to seat in the senate,	S	3	85

WM. B. STANTON.

1851.	Report on the right of, to seat in the senate,	S	3	85

STARKWEATHER, AVERY M.

1856.	Report on petition of,	A	4	129

STARR, FREDERICK.

1840.	Report on petition of, to grant power to the corporation of Rochester to pay him certain money,	A	3	71
1842.	Report of Mr. D. R. F. Jones, on petition of,	A	2	47
1842.	Report of committee on internal affairs of towns and counties, on petition of,	A	4	77

STATE AGRICULTURAL COLLEGE, *see* Agricultural College, State.

STATE AGRICULTURAL SOCIETY, *see* Agricultural Society, State.

STATE CABINET OF NATURAL HISTORY, *see* Natural History.

STATE COLONIZATION SOCIETY, *see* Colonization Society, State.

STATE CONVENTION AT POUGHKEEPSIE, for the purpose of adopting the Constitution of the United States.

1833.	Proceedings of,	A	1	111

STATE ENGINEER AND SURVEYOR.

CHARLES B. STUART:

1848.	Communication from, in relation to his duties, &c.,	S	2	63
1848.	Report of, as to amount of public lands,	A	3	104
1848.	Report of, on petition of Mary E. Edwards,	A	5	176
1849.	Report of, on the public lands,	S	1	27
1849.	Report of, on railroads,	S	3	84
1849.	Report of, relative to sale of certain salt lands at Syracuse,	A	3	130
1849.	Report of, on petition of John Randel, Jr.,	A	5	209

HEZEKIAH C. SEYMOUR:

1850.	Report on lands owned by the state,	A	5	88
1850.	Report on ventilation,	A	4	63
1851.	Annual report on railroads,	S	1	12
1851.	Report on the public lands of the state,	S	1	19

STATE ENGINEER AND SURVEYOR—*continued.*

		Doc.	Vol.	No.
1851.	Annual report,	A	3	45
1851.	Report in relation to lengthening locks,	A	3	67
	WILLIAM J. MCALPINE:			
1852.	Annual report of, on railroads,	A	1	27
1852.	Report of, on railroads,	A	1	27
1853.	do in answer to a resolution in relation to clerk hire,	S	1	18
1853.	do in relation to removing obstructions from channel of Hudson river,	S	1	23
1853.	do in relation to turnouts, switches, &c., on railroads,	S	1	31
1853.	do in relation to freight on railroads,	S	3	59
1853.	do relative to the cost of finishing the canals,	S	3	64
1853.	Annual report of, on the railroad statistics of the State,	A	1	10
1853.	Annual report of, on the canals for 1852,	A	2	28
1853.	Report of, under chapter 309, laws of 1852, in relation to plans and maps in reference to carrying out the objects of the act appropriating moneys to the Auburn prison,	A	2	37
1853.	Report of, in answer to a resolution in relation to persons employed in the engineer's department,	A	3	70
	JOHN T. CLARK:			
1854.	Report of, relative to grants of land under water near New York,	S	1, 12,	34
1854.	Annual report of, on canals,	S	1	60
1854.	Communication from, under resolution,	S	2	61
1854.	Communication from, relative to enlargement of canals,	S	2	109
1854.	Annual report of, on railroad statistics,	A	3	120
1855.	Annual report of, relative to railroad statistics,	S	2	35
1855.	Communication from, in reply to resolution of senate,	S	2	38
1855.	Annual report on canals,	A	2	50
1855.	Report of, in reference to certain canals,	A	2	58
1855.	do in reference to Crooked lake improvement,	A	5	117
1855.	Report from, in relation to new feeder for Genesee Valley canal,	A	7	146
	SILAS SEYMOUR:			
1856.	Report as to Seneca lake,	S	2	81
1856.	Communication from, relative to locks on Chemung canal,	A	4	113
1856.	Report on petition of, to repeal the act to establish a board of railroad commissioners,	A	4	123
1856.	Annual report of,	A	5	180
1857.	Report of, relative to Chemung canal,	S	3	87
1857.	do relative to Genesee Valley canal,	S	3	103
1857.	do relative to the same,	S	4	114
1857.	do relative to enlargement of Genesee Valley canal and canal commissioners,	A	1	35
1857.	Annual report of,	A	1	60
1857.	Report of, in reply to resolution relative to enlargement of Erie canal at Port Byron,	A	2	88
1857.	Report on map of the State in reply to resolution relative to,	A	2	114
1857.	Report of, and canal commissioner Sherrill in reply to resolution relative to the condition of the Champlain canal,	A	2	116
	VAN R. RICHMOND:			
1858.	Communication from, in relation to railroad commissioner,	S	1	9
1858.	Annual report of, on canals,	S	1	15
1858.	Report of, relative to channel of Hudson river near West Troy,	S	2	82
1858.	do relative to locks on Chemung canal,	S	3	124
1858.	do relative to enlargement of locks on Chemung canal,	S	3	133
1858.	do relative to incorporated navigation companies,	A	1	44
1858.	do on railroads,	A	4	89
1858.	do relative to amount necessary to complete the unfinished canals,	A	4	116

STATE ENGINEER AND SURVEYOR—*continued.*

		Doc.	Vol.	No.
1858.	Communication from, on petition of inhabitants residing in vicinity of Oneida lake,	A	4	121

STATE HALL, NEW.

		Doc.	Vol.	No.
1834.	Report of the trustees of the,	A	4	323
1835.	do do	S	1	21
1836.	do do	S	1	6
1837.	do do	S	1	28
1838.	do do	S	1	26
1839.	do do	S	1	15
1840.	do do	A	7	286
1841.	do do	A	3	66
1842.	Communication from comptroller in relation to,	A	7	134
1843.	Report of trustees of,	S	1	20

STATE HALL, OLD.

		Doc.	Vol.	No.
1853.	Report of committee on expenditures of the house relative to the,	A	3	69
1854.	Communication from commissioners of land office relative to,	A	3	89

STATE INSTITUTIONS.

		Doc.	Vol.	No.
1840.	Report relative to the hostility of the general government to,	A	8	344

STATE LIBRARIAN.

		Doc.	Vol.	No.
1830.	Report on bill fixing the salary of the,	S	4	401

STATE LIBRARY.

		Doc.	Vol.	No.
1830.	Annual report of the trustees of the,	A	2	190
1831.	do do do	S	1	7
1832.	do do do	S	1	3
1833.	do do do	S	1	3
1834.	do do do	A	1	3
1835.	do do do	S	1	3
1836.	do do do	S	1	3
1837.	do do do	S	1	2
1838.	do do do	S	1	3
1839.	do do do	S	1	3
1840.	do do do	S	1	6
1841.	do do do	S	1	4
1840.	Report of select joint committee on the state of the,	S	4	115
1841.	Report by same committee on same,	S	3	100
1842.	Annual report of trustees of the,	S	1	6
1842.	Report of joint committee on the,	S	4	104
1844.	do trustees of the,	S	1	50
1844.	do trustees of the,	S	3	114
1844.	do the minority of the library committee on an act relative to,	A	7	176
1845.	do trustees of,	S	1	10
1845.	do trustees of, relative to the purchase of Mr. Worden's library,	A	1	11
1846.	do trustees of,	S	1	4
1847.	do trustees of,	S	1	21
1847.	do trustees of, relative to exchanges,	S	4	129
1847.	do trustees of, donations,	A	8	227
1848.	Annual report of trustees of,	S	1	21
1849.	Annual report of trustees of,	A	1	21
1849.	Report of select committee on,	A	2	67
1849.	do joint committee on,	A	3	131

STATE LIBRARY—*continued.*

		Doc.	Vol.	No.
1849.	Report of Regents of University on the historical and other papers, &c., received from secretary's office for deposit in,....	A	3	148
1850.	Report of trustees of,....	S	1	29
1851.	Annual report of trustees of,....	S	2	25
1852.	Annual report of same,....	S	3	93
1852.	Report of trustees of building,....	A	2	42
1853.	Annual report of trustees of,....	S	1	25
1854.	Report of joint committee on state cabinet,....	S	1	48
1854.	Report of trustees of building,....	A	3	92
1854.	Annual report of trustees of,....	A	4	138
1855.	Report of trustees of,....	S	3	77
1856.	do do	S	1	29
1857.	Report of,....	1	1	37
1858.	Annual report of trustees of,....	S	3	139

STATE LOAN, *see* State Stock.

		Doc.	Vol.	No.
1834.	Message from the governor recommending a,....	A	4	326
1834.	Report of the joint committee on the same,....	A	4	350
1835.	Report of commissioners under the act authorizing a,....	S	1	25
1835.	Report on the report of said commissioners,....	A	2	144
1838.	Message from the governor recommending, to aid the banks in the resumption of specie payments,....	A	6	341
1838.	Report of select committee on same,....	A	6	352
1838.	Bill from the senate, with the amendments of the assembly,....	A	6	354
1838.	Report of committee of conference on said bill,....	A	6	358

STATE LUNATIC ASYLUM, *see* Asylum, State Lunatic.

STATE MEDICAL SOCIETY, *see* Medical Society, State.

STATEN ISLAND.

		Doc.	Vol.	No.
1830.	Report relative to the sale of the fortifications on, to the general government,....	S	4	434

CHARITABLE INSTITUTIONS, *see* New York.

MARINE HOSPITAL AT, *see* New York.

SEAMEN'S FUND AND RETREAT, *see* New York.

QUARANTINE AT, *see* New York.

STATEN ISLAND SOUND.

		Doc.	Vol.	No.
1830.	Report on petition for a law declaratory of the rights of the citizens of this State as it respects the taking of oysters in,....	A	3	242

STATE OFFICES.

		Doc.	Vol.	No.
1833.	Report as to the security of the documents of the, from fire,....	S	2	115

STATE OFFICERS.

		Doc.	Vol.	No.
1846.	Report on bill to reduce salaries of certain,....	S	3	79
1853.	Report of select committee to examine into the official conduct of certain,....	A	4	103
1853.	Report of majority of committee on the subject of impeachment of,....	A	5	130
1853.	Report of the minority on same,....	A	5	131

STATE PAPER.

		Doc.	Vol.	No.
1846.	Report of chancellor answering a resolution in relation to notices required to be published in,....	S	3	96
1846.	Report of committee on the judiciary relative to same,....	A	3	77

STATE PRINTER.

Year	Title	Doc.	Vol.	No.
1843.	Report of, relative to amount received for publishing legal and bankrupt notices,	S	1	14
1844.	Report of,	S	1	37
1845.	Annual report of,	A	3	34
1846.	Annual report of,	S	2	68

STATE PRINTING.

Year	Title	Doc.	Vol.	No.
1835.	Report of amount paid for the, in 1831, 1832, 1833 and 1834,	S	2	67
1838.	Report of select committee on the subject of the,	A	6	346
1838.	Communication from the state printer (E. Croswell) in relation to said report,	A	6	348
1840.	Report relative to the contract with Thurlow Weed for the,	A	2	47
1840.	Communication from Thurlow Weed in answer to a resolution requesting him to report the expense of printing for the legislature during the present session,	S	4	125
1841.	Report of state printer (Thurlow Weed) relative to the amount of printing done by him under his contract, and showing the amount which would have been paid under the old contract,	A	7	276
1843.	Report of the comptroller showing the sums paid for, from 1835 to 1842,	S	1	3
1843.	Report of the comptroller showing the sums paid for, from 1823 to 1839,	S	1	12
1842.	Message of governor returning bill to provide,	A	7	172
1843.	Report of committee on, on the resolution of inquiry relative to,	A	2	28
1845.	Report of committee on public expenditures answering a resolution of the senate in relation to,	S	1	31
1846.	Report of comptroller relative to,	S	2	56
1846.	Report of committee on, relative to engrossed bill from senate concerning,	A	3	86
1846.	Report of comptroller in answer to a resolution relative to,	A	4	91
1847.	Report of select committee, of 1846, to investigate frauds,	A	2	84
1847.	Report of expenses of,	A	4	130
1848.	Report of committee on, on subjects therein referred to,	A	5	162
1849.	Communication from secretary of state transmitting the contracts for,	S	1	15
1850.	Comptroller's return of cost,	S	2	47
1851.	Report of comptroller on expenses for printing, binding, engraving, &c.,	S	2	56
1854.	Report of committee on, on resolution relative to Jones' wood park,	A	2	46
1854.	Report of committee on, on memorial of Regents of University,	A	2	69
1856.	Report of the committee on, respecting the journals,	A	1	10
1856.	Report of comptroller relative to cost of,	A	3	33
1856.	Report of committee on grievances in relation to,	A	5	188
1858.	Extracts from contract to perform,	A	1	23

STATE PRISON INSPECTORS.

Year	Title	Doc.	Vol.	No.
1848.	Report of, under a resolution,	S	1	22
1849.	Communication from,	S	1	23
1849.	Annual report of,	S	1	30
1850.	Report of,	S	1	16
1851.	Annual report of,	S	1	13
1852.	Communication from,	S	1	33
1852.	Annual report of,	S	1	35
1853.	Report of committee on claims, on the application of the, for relief,	S	1	17
1853.	Annual report of,	S	1	30
1854.	do	A	2	40
1854.	do	A	2	55
1855.	do	A	4	85
1856.	Report of,	S	3	99

STATE PRISON INSPECTORS—*continued.*

		Doc.	Vol.	No.
1857.	Report of, relative to insubordination,	S	2	49
1857.	Annual report of,	S	3	110
1858.	Tenth annual report of,	S	1	4
1858.	Report of committee to which was referred annual report of,	A	4	129
1858.	Report of, relative to lime contract,	S	2	34
1858.	Report of, in answer to a resolution relative to Averill ore bed,	S	2	92

STATE PRISONS.

		Doc.	Vol.	No.
1832.	General report of the committee on,	S	2	74
1833.	General report of the committee on,	S	2	118
1833.	Convicts in, report on the propriety of providing for the discharge of certain,	A	3	203
1831.	Convict labor in the, report on petition for the abolishment of (Mr. Bogert),	A	3	279
1834.	Convict labor in the, report on petition for the abolishment of (Mr. Humphrey),	A	4	352
1834.	Convict labor in the, report on petition for the abolishment of (Mr. McDonald),	S	2	114
1835.	Convict labor in the, majority and minority reports on the same,	A	4	330
1835.	Convict labor in the, report of attorney-general in relation to contracts for,	A	2	106
1835.	Convict labor in the, report of commissioners under the act concerning state prisons, for the abolishment of,	A	2	135
1837.	Convict labor in the, minority report (Mr. Roosevelt),	A	3	169
1840.	Convict labor in the, report on the same (Mr. Sibley),	A	8	339
1841.	Convict labor in the, report on the same (Mr. Peck),	S	2	54
1841.	Convict labor in the, majority report on the same (Mr. Van Schoonhoven),	A	5	186
1841.	Convict labor in the, minority report on the same (Mr. Hotchkiss,)	A	7	286
1842.	Report of committee on, on numerous petitions for abolishing mechanical labor in,	A	4	65
1843.	Report of Ransom Cook, commissioner appointed under the act in relation to, passed April, 1842,	A	2	32
1843.	Report of the committee on,	A	3	72
1843.	Report of the committee on, with bill attached,	A	3	72
1843.	Resolutions on the subject of labor in, adopted at a meeting of the mechanics of the city of Albany,	A	5	156
1843.	Resolutions of a public meeting at Plattsburgh, county of Clinton, recommending the employment of convicts in mining and manufacturing iron,	A	5	157
1843.	Reply of R. Cook, Esq., to the Ausable memorial in relation to convict labor, &c.,	A	5	155
1843.	Report of the attorney-general in relation to contracts,	A	5	169
1843.	Report of the committee on, in relation to the employment of convicts,	S	3	99
1844.	Report of the committee on, on an act in relation to,	A	3	41
1845.	Report of the agent of the new,	S	1	16
1846.	Report of Mr. Backus, relative to discipline in,	S	4	120
1846.	Report of Mr. A. C. Hand on the same,	S	4	121
1847.	Report of committee on, for regulation of county and,	A	8	241
1848.	Report of expenses for transportation of convicts,	A	3	124
1850.	Report of committee on, in relation to lunatics in,	A	3	41
1850.	Communication from A. H. Wells,	A	5	134
1852.	Communication from inspectors of, respecting examination of prisons,	S	1	33
1852.	Report of committee to examine,	A	1	20
1852.	Report on reference of a resolution relating to,	A	5	114
1854.	Report of secretary of state respecting,	S	1	54
1854.	Report of Inspector Clark, relative to claims against,	S	2	66
1854.	Communication from H. Storms, relative to,	S	2	70
1854.	Communication relative to judgments against agent of,	S	2	92

STATE PRISONS—*continued.*

		Doc.	Vol.	No.
1854.	Report of T. Kirkpatrick, relative to indebtedness of,	S	2	98
1854.	Report of committee on, relative to Western House of Refuge,	S	2	107
1854.	Opinion of attorney-general, relative to judgments against agents,	A	3	121
1855.	Report of commissioners to investigate affairs of, relative to certain minutes and affidavits,	S	1	28
1855.	Report of committee on trades and manufactures on petitions relative to labor and competition,	S	3	71
1855.	Opinion of attorney-general as to judgments against agents,	A	2	28
1855.	Report of commissioners appointed to examine affairs of,	A	3	60
1855.	Report of committee in reference to debts of,	A	4	105
1858.	Report of inspectors of, relative to lime contract,	S	2	34
	AUBURN:			
1830.	Annual report of the inspectors of the,	A	1	38
1831.	do do	S	1	15
1832.	do do	S	1	31
1833.	do do	S	1	20
1834.	do do	S	1	39
1835.	do do	S	1	13
1836.	do do	A	3	133
1837.	do do	A	1	31
1838.	do do	A	3	86
1839.	do do	S	1	11
1840.	do do	A	1	18
1841.	do do	A	2	28
1830.	Message from the governor relative to altering the south wing of the,	S	3	220
1830.	Report on the same,	A	4	407
1832.	Report of inspectors relative to altering the south wing of said prison,	S	1	33
1834.	Agent of the, report of, relative to the terms of contracts for the labor of convicts, &c.,	A	4	289
1834.	Agent of the, report of, relative to the terms of contracts for the labor of convicts, &c.,	A	4	341
1833.	Investigation of the, report of an,	A	3	199
1838.	Investigation of the, report of an,	A	5	276
1840.	Majority report on same,	S	2	37
1840.	Minority report on same,	S	2	38
1840.	Testimony taken before said committee on same,	S	2	48
1834.	Officers of the, petition of, for an increase of salary,	A	1	20
1834.	Report on same,	A	3	161
1836.	Report on same,	A	4	226
1832.	Clerk of the, report relative to the accounts of the late,	S	1	51
1840.	Dam across the Owasco outlet adjacent to the, report relative to removing it,	A	7	301
1832.	Health, report relative to the preservation of, in the,	S	2	118
1836.	Manufacture of silk at the, report relative to the,	A	4	226
1842.	Report relative to the manufacture of silk in,	A	1	2
1842.	Annual report of,	A	2	31
1843.	Annual report of inspector of,	S	1	9
1843.	Report of the inspectors of, relative to silk manufacture,	S	1	23
1843.	Communication from governor relative to,	S	3	97
1844.	Report of the inspectors of,	S	1	18
1844.	Report of committee on state prisons relative to,	S	2	57
1846.	Annual report of inspector of,	S	2	46
1846.	Report of the agent of, answering a resolution relative to amount of earnings of convict labor, &c.,	S	3	87
1845.	Report of the inspectors of,	S	1	8
1846.	Report of inspector of, in answer to a resolution,	A	3	83
1846.	Report of inspector of, in answer to a resolution,	A	4	137
1846.	Report of agent,	S	3	87

STATE PRISONS—*continued.*

Year	Title	Doc.	Vol.	No.
1846.	Report of inspectors,	S	2	46
1847.	Report as to examination of,	S	1	11
1847.	Report of Luman Sherwood relative to,	S	1	12
1848.	Annual report of,	S	1	30
1853.	Report of state engineer in relation to plans and surveys in reference to appropriating moneys to the,	A	2	37
1858.	Report of committee relative to the affairs of,	A	4	143
	Sheriff's fees for transporting convicts to, *see* Sheriffs.			
	CLINTON:			
1846.	Report of agent of,	S	1	14
1846.	Communication from surveyor-general relative to road from, to Lake Champlain,	A	2	55
1857.	Report of committee on roads and bridges on an act for the laying out of and constructing a road from, to the town of Bellmont, &c.,	A	2	129
1846.	Report of agent of, in answer to a resolution,	A	4	138
1847.	Report of,	S	1	10
1848.	Report as to examination of,	S	1	18
1847.	Communication from keeper of,	A	4	105
1847.	Report of joint committee appointed to visit,	A	8	228
1847.	Report of Mr. Butrick, one of select committee to visit,	A	8	236
1852.	Report relative to iron works at,	A	2	62
1855.	Report of committee in reference to claims against,	A	4	98
1857.	Report of committee on state prisons favorable on petition of Green and Conro, for payment for castings furnished,	A	3	169
	FEMALE CONVICT:			
1830.	Report on the subject of erecting a,	S	3	238
1832.	do do	S	2	74
1833.	do do	S	1	32
1834.	do do	S	1	14
1835.	do do	S	2	68
1834.	Proposition from A. S. Blackman, and others, to build a, and to employ the convicts, &c.,	S	2	84
1834.	Proposition from W. Crabtree, to build a, and to employ the convicts, &c.,	S	2	86
1834.	Communication from E. B. Cobb relative to a,	S	2	103
	MOUNT PLEASANT:			
1834.	Agent of the, report of the, relative to contracts for the labor of the convicts, &c.,	A	4	288
1834.	Report of, of amount of pay received by the agents of, of the contractors, &c.,	A	4	333
1834.	Agent of the, report of, relative to the government and discipline of the prison,	S	2	92
1834.	Accounts of the late agent of, report concerning the,	S	2	63
1836.	Manufacture of silk at the, report relative to the,	A	4	266
1830.	Inspectors of the, annual report of the,	S	1	8
1830.	Supplementary report of the,	S	2	136
1831.	Annual report of the inspectors of the,	S	1	3
1832.	do do	S	1	14
1833.	do do	S	1	27
1834.	do do	S	1	14
1835.	do do	S	1	8
1836.	do do	S	1	23
1837.	do do	S	1	5
1838.	do do	S	1	7
1839.	do do	S	1	13
1840.	do do	S	1	17
1841.	do do	A	2	42

STATE PRISONS—*continued.*

		Doc.	Vol.	No.
1830.	Report of the, on petition of the Mount Pleasant Academy, ...	A	3	204
1833.	Report and resolution recommending to the inspectors to contract for the labor of the convicts at a per diem compensation, ...	A	4	330
1830.	Commissioners of the, report of amount paid the,............	A	1	52
1830.	Report on bill to repeal the law authorizing the commissioners to act as inspectors, ...	S	3	255
1832.	Preservation of health in the, report relative to the, ...	S	2	118
1830.	Guard of the, report on bill to increase the number of the, ...	A	3	276
1836.	Guard of the, report on petition to increase the salary of the,...	A	4	226
1834.	Land adjoining, report relative to purchasing, &c.,............	S	2	63
1830.	Keeper of the, Elam Lynds, communication from S. M. Hopkins, preferring charges against the, ...	S	2	118
1830.	Report of a select committee on the,........................	S	4	112
1831.	Report of a select committee on the,........................	S	1	60
1830.	Solitary cells, message from the governor relative to increasing the number of,......................................	S	3	220
1830.	Solitary cells, report of committee on state prisons on the same,.	A	4	407
1831.	Solitary cells, appropriation for building, &c., report relative to an, ...	A	1	32
1831.	Solitary cells, appropriation for building, &c., report relative to an, ...	A	3	215
1833.	Investigation of the, report of an, ...	A	3	199
1834.	do petition of Levi S. Burr for an,...........	A	3	211
1838.	do report of an,..........................	A	6	332
1839.	do report of an,..........................	A	6	335
1839.	do petition of the inspectors and agent for an,.	S	3	99
1840.	do majority report of an,..................	S	2	37
1840.	do minority report of an,..................	S	2	38
1840.	do testimony taken before said committee, ...	S	2	48
1842.	Annual report of inspectors of, and accompanying documents,..	S	2	39
1843.	Annual report of the inspectors of, ...	S	1	10
1843.	Report of finance committee on the payment of a judgment against the agent of, ...	S	3	83
1844.	Report of the inspectors of, ...	S	1	20
1844.	Communication from inspectors of, in regard to the contract for labor in that prison,..................................	A	5	113
1845.	Report of the inspectors of,...............................	S	1	9
1846.	Report of inspector of,..................................	S	1	16
1846.	Report of committee on state prisons, on so much of governor's message as relates to the financial concerns of, ...	S	4	111
1846.	Report of board of inspectors of, in answer to a resolution of the assembly, ...	A	4	139
1847.	Report of, ...	S	1	5
1847.	Report on affairs of, ...	S	4	153
1847.	Report of inspectors of, ...	A	8	258
1847.	Report as to the punishments at, ...	A	6	160
1847.	Report on bill relative to,..................................	A	8	243
1848.	Report of minority of inspectors of, ...	S	1	17
1848.	Annual report of,..	A	1	10
	SING SING :			
1843.	Memorial of the financial condition of,.......................	A	5	176
1846.	Report of inspectors of, in answer to a resolution,.............	A	4	139
1848.	Report of commissioners appointed to investigate the condition of,..	S	2	51
1849.	Report on the affairs of,..................................	S	2	69
1849.	Petition of Messrs. Hotchkiss and Smith, for the appointment of commissioners to examine and liquidate their claims against agent of, ...	A	2	85
1849.	Report of comptroller relative to draft paid by agents of, to Wm. Radford, ...	A	2	92

STATE PRISONS—*continued.*

		Doc.	Vol.	No.
1849.	Report of comptroller, of moneys drawn from treasury by Chauncey Smith, late agent of,	A	2	99
1850.	Report of inspectors in relation to fire at,	A	5	116
1851.	Remonstrance of inspectors against releasing Chauncey Smith,	S	2	57
1851.	Report of committee on construction of wall, &c.,	A	3	89
1851.	Report of committee on claims on petition of Chauncey Smith, late agent of,	A	4	105
1852.	Report of trustees, respecting assault and battery on H. Hagan,	S	3	95
1854.	Report of committee on judiciary relative to judgments against the agent,	S	2	75
1855.	Memorial of Fitch, Hunt and Cooley, relative to judgment, &c., against the agent of,	S	1	4
1857.	Report of committee on state prisons favorable on petition of Simeon D. Moody for payment for goods furnished to,	A	2	99
1857.	Report of committee on state prisons favorable on petition of Abraham Leggett for payment for goods furnished to,	A	3	168
1858.	Petition of Croton Aqueduct department for payment for water furnished to,	A	3	66

STATE REPORTER.

1841.	Report of the, in answer to a resolution of assembly,	A	2	36

STATE STOCK.

1834.	Message from the governor recommending the issue of,	A	4	326
1834.	Report of joint committee on same,	A	4	350
1835.	Report of the commissioners under the act authorizing the issue of,	S	1	25
1836.	Report on the report of the commissioners,	A	2	144
1838.	Message from the governor recommending the issue of, to aid the banks in resumption of specie payments,	A	6	341
1838.	Report of a select committee on same,	A	6	352
1838.	Bill from the senate to provide for the issue of, and amendments of the assembly to same,	A	6	354
1838.	Report of committee of conference on said bill,	A	6	358
1839.	Report on bill to allow banks to deal in,	S	3	87
1839.	Canal stock, report of unclaimed items of interest on, in the Manhattan Bank,	A	3	134
1839.	Railroads, report of amount of stock issued in aid of,	A	6	388
1841.	do do do do	A	7	273
1841.	do do do do	A	3	70
1840.	Railroads, report of amount issued to the New York and Erie Railroad Company,	A	4	127
1841.	Report on the same,	A	4	113
1841.	Resolutions proposed by Mr. Hoffman to require every law authorizing the borrowing money and the issuing of State stocks to be submitted to the people at the next election, &c.,	A	4	102
1842.	Report of the comptroller relative to interest paid on,	S	4	98
1843.	Report of comptroller in answer to a resolution of the assembly respecting the amount of appropriations for internal improvement, and amount of, issued, &c.,	A	3	65
1846.	do do relative to banks holding, in trust,	A	6	202
1849.	do do of the amount held by citizens of this country and of foreign countries,	S	1	29
1851.	Report on unclaimed interest on,	S	2	54

STATE TAX, *see* Tax, State.

STATIONERY.

1854.	Report of comptroller relative to,	A	1	9

STATISTICS OF THE STATE, *see* Census.

STAUNARD, ANN E.

		Doc.	Vol.	No.
1858.	Report on petition of,	A	4	153

STEAMBOATS.

		Doc.	Vol.	No.
1835.	Canal, report on petition of A. Plantou for an appropriation for building a,	A	5	385
1837.	Report on the same,	A	2	100
1831.	do petition to provide by law for the safety of passengers in,	A	3	271
1834.	do bill for the same,	A	2	70
1839.	do bill for the prevention of fires from,	A	5	301
1840.	do bill relative to the same,	A	5	164
1840.	Report in relation to a new plan for propelling, through the ice,	S	4	116
1834.	Plying between New York and Charleston, report on petition to place them on the same footing with steamboats from New Jersey, Connecticut, &c., in relation to the payment of hospital moneys,	S	2	96

STEAM DREDGING MACHINE (belonging to the State).

		Doc.	Vol.	No.
1830.	Report relative to the improvement of the Hudson river with the,	A	4	335
1835.	Report of comptroller in relation to the,	S	2	60
1837.	Report of comptroller in relation to the,	A	2	155

STEBBINS, AMAZIAH.

		Doc.	Vol.	No.
1838.	Report on petition of, for extra allowance for work done on the Chenango canal,	S	1	17

STEELE, ENOS.

		Doc.	Vol.	No.
1849.	Report on petition of,	S	1	19

STEEL ORE (at Duane).

		Doc.	Vol.	No.
1841.	Report of Professor Emmons in relation to the,	A	5	182

STEPHENS, JOHN, Jr., AND STEPHEN.

		Doc.	Vol.	No.
1830.	Executors, &c., of John Stephens, report on petition of,	A	1	35

STERNBURGH, HERKIMER.

		Doc.	Vol.	No.
1840.	Report on petition of, relative to certain funds in the court of chancery,	S	4	102

STERNBURGH, WILLIAM.

		Doc.	Vol.	No.
1838.	Report on petition of, for extra allowance for work done on the Erie canal,	A	5	223
1839.	Report of committee on claims on the same,	A	3	97
1840.	Report by same committee on the same,	A	4	133
1841.	Report of canal commissioners on the same,	A	5	190
1842.	do committee on claims on resolution of canal board on testimony taken before that board in the matter of,	S	3	75
1844.	do the canal board on the petition of,	A	3	55
1846.	do committee on claims on petition of,	A	4	106
1848.	Report on petition of,	A	2	43
1850.	Report on petition of,	A	4	71
1851.	Report on petition for relief,	A	1	10
1852.	Report on petition of,	A	2	30

STEUBEN COUNTY.

		Doc.	Vol.	No.
1839.	Courts, report on petition for an additional term of the,........	A	4	240
1840.	Poor-house system, report on petition to abolish the,...........	A	6	267
1836.	Bounty on wolves, panthers and foxes in, report relative to the,	A	2	89
1833.	Inspection of leather, report on petition to repeal the law requiring the,..	A	4	309
1830.	Report on petition to raise money for the improvement of the navigable waters in,..	A	4	302
1831.	New county from part of, report on petition for a,.............	A	3	277
1832.	New county from part of, report on petition for a,.............	A	2	169
1840.	Pulteney estate, report on petition for an investigation of the title of the,..	A	6	232
1840.	Report of attorney-general on the same, ...	A	8	342
1847.	Report on petition of inhabitants of Chemung, Tompkins, Yates and, for erection of a new county,.	A	2	62
1847.	Minority report on petitions for erection of a new county from parts of above counties,................................	A	2	81
1847.	Report on petition of citizens of, relative to the Pulteney estate,	A	4	121
1849.	Report relative to new county from parts of Allegany, and,......	A	3	136
1855.	Report of select committee on petitions to divide,..............	A	5	141
1856.	Report of select committee relative to the poor of,...............	A	3	15
1857.	Report of committee on erection and division of towns and counties, county from parts of Allegany and,....................	A	3	157

BANKS IN, *see* Banks—Steuben County,

STEUBEN, TOWN OF.

		Doc.	Vol.	No.
1833.	Town-house, report on petition to raise money to build a,......	A	4	301
1834.	Town-house, report on petition to raise money to build a,.......	A	1	18

STEVENS, A. H. (Dr.)

		Doc.	Vol.	No.
1849.	Communication from, relative to removal of quarantine establishment, ...	A	3	146

STEVENS, ALDEN S. (late sergeant-at-arms of the Assembly.)

		Doc.	Vol.	No.
1839.	Report on petition of, for extra pay for services in arresting Messrs. Jaques and Slam,................................	A	4	206

STEVENS, C. W., AND R. NELSON GERE.

		Doc.	Vol.	No.
1852.	Report on petition of, for relief,............................	S	1	49

STEVENS, GEORGE, AND ERASTUS WHISTON.

		Doc.	Vol.	No.
1836.	Report on petition of, for compensation for damages, by the sinking of their boat on the Erie canal,......................	A	4	220

STEVENS, GERSHOM.

		Doc.	Vol.	No.
1830.	Report on petition of, relative to a lot of land bought of the State,	A	1	157
1830.	Report on petition of, relative to a lot of land bought of the State,	A	3	209

STEVENS, JAMES, AND GEORGE TIBBITTS.

		Doc.	Vol.	No.
1843.	Report of committee on claims on petition of,.................	A	5	143

STEVENSON, DANIEL, AND OTHERS.

		Doc.	Vol.	No.
1830.	Sureties for R. M. Livingston and Thomas Wright, report on petition of, for relief,......................................	A	1	60

STEVENSON, JOHN L.

Year	Subject	Doc.	Vol.	No.
1847.	Report on petition of,......	A	2	65
1847.	Report of commissioners of land office on petition of, for relief,..	A	4	107

STEVENSON, WILLIAM.

Year	Subject	Doc.	Vol.	No.
1830.	Report on petition of, relative to certain land in the township of Lysander,......	S	4	396

STEVES, CHARLES W., AND OTHERS.

Year	Subject	Doc.	Vol.	No.
1852.	Report relative to,......	S	1	49

STEWARD, DANIEL.

Year	Subject	Doc.	Vol.	No.
1831.	Report on petition of, relative to the will of his father,......	S	1	

STEWART & CO.

Year	Subject	Doc.	Vol.	No.
1850.	Report of committee on canals on petition of,......	A	5	90

STEWART AND BARTLETT.

Year	Subject	Doc.	Vol.	No.
1854.	Report of committee on claims on petition of,......	A	2	48

STEWART, J.

Year	Subject	Doc.	Vol.	No.
1846.	Report of committee on grievances on petition of,......	A	5	165

STEWART, J., & CO.

Year	Subject	Doc.	Vol.	No.
1850.	Report on claim,......	S	2	64

STEWART, JAMES.

Year	Subject	Doc.	Vol.	No.
1839.	Report on petition of, for extra allowance,......	A	3	72
1845.	Report of canal board on petition of,......	A	4	125
1845.	Report of committee on claims on petition of,......	A	5	173
1855.	Report of committee of ways and means on petition of,......	A	2	42
1857.	Report of committee on claims on petition of,......	A	2	101

STEWART, JAMES, AND OTHERS.

Year	Subject	Doc.	Vol.	No.
1845.	Report of canal board on petition of,......	A	4	125

STEWART, JOHN, & CO.

Year	Subject	Doc.	Vol.	No.
1849.	Report of committee on claims on petition of,......	A	3	180

STEWART, JOHN, & CO., AND OTHERS.

Year	Subject	Doc.	Vol.	No.
1838.	Report on petition of, for extra allowance,......	A	3	120
1838.	Report on petition of, for extra allowance,......	A	5	215

STEWART, WILLIAM.

Year	Subject	Doc.	Vol.	No.
1849.	Report on petition of, for relief,......	A	3	133

STICKNEY, WASHINGTON.

Year	Subject	Doc.	Vol.	No.
1857.	Report of committee on claims on petition of,......	S	1	31

STILL, ELIZABETH, AND OTHERS.

Year	Subject	Doc.	Vol.	No.
1844.	Children of Thomas Mott, report of committee on claims on petition of,......	A	3	79

STILLMAN, SOUTHMAYD.

		Doc.	Vol.	No.
1837.	Report on petition of, relative to the property of Jonathan Morgan,....	A	4	310

STILLMAN, TIMOTHY.

1849.	Report on the memorial of,....	S	2	61

STILLWATER.

1841.	Side-cut from the Champlain canal at, report on petition for,....	A	6	232

STILLWATER AND SCHAGHTICOKE BRIDGE COMPANY.

1832.	Report on petition to renew the charter of the,....	A	1	22

STILLWELL AND BALDWIN.

1844.	Report on a bill to confirm the acts of,....	S	2	83

STILLWELL AND SMITH.

1853.	Report of committee on claims on petition of, for relief,....	S	1	22

STILLWELL, ELIAS, AND BENJ. SMITH.

1856.	Report on petition of,....	A	3	26

STITT, J. M.

1845.	Report of committee on claims on petition of,....	A	4	134

STITT, J. M., AND WIFE.

1846.	Report of committee on claims on petition of,....	A	4	100

STITT, JOHN M., AND WIFE.

1847.	Report on petitions of,....	A	1	33

STOCKBRIDGE INDIANS, *see* Indians—Stockbridge.

STOCK JOBBING, *see* New York Board of Brokers.

STOCKS, *see* State Stocks.

STOCKWELL, AUGUSTUS.

1850.	Report on petition,....	S	2	49

STONE AND CLARK'S ATLAS.

1839.	Report on petition for aid to,....	A	4	168

STONE, ASAHEL C.

1851.	Report of select committee in relation to charges,....	S	2	60

STONE, ENOS, AND OTHERS.

1834.	Report on petition of, to be released from the payment of a bond given to the state, as security for C. Van Slyck, a collector of canal tolls,....	A	3	116
1834.	Minority report on the same,....	A	3	121
1834.	Report of attorney-general on the same,....	A	4	381
1835.	do committee on claims,....	S	2	37
1836.	do committee on grievances,....	A	4	243
1838.	do select committee,....	A	5	204
1839.	do committee on claims,....	A	3	111
1841.	do committee on grievances,....	A	2	37

STONE, HENRY C.

		Doc.	Vol.	No.
1841	Report on petition of, relative to a contract for work on the Erie canal,	A	6	245

STONE, HIRAM.

1851.	Report of committee on petition for canal damages,	S	1	15

STONE, SAMUEL H., AND OTHERS.

1849.	Report of committee on judiciary on petition of,	A	3	104

STONE, WILLIAM A.

1831.	Report on petition of, for certain lands belonging to the Oneida Indians,	A	4	350
1836.	Report on petition of, for certain lands belonging to the Oneida Indians,	A	4	225
1846.	Report of the committee on claims on the petition of, for relief,	S	1	6

STONY CREEK.

1855.	Report of select committee on bill to build a bridge over,	A	4	106

STORING, ADAM.

1854.	Petition of, claiming seat in senate,	S	1	9

STORMS, H.

1854.	Communication from, respecting state prisons,	S	2	70

STORMS, HENRY.

1847.	Report on bill relative to,	A	8	249

STORY, AMOS, *see* W. L. Crossit, and others.

STRANGE, EDWIN B.

1846.	Report on the petition of,	S	3	100

STRATFORD, TOWN OF.

1838.	Report on petition to authorize the comptroller to receive the original tax list of non-resident lands in said town, and credit the treasurer of Montgomery county with the same,	A	5	208
1831.	Manufacturing company, report on petition to incorporate the,	A	3	251

STRATTONS, FRANCIS J.

1847.	Report of comptroller on petition of,	S	3	97

STREET CHILDREN.

1853.	Report of select committee on reference of the petitions concerning,	A	3	94

STRONG, BENJAMIN W.

1841.	Report on petition to allow him to rebuild a bridge over Flushing creek,	A	2	23

STRONG, CATHARINE, AND JANE NUGENT.

1834.	Report on bill for relief of,	A	1	26

STRONG, GEORGE W.

		Doc.	Vol.	No.
1844.	Petition on behalf of Madame Berthemy and children,.........	S	2	72

STRONG, JOSEPH, AND MALTBY, *see* Hervey Ely and others.

STRONG, THOMAS J.

1851.	Report of committee on ways and means,........................	A	1	18

STROUD, CHARLES, *see* Oscar Granger and others.

STROUD, CHARLES, AND OTHERS.

1844.	Report of committee on claims on the petition of,..	A	6	148
1845.	Report of canal commissioners on petition of,...................	S	1	14

STUART, JOSEPH (an alien).

1831.	Report on petition of, to hold and convey real estate, ...	S	1	59

STUYVESANT.

1841.	Report on petition of inhabitants of, to be relieved from the payment of one-half of the expense of maintaining a bridge on Kinderhook creek, ...	S	2	64

STUYVESANT, N. W.

1834.	Report on petition of the executors and heirs of, ...	S	1	36

SUB-TREASURY, *see* Independent Treasury.

SUFFOLK COUNTY.

1838.	Highways and bridges in, report on petition relative to,........	A	3	80
1833.	Loan officers, report on petition for a law to direct the collection of moneys secured by certain loan office mortgages,..........	A	1	18
1830.	Deer, report on petition relative to the hunting of,.............	S	4	394
1832.	Fish in, report on petition for a law for the preservation of,.....	A	4	337

SUFFRAGE, *see* Elective Franchise.

SUGAR.

1840.	Communication from the American Institute respecting manufacture of, from beet root,......................	A	4	134

SUITS.

1838.	Brought by executors, &c., report in relation to,...............	A	5	261

SULLIVAN COUNTY.

1832.	Records of, report in relation to the,......	A	3	224
1838.	And Lenox, great swamp in, report on petition to amend the law for draining the, ...	S	1	15
1840.	Report on petition to change the place of meeting of the proprietors of the,...	A	5	203
1842.	Petition of the New York and Erie Railroad Company relative to the different lines surveyed in Broome and, for the location of their road,..................	S	3	58
1842.	Report on the remonstrance of Orange, Ulster and, relative to the New York and Erie railroad,.............................	S	3	74
1845.	Report of committee on the judiciary on the petition of the inhabitants of, in reference to the naturalization of foreigners,.....	A	7	245

SUMMARY PROCEEDINGS.

Year	Subject	Doc.	Vol.	No.
1840.	To recover possession of land in certain cases, report on bill to amend the Revised Statutes in relation to,	S	3	65

SUNDAY, *see* Sabbath.

SUPERINTENDENT OF COMMON SCHOOLS, *see* Common Schools.

SUPERINTENDENTS OF POOR, *see* Poor, Superintendents of.

SUPERINTENDENT OF WEIGHTS AND MEASURES, *see* Weights and Measures.

SUPERIOR COURT OF COMMON PLEAS.

Resolutions for the creation of a, *see* Judicial System.

SUPERVISORS.

Year	Subject	Doc.	Vol.	No.
1834.	Report on bill to amend the law relative to the survey of non-resident lands by,	A	2	86
1839.	Report on petition to repeal the laws associating them with county judges in the appointment of county officers,	A	2	47
1839.	Boards of, report on petition to require them to publish their proceedings,	A	4	185
1839.	Report on petition to amend the law so that all officers connected with county poor-houses may be appointed by them,	A	6	384
1838.	And commissioners of loans, report on a resolution to inquire whether the offices of, ought to be vested in one person,	A	3	75
1847.	Reports of clerks of,	S	2	65
1849.	Memorial of inhabitants of Westchester county for a law on equalizing representation in,	A	2	74

SUPREME COURT.

Year	Subject	Doc.	Vol.	No.
1844.	Report of committee on the judiciary on an act in relation to the terms of,	A	3	89
1845.	Report on bill from the assembly entitled an act to provide for the removal of cases decided by canal board to, by certiorari,	S	3	103
1845.	Report of committee on canals, on the bill to provide for the removal of cases from canal board to,	A	5	195
1846.	Opinion of, in reference to convention apportionment,	A	5	181
1846.	Report of committee on judiciary, on petition of R. Balcom, relating to,	A	3	64
1849.	Opinions of Mr. Justice McLean, Mr. Justice Grier, and Mr. Justice Daniel,	S	3	74
1853.	Report of finance committee relative to compensation to constables attending the terms of the,	S	1	14
1858.	Communication from attorney-general in relation to payment of expenses of judges and justices of,	S	2	38

CHIEF JUSTICE OF:

Year	Subject	Doc.	Vol.	No.
1836.	Communication from the, relative to reorganizing the supreme court,	A	4	278
1838.	Communication from the, relative to reorganizing the supreme court,	A	1	58
1838.	Report of the, relative to the business of the court, the delay and the cause thereof, and the proper remedy,	A	1	58
1846.	Report of, relative to a resolution in relation to notices required to be published in the state paper,	S	3	85

SUPREME COURT—*continued.*

		Doc.	Vol.	No.
	CLERK OF, AT ALBANY:			
1832.	John Keyes Paige, report of amount of fees received by,........	A	2	267
1835.	Report of amount of fees received by,....................	A	3	241
1835.	do do	A	4	315
1836.	do do	A	3	145
1840.	Report of, relative to judgments docketed in his office,.....	A	7	80
1843.	Report of, ...	A	4	98
1846.	Report of,...	S	1	34
	CLERK OF, AT GENEVA:			
1832.	William N. Oliver, report of amount of fees received by,.......	A	3	270
1835.	Report of amount of fees received by Nathan Williams, ...	A	4	311
1836.	Report of amount of fees received by Jacob Sutherland,....	A	1	23
1840.	Report of, relative to judgments docketed in his office, ...	A	6	235
1846.	Report of,...	S	2	50
	CLERK OF, AT NEW YORK:			
1832.	W. P. Hallett, report of amount of fees received by,...........	A	3	202
1835.	Report of amount of fees received by him,................	A	4	310
1836.	Report of amount of fees received by him,................	A	3	146
1840.	Report of relative to judgments docketed in his office,......	A	7	274
1843.	Report of, ...	A	5	121
1843.	Report of, in answer to a resolution of the assembly relative to fees for searches of dockets of judgments in that court,	A	5	149
1846.	Report of,...	S	2	42
	CLERK OF, AT UTICA:			
1832.	T. H. Hubbard, report of amount of fees received by him,......	A	3	269
1835.	Report of amount of fees received by him, ...	A	4	312
1836.	Report of amount of fees received by him,................	A	2	83
1840.	I. Savage, report of, relative to judgments docketed in his office,	A	3	97
1843.	Denio, Hiram, report of, in answer to a resolution of assembly,..	A	4	92
1846.	Report of,...	S	2	44
	CLERK'S FEES, *see* Clerks:			
1832.	Report concerning, and statement showing the amount received in 1831,......................................	A	4	309
1833.	Report of comptroller relative to sums received for fees and the amount paid for salaries, &c., from 1810 to 1832,..........	A	4	303
1838.	Report on petition of Gary V. Sacket to fix by law the,........	A	5	273
1838.	Resolution to ascertain the amount received for, in 1837, ...	A	5	273
1838.	Report of amount of, received in 1837,.....................	A	6	351
1839.	Report of a select committee relative to,....................	A	4	186
1840.	Report of amount of, paid into the treasury forthe six months ending 31st December, 1839,.......................	A	3	77
1842.	Report of comptroller relative to the, and court of chancery,....	S	2	30
1846.	Report of comptroller in answer to a resolution respecting the, and salaries of, and others,.............................	S	1	10
1847.	Report of Robert Monell, as to,............................	S	1	19
1847.	Report of Jas. L. Beardsley, as to,....	S	1	22
1847.	Report of W. P. Hallett, as to, ...	S	1	23
1847.	Report of Chas. Humphrey, as to,.........................	S	1	24
	CLERKS:			
1843.	Report of,...	S	1	44, 48
	CLERK'S OFFICE, AT CANANDAIGUA:			
1830.	Report on petition for the removal of,.......	A	2	176
	CLERK'S OFFICE, AT GENEVA:			
1830.	Report on petition for the removal of the clerk's office from Canandaigua to Geneva,................................	A	2	176

SUPREME COURT—*continued.*

		Doc.	Vol.	No.
1834.	Report on petition for the removal of the, to Rochester,	A	1	33
1834.	Report relative to the business of the office at,	A	3	143
1835.	Report on petition for an appropriation to complete the,	A	1	15
1843.	Sutherland, Jacob, clerk of the supreme court at Geneva, report of,	A	4	96
	CLERK'S OFFICE, AT UTICA:			
1838.	Report on petition to rebuild the,	S	1	32
	CLERKS' OFFICES:			
1843.	Report of the select committee on petitions for the abolishing certain, &c.,	A	4	112
	CRIERS' FEES:			
1839.	Report on petition to abolish, &c.,	A	4	186
	DECISIONS UPON WRITS OF ERROR:			
1834.	Report on bill in relation to,	A	4	395
	JUSTICES OF THE:			
1836.	Report of the, relative to the business before them,	S	1	31
1839.	Report of the, relative to the business before them,	S	1	31
1840.	Opinion of the, relative to the constitutionality of the general banking law,	A	3	65
	RE-ORGANIZATION OF THE:			
1834.	Report of the committee on the judiciary on increasing the number of justices of the,	S	2	107
1835.	Resolutions proposed by Mr. Livingston to increase the number of justices of the,	A	3	193
1835.	Resolutions proposed by Mr. Livingston to increase the number of justices of the,	A	4	337
1835.	Resolution for the same,	A	4	338
1835.	Report of the select committee on the same,	A	4	370
1836.	Resolutions proposed by Mr. Gansevoort on the same,	S	1	22
1836.	Resolutions proposed by Mr. Powers on the same,	S	1	27
1836.	Report and resolutions by Mr. Edwards on the same,	S	2	66
1836.	Resolution proposed by the committee on the judiciary on the same,	A	4	265
1836.	Communication from the chief justice relative to the,	A	4	278
1837.	Resolutions proposed by Mr. Bradish relative to the,	A	3	173
1837.	Resolutions proposed by Mr. Edwards relative to the,	S	1	13
1837.	Resolutions proposed by Mr. Patterson relative to the,	A	1	24
1838.	Resolutions proposed by Mr. Ogden relative to the,	A	5	267
1838.	Communication from the chief justice relative to the,	A	1	58
1839.	Report and resolution by Mr. Edwards relative to the,	S	1	28
1839.	Resolutions proposed by Mr. Verplanck relative to the,	S	2	50
1839.	Resolutions proposed by Mr. Taylor relative to the,	A	1	15
1839.	Report on committee on the judiciary relative to the,	A	3	93
1840.	Resolutions proposed by Mr. Taylor relative to the,	A	6	273

SUPREME COURT DECISIONS, exchange of copies of.

		Doc.	Vol.	No.
1834.	Communication transmitting a set of supreme court decisions from Maryland,	A	1	11
1834.	Resolutions of the legislature of New Hampshire relative to the exchange of law reports,	A	1	11
1841.	Resolutions of the legislature of Alabama relative to the exchange of law reports,	A	4	138

SUPREME COURT OF THE UNITED STATES, *see* United States Supreme Court.

SURPLUS CANAL WATER, *see* Canals.

SURPLUS REVENUES OF THE UNITED STATES.

		Doc.	Vol.	No.
1831.	Report relative to the distribution of the, among the several states,	S	1	70
	Deposited with this state, *see* United States deposit fund.			

SURROGATES.

1834.	Courts, report relative to the proof of wills, executors and administrators, guardians and wards in,	S	2	118
1839.	Fees of, report in relation to the,	A	6	407
1844.	Report of Mr. Porter on the subject of their fees,	S	3	9
1844.	Report of a select committee on the subject of their fees,	S	3	100
1845.	Report of the secretary of state of the names of, who have not reported their fees and disbursements,	S	2	78
1845.	Report of the select committee on the report of,	S	3	106
1847.	Report as to, reporting fees received,	A	3	57

SURVEY OF NON-RESIDENT LANDS.

1834.	Report on bill to amend the law relative to the,	A	2	86

SURVEYOR-GENERAL.

SIMEON DE WITT:

1830.	Report of the, on petition of I. Sherwin for a grant of land,	S	1	58
1830.	Report on petition of John C. McLean relative to certain land,	S	2	77
1830.	Report on petition of Robert Fleming relative to certain land,	A	2	119
1830.	Report on petition of Gershom Stevens relative to certain land,	A	3	157
1830.	Report on bill for the relief of F. Stanley,	A	2	115
1830.	Report relative to the publication of a map and atlas of the state,	A	2	189
1830.	Report on petition of Andrew Phares relative to the salt lands at Geddes,	S	3	219
1830.	Report in relation to the military bounty lands,	S	2	82
1831.	Report in relation to the public lands,	S	1	19
1831.	Report on petition of the owners of lands in the old military tract,	S	1	31
1832.	Report in relation to the public lands,	S	1	12
1832.	Report on petition of Daty Allen relative to certain land,	A	3	235
1832.	Report on petition of W. Hotchkiss, and others, relative to certain land,	S	1	29
1833.	Report on petition of Daty Allen for certain land,	A	2	46
1833.	Report on petition of Jacob Shew for bounty lands,	S	1	26
1833.	Report on petition of school district No. 4 in Salina,	S	2	97
1833.	Report on petition of T. W. & D. Newcomb relative to certain land,	A	4	307
1834.	Report on petition of Benjamin Barton, and others, relative to certain land in Lewiston,	A	1	28
1834.	Report on petition of Henry Rice, and others, relative to certain land in the Oneida reservation,	A	2	76
1834.	Report on petition of Bates Cooke relative to certain land in Lewiston,	A	4	281
1834.	Report on petition of the directors of the Buffalo and Black Rock Harbor Company to construct a part of their road on land belonging to the state,	A	1	41
1834.	Report on petition of the Orchard party of Oneida Indians relative to the sale of their lands,	S	2	88
1834.	Report on petition of Simeon Veeder, relative to certain land,	S	2	101

W. CAMPBELL:

1835.	Report on petition of D. T. & T. Newcomb relative to certain land,	A	3	257
1836.	Report on petition of owners of lots at Oneida Castleton,	A	3	138

SURVEYOR-GENERAL—*continued.*

		Doc.	Vol.	No.
	O. L. HOLLEY:			
1838.	Report relative to the public lands,........................	S	2	63
1839.	Report of the, on bill for the relief of Marlett & Dunham,......	S	3	73
1839.	Report of the, on petition of Zebulon Ketchum,...............	S	3	75
1839.	Report of the, relative to the public lands in Hamilton, Essex, Clinton, Franklin and St. Lawrence counties, ...	A	6	382
1840.	Report on the same,..	S	2	61
1840.	Report of the, on petition of David L. Seymour, ...	A	3	64
1840.	Report of the, relative to the boundaries of the towns of Davenport and Oneonta,...	A	4	107
1840.	Report on the same, ...	A	4	124
1840.	Report of the, relative to the proposed road from Salisbury Centre to Racket lake, and the sale and settlement of the public lands,..	A	4	153
1841.	Report relative to the lands of the St. Regis Indians,...........	A	4	131
1841.	Report of the, on petition of Hiram Parsons and others,........	A	7	263
1841.	Report of the, on petition of Nathan Burchard,...............	A	4	139
	NATHANIEL JONES:			
1844.	Report of surveyor-general, of the amount of printing done for his office, ...	S	2	75
1844.	Report of, relative to lands in Totten & Crossfield's purchase,..	S	2	77
	HUGH HALSEY:			
1845.	Report of, relative to lands purchased by William Smith, Jr,...	A	6	212
1846.	Communication from, relative to road from Clinton prison to Lake Champlain,..	A	2	55

SURVEYS OF CANALS, *see* the different Canals.

SURVEYS OF RAILROADS, *see* the different Railroads.

SUSQUEHANNA AND CHEMUNG RIVERS.

		Doc.	Vol.	No.
1830.	Survey of the, report of select committee, relative to the, &c.,..	A	1	63
1831.	Survey of the, report of canal commissioners in relation to the,.	A	3	278

SUSQUEHANNA RIVER.

		Doc.	Vol.	No.
1831.	Dam across, in the town of Chenango, report on petition to repeal the law authorizing the erection of a,......................	S	1	65
1834.	Dam across, report on petition of Samuel Badger, to construct a,	A	1	60
1834.	Dam across, report on petition of David Mersereau, to construct a,	A	2	97
1834.	Dam across, report on petition of John A. Seaverson and others,.	A	3	159
1841.	Dam across, report on petition to extend an act authorizing Samuel Badger and others to build a,..........................	A	7	287
1841.	Dam across, report on petition to extend an act authorizing John W. Harper to build a,..................................	A	7	287
1835.	Dam across, report on petition of John Crockett to continue a,..	S	1	17

SUSQUEHANNA STEAM NAVIGATION COMPANY.

		Doc.	Vol.	No.
1835.	Report on petition to incorporate the,........................	A	4	339

SUTHERLAND, JACOB, *see* Supreme Court Clerks.

SWALLOW, STEAMER.

		Doc.	Vol.	No.
1845.	Report of select committee appointed to investigate the cause of the disaster to, on the Hudson river,........................	S	3	102

SWAN, RACHAEL, AND C. F. SEDGWICK.

		Doc.	Vol.	No.
1838.	Representative of Cyrus Swan, report on petition of, to sell real estate, ...	A	3	118

SWARTWOUT, BERNARDUS J.

		Doc.	Vol.	No.
1835.	Report on petition of, for a lease of surplus canal water, ...	A	4	341

SWEDEN, TOWN OF.

1831.	Report on petition for the sale of the school-house and lot in, ..	A	3	213

SWEET, E. SMITH.

1835.	Report on petition of, for the payment of certain counsel fees, ..	A	3	262
1835.	Report on petition of, for the payment of certain counsel fees, ..	A	4	307

SWEET, GERRETT C.

1844.	Report of canal commissioners on petition of, ...	A	5	137

SWEET, WATERMAN (a natural bone setter).

1839.	Report on petition to allow him to collect pay for his services, ..	S	3	82

SWEETING, JOHN.

1834.	Report on petition of, for compensation for damages by the Erie canal, ...	S	2	70

SWIFT, H. C.

1847.	Report on petition of, ...	S	3	105
1847.	Report on petition of, ...	A	2	58

SWIFT, JOHN.

1847.	Report on petition of, ...	S	2	67

SWIFT, JOHN C.

1847.	Report of committee on claims on petition of, for relief, ...	A	2	58

SYRACUSE, CITY OF.

1849.	Bill to sell certain salt lands, ...	S	3	81
1849.	Report on the abatement of a nuisance on lands in, ...	S	1	11

SYRACUSE, VILLAGE OF.

1836.	Eye and ear infirmary, report on petition for aid to, ...	A	4	303
1838.	Eye and ear infirmary, report of the trustees of, ...	S	1	30
1840.	Cemetery, report relative to granting land for a, ...	S	2	59
1832.	School district, No. 4, report relative to, ...	A	3	268
1838.	Supreme court commissioner, report on bill for the appointment of a, ...	A	4	196
1839.	Unitarian Congregational Church, report on petition of the, for a grant of land, ...	A	6	326
1842.	Report of committee on public lands on petition of, ...	A	5	106
1848.	Report on memorial of president of, ...	A	5	171
	Salt lands, *see* Salina.			

T.

TAFT, THOMAS J.

1856.	Report on petition of, for damages, ...	A	3	44

TALLMAN AND NOYES.

1844.	Report of canal board on the petition of, ...	A	3	46

TALLMAN, DARIUS, AND HENRY WILKINS.

		Doc.	Vol.	No.
1847.	Report of committee on claims on petition of,	A	2	49

TALLMAN, JOHN T., AND JONATHAN CHILD.

		Doc.	Vol.	No.
1841.	Report on petition of, for the payment of interest on the amount of damages awarded to them,	A	6	216
1841.	Report on the same,	A	6	249

TAMBLIN, JONATHAN, *see* David Harris and others.

TAPPAN, ARTHUR, AND OTHERS.

		Doc.	Vol.	No.
1842.	Report of committee on canals on petition of,	A	5	110

TARIFF.

		Doc.	Vol.	No.
1842.	Communication from the governor transmitting resolutions of council and general assembly of New Jersey, relative to a,	S	3	53
1844.	Resolution relative to,	S	3	93
1842.	Resolutions of Connecticut in relation to,	A	2	26
1842.	Resolution of Mr. D. S. Wright, relative to,	A	7	143
1843.	Resolution of Connecticut respecting,	A	1	11
1844.	Resolution relative to a protective,	S	3	93
1844.	Resolution of Connecticut concerning,	A	1	7

TARIFF LAWS.

		Doc.	Vol.	No.
1830.	Resolutions of the Legislature of Mississippi, relative to the,	A	1	13
1830.	Resolutions of the Legislature of Pennsylvania, relative to the,	A	2	120
1830.	Resolutions of the Legislature of Connecticut, relative to the,	A	2	123
1830.	Resolutions of the Legislatures of Delaware and Ohio, relative to the,	S	4	366
1831.	Resolutions of the Legislature of Louisiana, relative to the,	A	1	4
1832.	Resolutions of the Legislatures of Maine and Delaware, relative to the,	A	1	3
1833.	Resolutions of the Legislature of Alabama, relative to,	A	4	274
1833.	Resolutions of the Legislatures of North Carolina and Massachusetts, relative to the,	A	2	115
1833.	Resolutions of the Legislature of New York, relative to the,	A	3	163
1834.	Resolutions of the Legislatures of Connecticut and Maryland, relative to the,	A	1	11
1841.	Resolutions of the Legislature of Mississippi, relative to the,	A	6	235
1841.	Resolutions of the Legislature of Connecticut, relative to the,	A	1	14
1841.	Resolutions of the Legislature of Alabama, relative to the,	A	3	57

TAVERN LICENSES, *see* Excise.

TAXATION, *see* Assessments.

		Doc.	Vol.	No.
1835.	Of ground rents, quarter sales, &c., report on petition for the,	S	2	83
1835.	To pay school bills of indigent persons, report relative to,	A	4	281
1835.	To pay school bills of indigent persons, report relative to,	A	4	317
1845.	Report of comptroller relative to taxing quarter sales, &c., of,	A	6	228
1846.	Of interest of landholders, report relative to,	S	4	135
1846.	Of leasehold estates, report of Mr. Spencer on so much of governor's message as relates to, &c.,	S	3	92
1846.	Of leasehold estates, report relative to,	S	4	107
1846.	Of leasehold estates, report on so much of governor's message as relates to,	S	4	115
1847.	Memorial of Stephen Van Rensselaer respecting,	S	2	47
1847.	Report on law for equalization of,	S	2	56
1852.	Report relative to taxing real estate, mortgages, &c.,	S	1	28
1852.	Report of committee on internal affairs of towns and counties respecting,	S	1	28

TAXATION—*continued.*

		Doc.	Vol.	No.
1857.	Report of committee on ways and means favorable on petition of Sackett's Harbor and Saratoga Railroad Company to be released from, on its lands,..................................	A	1	53
1858.	Report of majority of select committee on communication from comptroller respecting assessments and,....................	S	2	95
1858.	Communication from comptroller relative to assessment and taxation, ...	S	3	103

EXEMPTION OF MINISTERS, &c., FROM, *see* Ministers.

TAXES.

1843.	Communication from commissioners of land office relative to over-payment of money for,..............................	S	1	8
1830.	Statement of amount paid by corporations in 1826 and 1827,....	A	1	32
1836.	Statement of amount paid by each county from 1816 to 1826,...	S	2	67
1840.	Bill to extend the time for the collection of, for 1839, report of the committee on conference on the same,.................	S	1	18
1840.	Report of Mr. Maynard on the same,.........................	S	1	21
1840.	Remonstrance against entrusting taxes to the custody of corporations,...	A	8	362
1848.	Report of comptroller on bill relative to lands sold for, ...	A	3	63
1848.	Report of unpaid, in Cortland county,.........................	A	5	126
1848.	Report of unpaid, in Cortland county, ...	A	5	136
1848.	Report of committee on internal affairs of towns and counties on petition from Ulster county to be relieved from, under certain law,...	A	5	175
1849.	Report of comptroller relative to printing certain statements of lands sold for,..	A	1	8
1849.	Report in answer to resolution of assembly relative to execution of deeds of lands sold for, in the name of the people, ...	A	3	160
1850.	Comptroller's report in relation to erroneous payments, ...	A	5	120
1850.	Report of committee on, and assessments,....................	S	1	19
1853.	Report of the comptroller in answer to a resolution in relation to the amount of, due the state treasury on lands sold in December, 1852, ...	A	2	25
1853.	Report of comptroller relative to unpaid taxes from certain counties, ...	S	2	49
1853.	Report of comptroller relative to unpaid, from counties, ...	S	3	78
1858.	Communication from comptroller respecting unpaid, due the state from treasurer of Livingston county,.......................	A	3	53

FOR MAKING AND REPAIRING HIGHWAY:

1830.	Report on petition to amend the law relative to the assessment of,	A	4	329

REDEMPTION OF LAND SOLD FOR:

1830.	Report of committee on the judiciary, relative to the,..........	A	3	237
1832.	Report of the comptroller relative to the,....................	A	1	37

REPAYMENT IN CERTAIN CASES OF MONEYS PAID FOR:

1830.	Report of commissioners of land office in relation to,...........	S	4	413
1832.	do do do	S	2	107
1833.	do do do	S	2	125
1835.	do do do	S	2	89
1836.	do do do	S	2	109
1837.	do do do	S	2	73
1838.	do do do	S	2	74
1840.	do do do	S	4	126
1841.	do do do	A	7	305
1842.	do do do	A	7	183

TAXES—*continued.*

		Doc.	Vol.	No.
	SALE OF LAND FOR ARREARS OF:			
1830.	Report of comptroller, on bill concerning the, ...	A	3	239
1831.	Report of expenses of the last sale, ...	A	3	264
1835.	Statement of all the sales (not heretofore reported), also the sales of land for the arrears of quit rent, &c., ...	A	5	380
1839.	Report of comptroller, on bill relative to the sale, &c., ...	A	6	340
1848.	Report on bill for, ...	A	3	63
1849.	Report on so much of governor's message as relates to, in the counties where such lands lie, ...	A	3	107
1852.	*See* report of comptroller relative to time of holding, ...	A	5	103
1856.	Report in relation to, ...	A	3	92

NON-RESIDENT, *see* Non-Residents.

ON BANKS, *see* Banks.

ON CORPORATIONS, *see* Corporations.

ON FOREIGN INSURANCE COMPANIES, *see* Insurance.

ON SALT, *see* Salt.

ON SEAMEN, *see* Seamen.

TAX, STATE.

		Doc.	Vol.	No.
1830.	Report of the committee on finance recommending, ...	A	3	205
1831.	do do do	A	3	224
1836.	do do do	S	1	35
1838.	Report of Mr. Ruggles on the recommendation of the comptroller to levy a direct, ...	A	5	242
1843.	Report of the comptroller in answer to a resolution of the assembly respecting the pledges of the proceeds of the mill, ...	A	3	66
1852.	Report on proposition to reduce the half-mill, ...	S	2	83
1853.	Report of comptroller in relation to the time when the, would be available for the improvement of the canals, ...	A	3	61
1853.	Report of comptroller in relation to the time when the, would be available for the improvement of the canals, ...	A	5	114

TAYLOR, GEORGE L.

		Doc.	Vol.	No.
1834.	Report on petition of, for compensation for damages by the canal,	S	2	69

TAYLOR, H. W.

		Doc.	Vol.	No.
1849.	Memorial of, on capital punishment, ...	S	1	10

TAYLOR, GEN. Z.

		Doc.	Vol.	No.
1848.	Communication from governor transmitting letter from, ...	A	6	212

TEAL, NATHAN, AND OTHERS.

		Doc.	Vol.	No.
1830.	Report of canal commissioners on petition of, relative to the waters of Seneca lake, ...	A	3	284

TEAL, O.

		Doc.	Vol.	No.
1854.	Report on petition of, ...	A	3	94

TEAL, OLIVER, AND OTHERS.

		Doc.	Vol.	No.
1853.	Report of committee on grievances on petition of, to amend seduction laws, ...	A	2	51
1853.	Report of committee on grievances on petition of, to amend the seduction laws, ...	A	3	61

TEFFT, A. C., AND OTHERS.

		Doc.	Vol.	No.
1844.	Report of canal committee on petition of,	S	3	106

TEMPERANCE, *see* Excise, Intoxicating Liquors.

1850.	Appeal of Charles J. Warner,	A	6	145

TEMPERANCE SOCIETY, STATE.

1848.	Remonstrance against bill legalizing sale of intoxicating drinks,	A	5	169
1850.	Memorial of,	S	1	10
1854.	Memorial of,	S	1	4

TEMPERANCE TAVERNS.

1834.	Report on petition to license, without paying excise,	A	3	250

TENANT, *see* Landlord and Tenant.

TEN BROECK, PETER B.

1837.	Report on petition of, for compensation for damages by the Chemung canal,	A	3	206
1837.	Report of committee on claims,	A	3	235
1838.	Report of committee on grievances,	A	3	89

TEN BROECK, WESSEL.

1832.	Report on petition of, for pay for work done on a road in the town of Edmeston,	A	4	281
1833.	Report of committee on claims,	A	3	175
1834.	Report of committee on claims,	A	3	192
1835.	Report of committee on grievances,	A	3	166

TENNESSEE, STATE OF.

1832.	Resolutions of the legislature of, relative to the exercise of certain powers of the general government, and relative to the public lands,	A	3	183

TERRILL, JEROME B.

1840.	Report on petition of, for a divorce,	A	8	323

TERRY, JOSEPH, AND OTHERS.

1835.	Report on petition of, to erect a wharf at Oyster pond village,	A	4	352

TERWILLIGER, HARMAN.

1843.	Report of committee on claims on his petition,	S	3	101
1844.	Report of committee on claims on petition of,	S	3	97
1848.	Report on petition of,	A	3	83

TESTIMONY (taken in foreign countries).

1836.	Report of committee on the judiciary in relation to,	A	3	135

TEXAS, REPUBLIC OF.

1838.	Resolutions of the legislature of Ohio against the annexation of, to the Union,	S	2	58
1838.	Resolutions of the legislature of Alabama in favor of the annexation of,	A	5	218
1838.	Report on the annexation of,	A	5	271
1842.	Resolution of general assembly of Alabama in favor of admitting, into the Union,	S	2	25

		Doc.	Vol.	No.
1842.	Resolution of Alabama in favor of admitting, into the Union,...	A	2	48
1842.	Resolution of Mississippi relative to the annexation of, to the United States,.. ...	A	7	199
1844.	Resolution relative to,..	S	3	107
1844.	Resolution of the legislature of South Carolina relative to the annexation of, to the Union, ...	A	1	5
1844.	Resolution of the Massachusetts legislature concerning,........	A	7	175
1844.	Communication from governor transmitting resolution of the legislature of Mississippi relative to,...........................	A	7	202
1845.	Report of majority of select committee on the annexation of,....	A	4	83
1845.	Report of minority of select committee relative to same,........	A	4	84

TEXAS, STATE OF.

1850.	Resolution of, concerning slavery,............................	A	8	193

THALIMER, PETER AND HENRY.

1832.	Report on petition of, for extra allowance for work done on the Champlain canal,..	A	2	179
1832.	Report of canal commissioners on the same,..................	A	1	56
1833.	Report of canal commissioners on the same,..................	S	2	109
1834.	Report of canal board on the same,..........................	A	4	338
1834.	Report of committee on claims on the same,..................	A	4	396
1837.	Report of committee on canals on the same,..................	S	1	44

THAYER, NANCY BLACKWOOD.

1842.	Report of judiciary committee on petition of, for a divorce,.....	S	2	45
1842.	Report on petition of, for a divorce, ...	S	2	103

THERMOMETER, CENTIGRADE.

1842.	Report of Regents of University relative to the,......	S	4	94

THOMAS & WORDEN.

1846.	Report on petition of,.. ...	S	1	31
1847.	Report of the testimony in case of,..........................	A	1	34

THOMAS BRIGGS.

1851.	Report on claim for canal damages,............................	S	2	29

THOMAS, MARY, AND ANN SMALLDEN.

1850.	Report on petition of,..	S	1	23

THOMPSON, ANSON.

1834.	Report on petition of, for pay for a horse lost in a ditch near the canal,...	A	4	398
1835.	Report relative to the same,..................................	A	3	161
1842.	Report of committee on claims on petition of,................	S	3	67

THOMPSON, CHARLES B., & HIRAM W. HASCALL.

1857.	Report of committee on claims on petition of,................	A	3	154

THOMPSON, GEORGE.

1831.	Report on petition of, for remuneration for a lot of land sold for taxes,...	A	1	22
1835.	Report on petition of, relative to the same,...................	A	4	293

THOMPSON, ISAAC, AND OTHERS.

		Doc.	Vol.	No.
1846.	Report of committee on claims in relation to claim of,	S	2	66
1846.	Report of canal commissioners in relation to claim of,	S	1	26

THOMPSON, JAMES, *see* Janet Hay, or McAndrew.

THOMPSON, W. AND M., *see* Daniel Cameron.

THOMPSON, WILLIAM, *see* Lewis Bebee and William Thompson.

THOMSONIAN MEDICAL SOCIETY.

1842.	Report of Mr. Taylor on petition for relief of,	A	7	142

THOMSONIAN PHYSICIANS, *see* Botanic Physicians.

1840.	Report on petition to allow them to collect pay for services,	S	4	107
1840.	Report of majority of select committee on the same,	A	8	340
1840.	do minority of select committee on the same,	A	8	354
1841.	do Mr. Hull,	A	4	94
1842.	do select committee on numerous petitions for relief of,	A	2	42
1842.	do committee on medical colleges and societies on petition for relief of,	A	7	142

THORP, EZRA.

1830.	A soldier of the revolution, report on petition for relief,	A	4	310

THROOP, ENOS T., *see* Governor.

THURMAN, JOHN.

1832.	Report on petition of the heirs, devisees and grantees of,	S	1	48
1855.	Report of commissioners of land office in relation to lands granted to,	A	5	140

THURMAN, W., AND OTHERS.

1852.	Report on petition of,	S	2	54
1854.	Report on petition of,	A	3	82

THURMAN, WASHINGTON.

1852.	Report on petition of, and others, for relief,	S	2	54

THURMAN, WASHINGTON, AND OTHERS.

1848.	Report of committee on claims on petition of,	A	5	150
1849.	do committee on claims on petition of,	A	2	59
1850.	do committee on grievances on petition of,	S	2	45

TIBBITTS, GEORGE.

1849.	Report of committee on claims on petition of,	A	3	106

TIBBITTS, GEORGE, AND JAMES STEVENS.

1843.	Report of committee on claims on petition of,	A	5	143

TICE, JOHN, AND OTHERS.

1848.	Report concerning,	A	3	102

TILLISTON, SPAFFORD, AND OTHERS.

		Doc.	Vol.	No.
1858.	Report of committee on finance on the petition of, for the repayment of moneys illegally collected,......................	S	3	115

TILLMAN, ANDREW P.

1830.	Report on petition of, for extra allowance for building locks on the Cayuga and Seneca canal,..............................	A	3	240
1830.	Report of committee on canals, on the same, ...	A	4	325
1831.	Report of committee on canals, on the same,..................	A	1	52
1841.	Report of canal board, on the same, ...	S	2	42
1841.	Report of committee on claims, on the same,..................	A	7	267
1857.	Report of committee on claims, favorable on petition of,........	A	3	174

TIMMERMAN, JACOB J.

1834.	Report on petition of, for remuneration for a lot of land sold by mistake for quit rent, ...	A	3	123
1835.	Report on the same, ...	A	1	37
1835.	Report on the same, ...	S	2	39

TIOGA COAL, IRON, MINING AND MANUFACTURING COMPANY.

1838.	Report on petition for a loan of the credit of the state,..........	S	2	45
1844.	Report of committee on the judiciary on a concurrent resolution directing the comptroller to suspend the sale of the road of,..	A	6	152

TIOGA COUNTY.

1833.	Commissioners of deeds, report on bill confirming the appointment of,..	A	3	208
1839.	County courts, report on petition to alter the time of holding the,	A	5	281
1833.	Courts of common pleas and general sessions, report on petition for an additional term of the,..............................	A	2	63
1834.	Race-course in, report on petition for a, ...	S	2	82
1833.	Supreme court commissioner, report in relation to the,.........	A	4	325
1840.	Sheriff of, Prentice Ransom, report on petition of, relative to the transportation of convicts, ...	A	3	75
1831.	New county from part of, Tompkins and Steuben, report on petition for a,...	A	3	277
1832.	Report on the same,......................................	A	2	169

TIOGA RIVER.

1833.	Dam across, report on petition of Isaac Gray and others, to construct and maintain a,....................................	A	2	82
1833.	Report on petition to prevent fishing with seines in the, ...	A	4	310

TOAN, ROBERT, *see* Josiah Rawson.

TOBACCO, INSPECTION OF, *see* New York.

TODD & GRANGER, AND OTHERS.

1848.	Report on petition of, ...	A	5	127

TODD, WALTER S.

1845.	Report of canal commissioners on the petition of,..............	S	1	13

TOLTS, GEORGE.

1855.	Report of committee on claims, in case of, ...	A	3	69

TOMLINSON, DAVID.

		Doc.	Vol.	No.
1855.	Report of committee on claims, on petition of, ...	A	5	131
1856.	Report on petition for relief, ...	A	4	102

TOMLINSON, DAVID, AND OTHERS.

		Doc.	Vol.	No.
1834.	Report on petition of, relative to the condition of the canal near Schenectady, ...	A	4	327
1849.	Report of committee on canals, on bill for the relief of,.........	A	2	63

TOMPKINS COUNTY.

		Doc.	Vol.	No.
1832.	Common pleas, report on petition to alter the terms of,.........	A	4	333
1833.	Leather manufactory, report on petition to incorporate the, ...	A	2	120
1831.	New county from parts of Tioga and Steuben, report on petition for a,...	A	3	277
1832.	New county from parts of Tioga and Steuben, report on petition for a, ...	A	2	196
1831.	Inspector of beef and pork, annual report of E. Warren,.......	A	2	98
1832.	do do do	S	1	36
1833.	do do do	A	3	160
1834.	do do do	A	3	169
1830.	Inspector of beef and pork, annual report of J. Potter,.........	A	2	111
1830.	Inspector of leather, annual report of E. Thayer,,.............	A	2	121
1831.	do do do	A	2	140
1832.	do do do	A	2	84
1833.	do do do	A	3	159
1833.	do do P. French,...............	A	3	195
1834.	do do do	A	2	73
1835.	do do do	A	1	7
1834.	do do H. F. Randolph,.........	A	2	72
1835.	do do do	A	1	9
1836.	do do do	A	3	148
1837.	do do do	A	2	95
1838.	do do do	A	3	98
1839.	do do do	A	4	191
1840.	do do do	A	2	49
1836.	do do John Van Houten,.......	A	3	177
1837.	do do do	S	1	12
1838.	do do do	A	3	93
1844.	Report of committee on medical societies, &c., on petition of physicians of,....	A	3	76
1847.	Report on petition of inhabitants of Chenango, Steuben, Yates and, for erection of a new county, ...	A	2	62
1847.	Minority report on petitions for the erection of a new county from parts of above counties,................................	A	2	81

TOMPKINS, DANIEL D.

		Doc.	Vol.	No.
1839.	Report relative to the erection of a monument to,..............	A	6	392

TOMPKINSVILLE, VILLAGE OF.

		Doc.	Vol.	No.
1834.	Church in, report on petition of St. Andrew and St. Paul's Church, to apply certain moneys toward the erection of a,....	S	1	20

TONAWANDA.

		Doc.	Vol.	No.
1846.	Report of canal commissioners relative to lock at, ...	A	4	117
1850.	Report of canal commissioners as to supply of water between and Montezuma, ...	S	2	41

TONAWANDA CREEK.

		Doc.	Vol.	No.
1831.	Bridge over, report on petition to raise money to build a, ...	A	4	358
1833.	Report on petition of inhabitants of Erie and Niagara, relative to damages caused by damming, ...	S	2	89
1838.	Lands overflowed by water on the, report of canal commissioners in relation to the, ...	A	3	124
1856.	Bridge across, ...	A	4	159

TONAWANDA INDIAN RESERVATION.

1831.	Road through, report on petition for power to lay out and open a,	A	4	318

TONAWANDA RAILROAD, *see* Railroads.

TONAWANDA SWAMP.

1855.	Report of select committee on bill to drain, ...	A	5	120

TOPOGRAPHICAL SURVEY.

1853.	Report of committee on colleges, academies and common schools, in relation to the, ...	A	2	32
1853.	Report of the committee on agriculture, in relation to the, ...	A	2	33

TORREY, JESSE, JR.

1834.	Report on petition of, relative to the manner of heating and ventilating the assembly chamber, ...	A	4	388
1835.	Report on petition of, relative to the manner of heating and ventilating the assembly chamber, ...	A	5	399

TOTTEN AND CROSSFIELD'S PURCHASE.

1843.	Report of commissioners of land office respecting the north gore, lying between townships Nos. 10 and 12 in, ...	A	5	161
1844.	Report of surveyor-general relative to land in, ...	S	2	77

TOWER, NATHANIEL, *see* E. Beebe.

TOWER, NEHEMIAH.

1835.	Report on petition of, relative to the sale of his land for taxes,..	S	2	57

TOWNS AND COUNTIES.

1850.	Report of attorney-general on division, alteration and erection of,	A	5	82

TOWN AUDITORS.

1830.	Report on petition for the creation of boards of, ...	A	1	30
1831.	do do do	A	3	222
1838.	do do do	A	4	160
1839.	do do do	A	2	23

TOWN CHARGES.

1838.	Statement of the charges levied on towns and counties, ...	A	4	183

TOWN EXPENSES.

1847.	Report on petitions relative to county and, ...	S	3	103

TOWN MEETINGS.

1839.	Report relative to changing the time for holding, ...	A	2	41

TOWN OFFICERS.

		Doc.	Vol.	No.
1838.	Report relative to the election of, for three years,	A	6	357
1839.	Report relative to the election of, for three years,	A	3	79

TOWNER, BENJAMIN, AND OTHERS.

		Doc.	Vol.	No.
1848.	Report of committee on claims on petition of,	A	5	150
1849.	Report of committee on claims on petition of,	A	2	59
1850.	Report of committee on grievances on petition of,	S	2	45

TOWNSEND AND BRITTON.

		Doc.	Vol.	No.
1858.	Report of committee on claims on petition of,	A	4	90

TOWNSEND, E. M., AND OTHERS.

		Doc.	Vol.	No.
1837.	Report on petition of, for extra allowance for work done on the Chenango canal,	A	3	184
1837.	Report on petition of, for extra allowance for work done on the Chenango canal,	A	3	220

TOWNSEND, JACOB.

		Doc.	Vol.	No.
1840.	Report on petition of, relative to a new plan of propelling steam-boats through the ice,	S	4	116

TOWNSEND, WILLIAM.

		Doc.	Vol.	No.
1849.	Report of committee on claims on petition of,	A	3	153

TOWNSEND, WM. B.

		Doc.	Vol.	No.
1849.	Remonstrance of, relative to removal of quarantine, &c.,	A	3	144

TRACY, FELIX.

		Doc.	Vol.	No.
1835.	Report on petition of, to build a dam and boat lock on the Genesee river in the town of Leicester,	A	4	295

TRACY, HENRY, AND ROBT. RENWICK, Jr.

		Doc.	Vol.	No.
1848.	Report on petition of,	A	5	179

TRAVIS AND BLOUNT.

		Doc.	Vol.	No.
1854.	Report on petition of,	S	2	106

TREASURER, STATE.

Abraham Keyser:

		Doc.	Vol.	No.
1830.	Annual report of the,	A	1	61
1831.	do do	A	1	34
1832.	do do	A	1	8
1833.	do do	A	1	12
1834.	do do	A	1	6
1835.	do do	A	1	6
1836.	do do	A	1	18
1837.	do do	A	1	9
1838.	do do	A	1	10
1833.	Report of the, on petition of Garret Quackenbush,	A	4	294

G. H. Barstow:

		Doc.	Vol.	No.
1839.	Annual report of the,	A	2	46

Jacob Haight:

		Doc.	Vol.	No.
1840.	Annual report of the,	A	1	17
1841.	Annual report of the,	A	1	6
1839.	Report on petition of, for extra allowance for clerk hire,	A	6	374

TREASURER, STATE—*continued.*

Year	Subject	Doc.	Vol.	No.
	THOMAS FARRINGTON:			
1842.	Report of,	A	2	32
1843.	Annual report of,	A	1	4
1843.	Communication from, relative to moneys received from the United States from the proceeds of the sales of public lands,	A	2	16
1843.	Report of, in answer to a resolution of the assembly relative to the moneys received on account of the sale of the public lands,	A	2	17
1844.	Report of, of the printing done for his department,	S	2	82
1844.	Annual report of,	A	1	12
	BENJAMIN ENOS:			
1845.	Annual report of,	A	1	6
	THOMAS FARRINGTON:			
1846.	Annual report of,	A	1	10
1847.	Annual report of,	A	1	26
	ALVAH HUNT:			
1848.	Annual report of,	A	2	22
1849.	Annual report of,	A	1	6
1850.	Annual report of,	A	3	20
1851.	Report of, on state finances,	S	3	93
1851.	Annual report,	A	1	6
	JAMES M. COOK:			
1852.	Annual report of,	A	1	6
	BENJAMIN WELCH:			
1853.	Communication from the, in answer to a resolution of the senate, in relation to clerk hire in his office,	S	1	7
1853.	Annual report of,	A	1	13
1853.	Report of, in answer to a resolution in relation to fees paid into the treasury by the attorney-general, since 1st January, 1848,	A	2	16
	ELBRIDGE G. SPAULDING:			
1854.	Report of, relative to fees paid by attorney-general,	S	1	60
1854.	Communication from, on same subject,	S	1	28
1854.	Annual report of,	A	1	14
	STEPHEN CLARK:			
1856.	Annual report of.	A	3	38
1857.	Annual report of,	A	1	18
	ISAAC V. VANDERPOEL:			
1858.	Annual report of,	A	1	34

TREASURER'S ACCOUNTS.

Year	Subject	Doc.	Vol.	No.
1830.	Report of the committee appointed to examine the,	S	1	14
1831.	do do do	S	1	6
1832.	do do do	S	2	77
1833.	do do do	S	1	12
1834.	do do do	S	1	30
1835.	do do do	S	2	32
1836.	do do. do	S	1	8
1837.	do do do	S	1	4
1838.	do do do	A	1	8
1838.	Report of committee appointed to examine the late treasurer's accounts,	A	6	347
1839.	Report of committee appointed to examine the,	A	1	8
1839.	Report of committee appointed to examine the late treasurer's accounts,	A	4	265
1840.	Report of committee appointed to examine the,	A	1	14
1841.	Report of committee appointed to examine the,	A	5	151

TREASURER'S ACCOUNTS—*continued.*

		Doc.	Vol.	No.
1842.	Report of the joint committee relative to the late,...............	S	3	65
1842.	Report of joint committee relative to the late,.................	S	3	71
1842.	Report of joint select committee relative to, and of commissioner of canal fund, &c.,..	A	1	4
1842.	Report of joint select committee appointed to examine, and of commissioners of the canal fuud,............................	A	7	4
1843.	Report of joint committee appointed to examine, &c.,............	A	1	13
1843.	Report relative to the condition of the banking department, the canal department and,....................................	A	2	18
1844.	Report of joint committee in relation to, and the banking and canal department,......................................	A	1	9
1844.	Report of joint committee in relation to, and the banking department,...	A	1	10
1845.	Report of joint committee on,................................	S	1	36
1845.	Report of the joint committee on,.............................	A	1	4
1846.	Report of joint committee to examine, and the banking and canal departments,...	A	1	7
1846.	Report of joint committee to examine, &c.,.....................	A	1	7
1846.	Report of joint committee to examine late,.....................	A	4	116
1847.	Report of committee appointed to examine accounts of,..........	A	1	21
1848.	Report of committee on,......................................	A	3	65
1849.	Report of joint committee to examine,.........................	A	2	83
1850.	Report of committee to examine,..............................	A	1	7
1851.	Report of committee on,......................................	A	2	23
1852.	Report of committee to examine,..............................	A	1	14
1853.	Annual report of committee to examine, and the canal and banking departments,.......................................	A	1	8
1855.	Report of committee appointed to examine,.....................	A	1	11
1856.	Report of committee to examine,..............................	A	4	173
1858.	Report of commissioners to examine, for 1856 and 1857,........	S	1	14
1858.	Report of commissioners to examine, and those of auditor, &c.,..	S	2	79
1858.	Report of commissioners appointed to examine, and those of the auditor, and securities in the bank department,.............	S	2	104

TREASURERS, COUNTY, *see* County Treasurers.

TREASURY.

1837.	Report of comptroller relative to drawing money from the, on a resolution of the assembly,...............................	A	2	74
1849.	Report of clerk of court of appeals as to paying into the sum of $35,181.50, ...	S	2	44
1849.	Report of comptroller of all moneys drawn from by Chauncey Smith, late agent of Sing Sing state prison,................	A	2	99
1853.	Report of committee on ways and means, on bill to provide means to pay present claims upon,..............................	A	2	48
1853.	Report of minority of committee in relation to, ...	A	2	54

TREAT, ASHBEL W.

1839.	A soldier of the revolution, report on petition for bounty lands,	A	3	159

TREAT, JAMES D., AND OTHERS.

1842.	Report of canal board on petition of,.........................	A	7	132
1844.	Report of committee on claims on an act for the relief of, ...	A	1	19
1845.	Report of canal commissioners on bill from the assembly, for the relief of,..	S	3	87

TREDWELL, F. C.

1838.	Memorial of, for an investigation of the affairs, &c., of the Brooklyn Bank, ...	S	3	83

TREDWELL, THOMAS, *see* H. F. Jones.

TRIALS BY JURY.

		Doc.	Vol.	No.
1834.	Report on bill in relation to,	A	4	376

TRINITY CHURCH, *see* New York.

TROUP, ROBERT, *see* Pulteney Estate, agent of the.

TROWBRIDGE, SAMUEL.

		Doc.	Vol.	No.
1835.	Report on petition of, relative to a tax paid by mistake,	A	3	230

TROY AND SCHENECTADY RAILROAD, *see* Railroads.

TROY, CITY OF.

		Doc.	Vol.	No.
1837.	Petition to allow banks to issue post notes,	A	4	293
1831.	Bridge over the Hudson at, report on petition for a,	A	1	29
1841.	Bridge at, majority report on petition for the removal of the,	A	7	299
1841.	Bridge at, minority report on petition for the removal of the,	A	7	300
1830.	College at, report on petition of the common council to raise money to establish a,	A	2	227
1837.	Corporation of, report on petition of the, to borrow money to aid in the construction of the Schenectady and Troy Railroad Company,	A	2	75
1831.	Macadam Turnpike and Railroad Company, report on petition to incorporate the,	A	2	186
1834.	Report on petition to amend the charter of the,	A	3	191
1834.	Memorial of inhabitants of Pittstown, relative to the,	A	3	204
1832.	And Lansingburgh Macadam road, report on petition to incorporate the,	A	1	34
1833.	And Lansingburgh Macadam road, report on petition to incorporate the,	A	3	219
1833.	Water works company, report on petition of the common council to purchase the works, &c., of the,	A	1	29
1845.	Report of committee on charitable and religious societies, on bill entitled "An act to prevent racing and trotting horses on Albany and Troy road," &c.,	S	3	88
1845.	Report of canal commissioners, relative to side-cut in Erie canal, at Troy,	A	3	57
1845.	Memorial of corporation of, on the Albany bridge question,	A	3	72
1846.	Report of attorney-general on petition of citizens of,	A	5	167
1850.	Report of committee on judiciary relative to Troy Art Union,	A	5	125

BANKS IN, *see* Banks.
DAM, *see* Amsden Manley and others.
REPORTS OF INSPECTORS OF LUMBER, &c., *see* Rensselaer county.
SLOOP LOCK DAM, *see* Henry James and others.

TROY FEMALE SEMINARY, *see* Academies, &c.

TRUAX, HENRY, *see* Maria Weaver.

TRUMPBOUR, JACOB.

		Doc.	Vol.	No.
1831.	Memorial of, for compensation for services rendered the state,	A	4	299
1832.	Report of canal board on the same,	A	3	188
1832.	Report of select committee on the same,	A	4	334
1832.	Documents accompanying the same,	A	4	335
1833.	Report of select committee on the same,	A	2	51
1834.	Report of committee on claims on the same,	A	1	37
1834.	Preamble and resolution on the same,	A	4	268
1835.	Report of committee on claims on the same,	A	4	266
1837.	Report of select committee on the same,	A	1	45

TRUMPBOUR, JACOB—*continued.*

		Doc.	Vol.	No.
1837.	Report of select committee on the same,	A	2	142
1837.	Report of canal board on the same,	A	3	181
1838.	Report of committee on canals on the same,	S	2	66
1838.	Report of committee on claims on the same,	A	4	182

TRUST COMPANIES, *see* Banks.

TRUSTS, *see* Powers and Trusts.

TRYON, AMOS S.

1847.	Report of comptroller on petition of,	S	1	35

TRYON, AMOS S., AND H. S. FRANKLIN.

1830.	Report on petition of, for a grant of land in Lewiston,	A	3	222

TUELL, AMASA.

1855.	Report of committee on claims, on petition of,	A	3	61

TUPPER, HARVEY N.

1856.	Report on petition for relief,	A	3	68

TUPPER, HARVEY N., AND C. L. KELSEY.

1855.	Report of committee on claims, in case of,	A	3	62
1857.	Report of committee on claims on petition of,	A	1	32

TURNER, AGNES C.

1856.	Report of judiciary committee on petition of,	S	2	67
1857.	Report of committee on petitions of aliens, favorable on petition of,	A	2	62

TURNER, BENJAMIN.

1852.	Report on assembly bill for relief of,	S	2	74

TURNER, BENJAMIN, AND OTHERS.

1848.	Report of committee on claims on petition of,	A	5	150
1849.	Report of committee on claims on petition of,	A	2	59
1850.	Report of committee on grievances on petition of,	S	2	45

TURNER, CAPT. DANIEL.

1836.	Report on the resolution relative to the naval services of,	A	4	325

TURNER, GRANT & RYAN.

1847.	Report of canal commissioners respecting moneys due,	A	7	212
1848.	Report on petition of,	A	2	42
1851.	Report of committee on canals on petition of,	A	3	78

TURNER, WILLIAM.

1849.	Report of committee on claims on petition of,	A	3	153

TURNPIKES.

1834.	Report on petition to amend the law relative to the laying out of,	S	2	122
1837.	Report on bill authorizing county judges to inspect, and to locate the gates thereon,	S	2	47

TUSCARORA INDIANS, *see* Indians—Tuscaroras.

TUTTLE, SALMON, AND WM. CLEAVELAND.

		Doc.	Vol.	No.
1857.	Report of committee on claims on petition of,	A	2	82

TUTTLE, STEPHEN, AND OTHERS.

1835.	Report on petition of, for remuneration for damages by the Chemung canal,	A	4	355

TUTTLE, WHITING.

1850.	Report on claim of,	A	3	40

TYLER, ORRIN.

1845.	Report of canal appraisers on the petition of,	A	3	46

TYRE, TOWN OF.

1845.	Report of canal commissioners respecting lot 63 in,	S	1	25

U.

UDALL, RICHARD.

1835.	Report on petition of, to erect a wharf in North Hempstead, Queens county,	A	4	305

UHLE, JOHN.

1857.	Report of committee on claims on petition of sureties of, to be released,	A	1	49

ULSTER COUNTY.

1840.	Bridge over Esopus creek, report on petition to raise money by tax to build a,	A	2	53
1834.	Bridge over Rondout creek, report on petition to raise money by tax to build a,	A	3	217
1832.	Superintendents of the poor, I. I. Schoonmaker and Joseph Hasbrouck, report on petition to confirm the appointment of,	A	2	76
1840.	New county from parts of, and Orange, report on petition for the erection of a,	A	8	312
1842.	Report of the committee on railroads on the remonstrance of Sullivan, Orange and, relative to the New York and Erie Railroad Company,	S	3	74
1847.	Report on contested election in,	A	1	16
1847.	Report of committee on privileges and elections on contested election in,	A	1	17
1848.	Report on petition from, to drain Pacama Fly, &c.,	A	2	34
1848.	Report on petition to be relieved from taxes under a certain law,	A	5	175
1852.	Erection of a new town in,	A	5	107
1856.	Report of committee on petition for a law to tax dogs in,	A	4	131

UNADILLA AND SCHOHARIE RAILROAD, *see* Railroads.

UNADILLA, COUNTY OF.

1845.	Report of minority of committee on erection of towns and villages, relative to,	A	4	107
1846.	Report of committee on erection and division of towns and counties, respecting proposed new,	A	4	97
1846.	Report of minority of committee on same,	A	4	105
1849.	Report of attorney-general on the constitutionality of erecting Patterson and, from parts of different senate and assembly districts,	A	3	123

UNADILLA, COUNTY OF—*continued.*

Year	Entry	Doc.	Vol.	No.
1856.	Report of committee on erection and division of towns and counties, as to erection of,	S	2	88
1837.	Report on petition for the erection of the,	A	2	131

UNADILLA, VILLAGE OF.

Year	Entry	Doc.	Vol.	No.
1836.	Supreme court commissioner at, report on petition for the appointment of a,	A	2	54
1840.	Report on petition for a new county from parts of Otsego, Delaware and Chenango, with the county seat at,	A	6	242

UNDERHILL, ABRAM S.

Year	Entry	Doc.	Vol.	No.
1845.	Report of committee on the judiciary on the petition of,	A	3	61

UNDERWOOD, JOHN.

Year	Entry	Doc.	Vol.	No.
1851.	Report of committee on contested seat,	A	3	55
1851.	Report of select committee on same,	A	4	128

UNDERWOOD, NATHAN.

Year	Entry	Doc.	Vol.	No.
1830.	Report on the claim of, to certain land in Freemasons' patent,	S	4	395
1837.	Report on the claim of, to certain land in Freemasons' patent,	A	3	192

UNIONDALE AND DOVER TURNPIKE COMPANY.

Year	Entry	Doc.	Vol.	No.
1830.	Report on petition to amend the charter of the,	A	3	288

UNITED STATES.

Year	Entry	Doc.	Vol.	No.
1839.	Courts, resolutions relative to plaintiffs in judgments in,	A	1	10
1830.	Accounts with the, for aid furnished during the late war, report relative to,	S	4	315
1832.	Judicial department, resolutions of Connecticut relative to the,	A	1	3
1830.	Cession of certain land at Watervliet to the, governor's message relative to the,	A	1	53
1841.	Land ceded to the, report relative to assessing the,	A	5	145
1836.	Mail, report on the subject of requiring railroads to convey the,	A	4	302
1836.	Mail, message from the governor returning a bill requiring railroads to convey the,	A	4	326
1839.	Ship canal around the Niagara Falls, report on bill authorizing the United States to construct a,	S	1	23
1840.	Memorial of Jesse Hawley against ceding to the United States the right to construct,	S	4	108
1834.	Public deposits, resolution approving of the removal of,	A	1	8
1834.	Public deposits, the president and secretary's reasons for the removal of the,	S	1	7
1839.	Senator, report on bill and resolutions from the assembly for the appointment of a,	S	3	77
1839.	Report on the resolutions of the senate relative to the appointment of a,	A	5	272
1839.	Senators, report on bill to provide for the election of,	A	6	404
1842.	Governor's letter to secretary of war,	A	1	2
1842.	Communication from secretary of state relative to digest of patents issued by,	A	5	123
1843.	Communication from secretary of war,	A	4	107
1843.	Report of commissioners of land office on the documents referred to them by the assembly, relative to ceding certain lands at the village of Black Rock to, for military works,	A	5	662
1844.	Joint resolution relative to the expenses of,	S	1	4
1845.	Report of comptroller relative to $84,000 received from government of,	A	3	75

UNITED STATES—*continued.*

		Doc.	Vol.	No.
1847.	Communication from secretary of navy,......................	A	2	96
1847.	Communication from secretary of navy,......................	A	6	156
1847.	Joint resolution of Missouri legislature respecting army of,......	A	6	164
1849.	Letter from secretary of war relative to annuities due from, to the Seneca Indians,...	A	5	205
1849.	Communication from secretary of navy respecting the purchase of certain land adjoining the navy yard in Brooklyn,.........	A	5	237
1850.	Letter from secretary of navy in regard to certain lands in Brooklyn,...	A	4	54
1850.	Letter from secretary of navy in regard to certain lands in Brooklyn,...	A	6	171
1850.	Report of select committee in relation to ceding land in Brooklyn to,..	A	8	183
1851.	Letter of secretary of the interior respecting the census,.........	S	2	63
1851.	Letters of secretary of war and Brevet Col. G. Wright relative to granting lands near Fort Ontario,.........................	S	3	82
1857.	Communication from the United States commissioners of Indian affairs relative to sales of land belonging to the Seneca Indians,	A	1	17
	PRESIDENT OF THE, *see* President.			

UNITED STATES BANK.

		Doc.	Vol.	No.
1832	Resolutions against rechartering,............................	S	1	28
1838.	do do offered by Mr. Mann,...........	A	3	94
1840.	do do offered by D. S. Dickinson,.....	S	1	30
1833.	Resolutions of the legislature of New Hampshire approving of the veto of the,..	A	2	115
1834.	Resolution approving the removal of the public deposits from the,..	A	1	8
1834.	Resolution approving the removal of the public deposits from the,..	S	1	6
1834.	Communication made by President Jackson to his cabinet, and the reasons given by the secretary of the treasury relative to the removal of the public deposits from the,................	S	1	7
1834.	Resolutions disapproving of the conduct of the,................	S	1	10
1841.	Resolutions of the general assembly of Rhode Island for the establishment of a,...	S	5	158

UNITED STATES CONSTITUTION.

CONVENTION OF STATES TO AMEND:

		Doc.	Vol.	No.
1833.	Resolution of the legislature of Georgia for a call for,...........	A	2	39
1833.	do do South Carolina for a call for,....	A	2	39
1833.	do do Delaware against,..............	A	2	135
1833.	do do Ohio against,...................	A	3	139
1833.	do do Massachusetts against,...........	A	4	291
1833.	do do Mississippi against,.............	A	4	291
1833.	do do Alabama against,...............	A	4	274
1833.	Resolution offered by Mr. Stilwell, to inquire into the expediency of establishing a supreme court of appeals,..................	A	2	107
1840.	Resolution to amend, relative to the appointment of members of congress to office, &c.,..................................	S	1	3
1840.	Report of joint committee on the same,.......................	S	1	29
1841.	Resolution to amend, relative to the appointment of members of congress to office, &c.,..................................	S	1	5
1841.	State stocks, resolution to amend the constitution so as to require every law for the issue of stock to be submitted to the people at the next election,......................................	A	4	102
1841.	Right of suffrage, resolution to extend the, to colored persons,...	A	5	183
1841.	Right of suffrage, resolution to amend, relative to the,...........	A	5	181
1842.	Amendment proposed by Connecticut,.........................	A	2	28

UNITED STATES CONSTITUTION—*continued.*

		Doc.	Vol.	No.
1842.	Amendment proposed by Maine,	A	2	28
1844.	Resolution of the legislature of Massachusetts relative to an amendment of,	A	3	52
	Resolutions of different states to amend, relative to the election of President and Vice-President, *see* President.			
	Amendments to, relative to the judiciary, &c., *see* Chancery, Supreme Court and Judicial System.			

UNITED STATES COURTS.

		Doc.	Vol.	No.
1839.	Plaintiffs in judgment in, resolution relative to,	A	1	10
1857.	Report of joint select committee relative to a certain decision of,	S	4	158

UNITED STATES DEPOSIT FUND.

		Doc.	Vol.	No.
1837.	Report of joint committee relative to the investment and distribution of the,	S	1	29
1838.	Report of Mr. Ruggles relative to the,	A	5	242
1839.	Report of comptroller relative to the application of the interest of the, while it remained in the banks, &c.,	A	6	403
1839.	Report of select committee relative to the fourth installment of the,	A	6	411
1840.	Report of comptroller relative to the investment of the,	S	4	122
1840.	Report of commissioners for loaning, on petition of citizens of New York to extend the time for the payment of the interest due the,	A	3	82
1841.	Report of comptroller relative to the commissioners for loaning the,	A	5	148
1841.	Report of select committee (Mr. Worden), relative to the,	A	4	104
1843.	Report of the comptroller in answer to a resolution of the assembly in relation to a call of twenty-five per cent of,	A	4	83
1843.	Resolution of town meeting in Bainbridge, Chenango county, relative to,	A	5	138
1847.	Report of comptroller respecting commissioners of loans of,	S	1	32
1849.	Report of comptroller in answer to resolution of assembly respecting certain balances due,	A	3	111

UNITED STATES LAND FUND.

		Doc.	Vol.	No.
1845.	Message from governor in answer to resolution as to whether $10,000 has been set apart from,	A	4	88

UNITED STATES MAIL STEAMSHIP COMPANY.

		Doc.	Vol.	No.
1850.	Majority and minority reports on,	S	3	79

UNITED STATES PUBLIC LANDS.

		Doc.	Vol.	No.
1832.	Resolutions of the legislature of Delaware relative to the,	A	1	3
1832.	do do Tennessee relative to the,	A	3	183
1833.	do do Massachusetts relative to the,	A	4	327
1834.	do do Georgia relative to the,	A	1	34
1834.	Mr. McKeon's report on the resolutions relative to the,	A	4	320
1834.	Message of President Jackson returning the bill relative to the distribution of the proceeds of the,	S	2	109
1836.	Resolutions of the legislature of Pennsylvania relative to the,	S	2	83
1838.	do do Arkansas relative to the,	A	6	365
1839.	do do Connecticut relative to the,	A	2	18
1839.	do do New Jersey relative to the,	A	4	211
1839.	do do Missouri relative to the,	A	6	328
1838.	Mr. C. E. Clarke's report relative to the distribution of the,	A	6	397
1840.	Mr. C. E. Clarke's report relative to the distribution of the,	A	6	234
1840.	Resolutions of the legislature of Vermont in relation to the,	A	3	73

UNITED STATES PUBLIC LANDS—*continued.*

		Doc.	Vol.	No.
1840.	Resolutions of the legislature of Maine in relation to the,........	A	4	139
1840.	do do Kentucky in relation to the,.....	A	7	285
1841.	do do Massachusetts in relation to the,	S	3	89
1841.	do do Connecticut in relation to the,...	A	2	24
1841.	do do Pennsylvania in relation to the,	A	4	109
1841.	do do Delaware in relation to the,.....	A	4	132
1841.	do do Rhode Island in relation to the,..	A	5	158
1841.	do do Indiana in relation to the,.......	A	5	168
1841.	Resolutions proposed by Mr. Root relative to the,........	S	1	32
1841.	Resolutions proposed by Mr. Worden protesting against the surrender of the, to the particular states in which said lands are situated,..	A	4	98
1841.	Report of select committee (Mr. Worden), relative to the,......	A	4	104
1842.	Message of the governor transmitting resolution of general assembly of Alabama relative to,....................................	S	1	19
1842.	Resolutions of South Carolina legislature concerning,..........	S	3	52
1842.	do Alabama relative to,........................	A	2	43
1842.	do Georgia relative to disposal of proceeds of,........	A	4	58
1842.	Report of select committee on so much of the governor's message as relates to the share of this state in the proceeds of,........	A	5	122
1842.	Report of minority of committee on same,........................	A	5	126
1843.	Report of select committee relative to the distribution of the proceeds of, by the general government,.........................	S	3	117
1843.	Letter from governor relative to proceeds of sale of,............	S	3	120
1843.	Resolution of Connecticut relative to,..........................	A	1	11
1843.	Communication from treasurer relative to moneys received from, from the proceeds of the sales of,............	A	2	16
1843.	Report of secretary of state transmitting correspondence in relation to,..	A	4	116
1843.	Report of the committee on ways and means in relation to the sum of $84,358.50, now deposited in the Commercial Bank of the City of Albany, part of the proceeds of the sales of,.... ..	A	5	144
1854.	Resolution of canal board relative to grants of,............. ...	S	1	13

UNITED STATES REVENUE LAWS.

1841.	Resolutions of the legislature of Massachusetts relative to the,...	S	3	89

UNITED STATES REVENUES.

1831.	Surplus revenues, report relative to the distribution of the, among the several states,...	S	1	70
1838.	Resolution protesting against the collection of, in specie,........	A	3	95
1838.	And of this state, resolution to collect them in notes of specie paying banks,...	A	6	328

UNITED STATES SENATORS, *see* Congress.

UNITED STATES STOCKS.

1849.	Report of committee on banks, &c., respecting the propriety of amending the general banking law so as to admit the deposits of, as a basis of circulation,..............................	S	1	22

UNITED STATES SUPREME COURT.

1842.	Message of the governor relative to certain decision of,.........	S	4	96
1857.	Report of joint committee of senate and assembly on decision of, in case of Dred Scott,................................	A	3	201

UNION ACADEMY, *see* Academies, &c.

UNION COLLEGE, *see* Colleges.

UNION HALL ACADEMY, *see* Academies, &c.

UNIVERSITIES, *see* Colleges, &c.

UNIVERSITY, REGENTS OF, *see* Regents of the University.

		Doc.	Vol.	No.
	URBANA, TOWN OF.			
1858.	Report of canal board as to propriety of legislature granting the petition of citizens of,	A	4	135
	USHER, ROBERT.			
1832.	Report on petition of, to be allowed to pack beef and pork for exportation, according to his own method,	A	1	28
	USURY.			
1837.	Jeremy Bentham's defence of,	S	1	7
1837.	Memorial of the Chamber of Commerce against the passage of the bill to prevent,	S	2	62
1837.	Report of the committee on the judiciary on bill to prevent,	S	2	64
1841.	Report on petition for the modification of the laws,	A	7	302
1847.	Report on act relative to,	S	2	42
1847.	Report on act relative to,	S	2	44
1850.	Report on bill prohibiting corporations from pleading,	S	3	112
1855.	Report of committee on judiciary in reference to,	A	3	78
	USURY LAWS.			
1850.	Report of committee respecting,	A	4	66
1855.	Report of committee on commerce and navigation on bill relative to,	S	2	58
1858.	Report of a minority on petitions for repeal or modification of,	A	4	118
	UTICA, CITY OF.			
1833.	Banks, memorial against incorporating more,	S	2	72
1830.	Bridge over the canal at, report of canal commissioners on petition for,	S	3	274
1839.	Citizens' corps report, on petition to incorporate,	A	6	409
1841.	Cotton manufacturing company, report on petition of, for compensation for damages by the obstruction of the water of Sauquoit creek, &c.,	A	3	52
1832.	Mechanics' Society, report on petition to incorporate,	A	4	325
1839.	McAdam road from, to Dearfield, report on petition for,	A	5	300
1834.	McAdam road from, to New Berlin, petition of inhabitants of Bridgewater relative to the construction of,	A	2	98
1830.	Memorial of inhabitants of, relative to Bartlett's School Manual,	A	1	65
1833.	Memorial of inhabitants of, against incorporating more banks,	S	2	72
1834.	Memorial of inhabitants of, for a ship canal from Utica to Oswego,	S	2	104
1835.	Memorial of inhabitants of, for a ship canal from Ontario to Albany,	A	2	158
1830.	Road from, to Sherburne, report on petition to lay out,	S	3	253
1831.	Road from, to Sherburne, report on petition to repeal act to lay out,	S	1	41
1835.	Termination of the Chenango canal at, report on petition to raise money by tax to defray the expense of, &c.,	A	4	368
1836.	Report on petition to be relieved from the expense of,	A	2	88
1838.	do do do	A	2	33
1838.	do do do	A	4	194
1843.	Report of canal commissioners respecting bridges between Little Falls and,	S	3	105
1844.	Report of the canal board on the petition of common council of,	A	1	30
1844.	Report of canal board on petition of common council of,	A	7	204

BANKS *see* Banks—Oneida County.

SUPREME COURT CLERK'S OFFICE AT, *see* Supreme Court.

UTTER, SOLOMON.

		Doc.	Vol.	No.
1831.	Report on petition of, for bounty lands, ...	A	4	295

V.

VAGRANCY.

1850.	Reply of governor to resolution and letters of judges relative to convictions for, ...	S	2	43

VAIL, ISAAC.

1836.	Report on petition of, for extra allowance for work done on the Champlain canal,..	A	4	230

VALUATION OF REAL AND PERSONAL ESTATE.

1834.	Report of comptroller giving the, ...	A	2	66
1835.	do do	S	2	40
1840.	do do	S	1	11

VAN ALLEN, DANIEL, AND ABRAHAM WAGNER.

1836.	Report of commissioners of land office on, petition of, relative to certain land, ...	A	4	297

VAN ALSTINE, C., AND A. MOSHER.

1854.	Report on petition of, ...	A	3	98

VAN ALSTINE, DAVID.

1848.	Report relative to petition of, ...	A	3	87
1849.	Report of committee on canals on petition of,................	A	2	96

VAN ALSTINE, JOHN C.

1849.	Report of committee on grievances on petition of,............	A	2	43

VAN ALSTYNE, CHARITY.

1852.	Report on petition of, for relief,..............................	A	1	19
1852.	Report on petition of, for relief,..............................	A	2	78

VAN ALSTYNE, JOHN C.

1854.	Report of committee on claims on petition of,................	A	1	23
1854.	Report of committee on claims on petition of, ...	A	1	29

VAN ALSTYNE, JOHN C., AND OTHERS.

1853.	Report of committee on claims on petition of, for canal damages,	S	2	39

VAN ALSTYNE, JOHN T.

1856.	Report on petition for relief of,..............................	A	3	39

VAN BUREN, HARMAN W.

1840.	Report on petition of, to authorize the commissioners of the land office to sell to him a portion of the salt lands,..........	A	7	284

VAN BUREN, MARTIN.

1845.	Communication from, declining office of Regent of University,..	A	5	196

VANDEBOGART AND YATES.

		Doc.	Vol.	No.
1844.	Report of canal board on petition of,	A	5	108
1844.	Report of committee on claims on petition of,	A	5	129
1845.	Report of committee on grievances on petition of,	A	3	65

VANDEMARK, JACOB.

1843.	Report of committee on claims on his petition,	S	3	95

VANDEMARK, JACOB, AND OTHERS.

1845.	Report of canal commissioners on petition of,	S	1	15
1847.	Report on petitions of,	A	2	33

VAN DEN HUEVEL, J.

1832.	Report on petition to change his name,	A	2	55

VANDERHEYDEN, ABRAHAM D.

1830.	Report on petition of, relative to certain land in the city of Troy,	A	4	428

VANDERHEYDEN, JACOB.

1840.	Report on petition of, for payment of a judgment recovered by him against Asa T. Smith for an injury by means of blasting frozen earth on the Erie canal,	A	3	88
1840.	Report of attorney-general on the same,	A	4	149
1841.	Report of committee on grievances on the same,	A	3	55

VANDERHEYDEN, LEVINUS, AND OTHERS.

1853.	Resolution of Mr. Beekman on petition of,	S	3	68

VAN DERKAR, RICHARD, *see* Gerrit Peebles.

VAN DERKEMP, JOHN J., *see* Holland Land Company Agent.

VANDERMARK, JACOB.

1841.	Report on petition of, for compensation for building culverts on the Black River canal,	A	4	96

VANDERMARK, JOHN.

1856.	Report on petition for relief,	A	3	81

VANDERPOEL, J.

1832.	Report of amount of fees received by him as circuit judge,	A	2	122

VANDERPOOL, AARON, AND JAMES McBRIDE, Jr.

1856.	Report on petition of, executors, &c.,	A	4	105
1857.	Report of committee on claims on petition of,	A	1	44

VANDERWORKEN, JOHN, *see* Oscar Granger, and others.

VAN DEUSEN, JOHN B., AND FRANCIS BATES.

1849.	Report of committee on petition of,	A	1	18

VAN DORN, JACOB.

1834.	Report on petition of, for compensation for damages by the Erie canal,	A	4	299

VAN DORN, JACOB—*continued.*

		Doc.	Vol.	No.
1837.	Report of committee on claims on the same,	A	3	255
1840.	Report of committee on claims on the same,	A	5	217

VAN EPPS, J. E.

1846.	Report of committee on grievances on petition of,	A	2	43
1848.	Report relative to petition of,	A	2	45
1852.	Report on petition of, for relief,	S	1	39
1853.	Report of committee on claims on petition of, for relief,	S	1	12

VAN HORNE, ABRAHAM A. AND JANE.

1836.	Report on claim of,	A	4	262
1836.	Report on claim of,	A	4	323

VAN HORNE, DANIEL.

1834.	Report on petition of, for a law authorizing the undersheriff of Niagara county to convey to him a certain lot of land,	A	3	193

VAN INWAGEN, ANTHONY.

1852.	Report on bill for relief of,	S	2	79

VAN PATTEN, H. N.

1832.	Report on petition of, for compensation for damages by the Erie canal,	A	3	254
1835.	Report on petition of, for compensation for damages by the Erie canal,	A	3	248

VAN NEST, T. V.

1836.	Report on petition of, for extra allowance for work done on the Chenango canal,	A	4	269

VAN NORTWICKE, WILLIAM.

1839.	Report of attorney-general in relation to the bail of,	A	3	123

VAN RENSSELAER, STEPHEN.

1847.	Memorial of, relative to taxation,	S	2	47

VAN RIPEN, MARY ANN.

1845.	Report of committee on the judiciary on petition of,	A	6	237

VAN SCHAICK, JOHN S., AND OTHERS.

1851.	Report of committee on claims,	A	4	108

VAN SCHOONHOVEN, J., AND OTHERS.

1846.	Report of committee on banks, &c., on petition of, on par redemptions,	A	4	131
1846.	Report of minority of committee on banks, &c., on petition of, on par redemptions,	A	5	145

VAN SLYCK, CORNELIUS A., *see* Enos Stone, Matthew Brown.

VAN SLYKE, ANTHONY H.

1857.	Report of committee on claims on petition of,	A	1	31

VAN STAPHORST, N., AND OTHERS.

1846.	Report relative to perpetuating evidence of the death of,	S	1	18

VAN TUYL, O. W., *see* Neversink Navigation Company.

VAN VALKENBURGH, RYNIER, AND OTHERS.

		Doc.	Vol.	No.
1832.	Owners of lots in Albany assessed for constructing a canal bridge, report on petition of,	A	3	190

VAN VORST, JAS. B.

1852.	Report on claim of,	S	2	62

VAN VRANKEN, C.

1845.	Report of canal board on petition of,	A	5	157

VAN VRANKEN, CORNELIUS C.

1843.	Report of the committee on grievances on petition of,	A	5	151

VAN WIE, HENRY A.

1856.	Report on petition of,	A	4	119
1857.	Report of committee on claims on petition of, for damages,	A	2	80

VARICK, ABRAHAM, *see* S. H. Addington.

1834.	Report on petition of, relative to the Marine Railway at Oswego,	A	3	201
1839.	Report on petition of, relative to the same,	A	4	181
1836.	Report on petition of, relative to certain lands in Freemasons' patent,	S	2	91
1836.	Report on petition of, relative to the same,	S	2	92

VATTEMARE, ALEXANDER, *see* International Exchanges.

1845.	Communication from, relative to international exchanges,	A	5	185
1847.	Report relative to donations through,	S	4	128
1847.	Report of donations from,	A	8	227
1849.	Message from governor transmitting report of, on the subject of international exchanges,	A	5	201
1849.	Communication from,	A	5	208
1850.	Second annual report of,	A	5	127
1850.	In relation to donations from France,	A	8	192
1856.	Report of, as commissioner, &c.,	S	3	108

VEDDER, JOHN H., AND OTHERS.

1846.	Reports on petition of,	S	1, 7,	29

VEDDER, JOHN M., AND OTHERS.

1846.	Report of committee on claims on petition of,	S	1	29

VEDDER, J. P.

1844.	Report of canal board on petition of,	A	4	135

VEEDER, SIMON.

1834.	Report on petition of, relative to certain land on the Mohawk river,	S	2	101

VERMONT, STATE OF.

1830.	Resolutions of the legislature of, relative to the election of president, and in relation to the tariff law,	A	2	123
1830.	do do relative to the fortifications on northern frontier,	S	4	366

VERMONT, STATE OF—*continued.*

Year	Subject	Doc.	Vol.	No.
1831.	Resolutions of the legislature of, relative to the election of president, &c.,	A	1	4
1837.	do do relative to slavery in the District of Columbia, &c.,	S	1	33
1840.	do do relative to the public lands,	A	3	73
1841.	do do relative to the re-eligibility of the president,	A	2	27
1842.	do do relative to time of holding election of president of the United States,	A	1	14
1843.	do do relative to the franking privilege and postage, transmitted by the governor,	A	2	15
1850.	do do on slavery,	A	8	181
1856.	Resolutions of,	A	4	124

VERONA, TOWN OF.

Year	Subject	Doc.	Vol.	No.
1840.	Report on petition of inhabitants of, for a law more effectually to secure the elective franchise,	A	5	185
1845.	Report of canal board on petition of inhabitants of,	A	5	193

VETERAN AND CATLIN, TOWNS OF.

Year	Subject	Doc.	Vol.	No.
1856.	Report of committee on erection and division of towns and counties on bill to alter lines of,	S	2	44
1846.	Minority report on same subject,	S	2	59

VICE-CHANCELLOR, *see* Chancellor.

VICTOR, TOWN OF.

Year	Subject	Doc.	Vol.	No.
1832.	Report on petition of the Northeast Congregational Society of Bloomfield in the town of, to change its name,	A	4	328

VIENNA, TOWN OF.

Year	Subject	Doc.	Vol.	No.
1836.	Report on petition to raise money by tax for the support of roads and bridges in the,	A	4	281

VIRGIL, TOWN OF.

Year	Subject	Doc.	Vol.	No.
1832.	Report on petition to divide the,	A	2	128

VIRGINIA AND KENTUCKY.

Year	Subject	Doc.	Vol.	No.
1833.	Resolutions of the legislatures of, of 1798 relative to the alien and sedition laws,	S	2	41

VIRGINIA, STATE OF.

Year	Subject	Doc.	Vol.	No.
1833.	Resolutions of the legislature of, relative to nullification in South Carolina,	A	3	211
1836.	Resolutions of the legislature of, in relation to slavery,	A	4	246
1840.	Fugitives from justice, controversy between New York and, in relation to certain, correspondence between the governor of New York and the lieutenant-governor of Virginia relative to,	S	1	1
1840.	Communication from the governor of, and the proceedings of the legislature on the same,	S	4	110
1840.	Report on the governor's message in relation to the same,	A	8	361
1841.	Correspondence between the governor of New York and,	S	1	1
1841.	Resolutions proposed by Mr. Paige,	S	2	47
1841.	Resolutions proposed by Mr. Lawrence,	A	2	30
1841.	Resolutions of the legislature of Mississippi,	S	2	56
1841.	Communication from the lieutenant-governor of,	S	3	71

VIRGINIA, STATE OF—*continued.*

		Doc.	Vol.	No.
1841.	Report and resolutions of the house of delegates of Maryland,..	S	3	88
1841.	Communication from the lieutenant-governor of,...............	S	3	94
1841.	Message from the governor relative to the requisition of the executive of, for the surrender of Robert F. Curry,.............	S	2	56
1842.	Message from the governor transmitting a law, a report and resolution of legislature of South Carolina relative to the controversy between, and New York,..........................	S	2	41
1842.	Message from the governor of, dissenting from the resolution of the legislature relative to the same,........................	S	4	102
1842.	Lieutenant-governor of, correspondence relative to fugitives from justice,..	A	1	2
1842.	Proceedings of municipal council of Alexandria in favor of retrocession to,...	A	4	53
1842.	Resolutions of South Carolina relative to the controversy between New York and,....................................	A	4	62
1842.	Report of judiciary committee on correspondence of the governor with executive of,.......................................	A	7	185
1842.	[Ex. Sess.] Communication relative to inspection laws,.........	A	7	195
1843.	Memorial of ship masters, &c., of Richmond county, in relation to the suspension law of,..................................	A	2	26
1843.	Report of committee on judiciary on the matters of difference between the States of New York and,........................	A	2	49
1844.	Communication from governor transmitting resolution of the legislature of Massachusetts relative to,.....................	A	7	170
1844.	Resolution of the general assembly of, in relation to the resolution of the general assembly of Massachusetts, proposing to amend the Constitution of the United States,................	A	7	190
1847.	Resolution of assembly of,.......................................	A	4	111

VISSCHER, GERRIT.

1841.	Report on petition of, for such portion of the bed of the Erie canal as may be abandoned,....................................	A	5	187

VOLUNTEERS, MEXICAN, *see* Mexican War.

VAN BECK, G. F.

1844.	Report of committee on the judiciary on petition of, ...	S	2	62

VOORHEES, JAMES L.

1839.	Report on petition of, relative to school district No. 25, in the town of Lysander,..	A	6	385
1840.	Report on petition of, relative to the same,.....................	S	3	89

VREELAND, JACOB.

1830.	Report on petition of, relative to the waters of Seneca lake,.....	A	3	284

VROMAN, CHARLES.

1852.	Report on petition of,..	A	2	58
1856.	Report of committee on finance on petition of,.................	S	1	23

VROOMAN & HULBERT.

1853.	Report of committee on claims on petition of, ...	S	1	19
1855.	Communication from auditor respecting award to,.............	A	5	138
1856.	Report of judiciary committee on bill to pay, ...	S	1	30

VROOMAN, ANN ALIDA, AND OTHERS.

1830.	Report on petition of, for certain escheated lands, ...	A	1	36

VROOMAN, B. E.

		Doc.	Vol.	No.
1830.	Report on petition of, for bounty lands,	A	2	93
1831.	Report on petition of, for bounty lands,	A	2	77

W.

WADDINGTON.

		Doc.	Vol.	No.
1855.	Report of committee on charitable and religious societies, on St. Paul's church at, St. Lawrence county,	S	2	47

WADSWORTH, BENJ.

		Doc.	Vol.	No.
1849.	Report of committee on claims on petition of,	A	2	48

WAGGONER, ABRAHAM, AND OTHERS.

		Doc.	Vol.	No.
1830.	Report on petition of, for the erection of a bridge over the Mohawk river,	A	4	332

WAGGONER, CHARLES.

		Doc.	Vol.	No.
1835.	Report on petition of, to allow him to take the oath of office of justice of the peace,	A	1	64

WAGGONER, JOSEPH.

		Doc.	Vol.	No.
1834.	Report on petition of, for compensation for damages by the canal dam at Otsquago creek,	A	4	383
1835.	Report of canal petitioners on same,	A	4	321
1835.	Report of committee on grievances on same,	A	4	362

WAGNER, PETER J.

		Doc.	Vol.	No.
1846.	Report on petition of,	S	3	84
1846.	Report committee on claims on petition of,	S	3	99

WAGONER, ABRAHAM.

		Doc.	Vol.	No.
1836.	Report on petition of, for compensation for damages to his mills by the construction of the Crooked Lake canal,	A	3	126

WAGONER, ABRAHAM, AND DAVID VAN ALLEN.

		Doc.	Vol.	No.
1836.	Report on petition of, relative to certain land,	A	4	297

WAINER, THOMAS.

		Doc.	Vol.	No.
1834.	Report on petition of, for indemnity for certain land sold by the state,	A	3	241

WALBRIDGE, SILAS.

		Doc.	Vol.	No.
1854.	Report on petition of,	S	1	59

WALKILL.

		Doc.	Vol.	No.
1831.	Bridge over the, near Hand's mills, report on bill authorizing the building of a,	A	4	328
1831.	Bridge over the, near Shawangunk kill, report on bill authorizing the building of a,	A	4	328

WALLABOUT BAY.

		Doc.	Vol.	No.
1856.	Report in reference to those revolutionary martyrs who died in,	A	4	111

WALLACE, SILAS, AND OTHERS.

		Doc.	Vol.	No.
1840.	Report on petition of, for compensation for damages by the construction of the tow-path on the Seneca river, ...	A	6	201
1842.	Report of committee on canals on petition of,.................	A	7	175

WALLER, PHINEAS, AND OTHERS.

1834.	Report on the claim of, to certain land in the Garnsey patent,...	A	4	371

WALLIS, JOHN, *see* L. Hildreth and others.

WALRATH, DANIEL.

1844.	Report of committee on claims on petition of,.................	S	1	21

WALRATH, JOHN I.

1843.	Report of the committee on claims on the petition of,..........	A	3	71
1844.	Report of committee on claims on petition of,.................	S	1	21
1845.	Report of committee on claims on bill for relief of,............	S	3	92
1845.	Report of majority of committee on claims on petition of,......	A	3	66
1845.	Report of minority of committee on claims on petition of,......	A	3	67
1848.	Report on petition of, ...	A	3	67
1851.	Report of committee on canal damages, ...	S	2	37

WALRATH, SAGE & DUNHAM, *see* Sage, Walrath & Dunham.

WALWORTH, CHANCELLOR.

1847.	Communication from, in answer to a resolution,..............	S	4	113

WALWORTH, CLINTON.

1842.	Report of committee on canals on petition of, for reduction of tolls on lead and copper, ...	A	7	158

WALWORTH, JOHN, *see* Chancery, Assistant Register in.

WALWORTH, R. H.

1847.	Letter from, ...	S	3	102

WALWORTH, REUBEN H.

1856.	Memorial of,..	S	1	37

WAPPINGER'S CREEK.

1842.	Report of committee on roads, &c., relative to a bridge across,..	S	3	79

WAR.

1841.	Resolutions proposed by Mr. O'Sullivan on the subject of, ...	A	5	154

WAR, MEXICAN, *see* Mexican War.

WAR OF 1812.

1853.	Report of comptroller in relation to pay, &c., of the officers and soldiers of the,..	S	2	52
1855.	Report of committee on militia, on petition of soldiers of,......	A	4	90
1856.	Report of committee on petition of veterans, ...	S	2	50
1856.	Memorial of the convention of veterans of,....................	A	3	96
1857.	Report on memorial of soldiers of, ...	S	1	36
1857.	Report of comptroller relative to moneys paid soldiers of, ...	S	2	81
1858.	Report of commissioners relative to soldiers of, ...	A	4	113

WAR OF THE REVOLUTION, *see* Revolution.

		Doc.	Vol.	No.
	WARD, ALEXIS.			
1833.	Report on petition of, to erect a dam across Oak Orchard creek,.	A	4	253
	WARD, ALEXIS, & THOS. WILSON.			
1853.	Report of committee on claims on petition of, for relief, ...	A	3	75
	WARD, ALVAH, AND OTHERS.			
1858.	Report on claim for relief of,......................................	A	3	58
	WARDEN'S LIBRARY.			
1845.	Report of trustees of state library relative to purchase of, ...	A	1	11
	WARD, JAMES, AND ELA MERRIAM.			
1857.	Report of committee on claims on petition of, for damages,.....	A	2	96
	WADSWORTH, E., AND OTHERS.			
1842.	Report of commissioners of land office on petition of,..........	A	4	68
	WARNER, ANDREW.			
1833.	Report on petition of, to change his name,.....................	A	3	154
	WARNER, A. S.			
1855.	Reports of majority and minority of committee on privileges and elections in reference to contested seat,.....................	A	2	37
1855.	Reports of majority and minority of committee on privileges and elections in reference to contested seat,.....................	A	2	47
1855.	Reports of majority and minority of committee on privileges and elections in reference to contested seat,.....................	A	2	59
	WARNER, CHAS. J.			
1850.	Appeal on temperance,..	A	6	145
	WARREN COUNTY.			
1835.	Clerk's office, report on petition to raise money to repair the,....	A	3	256
1837.	Poor law, report on petition to amend the,......................	A	1	41
1838.	Poor-house farm, report on petition to allow John B. Prosser to search for mines on the,..................................	A	3	148
1841.	Poor-house and farm, report on petition to sell the, and to revive the distinction between town and county poor,..............	A	7	265
1838.	Report on petition from, to encourage the growth of silk,.......	A	3	135
1844.	Report on the petition for aid to build a bridge in,.............	S	2	70
1857.	Report of committee on agriculture on bill to enable the Agricultural Society to draw their proportion of money from the state,	A	3	191
1857.	Report of select committee on petition of inhabitants of Essex, Franklin and,...	A	4	94
	BRIDGE OVER THE HUDSON, *see* Warrensburgh.			
	WARREN, LEMUEL.			
1831.	Report on petition for compensation for work done on a road through the St. Regis reservation, ...	A	3	226
	WARRENSBURGH AND ATHOL, TOWNS OF.			
1833.	Report on petition for an appropriation to build a bridge over the Hudson in the,...	A	3	157

WARRENSBURGH AND ATHOL, TOWNS OF—*continued.*

		Doc.	Vol.	No.
1833.	Report of committee on finance on the same,	S	2	117
1834.	Report of the committee on roads and bridges on the same,	A	3	168
1835.	Report of the committee on roads and bridges on the same,	A	2	126

WARRENSBURGH, ROAD FROM, *see* Lake George.

WARSAW, VILLAGE OF.

1831.	Commissioner of deeds, report on petition for the appointment of a,	A	2	131

WASHINGTON AND SARATOGA RAILROAD, *see* Railroads.

WASHINGTON COUNTY.

1836.	Clerk's office, report on petition to raise money by tax to erect a,	A	3	120
1840.	Commissioners for loaning money, report on petition relative to the place of meeting of the,	A	7	299
1830.	Foreign poor, report relative to the importation of, &c.,	A	4	330
1831.	Treasurer of, report on petition to credit the, with certain compound interest charged against him in the comptroller's office,	A	1	51
1832.	Northern turnpike road, report on petition to abandon part of the,	A	3	252
1832.	Accounts of officers for the support of the poor, &c., report on petition to amend the law relative to the auditing of,	A	1	12
1830.	Report on petition of the supervisors to raise on the county, and on the town of Kingsbury, a certain sum by tax,	A	4	362
1837.	Woolen and cotton manufacturing company, report on petition to incorporate,	A	2	150
1849.	Memorial of citizens of Rensselaer and, residing on the line of the Troy and Rutland railroad,	A	3	151
1849.	Report of committee on roads and bridges on petition of sundry citizens of Clinton, Essex and, relative to road from Whitehall to Plattsburgh,	A	3	186
1858.	Report of commissioners relative to bridge across South Bay in,.	A	6	167
	Roads, *see* Clinton County.			

WASHINGTON MONUMENT ASSOCIATION, NEWBURGH.

1838.	Report on petition to incorporate the,	A	6	320
1839.	Report on petition to incorporate the,	A	6	356
1840.	Report on petition to extend the time to organize the,	A	8	349
1851.	Communication of governor relative to,	A	5	144

WASHINGTON MONUMENT, NEW YORK.

1838.	Report on petition to incorporate an association to erect a,	A	3	144

WASHINGTON'S BIRTHDAY.

1832.	Report of a select committee appointed to make arrangements for the celebration of,	A	2	137
1832.	Report of a select committee appointed to make arrangements for the celebration of,	S	1	52
1832.	Oration delivered by the Hon. O. G. Otis on the centennial anniversary of,	A	4	306

WASHINGTON'S HEAD-QUARTERS.

1850.	Report,	A	5	122
1851.	Report of committee,	A	3	57

WATERBURY, N. J.

1846.	Communication from,	A	6	215

WATERFORD, VILLAGE OF.

		Doc.	Vol.	No.
1838.	Canal fences from, to the Saratoga dam, report in relation to,....	A	3	265

WATERHOUSE, M., AND OTHERS.

1858.	Report on claim for relief, ...	A	3	52

WATERLOO, TOWN OF.

1853.	Report of committee on grievances, on petition of sundry inhabitants for dyking and draining of certain lands in,...	A	4	96

WATERS, THOS. P.

1849.	Report of committee on canals on petition of,...	A	3	169

WATERS, THOS. P., AND J. H. ROOKER.

1857.	Report on claim of,...	S	2	57

WATERTOWN.

1841.	Academy, report on bill to repeal the charter of the,...	S	1	20
1832.	Water company, report on bill to incorporate the, ...	S	1	80
1834.	Report on petition to raise money for the support of roads and bridges in,...	A	2	63

WATERVILLE.

1831.	Fire company, report on petition to amend the act incorporating the,...	A	1	31

WATERVLIET, TOWN OF.

1830.	Turnpike road, report on petition of farmers of Watervliet to be restored to the free use of said road,...	A	3	229
1831.	Majority report on the same,...	A	2	92
1831.	Minority report on the same,...	A	2	93
1835.	Report of committee on roads and bridges, ...	S	2	59
1838.	Report of committee on roads and bridges,...	A	5	234
1839.	Report of committee on the judiciary, ...	S	3	66
1840.	Report of committee on roads and bridges,...	A	4	141
1830.	Cession of jurisdiction of certain lands in, to the United States, message from the governor relative to the,...	A	1	53
1832.	Surplus waters of the canal at, communication from Major Talcott relative to the,...	A	3	207
1832.	Street or highway, report on petition to open a,...	A	1	20
1832.	Street or highway, report on petition to open a,...	A	1	31
1832.	School district No. 2, report on petition of the trustees of,...	A	2	69
1843.	Report of committee on a petition from,...	S	1	30
1844.	Report of canal commissioners on the petition of the inhabitants of, for the construction of two bridges over the canal at West Troy, ...	A	6	149

WATKINS, JOHN.

1845.	Report of canal appraisers on the petition of, ...	A	3	41
1850.	Report of canal appraisers, of testimony,...	S	2	63

WATSON, ELKANAH.

1834.	Report on petition of, relative to the title of certain land,...	S	2	91

WATSON, MAJOR.

1835.	Report on petition of, for bounty lands,...	A	4	272

WATSON, MALBONE.

		Doc.	Vol.	No.
1857.	Report of committee on judiciary relative to,	A	3	188

WATSON, PLINY, *see* Livingston County Surrogate.

WAUMAKER, JOHN C.

1837.	Report on petition of, for compensation for damages by the Chemung canal,	A	3	207

WAYNE, COUNTY OF.

1837.	Clerk's office, report on petition to raise money by tax to build a,	A	3	262
1837.	Tax on dogs, report on petition to amend the law imposing a,	A	3	238
1834.	Beef and pork, annual report of E. Havens, an inspector of,	A	3	150
1834.	Beef and pork, amended report of E. Havens, an inspector of,	A	4	360
1835.	Beef and pork, annual report of E. Havens, an inspector of,	A	2	78
1836.	do do do	A	2	193
1838.	do do do	A	4	185
1839.	do do do	A	2	62
1851.	Report of committee on division, majority,	A	4	127
1851.	Report of committee on division, minority,	A	5	135
1852.	Report relative to division of,	A	2	55
1852.	Minority report relative to division of,	A	2	67
1853.	Report of committee on internal affairs of towns and counties, on petition of inhabitants of, praying for the removal of county buildings to Newark,	A	2	53

WEATHERHEAD, JOHN, *see* Lands, Freemasons' Patent.

WEAVER AND GEER.

1845.	Report of committee on claims on petition of,	A	3	32

WEAVER, MARIA, AND HENRY TRUAX.

1835.	Report on petition for remuneration for certain land sold by the attorney-general,	S	1	23
1839.	Report of committee on public lands on the same,	A	6	330
1841.	Report of comptroller on same,	A	3	79

WEBB, ISAAC, *see* N. Masters.

WEBBER, CHRISTIANA.

1853.	Report of committee on claims in relation to the claim of, for relief,	S	1	11

WEBSTER, DANIEL.

1842.	[Ex. Sess.] Letter of, to the governor transmitting apportionment law,	A	7	195

WEBSTER, HOSEA.

1857.	Report on bill relative to judgment in favor of,	S	4	170
1857.	Report of majority of judiciary committee favorable on bill authorizing an appeal by the state from a judgment in favor of, against the state,	A	3	186
1857.	Report of minority of committee on same subject,	A	3	178

WEBSTER, JOSHUA.

1848.	Report of committee on claims on petition of,	A	5	141

WEBSTER, P. G.

		Doc.	Vol.	No.
1844.	Report of committee on claims on petition of,	A	7	200

WEBSTER'S UNABRIDGED DICTIONARY.

		Doc.	Vol.	No.
1851.	Report of committee on furnishing, to common schools,	S	3	81
1851.	Report of committee on furnishing, to common schools,	S	3	89

WEED, NORMAN.

		Doc.	Vol.	No.
1838.	A sub-contractor on the Chenango canal, report on petition of, for relief,	A	2	29

WEEKS, GILBERT.

		Doc.	Vol.	No.
1839.	Report on petition of, to be indemnified for injuries received by falling from a wall constructed by the state,	A	6	336

WEIGHTS AND MEASURES, STANDARD.

		Doc.	Vol.	No.
1830.	Report of secretary of state relative to furnishing counties with,	S	2	188
1831.	Report of secretary of state relative to furnishing counties with,	A	1	5
1831.	Report on the same,	A	1	27
1839.	Communication from the secretary of state as state sealer of,	A	3	151
1845.	Report of secretary of state, relative to,	A	1	22
1849.	Report on, by W. H. Clark, of the State Normal School,	A	5	241
1854.	Memorial of superintendent of,	A	1	4
1856.	Communication from state sealer of,	S	2	63
1856.	Report relative to,	A	3	66
1857.	Communication from the superintendent of,	A	2	71

WELLS, A. H.

		Doc.	Vol.	No.
1850.	Communication from,	A	5	134

WELLS, ALBERT.

		Doc.	Vol.	No.
1847.	Report on petition of, for relief,	S	1	27

WELLS, GARDNER.

		Doc.	Vol.	No.
1832.	Report on petition of, to build a dam across Genesee river,	A	4	288

WELLS, REUBEN.

		Doc.	Vol.	No.
1834.	Report on petition of, relative to certain escheated lands,	A	2	53

WEMPLE, E.

		Doc.	Vol.	No.
1830.	Report on petition of, for compensation for damages to his lands by the Erie canal,	A	4	331

WENDELL, DANIEL T.

		Doc.	Vol.	No.
1837.	Report on petition of, for relief,	A	2	151

WENTWORTH, JOSEPH, AND OTHERS.

		Doc.	Vol.	No.
1842.	Report of committee on claims, on petition of,	S	3	57

WESTBROOK, JACOB, Jr.

		Doc.	Vol.	No.
1852.	Report to pay Job G. Elmore, Jr.,	A	2	65
1852.	*See* report of committee on petition of Job G. Elmore, claiming seat of,	A	2	28

WEST, C., AND OTHERS.

		Doc.	Vol.	No.
1842.	Report of commissioners of land office, on petition of, ...	A	4	68

WESTCHESTER COUNTY.

		Doc.	Vol.	No.
1831.	Beef and pork, annual report of Henry Strang, an inspector of, ..	A	2	175
1832.	do do ..	A	4	314
1834.	do do ..	A	3	186
1835.	do do ..	A	4	279
1832.	do Gilbert Oakley, ..	A	4	319
1833.	do do ..	A	3	146
1834.	do do ..	A	2	82
1835.	do do ..	A	2	71
1836.	do do ..	A	3	194
1837.	do do ..	A	2	124
1838.	do do ..	S	1	34
1837.	do Ebenezer Baldwin, ..	A	2	125
1838.	do do ..	A	3	153
1839.	do do ..	A	4	244
1840.	do do ..	A	5	208
1830.	County buildings, report relative to the location of the, ...	A	4	402
1838.	Court of common pleas, report on petition to try certain causes at the December term, ...	A	3	100
1838.	Croton aqueduct, report on petition relative to crossing the Harlem river with the, ...	A	6	319
1840.	Court-house, central, report on petition for a, ...	A	6	231
1841.	Court-house, central, report on petition for a, ...	A	6	255
1833.	Highway labor in, report on petition to amend the law relative to,	A	3	221
1835.	Ferries between, and Rockland, report in relation to, ...	A	4	313
1836.	Highway from Fishkill to the Croton river, report on petition for aid to improve a, ...	A	4	277
1832.	Superintendents of the poor, reports relative to granting additional powers to, ...	A	1	26
1832.	Surrogate's office, report on petition relative to the location of the, ...	A	2	133
1837.	Game in, report on petition for the preservation of, ...	A	3	196
1838.	Oysters, report on petition for a law to protect persons planting them in the East river, Long Island Sound, &c., ...	A	3	157
1840.	Division of the, report on petition to annex the four northern towns to Putnam county, ...	A	7	294
1833.	Report on petition from, relative to the Revised Statutes, ...	A	2	48
1834.	Society for the apprehension of horse thieves, report on petition to incorporate a, ...	A	4	310
	Roads, report relative to the alteration of, by the construction of the Croton Water Works, ...	A	3	175
1849.	Memorial of citizens of, for a law to equalize representation in boards of supervisors, ...	A	2	74
1858.	Report on petition of citizens of, living on line of New York and New Haven railroad, ...	A	5	158

Banks, *see* Banks—Westchester County.

Police, *see* Metropolitan Police.

WESTERN EYE AND EAR INFIRMARY, *see* Syracuse.

WESTERN HOSPITAL, at Geneva.

		Doc.	Vol.	No.
1839.	Report on petition to incorporate, and for aid to, ...	A	4	255
1840.	Report on petition for aid, ...	S	4	104

WESTERN HOUSE OF REFUGE, *see* Juvenile Delinquents.

WESTFIELD, TOWN OF.

		Doc.	Vol.	No.
1852.	Report of commissioner of land office, respecting the granting of lands under water at,	A	5	121

WEST GROVE, TOWN OF.

1838.	Report on petition to change the name of,	A	4	237

WESTLAKE AND McCONNELL.

1837.	Report on petition of, for extra allowance for work on the Chemung canal,	A	4	280
1837.	Report on the same,	A	2	63

WEST MENDON, VILLAGE OF.

1838.	Presbyterian congregation of, report on petition to legalize the acts of the trustees of the,	A	3	70

WESTMORELAND, TOWN OF.

1833.	Missionary lot in, report on petition of settlers, for the sale of the,	A	1	28
1833.	Missionary lot in, report of commissioners of the land office, on the same,	A	2	42

WEST POINT.

1832.	Report on petition to prohibit the sale of wine and liquors to the students and soldiers at,	A	3	228

WEST POINT MILITARY ACADEMY, *see* Military Academy, West Point.

WEST STOCKBRIDGE AND ALBANY RAILROAD, *see* Railroads.

WEST TROY.

1835.	Caoutchouc manufactory, report on petition to incorporate,	A	2	149
1838.	Level of the Erie canal at, report of canal commissioners, in relation to,	A	6	313
1838.	Level of the Erie canal at, report of committee on canals, in relation to,	A	6	333
1831.	Lumber, report on bill relative to the inspection of, at West Troy and Gibbonsville,	A	2	114
1844.	Report on petition of inhabitants of Watervliet for two canal bridges at,	A	6	149
1849.	Report of canal commissioners on the feasibility of constructing a basin at, or between Albany and,	S	2	65
1849.	Report of committee on canals, on bill and petition for constructing a basin at,	A	3	171
1857.	Report of canal commissioners, in reply to resolution relative to canal bridge in,	A	2	92
1858.	Report relative to channel of Hudson river, near,	S	2	82
	INSPECTORS' REPORTS, *see* Albany.			

WEST, W. C., AND OTHERS

1837.	Report on petition of, for pay for constructing a road from Cedar's point to Newcomb, Essex county,	A	3	176

WETHEY, PORTER.

1836.	Report on petition of, to construct a wing dam on the Seneca river,	A	1	32

WHALING COMPANIES, *see* Newburgh, Hudson.

		Doc.	Vol.	No.
	WHEAT, AMERICAN.			
1841.	Memorial of Joshua Leavitt, showing the importance of an equitable and adequate market for, with statistical tables, ...	A	7	295
	WHEATLAND, TOWN OF.			
1849.	Report of committee on claims, on petition of inhabitants of, ...	A	5	210
	WHEATON, HENRY G., *see* David G. Seger.			
	WHEATON, STEPHEN BRUSH.			
1836.	Report on petition of, to change his name, ...	A	3	167
	WHEEDON, A.			
1854.	Report on petition of, ...	A	3	86
	WHEADON, ALVA.			
1855.	Report of committee on claims, in case of, ...	A	3	71
	WHEELER, GEORGE.			
1846.	Report of committee on grievances, on petition of, ...	A	4	102
	WHEELER, GEORGE, AND OTHERS.			
1847.	Reports on petitions of, ...	A	2	92
	WHEELER, GEORGE P.			
1843.	Report of committee on claims, on petition of, ...	A	5	173
	WHEELER, THOMAS.			
1849.	Report of committee on the manufacture of salt, on petition of,	A	2	72
1851.	Administrator of John J. Mang, report of committee, ...	A	2	28
	WHEELER, THOMAS, AND HARVEY ALVORD.			
1845.	Report of committee on claims, on bill for relief of, ...	S	3	98
	WHEELOCK, J. G.			
1846.	Report of committee on grievances, on petition of, ...	A	3	76
	WHEELOCK, JOHN G.			
1836.	Report on petition of, for compensation for damages by the Erie canal, ...	A	4	284
	WHEELOCK, JOHN G., AND OTHERS.			
1844.	Report of canal board on the petition of, ...	A	1	27
1844.	Report of canal board on petition of, ...	A	7	203
1847.	Reports on petitions of, ...	A	4	127

WHIPPLE, J., *see* E. Cleaveland.

WHISTON, ERASTUS, *see* George Stevens.

WHITE CREEK, *see* Cambridge.

WHITEHALL, VILLAGE OF.

		Doc.	Vol.	No.
1832.	Water, report on petition of Justin Smith to supply the village with,	A	1	17
1834.	Report on the same,	A	2	74
1835.	Report of select committee on the same,	A	1	16
1832.	Road from, to the north bounds of Clinton county, report on petition for aid to open and improve a,	A	3	253
1834.	Report on the same,	A	3	110
1835.	Road from, to Port Henry, report of commissioners appointed to survey a,	S	1	14
1849.	Report on petitions for road from, to Plattsburgh,	A	3	186

BANKS, *see* Banks—Washington County.

WHITEHEAD, JOHN.

		Doc.	Vol.	No.
1845.	Report of committee on militia, &c., on the petition of,	A	4	93
1847.	Report on petition of,	A	1	30

WHITE, H., AND OTHERS.

		Doc.	Vol.	No.
1844.	Report of committee on claims on petition of,	S	1	23

WHITE, HENRY, AND JOHN WILLIAMS.

		Doc.	Vol.	No.
1841.	Report on petition of, for a re-appraisement of damages,	A	3	76
1842.	Report on petition of,	A	4	92
1843.	Report of committee on claims on petition of,	A	2	35

WHITE, H. H., AND OTHERS.

		Doc.	Vol.	No.
1844.	Report on petition of,	S	1	34

WHITE, SAMUEL.

		Doc.	Vol.	No.
1830.	Report on petition of, for aid to establish a lunatic asylum at Hudson,	A	4	316
1831.	Memorial of, for aid,	A	4	307
1832.	do	S	1	39
1834.	do	S	1	42

WHITE, STEPHEN, AND OTHERS.

		Doc.	Vol.	No.
1841.	Report on petition of, for an investigation into their acts and proceedings as directors of the City Bank of Buffalo,	A	7	290

WHITESBOROUGH, VILLAGE OF.

		Doc.	Vol.	No.
1832.	Report on petition for a supreme court commissioner to reside at,	S	1	63
1835.	Report on petition for a master in chancery at,	A	2	97

WHITESTOWN, TOWN OF.

		Doc.	Vol.	No.
1832.	Report on petition to raise money to repair roads, &c., in,	S	1	50

WHITING, ALEXANDER B.

		Doc.	Vol.	No.
1849.	Memorial of, relative to difficulty of enforcing the health laws of the state at the quarantine station, and asking an amendment of present law,	A	3	191

WHITING, BOWEN, AND OTHERS.

		Doc.	Vol.	No.
1841.	Report on petition of, for compensation for damages to their lands by the Erie canal,	S	2	62

	WHITNEY, JAS. F.	Doc.	Vol.	No.
1847.	Report on petition of,	A	7	186
1847.	Report on petition of,	A	8	239
	WIBERT AND SANFORD.			
1848.	Report of committee on canals on petition of,	A	3	90
	WICKAM, JAMES.			
1833.	Report on petition of, for compensation for a deficiency in a lot of land,	A	3	236
1833.	Report on the same,	A	4	250
	WICKWIRE, JARETT.			
1841.	Report on petition of, for compensation for damages to his lands, by the construction of the Woodman reservoir,	A	5	146
	WILCOX, S. S.			
1854.	Report on petition of,	A	2	43
	WILDS, OWEN.			
1835.	Report on petition of, for compensation for damages to his boat, while navigating the Erie canal,	A	5	395
	WILES AND FRITCHER.			
1840.	Report on petition of, for extra allowance for work done on the Erie canal,	A	3	85
	WILES, JOHN J.			
1857.	Report of committee on claims on petition of,	A	2	93
	WILKES, SAMUEL.			
1833.	Report on petition of, for compensation for damages by the canal,	A	4	273
	WILKINS & TALLMAN.			
1847.	Report on petition of,	A	2	49
	WILKINSON, JOHN.			
1846.	Report of, in answer to a resolution of the senate,	S	3	103
	WILLARD, EMMA, AND OTHERS.			
1852.	Memorial of, relative to female education, A 2 74,	5		117
	WILLARD, ERASTUS.			
1832.	Report on the claim of,	S	2	80
	WILLARD, G. W.			
1854.	Report on petition of,	A	3	91
	WILLARD, JAMES M., AND LEONARD J. EDGARTON.			
1840.	Report on petition of, for compensation for damages to their mill dike, &c., by the Chenango canal,	A	6	229
	WILLIAMS, A. K., AND OTHERS.			
1844.	Report of commissioners of land office on the petition of,	S	3	102

Year	Subject	Doc.	Vol.	No.
	WILLIAMS, DAVID.			
1848.	Report on bill to erect a monument to,	A	3	76
1856.	Report on erecting monument,	A	3	37
	WILLIAMS, EDWIN.			
1833.	Report on petition of, for aid to enable him to publish an improved Gazeteer of the state,	S	2	12
	WILLIAMS, ELEAZER.			
1845.	Report of commissioners of land office on petition of, a St. Regis Indian,	S	1	7
1855.	Memorial of, relative to St. Regis Indians,	S	2	43
	WILLIAMS, JAMES.			
1848.	Report on petition of,	A	5	155
	WILLIAMS, JOHN, *see* Henry White.			
	WILLIAMS, J. W., *see* Chancery, Clerk in.			
	WILLIAMS, NATHAN.			
1832.	Report of amount of fees received by him as circuit judge,	A	2	139
1835.	Report of amount of fees received by him as clerk of the supreme court,	A	4	311
1836.	Report on petition of the executors of,			
	WILLIAMS, PLATT.			
1846.	Report of commissioners of land office on petition of,	A	3	74
1847.	Report on petition of,	S	2	46
1850.	Report on canal claim,	A	5	109
	WILLIAMS, TOWN OF.			
1848.	Report relative to division of,	A	6	214
	WILLIAMS, R. G.			
1836.	Correspondence between the governors of Alabama and New York relative to the demand for the surrender of, a fugitive from justice,	S	1	1
	WILLIAMS, WM. B., AND BENJAMIN H. SAGE.			
1844.	Report of canal board on petition of,	A	5	121
	WILLIAMS, WM. H.			
1850.	Report on claim of,	A	5	114
1852.	Report on petition of, for relief,	A	2	81
	WILLIAMSBURGH & CYPRESS HILL PLANKROAD CO.			
1854.	Petition of, for increase of stock,	S	1	14
	WILLIAMSBURGH, VILLAGE OF.			
1833.	Wharf at, report on petition of E. Frost and P. Harmon to erect a,	A	4	311
1835.	Wharves at, report on petition of John Lorimer Graham and othe.s to erect, adjacent to their lands on the East river,	A	4	350
1837.	Wharves at, report on petition of Paul J. Fish and others for the same,	A	4	287
1851.	Report of select committee on union of New York, Brooklyn, and,	S	3	74

WILLIAMSON, CLARK & CO.

		Doc.	Vol.	No.
1830.	Report on petition of, for pay for manufacturing munitions of war for the State,	A	7	282

WILLIAMSON, MARIA H.

1847.	Report on petition of R. Colden and Maria Blakly, devisees of,..	A	2	94

WILLIAMSPORT AND ELMIRA RAILROAD, *see* Railroads.

WILLINK, WILHELM AND JAN, *see* Holland Land Co.

WILLIS, EVELINE, *see* David Frost.

WILLIS, JESSE E.

1854.	Report on petition of,	A	2	47

WILLIS, JOSEPH.

1852.	Report on assembly bill for relief of,	S	2	75

WILLS.

1838.	Executors of, report in relation to suits brought by,	A	5	261
1833.	Executors of, report on petition to enlarge the powers of,	S	2	94
1839.	Of real estate, report on bill giving jurisdiction to the court of chancery in cases of contested,	A	5	278
1830.	Proof of, and the probate of the same, report on bill relative to the,	S	2	158
1834.	Proof of, executors and administrators, &c., report of attorney-general relative to the,	S	2	118

WILNA, TOWN OF.

1840.	Report on petition for a loan to build bridges across the Black river,	A	8	336

WILSON, ALFRED, AND OTHERS.

1830.	Report on petition of, relative to the last will, &c., of William Wilson, deceased,	A	2	194

WILSON, JOHN.

1834.	A soldier of the revolution, report on petition of, for bounty lands,	A	3	216

WILSON, PETER, *see* Indians—Cayugas.

WILSON, ROBERT.

1849.	Report of committee on canals on petition of,	A	3	199
1856.	Report on memorial of,	S	1	16

WILSON, STEPHEN S.

1841.	Report on petition of, relative to certain land bought of the state,	A	4	134

WILSON, TOWN OF.

1832.	Report on petition for an additional bounty on wolves in,.	A	4	321

WILSON, WM.

1848.	Report on petition of,	A	3	55

WILTSE, THOMAS.

		Doc.	Vol.	No.
1856.	Report of committee on petition of,	A	3	23

WINDHAM AND DURHAM TURNPIKE COMPANY.

1831.	Report on petition to abandon part of their road,	A	2	113

WINDSOR, TOWN OF.

1831.	Report on petition for aid to improve a road in the,	A	4	311

WING, D. W.

1845.	Report of committee on claims on petition of, for relief,	S	2	81

WINSLOW, NATHANIEL.

1833.	Report on petition of, for a divorce,	A	2	97

WISNER, JEFFREY.

1838.	Report on petition of, for compensation for damages by the Chemung canal,	A	3	82

WISNER, JOHN W.

1835.	Report on petition of, for compensation for work done on the Chemung canal,	A	2	120
1835.	Report of committee on canals on the same,	A	3	192

WISNER, WILLIAM.

1840.	Report on petition of, praying for relief as surety of Matthew Carpenter, deceased,	A	4	104
1841.	Report of committee on grievances on the same,	A	4	101

WITNESSES, IMPRISONMENT OF.

1855.	Report of select committee in relation to,	A	3	68

WITNESSES IN CRIMINAL CASES.

1848.	Report relative to fees to,	A	3	95

WITNESSES IN JUSTICES' COURTS.

1833.	Report relative to increasing the compensation of,	A	3	180

WIVES.

1830.	Abandoned by their husbands, report relative to amending the Revised Statutes so as to give relief to,	A	3	214

WOLVEN, GILBERT.

1856.	Report on petition of,	A	4	140

WOLVES (bounty on).

1832.	Report on petition to increase the, in the town of Wilson,	A	4	321
1834.	do do in the town of Redfield,	A	4	378
1836.	do do in Franklin county,	A	1	39
1838.	do do in Lewis county,	A	6	325

WOMEN, MARRIED.

1842.	Report on petitions to extend and protect the rights of property of,	A	7	189

WOMEN, MARRIED—*continued.*

		Doc.	Vol.	No.
1842.	Report of judiciary committee on petitions to extend and protect the rights of property of,......	A	7	180
1844.	do committee on judiciary on petition asking for a law for the protection of,......	A	3	96
1846.	do committee on judiciary on rights of,......	A	6	219
1847.	Report on act to enable, to convey,......	S	1	37
1848.	Petition of, for repeal of certain laws,......	A	5	129

WOMEN'S RIGHTS.

1854.	Report of select committee on the extension of,......	A	4	129
1854.	Report of select committee relative to the same,......	A	5	149
1854.	Report of select committee relative to extension of certain,......	A	4	129
1855.	Report of select committee relative to the same,......	A	5	149
1855.	Report of select committee on petitions for,......	A	5	129
1856.	Report of judiciary committee on petition for,......	A	4	147

WOOD, ASA D.

1851.	Report of committee on petition,......	A	3	80

WOOD, ASA D., AND OTHERS.

1852.	Report on petition of,......	S	1	21
1856.	Report on petition of,......	A	3	45

WOOD CREEK.

1830.	Report of amount of damages awarded to owners of lands in the valley of, for injuries by the Champlain canal,......	S	4	360

WOOD CREEK AND DURHAMVILLE PLANKROADS.

1856.	Report respecting,......	A	4	152

WOOD CREEK TRACT OF LAND.

1831.	Communication from the surveyor-general relative to the,......	S	1	19
1832.	Communication from the surveyor-general relative to the,......	S	1	12
1832.	Report of the committee on finance on the same, and on the petitions of settlers for the conveyance of their respective lots to them, or that they may have the pre-emptive right,......	S	1	27

WOOD, EDWARD, AND OTHERS.

1848.	Report on petition of,......	A	5	138

WOOD, EZRA.

1848.	Report on petition of,......	A	2	49

WOOD, GEORGE.

1847.	Report on petition of,......	S	3	89

WOOD, HELEN A.

1856.	Report on petition of, for relief,......	A	3	49

WOOD, PERSON.

1837.	Report on petition of, to change his name,......	A	2	38

WOOD, SEYMOUR S.

1852.	Report on petition of,......	A	2	35

WOODRUFF, NORRIS M.

		Doc.	Vol.	No.
1837.	Affidavit of, relative to the Jefferson County Bank,............	A	4	299

WOODS, WILLIAM.

1835.	Report on petition of, to erect a dam across the Canisteo river,...	A	1	38

WOODS, I. L., *see* Chancery, clerks in.

WOODWARD, JAMES.

1851.	Report of committee on canal damages,.....................	A	1	19

WOODWORTH PATENT.

1852.	Minority report in relation to the extension of,...............	A	2	64

WOODWORTH, THOMAS, AND E. NEWLAND.

1850.	Report on petition of, for relief,..........................	A	4	177
1857.	Report of committee on claims on petition of,................	A	2	105

WOOLDRIDGE, GEORGE B.

1856.	Report for relief of,....................................	A	4	174

. WOOLSTEN, CHAS. W.

1851.	Report of committee on claims,...........................	A	3	47

WOOLSTEN, CHAS. W., AND VOLNEY HUGHES.

1851.	Report of committee on claims on petition of, for canal damages,	A	3	47
1852'	Report in relation to,..................................	S	1	38

WOOLSTON, COLLINS AND HUGHES.

1848.	Report on petition of,...................................	A	5	174

WORCESTER, TOWN OF.

1838.	Report on petition to extend the time for the collection of taxes in the,...	A	3	159

WORDEN & THOMAS.

1846.	Report on petition of,..................................	S	1	31
1851.	Report on claim for canal damages,........................	S	2	29

WORDEN, EBEN C., AND T. BRIGGS.

1847.	Report of canal board relative to testimony taken in case of,.....	A	1	34

WORDEN, WM. E., AND MORGAN L.

1851.	Report of the commissioners of the land office,...............	A	3	53
1857.	Report of committee on claims on petition of,................	A	2	139

WORKHOUSE, JAILS, &c.

1855.	Relative to commission to examine,........................	S	1	27

WORRELL, JOSHUA.

1852.	Report on the petition of,...............................	A	1	22

WORS, E.

1845.	Report of committee on aliens on the petition of,.............	A	3	35

WORTH, WILLIAM J.

		Doc.	Vol.	No.
1835.	Report on resolutions requesting the governor to procure a suitable sword to be presented to,	S	2	85
1855.	Petition of Thurlow Weed and others, for procurement of sword for,	A	3	65
1858.	Communication from J. W. Edmonds relative to sword of,	S	1	5

WRECKMASTERS IN QUEENS COUNTY, *see* Queens County.

WRIGHT, COUNTY OF.

1845.	Report of minority of committee on erection and division of towns and counties on proposed,	A	5	174

WRIGHT, ELIHU C.

1851.	Report of committee on canal damages,	A	4	104

WRIGHT, GEORGE.

1852.	Report on the petition of,	S	2	61

WRIGHT, GEORGE A., AND OTHERS.

1857.	Report of committee on claims favorable on petition of,	A	2	68

WRIGHT, JOHN.

1841.	Report on petition of, for the construction of a ditch near the Champlain canal,	A	5	156

WRITS OF ERROR.

1834.	Supreme court decisions upon, report on bill relative to,	A	4	395

Y.

YATES, A. J.

1845.	Report of canal board on petition of,	A	5	191

YATES AND McINTYRE.

1833.	Communication from, in relation to lotteries,	S	2	119

YATES, ANDREW, AND OTHERS.

1850.	Report of judiciary committee on petition of,	S	1	28

YATES, ANDREW J.

1856.	Report of judiciary committee on petition of,	S	1	7
1856.	Report of judiciary committee on petition of,	S	1	19

YATES AND VANDEBOGERT.

1844.	Report of the canal board on petition of,	A	5	108
1844.	Report of the committee on claims on petition of,	A	5	129
1845.	Report of committee on grievances on petition of,	A	3	65

YATES COUNTY.

1835.	Court-house and jail, report on petition to increase the number of commissioners for building the, and to raise money to complete the same,	A	1	21

YATES COUNTY—*continued.*

Year	Subject	Doc.	Vol.	No.
1835.	Report of select committee on the same,	A	3	255
1831.	Board of town auditors, report on petition to create,	A	3	222
1831.	Domestic spirits, report relative to the inspection of,	A	1	33
1837.	Tax on dogs, report on petition to amend the law imposing a,	A	3	238
1835.	Sole leather, annual report of I. B. Grant, inspector of,	A	4	277
1836.	Sole leather, annual report of I. B. Grant, inspector of,	A	4	256

YATES, EVERT.

Year	Subject	Doc.	Vol.	No.
1844.	Report of canal board on petition of,	A	3	73

YATES, EVERT L.

Year	Subject	Doc.	Vol.	No.
1855.	Report of committee on claims on petition of,	A	1	19
1856.	Report on petition of,	S	2	65
1856.	Report on claim of,	S	3	65

YATES, ISAAC I.

Year	Subject	Doc.	Vol.	No.
1845.	Report of committee on canals on petition of,	A	6	221

YATES, ISRAEL I.

Year	Subject	Doc.	Vol.	No.
1845.	Report of committee on canals on petition of,	A	6	221

YATES, JOHN B.

Year	Subject	Doc.	Vol.	No.
1830.	Memorial of, relative to the Chittenango Literary Institution,	S	1	39
1830.	Report on the same,	S	2	124

YATES, J. P.

Year	Subject	Doc.	Vol.	No.
1845.	Report of canal board on petition of,	A	6	214

YORK, TOWN OF.

Year	Subject	Doc.	Vol.	No.
1836.	Report on petition of trustees of school district No. 8 in the,	A	1	20

YORKTOWN.

Year	Subject	Doc.	Vol.	No.
1850.	Report on petition in regard to a certain road,	S	3	100

YOUELLS, NEIL H.

Year	Subject	Doc.	Vol.	No.
1847.	Report on petition of,	A	8	229
1848.	Report on petition of,	A	3	101

YOUNGSTOWN, FERRY AT.

Year	Subject	Doc.	Vol.	No.
1836.	Majority report on petition of John Phillips for a grant of,	A	2	63
1836.	Minority report on the same,	A	2	62

YOUNG, WILLIAM.

Year	Subject	Doc.	Vol.	No.
1834.	Report on petition of, for compensation for damages by the Erie canal,	A	3	208
1834.	Report of canal commissioners on the same,	A	4	330

YOUNG, WM., AND OTHERS.

Year	Subject	Doc.	Vol.	No.
1847.	Report on petition of,	A	2	97

YOUNG, WILLIAM C.

Year	Subject	Doc.	Vol.	No.
1830.	Report on petition of, for compensation for surveying a route for a railroad from Boston to Hudson river,	A	2	181

YOUNG, WILLIAM C.—*continued.*

		Doc.	Vol.	No.
1831.	Report on petition of, for compensation for surveying a route for a railroad from Boston to Hudson river, ...	A	1	24

YOUNG, SAMUEL.

1837.	Report of a select committee in relation to the sale of his stock in the Saratoga County Bank, ...	S	2	66

Z.

ZOAR.

1836.	Bridge across Cattaraugus creek at, report in relation to, ...	A	4	241

www.ingramcontent.com/pod-product-compliance
Lightning Source LLC
LaVergne TN
LVHW021312110826
845150LV00003B/547

* 9 7 8 1 4 2 5 5 5 8 1 4 7 *